OBJECT-ORIENTED PROGRAMMING LANGUAGES AND EVENT-DRIVEN PROGRAMMING

OBJECT-ORIENTED PROGRAMMING LANGUAGES AND EVENT-DRIVEN PROGRAMMING

Dorian P. Yeager

MERCURY LEARNING AND INFORMATION

Dulles, Virginia
Boston, Massachusetts
New Delhi

Publisher: David Pallai
MERCURY LEARNING AND INFORMATION
22841 Quicksilver Drive
Dulles, VA 20166
info@merclearning.com
www.merclearning.com
1-800-758-3756

This book is printed on acid-free paper.

Dorian P. Yeager, *Object-Oriented Programming Languages and Event-Driven Programming*.
ISBN: 978-1-936420-37-7

Library of Congress Control Number: 2012952666

131415321   Printed in the United States of America
This book is printed on acid-free paper.

CONTENTS

PREFACE

TO THE STUDENT

Each of you brings to the table a year or more of study in a particular object-oriented programming language. Some of the subtleties of those languages you have already encountered, probably enough of them so that you have already experienced the difficulty of mastering some of the intricate concepts of object-oriented programming languages. Mixed in with the concepts of inheritance, polymorphism, generic programming, and several variants of information hiding and access control, there are hundreds of smaller design decisions which impact these larger issues and impact each other as well. Most of these design decisions are treading in well-worn paths, because imbedded in these newer languages are myriad concepts which have been used in languages of the past.

Your instructor has carefully selected those chapters on which you are going to concentrate, but I encourage you to read and study the other chapters as time permits. There is great beauty in a consistent programming language design, and there is much to be learned even from some of the apparently poor design decisions which were made. All programming languages have flaws, but usually those flaws were deliberately accepted by the designer in order to achieve a specific goal. You may agree or disagree with the goal, but it is important to grasp the reasons why a design decision was made.

Event-driven programming can be frustrating and challenging, and certainly great fun. It is included here because it is an important tool for producing more useful and creative software, but also because it is a showcase for the advantages of object-oriented design. From the beginning graphical user interfaces were a major motivation for the design of object-oriented languages, because the hierarchy of types of objects seen on a display device (and interacted with using a mouse and keyboard) strongly suggests a hierarchy of software types. We dip into several EDP environments in this text, and our purpose is always to not only give the reader the flavor of how it feels to develop applications in that environment, but to actually cover enough of the details so that medium-sized projects can be undertaken and completed by the student within the framework of a semester of college.

Omitted from the historical context presented in this text are a great variety of languages with unique and creative designs which have motivated today's designs. A short list of missing languages includes APL, LISP, PROLOG, FOR-TRAN, COBOL, Snobol, Pascal, and Ada. Contrary to popular opinion, *none* of these languages is "dead." Variants of them are still in use, and it is likely that they will continue to grow and evolve and be of continuing usefulness indefinitely. The reason for their longevity lies in their inventiveness. At the core of each lies an idea that motivated the design, and in all cases where the idea was clear and communicated well, there was staying power.

If you enjoy this text, you will also enjoy studying the design and implementation issues encountered in other languages, object-oriented or otherwise, and you are strongly encouraged to do so. It is likely that during that study some new types of design solutions will take shape in your mind that would otherwise never have occurred to you. Since the invention of the wheel, our tools have shaped our thinking. For this reason, programming language design lies at the heart of the discipline of computer science. I hope this text motivates you to continue your study in this very important area.

TO THE INSTRUCTOR

The last twenty years have seen a dramatic change in computer science curricula, engendered in part by the introduction of object-oriented languages into those curricula and by the near-universal use of such languages as a tool for teaching software design and construction principles to Computer Science majors. The large majority of departments use either Java or C++ as the major teaching language in their curricula, and object-oriented (OO) programming languages (OOPLs) as a whole have become very important in our curricula. Because of the breadth and density of concepts in this set of languages, and the fact that each is accompanied by a sophisticated library of container classes, classes for graphics and event-driven programming, and other concept-heavy classes, there is now room within the OO paradigm to discuss a large part of what we have always taught in the Programming Languages course, while building on a broad, established base of familiarity on the part of our students. This text is meant to be a resource for instructors wishing to teach programming language design and implementation from that perspective.

The student using this text should have completed a year of study in an object-oriented programming language. The text generalizes from that year of experience in order to present the foundational principles of programming languages, drawing on the students' OO background while widening their perspectives. It uses a historical approach to link the older procedural languages to current object-oriented languages, tracing the roots of the latter to their origins in Simula 67. The main body of the text teaches a selected set of object-oriented languages from the standpoint of language design and implementation, beginning with the historically significant and highly original Smalltalk language. Enough information is presented to allow the students to see the depth and power of each language, and to be able to write some interesting programs.

Recognizing the growing importance of language-integrated libraries, the author presents in the context of each language a sampling of library types, including the standard types of container classes and associated iterators. In the same way, in keeping with the historical and current symbiosis between OO languages and event-driven programming (EDP), the text includes an early chapter on the basics of EDP, and follows up on that theme by including a detailed introduction to an EDP library for each of the languages covered.

The historical theme is reinforced in a pivotal chapter on C++ and Java similarities, tracing those languages back to their roots in C. The student is made to see how dramatically two languages can diverge from a common base, given two different sets of design goals. Further chapters complete the study of C++ and Java and provide a detailed and critical introduction to C# and Python. Common EDP themes such as graphics, animation, and user controls are introduced for each language, using as vehicles the MFC library (C++), Swing (Java), Windows Forms (C#), and Tkinter (Python).

The object-oriented paradigm isn't perfect, and it is certainly true that a design is not necessarily good just because it is object oriented. But the object-oriented languages taken as a group are a very rich and rewarding study. The sheer number of concepts involved in learning Java or C++ or any other object-oriented language, and the requirement we now place on our students to learn those concepts early in the curriculum, has enriched our curricula. The accompanying demand on our students for a higher degree of sophistication has changed the way we teach programming and software engineering.

A course based on this text makes a natural alternative or companion to the traditional Programming Languages course. A variety of ways suggest themselves to accommodate such a course into the curriculum. One idea is to offer a two-course sequence in Programming Languages, using this as either the first or the second course. Or two alternative courses could be offered, perhaps during alternate years. On the other hand, if this course is used as the only Programming Languages course at the undergraduate level, there is ample material in it to satisfy the ACM curriculum requirements. Along with a good theory course, it should prepare the student well for the study of the theory, design, and implementation of programming languages at the graduate level.

ACKNOWLEDGMENTS

I wish to thank my mother, for always believing in me, for failing to see my shortcomings, and for never being surprised at my successes. I also wish to thank my wife, Carol, and son, John, and various members of my extended family, for their patience as I have shortened my times of fellowship with them, and perhaps also shirked a few duties, in order to do this work. Professionally, I wish to thank Terrence Pratt, out of whose classic textbook I taught for many years, for first opening my eyes to the richness of programming language design. My colleagues in the Computer Science department at Grove City College have sacrificed to give me the time to write, and I will always be grateful for their unanimous support. Grove City College as an institution has done far more than provide me with an office, computer, and network. It has provided a unique atmosphere, a positive influence coming at me from all directions, which makes it a joy for me to go to work each day. The faculty and the student body are the largest part of that, but sound institutional principles and an honest desire to remain true to those principles are the guiding force. Thanks also go to the Coffee Grove (now Beans on Broad), Purdy's, and various other coffee shops, for putting up with my Spartan patronage and allowing me to use their space and wireless network when I wanted a change of scenery as I worked.

CHAPTER 1

A CONTEXT-SENSITIVE INTRODUCTION

B ecause this text is chiefly concerned with object-oriented programming languages (OOPLs), we will begin it with an attempt to characterize exactly what is meant by the term and to supply a framework into which we can fit our study of OOPLs. We assume up front that the reader already has a good foundation in one such language. We cannot assume, however, that the reader has a complete overview of where these languages fit in the design space, their historical context, the elements of programming language design, or even of what one means when one speaks of "good" design. We also cannot assume that the reader has seen all the concepts necessary for a broad comprehension of the design and implementation issues encountered in a wider study of programming languages. This chapter is meant to supply an overview of these issues, and to provide a context for our study of the widely and wildly varying possibilities which exist in the design of an object-oriented language.

NOTE

Throughout the text we will try to relate the language elements we discuss to the people who will be affected by their use. For greater clarity, we will standardize our use of the terms "programmer," "client," and "user." The first term, programmer, relates to you, our reader, as one who designs software using a particular programming language. The second, client, refers to another programmer who will be the direct consumer of the software module you are producing and whose work cannot proceed without that module. The term user is the (probably nontechnically oriented) user of a program written in the language. We will also use the term "client" to refer to software modules, so that program component A is a client of program component B if it makes reference to B or its contents in any way.

1.1   WHAT IS OBJECT-ORIENTED PROGRAMMING?

"Object-oriented" is a style of programming that has come into its own in business, government, industry, and academic circles. It promises a more natural, and therefore a more powerful, design paradigm, to the extent that a programmer is more productive if his software-constructed model conforms closely to the structure of the problem being solved. To amplify this statement, let us say that we equate "power" in a language with the ability that language has to inspire good solutions in the mind of the programmer. What we mean, then, by saying that an object-oriented language is more powerful, is that its features allow the programmer solving a problem to build constructs that reflect the structure of the world within which that problem arose. The idea here is that familiarity with such a language will be likely to open up avenues to a clear and natural solution in the programmer's mind. Whether or not this is the case is still being debated [Hadar08], but the paradigm has enough of a track record to establish it as a powerful force, and it is likely to be a dominant force in the programming world for many years to come.

NOTE

The domination of object-oriented programming (OOP) began with the rise of C++ and Java™ in academic circles in the nineties. In 1990, a panel discussion at a national meeting for Computer Science educators ([Bierbauer90]) was introduced with the statement, "As object-oriented programming becomes a main-stream technology, instructors are wrestling with how to incorporate it into the Computer Science curriculum." This uncertainty on the part of academic professionals did not last long. By 1998, there was no longer any doubt that OOP was to be the primary paradigm on which the curriculum would be based in an overwhelming majority of computer science departments around the country. That year was the year that the College Board's Advanced Placement (AP) computer science test was redesigned to test proficiency in the C++ language. (Before that date the test had been based on the procedural language Pascal.) Today the

> *OOP paradigm remains dominant, but for a large number of college and university computer science departments the preferred teaching tool is Java.*

In this section, we will take some time to review the primary qualifications that a programming language must have before it can be said to be object-oriented. Some of the discussion here anticipates material to be encountered later in the chapter, where we will go back and lay a more careful foundation for some of the terms in this section. Our purpose at this stage is to carefully define what we mean by an object-oriented programming language.

1.1.1 Data Abstraction and Information Hiding

A major breakthrough in programming language design occurred when programmers were allowed to define their own data types. C. A. R. Hoare's record class was the source of the idea and influenced the design of the class construct in the Simula 67 language. But initially few people knew of or cared for Simula; the version of the programmer-defined data type used in the teaching language Pascal ([Wirth70]) was much more widely used and accepted.

Pascal's data types incorporate *only* data. Actions performed on the data are considered external to the data type itself, so that the syntax of the language indicates only a grouping of data, as in the following example.

```
type Point =
    Record
        x, y: integer;
    end;
```

The above Pascal declaration introduces a data type called `Point` which incorporates two integer components named x and y. (A similar data type appears in every library for event-driven programming (EDP) discussed in this text.) Thus, once the above declaration has been made the Pascal programmer can use the type name `Point` to instantiate as many data entities as desired. For example, the following code declares two variables and an array, all of type `Point`.

```
var
    basepoint, corner: Point;
    vertices: array [1..20] of Point;
```

The `Point` data type as given here is *homogeneous*, meaning that all of its components are of the same type (`integer` in this case). Pascal, however, does not restrict itself to homogeneous data types, and indeed the `record...end` construct lends itself quite well to the encapsulation of a variety of different types of components. In other words, Pascal allows the creation of data types which are *heterogeneous*, i.e., are aggregates whose individual elements can be of different types. Pascal does *not* have the ability to incorporate *operations*, as does the following Java segment.

```
class Point {
    private int x, y;
    public int getX() { return x; }
    public int getY() { return y; }
    public void setXY(int x, int y) {
        if (x >= 0 && y >= 0) {
            this.x = x;
            this.y = y;
        }
    }
}
```

The above example illustrates another capability associated with object-oriented languages, which is the ability to define an interface, i.e., to specify the portions of the data type that are accessible from outside. In the above example, public write access to x and y is limited to the setXY() member function, because x and y themselves are declared private. Thus, a language with true data abstraction must have *explicit interfaces*.

There are, of course, two sides to this coin. As soon as we state that a choice can be made as to what is visible from outside, we are implying that what remains is *hidden*, in some sense. Thus, *information hiding* goes hand in hand with the idea of explicit interfaces.

Definition

A term which we define up front, in a very general fashion, is the term *encapsulate*. Whereas many texts provide a rather specialized meaning of this term, with many connotations, we will restrict our definition to the simple statement that to *encapsulate* a series of program elements is to provide bracketing syntax that allows us to group those elements and to think of the encapsulated set as a single entity. Such encapsulation may or may not involve defining an interface, or even naming the entity. An example of an encapsulation is the C compound statement, in which a series of statements preceded by the left set bracket ("{") and followed by the right set bracket ("}") is considered to be a single statement in the syntax of the language. Function and class definitions are also examples of encapsulation.

Data abstraction, then, in its full power as a programming language capability, requires (1) the ability of the programmer to define and name his own data types, (2) the ability to incorporate heterogeneous data structures into such data types, (3) the ability to specify a set of operations included *within* the data type, and (4) the ability to specify which portions of the data type are available to be accessed from outside.

NOTE *The term abstract data type (ADT) is often used to refer to a data type that is constructed using the data abstraction capabilities of some programming language, but such a data type can be, and often is, described and discussed in a totally language-independent fashion, and used as a program design tool whether or not the target language provides complete support for data abstraction.*

Here we introduce the term *object*. If we use the term in its most general sense, we can call any data entity an object. In fact, the term *data object* has been around a long time and has been used to mean nothing more than a stored data value or aggregate of values, to which a specific type has been assigned. But in the context of object-oriented programming the term takes on additional connotations. In that context, we speak of an object as consisting of two parts: its *attributes* and its *behaviors*. Such an object is an instantiation of an abstract data type, and in that context the attributes are the data components of the ADT and the behaviors are the included operations. But the strongest sense of the term *object* is in the context of object-oriented languages, where more is required to use the term than a simple abstract data type.

NOTE *In this text, we will use the term object in both its weak sense, i.e., as a stored data item, and also in its strong, object-oriented sense. The context of the discussion should always be more than sufficient to distinguish the sense in which we use the term.*

The active components of an ADT, in the context of object-oriented programming languages, can be referred to using a number of different terms. We have already used the terms *operation* and *behavior*, which are somewhat abstract and refer to "capabilities" of an object, but in the context of specific languages we may use the term *method* or *member function*, both of which refer to the specific program unit which defines the details of the way the behavior is achieved. We use the term *message*, or a term such as *method call*, *method invocation*, or *member function call*, to refer to the program element which invokes the corresponding behavior for a given object.

1.1.2 Inheritance

Relationships between types are important in a language. The *type equivalence* relation, for example, establishes two types as exactly the same, meaning not only that each type represents the same set of possible data values, but also that two objects of the two respective types are compatible across assignment statements, at the parameter transmission and return level, and in comparisons for equality.

NOTE

One example of an early and persistent issue concerning the relationship between types in a language is the issue of structural equivalence versus name equivalence. A language which uses structural equivalence considers two types the same if they have the same types of components in the same order. Name equivalence is stricter and never considers two types of different names to be equivalent no matter what their internal structure. Often a particular programming language design will use a combination of these; using pure name equivalence is too restrictive, and unrestricted structural equivalence is insecure and complex.

Type relationships in object-oriented languages are enriched by the presence of the *inheritance* and *subtype* relationships. These add a new complexity to the type structure of a language. We say that type B is *derived* from type A, or that B is a *derived type* of A, provided that in the program some syntax has been employed which guarantees that objects of type B have all the same attributes and behaviors as objects of type A, possibly with some more of their own. This relationship is the inheritance relationship, and we say that B *inherits* these attributes and behaviors from A. We say that A is the *base type*, or *base class*, from which B is derived. The terms *superclass* and *subclass* are used interchangeably with the terms base class and derived class, respectively.

The *subtype* relationship is similar to the inheritance relationship, and in some languages it turns out to be equivalent. In order for a subtype relationship to hold, objects of type B must be considered to also be objects of type A. This means more than just saying that B objects have all the same attributes as A objects; it means that B's public interface is a superset of A's public interface. In other words, whatever attributes and behaviors of type A are accessible to client programmers are also accessible in type B. With this stipulation, B objects can serve as arguments passed to parameters of type A. We say that B is a *subtype* of A, or that A is a *supertype* of B.

Be careful of a common source of confusion here—it seems counterintuitive that the subtype relationship should apply in the direction given. Because B has more attributes it would seem more intuitive to say that B was the supertype. In fact, having a larger set of attributes and behaviors makes B more specialized and less general, and therefore representative of a more constrained set of values. It is in that sense that B is said to be a subtype of A.

We make two observations for clarity and further guidance here. The first observation is that neither inheritance nor subtyping reaches the level of type equivalence, because the relationships are not symmetric. In neither case are objects of type *A* considered to be objects of type *B*. The second observation is that in common usage of the features of an object-oriented programming language, wherever there is inheritance there is subtyping. We will not again make an explicit distinction between the two until we encounter cases where the distinction exists in specific languages.

A data type construction facility which incorporates inheritance is universally referred to as a *class* construct, and such a data type is called a *class*. For example, consider the class Point defined above using the Java language. If we "fatten up" a point, we could call it a Disk. For this, all we need are two more attributes: a radius and a color. We still need the x and y attributes and the behaviors that allow us to manipulate those attributes, but the point (x, y) is now taken to be the coordinates of the center of the disk. We add to these the two additional attributes and some other behaviors for the purpose of manipulating the two new attributes. The result in Java might be the following class description.

```
class Disk extends Point {
    private double radius;
    private Color color;
    public double getRadius() { return radius; }
    public void setRadius(double radius) {
        if (radius > 0) this.radius = radius;
    }
    public Color getColor() { return color; }
    public void setColor(Color color) { this.color = color; }
}
```

Inheritance does not necessarily change the way we use a specific class. As with any class, using the above requires that we (1) instantiate an object of the type represented by the class and (2) use its public members and methods to modify it and access its parts. Here is an example Java code sequence:

```
Disk d = new Disk();
d.setXY(100,210);
d.setRadius(25.7);
d.setColor(Color.red);
```

The act of executing the method call d.setXY(100,210) can be referred to as *sending a message* to the object d. In particular, we are sending d the setXY message with arguments 100 and 210. Note that setXY() is a method in the base class, but the derived class object d understands and is able to respond to it.

Most methods are instance methods, meaning that when we use one of them to send a message that message is sent to an instance of the class (an object), not to the class itself. When a message is sent to the class instead of the object, we call the method associated with that message a *static method*, or a *class method*, and the language or its implementation must provide a way to identify the method definition as being associated with the class, not with objects instantiated from the class. In Java, C++, and C# we use the attribute *static* to identify a class method. Smalltalk, a minimalist language which is rather stingy with its allocation of keywords, assumes the development environment will provide a way to distinguish between class and instance methods.

NOTE

As the usage given here illustrates, the keyword static in many languages has a number of very specialized meanings, but there is another quite general and widely accepted meaning of the word. Accordingly, the term static is generally used, and will consistently be used throughout this text, in opposition to the word dynamic. Generally speaking, "static" refers to translation time and "dynamic" refers to run-time. Thus, an expression which is "statically evaluable" is an expression that can be evaluated by a compiler once and for all; this situation is potentially advantageous because the translator can substitute the computed value for any occurrence in the translated code and will not have to generate executable object code to evaluate the expression dynamically.

The addition of an inheritance mechanism to a data abstraction facility carries with it immense power and proportionate complications. Now instead of a collection of types which are unrelated or related only by type equivalence we have the potential for a complex *hierarchy* of types related by inheritance. Now in describing the syntactic and semantic rules which define the language we must potentially consider type-theoretic terms like *direct base class*, *indirect base class*, *common base class*, etc. These terms will be discussed in the remainder of the text, in the contexts of the specific languages to which they are relevant.

1.1.3 Polymorphism

Considering that there are behaviors anyone would expect from a certain class of objects, but that often a more specialized object would perform that behavior in a different way, we are led inexorably to the necessity to *override* base class behaviors. For example, let us suppose we have a class called `Automobile` with a behavior called `accelerate`. The base class might not support an acceleration any faster than five miles per hour per second. So if `familyCar` is an object of type `Automobile`, and one issues the message `familyCar.accelerate(60,3)`, requesting a total acceleration of 60 miles per hour in 3 seconds, the result might only be a total speed increase of 30 miles per hour in the time specified. If on the other hand `familyCar` was an object of the subtype `Corvette`, one might be more realistic in expecting the command to be followed precisely. Here we say that the definition of `accelerate` in the derived class `Corvette` overrides the definition of that method in the base class `Automobile`.

Let us consider an example of a more prosaic nature, this time using C++ syntax. Suppose we have a base type `Animal`, with a behavior called `soundMade()`, described as follows:

```
class Animal {
public:
    char * soundMade() { return "generic animal sound"; }
};
```

Then when an object `pet` of type `Animal` is expected to furnish a C-style string with the call `pet.soundMade()`, it will return a pointer to a character location where the string `"generic animal sound"` is stored. It is not much of a stretch to imagine the need for the derived class (subclass) `Cat`, defined as follows:

```
class Cat: public Animal {
public:
    char * soundMade() { return "meow"; }
};
```

After this declaration, if `pet` is declared to be of type `Cat`, the pointer returned by `pet.soundMade()` is pointing to the string `"meow"`.

Consider now the situation in which `pet` refers to a `Cat` object, but in fact is only known to be an `Animal`. (In other words, the only declaration for `pet` assigns `Animal` as its type.) This can happen in several ways. For example, `pet` could be a parameter of type `Animal` to which has been transmitted an argument of type `Cat`. There are two things that one might reasonably expect to happen:

1. Because the parameter is of type `Animal`, and the compiler is able to statically ascertain this fact, it could simply generate code to call the member function declared with that class (in C++, the function `Animal::soundMade()`), resulting in a pointer to the string "`generic animal sound`".

2. Because the object transmitted is of type `Cat`, the compiler might initiate some run-time actions to determine the location of a compiled `Cat::soundMade()` function, and call that function, which would return the result as a pointer to the literal "`meow`".

It is response (2) above which we would label *polymorphic* behavior. Interestingly enough, polymorphism is not the default behavior in C++, and we would actually get response (1) in that language. We can, however, request polymorphic behavior on a method-by-method basis in the language by using the keyword *virtual* in the base class as an attribute of the method, as follows:

```
class Animal {
public:
        virtual char * soundMade() { return "generic animal
sound"; }
        };
```

This one declaration makes the `soundMade()` method exhibit polymorphic behavior in all overrides of all derived classes, direct or indirect. So if this one addition is made to the declaration in the base class, we would get behavior (2) and the call `pet.soundMade()` would return "meow."

NOTE

> *What is polymorphism? Literally, it means "many forms." In this setting, it means that the one method name may result in many forms of response depending on where in the inheritance hierarchy we happen to be, and the key ingredient is that the form of response rests with the object, not the static type structure of the language. It is the object, not a set of statically determined characteristics of the variable by which that object is referenced, which governs the response to a message. This type of polymorphism is an essential ingredient of object-oriented programming as it is understood by the programming community.*

1.1.4 Related Concepts—Overloading and Generic Programming

Taking polymorphism in its most general sense (which is not the sense in which the term is usually applied), we can say that it involves similar syntax causing different forms of run-time actions depending on context, whether that context is determined by static program structure or by run-time history. Two language features which are important, but are features for achieving "polymorphism" only if we use the more general view, are overloading and generic programming.

Definition

Overloading is the act of providing additional meanings for an identifier, reserved word, or operator symbol, combined with a plan for using context to resolve the question of which meaning is needed in a particular circumstance. Overloading adds additional meaning to a name and does not remove its old meaning. The practice of introducing a new meaning for a name that masks, or makes inaccessible, the old meaning is called *overriding*. Overriding plays a prominent role in the example of Section 1.1.3; indeed, the style of polymorphism described there cannot be accomplished in a language that does not permit overriding.

Although overloading is not polymorphism and technically has nothing to do with object-orientation in a language, it needs to be mentioned here because of its strong relationship with overriding and polymorphism. Overloading a term has the result that it means different things depending on the context in which it is used. Consider, for example, the + symbol in just about any language with which the reader is familiar. That symbol usually comes with an overloaded meaning; that is, $x + y$ means different things depending on the types of the objects named by x and y. If they are both integers, then the expression denotes integer addition. If they are both floating point numbers, the expression denotes floating point addition. If one is of an integer type and the other of a floating point type, then the expression usually denotes a type conversion (integer to float) followed by floating point addition. In some languages the same + symbol might mean concatenation if one or both of x and y happened to be a string.

Programmer-defined overloading takes this idea to the extreme, and it is the key to another kind of polymorphism. If the programmer is able to associate new meanings with, say, the + symbol, or with an identifier which names one of the methods of a class, then the programmer is introducing multiple behaviors identified with the same name. This type of overloading is usually permitted in object-oriented languages for methods named with identifiers. However, whether or not overloading of operator symbols is allowed depends on the language.

Let us turn now to a consideration of generic programming, our second "polymorphic" language feature which does not fit the usual definition of polymorphism. We begin with a discussion of how to make method definitions "generic."

Method definitions are a form of algorithm, and so a method represents a prescribed sequence of actions which, taken in concert, return a result or produce an internal change in the state of an object. Let us take, for example, the following Java method for the `Point` class above:

```
public void translate(int delta_x, int delta_y) {
    x += delta_x;
    y += delta_y;
}
```

The algorithm is simple. To translate a point (x, y) to a new position in the coordinate plane, simply add a specific amount `delta_x` to the x-coordinate and another amount `delta_y` to the y-coordinate. But notice that although the method specifically uses the integer data type for its parameters, the algorithm is in fact more general than that. Addition makes sense across a range of several different numeric types, so the pair `(delta_x, delta_y)` could be assigned any combination of those types and the algorithm would make perfectly good sense. Why then are the parameters declared to be integers? It is because the syntax of the language requires the assignment of a specific type to every parameter of a method.

Consider, by way of contrast, the Python method below, assuming the `Point` class to be set up in a similar way in that language:

```
def translate(self, delta_x, delta_y):
    self.x += delta_x
    self.y += delta_y
```

Notice that `delta_x` and `delta_y` are not assigned a type by the syntax of the language. In fact, the success or failure of a call to this method depends not on whether the correct types of arguments are passed to it but rather on whether or not the `+=` operation makes sense when it is applied to each of those arguments.

Python achieves this degree of generality by delaying its decision about what to do in response to the `+=` operation until run-time. This incurs a cost which languages like C++, and to a lesser extent Java, cannot afford. The more decisions a language postpones until run-time, the more slowly programs in that language tend to run, simply because the decision must be made over and over while the program executes. C++ puts a premium on fast execution speeds; therefore, utilizing a design such as Python employs is not an option.

C++ offers a variety of solutions to this problem. For example, using a C++ version of the `translate` method above with arguments which are not integer but are primitive numeric types would trigger a coercion and produce at most a warning at compile time. But the most general C++ solution to such problems is to use a construct called a *template*, which allows automatic compile-time generation of a new version of the method which fits each different use of that method. The method itself is defined as a method template, not an ordinary method, and its definition looks as follows:

```
template<class NumericType1, class NumericType2>
void translate(NumericType1 delta_x, NumericType2 delta_y) {
    x += static_cast<int>(delta_x);
    y += static_cast<int>(delta_y);
}
```

Here, NumericType1 and NumericType2 are template parameters for which the call on translate will implicitly determine and transmit actual types. Supposing, then, that p is a Point object, the two calls p.translate(20,30) and p.translate(21.5,45.7) would actually call into play two different functions, both named *translate* and both generated from the template above. Because the types of the two literals 20 and 30 are both int and those of 21.5 and 45.7 are double, the effect is as if we had coded two functions, one with the interface void translate(int,int) and the other with the interface void translate(double,double). The template mechanism will, in fact, generate as many different versions of the method as are needed.

This mechanism is clearly unrelated to the style of polymorphism we described in Section 1.3, and it is not necessarily associated with object-oriented programming. But it is nevertheless a very strong kind of polymorphism. Because it is a compile-time mechanism, it is often called "compile-time polymorphism." Because templates work by generating different versions of the same construct, all named identically, compile-time polymorphism cannot be implemented in a language that does not permit programmer-defined overloading.

NOTE

Note the complementary sets of characteristics applying to run-time and compile-time polymorphism. With the first, we are able to define a large number of different methods, all having the same interface, and a run-time mechanism is used to select between those methods. Each new method, however, requires a separate definition and may use a totally different algorithm. With the second, there is only one definition of a construct (typically a method, function, or class) in the program, yet all the different compile-time-generated versions of the construct employ different interfaces.

We use the term *generic* to refer to nontype-specific code. By defining the term as the opposite of "type-specific," we are admitting the above Python method definition as a generic method, and the reader should be aware that to some programmers the term would not be used in this way. But by making our definitions language-independent, we allow a broader discussion and room to compare different ways of achieving the goals of a programming language design. Using this definition allows us to state clearly that all the languages discussed in this text provide some facilities for generic programming. The thing that C++ templates (and Java generics as well) provide is the ability to use a generic program construct to generate at compile time multiple type-specific versions of that construct.

Generic method definitions using type parameters are only one way of using compile-time polymorphism. Once one admits the concept of a parameter whose argument can be a type, any encapsulated program unit potentially could be generalized to a generic form. Commonly encountered examples of this are generic classes and generic stand-alone procedures.

1.2 ALTERNATIVE LANGUAGE PARADIGMS

Higher-level languages structure the way we think about solving problems, and each such language puts forth one or more *paradigms*, or central ideas, about how to construct problem solutions. Object-oriented is certainly not the first paradigm, nor will it likely be the last. In this section, we will briefly discuss the major alternatives which pre-date the object-oriented paradigm and are still in use today.

1.2.1 Introduction—Some Basic Terminology

In the same sense as *point* and *line* are used as undefined terms in geometry, we will start here with some undefined, or vaguely defined, terms. To begin with, we will use the term *symbol* with only the vague definition that it is a name with a meaning, either predefined or programmer-defined. We use the term *identifier* to mean a symbol with a name which is allowed to be multi-character, which is used by the programmer for his own purposes, and which is atomic, i.e., not divisible into component parts. An identifier might be used, for example, to name a stored object or a type. There are in any given language some simple formation rules for what constitutes a valid identifier, and we will assume the reader has experience using identifiers. A *keyword* is a symbol that may conform to the rules for formation of identifiers, but which has a language-defined meaning in certain contexts. Examples of symbols often used as keywords are `if`, `else`, and `while`. A keyword which cannot be used for any other purpose than its language-defined meaning is called a *reserved word*.

We make only a weak attempt to define the term *value*. The term is general enough to apply to a wide range of well-conceived and rigorously defined entities, but in general it has two essential aspects: it has meaning in some context, and it can be represented by an encoding into a string of binary digits. A *literal* is a self-defining symbol, i.e., one which has a value and whose name describes its value. Some examples taken from the C-derived languages are the character string literal "`A string literal`" and the double-precision floating point literal `25.7`. The term *token* is used to refer to an indivisible symbol in the text of a program. Examples are identifiers, keywords, operator symbols, literals, and bracketing symbols (e.g., parenthesis characters and square bracket characters).

A *constant* is a named, immutable value. Depending on the implementation, the name of a constant refers to either (1) a storage address which is initialized with the particular value at the time the constant is defined and for which an attempt to change its value causes an error condition, or (2) the value itself, which replaces the name wherever it is used. A *variable* is a named storage location whose value is subject to change.

An *association* is a (*symbol, meaning*) pair. In most languages the only associations under the programmer's control are *identifier* associations, in which the symbol used is formed as a valid identifier in the language. In a few languages the programmer may also introduce his own associations for operator symbols, such as the plus sign. A *scope rule* is a rule for determining at any given time, or at any given location in the text of a program, the set of associations which currently applies.

NOTE

> *The meaning of a symbol is in some languages totally unambiguous at all points in the text of a program, meaning that it can be traced back to exactly one definition without examining its context in any detail. That is not usually the case in modern object-oriented languages, however. Most such languages allow the programmer to overload the meanings of symbols, so that multiple associations can exist at the same time for one symbol, with detailed considerations of context determining the precise meaning.*

A *symbol table* is a table of associations. Symbol tables are used in all language implementations, either during the translation of source code, at run-time, or both. The structure of a symbol table is typically that of a hash table, because it is necessary to fetch the meaning of the identifier quickly and no advantage accrues by keeping any particular order in the storing of associations, other than a natural hierarchy imposed by the program structure itself. If such a hierarchy exists, as it does in any language with any degree of sophistication, then the symbol table will typically be a collection of hash tables, the structure of which is dictated by the structure of programs in the language, or a single hash table for which an access using a particular symbol as key calls up an ordered list of associations for that symbol.

A *declaration* is a program statement which provides information concerning an association, information which can be recorded in a symbol table. A *definition* is a declaration which provides a precise and complete meaning for a symbol. A *reference* to an association is a usage of the associated symbol in the text of a source code unit which calls forth the particular meaning specified in the association. The word "reference" can also be used as a verb, meaning to use a symbol in a way which calls forth an association. The *referencing environment* at any given time is the set of all associations which are currently available for referencing.

A *block* is a sequence of executable statements, possibly including some declarations, which is encapsulated by a procedure definition framework or by bracketing symbols (*begin* and *end*, for example, or C-style set braces). In most programming languages, a block is considered a statement, so that the syntactic category "statement" is recursively defined and therefore a block can be nested inside a block, inside a block, etc., to any nesting level.

A *static* scope rule is a scope rule which is defined using textual position. In other words, the meaning of a reference to a symbol x depends on where x occurs in the text of the program unit. A *dynamic* scope rule is a scope rule which is defined based on a history of run-time actions. In this case, the meaning of x depends on the particular pattern of the program's execution. The scope of an association is therefore either the extent of program text at which a reference to the given identifier or other symbol could be resolved using that association (in the case of static scope rules) or the span of program execution time during which a reference to the identifier could be so resolved (in the case of dynamic scope rules).

_____

NOTE

Most languages which are currently in widespread use employ static scope rules. An exception is the special-purpose language Mathematica [Wolfram10], whose programs are actually mathematical documents with embedded, separately executable cells. A Mathematica document has a single global scope, and the meaning of any identifier at any point in the document depends on which cells have been evaluated and in what order.

A *global association* is one that applies in all contexts of the program. The term *local association* can best be defined as one which is not global, but it usually refers to an association with a very limited scope, often qualified by a description of that program unit to which it is local; for example, we could say that x is *local to* method $f()$, or to a block within that method. In the same way, associations which are not local in the most restrictive sense may be called simply "nonlocal" or "local to" some program unit of intermediate size.

1.2.2 The Imperative Programming Paradigm

The classical procedural languages (Algol, Fortran, Pascal, C, etc.) are first of all *imperative* languages, meaning that work is accomplished by the sequential execution of commands, each of which may require the evaluation of one or more operations. Each command changes the state of the executing program and its environment, so that a correctly constructed program steers the system into a sequence of target states which serve the purposes of the user. The way that control is exerted over the sequence in which those commands and operations are executed and evaluated (the *sequence control* mechanisms of the language) varies somewhat between imperative languages, but falls generally into two categories: *expression-level* sequence control and *statement-level* sequence control.

Definition

The *arity* of an operation is the number of operands it has. For example, the prefix negation operation seen in the expression $-a$ has arity 1, whereas the same symbol denotes an arity 2 operation in the expression $a - b$. An arity 2 expression formatted in this way, i.e., so that the operator symbol is positioned between the two operands, is called an *infix* expression.

The mechanisms typically used for expression-level sequence control are operator precedence and associativity rules, which along with the use of parentheses for overriding those rules will define the order of execution down to the *expression tree* level. For example, in most imperative languages the expression

$$a + b * (c + d)/(7 * n)$$

defines the expression tree in Figure 1.1. This tree does not provide all the details of evaluation order, because the two multiplications could take place in either order and still satisfy the requirements of the tree. The choice of which multiplication to evaluate first is typically up to the implementer of the language, not its designer. There are some notable exceptions to this rule, in which the precise order of evaluation of the nodes of the tree is specified in the language definition, but such a policy hampers optimization of the generated code by the compiler.

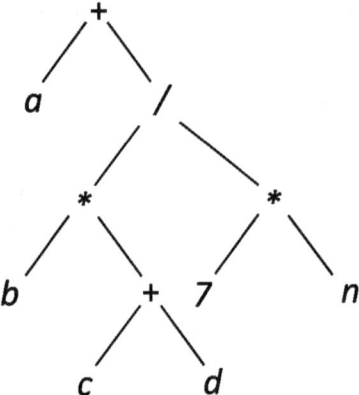

FIGURE 1.1 An expression tree.

In rare cases in practical programming, the programmer may be vitally interested in knowing the order of evaluation beyond that specified by the tree. If a function call is made which causes *side effects*, that is, changes to the machine state that are not apparent in the function's interface, then it may matter greatly whether a given function has been called at a particular time. A case in point is *short-circuit Boolean operations*, versions of the logical "and" and "or" operations that sometimes evaluate only the left-hand operand. Using "or" as an example, the Java or C++ expression `pred(a,b)||pred(c,d)` evaluates `pred(a,b)` first, and if it is true skips the second evaluation `pred(c,d)`. This causes problems if the programmer meant to take advantage of some side effect (such as output to the screen) expected to be caused by that evaluation.

NOTE

Side effects excepted, expression-level programming language operations are all essentially just function applications, and precedence and associativity rules are there to guide the order in which composition of functions occurs. But the only reason such guides to evaluation order are necessary is because of the widespread use of infix notation for operations such as addition and multiplication.

Besides infix, there are two other notational conventions which can be used for *any* function, no matter what its arity. These are *prefix*, in which the operator symbol precedes its operands, and *postfix*, in which the operator follows its operands. As an example, consider the infix expression $a + b$. Using prefix it might appear as $+(a\ b)$ or $(+a\ b)$. Using postfix it might appear as $(a, b) +$ or even $a\ b\ +$. Note that both of these notational conventions are totally general, representing a function call of arity 3 as $f(x, y, z)$ or $x\ y\ z\ f$, for example. (An interesting thing here is that postfix does not require any parentheses or other grouping tokens as long as the arity of each function can be determined without ambiguity.) Both postfix and prefix precisely specify the order of function composition without using precedence or associativity rules.

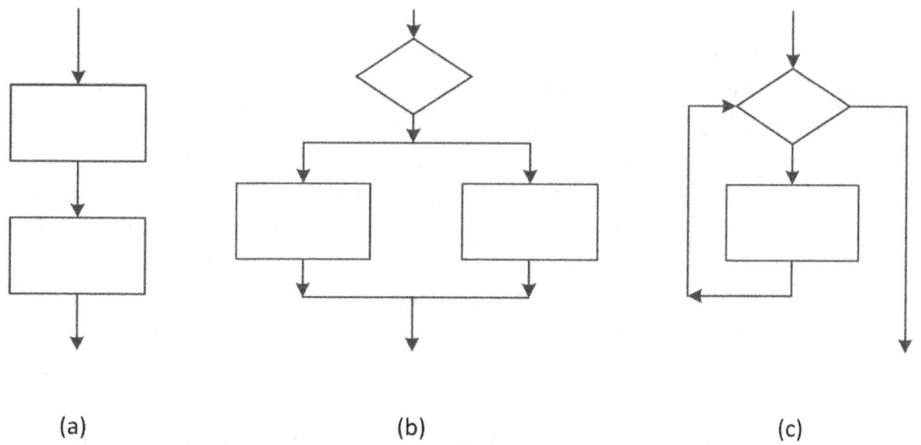

(a) (b) (c)

FIGURE 1.2 The three structured programming constructs: (a) Sequence, (b) Selection, and (c) Iteration.

Modern programming languages base statement-level sequence control on the structured programming mechanisms of *sequence, selection*, and *repetition*. The *sequence* principle simply codifies what we universally assume in western cultures is the natural order of things: left to right and top to bottom. It states that a sequentially arranged block of statements will be executed in order, from first to last. This is the default control mechanism in most languages. For this reason, a sequence of consecutive statements in an imperative language is represented in flow diagrams as a linear graph such as that in Figure 1.2(a), where the nodes are program statements and the arrows provide a visual representation of the order of execution. The sequence mechanism, like the other mechanisms, applies not only to individual statements but also to encapsulated blocks of statements. In structured languages such an encapsulated block satisfies the technical definition of a statement. Thus each rectangle in the above diagram could represent not just a single statement but another structured program unit, such as a block. All three of the structured programming constructs are typically classified as statements in the language, and therefore in any of the sequence diagrams here we can replace any rectangle with one of these structured constructs.

A language feature which implements the *selection* control structuring principle will allow execution to proceed to exactly one of two statements, or one of two structured program units, based on the truth or falsity of a Boolean condition. The keyword universally used to introduce such a structure is *if*, and its flow diagram appears in Figure 1.2(b), where the Boolean condition is represented by the diamond-shaped box. Sometimes this structure is referred to as a *two-way* selection, as opposed to a *one-way* selection, in which the "false branch" is empty.

Finally, *repetition* shows up in procedural and other styles of programming languages as a control structure introduced, usually, with the keyword *while*. It is a simple looping construct which is entered in the same way a selection construct is entered, i.e., by testing the truth value of some Boolean expression. In the classic *while* construct, if the expression evaluates to *true* then a particular statement (or structured program unit) called the *loop body* is executed and control returns to the same Boolean expression afterwards. If the expression evaluates to *false*, then control proceeds to the next statement, as indicated by the flow diagram in Figure 1.2(c). We call this a *pretest* loop because a "test," in the form of the above-mentioned Boolean expression, guards its entry.

These are the three structured programming principles, and all modern imperative programming languages support them. In addition, one usually finds a multiway selection structure, typically called a *case* or a *switch* construct, and additional looping constructs. *Post-test* loops, where the test is executed after the body of the loop instead of before, are common, as are iterated loops which use an integer counter or some more general control strategy, but which always have an *increment* step which presumably brings the program state closer to the exit condition of the loop with each execution.

NOTE

An alternative to structuring imperative programs with the structured programming principles is simply to import from the machine level of abstraction the jump instruction (referred to in high-level languages as the "goto") and the "test and branch" operation. The latter strategy is illustrated by the Dartmouth BASIC code

```
IF X>=0 THEN 400
```

which tests to see if variable X's value is non-negative, then does one of two things. If X is indeed non-negative, the next instruction to be executed will be the instruction labeled 400. If that is not the case, then no interruption in the default instruction sequence will occur.

Early languages like BASIC and FORTRAN depended heavily on gotos and on test and branch, and the programming community resisted moving to languages which did not incorporate it. Two publications ensured the ultimate rejection of such primitive control structures. First, a theoretical result of Böhm and Jocopini [Böhm66] was published which proved that the three structured programming constructs were sufficient for constructing an equivalent flow graph for any program. Second, influential computer scientist Edsger Dijkstra published a letter in the *Communications of the ACM* which the editors titled "Goto considered harmful" [Dijkstra68], in which Dijkstra argued not only that branch instructions were unnecessary in a high-level language, but that a heavy reliance on them results in programs that are harder to read, and therefore harder to maintain. That letter generated much acrimony, but its good sense and the highly regarded status of the writer ultimately carried the day.

1.2.3   Procedural Programming Languages

Serious imperative languages are based on an abstraction called the *procedure*. A procedure is like a disembodied method, meaning that it is an active, encapsulated program unit which is like a method but does not belong to a higher-level structure. The only things which give a procedure a context in which to execute are the parameters which were passed to it and any global associations that may apply. The procedure has two possible forms, one which explicitly returns a value and one which does not. Procedures which do not return a value are assumed to perform their work by causing side effects. Such side effects are usually changes in the value or the internal state of one or more data items or data aggregates, but may also be changes in the external environment. Examples of the latter would be changes to data files, display changes, or file system modifications.

A procedure which has no side effects and does its work only by returning a value is a *pure function*, and often the term *function* is employed to mean a pure function. Pure functions work without causing side effects, so that the only work they do (from the standpoint of the client) is to compute and return that value. Theoretically, any state change can be modeled as a returned value, if we broaden our concept of a "value" to include all the encoded state information for a large and complex object. This fact has caused purists to argue against side effects, because side effects make programs more difficult to read and maintain, and functions have much better qualities for the purpose of constructing correctness proofs. We will say more about this point of view in the next section, in which we cover functional programming.

Traditionally, we speak of the procedure in which execution first begins as the *main program*. Thus, a procedural program consists of one main program and a collection of procedures and functions, viewed as *subprograms*. We will often use the more general term *program unit* to refer to a subprogram, a method, or an object with active content. The act of one program unit in transferring control to another is called a *call*. The program unit which relinquishes control is the *caller*, and the program unit which receives control is the *callee*, or the *called* unit.

An essential part of the communication between caller and callee is the transmission of a portion of the state of the caller into that of the callee by means of parameter passing. To make our terminology specific, we will refer to a variable receiving the state information during a call as a *parameter*, and we will refer to the value, object, or address being transmitted as the *argument*. Both these terms are specializations of the more generic term *operand*, which is used to refer to any entity serving as data for a computation.

Implementation of procedures is based on a machine-level concept, namely the *subroutine*. A machine-language subroutine is a block of machine-executable instructions, identified by the address of the first instruction, to which control is transferred using a machine-level mechanism that "remembers" the context in which it was executing when the transfer occurred. This transfer of control is a primitive call mechanism. Arguments of such a call have historically been passed by placing values or addresses in registers or on a hardware-defined stack, or by placing the address of a parameter block in a register. Thus, a statement which calls procedure *init*, coded in FORTRAN as

```
call init(a,b,c)
```

or in Pascal or Algol as

```
init(a,b,c)
```

might be translated into the sequence

```
push a
push b
push c
jsub init
```

on a machine with a hardware stack and a *jsub* instruction which implements a low-level "jump to subroutine" operation. Whereas the language must associate types with variables *a*, *b*, and *c*, and an abstractly defined procedure with *init*, the machine language equivalents of the above four statements will replace all four symbols with memory addresses (or with computations yielding memory addresses) which are ultimately typeless.

1.2.4 Functional Programming Languages

To most programmers, the notion of basing a language design on nothing but value-returning functions would seem ludicrous. We think of a program as supervising a *process*, not as computing a single value. Yet every program does in fact compute a value, and most of the states reached along the way to that computation are unimportant. For every "important" state the machine achieves along the way to the completion of its computation, there are usually only a few components of that state in which the programmer is interested, and which taken in their entirety characterize that state. So the "value" computed by a program, which characterizes the purpose of the program, can be thought of as a vector of encapsulated chunks of state information. That vector may be quite simple or quite complex, but it can certainly be considered a value. It is for this reason that the functional style of programming is in fact a general-purpose programming paradigm.

The notion of functional programming (*FP*) arose from a paper by John Backus [Backus78], in which he introduces a series of *combining forms* for constructing a program from basic functions such as constant functions and identity functions. For example, two single-valued functions can be combined using a vector-forming combining form, thus constructing a vector-valued function. Conversely, a vector-valued function can be projected into one dimension to produce a single-valued function. An *FP* environment needs only a set of precompiled elementary functions, a set of rules and notations for managing identifier (and/or operator symbol) associations, and a set of notations for applying the necessary combining forms.

One early realization of Backus' ideas was the *ifp* language (Illinois functional programming), which used postfix notation for function application and denoted the composition of two functions *f* and *g* using the Unix-like notation *f* | *g*. It could convert a single-valued function *f* of one variable into a vector-valued function of *n* variables using the notation *each f end*. Thus, the notation $<x_1, x_2>$: *each f end* stands for a computation which returns the value$<x_1:f, x_2:f>$. The built-in function *trans* applies to *n* vectors, each of size *m*, and computes an *n* by *m* "transpose," so that for example the expression

$$<<x_1, x_2><y_1, y_2>>: \text{trans}$$

yields the result $<<x_1, y_1><y_2, x_2>>$. The function *trans* | *each* ∗ *end* | *insert* + *end* computes the inner product of two vectors.

Actually, most languages which are thought of as "functional" involve some aspects of other programming language paradigms, usually allowing the programmer to construct sequences of expressions with side effects in order to mimic the imperative paradigm in places where it is convenient to do so.

NOTE

The LISP language or one of its variants is often used to teach functional programming, and instructors initially avoid teaching the imperative aspects of the language. De-emphasizing these "corrupting" features allows the instructor to show students the full power of the functional paradigm, in which recursion replaces looping as a mechanism for causing and controlling repetitive actions.

One feature commonly encountered in functional languages is the dynamic binding of identifiers or operator symbols to functions, thus permitting function-valued variables. Along with some form of "apply" operation, illustrated in Figure 1.3, this capability allows the programmer to associate different actions with the same program text at different times.

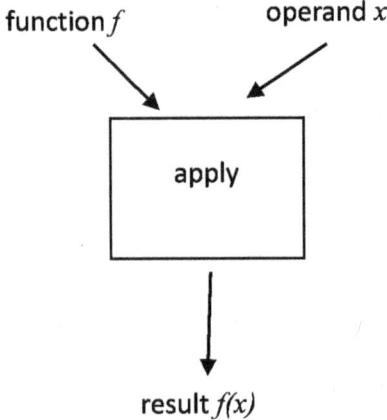

FIGURE 1.3 The "apply" operation.

Some functional languages go so far as to provide data types whose values can be dynamically altered then executed as functions. For example, in LISP the most prominent data structure is that of a linked list, and that structure is also the form of an uncompiled function definition. The definition can be dynamically manipulated as a data structure, after which it can be compiled and executed.

Let us elaborate on the example set by LISP. The LISP language has a form of literal which represents a linked list as a space-separated list of tokens enclosed by parentheses, so that (25 X 1.7) is a linked list with three elements: the integer 25, the symbol X, and the floating point number 1.7. Such lists can be assigned to variables and manipulated at run-time. Interestingly, such lists are also the run-time representation of program code, so that (+ 27 48), if compiled and evaluated, will yield the value 75. But both the "compile" and "evaluate" operations are actually LISP primitives available for the programmer to incorporate into a program, so that if a variable is initialized *at run-time* to the empty list and to that list are added, in turn, the + symbol, the value 27, and the value 48, then the resulting data object can be dynamically compiled and evaluated, again yielding the value 75.

Functional programming languages often give dual citizenship to functions, viewing them both as active program components and as values which can be assigned. They therefore go at least part-way along the road to considering functions as *first-class objects*. A precise definition of this term is given in Section 1.5, but the short definition is that a first-class object not only can be bound as the value of a variable, as discussed in the previous paragraph, but can be sent messages and has a type which is a class in the object-oriented sense. A function with such qualities might seem to be a rare bird, but there are settings in which those qualities can be quite useful, one of which is that in which a function is dynamically associated with an event, as an event handler. The *delegate* type in C#, for example, takes a view of functions which approximates this ideal. C++ has "function objects," which are not functions at all but objects of a class type which has been given a programmer-defined "function application" operation.

1.2.5 Modular Programming Languages

Sandwiched between the purely procedural languages and what we would consider the "modern" object-oriented languages are the *modular* languages. The term *module* has been used in several ways throughout the history of programming languages, and generally refers to a named program unit, encompassing both code and data, which has a well-defined purpose and an explicit interface. In the broadest sense of the term, "module" could refer to anything that could be used as a "building block" for modular construction of programs, including a simple procedure or function definition. The Modula 2 language makes the term more specific, and gives it more power. A Modula 2 module encapsulates, on an equal basis, a collection of types, variables, constants, and procedures, along with some initialization code. Such a module must explicitly "export" all such items which it wishes to make available for public use, and all modules which use those items must explicitly "import" them. All items in a module which are not exported are "hidden" by default.

To illustrate the structure of a Modula 2 module, we present the following piece of code. This code is simple but a bit wordy, because it is specifically constructed to attempt to illustrate a point. The point is that, omitting inheritance considerations, all one needs in order to achieve the same purpose in Modula 2 as is achieved by a class in an object-oriented language is to have the module export a type along with operations which manipulate objects of that type.

```
MODULE PointOps;
    EXPORT Point, getX, getY, setXY;
    TYPE Point =
        RECORD
            x, y: INTEGER;
        END;
    PROCEDURE getX(p: Point): INTEGER;
    BEGIN
        RETURN p.x;
    END getX;
    PROCEDURE getY(p: Point): INTEGER;
    BEGIN
        RETURN p.y;
    END getY;
    PROCEDURE setXY(VAR p: Point; x, y: INTEGER);
    BEGIN
        IF (x >= 0 AND y >= 0) THEN
            p.x := x;
            p.y := y;
        END;
    END setXY;
END PointOps.
```

The code is somewhat absurd because of the difference in information hiding characteristics. Records do not have any ability to separate public items from private items, so that by exporting the type Point our PointOps module is also exporting public access to that type's x and y components. So a call like getX(p) looks silly to a Modula 2 programmer, who could much more naturally code p.x. In fact, a sequence of Java code such as the following will look awkward when translated directly into Modula 2.

```
Point p = new Point();
p.setXY(25,37);
...
```

```
int baseX = p.getX();
int baseY = p.getY();
```

The translation, put into the context of a Modula 2 main module, is as follows:

```
MODULE PointMain;
    FROM PointOps IMPORT Point, getX, getY, setXY;
    ...
    VAR
        p:  Point;
        baseX, baseY: INTEGER;
    BEGIN
        setXY(p,25,37);
        ...
        baseX := getX(p);
        baseY := getY(p);
        ...
END PointMain.
```

The point of view of the modular programmer, who has never directly experienced the benefits of inheritance and polymorphism and has a different view of information hiding, is that the association of types with the operations on those types can be done with the "more general" module structuring concept, and that much more can be done with that concept. In fact, if all we are looking for is a facility for constructing abstract data types the argument deserves to be heard. There is a conceptual shortcoming to this approach, however, which has to do with *ownership*. With the class concept each type *owns* not only its associated data components but also the operations which manipulate that data. With the module concept, the association is weaker and is imposed artificially by the programmer using a structuring concept not precisely intended for that purpose.

Ada provides a nearly identical program organization tool with its *package* construct. The only difference between an Ada package and a Modula 2 module is that instead of explicitly selecting identifier associations to be exported, the package must explicitly select those which are to be hidden. The C++ *namespace* is very similar, except that all the code for a namespace does not have to be included in a single source file, nor even in a contiguous area of program text.

1.2.6 Declarative Programming Languages

Opposed to the idea of *imperative* programming is that of *declarative* programming. A declarative program defines relationships and provides the programmer the opportunity to search for entities satisfying those relationships, rather than explicitly specifying a sequence of program steps. Like any useful language, a declarative language has a library of functions which are predefined. Those which return Boolean results are called *predicates*, and the programmer is allowed to define his own predicates. In fact, the process of writing a declarative program is precisely that of defining predicates, either by making simple assertions or by specifying rules which the run-time system (sometimes called an *inference engine*) can use for its reasoning processes.

The most prevalent form of declarative programming is based on the *Horn clause*, which is an *if...then* statement consisting of a conjunction of conditions and a conclusion. In the Prolog language, the conclusion is stated first and the separate clauses in the conjunction are separated by commas. For example, given that the predicate `parent(a,b)` states that a is a parent of b, a statement that indicates two people are first cousins if one has a parent who is a sibling of the other's parent could be made as follows:

```
firstcousins(X,Y)  :-
     parent(P1,X), parent(P2,Y), siblings(P1,P2), X \= Y.
```

Here X, Y, P1, and P2 are typeless variables which can be bound by a pattern-matching process called *unification*. We can add the following Horn clauses to our program in order to provide it with enough information to answer a query.

```
parent(linda,george).
parent(bob,george).
parent(linda,michael).
parent(bob,michael).
parent(sue,fred).
parent(george,fred).
parent(jane,jennifer).
parent(michael,jennifer).
siblings(X,Y)  :- parent(P,X), parent(P,Y), X \= Y.
```

Now the query

```
siblings(X,george).
```

yields the result

```
X = michael
```

Prolog will find as many correct answers as it can to a given query, so that if we were to add

```
parent(linda,bill).
parent(bob,bill).
```

to the program, then the same query would get the two results

```
X = michael
X = bill
```

The query

```
firstcousins(X,Y).
```

yields the results

```
X = fred, Y = jennifer
X = jennifer, Y = fred
```

A pure declarative program does not specify any order in which to search for the results of a query, but obviously an implementation must choose such an order. A declarative program based on Horn clauses is a directed graph, enabling many different search strategies. Typically, a Prolog query such as the one above invokes a *backward chaining* process, which is a goal-oriented search that uses the query itself as its initial goal and begins the search by looking for Horn clauses whose conclusions match that query. For all such clauses, Prolog unifies the variables involved and adds all the premises on the right of the clause to its list of goals. Every time it finishes such an investigation for a given goal, it deletes the goal it has just investigated from that list and selects another goal. At that point in time, it matters greatly which of the goals it attempts to match next.

NOTE

Programmers who are new to this paradigm mistakenly assume that they should not worry about the particularities of the engine which conducts the search. As they gain experience, they become informed of those particularities and of ways to affect the order in which rules are applied. They become better informed about ways to optimize the search, to prune unproductive search directions, or to find certain solutions before others. In other words, programmers in such languages begin to think like the search algorithm, so that they become keenly aware of the sequence of pattern-matching and inference steps that make the program work.

A difficult problem to surmount in using Prolog and languages like it is that there is no way to assert in a Prolog program that a given predicate is false. All assertions are true assertions. Certainly one can try to fashion predicates in pairs such as pred(X,Y) and notpred(X,Y), and such an approach sometimes works, but typically the only way for a Prolog program to detect that a statement is false is to attempt to use the assertions it has to prove it true, and then to fail. This is logically acceptable only if complete information on the entities involved is included in the database. Moreover, the "negation as failure" policy may be unacceptable in practice because of performance constraints.

In spite of its problems, a programmer with the right goals and attitudes can make very good use of a declarative language. Like the other paradigms we have discussed in this section, it will be a significant force in the programming language field for the foreseeable future, and a programmer having no familiarity with it may pass up the chance at finding elegant and useful solutions to some common problems. Moreover, a familiarity with this paradigm will educate the programmer to a way of thinking about relationships which will enrich the solution space no matter what programming tools are available.

1.3   RELEVANT PROGRAMMING LANGUAGE CONCEPTS

We review in this section some of the concepts to which the student should have been exposed in previous courses, but for which the instruction may not have been explicit or may have been specifically targeted for one language and/or environment. We will attempt to give a broader and more explicit introduction to these topics. We begin with the most fundamental, and perhaps the most important, term in this text.

1.3.1 Abstraction

Computer Science shares with Mathematics a preoccupation with the process of creating and defining the properties of abstractions. But abstraction is not solely the domain of those two fields of study; it lies at the core of all intellectual endeavors. At the most fundamental level, an *abstraction* is a scheme for substituting symbols (and sometimes also a set of artificially defined rules for manipulating those symbols) for objects or concepts. We say that the objects or concepts come from a *semantic* domain, a concrete or abstract domain from which a person selects the *meaning* of the abstraction.

To the person creating an abstraction, the denizens of the semantic domain are usually considered to exist in a way which is to some extent independent of that person's creative input, and may in fact be only partially understood by him. The intention in defining the abstraction is to rigidly specify the properties and rules for manipulating the abstraction in ways totally understood by the creator, properties and manipulations that are at least analogous to the properties and behaviors of the semantic counterpart. The hope is that by analyzing the properties or performing the manipulations, conclusions may be reached, or work may be accomplished, and that the conclusions will be relevant or the work will be of benefit to those who have an interest in the semantic domain.

If we have properly constructed the abstraction and followed our rules in manipulating it, we may say that the results of manipulating the abstraction are *consistent*. We cannot say that those conclusions are *relevant* in the semantic domain, however, unless we can independently confirm those results by our own observation. The measure of goodness of an abstraction is the extent to which consistent and valid conclusions tend to be reliably relevant. Computer programs and their various named components are such abstractions, as are the names introduced in mathematical theorems and proofs. The Calculus of Leibniz and Newton and the lambda calculus of Church and Kleene introduce several celebrated and highly useful higher-level abstractions.

An abstraction is usually simpler than its corresponding semantic entity. That entity may in fact have far more properties and capabilities than those which have been incorporated into the corresponding abstraction. For example, a note sung by a human voice is far more complex than the simple wave form with which we abstract it, but without substituting the simpler, better understood abstraction there is no way a proper study could be made of music. This *hiding of irrelevant detail* is an essential ingredient of the abstraction process.

The central activity of the abstraction process is that of *naming*. We name things we understand well, and we (sometimes superstitiously) give names to things we do not quite understand. We manipulate the name itself, by using it in conversation or in writing or in hand or machine computations and manipulations, subconsciously associating it with other names that have meaning to us. As others listen, read, interpret the results of a computation or a series of mathematical derivations, or interact with a computer program, the abstractions they observe communicate to them the ideas and concepts that are embodied there. This is the way knowledge advances, and in the world of the computer scientist this is the way actual work can be accomplished.

NOTE

Mathematicians are very parsimonious with their names, using typically less than half a dozen in a proof or discussion, some of them persistent names ("By the Pythagorean Theorem, …") and some of them useful only for a paragraph or two ("Let x be the distance travelled…"). Computer scientists and software engineers, on the other hand, may use many thousands of names in constructing a large and complex software system. In doing so, they create some of the most complex artifacts known to man, artifacts that dramatically affect the lives of human beings all over the planet. These artifacts, computer programs, can become so complex in their design that they baffle the most brilliant of individuals. Hierarchically structuring and modularizing the system, giving names to key elements and making sure those names are understood by key individuals, makes it possible for many minds to be brought to bear on the understanding, construction, and maintenance of the

> *system. That is why the building of useful abstractions must be a*
> *central activity for us, and why the study of languages for coher-*
> *ently building layered abstractions (i.e., programming languages)*
> *is central to the discipline of computer science.*

Let us bring to an end our greatly prolonged discourse on abstraction and make the specific application. In programming language terms, abstraction is nothing more than a technique. The higher level discussion above provides us a clue to its meaning, however. When a scientist creates a simple abstraction, such as a name for a species, we put the name up front and use it instead of lower level abstractions (omnivorous bipedal marsupial with prehensile tail). Although we are generally aware of its meaning, we use the name as an "interface" to that meaning, hiding the details of the definition behind the name. Thus, for us abstraction consists of (1) creating a name for some program entity, (2) defining an interface through which the entity can be accessed and manipulated, and (3) hiding all details from view which have no explicit representation in the interface. It can accurately be stated that the true power of a programming language is most fairly measured by the degree to which it gives the programmer the ability to create useful abstractions in an easy and natural way.

1.3.2 Syntax and Semantics

The rules for constructing abstractions in a computer program are called *syntax rules*, and a collection of symbols consisting of a properly ordered sequence of simple and complex names, bracketing symbols, operator symbols, and keywords, is referred to as a *syntactic construct*. The aspects of a language which govern the correct formation of syntactic constructs are called its *syntax*, and the meaning of that syntax is referred to as *semantics*. The latter as a general term is of necessity very loosely defined, but can for a specific language be precisely defined in terms of mathematical sets called *semantic domains*. In the discussion of the semantics of programming languages the semantic domains, although idealized as abstract domains such as the integers, real numbers, and free semigroups (strings and concatenation), are actually comparatively limited finite machine implementations of those domains. These limitations mean that we either have to lie about the meaning of an operation by speaking only of its usual effects, or we must continually be bogging down the discussion with the introduction of exceptional conditions such as integer overflow or insufficient space.

The syntax of a programming language is more easily described than its semantics, and can effectively be communicated using examples and discussions, but these discussions are usually supplemented with precise, formal notations. A formal description of syntax has two components. The simpler of those two components consists of *lexical* rules, i.e., rules for forming *tokens*, a term we first encountered in Section 1.2.1. Each token in a program is composed of a sequence of one or more characters, and the rules for forming tokens are usually very clear and easily checked. For example, we might say, "An identifier must consist of a single letter followed by a finite sequence of letters and digits."

Regular expressions are often used for specifying lexical rules, for example:

```
letter =
    a + b + c + d + e + f + g + h + i + j + k + l + m + n +
    o + p + q + r + s + t + u + v + w + x + y + z
digit = 0 + 1 + 2 + 3 + 4 + 5 + 6 + 7 + 8 + 9

identifier = letter (letter + digit)*
```

Here we are using the plus symbol (+) to mean "or" and the asterisk (*) to mean zero or more copies of the preceding element. Juxtaposition of two lexical elements indicates concatenation. The three operations of concatenation, +, and * are sufficient to fully describe the lexical rules of a language, but many lexical specification schemes introduce additional, more powerful operators in order to shorten the task of specifying the lexical structure of the language.

Once the tokens of the language have been fully specified, most of the higher-level syntactic rules can be specified using "context-free" productions which specify how the tokens of the language may be used to form correctly composed expressions, statements, and higher-level structures such as methods and classes. A context-free production is a rule for defining syntax elements, consisting of the name of the syntax element and a pattern which describes the correct formation of that element. A production in *Backus-Naur form* (BNF) consists of the name of a syntactic element, followed by the symbol "::=", followed by a collection of alternative patterns on the right, separated by "|" vertical slash symbols. In order to make the names of syntactic elements stand out, BNF notation encloses them in angular brackets, for example <*switch statement*> or <*identifier*>. An example follows:

```
<if statement prefix> ::= IF <Boolean expression>
                         THEN <statement sequence>
<if statement> ::= <if statement prefix> ENDIF |
                   <if statement prefix>
                      ELSE <statement sequence> ENDIF
```

Symbols not enclosed in angular brackets typically are keywords, bracketing symbols, or operator symbols of the language (such as *IF* in the example above) and are BNF literals, i.e., symbols representing themselves. The vertical slash connector connects two mutually exclusive alternatives.

Many variants of BNF exist; for example, some use different type faces instead of angular brackets, some use arrows instead of the ":: =" symbol, and some use flow-graph depictions instead of | and *. All of these various notations are logically equivalent.

Syntax rules which cannot be expressed with BNF are *context-sensitive* rules, and are typically not formalized but informally described with a narrative specification, such as "A variable must be declared before it is used."

NOTE
The syntax of the language is typically described in parallel with its semantics, meaning that as the proper forms are introduced and described syntactically the meaning of each form is specified with a narrative description and examples. The syntactic forms should be rigorously described, but that formal description is usually kept as a separate document for use by implementers, while the manuals for use by programmers are a mixture of informal syntax descriptions and semantic discussions. The case studies in this text follow the latter form.

Although the deeper issues of a language are to be found in the semantics, an understanding of the language must always begin with and be built around its syntax. Syntax is the "skeletal system" around which a language is built, and knowing the language syntax is essential to the serious programmer in that language.

1.3.3 Target Machines

An experienced student of languages will be able to examine the syntax rules and infer much of the semantics of the language. Simple syntax with few rules indicates a *software-simulated* language with dynamic binding of types to variables, possibly with dynamic scope rules, and with a semantics which is not easily mapped into features available on commonly encountered hardware machines. A language with a large number of syntax rules generally indicates a *compiled* language with features that, although radically more elaborate than those furnished by any hardware machine, are carefully designed to allow an efficient mapping onto the features of such a machine.

There is an intricate relationship between machines and the languages they are designed to understand and execute, a relationship which goes to the core of the idea of semantics. As we describe in detail the semantics of a language, we are in fact describing a machine. That machine is the *virtual machine* defined by the language, the one whose "machine language" is the programming language itself. The language implementation has as its task the "building" of the virtual machine, using a combination of two techniques: translation and execution. Translation transforms a syntactic structure into a different form, whereas execution uses the translated forms to direct the progress of an actual computation.

Translation transforms a program written in a *source language* into an equivalent program in a *target language*. The set of files containing the source language program is called the *source code*, and the file containing the translation is said to consist of *object code* and is called an *object file*.

If the target language is already recognizable to a particular operating system as "native code," then the language implementation consists only of a translator. On the other hand, if the object code is an artificial code unrecognizable in any already existing environment, then a *software interpreter* must be written for that code. A software interpreter is a program which mimics the operation of a CPU control register. In other words, it reads the individual instructions of the object code and executes those instructions, in much the same way as a real machine would execute them. It runs on an existing machine and implements the virtual machine defined by the language of the translated code.

NOTE

The extent and difficulty of translation depends on the gap between the form of the source language and that of the target language. The source language is simply that defined by the language reference manual, but the target language, that into which the language is translated for execution, may be radically different from the source language or may only be a simple, more compact translation and reordering of the source code elements.

Generally speaking, we say that a language is a *low-level* language if it is difficult for a human reader to understand but easy for a machine to read and execute. A language is *high-level* if it is designed for humans to understand more so than machines. The best definition we can make of a *compiled* language is that it is a high-level language intended for translation into low-level code. Because low-level machines have rigid expectations owing to the type-specific nature of the operations of which they are capable (integer division, floating point addition, etc.), a compiled language must specify in advance the types of operands in its various operations, and it must be possible by examining the source text to infer a sequence of low-level machine operations which constitutes an appropriate translation of that text.

There are two cases where the semantic gap between source and target languages is small: (a) low-level to low-level and (b) high-level to high-level. Some representatives of translators in class (a) are assemblers, linkage editors, and loaders. Class (b) translators are the rudimentary first step in *software simulation*, in which the target machine is not a hardware machine but a machine defined by a software interpreter. Languages which use the latter strategy tend to be languages that present an unusual execution paradigm, and include LISP, Snobol (a string processing language), APL, and Prolog. The translation of a program in such a language tends to be not much more than a compactification (a.k.a. *tokenization*) of the source program, replacing operators and certain keywords with integer codes, and replacing other identifiers with pointers into a symbol table. Even with such languages, compiling to native code is possible and may speed up execution because the software interpreter has been eliminated; however, if the basic operations of the language itself are radically different from those provided by the machine on which it runs, the "compiled" program will consist largely of calls to the same machine language subroutines which would have been invoked by the software interpreter. Consequently, such compilation may not greatly speed up execution.

In some cases, the language definition rigidly specifies the target machine and its language, to the extent that the precise mapping of syntax to semantics can be done once and for all. In these cases, the target machine is not an actual hardware machine but a virtual machine. Nonetheless, a virtual machine may have much in common with hardware machines. Indeed, just because a machine is software-simulated, it does not follow that its design must be radically different from that of a hardware machine. Regardless, once a translator is written for a language with a precisely specified target machine, that same translator can be easily ported at the source code level to another machine. In this case, the only step remaining in order to implement the language on the new machine is to write a software interpreter for the target language, effectively simulating the abstractly defined target machine on the actual machine. Two languages which use this approach are Java and C#.

NOTE
An alternative to software interpretation is just in time (JIT) compilation. In this case, the translator targets a low-level virtual machine, but when it is time to execute the translated program the code for the virtual machine is "compiled" into native code for the actual physical machine. (Here the quotes are to remind the reader that the translation is low-level to low-level and hence is not compilation by the definition given in this book.) Only the

code that is actually used in the particular run of the program is compiled, and when such code is revisited during that run the native code translation produced earlier will execute.

1.3.4 The Semantic Mapping, Parsing, and Syntactic Discontinuities

The semantic domain of a language implementation is the set of abstractions that are necessary for a programmer to understand in order to use the language. It is this semantic domain which must be implemented by the construction of a virtual machine, i.e., an implementation, for the language. The correspondence of a syntactic construct with its associated meaning in the semantic domain, an association which is largely prearranged by the language definition, is called the *semantic mapping*. The implementation of the language must actualize this mapping by (1) using the syntax rules to detect the structure of the program element to be translated, and then (2) using the semantic rules of the language and its own internal tables to associate meaning with that structure. Among other things, this means that the implementation must plan for static storage layout and for dynamic patterns of allocation and deallocation of storage, and it must also plan for the proper actions to occur at run-time, by generating code for the target machine.

The process of detecting syntactic structure is called *parsing*. The parsing of a syntactic construct is a sophisticated but well understood process, and its result may be an explicit data structure or a sequence of translation actions. For example, the expression from Section 1.2.2 could be translated into a data structure such as the one in Figure 1.4.

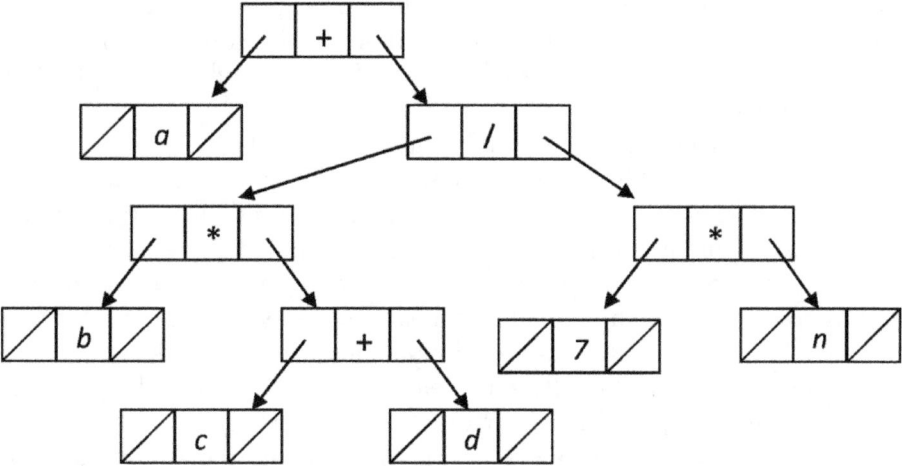

FIGURE 1.4 A run-time representation of an arithmetic expression.

Alternatively, the translated form of the expression could be a series of machine or assembly language statements such as the following.

```
Load    R1,c
Add     R1,d
Mul     R1,b
LI      R2,7
Load    R3,n
Mul     R2,R3
Div     R1,R2
Load    R3,a
Add     R1,R3
```

NOTE

In the process of generating such code it might be convenient to build a data structure as an intermediate form of the expression, or it might be preferred to generate the code in parallel with parsing, as the running translation program detects the structure of the expression. Much depends on the type structure of the language, the desired level of optimization, and the extent to which the set of primitive types of the programming language compares to the set of types provided by the target machine.

With the proliferation of more powerful processors, ease of translation is not nearly as important as it used to be, as a "beneficial" characteristic of languages. It could be said that the difficulty of translation was one of the drawbacks to the design of the Ada language, but the real issue in those days was its slow compilation speed on the new personal computers. Current personal machines are powerful enough so that a complex and difficult translation step is accomplished relatively quickly. Having the freedom to ask more of the compiler writer was an essential ingredient in the success of the C++ language, whose complexities easily match those of Ada.

Although ease of translation is not as great an issue in language design as it once was, there is a related issue which continues to be quite significant, which is the ease with which a program can be composed, read, and understood by the human reader. Helpful in that process is a design which makes it easy for translators to point out syntax errors accurately. Perhaps the most egregious design flaw relating to this point is the *syntactic discontinuity*. A syntactic discontinuity occurs when a small modification to a valid syntactic construct produces another valid construct with a radically different meaning. In some cases, the program containing the error compiles with no error messages and the resulting program executes in a subtly incorrect manner, causing infinitely more harm by this subterfuge than the few minutes time that would have been required to find and fix the syntax error had there been one. Such discontinuities are the fault not of the compiler but of the language design. The C and C++ languages are notorious for their syntactic discontinuities, where the use of the = operator in place of the == operator, the presence or absence of a semicolon, or the permutation of two items in a list can cause errors which may take days to find. Current compilers will by default issue warnings when they encounter certain patterns of usage that indicate the programmer is likely to fall victim to the effects of a syntactic discontinuity.

1.3.5 Binding Times and Translation Strategies

A *binding* is an association of a program or language entity with one of its attributes. Some examples are the binding of a variable to its type, the binding of a class to its base class, and the binding of a parameter to its associated argument. Some bindings occur exactly once during the execution of a program, and some bindings are destroyed and replaced with new bindings. An example of the former is the location within a program's memory map at which a compiled procedure's machine language translation is stored, and an example of the latter is the binding of a variable to its value.

The time at which a binding occurs is one of the crucial decisions in programming language design. Let us categorize the list of *binding times* we might expect to see:

1. Some bindings are made at *language definition* time. This is obviously the earliest possible binding, and it applies to things like the binding of built-in types to some or all of their attributes. For example, the Java language definition binds the *float* type to the single-precision 32-bit IEEE 754 representation, which predetermines its range and precision, leaving no decisions to be made by the language implementation.

2. A binding may be made at *language implementation* time. For example, the C++ *float* data type is only loosely described in the language definition and is typically bound by the language implementation to a floating point data type which is built into the target machine.

3. The binding of a C++ variable to its type is made at *translation time*, which in this case is also known as *compile time*.

4. For languages that use separate compilation, a binding may be made at *link time*; that is, it may be made when the various separately compiled modules are linked together into one executable file. For example, a ref-

erence to a variable made inside one source file may be bound to the definition of the variable in another source file.

5. Some storage location bindings are made at *load time*; that is, they are made when the executable file is loaded into memory and readied for execution. (We speak here of *logical* locations, because operating systems which use paging and segmentation play havoc with our notions of actual physical address. We will throughout this text ignore any of these relocation tricks the operating system may play, because they are transparent to the language implementation.)

6. *Dynamic bindings* are made during execution time. Here are some examples:

   a. Bindings may be made *at block entry time*. For example, the actual locations of most variables defined inside a block will be determined at the time the block is entered.
   b. A related binding is one made at *call time*, for example the binding of a value parameter to its initial value. Similar bindings are sometimes made at *exception time*, which is the time at which an exception handler is called.
   c. Bindings may be made at *unspecified times* during execution. For example, in C and C++ the binding of a variable declared inside a block to its first useful value is not necessarily made at block entry time but may be made at some time during the execution of that block.

A binding made at execution time is called a *late binding*. All languages have some late bindings, or they would be useless. But languages with a large number of late bindings fall into a different classification entirely, as they may allow such bizarre behavior as variables which dynamically change their types, strings which can be converted to variables and then dereferenced dynamically, or even procedures that dynamically change their own behavior.

One particular binding is problematic and requires a great deal of sophistication on the part of the language implementation. We said above that the binding of a function or procedure to its location in memory is typically done at load time. On the other hand, this is a binding that may in some cases not be made at all. Storing a target machine-language representation of a subprogram in a particular place in memory, then branching to it and transmitting arguments every time it is called, involves a certain amount of overhead with every call. A return address must be stored, register contents must be saved at call time and restored at return time, arguments must be transmitted to their corresponding parameters, local variables must be allocated at call time and deallocated at return time, and a return value may need to be transmitted back to the caller at return time. Most or all of this overhead can be eliminated by doing an *inline translation* of every call to the procedure. This technique involves the compiler keeping the procedure definition in a memory buffer and doing a new translation with each call, substituting the appropriate value of, or reference to, the corresponding argument for each reference to a parameter. Notice that besides nullifying the need for a location binding, inline translation may affect the binding time of arguments to parameters, by making that binding at translation time rather than at procedure invocation time.

NOTE

Inline translation is very appropriate if the procedure is short, and may actually save both space and time in that case. In fact, inline translation is always more efficient in terms of execution speed, but it may sometimes waste space. If the procedure has a definition which will expand into a large code segment, and if the procedure is called from many different locations in the code, there is a potential for code bloat, causing the translated code to be much larger than it would have been if the usual translation strategy had been employed.

Inline translation is not an option in some situations. For example, if there is a specific need for the procedure to have a location binding then the technique cannot be used. In particular, if there is a procedure pointer or reference type in the language, and if the procedure's location is assigned to a variable of one of those types, then an explicit translation of the procedure into target code is required. For similar reasons, if a method is polymorphic then it will not be possible to do a strictly inline translation of it because the mechanisms for finding the appropriate version of the method are brought to bear at run-time and invariably use code pointers. Inline translation of recursive procedures, although possible in restricted situations, is usually not performed.

For all the above reasons, languages which do inline translation make it a decision by the compiler, not the programmer. Notations may be provided for the programmer to *request* inline translation, but the compiler may reject the request.

1.3.6 Storage Classes and Storage Management

In spite of all the advances in recent years in programming languages, no one has introduced any drastically new ways to manage storage during the execution of a computer program. In any language, interpreted or compiled, one encounters at most three approaches to storage management. The storage either (1) resides in a fixed, static location which does not change during the execution of the program, (2) resides on a stack and is allocated when a block is entered and deallocated when it is exited, or (3) is allocated from a linked list of variable sized blocks of storage and is managed dynamically. These three management techniques partition into the static category (option 1) and the dynamic categories (options 2 and 3).

Among the very earliest languages, the older versions of FORTRAN and COBOL used solely static storage management. Because data items in early versions of those languages were allocated space at load time along with the executable code, storage management could be handled statically via the combined efforts of the compiler, linkage editor, and loader.

Algol 60's block structure and its incorporation of stack-based storage management were considered exotic, and the language got little attention in the United States outside academic circles. Unlike FORTRAN and COBOL, however, Algol 60 allowed procedures to call themselves, a fact that made stack-based storage management absolutely necessary, because a routine which calls itself, either directly or indirectly, must maintain multiple copies of its set of local variables, with the most recent set being the currently active one. This pattern of usage is ideally suited to a stack, and today nearly all machines have hardware support for stack operations.

NOTE

To be more precise about stack storage management, what actually happens is that the compiler is able to statically assess what the storage needs for a given block are, say n bytes, so that it may generate code to increment the stack pointer (which is usually a hardware register) by n at block entry time. It also must make sure that when the block is exited the stack pointer is decremented by that amount. Inside the block, a reference to a block scope variable can then be compiled to compute the appropriate address as a fixed displacement from the address stored in the stack pointer. The block of n bytes is called a stack frame, or activation record, for the block.

For situations in which the allocation of space occurs at random during execution and is not synchronized with block entry, the stack is not available to meet those needs. (The reason is that for efficiency's sake a variable which is allocated on the stack should always remain at the same position within the stack while execution is taking place within the block to which the variable belongs. If this invariant is maintained, then references to the variable may be mapped to efficient machine-level addressing operations.) Because the stack cannot be used, a separate mechanism must be called upon to manage this less predictable space allocation. The mechanism employed in such languages is the *free space list*, and has as its basic form a list of memory blocks which are not currently being used. A variable being bound dynamically to storage of a given size is allocated space from the list, and at the same time that space is deleted from the list. When the space is no longer needed, it is returned to the list.

NOTE *The first widely used language to use a free space list for dynamic allocation and deallocation of storage was LISP, and early versions of that language had an easy time of it because the chunks of memory which they were managing were fixed-size. Algol, with its dynamically allocated arrays, was the first widely used language to incorporate a free space list with variable-sized memory blocks (a heap). Simula 67 expanded Algol's heap usage by placing the activation records of objects on the heap rather than the stack.*

For languages that use a free space list, there is an important issue to be decided. Is the allocation and deallocation of space from that list to be managed manually by the programmer, or is the language run-time to assume responsibility? The language definition makes this decision by either providing or not providing a space deallocation facility. Obviously a space allocation capability must be provided to the programmer regardless of the way the above question is answered. But if the language provides a deallocation operation such as C++'s *delete* operator, then the programmer has direct control of heap operation and the heap becomes a passive object. If the heap is mismanaged, it is the fault of the programmer.

Two important terms involved in the operation of a heap are *garbage* and *dangling reference*. Both can be a problem, but garbage is by far the lesser problem in terms of negative impact, and in some systems is not considered pathological at all. Garbage is storage which has been dynamically allocated from the heap, but which is no longer accessible from the program and has not been returned to the heap. Because it is not a part of the free space list, it is both no longer in use and unavailable for reuse. It does not cause problems unless there is a lot of memory involved, but in extreme cases it can cause a program to crash.

Dangling references are the opposite problem, and only occur in systems where there is an explicit deallocation operation. A dangling reference occurs when storage which has been returned to the heap is still accessible from program variables. If such storage is written to, then the links, counts, flags, or other items of overhead employed by the heap to manage its operation may be compromised and the heap may become unusable. This is a catastrophic error and is one reason that programming in C++ is considered risky. See Section 5.2 for a code example showing how a dangling reference can be created.

On the other hand, if no deallocation operation is provided by the language, then dangling references cannot be a problem, but garbage will likely be generated in large quantities. For such languages it is unacceptable to simply ignore garbage. A scheme for reclaiming garbage must be employed by the language's run-time system.

1.3.7 Dealing with Garbage

Garbage can be automatically reclaimed if there is a way of finding those chunks of memory within the heap which are no longer accessible from program variables and yet are not part of the free space list. The simplest way to approach this operation is through *reference counts*. A reference count is an integer field within an allocated block of storage which records the number of pointer fields which reference that storage. At the point when the storage is first removed from the heap and allocated (made accessible to a program variable), say in response to the instruction

```
widget = new Widget();
```

a block of storage is allocated sufficient to handle both the data requirements of a `Widget` object and the reference count (and possible additional items of overhead). In the reference count is placed the number 1, because the only way of gaining access to the allocated space is via the program variable `widget`. If an assignment is made which establishes two different access paths to the allocated storage, say

```
node.link = widget;
```

then the reference count is given the value 2. When one of those access paths is overwritten, as in

```
widget = null;
```

then the reference count goes back to 1. When the reference count reaches zero, the block is no longer accessible from the program, but has become garbage. At that point the space can be returned to the heap's free space list.

_____

NOTE

The difficulty with reference counts is that they are useless if a chain of pointers becomes circular, because at that point in time no reference count in the circularly linked set of storage blocks can possibly decrease to zero. Detecting circularity with cycle-detection algorithms is possible, but those algorithms are time-consuming when compared to the simple checking and maintenance of reference counts. Cycle-detection algorithms are worth considering, however; they are employed with great effectiveness in the language Python. (See [VonRossum11].)

A complete solution to the garbage problem is available by means of a process called *garbage collection*. On the surface, this process is easily understood and explained. It proceeds in two phases: a *marking* phase, followed by a *collection* phase.

A naïve assumption would be that the marking phase of garbage collection would traverse the entirety of the physical storage assigned to the heap and identify and mark the garbage blocks. Actually, the opposite is true. The marking phase actually starts by marking *all* blocks of storage in the heap as garbage; it then chases down all access paths from program variables and marks the blocks which are *in use* by the program. The collection phase then returns all blocks which are not in use to the heap. The garbage blocks are never actually directly identified.

An important side effect in garbage collection is often the *coalescing* and/or *compaction* of storage. If two blocks of storage which are both inaccessible to program variables are found to occupy contiguous space, then they can be coalesced into one block. A more extreme operation, compaction, actually moves values around in memory in such a way that more nodes can be coalesced. The extreme example is that in which all the space accessible to program variables is moved to one end of the heap so that all the nodes in the free space list can be coalesced into one large block, which is the ideal state from which to allocate space.

How much overhead accompanies a heap? We have already alluded to some items of storage overhead, such as links to support the free space list, reference counts, and flags to be used for marking. Additional storage overhead would involve block byte counts or pointers from one end of a block to the other for better navigation in heap maintenance operations. Reference counts place a performance tax on every pointer assignment. In order to be able to track down all heap references from program variables it may be necessary to route all pointer references indirectly through some central bank of pointers. All this pales, however, in comparison to the cost involved in marking and compaction. The heap space accessible to program variables in a large program may constitute a very large directed graph, and that graph must be traversed quickly to avoid a painful performance hit. Compaction may involve moving large blocks of memory around in real time. For that reason, mission critical systems which have real-time performance constraints are often written in languages like C++, whose run-time system does not normally employ garbage collection.

1.3.8 Scope, Visibility, Accessibility, and Lifetime

We introduced the notion of *scope* when we defined the term *association* in Section 1.2.1. In this section, we expand on the term, differentiating it from the terms *visibility* and *accessibility*, and relating it to the issue of *lifetime*.

A name which is associated with some program entity has a scope, and often that scope can be determined by a static examination of its pattern of definition and usage. For example, if it is defined inside a block we say that it has *block scope*, meaning it will not be legal to reference that name with that same meaning outside the block. If it is defined inside a class we say that it has *class scope*, meaning it can be referenced inside that class and its methods. We say that the named entity is *accessible* within a given (statically defined) program context if the name can be legally referenced there and provides access to the given entity (although it may need some qualification).

NOTE
There is a fundamental difference between block scope names and class scope names, as the latter can actually be made accessible, using a qualification scheme, outside the class. For example, in most of the languages discussed in this book, if x is a class scope variable inside class C belonging to object o, and certain access rights have been associated with x which apply to a given segment of code, then inside that code segment the notation o.x provides access to the entity named x inside o. If x belongs to the class, and not to individual objects of the class, then the notation which succeeds is usually C.x.

Three levels of access are commonly associated with class scope names: *public*, *private*, and *protected*. Typically, public names provide access to the named entity in any context in which the containing object or class is accessible, whereas private names provide such access only inside the class itself. Intermediate between these two extremes, protected access means the name can be used for the purpose of accessing the class-scope entity only inside the class and any class which is derived from it.

NOTE *Access level is a related but separate issue from inheritance type, which also can be characterized as public, private, or protected. In practice, most inheritance is public, meaning that all entities in the base class have the same accessibility to clients of the derived class as they did to clients of the base class. In most of the languages in the book, the only way to create a derived class is to do a public derivation. See Chapter 5, "Additional Concepts from the C++ Language," for alternative ways of deriving classes.*

Named entities defined in packages, modules, or namespaces typically are accessible only through qualification using the name of the enclosing scope. Thus, a type name `MyType` inside namespace `N1` is referred to as `N1.MyType`. Some languages allow the qualifying name to be dropped if there is an `import` or a `using` statement or the equivalent. All these hierarchical structuring principles are recursively applied, so that there is no limit to the extent to which one can, for example, nest namespace inside namespace inside namespace, etc. Some restrict accessibility by default, while others require a specific attribute in order to restrict accessibility. For example, C++ namespaces allow the `static` attribute to be applied to a name inside a namespace for the purpose of making it inaccessible to scopes outside the namespace.

Static scopes are usually established using bracketing notations, which associate a closing "bracket" (right parenthesis, right set brace, or the *end* keyword, for example) with the most recent unmatched opening bracket (left parenthesis, left set brace, or the *begin* keyword, for example). For that reason, two static portions of program text both of which define a scope cannot intersect without one being nested inside the other. This would seem to imply that if two such scopes have a nonempty segment of program text in common, then the set of associations accessible in the smaller textual element should be a superset of the associations accessible in the larger textual element. One issue complicates this simple conclusion, however, and that is the introduction of new associations for a name inside the scope of that name. If one block, for example, is nested inside another, and if the inner block and the outer block both have an association for a variable named x, then although the mechanisms of the language ensure that the outer association will *exist* inside the inner block, it will not be accessible there because it is *hidden* by the inner association. The *scope* of the name declared in the outer block remains the same, but its *visibility* has been curtailed. Some language designers have considered this an evil and have placed limitations on the ability to hide associations for names.

Storage management is usually associated with scope, and thus usually correlates with the *lifetime* of a variable. Most block scope variables have a lifetime which begins with block entry and ends with block exit, so that whether a block is exited by execution flowing out through the bottom, via a *break* or *return* statement, or with a *goto* statement, the stack frame on which it resides will be popped off the stack at the time the block is exited. The exception is that some languages allow block scope variables to be explicitly declared as static (although the keyword *static* is not always used. Algol uses the keyword *own* for this purpose), so that their scope and their lifetime do not correlate. A static variable inside a block is actually not stored on the block's stack frame but in a separate storage area which is usually allocated at load time. The lifetime of this type of variable is said to begin upon the first entry into the block and to end with the end of program execution. In reality, the storage for a static local variable is usually allocated *before* that first block entry event. (If there is an initialization required, however, such as the assignment of an initial value or a constructor call, that initialization typically will not take place until the first time the block is entered.)

The stack frame for a simple inline block contains only local variables, such as x and y in the following example (which could come from C or any of the C-derived languages), which also references variables w, n, r, and s from larger enclosing scopes.

```
{ int x; float y; x = w + n; y = r - s; z = x + y; }
```

In the above case, each time the block is entered, a stack frame containing at least enough newly allocated space for x and y is pushed on the stack. That stack frame may also contain space for the temporary results w + n, r - s, and x + y. On the other hand, if this code appears as the active part of a procedure, then space may have to be allocated on that same stack frame for value parameters, for addresses of reference parameters, for return values, for a return address, and possibly also a register save area.

NOTE

Interestingly enough, objects allocated on the heap typically have lifetimes unrelated to scope, and are usually accessible only via a static or local association which is a pointer or reference variable. The object's lifetime often goes beyond that of the variable via which it was initially accessible, as its address may be copied into a variable with a wider scope or returned as the result of a function call, and in that case it will become accessible inside a totally different scope.

1.3.9 Types, Type Checking, and Type Transfers

Physical machines have a very crude notion of types. Most machine instruction sets account for a dozen or fewer types, and the types involved are characterized by the set of hardware operations that are available to perform on values stored at untyped memory locations. Nothing prevents a machine language program from sending the same 32-bit quantity from the same location in memory to the integer addition operation at one time and to the floating point addition operation at another. The virtual machine defined by a programming language must be more sophisticated than this. Binding of names and/or objects to their types is done in a more serious fashion in high-level languages for exactly the reason that the above-described abuse of CPU hardware is a bad idea. It simply is not reasonable that the same bit pattern stored in the same block of memory should be expected to be used in a meaningful way by two different operations, each of which expects its operand to be of a radically different type from that expected by the other. Hence high-level languages incorporate *type checking* to attempt to ensure that this kind of error never occurs.

A type check is an operation performed before some other operation in order to make sure the operands for the latter are of the correct type. The precise time when this type check occurs depends on when the needed type information is available. Some languages are designed in such a way that the type check can only occur at run-time, while others provide sufficient static information that the check can be done at compile time. Compile-time type checking is by far the more efficient, because the check is only done once and does not retard execution speed because it is done before the program executes.

Languages that provide sufficient information to allow compile-time type checking are said to be *strongly typed*. In *weakly typed* languages there is no such information; typically in such languages, identifiers may be statically bound to a scope but not to a type. Because it is not an option to attempt to invoke operations which are not applicable to a given type, the language implementation must ensure that the operations in the program are being applied to the proper types of operands by means of run-time checks. There are at least three ways this can happen. First, the type-checking code can be inserted into the translated form of the program and executed prior to the code which implements the operation. Second, the operation itself can be implemented as a call on a run-time routine, and that routine can itself be given the responsibility to do the type checking. Third and finally, in the case of an operation being invoked by sending a message to an object, the run-time system can turn the problem inside-out by asking not whether the object is an appropriate target for the message but whether the message is an appropriate message for the object. In other words, the run-time system can ask the object if it has a method corresponding to the message. If it does not have such a method then there is a run-time error. This approach is actually a form of *existence checking*, to be discussed in the next section.

If an operand type does not match that of the corresponding argument being supplied, that does not always mean that an error condition results. Often the language definition or the programmer supplies a *coercion*, or an implied type transfer, by which an operand of the appropriate type can be computed from the original operand. The most common instance of this is the situation in which one of the operands should be of a floating point type, and an operand of an integer type is supplied instead, or vice versa. In those cases either the compiler generates code to make the type transfer or the run-time system calculates the corresponding value. If the parameter transmission requires an address, not a value, and if the argument denotes only a value, then the compiler will often generate a *dummy argument*, which is a nameless stored value. Because it is stored, it has an address which can be transmitted to the parameter. Such a technique can be allowed only with parameter transmission techniques which do not attempt to change the argument's value. If that is the case, dummy arguments can also be used when the type of the argument does not match that of the parameter and the latter requires an address. The dummy argument's type matches that of the parameter, and the argument is coerced to that type when it is copied into the dummy's location.

NOTE

Programmer-defined type transfers are common in object-oriented languages, and typically are performed in one of two ways: either a conversion constructor is provided which converts a single object of the supplied type into an object of the desired type, or the class of the supplied argument has an instance method specifically designed to convert its own value into a value of the desired type. Such type transfers may be explicitly invoked by the programmer, or may implicitly be called by the compiler or run-time system, in which case we have what amounts to a programmer-defined coercion.

1.3.10 Uninitialized Variables and Existence Checking

Often errors in programs result when an attempt is made to invoke an operation which does not exist, or to send a message to a nonexistent object, or to supply an object which does not exist as an operand of some operation. This particular kind of error often goes undetected at translation time, even in a compiled language.

A common source of existence errors is uninitialized variables. Historically, compiled languages have suffered from the inability to detect whether or not a variable being referenced in a given operation has been properly initialized, and when uninitialized variables are used in an operation there is no way to predict what will be the result of that use. So from a software engineering standpoint, uninitialized variables are disastrous.

> **NOTE** *It can be argued here, and it is in the C tradition to do so, that the initialization of variables is the responsibility of the programmer, not the language designer. However, the language designer is in a position to save untold thousands of hours of wasted programmer time by making it difficult or impossible to have an uninitialized variable.*

There are several possible solutions to the uninitialized variable problem, and whether or not each is acceptable to the language designer depends on his philosophy of language design. The first possible solution is to require an initializer be applied to all variables when they are created (instantiated). The initializer can either be explicitly furnished with initialization syntax or established by default actions taken by the language implementation. For primitive types, an arbitrary decision would have to be made about a default value, say zero for numeric types, the null pointer for pointer or reference types, the null character for character types, *false* for Boolean types, etc. For programmer-defined types, a constructor would have to be called, either explicitly or by default.

There are a couple of objections to requiring an initializer. The first objection is that initialization takes time, and in languages like C and C++ that time is begrudged, rightly or wrongly. The second is related to the first, and it is that often there is no reasonable initial value to be assigned at the point of definition, because the correct initial value may depend on actions taken in some other context than that in which the definition must occur. In that case, requiring an initializer means that a default value must be constructed, and then later discarded without ever being used.

The other extreme is to require a run-time existence check. In this case, *every* reference to the variable's value must run such a check, and the resulting cost in performance is not acceptable to any compiled language. It is, however, acceptable in highly software-simulated languages which have already conceded a certain amount of performance degradation.

Somewhere between these two extremes is the option of not requiring explicit initializers with each declaration, but nonetheless requiring that each variable be initialized before it is used. This requirement is enforced by doing a sophisticated code analysis at compile time to ensure that no part of the code requires the value of a variable in any setting where it might not yet have been initialized. Such analysis might sometimes yield a false negative, in response to which the programmer is forced to provide an initial value at an earlier time than is needed, a value destined to be overwritten before it is used. The performance hit here is likely to be insignificant, and the annoyance factor is small.

Two particular kinds of existence error need explicit discussion: null pointer references and out-of-bounds subscripts on an array. Let us handle each in turn.

A null pointer reference occurs when an object to which indirect reference is made through a pointer or reference variable does not exist because the address stored in the variable is a null pointer. Such an error, technically, does not occur because a variable was uninitialized; it occurs because the variable was initialized to the null pointer value. Thus, we encounter the same problem as that of an uninitialized variable, but we cannot solve it in the same way.

NOTE

Again some languages take the laissez-faire approach to null pointer references, which is to insist that such errors are the responsibility of the programmer. There is more of a legitimate argument for this approach in this case, because most machines will have hardware support for detecting a null pointer reference. Still, inadequate testing may cause null pointer references to be present in delivered code, a disastrous situation. The code analysis approach works here, and makes good sense. Run-time checking is invariably the solution with interpreted languages.

Finally, the problem of subscripts out of range has a similar set of solutions. The actual numerical range of allowable subscript values for an instantiated array will either be statically discernible using the declared size of the array, as in the C-derived languages, or it will be ascertainable at run-time using information obtained from a declaration or an initializer. Any value outside that range is an error. Sometimes a static code analysis will tell us that a particular subscript value is going to be out of range, but that is the exception. No generally applicable compile-time solution exists for this problem.

C and C++ ignore the problem, partly because the designers were not willing to put additional range-checking instructions in the code for every subscripting operation. There is more to their motivation than this, however, because other primitive types besides arrays allow subscripting. Specifically, these languages allow pointer variables to be subscripted. Granted that such a variable *should* be pointing into an array, such a requirement is not enforced. Even if it were, there is no way to know where in the array the pointer points, and if there was it would not be possible to ask the array object what its bounds were because the array representation does not include run-time size information. (In fact, in C and C++ arrays are not objects in the object-oriented sense and cannot be "asked" anything at run-time.)

In languages which have a more sophisticated run-time representation for arrays, such as Java and C#, run-time range checking is an option. In the case where complete information is available statically, such checking can be done efficiently by code generated at compile time. In software-simulated languages, the checking can be done by the subscripting operation itself. When subscripting is an operation added by the programmer to a programmer-defined type, the subscript operation code can usually be written to do or not to do range checking. The array-like library types `Vector<>` from the Java library and `vector<>` from the C++ standard library, differ in their choices here. Java does range checking routinely, whereas C++ offers the programmer the choice of unchecked subscripting or checked access using the `at()` method.

1.3.11 Pointer Semantics versus Value Semantics

Identifiers which name objects of a built-in, primitive type are usually (but not always) names of *values*, or more accurately of storage locations that store values, and everywhere they appear they represent either those values or those locations. Conventionally, in an assignment operation, say x = y, involving two values of the same primitive type, the variable y on the right denotes a value, whereas x, the variable on the left, denotes a location. The result of executing the operation is that the value of y is stored at the location x. If the operation is allowed to appear as a subexpression of a larger expression, then typically that subexpression denotes a value, namely the value stored by the assignment.

When the objects associated with those identifiers are objects of a first-class type, then there are two language design paradigms which may be used to explain assignment semantics: *pointer semantics* and *value semantics*. The latter is precisely the interpretation given in the preceding paragraph, and in this case the "value" stored at y is a potentially large area of storage containing an object. The result of the assignment operation, then, would be to copy that large object from the location y to the location x. After the assignment, the values stored at the two locations will be identical, but the copy will be a *shallow copy*, meaning that an imbedded pointer or reference field p in the value stored at y will have as its counterpart another field x.p containing exactly the same pointer or reference. The assignment will not cause the actual object pointed to by y.p to be copied. In other words, the value copying procedure invoked by such an assignment stops at the top level.

If the pointer semantics approach is being used, then no copying of values occurs at all. In this case the identifiers *x* and *y* never denote a complex value at all. They denote either a stored *pointer value*, sometimes called a *handle*, or the location at which that pointer value is stored, depending on the way they are used. Thus, the result of the assignment x = y is to copy that pointer value and *not* the value of a large and complex object. This interpretation is radically different from value semantics and should be thoroughly understood or severe errors will be made.

Of course, the pointers stored at x and y are allowed to point to large and complex objects, and those variables can be used as qualifiers for field names. For example, if there is a field called *name* in the type associated with variable x, then x.name refers to that field. This seems contradictory to the statement we made in the previous paragraph that x does not denote a complex value, but rather a pointer or handle. The key idea in this type of semantics, as it occurs in Java and C#, is that when the name x is used in this fashion there is an extra level of indirection and the pointer is automatically dereferenced to obtain the object pointed to.

1.3.12 Parameter Passing Mechanisms

Over the last sixty years, some pretty creative ways have been devised for transmitting arguments in a function or procedure call to their corresponding parameters. Let us classify the kinds of communication which take place in parameter transmission, then we will try to summarize the ways in which such communication can be effected.

There are three ways a parameter of a function or procedure which is responsible for some computation can be used: (1) as an *input* to the computation; (2) as a result, i.e., an *output*, of the computation, or (3) as *both* an input and an output. The Ada language makes this beautifully clear by simply using the attributes *in*, *out*, or *in out* on its parameters. Other languages are often more cryptic in their notations.

The simplest category is the *in* parameter. If the parameter is only an input to the computation, then that parameter can be implemented as a local variable of the procedure, and the value of the corresponding argument can be copied into the storage for the parameter incident to the call. This simple scheme is called *call by value*, and it is the *only* mechanism used by the procedural language C and the object-oriented language Java. All the same, both languages are able to achieve the modification of objects which reside in the calling environment. In C, that goal is achieved by the simple device of passing in a pointer argument, which can then be dereferenced and used to overwrite the value pointed to. In Java, all first-class objects are actually represented as handles, which are pointers that are conveniently dereferenced when necessary. Thus, if we transmit a handle by value, then in the called environment we can transmit a message to the object to which the handle refers. The message may then cause the object to modify itself or some other object to which it has access.

An *out* parameter does not actually need the argument to transmit its value when the call is made. The parameter is either uninitialized or initialized to a default value, and is given a meaningful value by the action of the called routine. The burden in this case is not on the caller but on the procedure itself, to transmit the final value of the parameter back to the caller, to be copied into the actual argument location as a side effect of returning from the procedure. Obviously, then, the argument should be a variable or some other expression which denotes a location, and not a value, a constant, or a literal.

The effect of an *in out* parameter can be achieved in various ways. The simplest approach is to transmit the value of the argument at call time, and then to transmit the final value of the parameter back to the argument location at return time. Ada takes this approach, which is referred to as *call by value/return*.

More commonly *in out* transmission is accomplished by making the parameter a *reference parameter*. In this case, the parameter is represented by a pointer at run-time, but syntactically it is declared with the same type as that of the argument, with an extra attribute which indicates that it is a reference parameter. (For example, Pascal uses the `var` attribute, and C# uses `ref`.) Wherever the parameter appears in the procedure's text it has the properties of a variable with the same type as that of the transmitted argument. This is achieved in the implementation by automatically dereferencing the pointer stored as the parameter's value every time the parameter is used. Consequently, every time there is a change made to the parameter the same change occurs in the corresponding argument. This technique is called *call by reference*. Call by reference may on rare occasions produce a different result from call by value/return, some examples being when (a) the procedure is interrupted without doing a normal return, and when (b) the reference is to a nonlocal variable whose scope overlaps that of the procedure being called.

An interesting *in* parameter transmission technique is *call by constant reference*. This technique transmits the argument in exactly the same way as call by reference, but a compile-time restriction effectively gives the technique precisely the same effect as call by value, logically speaking. Specifically, the compiler is informed by the syntax of the parameter declaration that the parameter receives its argument by constant reference, and in response the compiler specifically marks as an error any part of the procedure definition in which the parameter name is used in a way which could result in a change in that parameter's value. Call by constant reference usually saves space over call by value, because the parameter's run-time representation is that of a memory address, not a copy of the argument value.

Another exotic *in out* transmission technique is the old Algol 60 *call by name*. This mechanism was the default mechanism for parameter transmission in that language. We will begin by describing the effect of call by name, then we will talk briefly about how the technique can be implemented.

Unlike arguments corresponding to reference parameters, the argument for a name parameter is not required to be a variable. It may be any arbitrary expression. When the parameter is referenced in the called procedure, its corresponding argument will be evaluated in the calling procedure, and the value thus obtained will be used. This evaluation will take place every time the parameter is referenced. The effect is almost as if the parameter were replaced by the corresponding argument wherever it appears in the called procedure. This is not the case, however, because when the argument is evaluated it is evaluated *in the context of the calling procedure*. In fact, this must be the case, because it is in that context that the argument was syntactically placed, and it is only in that context that we can even be sure that it will make sense.

So how is it possible to implement call by name? There is only one way. Because every use of the parameter corresponds to the execution of a segment of code, the parameter has become a sort of procedure. The compiler, then, must cause the argument to be transmitted to the called procedure as a pointer to a segment of code which executes in the caller's environment and returns a value or a location. Every reference to the parameter causes that code segment, actually an anonymous procedure called a *thunk*, to execute and deliver a quantity consistent with the form of the argument. If the parameter is used in such a way as to require a store, then the thunk should evaluate to an address. As in other *in out* methods, there should be an error condition if a store occurs to a parameter and the transmitted argument is a computed value which cannot be interpreted as a location.

NOTE

As a sidelight to the discussion on call by name we should mention the "parameter-passing" mechanisms associated with text-substitution macros (used by the C and C++ pre-processors and other text-processing applications). For the novice attempting to understand call by name it is tempting to think of the call by name parameter transmission technique as a text substitution facility, as is the transmission of macro parameters. The difference is that the text substitution for a macro takes place in-line at the point of call, so that there is no opportunity to confuse the meanings of names—the meaning of a name is simply that given to it by the context encountered at the point where the macro was used. With call by name, simple text substitution would not succeed because some of the names in the called procedure would need to be resolved as local and nonlocal references in the context of the procedure and some would need to be resolved in the calling environment. (See Section 5.14 for a discussion of C++ macros.)

1.3.13 Aliasing

In our use of natural languages, we are accustomed to encountering many different names for the same thing. We call them synonyms, and they help to make our writing more interesting and meaningful. In a computer program, two names which mean the same thing are called *aliases*, and whether or not they are a good thing depends on the potential they present for error. The most commonly used example of where aliases cause problems involves overlapping scopes. Specifically, it is the example in which a nonlocal variable is transmitted as the argument to a reference parameter in a procedure in which the variable in question is visible. The situation is illustrated by the following C++ code.

```
class A {
public:
    int x;
    A() { x = 0; }
    int f(int &y) {
        // Increment parameter y, then add the incremented
        //value to class
        // scope variable x.
        x = ++y + x;
        return y;
    }
    int g() {
```

```
        return f(x);
    }
};
```

Now study the code below carefully.

```
int r = 0;
A a, b;
cout << a.g() << endl;
cout << b.f(r) << endl;
```

We might reason that the two lines of output would be identical, because in both cases the value output is obtained by calling member function f of a default-constructed object of type A, so that in either case when f is called its argument is a variable whose initial value is zero. In fact, however, the first line outputs 2 and the second outputs 1. The difference is that in the first case the class scope variable x and the parameter y are *aliases*, and in the second they are not. This is a contrived example, but overlapping scopes and reference parameters are so commonly used in C++ programs that the above situation often does arise, and it allows the careless programmer to make a very subtle error.

C++ is particularly adept at creating aliases because of its heavy use of explicit pointer variables and its permissiveness concerning what constitutes legitimate use of an address. In C++, the location of any variable x can be ascertained using the prefix & operator, and that address can be stored in a pointer variable p, as in the following:

```
int x;
int *p = &x;
```

After these declarations the expression *p denotes the object to which p points, as does p[0]. Thus, *p, p[0], and x are aliases of each other. In general, if x is a C++ variable, then *x* and *&x are aliases.

> *Aliases are created wholesale in languages that use pointer semantics. The assignment x = y, if it is executed using pointer semantics, causes the variables x and y to be aliases when used in a situation which requires their values. Thus, sending a message to x which makes an alteration to the value it references, say x.setName("Dolores"), will make a change in the object referenced by y, because it is the same object. This is business as usual in Java, and the C++ programmer migrating to that language can make some deadly mistakes if he does not realize this.*

NOTE

1.3.14 I/O and the External Environment

Every language must include facilities for communicating with the outside world. There are many ways of doing this, and much of this text is concerned with describing creative ways of using event-oriented library facilities and language features for this purpose. In this section, we concentrate on the most universal way of making the results of a series of computations visible to the outside world, and of obtaining data from that world. Specifically, we concentrate here on sequential input and output (I/O).

There are two kinds of sequential I/O: binary and text. Binary I/O stores and retrieves data to and from external devices in exactly the same format in which that data is stored in memory. This is in some sense the simplest idea, but to the naïve human user it seems quite complex. So if we wish to make our communication with the outside world understandable to human beings we must use text I/O, not binary; therefore, we must provide for the translation of internal binary forms to text and vice versa. There are two main schools of thought about how to do this, and both are represented in the object-oriented world.

Let us begin with a discussion of text *output*. To have a comprehensive facility for converting a stored binary representation into text to be displayed on a screen, to be output to a printer, or to be stored in a text file, we must first furnish such a capability for all primitive types. There are two widely used strategies for doing this.

The first idea is to have a single function or method name which is overloaded once for each such primitive type. For example, if the name of the function is `write`, then that function is overloaded multiple times, so that no matter what primitive type is assigned to variable x the call `write(x)` will place a recognizable literal on the output device or file which represents x's value. (Variants usually exist which attempt to give specific control over how that literal is formatted and whether or not a new line begins after the literal.) This solution appears ugly because of the proliferation of a large number of calls on this one output routine. C++ offers a nice solution by making its generic output method an operator << belonging to one of its stream classes. When the operator is used it causes the desired output as a side effect but returns the stream object as its value, so that additional messages may be issued to it in a cascading fashion. Thus, if *out* is the name of the stream object, then instead of coding

```
    out << x;
    out << y;
we can code
    out << x << y;
```

Long chains of C++ streaming operations can be formed for the purpose of producing lines of text with multiple data items having various types represented. New data types can simply overload the << operator and blend seamlessly into the same pattern. Refer to Chapter 5 for more details.

The second approach is to supply output routines only for characters and character strings, but to make each data type responsible for its own conversion routine, a method which has been called `asString()` or `toString()` in some languages. This is the approach often taken in languages with a unified type system based on inheritance and polymorphism. The resulting code has a superficially similar appearance to the first approach, in the case where the language uses the conversion method implicitly in cases (perhaps not all cases) where a string is needed. On the other hand, the approach to eliminating the proliferation of calls on a single output primitive is different and is based on the use of string concatenation rather than cascading method calls.

Regarding text input, it matters very much whether your programming language supports call by reference. If it does not, then it likely does not support *any* of the *in out* parameter transmission techniques, because none of those are in use in more recent languages. In that case, the most prevalent form of input is by simple value return. A parameterless routine (a commonly used name is `read()`) picks up some portion of the input text and returns it as a string or a character, along the way advancing the input pointer so that the same data will not be picked up again.

The input of whitespace is often a case which requires special handling. This commonly occurring problem is made annoying by the almost universal use of whitespace as delimiting text without any semantic content. When there is an exception to that usage, a different technique must be used. One way is to provide the language or a library with a *readLine()* primitive, which returns a string containing everything on the line beginning at the current input pointer and ending at, but probably not including, the next end of line character. The other way is to read one character at a time. Both typically require an application-level parse to mine the input line for its content.

If the input routines are only capable of inputting strings or single characters, then the onus of converting those strings into stored values of various types lies on other facilities than I/O. This involves a kind of lexical analysis which is typically misnamed a "parsing" operation. The parse is either performed individually for each of the various primitive data types, as in the Java

```
int x = Integer.parseInt("123");
```

or it is the responsibility of one particular class.

On the other hand, if the language does support some form of *in out* parameter transmission, then overloading a single input operator or method name makes sense again. The generic-looking method call `read(x)` would then use overload resolution to invoke a specific input routine tailored for *x*'s data type. C++'s operator >> is overloaded in this way, and typically the programmer overloads it again for any data type for which he wishes to have text input capability.

Binary I/O is useful for one very important programming technique, highly used by object-oriented applications, namely *serialization*. Serialization makes a deep copy of a complex internally stored object on an external device. It is important because *persistence*, the ability of an object to outlive any particular execution of the applications that create and maintain it, is essential in many situations. Serialization can either be directly supported by the language, or the language can by more primitive methods encourage its use. Smalltalk, Java, C#, and Python provide support for serialization by building it into the library framework, whereas serialization in C++ must be achieved from the bottom up unless it is furnished by a third-party library. In either case, the path toward extending existing serialization facilities to new types defined by the programmer may not be simple.

1.3.15 Exception Handling

During the execution of most programs of any degree of sophistication, conditions arise which do not fit the normally expected sequence of operations, and which need special handling by code which has a purpose orthogonally opposed to that of the program proper. Such a condition is called an *exception*, the purpose is *exception handling*, and the block of code which responds to the condition is called an *exception handler*. Exceptions do not have to be errors, just conditions that do not arise with every execution of the code, in fact which arise rarely, but which need handling of a quite different nature than the normal sequence of computation states for that routine.

NOTE

> *The problem of exception handling is largely a software engineering problem: how do we provide the appropriate response to exceptional conditions and still keep source code readable? The challenge to the language definition is to provide immediate response to exceptions while physically separating the exception handling code from the code which handles the normal states of program execution.*

The solution offered by the Ada language was to provide a special language primitive, the *raise* operation, which functioned as a limited type of *goto* instruction. This was paired with the ability to divide any *begin…end* block of statements, if desired, into two portions, the top for normal processing and the bottom for exceptional conditions. The division was achieved by inserting the keyword *exception* in the middle, to obtain a *begin…exception…end* block. This facility was a forerunner of the *try…catch…* scheme used with very little variation in C++, Java, and C#.

1.3.16 Threading

A *thread* is an execution sequence. Typically, a program begins execution with a single thread, called the *main thread*. When we say that an execution environment supports threads, we are really saying that it supports multiple threads, so that once the main thread begins it may spawn new threads. For example, event-driven environments often do not use the main thread for event handling but rather use a special dispatch thread which removes events from a queue and executes their handlers.

Essentially all that is needed to characterize a thread in the context of an active program is a code pointer and a stack. Each thread must have its own stack, because each entry into a new block scope by a thread must push a new stack frame, a stack frame that cannot have any relevance to any other thread. On the other hand, all other aspects of the referencing environment are shared by all threads taking part in the application. Static members of classes, objects aliased from two separate locations in the program text, members of such aliased objects, and objects accessible via links stored in static data members, are some examples of data that might be shared between threads.

Support for threads is usually not language-defined, but rather it is library-defined. In an object-oriented language, it is natural for a thread to simply be another type of object, typically a library type. For languages that compile to native code, a thread will usually be an operating-system–defined entity and will only need a wrapper class to interface with the language. For languages that compile to a virtual target machine, that virtual machine must provide a thread facility (perhaps implemented using the operating system's facilities for thread management) and the language facilities will map to it.

> *Two threads which have access to the same object or data member must synchronize in order to avoid interfering with each other in unsafe ways. Facilities for doing this may again have to be furnished by the operating system and provided with object-oriented wrappers, but often synchronization is language-defined.*

NOTE

The line between library facilities and built-in language facilities continues to be blurred, however, and that line has become even less distinct in the newer language designs. In the case of Java, the library class Object is language-integrated because all first-class objects must be of a class which has Object as its ultimate base class. This effectively melds the library and the language into a seamless whole, because some of the behaviors implemented as polymorphic overrides of Object methods are routinely and implicitly invoked by the language runtime. For example, the toString() method is implicitly invoked when a string is needed for the right-hand operand of the language-defined concatenation operation but another type of object is supplied instead. Also present in the Object base class of Java are synchronization primitives notify(), notifyAll(), and several overloaded versions of the wait() operation. Similar thread synchronization facilities are supplied by the Object base class of C#.

1.4   SIMULA 67 AND ITS HISTORICAL SIGNIFICANCE

A very early Algol-based language, Simula 67, has had far-reaching effects on programming language design. Simula 67 had classes, inheritance, and run-time polymorphism, and it relied heavily on heap-based storage management at a time when most other languages were using only static, or only static and stack-based, storage management.

> *Originally conceived as a "niche language" and used primarily by the modeling and simulation community, Simula 67 was in fact a (dramatically different) general-purpose programming language. The key to its having such a long-term effect on the way programming language thought has evolved is the fact that "modeling" is not a niche activity. Now that we understand more about the ways in which software can be constructed for understandability and long-term maintenance, we know that we must construct clear models of real-world inspired entities in our programs in order to have any hope of those programs being able to adapt and grow as*

NOTE

their application area changes. Languages which do not support this modeling activity well are no longer considered viable languages for medium-scale to large-scale applications. The Simula class concept was exactly the right idea, filling a need which few contemporary researchers anticipated, long before its time.

1.4.1 Generalizing the Procedure Call

What Simula did was to extend the Algol idea of an activation record, or stack frame, by not popping the stack when a return occurred (in fact by not keeping the activation record on a stack at all!). The central idea was that after a procedure's work had been accomplished, the results of that work would not be returned all at once, via arguments and a return value, but that they would remain behind for future access, inside the referencing environment of the still-extant "procedure." This was clearly, however, quite a bit beyond the current concept of a procedure, so the designers (Ole Johan Dahl and Kristen Nygaard) invented a new term: *class*. Algol-style procedures were also allowed by Simula 67, of course, and the class was just considered a more sophisticated cousin of the procedure.

Not only was it deemed necessary to keep the activation record around, so that the "objects" thus created could continue to inform the caller on various aspects of their final states at "return time," but because of the simulation flavor of the language it was of course necessary to create more than one object of the same kind. (How many bank teller queues have only one customer waiting in line at a time?) Thus, a class had to allow multiple activations. The result of this constraint was a design that was not at the time viewed as a facility to allow programmer-defined data types, but that is what it was, and more. Consider the following sample Simula 67 program.

```
Begin ! Stooge denial of service program. ;

    Integer TimeStamp;
    Ref(Customer) Larry, Moe, Curly;

    Class Customer(Name, Patience);
    Text Name; Integer Patience;
    Begin
        Integer ArrivalTime, WaitTime;

        Procedure AngerWarning;
        Begin
```

```
        OutText(Name);
        OutText(" is getting angry.");
    End of AngerWarning;

    Procedure Wait(Interval);
        Integer Interval;
    Begin
        WaitTime = WaitTime + Interval;
    End of Wait;

    Procedure ReportStatus;
    Begin
        OutText(Name);
        OutText(" arrived at time ");
        OutInt(ArrivalTime);
        OutText(" and has been waiting ");
        OutInt(WaitTime,3);
        OutText(" minutes.");
        OutImage;
    End of ReportStatus;

    WaitTime := 0;
    OutText(Name);
    OutText(" has joined the queue.");

  End of Class Customer;

TimeStamp := 0;
Larry :- new Customer("Larry", 50);
Larry.ArrivalTime := TimeStamp;
Larry.Wait(5);
TimeStamp := TimeStamp + 5;
Curly :- new Customer("Curly", 200);
Curly.ArrivalTime := TimeStamp;
Curly.Wait(5);
Larry.Wait(5);
TimeStamp := TimeStamp + 5;
Moe :- new Customer("Moe", 10);
Moe.ArrivalTime := TimeStamp;

While TimeStamp lt 300 do
    Begin
        TimeStamp := TimeStamp + 5;
        Moe.Wait(5); Moe.ReportStatus;
        Curly.Wait(5); Curly.ReportStatus;
```

```
          Larry.Wait(5); Larry.ReportStatus;
          If (Moe.WaitTime gt Moe.Patience) Moe.AngerWarning;
          If (Curly.WaitTime gt Curly.Patience)
              Curly.AngerWarning;
          If (Larry.WaitTime gt Larry.Patience)
              Larry.AngerWarning;
      End of While;

  End of Program;
```

The action taken by the program is to initialize the `TimeStamp` variable to zero, then to instantiate three `Customer` references (of type `Ref(Customer)`) named `Larry`, `Curly`, and `Moe`, in that order, giving them arrival times five minutes apart. Each customer has a different patience level, with `Curly` being the most patient and `Moe` the least patient. The program "simulates" five hours of elapsed time, in which no one actually gets served, and for the last 95 minutes all the customers are angry. (Much better facilities are provided in the language for serious simulations; the intent here is not to give a detailed summary of the language but rather to introduce enough features for the reader to get an idea of its "flavor.")

1.4.2 Inheritance in Simula

The above program is not a model of good abstraction, nor is it intended to be. It declares a class `Customer`, but note that the class has no access level designations to provide for information hiding. Simula 67 did not provide such features, a fact that in this case encouraged the programmer to directly access the `ArrivalTime` member for initialization instead of building the initialization into the instantiation process by making `ArrivalTime` a parameter of that initialization. Having to separately command each customer to wait five minutes is also not good abstraction, and of course was not necessary, because Simula 67 has a perfectly good array construct. The program could have kept references to all its customers in an array, and a single wait procedure could have been written which cycled through that array.

NOTE

There are some syntax oddities due to the age of the language and its pioneering nature. For example, the operator for "less than" is lt, not <, and there are two different kinds of assignment operations: the := operator is used for value assignments and :- is used for reference assignments. The language is case-insensitive, and any text between the keyword End and the semicolon following it is considered a comment.

Inheritance was built into the language, and could be applied not only to new types but to blocks. For example, to make class B inherit the attributes of class A it was only necessary to preface the definition of the subclass with the name of the base class, as follows:

```
A Class B;
Begin
    ! New attributes and behaviors in addition to those ;
    ! inherited from A go here.                         ;
    ! Initialization code ends the block, and will      ;
    ! execute after the initialization code for A.      ;
End of Class B;
```

To cause all the attributes of an A object to be made available in a block, we prefix the block with the name A:

```
A Begin
    ! An anonymous A object is instantiated upon entry into   ;
    ! this block.  Its initialization code will execute before ;
    ! the statements in the block, and the data members and    ;
    ! procedures of A can be referenced in the block without   ;
    ! qualification.                                           ;
End of block;
```

Finally, we can declare virtual procedures in the following manner:

```
Virtual:  Procedure AngerWarning; Begin   statements  End;
```

In derived classes, now, we can override the virtual procedure. For example,

```
Customer Class Stooge(Selector);
     Integer Selector;
Begin
     Procedure AngerWarning;
     ! Override of virtual procedure;
     Begin
         OutText(Name);
         If Selector eq 1 then
             OutText(" is about to start hitting people.");
         Else if Selector eq 2 then
             OutText(" is running around in circles.");
         Else
             OutText(" is yelling 'yip, yip, yip, yip!'");
             OutImage;
     End of AngerWarning override;
End of Class Stooge;
```

Interestingly, because `Stooge` inherits the *parameters* of the base class `Cus-tomer`, and those parameters must be supplied at instantiation, we must provide three parameters per each such instantiation, as in

```
Larry :- new Stooge("Larry", 50, 2);   ! A runner;
Curly :- new Stooge("Curly", 200, 3);  ! A yeller;
Moe :- new Stooge("Moe", 10, 1);       ! A hitter;
```

Assuming `Larry`, `Moe`, and `Curly` were defined as `Ref(Customer)`, the `Anger-Warning` procedure will exhibit polymorphism when it is called via those identifiers, because it is the object which was instantiated, not the type of the variable providing access, which responds to the procedure call. The call

```
Curly.AngerWarning;
```

thus produces the output

```
Curly is yelling 'yip, yip, yip, yip!'
```

So here we already had programmer-defined data types, classes and objects, inheritance, sophisticated memory management, and polymorphism. What we did not have was abstract data types which clearly defined a public interface and hid everything else from view. What Simula 67 did was to prepare a foundation for later development of more sophisticated object-oriented languages, with better information-hiding characteristics. The object-oriented paradigm really began here, however, and no one seriously disputes that point.

1.4.3 Coroutines

A very important idea used in the Simula 67 language was the *coroutine*, another concept initially viewed as a generalization of the procedure call. Without going into specific syntax, it is possible to quickly and easily explain the interaction of coroutines. A coroutine is an ordinary procedure—the only difference is that instead of the usual caller-callee hierarchy, a set of coroutines is able to actively share processing time via voluntary control transfers. These transfers are not primitive gotos, however, but an odd combination of aspects of a call operation and a return operation. We call such a transfer a *resume* operation. When coroutine *A* actively resumes coroutine *B*, the latter resumes execution at the point at which control was last suspended. If *B* then resumes *A*, that routine picks up execution immediately after the code which had caused *B* to resume. Coroutines, like objects, cannot use the stack to save and restore referencing environments. Instead, each coroutine must "own" its context information.

Although few modern languages implement coroutines in their full generality, there are aspects of this control paradigm which are ideally suited to a usage pattern seen in two of the languages covered in this book—Python and C#. Both of these have a specialized form of coroutine transfer called the *yield* transfer, which allows those languages to blur the lines between passive data structures and active algorithms. See Chapter 8, "C# and the Common Language Infrastructure," and Chapter 9, "Python," for details.

1.5 SETTING THE STAGE: OBJECT-ORIENTED TERMINOLOGY

In this section, we prepare for the remaining chapters of the book by standardizing some important object-oriented terms which were not discussed in Section 1.1. We take terms like *class* and *object* for granted, as they will mean slightly different things with different languages, and the reader should already have a strong idea of their meaning which will not conflict with anything we have to say now and will be somewhat adjusted by that reader if he is successful in mastering some of the case studies in this book.

The first order of business is the classification of constructors. Interestingly enough, Simula did not contain an explicit concept of a constructor, because there was never more than one way to instantiate an object. Specifically, a Simula object had to be supplied at its instantiation with all the arguments which were necessary for the instantiation of all the base classes, in order. The "construction code" was actually the "life code" which ended the class block, and all the life code from all base classes executed with each instantiation, starting with the ultimate base class. There was no way to provide multiple choices for construction code.

All other languages discussed, from this point on in the text, provide multiple constructors for their classes. A simple classification of such constructors goes as follows: (1) if a constructor has no parameters, or if all its parameters have default arguments, then it is a *default constructor*; (2) if a constructor's parameter is an object of the same type as is about to be constructed, then we call that constructor a *copy constructor*; (3) finally, all other constructors will in this text be referred to as *conversion constructors*, because they take a list of arguments and "convert" that list into an object of the desired type. (This usage of the term differs from some other sources, which prefer to restrict the term to one-parameter constructors.)

The term *first-class object* is an interesting term, because there is not complete agreement as to its meaning. The general meaning is that there are no restrictions on what can be done with such objects. In this text, we will define a first-class object to be an object satisfying the following requirements: we can (1) instantiate the object at run-time, (2) assign that object or a reference to it to a variable of the given type, (3) transmit the object as a parameter, (4) return the object or a reference to it as the result of a function or method call, and (5) send messages to the object as method calls. We do not require by this definition that a first-class object be an object of a class type.

Two important terms, accessor and mutator, have broad application across all OOPLs. An *accessor* is an instance method of a class which provides access to a specific attribute of an object of the class type. That attribute may be a stored attribute or it may be computed as needed, but to the client who is using the method there is the strong impression that it is fetching stored data. Conversely, a *mutator* is an instance method that is used to *change* an attribute of a class instance.

A *descriptor* is a data structure which contains type information. For example, for an array a descriptor would contain an integer code indicating the type *array*, perhaps another code indicating the type of elements stored in the array, and upper and lower bounds on subscripts. Often descriptors are incorporated into symbol tables at translation time and are discarded at run-time. *Run-time descriptors*, which can be dynamically accessed to obtain information on an object of unknown type, are used to a greater or lesser extent for some or all class types in most object-oriented languages, even compiled ones. A class which not only provides *complete* run-time information about itself but allows itself to be manipulated at run-time by a program which has no static information concerning the class, to the extent that such a program can instantiate its objects and invoke their methods, is said to be *reflective*.

A *container class* is a class whose objects have as their primary purpose the storage and retrieval of other objects. A *queue* class is a container class whose objects allow access to their contents in "first in, first out" fashion, meaning that the object which has been stored there longest is retrieved first. A *stack* class is a container class whose objects allow access in "last in, first out" fashion. A *vector* class is a container class whose objects allow constant-time random access to their contents by position; in other words, for any positive (or non-negative, depending on the language or library) integer n within a certain range, the container is able to honor a request to store a new object as the nth object in the container, or to fetch either the value of the nth object or a pointer to the nth object. A *list* class is a container class which allows traversal of elements in order and constant-time insertions of new elements and deletions of old elements at positions defined in terms of the progress of that traversal.

1.6   SUMMARY

Object-oriented languages, like all programming languages, are categorized in terms of the features they support. In particular, an OOPL should provide features which support data abstraction, inheritance, and polymorphism.

Data abstraction facilities should provide the programmer with the ability to create and name a heterogeneous data type and to strongly associate with that type the operations which one might naturally desire to perform on its objects. In object-oriented terms, we say that the programmer should be able to specify the *attributes* and *behaviors* of objects of the given type. Also desired in an OOPL are facilities to explicitly describe an *interface*, i.e., a subset of attributes and behaviors which defines the client interface to the class and to objects of the class. Such an interface may or may not provide for *information hiding*; attributes and behaviors not explicitly included in the interface are not always made inaccessible to the client programmer by the mechanisms of the language implementation.

An *inheritance* facility allows the programmer to build *derived types*, i.e., types that build on existing parent types. In most cases, such types are *subtypes* of the parent type, meaning that objects of the derived type can be used in places where an object of the parent type is required. Behaviors already defined in the parent class can be overloaded or overridden by redefining them in the derived class. *Overloading* simply defines an additional meaning, whereas overriding provides a new meaning that supersedes the old. If overloading a method in a derived class forces method calls to a derived class object to always invoke the overload, then the method is *overridden* for objects of the derived class, and the type is said to be *run-time polymorphic*.

In general, the term "polymorphic" is applied to any construct which is capable of taking on many different forms depending on how it is used. While run-time polymorphism is an essential ingredient for an OOPL, some languages also employ a kind of *compile-time polymorphism*, in which static context is enough to allow the compiler to translate the polymorphic construct into the appropriate run-time representation. Examples of this are the generic constructs of Java and C# and the templates of C++.

Alternatives to the object-oriented paradigm include the *imperative*, the *procedural*, the *modular*, the *functional*, and the *declarative* paradigms. The first two are related; the imperative paradigm views a program as a sequence of commands, and the procedural paradigm builds on that view by allowing the programmer to invoke by name an encapsulated sequence of commands called a *procedure*. The functional paradigm views a program as a collection of coordinated functions which are combined using a built-in set of combining forms, such as composition and projection. The modular paradigm sees a program as a collection of modules, each of which is a named collection of types, procedures, and data. Finally, the declarative paradigm views a program as a collection of facts and rules, along with a query to be answered using the "knowledge" embodied in those facts and rules.

All of the above paradigms for programming share some cross-cutting concerns, with regard to naming and the maintenance of associations. An *association* is a (*symbol, meaning*) pair, and is typically introduced either through a run-time creation operation or a *declaration*. A declaration is a syntactic construct which provides information about the meaning of a symbol; a *definition* is a declaration which provides *complete* information on the meaning of a symbol. Related terms are: the term *literal*, which is a symbol whose name communicates its value; the term *identifier*, which is a language-dependent multi-character symbol usually consisting of mostly alphabetic and numeric characters; the term *constant*, which is a symbol whose meaning is a value assigned at creation time, a value which is unchangeable after it is assigned; and finally the term *token*, which is an indivisible unit of syntax.

The maintenance of associations requires the use of one or more *symbol tables*, either at run-time or at compile time. The tables implement the idea of a *referencing environment*, i.e., a set of associations. Logically, the referencing environment at any given time during the execution of a program is determined by the *scope rules* of the language. Static scope rules are rules that define the *scope* of an association to be a particular segment of program text, whereas dynamic scope rules define that scope to be a period of time during the execution of a program. A *global* association is one which encompasses the entire program, while a *local* association is one which encompasses only a limited portion of the program, typically a block, subprogram, or class.

For procedural languages, *sequence control* is an issue, and must be understood on two levels: the expression level and the statement level. Expression-level sequence control typically depends on associativity and precedence rules, whereas statement-level sequence control is almost universally achieved in modern imperative languages using the "structured programming" mechanisms known as *sequence*, *selection*, and *repetition*.

The *syntax* and *semantics* of a language are communicated via formal description languages like regular expressions and Backus-Naur Form (BNF) and through less formal explanations of the meaning of the syntactic elements. *Implementing* a language involves planning for the mapping of the syntactic elements of a program into the domains which match or approximate its semantic model, which we call the *semantic mapping*. That mapping can be implemented using a combination of two techniques—*translation* and *simulation*.

A *binding* associates a program or language entity with one of its attributes. Binding times in early-to-late order are *language definition time, language implementation time, translation time, load time,* and *run-time*. Run-time bindings are called *late bindings*; some late bindings are only made at *call time* or *block entry time,* but some are made at arbitrary times during execution.

Storage management includes mechanisms which make sure that the storage is available when local environments must be created. These mechanisms fall into three categories: *static, stack-based (automatic),* and *heap-based*. Static storage management must be planned at an early stage, and consists of the allocation of storage which is needed for the duration of the program. Automatic storage is allocated on a stack when a block is entered or a subprogram is called, and it is deallocated when the block is exited or the subprogram returns. Heap-based storage can be allocated at any time, and its deallocation is problematic. If the programmer is given the power to explicitly free storage, then that storage may become unfreeable *garbage* or the access path to it may become a *dangling reference*. If the programmer is not allowed to free dynamically allocated memory, then the language run-time must be able to recognize when that memory is no longer accessible and specifically take action to free it. Two techniques which come into play here are *reference counts* and *garbage collection*.

The issue of scope differs from that of *visibility* and *lifetime*. An association which is in scope may still not be visible because inner declarations may introduce new associations which hide it from view. The lifetime of an association is measured in dynamic terms, and whether an association which goes out of scope is destroyed or simply hidden determines its lifetime.

Types can be statically or dynamically assigned to a variable, but mechanisms must be in place to make sure that the values assigned to a variable come from the appropriate domain. This means that type checking is often necessary, in order to prevent a value of one type from being assigned to a variable of a different type, or to make sure that all operands of an operation are of the appropriate type. In *strongly typed* languages, there are sufficient declarations to allow type checking to occur at translation time. In *weakly typed* languages, this checking must be done at run-time. A related mechanism is *existence checking*, which checks to see if an operand exists or if an operation exists. Resolving these issues may involve *coercions*, which are implicit forced type changes.

One form of existence checking is checking to see if a variable has been initialized before it is used. Some languages have enforced initialization rules, and check them actively using translation-time or run-time mechanisms. Others see the initialization of variables as the responsibility of the programmer. Subscript *range-checking* is another type of existence checking, which may or may not be employed at run-time.

Value semantics sees the assignment a = b as the copying of b's value into a's location, whereas *pointer semantics* makes a and b aliases for each other after the assignment, so that sending a message to a can change the values of both a and b.

Parameter-passing mechanisms match the operands on the call side, called *arguments*, with the operands on the called side, called *parameters*. Such mechanisms fall into three categories: *in*, *out*, and *in out*. An "in" mechanism ensures that the parameter receives the argument as a side effect of the call, and that no transmission is made back to the argument upon return. Conversely, an "out" mechanism makes the initial value of the parameter irrelevant while ensuring that the corresponding argument receives a value upon return. Finally, an "in out" mechanism ensures two-way communication between argument and parameter. Some "in out" mechanisms are *call by value/return*, *call by reference*, and *call by name*.

Sequential input and output facilities may be constructed in two ways, depending on whether overloading is permitted. If it is, then I/O facilities can be built around a set of overloaded type-specific operations which provide for the input and output of primitive values. If not, then I/O will be built around character-oriented and/or string-oriented routines and implicit or explicit type conversion facilities—from string to primitive value and vice-versa.

Exception handling is a software engineering problem, namely how to construct clear and readable code yet manage all the contingency issues in a complex program. The language can help this issue greatly with explicit mechanisms which provide for a "limited goto" capability, transferring control to an exception handler in a way which preserves essential information and allows a graceful exit from an offending routine. Variants of the *try…catch* block included in most major OOPLs accomplish this in an elegant fashion.

A *thread* is an execution sequence, consisting of a code pointer and a stack of activation records. Threading is typically a library issue, but often the library facilities for threading are language-integrated, with synchronization primitives defined by the language using inheritance and polymorphism and a unified type system organized around a common base class.

Most of the features we think of as characterizing an OOPL were incorporated into the pioneering simulation language, Simula 67. Simula employed a class concept as a generalization of the procedure, in which the "procedure call" created and initialized an object. The activation record was not destroyed upon the return, however, but "stayed around for questioning" on the heap after the call was completed. Simula 67 incorporated data abstraction (without information hiding), inheritance, and polymorphism.

Some terms which are standardized for further study in this text are the terms *default constructor, copy constructor, conversion constructor, first-class object, descriptor, run-time descriptor, reflective type, container class, queue, vector,* and *list*. These are defined in the previous section.

REVIEW QUESTIONS

1. In what context would one use each of the following adjectives? What programming language entities would they be applied to, and what would the terms mean in that context?
   a. Static
   b. Dynamic
   c. Homogeneous
   d. Heterogeneous
   e. Polymorphic
2. What is the essential difference between programmer-defined data types as they were conceived in the Pascal language and programmer-defined data types in a modern object-oriented language?
3. List and describe the qualities a language should have before it can be called an object-oriented language.
4. Give two different usages of the term *object*, and clarify the difference between those two usages.
5. Define each of the following in your own words:
   a. Data abstraction
   b. Information hiding
   c. Abstract data type
   d. Base class
   e. Derived class
   f. Attribute
   g. Behavior
   h. Method
   i. Message
   j. Type equivalence

    k. Structural equivalence

    l. Name equivalence

6. Explain what we mean when we say that most languages employ a combination of structural and name equivalence.

7. Distinguish between the terms subtype and derived type.

8. Explain why, when class D is derived from class B, class B is often referred to as a "supertype," even though it usually has fewer attributes and behaviors.

9. Describe the difference between overloading and overriding.

10. Describe two possible responses when a parameter declared to be of a base class type is sent a message to a method which is overridden in the derived class, given that the argument is of the derived class type. Which response is considered "polymorphic"? Why?

11. What is the most general interpretation of the term polymorphism, and how can we apply that more general interpretation in the context of programming languages?

12. List and describe some alternatives to the object-oriented paradigm.

13. Describe how the terms symbol, identifier, keyword, and reserved word relate to each other.

14. Describe how the terms value, literal, constant, and variable relate to each other.

15. Define each of the following terms:

    a. Identifier association

    b. Reference

    c. Scope rule

    d. Dynamic scope rule

    e. Static scope rule

    f. Symbol table

    g. Global association

    h. Local association

16. Describe the imperative programming language paradigm.

17. What mechanisms dictate sequence control at the expression level?

18. To what extent does the tree representation of an expression determine an exact sequence in which the operations in an expression must be performed? Explain.

19. Describe the three possible notational conventions for the design of expressions in a programming language. Which is the most limited? Why? Which is the most predominant? Why?

20. Describe the three structured programming principles for controlling flow of execution and imparting structure to an imperative program at the statement level.

21. What two things are credited in the text as leading to the ultimate rejection of primitive control features in the design of programming languages?

22. Relate the two terms function and side effect to each other.

23. Describe the difference between a high-level language procedure and a machine-level subroutine.

24. Describe the functional programming paradigm.

25. What mechanism is used to achieve looping in a purely functional language?

26. What capability do you think is implied by the term self-modifying code? What features commonly encountered in functional languages might enable such a capability?

27. Describe all the differences between a module, as defined in Modula 2, and a class in an object-oriented language. Be sure to mention the role of ownership in making that distinction.

28. Differentiate between the generic use of the term "module" and its use in modular programming languages.

29. What is a declarative language? What is the central activity of the programmer who is using a declarative language?

30. What is the name for the engine at the center of a run-time system for a declarative language?

31. What is a Horn clause? Describe the Prolog notation for Horn clauses.

32. Describe the backward-chaining search strategy for goal resolution in Prolog.

33. Two difficulties which often come up in declarative languages are search order and negation as failure. Describe each and explain why each can be a problem.

34. Define the term *abstraction* in a general sense. When are the results of manipulating an abstraction consistent? When are they relevant?

35. Relate the two terms *abstraction* and *information hiding*.

36. What is the central activity of the abstraction process? How is that activity different for the computer scientist, as opposed to the mathematician, the scientist, the historian, or the artist, for example? What are the implications of that difference for the design of complex systems and for the design of programming languages?

37. Describe the three main activities engaged in by a programmer who creates an abstraction using a programming language. Describe from your experience some of the ways a good language can support these abstraction activities.

38. Give an example of a context-sensitive syntax rule.

39. Explain the difference between low-level and high-level languages.

40. What is a language translator called if its source language is high level and its target language is low level?

41. Give some examples of low-level to low-level language translators.

42. Define *just-in-time compilation*. What language is being "compiled," and why do we enclose the term in quotes?

43. Define the term *semantic mapping*. Describe the two-step procedure used by a language implementation to actualize the semantic mapping.

44. What is the purpose of parsing? Give two possible ways to represent the results of the parsing process.

45. Which is more important in a programming language: (1) the ease with which a translator can be written, or (2) the ease with which programs in the language can be read, composed, and understood by a human reader? Explain.

46. What is a syntactic discontinuity? Give an example from a language with which you are familiar.

47. Give some examples of bindings in a programming language, and their associated binding times.

48. What do we mean by a late binding? Give some examples.

49. Describe the inline translation strategy? How does it differ from the standard translation strategy for procedure and/or method calls? Why, and under what circumstances, can it sometimes cause code bloat?

50. When is inline translation not an option? How does the compiler respond to programming language notations which explicitly or implicitly request inline translation? Explain.

51. Describe three approaches to storage management in a programming language.

52. Define the term *stack frame*. Why, how, and when is a stack frame created? What is another name for a stack frame, and why is it called that?

53. Describe heap-based storage management.

54. Relate the terms scope, visibility, accessibility, and lifetime to each other.

55. Describe the access levels public, private, and protected for named entities at class scope.

56. Do the three access levels in the previous question typically have any impact for references to those entities made at class scope within the given class or classes derived from it? Explain.

57. Discuss the accessibility of members of a namespace or package.

58. Describe the implications for visibility of nested scopes. How can nested scopes "hide" an identifier association? Should such hiding be restricted? Does your previous experience with languages suggest that such restrictions are made? Is this a good thing?

59. Explain how storage is allocated for a static variable inside a block, and why and how its lifetime differs from its scope.

60. What run-time entities may need to be allocated space on a stack frame?

61. How do scope and lifetime correlate for objects allocated on the heap?

62. Contrast the set of types available on a typical physical machine to those available in a compiled high-level language. What protections relating to type are available on each of these two types of machines?

63. Define the term *type check*. What determines whether a type check is done at compile time or at run-time?

64. When is a language said to be strongly typed?

65. Describe three ways in which a weakly typed language can perform a run-time type check.

66. Define the term *coercion*. How does the term relate to type checking and to programmer-defined type conversion operations?

67. Describe and give three solutions to the uninitialized variable problem.

68. Define the term null pointer reference. How is the problem of null pointer references related to that of uninitialized variables? Describe some approaches at the language definition and implementation level for solving this problem.

69. Why is there no way of detecting subscript out of range errors at compile-time?

70. Practically speaking, why do C and C++ fail to do run-time checking for subscript out of range errors?

71. Describe both the pointer semantics and the value semantics interpretation of the assignment x = y.

72. Describe the difference between a shallow copy and a deep copy.

73. Name and describe the three usage patterns for parameters of a function or procedure.

74. Name and provide descriptions for two different mechanisms for transmitting an argument to an *in* parameter.

75. Name and provide descriptions for three different mechanisms for transmitting an argument to an *in out* parameter.

76. Define the term *thunk*. What is a thunk used for?

77. Define the term *alias*, and describe a situation where aliases cause difficulties for the programmer.

78. Why do languages that define assignment in terms of pointer semantics create a lot of aliases? Why is this type of aliasing a trap for novice programmers in the language who are accustomed to value semantics?

79. Describe the difference between binary I/O and text I/O.

80. Describe two distinctly different approaches to the design of a text output facility in a language.

81. Describe two distinctly different approaches to the design of a text input facility in a language.

82. Discuss binary I/O, serialization, and persistence.

83. Briefly describe the Ada facilities for exception handling, and relate them to facilities in an object-oriented language with which you are familiar.

84. What is a thread? Describe how facilities for threading are integrated into the Java language by means of the library class Object.

85. Why did the so-called "niche language" Simula 67 have such a profound effect on the design of future programming languages?

86. Explain how the Simula 67 concept of a class evolved from the Algol 60 concept of a procedure.

87. Which of the following OOPL features were present in Simula 67?
    a. Construction code for new instances of a class
    b. Multiple constructors
    c. Inheritance
    d. Polymorphism
    e. Access control for class members

88. Explain how parameters were passed to a Simula 67 derived class at instantiation time. How does that differ from the pattern used in modern OOPLs?

89. Explain how ordinary blocks in Simula 67 can inherit the attributes of a class. Give the syntax and describe its meaning.

90. Describe the three categories of constructors in an OOPL.

91. Give a definition for each of the following terms:
    a. First-class object
    b. Descriptor
    c. Reflective class
    d. Container class
    e. Queue
    f. Stack
    g. Vector
    h. List

EXERCISES

1. In a language of your choice, give some examples of (a) overloading and (b) overriding. Explain the difference between the two terms using your examples.

2. Again in a language of your choice, give some examples of polymorphic constructs. Illustrate two different kinds of polymorphism with your examples.

3. If function names cannot be overloaded and each reference to a function is preceded by a declaration specifying its arity, then a postfix expression needs neither precedence rules nor parentheses in order to be unam-

biguous. Why? Explain carefully and give an example.

4. In a language with which you are familiar, give an example of a function or method which both returns a value and has a side effect. Is the use of such functions considered good software engineering practice? Why or why not?

5. Function gcd, written below in Python, incorporates simple looping in order to compute the greatest common divisor of two integers. In Python or any other language you choose, rewrite gcd as a stand-alone function or as a static method of a class, and write it so that it uses recursion instead of an explicit loop.

```
def gcd(m,n):
    large = max(m,n)
    small = min(m,n)
    while small > 0:
        temp = small
        small = min(large - small, temp)
        large = max(large - small, temp)
    return large
```

6. In most cases with which we are familiar, the "interface" to an abstraction is simply its name, in the sense that the use of the name calls forth its meaning in some context. How complex can an interface get? Give code examples of interfaces in a language familiar to you.

7. Give a set of lexical rules specifying the correct formation, in a typical object-oriented language such as C++ or Java, of...

   a. An integer literal.
   b. A floating point or double literal.

8. Give a set of context-free productions in BNF notation, in a typical object-oriented language such as C++ or Java, for...

   a. A while loop.
   b. A switch construct.

9. Construct some code in a language familiar to you which constructs an array and stores a zero in every element of that array, but goes beyond the bounds of the array storing extra zeros in nonexistent elements. If an error is detected, describe the way in which the error is reported and whether it was reported at run-time or at compile time. If it is clear that no error has been detected, augment the code with tests to see if "dam-

age" has been done by over-writing elements which should not logically have been involved in the initialization. Execute the code and report on the results.

10. Investigate the use of "shallow copies" and "deep copies" of first class objects in your favorite object-oriented language. Which kind of copy is typically made when an assignment statement is executed? How much trouble is it to achieve the alternative behavior? Give code examples along with your discussion.

11. Does your favorite language allow *in out* parameters? If so, describe the language's facilities for doing so. If not, describe how the effect of *in out* parameters can be achieved in their absence.

12. Answer Question 11 for *in* parameters.

13. Answer Question 11 for *out* parameters.

14. Using your favorite language, describe ways in which aliases may be created. Describe as many different ways as you can, and give code examples to illustrate each.

15. Demonstrate with code the manner in which text output of nontext values (e.g., integer and real) is achieved in your favorite language. Now do the same with binary output.

16. Demonstrate with code the manner in which text input of nontext values is achieved in your favorite language. Now do the same for binary input.

17. Using your favorite OOPL, design a class for a dynamic array of integers. Give your class a default constructor, a copy constructor, and at least one conversion constructor. (Your language's container library may already have some sort of dynamic array type. Try to give your homemade class some specific advantage which makes it more desirable in some situations.)

REFERENCES

[Backus78] Backus, John, *Can Programming be Liberated from the Von Neumann Style? A Functional Style and its Algebra of Programs*, Communications of the ACM, vol. 21, no. 8, (August 1978): pp. 613–641.

[Bierbauer90] Bierbauer, John et al., *Object-Oriented Programming in the Computer Science Curriculum*, SIGCSE Bulletin, Volume 22, no 1, (February 22, 1990): p. 260.

[Böhm66] Böhm, Corrado, and Giuseppe Jacopini, *Flow Diagrams, Turing Machines and Languages with Only Two Formation Rules*, Communications of the ACM , vol. 9, no. 5, (May 1966): pp. 366–371.

[Dijkstra68] Dijkstra, Edsger. *Go To Statement Considered Harmful*, Communications of the ACM, vol. 11, no. 3, (March 1968): pp. 147–148.

[Hadar08] Hadar, Irit, and Leron, Uri, *How Intuitive is Object-oriented Design*, Communications of the ACM, vol. 51, no. 5, (May 2008): pp. 41–46.

[VonRossum11] Von Rossum, Guido, et al., *Python v3.1.3 Documentation*, available online at http://docs.python.org/py3k/, August 2012.

[Wirth70] Wirth, Niklaus. 1970. "The Programming Language Pascal," *Acta Informatica 1*, (Jun 1971): pp. 35–63.

[Wolfram10] Wolfram Research, Inc., *Mathematica*, Version 8.0, Champaign, IL (2010).

2

EVENT-DRIVEN PROGRAMMING

We will begin our study of OOPLs in earnest in the next chapter, in which we will introduce the Smalltalk language, but this chapter is a necessary prerequisite in order for the reader to understand the context into which Smalltalk fits. Smalltalk had several motivating factors, but a key factor in its design and in its ultimate success was its more sophisticated set of assumptions concerning the external environment. Just as the introduction of interactive environments based on time-sharing in the 1960s ultimately required programmers to accommodate screens and keyboards into their design universe, so the introduction of the mouse and bit-mapped graphics would ultimately cause programmers to think in terms of event-driven programming (EDP). In this chapter, we will set the stage for our discussion, throughout the text, of event-driven library and programming language features by defining the relevant terms, giving some examples, and describing the qualities common to event-driven programming environments.

NOTE

The ultimate foundation for the idea of objects came from the class concept in the Simula 67 language, but a more compelling picture is seen in the direct manipulation of screen artifacts using a mouse. It was the need for a language that facilitated working with such an interface that led to the first truly object-oriented language, Smalltalk. Although the kernel of that language is quite small and has nothing to do with EDP, the strongly language-integrated library which was developed in parallel with Smalltalk was necessarily rich in event-driven concepts.

Many things enter into the design of an event-driven programming environment, but the essentials are always the same. Program actions are initiated based on scheduled events, hardware events, operating system events, language run-time events, or events triggered by the user's direct manipulation of a graphical interface. The programmer is given tools to specify these program actions in the form of event handlers. The programmer's mindset must center on a machine state that adapts and changes based on the occurrence of these events. No longer is the programmer concerned with managing a single thread of execution from start to finish. Here a program design activity typically begins with the question, "What needs to happen when this particular event occurs?" The mindset is that of a server—a set of capabilities is to be furnished, and happenings initiating in the external environment dictate which of those capabilities will be needed. The inspiration for this view of program execution comes from an unlikely source: hardware interrupts and interrupt handlers.

2.1   BASIC DEFINITIONS

An *event* is a condition that arises during the lifetime of a program, which requires the initiation of program actions by the run-time system. The event may simply cause information to be read from the machine state and displayed on the screen, or it may cause a computation to be performed, or it may result in a change in state. Events are often represented at run-time by a data structure called a *message*, which provides information detailing (1) the type of event (usually encoded as a small integer) and (2) the parameters needed to handle the event. An *event handler* is an active program unit which is invoked in response to the event. An *event queue* or *message queue* is a queue of messages representing events that have occurred but that have not yet been handled.

A commonly used technique for implementing event-driven programs is the *message loop*. This is a polling algorithm that continually examines a message queue and routes traffic to event handlers. At each iteration of the loop, the queue is examined; if the queue is not empty, the first message is removed and interpreted and an event handler is called to respond to the event the message represents. In the process, the parameters are unpacked from the message and passed as procedure parameters to the event handler. The programmer is typically not involved in writing a message loop. Most event-driven programmers write only initiation code and message handlers and ancillary routines in support of message handlers. The programmer assumes the message loop will be provided, either by the operating system, by the language run-time, or by automatically generated source code.

Not all events are handled as messages stored in a message queue. When events are generated synchronously by the programmer, they may cause immediate actions to occur by indirectly invoking an event handler. There are various means of achieving the indirection, but indirection is crucial in order to maintain the flexibility of the event handling mechanism. This is because, as an event-driven program executes, the set of objects interested in an event is subject to change, and the occurrence of a given event may cause different actions to be taken depending on when the event occurred. In order to enable the dynamic nature of the association of events with their handlers, the programmer must route event notifications through at least one level of indirection, perhaps by something as simple as a function-valued variable (the value of the variable being either a primitive pointer or a first-class object). More elaborate mechanisms include callback tables, message queues, and/or variables whose values are first-class objects incorporating specific interfaces.

2.2   THE HARDWARE MODEL: INTERRUPTS AND INTERRUPT HANDLERS

The archetypal event-driven model is the hardware model. A central processing unit with any degree of sophistication is capable of being *interrupted*, which is to say that it can suspend normal operation in order to respond to some external stimulus. That stimulus is a primitive event and may be, for example, the pressing or releasing of a key, the click of a mouse, or the arrival of data on a serial line. On this level very little processing is done in response to the event, so as to minimize overhead which might interfere with the efficient conduct of higher-level functions of the operating system. The event handler in this case is termed an *interrupt handler*, and the mechanism that invokes it is a hardware mechanism. Let us briefly examine that mechanism.

A common hardware model for interrupt handling centers on the idea of an *interrupt vector*. In processors that employ this model, there is an area of memory set aside for an array of interrupt vectors (more properly called *interrupt descriptors*), each of which provides sufficient information to compute a memory address. Following the memory address brings us to a place in memory where a machine language program unit called an interrupt handler is stored. This array of interrupt vectors is called the *interrupt table*, or the *interrupt vector table*. Each of a selected set of events is associated by the design of the hardware with a position in the interrupt vector table, and the occurrence of the event triggers a sequence of actions which is summarized as follows: (1) the essentials of the current machine state are saved, usually on a stack; (2) the program counter is loaded with the machine address stored in the interrupt vector table at the position associated with the particular kind of interrupt; (3) the change in the program counter automatically causes the code in the interrupt handler to be executed, the last instruction of which will be a "return from interrupt" instruction; and (4) the machine state will be returned to its former condition from the place where it was saved. This mechanism is somewhat similar to a procedure call, but the procedure being called, i.e., the interrupt handler, is invoked indirectly via the interrupt vector.

A central part of hardware processing unit design is the assignment of specific hardware events to specific locations in the interrupt vector table. For example, in the Intel x86 architecture, interrupt vector 00 (i.e., the vector stored at the first position in the table) points to a handler which is called when division by zero occurs.

An important point about the interrupt vector model is that it is often extended beyond the necessary hardware events to software-defined events. The method of handler invocation is so simple and flexible that it is easily extended to incorporate events that cannot be explained in pure hardware terms. In the same way that programming languages provide features to supply language extensibility, making features provided by the programmer integrate so seamlessly that they appear to have been designed into the language, so does a good hardware design provide ways of extending the hardware model. In the case of the interrupt vector model, all that is necessary to extend the basic idea of hardware interrupts is to include a kind of "software interrupt" as an operation in the machine instruction set, needing only a single integer operand. That one operand is nothing but an index into the interrupt vector table, and executing a software interrupt instruction from a machine language program simply initiates steps 1–4 as described above. By writing an interrupt handler and storing its address in the appropriate place in the interrupt vector table, the system programmer can extend the basic machine model to include behaviors that were not envisioned by the machine's original designers.

It is important to note here that this hardware model is different in kind from the models used in event-driven programming systems. In the hardware model there is no message queue, and the occurrence of the event causes an immediate response. However, all that is necessary to make a hardware event integrate into a higher-level event model is to install an interrupt handler that gives notice of an event on a higher level, for example by crafting a message corresponding to the event and placing that message into the appropriate queue.

2.3 OPERATING SYSTEM SUPPORT

In our discussion, we have been using the term "message" in a specific way, but like so many other terms in computer science, this term has alter egos. The two primary meanings of the term in a programming languages context are (a) a method call, and (b) a data structure containing a notification of some event. Generally speaking, a "message" is an encapsulated set of data that is transmitted from one program entity to another program entity. Messages are often used for communication between two objects that do not share state. This use of the term has its roots in operating system (OS) design, where it is often the primary means for communication between tasks.

One of the most important concepts in the study of operating systems is *concurrency*, which is the actual or apparent ability of two program entities to execute simultaneously on the same machine. If these program entities share memory, they are called *threads*. If not, then they are typically called *processes* or *tasks*. If the machine has two or more processors, *actual* concurrency is possible. However, using timer interrupts (which are in fact low-level events) and schedulers, *apparent* concurrency is possible even with uniprocessor machines. The timer interrupt handler in this case does not immediately return control to the interrupted task or thread entity; instead, it saves a data block encapsulating the state of that entity in a queue and invokes a scheduler. The scheduler uses some system-defined policy to choose the next entity from the queue and gives that entity control of the processor. Because execution is interrupted many times per second, and each scheduled entity receives a "fair" share of the processor during each second of its lifetime, the effect can often be the same as if each task or thread was allocated its own processor.

In many operating systems, messages are a means of communication between independently executing tasks, or between the operating system and the tasks that dwell in it. For this reason, when an EDP environment is designed, it becomes an important decision precisely how to use the OS-defined message facility. Often a new message format with its own approach to message passing must be constructed, and a protocol must be established to translate OS messages into the new format. Like so many other issues in programming language design, a key question is whether or not the language is designed primarily for native code compilation. If it is not so designed, then a very active and sophisticated run-time system will be constructed as part of the language implementation, and the message passing facility will be designed into that system. The run-time system becomes a new layer of software which completely or partially hides the machine and its operating system from the programmer's view. This new layer of software may include its own scheduler, its own message format, and its own policies for routing messages. Any message from the OS with relevance to a program running within the language run-time environment must be intercepted by that run-time environment, reformatted to conform to the implementation-defined standard, and placed in the appropriate message queue.

Just as machines are designed for extensibility via the interrupt vector table, operating systems are made more flexible by the message passing paradigm. Each copy of an OS can be customized by adding new messages and message handling tasks, or by designing a new message type. Operating systems allow scheduling policies to be modified as well, so that the same type of task would have higher priority in some installations of an OS than in others. Language implementations can take advantage of this extensibility to bend the OS to their own purposes and make them conform to their own event models.

2.4 CALLBACK FUNCTIONS

One of the oldest tools for event handling is the callback function. This is a procedural model for event-driven programming, strongly based on the interrupt vector table model. The callback function must have a prescribed interface, but the precise interface may be different depending on the type of event. The event type, or message type, is at run-time a small integer. That integer is used to compute a position in a callback table (just as the interrupt type is used at the hardware level to compute a position in the interrupt vector table). At this position is stored a pointer to the appropriate callback function. The callback function is invoked by the message loop using the callback table when it discovers a message at the head of the queue corresponding to that particular type of event. When the function has executed, it simply returns control to the message loop. The run-time representation of the callback function is a code pointer; in C and C++, for which there is an actual function pointer data type, the message loop is not a part of the run-time model—the message queue and the message loop are written by the programmer or generated by a code generator. In languages that do not supply a function pointer type there must be other built-in mechanisms for associating functions with events, and the run-time system must implement those mechanisms.

To implement an event-driven model with callback functions, there must be a method of associating a particular event type with a specific callback function. It is too primitive and error-prone to rely on the programmer to directly manipulate the callback table by storing function pointers, even if it is compatible with the language model to do so. In any EDP environment, there will either be library facilities for making the association, or there will be facilities built into the language itself.

2.5   OBJECT-ORIENTED MODELS FOR EDP

In an object-oriented setting, the question of what handler should respond to an event is somewhat more complicated. In this setting, two questions must be answered when an event occurs. The first is, "What objects have an interest in the event?," and the second is, "What specific behaviors (represented as methods, or member functions, of the object's class) of those objects should be invoked in order to respond to the event?" So we see that it takes more than a function pointer to represent the event handler at run-time—the handler must in fact be an (object, method) pair. What this means at run-time is that enough information must be present in the run-time representation of the event handler to specify both the object and its method. In a compiled language like C++, this will require a data pointer to furnish a referencing environment and a code pointer to represent the actions to be taken in response to the event. (Note that static methods used as event handlers do not fall into this category. They are essentially callback functions, because their referencing environments are static.)

For a language with a highly simulated environment, a single pointer or reference may be sufficient because run-time actions can be used to traverse a single structure in order to identify both the object and the method. For example, the Java Swing library provides a *listener list* for each type of event, consisting of objects which are able to respond to the event. When the event occurs, the list is traversed and each object on the list is sent the same message. For example, if the event is an "action event" (a button was pushed or a menu item was selected, for example) then each object will be sent the *ActionPerformed* message along with a single *ActionEvent* argument.

Again, each event type must be associated with a particular method interface. The essential ingredients in this type of EDP environment are that (a) the programmer is somehow allowed to specify which objects are able to handle events of a given type and (b) there is a protocol or mechanism for assigning one of the methods of that object to the event.

Although an event must be associated with a particular method interface, it does not necessarily follow that all handlers for a specific event must come from a specific class of objects. Two methods from two quite different classes may be associated with the same event at different times or even at the same time. All that is necessary is that the two methods have the prescribed number and types of parameters, in the same order, and that they return the prescribed type of result.

2.6   AN EXAMPLE OF AN EVENT AND ITS LIFETIME

For a specific example, let us consider mouse actions. If a mouse button is pressed, and the user expects some program action to occur as a result, how might the hardware, the operating system, and the programming language run-time system in concert communicate to the running program the fact that the button was pressed? What information might be transmitted to the program in order for the correct response to occur? How might that information be transmitted? Let us try to break down in time sequence what internal actions might occur, and answer these questions as these actions unfold.

On a hardware level, the pressing of the mouse button typically causes an interrupt to occur. But the EDP programmer does not program the response to the mouse click by writing an interrupt handler in machine language—that is far too inflexible, especially when you consider that there may be several independently running tasks which are interested in mouse clicks. Typically, the interrupt handler is generic and does nothing more than fashion a message with encoded information about the mouse click and place that message in a buffer. On a hardware level, too little is known about the context of the mouse click to completely handle the event.

What does the generic interrupt handler place into its message? There are only two things at that level which need to be known. The first is simply that a mouse click has indeed occurred. This fact can be communicated as a message type. In other words, the encoded message contains an unsigned integer type ID code, and that code communicates the type of message. The message type might at that level be quite generic, and might simply denote the arrival of data on a serial line. But for simplification let us assume that the type of the message is that of a mouse click. The second vital piece of information is an indication of *where* the mouse click occurred. This information is stored in low-level registers or memory and can be transcribed into a message. The location of the mouse click is communicated on the most basic level as a pair of absolute mouse cursor coordinates, an (x, y) pair with the x value giving the number of pixels from the leftmost edge of the screen and the y value giving the number of pixels from the top edge of the screen.

Thus, the interrupt handler need only fashion a message with three components: the "mouse click" message ID code, the absolute x coordinate of the mouse cursor, and the absolute y coordinate of the mouse cursor. Is this message then sent on to the message loop of the application? Not without alteration. The message encoded as stated does not contain enough information to identify what task or tasks might be interested in the event, nor does it allow for relative coordinates within a screen window. Because of overlapping windows, a given set of absolute screen coordinates for a mouse cursor may in fact be mapped to several independently running tasks. In order for a task to lay claim to a specific mouse click, that task must be associated with a window which both contains the mouse cursor and is positioned in front of all other windows which contain the mouse cursor. The hardware interrupt handler is too low-level a routine to be interested in these details. Higher level window management software must pick up the message from where it was left by the interrupt handler and identify which window has the focus and which task handles messages associated with that window. It must then reformulate the absolute mouse coordinates as coordinates relative to a specific window and fashion a new message for the active task. The new message is then placed in a queue associated with that task.

The above scenario is not a case study but an illustration. The actual details of how the mouse cursor is maintained and updated in response to mouse movements are much more complex and are not the point here. The point is that in order for the EDP run-time to function effectively, low-level hardware events must be passed along to higher and higher levels of software until sufficient information is brought together to form a message relevant to the EDP environment. That message is then delivered to a high-level queue associated with a program unit which has the responsibility for responding to that particular message. Ultimately a message loop discovers the message and invokes the appropriate event handler. All this typically occurs in a small enough fraction of a second so that the user who clicked the mouse button perceives no delay before seeing the desired effects take place on the screen, effects that in fact were programmed into the mouse click event handler.

2.7 PROGRAMMING IN AN OBJECT-ORIENTED WINDOWING ENVIRONMENT

The most obvious place where we encounter events and their handlers is in designing applications for direct manipulation of graphics displays. Accordingly, we will spend some time discussing common characteristics of those displays and the keyboard and mouse events which are associated with them, and of environments for constructing applications for them. Many integrated development environments (IDEs) are available for programming graphical user interfaces (GUIs), and virtually all of them are built around an object-oriented programming language (OOPL). There are a variety of language designs within that general category, and there is a corresponding richness of choice in the IDEs and the associated libraries which support GUI development. There are, however, also a number of commonalities, which we will try to summarize.

2.7.1 Bitmapped Graphics Displays

All GUI development environments provide some basic tools, and once a programmer has written programs in one such environment it becomes easier to move to a new environment of the same type, because there are specific tools one looks for and expects to find. All of these tools have as their central focus a high-resolution graphics display.

Modern display devices are bitmapped, meaning that the display consists of a rectangular arrangement of tiny *pixels*, or points of color on the screen, and that the determination of how to paint each pixel is dependent upon an underlying data structure called a *bitmap*. The bitmap contains enough information to determine how to paint each pixel. This determination is done in hardware by a graphics card, and is extremely sophisticated—the correct drawing of hundreds of thousands, or millions, of pixels on the screen seems to our slow eyes to occur instantaneously.

The best way to understand a bitmap is to realize that (1) corresponding to each pixel on the screen there is a small contiguous block of memory somewhere in the bitmap containing all the necessary information about that pixel, and that (2) the larger this block is, all other things being equal, the richer the capabilities of the corresponding display. If there is only one bit behind each pixel, then only a newspaper-like black and white pixilated display is possible. That is true because if there is only one bit, then each pixel is either "on" (white) or "off" (black). On the other hand, if there are eight bits behind each pixel then each pixel can be in one of 2^8, or 256, states. A bitmap design of this type would usually mean a display was capable of exhibiting 256 colors at the same time. Early versions of MS Windows used this scheme. A typical current design uses either 24 bits or 32 bits to define the state of a pixel. The latter type of bitmap uses 24 bits to determine color and an additional eight bits to define the "transparency" of a pixel. We will concentrate only on color in this discussion.

The 24-bit pixel can be viewed as being made up of three 8-bit parts, corresponding to the colors red, green, and blue: the larger the value, the lighter the color. These three values are often called the RGB coordinates. A zero in all three coordinates corresponds to black, and a value of 255 in all three coordinates is the color white. There are some interesting counterintuitive things that happen because we are mixing light, not pigment. An RGB coordinate combination of (255, 255, 0), i.e., full-intensity red combined with full-intensity green, gives us yellow. And how do we achieve the color brown? Well, as it turns out brown is best approximated as "dark yellow." The coordinate combination (140, 100, 0), for example, makes a very nice milk-chocolate brown.

The gross structure of the bitmap, like that of the display itself, is rectangular. For example, a display with dimensions 1024 by 768 (horizontal by vertical) would incorporate $1024 \times 768 = 786,432$ pixels. Many configurations, with finer resolutions and millions of pixels, are within the capabilities of current graphics cards, as bigger and better displays continue to be seen on the market.

2.7.2 Partitioning the Display

A bit-mapped graphics display is a very flexible thing. Because of the large amount of "screen real estate," we are able to keep track of a number of different processes by fixing our attention on different parts of the screen, where various visual displays offer us specific views of the states of those processes. The traditional "windowing" environment gives each of those views a rectangular form, typically with a "frame," or border, delineating the boundary of the view and with a title bar announcing the contents of the window in summary form. The reader should keep in mind, though, that the restriction to a rectangular appearance is not necessary, nor is it universal.

Whatever one calls these depictions of process states, whether "windows" or "views" or "worlds," it is clear that a major function of an IDE for GUI development should be to enable the programmer to craft them, draw them as he sees fit, and place them on the display for the enlightenment of the user. We will use the term "view" for these depictions throughout this chapter, partly because the more common term, "window," implies a specific kind of rectangular display, and we wish our discussion to be more general.

2.7.3 Mice, Cursors, and the "Focus"

To navigate the bit-mapped graphics display requires a pointing device, such as a mouse, a pen, a touch pad, or a human finger and a touch-sensitive display. No matter how the technology enables it, there must be some visual feedback to allow the user to properly manipulate the display. Accordingly, the operating system maintains two things: (1) an internal (x, y) integer pair which is a record of the last known mouse location, and (2) a "mouse cursor" which provides visual feedback to inform the user concerning where the system declares the mouse to be positioned. A system-level event handling facility underlies the coordination of these two entities. Specifically, it is the primitive mouse "move" event which continually fires and keeps this information current. When a mouse "click" event occurs, however, a totally different type of cursor may be brought into play.

In the old days of purely text-oriented displays, it was typically only possible to view the output of one process at a time. If the process invited input from the user, it displayed a cursor, indicating a spot on the screen at which keyboard input would be displayed as it was entered. Such a cursor would today be referred to as a "text cursor," to distinguish it from the mouse cursor. The text cursor usually takes the form of a short blinking line or a blinking rectangular background surrounding a single character in the display. Usually, if there is a text cursor to be seen in a view, it signifies that the view has the "focus," meaning that it will respond to keyboard events. It is usually the click event, however, that "gives the focus" to the view.

Commonly, there are several views on the screen at any time that are capable of responding to click events. Any such view has an area of the screen which it "owns," for the sake of responding to such events. If one clicks in this area, then the view receives the focus. A view that has the focus often also has a text cursor and has been enabled to respond to keyboard events, which means something similar to what the old-style cursor meant: if you press a key, something will happen, and usually that just means that (a) the character corresponding to the key will echo on the screen and (b) that character will be inserted into some text buffer being maintained by the corresponding process. However, it is totally up to the programmer of the view and its underlying process to determine how to respond to particular mouse and keyboard events.

2.8   TWO-STAGE VIEW CREATION

In an object-oriented programming environment, the creation of a view means the creation of a program object. This may not be as simple as it sounds, however. Normally an "object," in the programming language sense of the word, is created by simply calling a constructor or issuing a message to the corresponding class that a new instance is needed. But there is a problem with that simplistic idea of view creation. The operating system, or the language run-time system, will typically not give the programmer direct control of the visual appearance of the view. Instead, it will maintain a bitmap and other essential pieces of information, such as the current location on the screen and whether or not the view has the focus, in its own separately maintained data structures. This means that no matter how artfully one crafts the constructor, the result of calling that constructor will be totally invisible to the user. If the programmer does attempt to "draw" the view inside the constructor, he may quickly discover that he does not have sufficient information for properly doing so. This is because some of the decisions about how to draw that view will reside with the language run-time or the operating system. In this case, some separate action must be taken in the form of a system call or a separate message to some run-time object in order to create the visible manifestation of the view.

Thus, there are two stages in the creation of a view: (1) the creation of the internal object (the "view object," as we will refer to it) which the corresponding process will be manipulating, and (2) the creation of its visible manifestation (which we will simply call the "view"). These two may need to be created separately, with each having at most partial information about the other. Once both have been created, they must be coordinated so that the visible view is "true," i.e., so that the view on the screen gives an accurate representation of the internal state of the view object. This accuracy then must be maintained, and a major responsibility of the programmer in a GUI environment is to keep the two objects coordinated.

The above considerations mean that there are two events which must be uppermost in the mind of the GUI programmer. First is the "load," or "initial update" event, which is the first point in time at which full information is available about both the underlying view object and the view on the screen. Until this event occurs, the view object is incomplete and cannot perform the program actions required to draw the view. The second event is the "paint" event, in which the view is updated, i.e., redrawn using current information. Often, the states of one or more view objects depend on those of other program objects, and it is up to the programmer to keep in mind that when an internal object changes in such a way as to affect any of its views, the affected views must be redrawn. This redrawing may occur outside the paint event handler, and may only consist of making a localized change in the view, using graphics primitives. However, updating the display often means that the programmer himself must generate a paint event. GUI libraries will usually provide a generic view class and a method call within that view class which "raises" the paint event, indirectly invoking the event handler and causing the view to be redrawn.

However, the programmer chooses to do it, he must be responsible for the maintenance of the display. This typically means that he must, at a minimum, provide an event handler for the "paint" event, and that this event handler must regenerate at least a portion, and often the entire displayed view from scratch. But if the only place where any drawing takes place is within the paint event handler, then the paint event must typically be raised in several places throughout the GUI application. If multiple repaints of this nature are rapidly queued, then the screen may begin to flicker and, if so, the resulting display will not present a pleasant appearance to the user. For this reason, it is often desirable to either (a) find ways to draw only those segments of the display which are affected, or to (b) draw the changes on a separate bitmap and periodically "blit" them onto the screen (see Section 2.10 below).

2.9   A WARNING ABOUT CODE GENERATORS

Much of the code which creates a message loop, creates a view object, creates the external manifestation of a view, and keeps the display true is repetitive in nature and appears much the same from application to application. This fact has led to routine usage of code generators to lessen the overhead of beginning a new GUI application and adding additional event handlers. The programmer invokes a code generator of a specific type and is prompted for some generic information concerning the type of application or component he wishes to create, and the skeleton, or shell, of a program for that specific type of application is generated for him. This saves him from continually "reinventing the wheel" every time he begins coding a new application or program component, because he is spared from generating "by hand" a body of code which would be very similar to the skeletal code for any other project of the given type.

There are two caveats that need to be considered when working with code generators. The first concerns the diluting of intellectual property. A carefully designed program is the property of its creator, and the programmer has copyright protection in the same sense that the author of a literary work has copyright protection. But if the programmer's creative input consists of the modification of a template, the establishment of rights is more complicated. The second problem is the problem of maintenance. When the code generator's initial interview with the programmer is conducted, a series of decisions are made which affect the resources available to the programmer in the constructed framework. Subsequently, after the programmer has made wholesale changes to the code which was constructed, he often will find that he failed to request a resource which is highly desired, or is essential to the application. This unfortunate circumstance may be due to poor planning or a change in specifications, but it is a very common happening. At any rate, the programmer may be faced with the difficult choice of (a) doing without the resource, (b) inserting by hand the code and/or data necessary to make the resource available (often a highly technical and difficult task), or (c) regenerating the code and reinserting the same changes in the newly generated code which were inserted in the original skeleton.

Even if the programmer plans exceptionally well and specifications are stable, the scenario above can and often does result when new versions of an IDE and its accompanying code generators are released. A high premium is placed on upgrading to the new environment, but the code generated by the old version of the IDE may not be compatible with the support framework of the new IDE. In this case, the code may in fact be relatively mature code, with the programmer's creative inputs hopelessly intertwined with the generated code.

Is there any way out of this dilemma? Yes, but the solution is largely not language-theoretic. The insertion of changes into generated code files must be done very carefully, and if there are wholesale changes, they should be documented well enough to be reproducible in a routine fashion. The best kinds of changes are those which are minimal and which make reference to code which resides in separate hand-coded files; inserting hundreds of lines of code into a generated code file is asking for trouble.

2.10   GENERIC GRAPHICS OVERVIEW

This textbook is not primarily concerned with graphics, but some minimal set of graphics capabilities needs to be described here in order to give us a foundation upon which to build our examples. Constructing a GUI application does not have to involve drawing directly onto the screen, because much of what is needed in the construction of a GUI has usually already been developed and in fact is available in the IDE in "drag and drop" form. But some of the most compelling and interesting examples are obtained by assuming that the programmer has a blank canvas on which to paint at load time and at paint time.

Any graphics primitive in a purely object-oriented environment will be an instance method of a class and will do its work in response to messages sent to objects of that class. It is usually not the view object, however, that alters the display. There typically will be another object which is associated with the view, knows its boundaries, knows its defaults, and is able to draw on it. For the sake of this brief discussion we will call this the *drawing object*. Being an object, it has state, meaning that it remembers things like what color it is currently drawing with, what color it is filling regions with (if that happens to be a different color), at what point in the view it is currently positioned, etc.

Before we talk about the typical capabilities of a drawing object, we must understand what the drawing object means by screen position, or pixel position. Fortunately, the coordinatizing of a screen is fairly standard, but programmers often find that standard initially difficult to accommodate because it fails to conform to either of the two most natural mental models. The first natural model views a pixel as an (x, y) pair, but in fact the orientation of the rectangle being coordinatized is not the same as that encountered in coordinate geometry. Instead of having $(0, 0)$ at the lower left-hand corner, it is always found at the upper left-hand corner. In other words, the positive direction on the y-axis is down, not up, so that in coordinate geometry terms the quadrant represented in Figure 1 is actually what we would refer to as the "first quadrant," i.e., the quadrant where all coordinate values are positive. So the programmer must modify his mental picture of a coordinatized plane.

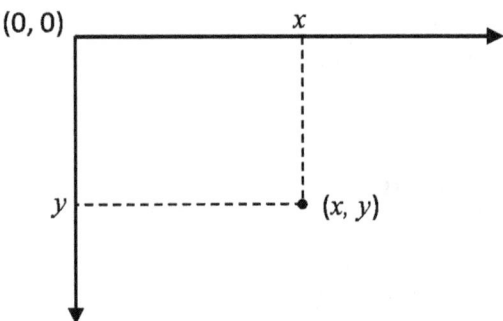

FIGURE 2.1 Coordinate Scheme for a View

The second natural model, which also fails to apply, is that of an indexed matrix, or doubly subscripted array. In a real sense, it is true that a bitmap can be thought of as a rectangular array of pixels, but as soon as we start to think of it in those terms we run afoul of the conflicting standard that in such an array subscripting scheme it is the row subscript that comes first. If we are using (x, y) pairs (and we are), then it is in fact the column subscript which comes first.

The fact that the coordinatization of a view runs afoul of both mental models which the programmer might bring with him when learning a set of graphics primitives would seem to be a minor problem, and it is. After working with the coordinate scheme for a while, it becomes a perfectly comfortable orientation. However, the mapping of the internal state of a view object into its on-screen manifestation often is complicated by the fact that the natural organization of the internal data structures in the view object follows one or the other of these older, well-established conventions. A straightforward mapping may render an image which is upside-down or reflected.

Another issue is the standardization of the idea of the "position" within the display of an object that is larger than one pixel. We typically must consider such an object as being drawn inside a containing (or bounding, or circumscribing) rectangle. But because of the convention that the two positive directions are left to right and top to bottom, the *base position* of a drawn object is usually (but not always) considered to be the upper left-hand corner of its containing rectangle.

All the above having been said, it is a relatively simple matter to summarize some commonly encountered basic capabilities of a drawing object:

1. Draw a line of a given color and thickness from one pixel location to another.

2. Draw a rectangle with its base position at a particular pixel position and with a specific width and height (or alternatively with its opposite corner positioned at a specific pixel location). Here various schemes are employed for specifying the color and thickness of the border, and for the color of the interior.

3. Draw an oval (as used here, "oval" is synonymous with "ellipse") inscribed in a specific rectangle. The interface for this capability is usually identical to that for drawing a rectangle.

4. Draw a polygon with a given set of vertices, using an array of pixel coordinates to specify those vertices. Typically this algorithm can detect the "interior" of the polygon, and so the same considerations apply for drawing and filling as apply in the case of rectangles or ovals.

5. Draw a text string with a specific font and a specific base position.

6. Given a base position and a (language-, library-, or operating-system-specific) bitmap data structure, draw the indicated bitmap at that position. (This operation is often called "blitting," and all graphics cards are designed to accomplish this type of action very efficiently.)

Each language and/or graphics library adds many more drawing methods to the basic list given here. Colors to be used either for drawing a boundary or filling an interior may be passed as parameters to the method call or, more commonly, taken from the current internal state of the drawing object. The details of how to perform some of the above actions and other drawing actions in specific languages and environments will be given in succeeding chapters of this text.

2.11   PRIMITIVE EVENTS AND THEIR HANDLERS

In this section, we catalog and discuss the more primitive basic events to which the EDP programmer might need to respond by supplying event handlers. Some of those have already been mentioned above, but we need to discuss them in greater detail.

2.11.1 Mouse Events

These events are all primitive, in the sense that they have their origins in hardware interrupts. For example, "mouse move" occurs one or more times every time the user moves the mouse. The event will often occur on a primitive level as a data event on a serial line, but by the time it has been processed by the operating system and the language run-time system, it will have been crafted into an event which can be of use to the high-level language programmer. The event in this more abstracted form will encapsulate only one essential piece of information: the (x, y) coordinates of the mouse at the time the event occurred. If the application wishes to use a whole series of mouse move events, for example, in order to draw a scribbled line on the screen, then the application must save each of the reported mouse positions in a data structure. The paint event handler can then use this recorded history of mouse positions in a manner consistent with the desired effect.

Mouse "click" events have many variations, depending on whether the mouse has one, two, or three buttons and on whether multiple clicks are treated as a different type of event. Thus, we can have simple "click" events, "left click" events, "right click" events, or even "double click" events. Some systems allow the programmer to break down a mouse click into a "mouse button down" and a "mouse button up" event. All of these events will encapsulate the pixel position at which the event occurred, and in systems where there is not a separate multiple click event it may be the case that some or all of the click events also encapsulate a "click count." Thus, in the latter case, if the programmer wishes to specify what is to happen when the user "double clicks," he must write the click event handler to check the click count and invoke the desired action only in the case where the click count is two or greater.

2.11.2 Keyboard Events

Events associated with the keyboard are more sophisticated than one might suppose. Like mouse events, they originate as hardware interrupts, but by the time they have been screened by the underlying layers of support software they will be presented to the application as very cleanly specified abstract events. Some systems supply only a simple "key" or "key pressed" event, along with an ASCII or Unicode representation of the character or control code associated with the key or key combination. Others have both a "key up" and a "key down" event in addition to or instead of the basic event. Also, some way must be worked out to deal with keys which are not associated with specific characters, such as shift keys, control keys, etc. In some programming environments, the programmer may simply not be informed when such keys are pressed, and instead a "cooked" event, such as a key pressed event and a "capital A" code or a "control C" code, may be generated by the run-time system when appropriate. This type of event will not reach the program until all the necessary keys have been pressed.

Keyboards are sophisticated devices, and in spite of the prevailing "qwerty" standard they are not all alike. There are other standards, and even within a basic standard there are myriad differences in the placement of control and function keys and even in the number of such keys. (Consider that it may be important to a given application to be able to discern whether the left shift key is down or up, and whether the right shift key is down or up, and that the response in each of the four possible situations may need to be different.) To deal with these differences in a flexible way, the hardware keyboard interrupt reports only "scan codes," which essentially specify only the position of the key in the keyboard layout. The hardware interrupt handler and other lower level event handlers will do a substantial amount of translation and will ultimately determine the amount of information which the application's own event handler will have at its disposal.

2.11.3 Timer Events

Timer interrupts for hardware processors can occur at a dizzying rate, and it is clear that responding too often to such primitive events and/or asking for too much to happen in response to those events could cause much harm. So, just as is the case with mouse and keyboard events, there is a huge difference between a timer interrupt on the hardware level and a timer event on the application level. But the basic capability to construct and respond to such events rests on the more primitive capability of processors to generate timer interrupts.

Unlike keyboard and mouse events, timer events do not occur automatically. In order to begin receiving such events, the application must ask for them. In order to do this in an OOP environment, this usually means (a) instantiating a timer object, (b) informing this object how often timer events are to be generated, and (c) explicitly issuing a command to start generating timer interrupts. These actions are typically undertaken either in a constructor for some run-time object or in the "load" event handler for the view object.

For basic functionality, there is no information needed in a timer event beyond the fact that an event of that type has occurred. The effect of a timer event handler, like that of a mouse move handler, is achieved via multiple invocations, and often the correct response to a series of such events depends on the accumulation of historical data. Multiple timer events are often possible, however, using multiple timer objects, and the event handler in that case will be told which timer object caused the event and can respond accordingly. For example, in an arcade game application new monsters of type A may be generated every five seconds, and new monsters of type B may be generated every three seconds. One way to achieve this effect is to use two timer objects and write the event handler so that it queries the event object to see which timer object generated the interrupt.

The timer event handler must be written carefully. For example, if the timer object has been told to generate timer events every ten milliseconds, then it is obviously vital that the event handler not use more than ten milliseconds of processing time. This restriction is far too weak, however, because any amount of processing amounting to a significant fraction of ten milliseconds is likely to cause an intolerable overhead which can cripple the application and other applications running concurrently with it.

Just as it is good citizenship for an application which opens a file to close it before it ends, it is good citizenship for an application to stop any timers which it has started before exiting. The run-time system may or may not quickly and efficiently stop the timer, and if the timer event handler is not stopped at the correct time it may attempt to access data that logically no longer exists because the containing object has been destroyed. Often the view object has an associated "destroy" event (see below) which is generated before the view is removed from the display, and one thing that should happen in response to this event is that all timers associated with the view should be stopped.

2.12   HIGHER-LEVEL EVENTS

Not all events can be traced to a hardware interrupt. Just as the hardware interrupt mechanism is too convenient an abstraction to be used solely for its original purpose but has been altered to allow it to be synchronously invoked in software, so the event handling mechanism has been elaborated to the extent that most events have nothing to do with hardware components such as mice, keyboards, and CPU clocks. We have already mentioned some of these "higher level" events, specifically the "load," "paint," and "destroy" events. We will begin with these events, and then discuss programmer-supplied events in general.

2.12.1 The Load Event

The load event is raised by the run-time system or by an explicit program action sometime after the view object has been instantiated and before the first paint event for that view occurs. The event handler for the load event is the first place from which complete information about both the application-level view object and the manifestation of that object on the screen can be ascertained. Some of the actions that might occur inside this handler are to (a) instantiate and/or initialize any objects which will be needed for the initial paint event, (b) instantiate any timers needed for animation or other purposes, and (c) place essential information about the view's screen manifestation at class scope for event handlers or other methods in the view class to use as needed.

2.12.2 The Paint Event

In windowing environments, the various views on the screen must be coordinated by the windowing system in such a way that the focus can be moved from view to view (with an associated change in the screen display), and in such a way that the view with the focus can be reduced or expanded in size, moved, minimized, maximized, dragged, etc. The system may not have enough information to keep in a current state all the bitmaps which are affected by these actions, and which are necessary to draw all the attached displays. Each of those displays is in fact patched together using application-specific views, each of which depends on view objects which may not be part of the windowing system's level of abstraction.

So the system may need to rely on all of its application processes to keep track of their own sets of views and view objects. This means that the best it can do to keep its own bitmaps current is to raise the paint event for each of the views it is currently maintaining, and to count on the applications themselves to draw those views.

The paint event handler receives some or all of the information encapsulated in the paint event, and that information usually comes to the handler in the form of a drawing object which is ready to respond to the commands needed to regenerate the view. Through a series of commands to this drawing object, the paint event handler constructs an accurate depiction of the current state of the view object.

2.12.3 Focus Gained and Focus Lost

A common reaction to a mouse move or click event is to give the keyboard focus to the view object, or to remove the focus from the object. Commonly one of the actions of these mouse event handlers is to raise a "focus gained" or a "focus lost" event, because it is important that the program be informed of these occurrences. Such an event often requires a state change in the view object, for the purpose of making ready for keyboard event handling. If there is a text area to be maintained, the underlying system may respond to the event by displaying a text cursor in the appropriate position (in the case of a "focus gained" event), but the application programmer may want to add his own event handler.

2.12.4 The Destroy Event

When a view is permanently removed from the screen, we say that it has been destroyed. The destruction of the view typically immediately precedes the destruction of the view object behind it, but not always. A notable exception is when the view is a *modal dialog box*, meaning that (1) it is a view generated dynamically by some other object, for the purpose of obtaining some kind of information from the user, and that (2) when it appears on the screen it makes it impossible for the view which spawned it to obtain the focus until the dialog is destroyed. In this case, the dialog box's view is destroyed before its corresponding dialog object, and the process which created the dialog can continue to send and receive messages to and from the dialog object after the dialog box itself has disappeared from the screen. Here the work of the "destroy" event handler is to make sure that whatever information has been entered by the user in his interaction with the dialog box view is available inside the dialog object for the purpose of answering the queries of the parent process. So a large part of the code in the destroy event handler consists of copying data from entities which are part of the dialog box view into data members within the dialog object.

Generally speaking, the actions performed by the destroy event handler include actions similar to those performed by a destructor for a program object— release resources which were tied up by the object during its lifetime. But there may also be a need to transmit information to the underlying view object or to some other program object before the view object itself is destroyed.

2.12.5 Programmer-Defined Events

Events are usually objects of a library type, meaning that they are described as programmer-defined types in the given programming language, and their description is available, if not as source code then as part of the documentation of an EDP library associated with the IDE. New event types can usually be created by the programmer using some language-defined mechanism, such as inheritance. Those events then are typically "raised" in response to synchronous tests at appropriate times during the execution of an application.

It is natural, then, that some program objects might have associated with them one or more events of a programmer-defined type, events that make sense in the context of the application or its user interface. For example, a producer process might raise a "new consumable object" event every time it placed a new consumable object in some queue. A consumer process could then raise an "object consumed" event every time it had finished using one of those objects for its particular purposes.

The advantage of the event model in this setting is that it only very loosely couples the data condition with the actions taken in response to that condition. In contrast to a method call, raising an event *indirectly* invokes the event handler, and the code that raises the event need not be modified nor recompiled when a new event handler is installed.

2.13 GUI COMPONENT EXAMPLES

A GUI component is an encapsulated object that has a representation on the screen which the user identifies as part of a larger view. The component has been programmed to react to certain events and also to raise its own events as notifications to the containing view object. There are a large number of more-or-less standard types of components, and we will present and discuss a few of them here.

2.13.1 Push Buttons and Menu Choices

The simplest active component of a GUI is the push button. It typically has been programmed to respond only to a mouse click event, and in response raises a "button pushed" event in the view object. That event might be specific to the particular button pushed, or it might be a generic push event. In the latter case, the event handler, like a timer event handler, can simply query the event object to determine which button was the source of the event. From the user's point of view, the most important attribute of the push button is a text string or bitmap which appears as part of its on-screen display and (hopefully) accurately describes the button's purpose.

Various responses may be taken to the button push event once the application determines which button was pushed. A Boolean variable might be toggled, a counter might be incremented, a text string might be copied from one place to another in a display, or the view itself might be destroyed.

Logically speaking, a menu choice behaves exactly as a push button behaves, meaning that a "menu item selected" event would be handled in exactly the same manner as a button push event. Like buttons, menu items have a run-time identity, usually expressed as a small integer ID code or a symbol, so that a generic menu item event handler would be possible, but that is not usually the case. Normally, there is more or less a one-to-one correspondence of menu choices to event handlers.

2.13.2 Edit Boxes

An edit box is a rectangular component containing a character string. The contained string is an attribute of the component object and is accessible for reading and writing via public access methods. The component typically is preprogrammed to react to a mouse click event by giving the edit box the focus, and once it has the focus it displays a text cursor and reacts to keyboard events, for the purpose of storing text in the accompanying string buffer and keeping the displayed text consistent with the contents of the buffer.

A selected set of high-level events is used to inform the containing view object about changes in the state of the edit box. Minimally, there are the "focus gained" and "focus lost" events, which fire when the edit box receives the focus and when it loses the focus, respectively. A reasonable response to "focus gained" might be to set the text associated with the box to some default value, or to a value dependent on the current state of some application object. In response to "focus lost," the text of the box might be copied elsewhere, either to another part of the display or to some program object, or both.

For situations in which fragments of a user's input must cause immediate response, before the focus lost event fires, some edit boxes will raise a "text changed" event every time there is any change in the contents of the text string.

A distinction is often made between edit boxes which only display one line of text and those which "wrap" and are able to display multiple lines. From the standpoint of the event programmer, there is no difference. The multiple line display was of course more difficult for the component designer to achieve, but that capability has now been encapsulated and does not affect the client programmer, for whom a simple character string remains as the only essential attribute at run-time.

2.13.3 List Boxes

A list box is a list of strings, again displayed in a rectangular area of a containing view. Here, as in the case of the edit box, it may be that the actual data which accompanies the visual display is larger than the capacity of the component to display it. That is not a problem with the single-line text box, because it is programmed to display a text cursor and to always keep that cursor in view while the edit box has the focus, so that the user can see any part of the string by giving the edit box the focus and then moving the text cursor through the string. But although a list box can certainly receive the focus, it typically will not display a text cursor but only highlights a selected string in response to a mouse click. Hence, a list box is often accompanied by a vertical scroll bar (see Section 2.13.4), so that the user can scan the contents of the list box by dragging the button on the scroll bar.

As indicated above, the most important attributes of a list box are its list of strings and the location of the string which is currently selected. The latter is most likely indicated by an integer attribute, which is either a one-based or a zero-based index into the collection of strings.

Events commonly raised by a list box in the containing view object include the "selection changed" event, as well as some more primitive events that are passed on, such as mouse clicks and double clicks, and keyboard events used as "hot key" actions. For example, a common set of user actions is to click on a particular line of the list box, then press the "delete" key. To the programmer this appears as two consecutive events: a "selection changed" event, followed by the more primitive keyboard event. In response to the latter, the programmer tests to determine which key was pressed. Finding that it is a delete key, the programmer removes the line of text from the screen and from the underlying data structure. An alternate approach is to make the delete key a "hot key," meaning that pressing that key raises a "delete" event, and the necessary actions take place in the handler for that more specific event.

2.13.4 Scroll Bars

A scroll bar seldom appears by itself; it is commonly "attached" to other components or to the view itself. The interaction of such a scroll bar when it is attached, say, to a list box, has been preprogrammed and encapsulated. Scroll bars can, of course, be used as stand-alone components, in which case they usually signify to the user the capability of moving swiftly through some aspect of the display, such as a bitmap or text object.

When scroll bars are used as stand-alone components, they are somewhat complex. They are already programmed to react to primitive mouse events in order to achieve a "click and drag" effect, but how is that effect to be passed on by the programmer to the other parts of the display which he intends to control? Before we answer this question, we must answer the question of what higher-level events might be raised by the user's manipulation of the scroll bar.

The scroll bar has two essential parts: (1) the "button," and (2) the "track" on which the button slides. The user interacts with the scroll bar by clicking on the track, or by clicking on the button and dragging it along the track. The only absolutely essential piece of information the programmer needs is a precise indication of where on the track the button is positioned at any given time. This information could be communicated to the programmer by a simple readable attribute, say a fraction (a floating point number between 0 and 1) or a small integer. In the latter case, the range of integers represented by the scroll bar could be specified in a constructor or in a method call. It is then up to the programmer to map the values which fall between the upper and lower limits of the scroll bar's range into intermediate states of the display and render that display correctly for each position along the scroll bar.

Passive access functions are not enough, of course. The containing view object should be notified concerning the user's interactions with the scroll bar. The simplest way to do this would be with a "position changed" event (a modified pass-through of the mouse move event), in response to which the programmer could simply query the scroll bar object concerning its current position and modify the display accordingly. However, if such modification is complex, the programmer should consider the likelihood that the change of position event might fire with great rapidity, causing a significant processor load.

If the programmer wishes the freedom to wait until the user has reached the desired final position of the button on the scroll bar before taking action, he may choose to ignore the "position changed" event and to react to some other more informative combination of events. A button push event and a button release event might be all that is necessary, after which the programmer can query the scroll bar object and paint the affected area of the display (and make corresponding changes in the affected program objects) accordingly. In practice, however, the events and attributes associated with scroll bars vary widely, and each of the incarnations of this standard component merits a separate, careful study.

2.14   GUIS AND THREADING

Threads are often an essential part of the design of an application with a graphical user interface for one important reason. When a user causes an event for which the handler (a) is computationally time-consuming and (b) can reasonably be expected by the user to execute in the background and leave the interface operational, then the event handler should do most of its processing in a separate thread. Often, the EDP environment enforces this actively, routinely creating a new thread for each invocation of an event handler. If not, the programmer will need to create the thread using other language or library facilities. Regardless, if threading is used then the programmer's task may become more difficult, because race conditions could be introduced. Some events should be disabled, and some menu items should be "grayed out," to avoid giving the appearance to the user that the event caused by the menu choice is operational.

2.15   SUMMARY

Programming in a windowing environment means programming for the purpose of causing, and reacting to, events. It often also means constructing some or all of the elements of the display using graphics primitives. A graphics display in such an environment consists of a rectangular arrangement of *pixels*, and is maintained through the manipulation of a *bitmap*, which is the internal data structure underlying the pixel arrangement. Each pixel is assigned a color which is determined by a fixed-length element of the bitmap which corresponds to that pixel.

Some objects within a program with a graphical user interface (GUI) have the specific purpose to provide the user with an external representation of some part of the state of that program. We call these objects *view objects*, and their screen representations we call *views*. Views often require a two-stage construction regimen, consisting of synchronous actions taken by the program and event-driven actions determined by the operating system or language run-time system.

By reacting to mouse move events which track the movement of the mouse by the user, the system maintains an (x, y) pair representing the position of a mouse cursor, and draws the cursor in the correct position. The mouse move event can be handled also by user programs, as can various forms of the mouse "click" event. A common response to a mouse click event is to give to a view the keyboard "focus," meaning that keyboard actions by the user will now raise events such as "key up," "key down," or "key pressed" in the application. Such events can be "cooked," meaning they take into account shift keys and control keys by encapsulating a single character code, or they can be "raw," meaning that every key causes its own event, including shift, control, and function keys. Focus gained and focus lost events are typically raised as a result of mouse movements and/or clicks.

The "load" event occurs when a view first appears on the screen, and the view object may need to react to that event in some way in order to match its internal state and the appearance of the view. The "destroy" event occurs when the view is removed from the screen, and may or may not coincide with the destruction of the view object. Timer events are typically achieved by constructing and/or initializing a timer object, and occur at regularly spaced intervals of time.

In a windowing library, an event is usually defined as a class, and programmers typically can define and use their own event types. Standard GUI components such as menu items, push buttons, text boxes, list boxes, and scroll bars both consume and produce such higher-level events.

Code generators are usually integrated into IDEs for windowing applications, and can automatically generate skeleton code for various types of applications and components. The programmer should use these with caution, making sure to document carefully the changes needed in the skeleton in order to produce the finished source code.

Graphics commands which affect the display are typically issued as messages to a drawing object which encapsulates a bitmap and various attributes and tools for drawing. Such graphics commands assume a coordinate system which places the origin at the upper left corner of the bounding rectangle of the view. Commands which draw geometric figures such as ellipses, rectangles, lines, and arbitrary polygons are among the essential capabilities of a drawing object.

REVIEW QUESTIONS

1. What is the nature of event-driven programming? Describe the mindset of the programmer who is writing an event-driven program.

2. Define each of the following terms:
   a. Event
   b. Message
   c. Message queue
   d. Event handler
   e. Message loop

3. Describe the idea of a hardware interrupt. What external stimuli might cause a hardware interrupt?

4. Define the terms *interrupt vector* and *interrupt vector table*, and *interrupt handler*. How is an interrupt vector table used by a CPU with an interruptible processor?

5. Discuss in detail the steps involved in handling a hardware interrupt.

6. Describe what is meant by a *software interrupt*.

7. Give two meanings for the term *message*. How do the two usages of the term relate to each other?

8. What is the difference between a thread and a process? How are interrupts and interrupt handlers involved in the implementation of threads and processes?

9. Describe the procedural event-handling model which centers around callback functions and a callback table.

10. When an event occurs in an object-oriented EDP environment, what two questions must be answered in order to handle the event?

11. Describe in general terms the process by which a mouse action is translated from a low-level interrupt into a message on the message queue of an application.

12. Explain what is meant by a bitmapped graphics display.

13. Describe the memory organization of a color corresponding to a 24-bit pixel.

14. The "mouse move" hardware event allows a windowing system to keep what kind of information current?

15. What is the "focus"? How does a view obtain the focus? What changes may occur when a view obtains the focus?

16. Explain why a view often needs to be constructed in two stages.

17. Describe two ways to combat "flicker" due to frequent, complex screen updates.

18. Explain why code generators are useful, and why they tend to be widely used in an EDP programming environment.

19. Describe two disadvantages or difficulties which accrue when a programmer constructs his program by editing a generated code file.

20. Is the graphical construction of a representation of process state in a view

allocated for that purpose on the screen accomplished by sending a series of messages to the view object? How is it accomplished?

21. Describe some attributes which are likely to be part of the internal state of a drawing object.

22. Describe the typical coordinatization scheme for pixels in a view.

23. How does the Cartesian coordinate system differ from pixel coordinates? How do row and column indices for a matrix differ from pixel coordinates?

24. The pixel coordinates at what location on the screen are usually referred to as those of the "base position" of a screen object?

25. Describe some commonly encountered capabilities of a drawing object.

26. What must be done to maintain a display consisting of a scribbled line input by the user using mouse actions? What events are involved, and what information must be stored?

27. Describe two ways a mouse event handler interface could be constructed to detect and respond to "double-click" events.

28. Describe several approaches to keyboard event handling. What specific kinds of events might be generated, and what information would be transmitted to the event handler?

29. What are keyboard "scan codes," and why are they needed?

30. Describe a protocol for setting up and responding to timer events.

31. Why is a "mouse move" event handler often constructed in a way similar to that in which a timer event handler is constructed?

32. How can one timer event handler process events from more than one timer?

33. Why must timer event handlers be written very carefully, and why is brevity important?

34. How is the stopping of a timer similar to the closing of a file? Describe a typical timer "lifetime," in terms of when timer events usually begin and when they end.

35. Describe the *load* (or "initial update") event. When might it occur, and what things are often accomplished by a load event handler?

36. Describe the *paint* event. When might it occur, and what is accomplished by a paint event handler?

37. Describe the *focus gained* event. When might it occur, and what things might be accomplished by its event handler?

38. Describe the *focus lost* event. When might it occur, and what things might be accomplished by its event handler?

39. Describe the *destroy* event. When might it occur, and what might be accomplished by its event handler?

40. Describe the concept of programmer-defined events. How are they similar to software interrupts?

41. Since a programmer-defined event occurs synchronously, it is a fair question to ask why a simple procedure call would not do just as well as "raising" an event. What is the advantage of an event handling mechanism over a procedure call?

42. From an event handler's perspective, why is a button push event similar to a menu selection event?

43. Describe some events often associated with text boxes, both events that are handled by the text box itself and those which it might raise in the containing view object.

44. Describe some events which a list box might raise in the containing view object.

45. Describe the parts of a scroll bar, its attributes, and the events it might raise in the containing view object, along with a general description of how the programmer might have the corresponding event handler react to those events.

46. Why are threads often an essential part of the design of an application with a graphical user interface?

EXERCISES

1. In your favorite language, describe what facilities are available for an indirect procedure call. Can you construct a callback table? Describe carefully and give code examples, and mention whether the language's support for EDP has any inherent limitations.

2. Write a procedure p with one integer parameter n with at least quadratic complexity. (A selection sort is an example, but if you use it you will also need to write a routine which can randomly generate large amounts of

data.) Write a driver which calls the procedure with varying values of n and times the execution of each call down to one microsecond. Through experimentation, determine the largest value of n for which your procedure will run in...

a. 10 microseconds.
b. 100 microseconds.
c. 500 microseconds.
d. 1 millisecond.

3. Using interpolation in the data from Exercise 2 and assuming the procedure p is to be used as a timer event handler, estimate the largest value of n for which the event will be handled using no more than one-third of a time slice, assuming...

a. A time slice is 500 microseconds.
b. A time slice is 1 millisecond.
c. A time slice is 10 milliseconds.

4. Let's say a certain program holds integer data in a standard two-dimensional array A with m rows and n columns. The data is to be pictured on the screen as a bitmap. You have written a function called colorOf() which takes row index i and column index j as its parameters (in that order) and returns a 24-bit integer value which is the color you want to use to represent the value in A[i][j]. Write a code segment in your favorite language that will draw the screen in such a way that each entry in A is represented as a single pixel on the screen, with A[0][0] placed at the bottom left, with each row in the array corresponding to a single y coordinate on the screen, and with each column in the array corresponding to a single x coordinate. Assume the drawing object is called drawer and you can paint a single pixel at location (x,y) by sending drawer the message drawPixel(x,y,color), where color is represented in the standard way as a 24-bit integer.

5. Write a method, function, or procedure called separate in your favorite language that takes a single integer parameter and returns three results. (Returning three separate results is tricky and the best way to do it depends on the language you are using. Use your best judgment.) Precisely, separate takes one 24-bit integer and returns the three 8-bit color components red level, green level, and blue level. Assume that red is in the low-order bits, blue in the high-order bits, and green in the middle. For example, separate(1000000) should return a red level of 64, a green level of 66, and a blue level of 15. This is because 1000000 is $15 \cdot 256^2 + 66 \cdot 256 + 64$.

3

SMALLTALK AND THE SQUEAK ENVIRONMENT

A lthough Simula clearly initiated the object-oriented idea, the first modern OOPL did not appear on the scene until the Dynabook group at Xerox Palo Alto Research Center (PARC) developed the Smalltalk programming language. Smalltalk was intended to be interpreted, and its design is elegant and simple, with few syntax rules. Way ahead of its time, it was designed around a direct-manipulation graphical development environment and provided tools for the programmer to construct sophisticated interfaces based on mouse and keyboard events. The Squeak implementation, which we will introduce and use in this chapter, is the direct descendant of the original Smalltalk-80 environment and continues the admirable educational ideals of *Dynabook*.

3.1 A BRIEF HISTORY OF SMALLTALK

Alan Kay was in the right place at the right time. The '60s and '70s seem to have supplied the "meme pool" from which most good ideas in Computer Science have sprung, and Kay had the good fortune to be fully immersed in that deep pool. In the early '60s as a programmer in the military, then later as a graduate student at the University of Utah, and through consulting work on a variety of projects, Kay was exposed to a dizzying array of seminal ideas. Somewhere in his head he knew these ideas needed clarification and crystallization. He was struck early on with the idea that the computer would eventually become personal and that there would be more power in a computer the size of a notebook than there was at that time in the largest and most powerful mainframes. He was exposed to the idea of objects through his work at Utah with the Simula language, but he knew that what he needed went beyond what that language provided. What was needed was a metaphor powerful enough to be understood quickly not just by programmers but by naïve users, even very young users. His work on the early Sketchpad system of Evans and Sutherland showed him how powerfully on-screen graphics could pull the user into a virtual world. Others around him were talking about the computer as an augmentation to the human brain. All this was happening at a time when most programming was done without interactive displays. Most of the computing world had no notion that direct interaction between the computer and a human being could ever be a practical, or even a desirable, goal.

But Kay latched onto the vision that computers could be personalized, even individually programmed, by their users in a straightforward fashion. In a way, he anticipated the world in which we now live, where children are exposed to computers in an interactive way and naturally and effortlessly become proficient as they mature. When he went to the newly formed Xerox PARC and established the Learning Research Group, he presented each of his new hires with the notebook computer idea and centered all the efforts of the group on that idea. The eventual result was the Dynabook project and the Smalltalk language, a vision communicated by Kay and implemented and embellished by two prominent members of his group, Dan Ingalls and Adele Goldberg.

3.2 "EVERYTHING IS AN OBJECT"—BASIC SMALLTALK SYNTAX AND SEMANTICS

Smalltalk is radically object-oriented. When we say that everything is an object in this language, we mean that all data types in the language participate in the same inheritance hierarchy. Specifically, all types are classes and descend from a common base class (*ProtoObject*), even the numeric types. Moreover, the only way any work gets done in this language is by sending messages to objects.

Code samples for this chapter are located on the companion CD-ROM.

For example, the expression 2+2 gets turned on its head. Instead of viewing this as an invocation of a primitive addition operation, with both operands being the value 2, we view it as an "add" message transmitted to object 2 (the left-hand side of the expression) with 2 (the right-hand side) as an operand. This is true uniformly, meaning that almost all binary operations are viewed as a message being sent to the left-hand operand with the right-hand operand being an argument of the message. The one exception is assignment (we will use the operator symbol := for assignment here, one of the notations which works in Squeak, but some systems use a leftward-pointing arrow), in which the left-hand argument is not an object but a name.

3.2.1 Messages

Let's begin, then, by talking about messages, i.e., method calls. There are three message classifications in Smalltalk: unary, binary, and keyword. A *unary* message is named by an identifier and has a postfix-style notation, as in n **negated**, which returns a number having the same magnitude as the number n but the opposite sign. A *binary* message is an operator (for example, the asterisk symbol for multiplication) which has two operands. The left-hand operand is actually the object receiving the message, and the right-hand operand is the argument of the message. The example 2+2, given above, illustrates this type of message. Finally, a *keyword message* may have two or more operands and is named by a series of identifiers, each followed by a colon. Thus, the syntax

```
(a < b) ifTrue:[x:=1] ifFalse:[x:=2]
```

is interpreted as follows. First, the binary message < is sent to the number a with operand b. If b is a number, as required, this will return either the object true or the object false. Both of the latter objects are capable of understanding the message **ifTrue:ifFalse:** – the object true reacts to the message by evaluating the first block ([x: = 1]) and the object false reacts by evaluating the second block ([x:=2]).

Think about what this means in terms of the design of methods. If a programmer needs to define a new method with two or more parameters, the only choices available to that programmer are to define the method with an operator symbol or to construct a keyword message. A method call that in C++ or Java would have the form obj.f(x,y,z) must in Smalltalk be designed using three names—one to separate the object from its first parameter, one to separate the first two parameters, and one to separate the last two parameters. We can use a single identifier for all three, as in

```
obj f: x f: y f: z
```

but this is at best awkward. On the other hand, the conscientious programmer can always find ways to make his code self-documenting. For example, a program action that requests an employee data collection called empBase to add employee a to department b with pay classification 4 might be coded as

```
empBase add: a toDepartment: b withPayClass: 4
```

As you can see from the example, sometimes this naming convention can be used to make the meaning of a program statement quite clear.

Precedence rules in the Smalltalk language are simple. Unary messages have the highest priority, then binary operators, and finally keyword messages. Parentheses can be used to modify order of execution, in the usual way. Multiple unary messages are evaluated from left to right, as are multiple binary operators.

NOTE *It is helpful to look at a couple of examples. (1) The formula $\sqrt{e^{\sin x}}$ involves three successive applications of unary messages, and would be coded as x **sin exp sqrt**. The postfix syntax here makes for an odd-looking but unambiguous expression. (2) On the other hand, we are surprised when we think through the repercussions of Smalltalk's simple precedence rules and realize that the value of 3+4*2 is 14, not 11, as both + and * are binary operators and have the same precedence.*

Keyword messages cannot be nested without the use of parentheses, for obvious reasons. Consider, for example, the application of two keyword messages `f:` and `g:`, in sequence, with object x receiving the initial message and parameters y and z being supplied to each method call in turn. Without the parentheses, this would appear as x `f:` y `g:` z. Unfortunately, however, Smalltalk would parse that as a single keyword message `f:g:`. The correct call should be coded as (x `f:`y) `g:`z.

3.2.2 Symbols

Smalltalk maintains dynamic run-time information on all accessible entities, and does so by making the names of objects and classes available as keys for a lookup, so that their attributes can be quickly determined. A name used in this way as a key is called a *symbol*, and any string can be used as a symbol by prefixing it with the # character. For example, the type of the expression `'Colonel Sanders'` is `ByteString`, but that of `#'Colonel Sanders'` is `ByteSymbol`, the type given to symbols. If a string is a valid identifier or method name, then no quotes are required; for instance, `#KFC` and `#ifTrue:ifFalse:` represent the same symbols as `#'KFC'` and `#'ifTrue:ifFalse:'`, respectively.

This is another source of Smalltalk's flexibility. Any object can be sent the message **perform:**, or the message **perform:with:**, or any of a series of similar messages, where the first argument is a symbol representing one of the methods of the object receiving the message. For example, x **negated** can be coded as x **perform:** `#negated`. Also, 2 + 2 can be coded as 2 **perform:** `#+` **with:** 2. The net effect is that we can use a symbol as a *selector* for the purpose of dynamically determining what actions we wish to see an object perform.

Because a symbol is data, then in particular we can use the name of a method as data. Such an item of data can be passed as a parameter to a method, and we can use one of the **perform:** family of messages to dynamically look up the method represented by the symbol. This ability is very useful for the implementation of event handling.

3.3 NAMES AND TYPES

Names in Smalltalk are run-time entities, meaning that the translation step is rudimentary and does not destroy names. Instead all names are entered into tables along with their attributes, and the name can be used at run-time as a key by which the object, method, class, or other association can be looked up and its attributes determined.

3.3.1 Dynamic Bindings and the Referencing Environment

Identifiers in Smalltalk are not statically bound to a type. The type of an object resides with its value, not with any particular name. Thus, the assignment $x := y$ is always a legal statement and does not cause any type checking to occur. After the assignment takes place, the names x and y will simply refer to the same object. (In other words, Smalltalk uses pointer semantics: after the assignment x and y are aliases.) The type of the old value held by variable x is irrelevant, because that value will no longer be associated with x.

Smalltalk partitions its name space in a few very simple ways. Type names (i.e., class names) reside at the global level and are placed in the global dictionary whose name is Smalltalk. Other names can also be stored globally by placing them in the Smalltalk dictionary. A variable name may always be introduced into a block, either as a temporary variable or as a parameter. Similarly, method definitions can incorporate temporary variables as well as parameters. Finally, each class defines a set of class variables and a set of instance variables. Instance variables are visible inside instance methods, whereas class variables are visible inside both class methods and instance methods.

Let us say again, for emphasis, that at all levels of the referencing environment the only lasting attribute of a variable is its name. There are no static bindings of variables to types or values. The type of a variable is an attribute of its value, and that value may change as program execution progresses. That does not mean types themselves play a minor role. In fact, just the opposite is true.

3.3.2 Types

A Smalltalk environment always incorporates a rich variety of types, some of which are primitive but most of which are library types defined completely in Smalltalk as Smalltalk classes. All Smalltalk types are classes; most descend from the base class `Object`, and all types descend from the common library class `ProtoObject`.

Distinguishing between primitive types and library types is both difficult and unnecessary. For example, a rich set of numeric types is available in the Squeak environment, including `SmallInteger`, `Integer`, `Float`, `Fraction`, and `ScaledDecimal`. Because each method has the opportunity of deciding for itself the type of the object returned, we get interesting results such as the fact that `5/2` returns a `Fraction` instance, but `4/2` returns a `SmallInteger` instance. The distinction between primitive types and library types is further blurred by the facts that (a) one can add new methods to a so-called primitive type, and that (b) some of the methods which one might consider 'primitive' are actually written in Smalltalk and their definitions can be inspected by the programmer.

Literals are for the most part formed in the standard ways, but the fluidity of type transfers obscures the distinction between different types of literals. The type of an integer literal depends on the number of digits it contains, for example. String literals are unconventional in that they are enclosed in single quotes, not double. Double quotes enclose comments, which can appear anywhere. Both string literals and comments can span multiple lines without any special characters needed. Character literals use a `$` prefix, so that the character corresponding to a capital `'a'` is coded as `$A`, a dollar sign is `$$`, and a space is a dollar sign followed by a space. The last convention being somewhat odd, one might be better advised to use the expression

   ` ' ' `**asCharacter**

or

   `Character` **cr**

instead, because they are more readable, though also more wordy!

Array literals are easy to form and use, because arrays in Smalltalk are heterogeneous and the type of such a literal is simply `Array`. The syntax of an array literal is a series of Smalltalk tokens preceded by the `#(` delimiter and ended by the right parenthesis `)`. For example, `#(23 25 32)` is an array containing three `SmallInteger` values. What actually happens is that everything that comes between these two delimiters is lexically analyzed and translated into an array of tokens. Thus, `#(67 frank [x:=3])` is stored as a seven-element array with values `67`, `#frank`, `#'['`, `#x`, `#':='`, `3`, and `#']'`.

Squeak Smalltalk adds a second notation for constructing arrays, namely a sequence of expressions enclosed in curly braces and separated by periods. For example, if `y` currently has the value binding `55` then the notation `{21.7 . y+1 . 'Thelma'}` evaluates to a three-element array whose elements are the objects `21.7`, `56`, and `'Thelma'`. Each element of the period-separated list is evaluated at run-time, not at compile time.

3.3.3 Type BlockContext

The type `BlockContext` is an extremely important data type in Smalltalk. Having such a data type places Smalltalk in an unusual category where programming languages are concerned: the category of languages in which *executable code* can be used as data. A `BlockContext` literal consists of a sequence of Smalltalk expressions separated by periods and enclosed in square brackets. Such a literal denotes an unevaluated code sequence. When the message **value** is sent to such an object, the expressions it contains are evaluated in order, and the value of the last expression is returned.

NOTE

*As an example consider the assignment f := [25 **sqrt** + 4], which causes the variable f to be assigned an unevaluated Smalltalk expression (a BlockContext object). Evaluation is accomplished by sending the **value** message; for instance, the assignment g := f **value** would place in g the value 9.*

Here the language takes on somewhat of a functional appearance. We can introduce a named parameter into a `BlockContext` object by preceding the parameter's name by a colon at the very beginning of a `BlockContext` literal, just inside the left brace, and separating the parameter from the first expression with a vertical line, as follows:

```
h := [:x | x*x +(38*x) -12]
```

Such a parameterized block can be evaluated by sending it the **value:** message, as follows:

```
h value: 2
```

The value of the latter expression is the value of the polynomial $x^2 + 38x -12$ at $x = 2$.

Two or more parameters can be used in a parameterized block. To implement the function $C(m, n)$, the number of combinations of m things taken n at a time, we might use the following assignment:

```
comb:= [:m :n | m factorial / ((n factorial)*((m-n)factorial))]
```

The value $C(9, 5)$ could then be (very inefficiently) computed as

```
comb value: 9 value: 5
```

Temporary variables can be used inside a `BlockContext` object by enclosing them in a space-separated list inside vertical bars. An example follows, where `temp` and `swapped` are temporaries and `a` and `b` appear as free variables.

```
swapper := [ | temp swapped |
    swapped:= false.
    (a < b) ifTrue: [temp:=a.  a:=b.  b:=temp.  swapped:=true].
    swapped
]
```

The above `BlockContext` object can only be coded in a setting in which variables `a` and `b` exist, and those variables should be bound to numerical values before the `value` message is sent to the object. Sending the message `swapper value` causes the values associated with variables `a` and `b` to be swapped if `a`'s current value is smaller than `b`'s, and the value `true` returned if a swap actually occurred. But be careful here. If `swapper` is returned as the value of a method, and the `value` message is sent to that object in a different setting, the associations used for variables `a` and `b` will be those for the original context in which the `BlockContext` object was created, even if the host environment now has different associations for those variables. Thus, a `BlockContext` object represents a *closure*, i.e., an expression in which all variables have been replaced by references (pointers) to the symbol table entries which those variables were bound to when the expression was created. Note that if `a` and `b` are bound to temporaries or local variables, this means those variables will now outlive the context in which they were created. Even if the symbol table in which they were originally installed has been destroyed, these two entries will be preserved as long as the `BlockContext` object to which they are bound exists. We say that the object has *captured* the variables `a` and `b`.

3.3.4 Basic Operators

Operator symbols in Smalltalk are not special in any way other than their syntax. They are simply names that come with prepackaged bindings which can, like just about any binding in this language, be changed. Because every type in the language is open to inspection, and every type is part of a unified hierarchy, most definitions of most operators can and should be redefined as new types are added or old definitions are changed or refactored. There are a few bindings which are special, however, in the sense that there are precise conventions concerning their meanings.

In class `ProtoObject`, we see the definitions of operators `==` and `~~`. Because this class is the ultimate base class for all types, we can use these comparison operators to compare any two objects for equality or inequality, respectively. But this is not a value comparison. At this level, we are asking whether or not the objects referred to on either side of the operator symbol are actually *the same object*. These operations are defined on a primitive level, and should never be overridden or redefined.

One step down in the type hierarchy, in class `Object`, we encounter the definitions of operators `=` and `~=`, the value equality and inequality operators. Unlike the operators in `ProtoObject`, these operators are routinely overridden. Each new type defines a new universe of possible values, and what it means for two objects to have the same value must be carefully considered when such types are defined.

In class `Magnitude`, we encounter for the first time the order comparison operators `<`, `>`, `<=`, and `>=`. Again, these are redefined several times in the set of types which descend from it, which includes all the library numeric types.

Finally, the type `Boolean` includes the `&` and `|` operators, which we know as "and" and "or," respectively, as well as a series of keyword messages which have similar functionality, such as **and:**, **and:and:**, **or:**, **or:or:**, etc.

3.3.5 The nil Object

The object `nil`, like all other objects in Smalltalk, is a first-class object. Its type is `UndefinedObject`, which inherits directly from `Object`. All class, temporary, and instance variables have `nil` as their initial value.

Because `nil` is an object, however, it can receive messages. This is not to say that any method in class `Object` can legitimately be sent to the `nil` object (some will be rejected by run-time checks), but `nil` is able to successfully handle several methods in that class. For example, a programmer designing a method cannot err by comparing `a` and `b` with the expression `a = b`. Even if `a` has not been initialized, the message is correctly executed, because `nil` is able to compare itself with other objects.

3.3.6 Storage Management

A consequence of Smalltalk's pointer semantics is that objects are routinely created and destroyed, and the programmer is not bothered with the details of destruction. However, there is always at least one creation operation for each class (class method **new**, to be overridden by the programmer at his own risk), and often there is a rich variety of such instance creation capabilities (see class `Rectangle` below, for example).

All the realities of heap storage management come into play, of course, but they are dealt with by the language run-time. Garbage collection of some sort is required, and the timing and details of object destruction are determined by the whims of the garbage collector.

3.4   CONTROL FLOW IN A SMALLTALK PROGRAM

Control flow in Smalltalk is dictated by two things: function composition and inheritance hierarchy. Messages like `ifTrue:` are sent to objects and those objects then have the opportunity to evaluate or not to evaluate an operand. For example, two of the classes which implement the `ifTrue:` instance method are classes `True` and `False`, each of which is a subclass of class `Boolean`, and each of which is a singleton with only one instance. If the instance `true` receives the message, it evaluates the operand. If the instance `false` receives the message, it simply ignores it.

When we speak of "evaluating," we truly mean that the object receiving the message does itself "evaluate" the block of code passed as an operand. For example, in response to the `ifTrue:` message the object `true` would send the **value** message to the `BlockContext` operand.

In addition to the `ifTrue:` method, the class Boolean also has the **ifTrue:ifFalse:** method and the `ifFalse:` method. These methods are defined in Smalltalk; the programmer can examine the code and add similar methods of his own, as desired.

Constructing the standard *if...elseif...elseif...endif* control structure is awkward in this language. For this reason, the Squeak dialect adds a new control structure as a message to instances of class `Object`, namely the **caseOf:** message. In order to do this, Squeak adds a new primitive data type called `Association` and an operation in class `Object` with operator symbol `->`. An instance of class `Association` is a *(key, value)* pair. In response to a message sent with operator `->`, an instance of `Object` returns an association having itself as key and the operand as value. The operand supplied to **caseOf:** is an object of the class `Collection`, every element of which must be an instance of `Association` where both the key and the value are `BlockContext` objects. An example follows:

```
dayNumber caseOf: {
        [1] -> ['Sunday'].
        [2] -> ['Monday'].
        [3] -> ['Tuesday'].
        [4] -> ['Wednesday'].
```

```
    [5] -> ['Thursday'].
    [6] -> ['Friday'].
    [7] -> ['Saturday']
}
```

In the above example, the collection of associations is inspected one at a time as the object receiving the **caseOf:** message (i.e., dayNumber) searches for an association which has a key which is equal to itself. When such an association is found, the value portion of that association (a BlockContext object) is evaluated and its value is returned as the value of the method call. Note that there is the potential for additional side effects, because each 'key' is actually a BlockContext object which must be evaluated.

The equivalent code using **ifTrue:ifFalse:** messages sent to Boolean objects would appear as follows:

```
dayNumber = 1 ifTrue: ['Sunday']
ifFalse: [ dayNumber = 2 ifTrue: ['Monday']
ifFalse: [ dayNumber = 3 ifTrue: ['Tuesday']
ifFalse: [ dayNumber = 4 ifTrue: ['Wednesday']
ifFalse: [ dayNumber = 5 ifTrue: ['Thursday']
ifFalse: [ dayNumber = 6 ifTrue: ['Friday']
ifFalse: [ dayNumber = 7 ifTrue: ['Saturday']
]]]]]]
```

The code which might appear in a more conventional language as

```
if a < b then c := d
else if a < c then d := e
else e := f
```

would appear as follows:

```
true caseOf: {
    [a<b] -> [c := d].
    [a<c] -> [d := e].
}
otherwise: [e := f]
```

Loops are also achieved by sending the appropriate messages to objects. For example, the **whileTrue:** message can be sent to a BlockContext object to achieve a while loop effect, as the following example shows:

```
[x < limit] whileTrue: [x := x + 0.05]
```

The block context object receiving the message evaluates itself, and if the value is true it evaluates the argument and resends the same message to itself. If the value it obtains by evaluating itself is false, it simply returns false and the loop ends. Thus, looping is actually achieved via recursive calls on the **whileTrue:** method.

Iterative loops are implemented as messages sent to numbers. For example, to construct a `BlockContext` object which when evaluated computes and returns the sum of the square roots of all the integers from 1 to 100, one could write...

```
[ |sum|
    sum := 0.
    1 to: 100 do: [:n |
        sum := sum + n sqrt
    ].
    sum
]
```

3.5 THE SQUEAK DIALECT AND ENVIRONMENT

The Squeak programming environment is open-source, and is available as a free download. Squeak is a direct descendant of the original groundbreaking Smalltalk-80 environment at Xerox PARC. It is more than a programming environment; it is also a dialect of the Smalltalk language, a large and growing class library, and a means of access to a vast body of open source code. Most of Squeak is written in Smalltalk, and all of that code is visible using the Squeak browser tool.

3.5.1 Navigating Squeak

The reader should of course familiarize himself with Squeak, a task which is easily accomplished using the online helps and tutorials that are available. In particular, upon installing Squeak you will be given several simple tutorial windows which acquaint you with the menu system and the specific ways one can use the mouse buttons and keyboard. It is important to read this brief tutorial material, because some things commonly assumed about what various mouse actions should do are not valid in this environment. Remember, however, that this is the original mouse-and-bitmapped-graphics environment, and was the test bed for developing all the interactions with which we are now so familiar.

The feel of the environment is somewhat odd but well worth mastering. Important tools to which we will be referring throughout this chapter include: (a) the workspace window, in which code fragments can be entered and executed; (b) the transcript window, in which simple text output can be made to appear; and (c) the browser window, in which relationships between classes can be examined, code from the library can be looked up and displayed, and new code can be entered. The user actively experimenting with the Squeak development environment should always have at least one workspace window and one transcript window open. (Having more than one transcript window is unnecessary, because there is only one `Transcript` object, and every transcript window is sent the same text in response to messages to that object.)

The workspace and transcript windows can be employed by the user to familiarize herself with Smalltalk's semantics. A piece of code of the form

```
Transcript show: <Smalltalk expression>
```

can be typed into the workspace window and executed, whereupon the value of the expression will be seen in the transcript window. However, just typing the desired command and pressing the "Enter" key will not cause the command to be executed. To execute the command, the user should select the entire text of the command with the mouse (using a "click and drag" motion) then press "Ctrl-D" (for "do it"). Only then will the output be seen in the transcript window.

3.5.2 The Squeak Browser Window

The lower pane of the Squeak browser, besides being a window into the source code, is also the means of adding to that body of source code. To install a new class definition one overtypes an old one or a template and "accepts" the new definition, which immediately becomes a part of the user's local copy of the library (*without* erasing the class whose definition was overtyped).

Fileout and *Filein* operations are available via menu choices, for the purpose of saving and restoring source code in text files. This capability is essential, but the more usual manner of updating code during development is simply to save and restore the state of the entire environment as a community of persistent communicating objects.

An example of a class definition follows:

```
Object subclass: #Gadget
    instanceVariableNames: 'cog gear numCogs numGears'
    classVariableNames: 'DefaultNumCogs DefaultNumGears'
```

```
poolDictionaries: ''
category: 'Application-Classes'
```

This definition is for class `Gadget`, a subclass of `Object`. The class definition is established by sending a message to its superclass (the keyword message `subclass:instanceVariableNames:` etc.). Two of the arguments in that message are a string containing a space-separated list of instance variable names and a similar string of class variable names. (Class variables, like class names, must start with a capital letter.) The class is placed in category `Application-Classes`, but the category has no language-theoretic impact. Categories are only useful for the purpose of arranging class definitions inside the browser for organizational and search purposes. In this particular case, if the category `Application-Classes` does not already exist it will be created as a side effect of installing the above definition.

Pool dictionaries allow the programmer to set up a series of identifier associations and make those associations available to the class. A pool dictionary is simply an object of type `Dictionary`, which is a collection of (*key, value*) pairs, the key always being a symbol. Recording the name of the dictionary in this fashion in the class definition is all that is necessary to allow class methods and instance methods to use the names from that dictionary without qualification. No pool dictionary is associated with the example class.

Figure 3.1 is a screen shot of a browser window. (To reiterate, the window was obtained by clicking on the 'tools' tab to the right in a Squeak project pane, then dragging the browser icon onto the larger pane.) The window entered the state below after the user clicked on the category `Kernel-Chronology` in the upper-left pane.

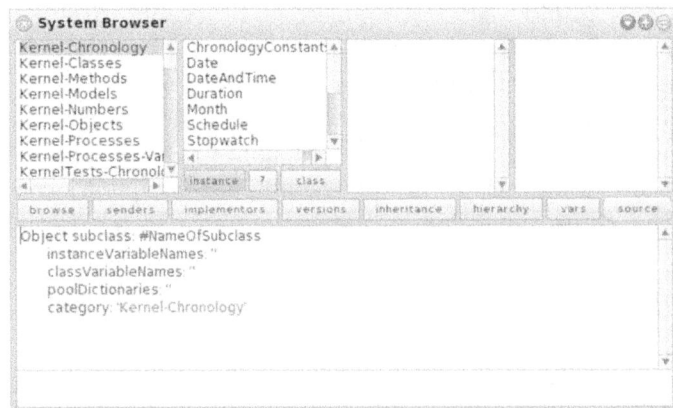

FIGURE 3.1 A Squeak browser window.

If at this point we wish to create the `Gadget` class mentioned above, we can selectively overtype portions of the lower pane, producing the window state pictured in Figure 3.2.

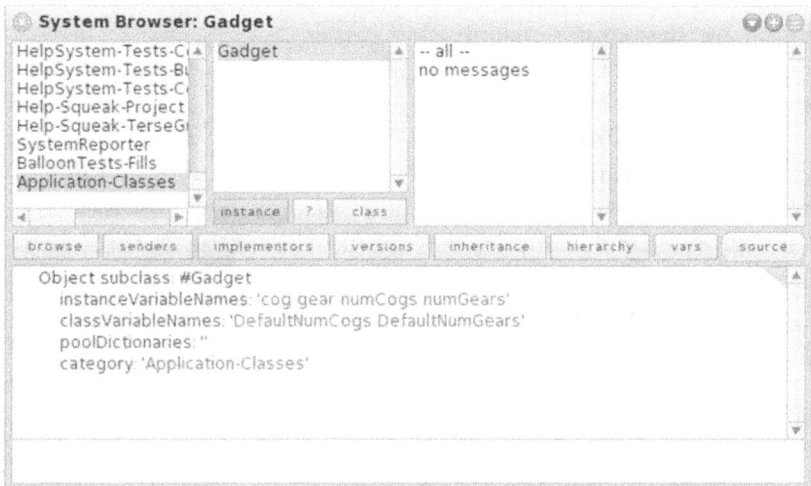

FIGURE 3.2 The browser window from Figure 3.1 after the `Gadget` class creation code has been inserted.

Now we can make the new class part of the library by selecting all the text in the lower panel (ctrl-a), then accepting the definition with the ctrl-s keystroke.

To install a new method, one uses an approach similar to that for adding a new class—the browser displays a template in its bottom frame, and the user overtypes the template and requests that Squeak accept the new method. The association of method with class is done not with static syntax but in a dynamic, context-sensitive way, by selecting the class from a list in a separate pane, selecting either "instance" or "class" to indicate which type of method, specifying in another pane the category of the new method, and finally overtyping a template or an existing method definition with the new definition. An example of an instance method definition for class `Integer` is as follows:

```
divides: anInteger
    "Answer true if self goes evenly into anInteger"
    self = 0 ifTrue: [^false].
    ^anInteger \\ self abs = 0
```

In the example, the operator `\\` is the integer "mod" operator. The value of m **divides:** n will be true provided that m is not zero and n **mod** |m| is zero.

The first line of the definition is the method's explanatory comment. In the second line, the binary operator `=` is used and constitutes a message to self, i.e., to the object (the `Integer` instance) receiving the message. Here `self` must decide if its own value is zero, and if so it returns `false`. On the other hand, if it is not then `self` receives the **abs** message, and returns a positive nonzero value, its magnitude. The function then returns `true` if and only if the remainder upon dividing `anInteger` by that positive magnitude.

Here the symbol ^ appears for the first time in our discussion. Its usage makes it appear to be a prefix operator, yet we made no reference to such an operator above, insisting that all operators are infix. In that discussion, we were talking about operators considered as methods in a class. The ^ symbol does not denote a method of any particular class, but is simply the syntax for specifying a value to be returned from a method call. Thus, its usage is like that of the "return" statement in the C-derived languages.

The browser window in Figure 3.3 was produced after the user (a) selected the category `Kernel-Numbers` from the list box in the top left pane, (b) selected the class `Integer` from the second pane, (c) selected `mathematical functions` from the third pane, and (d) selected `factorial` from the fourth pane. As a consequence of the last action, the source code for the `Integer` instance method **factorial** appears in the bottom pane.

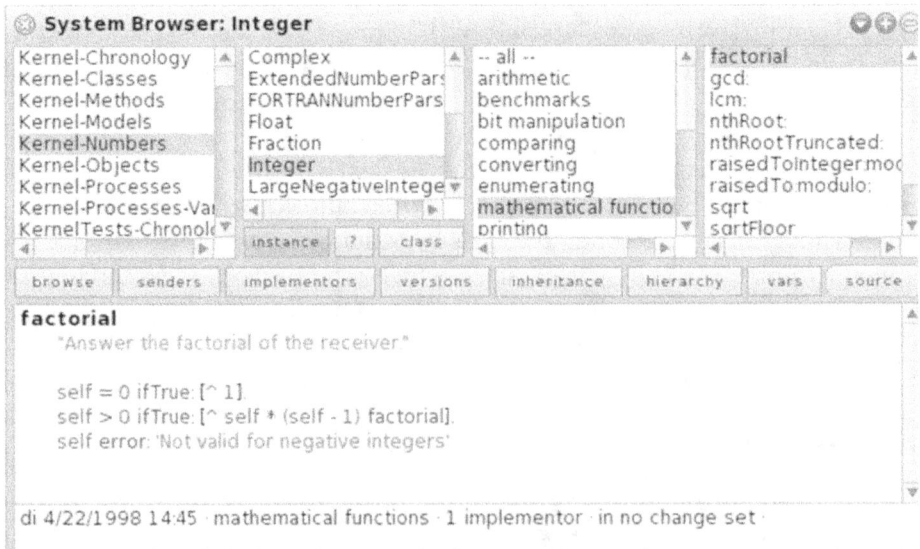

FIGURE 3.3 A browser window displaying the library source code for method **factorial** of class `Integer`.

The new **divides:** method can now be added to class `Integer` by typing its definition in place of that of the factorial function, then pressing the *ctrl-a,* *ctrl-s* sequence. Once that is done, all integers will respond to the **divides:** message. For example, 5 **divides:** 10 will respond `true`, and 2 **divides:** 7 will respond `false`.

If the user wishes to examine the code for a class method (static member function) of a class, then it will be necessary to click on the "class" button. For example, clicking on the class button in Figure 3.3 produces the browser window in Figure 3.4.

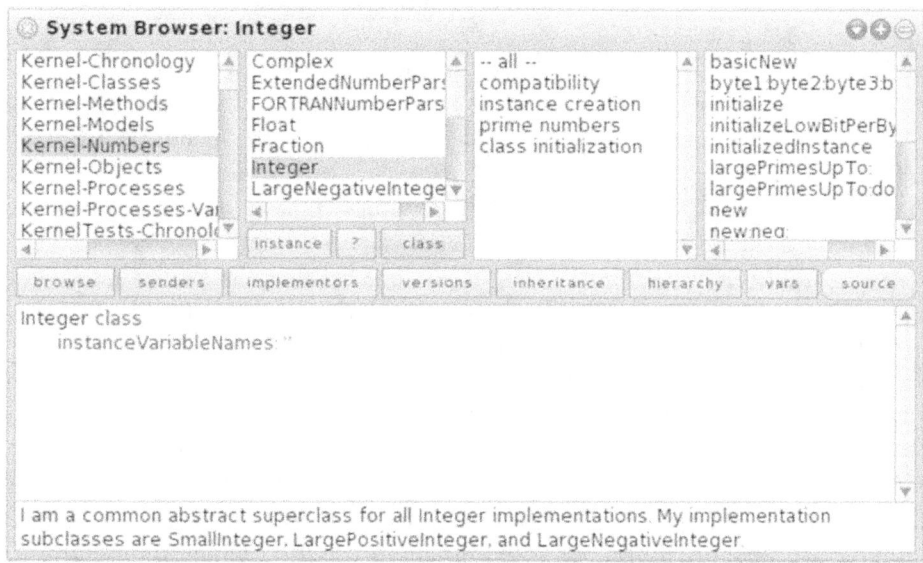

FIGURE 3.4 A browser window displaying the class methods of of class `Integer`.

We now see in the third and fourth panes a totally different set of method categories and methods, all of which are used to send messages to the class itself, as opposed to sending messages to instances. The reader should investigate some of these method definitions. An interesting example is the **new** message, which ordinarily would be used to create new instances of the class, but in this case would cause an error. Because there is not enough static structure to the language to discover at translation time that `Integer` cannot handle the **new** message (being "abstract"), it is up to the **new** method itself to inform the user of the error, at run-time. Thus, the concept of an abstract class is implemented as a coding convention, not as a language feature.

To install a new class method involves the same actions as those which were used to install a new instance method: overtype any of the existing methods, select, and accept.

A highly detailed menu is available at any time by clicking on any part of the screen inside the Smalltalk window which is not occupied by another object with its own mouse event handler. This menu will offer the important option to save the state of your Smalltalk session, to quit without saving, or to save and then quit.

3.6 INFORMATION HIDING IN SMALLTALK

Recall that in Simula 67 there was no information hiding. Every data member and every member function of a class was accessible to clients. Smalltalk took a radically different approach, completely hiding all its data from clients! A Smalltalk class variable is visible only from within a class or instance method of that class or one of its subclasses, and an instance variable is visible only from within an instance method of the class or one of its subclasses. (There is, in fact, no syntax for referring to data members of an object or class from outside that object or class!) This policy enforces strictly the use of accessor and mutator functions. The programmer must make a conscious decision to make a data member accessible (by writing an accessor and/or a mutator), or it will not in fact be accessible.

On the other hand, all methods, class or instance, are public. This is a point on which one could criticize the language on principle, but the designers decided to keep the number of restrictive rules to a minimum. This design decision in favor of simplicity, however, means that if a method is highly technical and is included only for the purpose of supplying some auxiliary function to another method, then that technical method will appear on the public interface and could likely be terribly misused by the client programmer. It is considered good citizenship to place such a method in the "private" category, but categories in Smalltalk have nothing to do with access rights, so placing a method in a particular category cannot prevent that method from being invoked from outside the class.

3.7 POLYMORPHISM IN SMALLTALK

Polymorphism is another area where Smalltalk broke with its predecessor, Simula 67. In the latter language, we could use the keyword *virtual* to make a method polymorphic, and if we did not use that attribute all calls to that method would be resolved statically. In contrast, polymorphism is not optional in Smalltalk. Each message sent is sent to a run-time object, and that object will respond to the message if its class has an appropriate method. If the object has no methods that can receive the message, then the message will be sent to the object considered as an instance of its superclass. This procedure continues until an appropriate method is found to respond to the message, or until there are no more superclasses to check, whereupon an exception is generated.

There is one exception to this rule, which requires careful study to understand well. From within a method definition, the pseudovariable `super` refers to the current object considered as an instance of its superclass. So messages sent to `super` will never be responded to by instance methods of the current object's own class. But this exception to polymorphism is only temporary. Consider the following method definition:

```
f
    super f f
```

Here the first call on `f` is not recursive, because it is fielded by a method either in the superclass or some indirect base class further back in the hierarchy. On the other hand, assuming the method handling the call returned `self`, as is usually the case because that is the default return value, the second call on `f` is in fact *directly* recursive because of polymorphism. As a result, under the stated assumptions the above method will cause an infinite loop, if invoked.

3.8   SMALLTALK CONTAINERS

`Array` is one of those types that seems to be a mixture of primitives and library code. The **at:** and the **at:put:** methods are primitives, meaning that they are not written in Smalltalk and their complete definitions cannot be examined from within the Squeak environment. It is these two methods that furnish the basic capabilities we expect from an array, i.e., to be able to store items at specific numbered locations and to be able to retrieve those items when they are needed. Interestingly, these capabilities are implemented in the base class `Object`, not in `Array` itself.

This basic `Array` data type is greatly embellished, however, in Squeak. To these simple capabilities is added a long list of additional methods, some of which appear quite special-purpose and strange. Moreover, `Array` as a class appears fairly deep in the inheritance hierarchy. As a matter of fact, it is six levels deep, as illustrated below:

```
ProtoObject
```

```
Object
    Collection
        SequenceableCollection
            ArrayedCollection
                Array
```

Even though the **at:** message appears in the penultimate superclass `Object`, Smalltalk does not allow this access function to be invoked for every class derived from `Object`. It performs a run-time type check to ensure that the object receiving the message is "indexable." An exception occurs when that is not the case. Many such examples of run-time checks can be found in this language—with only a perfunctory translation step and a scarcity of translation-time information, run-time checks are usually the only option. Thus, the only teeth in the notion of an "abstract class" is a special-purpose class method which returns `true` or `false`. Examples are **isArray**, **isCollection**, and **isDictionary**, all three of which methods are defined at the `Object` level, and all of which return `false` at that level. Inheritance and polymorphism guarantee that any subclass can qualify as that particular type of container simply by redefining the appropriate method at the subclass level.

In fact, all of the intervening container classes `Collection`, `Sequenceable-Collection`, and `ArrayedCollection` are abstract in that sense, meaning that an attempt to instantiate an object of any of these types causes a run-time check to discover that a certain method has not been overridden, resulting in the throwing of an exception.

`Collection` is the base class for all container classes. Some concrete classes that derive directly from `Collection` include `Set`, `Bag`, `CharacterSet`, and `Matrix`. `Bag` objects are multisets, meaning they are sets capable of storing the same object more than once. `CharacterSet` objects are sets of characters optimized for quick storage and retrieval. Finally, a `Matrix` is a two-dimensional array; interestingly, it does not inherit from `Array`.

`SequenceableCollection` is the base class for container classes whose elements are stored with a defined order. Examples of concrete classes derived from `SequenceableCollection` are `Heap`, `LinkedList`, and `OrderedCollection`. All these are variable-sized lists with an **add:** method. `OrderedCollection` combines the array operations **at:** and **at:put:** with an extensible size, with a resulting decrease in efficiency.

Finally, `ArrayedCollection` includes as subclasses not only the familiar fixed-size array type `Array`, but also its sister classes `Bitmap`, `String`, and `Text`.

3.9 THE MODEL, VIEW, CONTROLLER (MVC) AND MORPHIC PATTERNS

The term "design pattern" was coined recently [Gamma95] to describe any pattern of class and object relationships which tends to suggest itself again and again across a large number of applications. One such pattern, introduced before the term 'pattern' was widely used, was the Smalltalk 80 "Model, View, Controller" (MVC) pattern. Experimenting with direct-manipulation interfaces led the Smalltalk developers naturally to the separation of certain applications into a business class (the 'Model'), a display or window class (the 'View'), and a 'Controller' class. In the Smalltalk MVC framework, a model class need have no particular interface; rather, the view class is designed around the model class and is specialized for the purpose of examining the state of model objects and building some on-screen representation of that state. The controller class implements the event model, routes messages to the appropriate objects, and maintains the display by coordinating the various views.

The Squeak implementation of Smalltalk provides a more streamlined method of building event-driven user interfaces: a recursive design pattern called "Morphic." In this pattern, interface elements are built from objects called morphs, whose classes are derived from class `Morph`. A morph typically is both a model and a view, in the MVC sense, and all morphs can be configured to respond to events. The programmer builds complex user interfaces by placing morphs inside morphs inside morphs, to any level of nesting.

3.10 PIXELS, GRAPHICS OBJECTS, AND DRAWING

Drawing on morphs involves the use of a number of data types and primitives, some of which are quite straightforward. Remember, however, that this is a large and complex library, and there are many subtleties. We will skim lightly over the surface with our examples.

3.10.1 Important Data Types for Drawing

A pixel location in Smalltalk is an object of type `Point`. The `Point` class is essentially identical to other data types we will see in all the languages we will discuss in this text. It has two important instance variables, named `x` and `y`, which are pixel coordinates. For example, one could instantiate such a `Point` object, representing location (80,120), as `Point` **x:** 80 **y:** 120. On the other hand, the expression 80@120 has the same type and value. In other words, the operator @

can be sent as a message to an object of type `Number`, with a `Number` operand, and will return a `Point` object.

As in all graphics libraries, the rectangle is an important abstraction here. Data type `Rectangle` has a number of instance creation primitives, many of which use `Point` objects as parameters. For example, all of the following create and return the rectangle seen in Figure 3.5.

```
Rectangle origin: 20@50 extent: 200@100
Rectangle left: 20 right: 220 top: 50 bottom: 150
Rectangle origin: 20@50 corner: 220@150
Rectangle center: 120@100 extent: 200@100
```

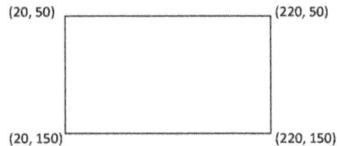

FIGURE 3.5 A rectangle with pixel coordinates for each corner.

Besides these instance creation facilities, a *Point* object is capable of constructing the rectangle in question in response to the **corner:** message, as follows:

```
20@50 corner: 220@150
```

The data type `Color` encapsulates a color which may be specified as either a (red, green, blue) triple or a (hue, saturation, brightness) combination. These two ways of specifying color are equivalent, and we will restrict our attention to the former, in which each color level is expressed as a fraction. Our milk chocolate color can thus be instantiated with the **r:g:b:** class method, then, as

```
Color r: 140.0/255 g: 100.0/255 b: 0
```

A number of premixed colors can be obtained by sending messages to the class `Color`. For example, there are class methods named **red**, **green**, **black**, **white**, **magenta**, and **paleOrange**.

3.10.2 Drawing on a Canvas

To draw on a morph requires a `Canvas` drawing object. This object has all the capabilities described in Section 2.10. For example, if `aCanvas` is a `Canvas` object, then

```
aCanvas line: 50@75 to: 300@800 color: Color black
```

draws a black line from pixel position (50, 75) to pixel position (300, 800). To draw the outline of a rectangle requires the **frameRectangle:color:** method, as for example:

```
aCanvas
    frameRectangle: (Rectangle origin: 0@0 extent: 300@200)
        color: Color black
```

If we desire instead to paint the interior of a rectangle, we use the **fillRectangle:color:** message.

Ellipses are called ovals in this library, and as in other such libraries they are specified using their circumscribing rectangles. We simply use the messages **frameOval:color:** and **fillOval:color:** in a similar way to that just described for rectangles.

To draw a polygon requires the creation of an array of vertices. We can use the methods we have already discussed to construct this array inline, as for example:

```
aCanvas
    drawPolygon: {50@50.100@100.50@100.100@70.200@30}
    color: Color transparent
    borderWidth: 2
    borderColor: Color black
```

Drawing strings is simple, and if one is willing to use the default font, it only involves specifying the base point and the contents of the string, as follows:

```
aCanvas
    drawString: 'Please deposit trash in receptacle'
    at: 70@50
```

Remember that the base position is the upper-left corner of the rectangle in which the string is drawn. So the text above will be drawn below and to the right of pixel position (70, 50).

3.10.3 Default Drawing Attributes

Two important attributes of a morph are its background color and the size of its bounding rectangle. These have default values which are not usually suitable, namely a dark blue background and a rather small rectangle positioned at the top left corner of the containing world. (The "world" at any given time is determined by the global variable `World`. It is simply a morph that contains all other visible morphs). The functionality for making a morph visible in the world is encapsulated in the `Morph` base class by the **openInWorld** method. This method can be overridden, but the overriding method should always contain the following invocation of the superclass method:

```
super openInWorld
```

After issuing this command, attributes of the morph's visible manifestation on the screen can be set in order to configure its appearance, for example with...

```
self bounds: (90@90 corner: 590@390).
self color: Color transparent.
```

The same types of statements can be used to dynamically reconfigure the morph at any time while it is visible. If it is desired that it should have a border, that border can be attached in a manner similar to the following:

```
self borderColor: Color black.
self borderWidth: 2.
```

Or one can use `BorderedMorph` as a base class. Objects of the `BorderedMorph` class come with a default border color, size, and style.

Collecting all the above into one method definition gives the following:

```
openInWorld
    super openInWorld.
    self bounds: (90@90 corner: 590@390).
    self color: Color transparent.
    self borderColor: Color black.
    self borderWidth: 2.
```

3.11   THE MORPHIC EVENT MODEL

Mouse and keyboard events in the morphic system of classes begin with the *hand*. The hand is an abstraction of the mouse cursor, and is an object of type `HandMorph`. The hand encapsulates a cursor position and a bitmap for drawing the cursor, as one might expect. But the hand also keeps with it one or more lists of morphs called *listeners*. There are mouse listeners, which are informed when mouse events occur, and there are keyboard listeners, and there are generic event listeners which are informed about all events. Let us illustrate how this works by using a mouse click as an example. Clicking the mouse sets in motion operating system actions such as those that we have already discussed in Chapter 2, "Event-Driven Programming (EDP)." Ultimately, Squeak packages the mouse click event into an object of type `MouseButtonEvent`, which contains information about which button was involved and whether it was pushed or released. This event is delivered to the hand, which passes it on to the appropriate mouse listener(s). The mouse listener is galvanized into action when the mouse event calls the listener's **handleMouseDown:** method, to which the event passes itself as a parameter. The morph acting as mouse listener, after some initial housekeeping, passes the event on to the **mouseDown:** method.

From the application programmer's point of view, this means that in order to handle mouse clicks of this nature, he must craft a subclass of `Morph` which (a) allows itself to be placed on the hand's mouse listener list and (b) supplies a definition for the **mouseDown:** method. To satisfy requirement (a) it is necessary that the programmer supply an override of the **handlesMouseDown:** method which simply returns `true`.

3.11.1 A First Exercise in the Use of the Morphic Framework

In this section, we will illustrate the use of the `Morph` class through the construction of some derived classes with specific drawing patterns. We will start with a morph which draws a green-filled circle in response to each mouse click.

Let us call our new subclass `GreenSpotsMorph`. In order to begin developing the class, the reader should open a browser window and click on any one of the categories in the upper-left pane. A template for class definitions will appear which can be edited in order to define a new class. The class description we want is as follows:

```
BorderedMorph subclass: #GreenSpotsMorph
    instanceVariableNames: ''
    classVariableNames: 'Radius'
    poolDictionaries: ''
    category: 'Morphic-Examples'
```

The above description includes the class variable name `Radius`. Each spot drawn in the morph will have the same radius, and the most convenient way in this language to establish this common value is through the use of a class variable name. Because there is not enough static structure to the language to allow us to declare a named constant, we must choose a binding time at which this class variable can be given a value. An often-used device for making such bindings is to include a class initialization method, as a message to the class itself. Such an initialization routine would have the opportunity, if called before any instantiations of objects of the corresponding type, to make whatever bindings should be common across all class and instance methods. This scheme, however, depends on some external object to invoke the class initialization routine before any instances of the class are created. If we cannot depend on the existence of such an object, then we must initialize the class variable at instance creation time, as follows:

```
new
    Radius := 10.
    ^super new
```

The above should be entered as a class method, whereupon Squeak will seek confirmation that we do indeed wish to override new. We can answer yes confidently, because the last line of our method ensures that we will properly invoke the **new** class method in the base class and return the object it produces.

The remaining methods are all overrides of base class instance methods, as follows:

```
openInWorld
    super openInWorld.
    self bounds: (Rectangle origin: 50@50 extent: 700@500).
    self color: Color white.

handlesMouseDown: evt
    ^true.

mouseDown: evt
    | center rect cvas |
    center := evt cursorPoint.
    ((self bounds insetBy: Radius) containsPoint: center)
        ifTrue: [
            rect := Rectangle origin: 0@0
                extent: (2*Radius) @ (2*Radius).
            cvas := FormCanvas extent: (2*Radius)@(2*Radius).
            cvas fillRectangle: rect color: Color white.
            cvas fillOval: rect color: Color green.
            cvas showAt:
```

```
                    (center x - Radius) @ (center y - Radius).
        ]
```

In response to a **mouseDown:** message, a GreenSpotsMorph first captures the coordinates of the mouse click in a local variable called center. It then determines whether the mouse click is far enough inside the morph's bounding rectangle so that it can be drawn without spilling outside that rectangle. If so, it draws a green spot centered at center. The type of canvas used above for the purpose of drawing a green circle, i.e., type FormCanvas, is instantiated with the **extent:** class method. Our use of this method creates a bitmap of a specified size (the size of the circle's bounding rectangle) upon which the resulting canvas object does its drawing. This canvas is filled with white, and the green spot is drawn inside it. Nothing appears on the morph, however, until the **showAt:** message is sent to the canvas object.

In order to see and interact with a GreenSpotsMorph, it is necessary to instantiate an object of that type, and then to send it an **openInWorld** message. This can be done by typing the command

```
    GreenSpotsMorph new openInWorld
```

in a workspace window, selecting the command, and pressing ctrl-d. The effect the user will observe, however, is far from satisfying. We explain the problem, and how to fix it, in the following section.

3.11.2 Maintaining a Persistent Display

There is a problem with the drawing scheme described in the previous section. As soon as we attempt to move or resize the morph on the screen, the green spots disappear. Indeed, any spot may seemingly decide to disappear at any time. This is because no information is being kept for the purpose of redrawing the spots, and because the paint event is being handled by a generic method in the BorderedMorph base class. So we must do two things to remedy the situation: we must keep a collection of points to aid us in recalling where our spots are to be drawn, and we must write a **drawOn:** method in our GreenSpotsMorph class which overrides the method by the same name in the base class.

Accordingly, we add an instance variable called spots to the class description, and instantiate it with the following line of code:

```
    spots := OrderedCollection new.
```

The difficulty with this line of code, however, is that it seems to have no natural setting within the methods we have designed. One might think it should go in the **new** class method, but the instance variable `spots` is not visible there. Instead, we will add an **initialize** instance method, as follows:

```
initialize
    super initialize.
    spots := OrderedCollection new.
```

At this point, a natural question to ask is, "From where do we call this initialization routine?" We do not call it at all. As it turns out, the call occurs as a side effect of the instance creation method **new**, which normally would call the **initialize** instance method in the superclass, but instead, because of polymorphism, will call our method defined above. For this reason, it is essential that the first line of our initialization routine perform the duty now short-circuited by the override.

To the **mouseDown:** routine we add a line of code which saves the offset of the mouse position from the upper left-hand corner (the "origin") of the bounding rectangle:

```
spots add: center - self bounds origin.
```

Note that the above code works because the subtraction operation has been defined as coordinate-wise subtraction in class `Point`. There is a corresponding addition operator, which we use in our override of the **drawOn:** method, as follows:

```
drawOn: aCanvas
    super drawOn: aCanvas.
    spots do: [:pt |  |rect|
        rect := Rectangle
            center: (self bounds origin + pt)
            extent: (2*Radius)@(2*Radius).
        aCanvas fillOval: rect color: Color green
    ]
```

We can test the new version of the `GreenSpotsMorph` class with the same code as before, executed from a workspace window:

```
GreenSpotsMorph new openInWorld
```

The user will see a rectangular view with a black border and white background. A new spot will appear with each mouse click inside the window. Minimizing and restoring the window, resizing the window, and dragging it to a new position will demonstrate the fact that the green spots are persistent.

In the above scenario, the repainting of the morph occurs because of external events. If the programmer desires to synchronously raise a paint event (and therefore indirectly call the **drawOn:** method), that can be accomplished anywhere within an instance method of the class using the **changed** message, as in

```
self changed
```

This method is intended to be called when the morph changes in a way that should affect its external appearance. For example, using this technique allows us to greatly simplify our **mouseDown:** event handler, as follows:

```
mouseDown: evt
    | center |
    center := evt cursorPoint.
    spots add: center - self bounds origin.
    self changed.
```

3.11.3 Subclass for a Bouncing Ball

In this section, we design BouncingBallMorph, another subclass of Bordered-Morph. Each new instantiation of this morph will encapsulate a rectangular view with a magenta color and a yellow ball (filled circle). To draw and animate a bouncing ball, we need to know three things: (a) the location (x, y) of its center, (b) its speed dx in the x direction, and (c) its speed dy in the y direction. We will use four instance variables for that purpose. Our units of speed will be pixels per second, and we will use timer events to update the location (x, y) and thereby animate the ball.

Timer events are handled in classes derived from Morph by overriding the methods **step** and **stepTime**. The former specifies actions to occur with every timer event, and the latter returns an integer which is the number of milliseconds between consecutive timer events. The programmer has the option of using an existing morph for the timer or instantiating another morph to act as timer. The latter technique can be used as many times as is necessary, for the purpose of having multiple timers. In our case, we only need one timer (for the animation of the ball), so we will use the containing morph as the timer. The generation of timer events starts when the morph is sent the **startStepping** message, and it ends when **stopStepping** is received or when the morph is destroyed. Below is the definition of the class:

```
BorderedMorph subclass: #BouncingBallMorph
    instanceVariableNames: 'x y dx dy radius ballColor'
    classVariableNames: 'DefBallColor DefColor MaxSpeed'
    poolDictionaries: ''
    category: 'Morphic-Examples'
```

Instance creation will establish the values of the class variables:

```
new
    DefColor := Color magenta. "Default background color"
    DefBallColor := Color yellow. "Default ball color"
    MaxSpeed := 200. "Maximum ball speed in pixels per second"
    ^super new.
```

The **initialize** method passes on the default colors to the corresponding instance variables. Again, recall that the **initialize** instance method will be called by the base class instance creation method, and our code does not explicitly invoke it.

```
initialize
    super initialize.
    color := DefColor.
    ballColor := DefBallColor.
    x := 0. y := 0. dx := 0. dy := 0.
```

In our **openInWorld** method, we will create a view of maximum size and turn our bouncing ball loose. For this purpose, we instantiate a random number generator as a temporary variable and use it to (1) randomly choose a ball radius between 10 and 30 pixels, (2) randomly choose initial values of x and y so that the ball is totally contained within the bounding rectangle of the morph, and (3) randomly choose speeds dx and dy, each between MaxSpeed and MaxSpeed in value. For the purpose of making these choices, we will use the **next** instance method of class Random, which returns a randomly chosen floating point number taken from the half-open interval [0, 1).

```
openInWorld
    | ran |
    super openInWorld.
    self bounds: self world bounds.
```

```
ran := Random new.
radius := 10 + (ran next * 21) asInteger.
x := (self bounds extent x - (2* radius)) * ran next
     + radius.
y := (self bounds extent y - (2* radius)) * ran next
     + radius.
dx := ((2*MaxSpeed + 1) * ran next) asInteger - MaxSpeed.
dy := ((2*MaxSpeed + 1) * ran next) asInteger - MaxSpeed.
(dx = 0) & (dy = 0) ifTrue: [dx := 1. dy := 1].
```

Because the morph involves animation, one would expect to see the command

```
self startStepping
```

in our version of **openInWorld**, but this has been omitted for good reason—the superclass version of **openInWorld** issues that command as a matter of course if it detects a **step** method in the morph.

Drawing is quite simple. First, we make sure to call the base class **drawOn:** method, and then we need only to frame the circle in black and fill it (with the color bound to variable `ballColor`).

```
drawOn: aCanvas
    |rect|
    super drawOn: aCanvas.
    rect := Rectangle
        center: ((x@y)+ self bounds origin)
        extent: (2*radius)@(2*radius).
    aCanvas fillOval: rect color: ballColor.
    aCanvas frameOval: rect color: Color black.
```

There remain only the **step** and **stepTime** events. We shall schedule timer events every 50 milliseconds, and base our adjustment of the `x` and `y` values on the assumption that 1/20 of a second ((self **stepTime**) / 1000) elapses between timer events. Note that the new computed values of `x` and `y` are floating point values, to ensure a smooth motion and to ensure that the ball actually moves. (Actually, leaving them as rational numbers would achieve that same goal, but for debugging purposes, it is easier to inspect floating point values.)

```
stepTime
    ^50
```

```
step
    x := (x + (dx * (self stepTime / 1000))) asFloat.
    y := (y + (dy * (self stepTime / 1000))) asFloat.
    x + radius >= self bounds extent x
        ifTrue: [dx := dx negated].
    x - radius <= 0
        ifTrue: [dx := dx negated].
    y + radius >= self bounds extent y
        ifTrue: [dy := dy negated].
    y - radius <= 0
        ifTrue: [dy := dy negated].
    self changed.
```

Making the ball bounce, then, is just a matter of testing to see if its center is within `radius` pixels of the left, right, top, or bottom edges of the bounding rectangle, and reversing the sign of either `dx` or `dy`, if that is the case.

Note that the last action of the **step** method is to raise a paint event by sending the **changed** message to the morph. This completes the scheme for making the ball move.

Finally, should we tire of magenta and yellow, some access functions might be useful. The `color` and `color:` methods are already present in the base class, so we will add the capability for clients to read from and write to the `ballColor` attribute.

```
ballColor
    ^ballColor

ballColor: newColor
    ballColor := newColor
```

3.11.4 Adding a Slider Component

Many morphs come preprogrammed in Squeak, and as we have seen the programmer can create new morphs as subclasses of existing morphic classes. Preprogrammed components such as edit boxes, buttons, scroll bars (called *sliders* here), and list boxes are all available as descendants of class `Morph`. Let us illustrate the use of a slider by adding a slider control to our `BouncingBallMorph`.

An object of type `Slider` is programmed to react to mouse events by changing its value, which is always a number between zero and one, inclusively. Mapping this fractional value into a value which makes sense in the containing morph and causing the appropriate changes in that morph is the job of the client programmer. The programmer can accomplish that work by creating subclasses of Morph and possibly of Slider which are specialized for a particular purpose. In our case, we wish to increase or decrease the speed of the ball in response to the dragging of the slider button. We will do so by using the slider button position to compute a new speed while keeping the "ball" moving in the same direction.

The simplest way to make this morph work is to make a smarter slider. We will do this by deriving a new class from Slider called BouncingBallSlider. The only thing our new slider does which is different from the superclass is that it overrides a method called **scrollAbsolute:**, which is called by the slider in response to mouse events. By notifying the containing BouncingBallMorph object every time the slider moves in this way, we can have that object react in the appropriate way. The way we will perform this notification is by calling a method called **onSliderMove**, which we will add to BouncingBallMorph. The (only) new method, then, in BouncingBallSlider, is the following:

```
scrollAbsolute: anEvent
    super scrollAbsolute: anEvent.
    owner onSliderMove
```

The owner attribute of a morph gets bound to that morph's containing morph when **addMorph:** is called to establish this relationship. We will issue that call in our **openInWorld** override, but first note that our changed BouncingBall-Morph class must implement the **onSliderMove** method, as follows:

```
onSliderMove
    | speed newSpeed |
    speed := ((dx*dx)+(dy*dy)) sqrt.
    speed=0 ifTrue: speed := 1.
    newSpeed := slider value * MaxSpeed.
    dx := dx / speed * newSpeed.
    dy := dy / speed * newSpeed.
```

The instance variable slider must be added to the class definition, and will be initialized in **openInWorld**. It denotes the slider object we will instantiate from BouncingBallSlider and add as a submorph to our BouncingBallMorph object. We see it being used in the above method to compute the value of the temporary variable newSpeed.

The other methods from BouncingBallMorph that must change are **openIn-World** and **drawOn:**. The former changes only by the addition of the following four lines of code:

```
slider := BouncingBallSlider new.
slider bounds:
    (self bounds origin corner: 20 @ self bounds corner y).
self addMorph: slider.
slider value:
    ((dx*dx)+(dy*dy)) sqrt / (2 sqrt * MaxSpeed) asFloat.
```

Note that we have positioned the slider morph to have the same base point as the containing morph and a width of 20 pixels, and to extend down the entire length of the left-hand side. Moving the containing morph around on the screen will, because of our use of the **addMorph:** method, also move the slider, so that the slider remains attached to the bouncing ball morph.

The initial value of the slider is computed and installed here with the **value:** message, and again is an approximation which should suit our needs well.

We have a problem, however, when the morph is resized. Note that the slider keeps its same relative base point when a resize of the bouncing ball morph takes place, but it does not change its own size, as we would like. We can detect a change in size in the **drawOn:** routine by remembering the size of the morph from the last time it was drawn, and if the new bounds are different we will re-size the slider. The new **drawOn:** routine, then, looks like this:

```
drawOn: aCanvas
    |rect|
    super drawOn: aCanvas.
    rect := Rectangle
        center: ((x@y)+ self bounds origin)
        extent: (2*radius)@(2*radius).
    aCanvas fillOval: rect color: ballColor.
    aCanvas frameOval: rect color: Color black.
    oldBounds ~= self bounds ifTrue: [
        slider bounds:
            (self bounds origin corner:
                (self bounds origin x + 20) @
                self bounds corner y).
    ].
    oldBounds := self bounds.
```

It is, of course, essential that oldBounds appears as an instance variable of the class. We instantiate the morph and invoke **openInWorld** from a workspace window again, as follows:

```
BouncingBallMorph new openInWorld
```

We now find that we are able to slow down or speed up the ball at will by dragging the button on the slider up or down, respectively.

3.12 CASE STUDY: SCORING A BOWLING GAME

We now illustrate an application with a substantial amount of "business logic," which we will not cover in this text, but for which the source code is provided to the reader. Our goal in this section is to program an interactive "view" of the business logic object, in the form of a morphic class. The application is to the problem of scoring a bowling game.

3.12.1 The Interface to the Business Class

The `BowlingScore` class is available as a resource on the textbook's accompanying CD. The object of the class is to keep score for a single bowler in a bowling game. For example, to instantiate from the workspace window a `BowlingScore` object for a bowler named `Lucy`, we would use...

```
lucyScore := BowlingScore new initialize: 'Lucy'
```

Methods of the class are described in Table 3.1 using messages to `lucyScore`.

TABLE 3.1 Messages to a `BowlingScore` object

Message	Effect of Message
lucyScore **ball**	Returns 1, 2, or 3, depending on which ball Lucy is about to bowl in the current frame.
lucyScore **displayScore**	Displays Lucy's score in the Transcript window.
lucyScore **bowlerIsPast:** 7	Returns true or false, depending on whether or not Lucy has bowled through the seventh frame.
lucyScore **bowlerIsPast:** 5 **ball:** 1	Returns true or false, depending on whether or not Lucy has already bowled the first ball of the fifth frame.
lucyScore **bowlerName**	Returns 'Lucy'.

Message	Effect of Message
lucyScore **frame**	Returns a number from 1 to 10, indicating the current frame.
lucyScore **gameFinished**	Returns true if the game is over, false otherwise.
lucyScore **getLastPinCount**	Returns the pin count from the last ball.
lucyScore **getPinCountList**	Returns an OrderedCollection object which contains all the pin counts, in order, from all the balls Lucy has bowled so far in the game.
lucyScore **isOpenFrame:** 3	Returns true if the third frame is an open frame, false otherwise.
lucyScore **isSpare:** 6	Returns true if the sixth frame is a spare, false otherwise.
lucyScore **isStrike:** 2	Returns true if the second frame is a strike, false otherwise.
lucyScore **lastFrameScored**	Returns a number between 0 and 10, indicating the last frame for which a cumulative score through that frame could be computed.
lucyScore **pinsAt:** 5 **at:** 1	Returns the number of pins knocked down by Lucy's first ball in the fifth frame.
lucyScore **putBall:** 7	Record a count of seven pins for the current ball of the current frame, if that count makes sense. Ignore the message if it does not make sense.
lucyScore **putSpare**	If a spare can be earned on the current ball, record the correct amount of pins to complete a spare.
lucyScore **scoreInFrame:** 8	If frame 8 has been scored, return the score through that frame. If not, return the score through the last frame scored.

The transcript display of a bowler's score leaves something to be desired. Suppose we give the following command sequence on the workspace window:

```
lucyScore putBall: 7.  lucyScore putBall: 2.
lucyScore putBall: 10.
```

```
lucyScore putBall: 5.  lucyScore putBall: 5.
lucyScore putBall: 7.  lucyScore putSpare.
lucyScore putBall: 5.  lucyScore putBall: 3.
lucyScore displayScore
```

The output in the transcript window would look something like this:

```
            7 2    X    5 /  7 /   5 3
Lucy      9  29   46   61   69
```

We wish to improve on this display by drawing a morph, and, furthermore, we want our morph to interact with the user to keep score using keyboard and mouse events. We will take a straightforward graphics-oriented approach, using no submorphs. The class we develop will be called BowlingScoreMorph. But before we introduce its class description let us develop an essential supporting class.

3.12.2 The BowlingFrameMorph Class

The BowlingFrameMorph class, which encapsulates all the attributes necessary to represent a single frame of a score sheet, has an on-screen representation similar to that shown in Figure 3.6.

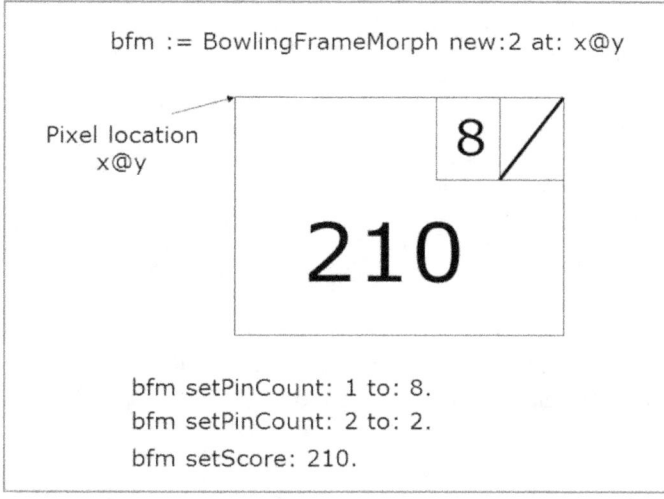

FIGURE 3.6 An on-screen representation of a BowlingFrameMorph object.

Its class description is as follows:

```
Morph subclass: #BowlingFrameMorph
```

```
instanceVariableNames:
    'score pins numBalls basePoint digitWidth digitHeight'
classVariableNames: 'FrameHeight FrameWidth'
poolDictionaries: ''
category: 'Morphic-Examples'
```

There are four class methods for BowlingFrameMorph, the first three of which are simple initialization and access methods. (For emphasis, let us repeat again that these are class methods. Be sure you press the 'class' button in the browser window before entering them.)

```
initialize
    FrameHeight := 50.
    FrameWidth := 40

height
    ^FrameHeight

width
    ^FrameWidth
```

The **initialize** message should be sent to class **BowlingFrameMorph** before the first such morph is instantiated. An example instantiation with **new:at:** is shown in Figure 3.1. The object creation method first calls **new**, then calls the following instance method:

```
initialize: twoOrThree at: aPoint
    super initialize.
    numBalls := twoOrThree.
    pins := Array new: numBalls.
    digitWidth := 12.  "The extent of a pin count box"
    digitHeight := 19. "is digitWidth by digitHeight"
    basePoint := aPoint.
```

Once the above method is in place, we can press the 'class' button again and enter our final class method, a specialized **new:** method.

```
new: twoOrThree at: aPoint
    "The first operand must be either 2 or 3 and determines"
    "how many pin counts are needed by the morph."
    ^super new initialize: twoOrThree at: aPoint.
```

Because our bowling frame morphs are not going to be submorphs, we need to teach them to reposition themselves so as to keep their proper places within the bowling score morph. The following instance method will be used to achieve that purpose:

```
moveTo: newBasePoint
    basePoint := newBasePoint.
    self changed
```

The following instance method gives a client the ability to change the pin counts in a bowling frame morph:

```
setPinCount: anInteger to: aCount
    pins at: anInteger put: aCount.
    self changed
```

Similarly, we change the score field by calling the following instance method:

```
setScore: anInteger
    score := anInteger.
    self changed
```

The drawing of the morph is shown below.

```
drawOn: aCanvas
    |upper lower right left rect|
    upper := basePoint y.
    lower := basePoint y + BowlingFrameMorph height.
    left := basePoint x.
    right := basePoint x + BowlingFrameMorph width.
    rect := Rectangle left: left right: right
        top: upper bottom: lower.
    self bounds: rect.
    aCanvas frameRectangle: self bounds color: Color black.
    score ifNotNil: [
        aCanvas
            drawString: score printString
            at: (left+15)@(upper+25).
    ].
    rect := Rectangle
        left: right-(numBalls*digitWidth)-1
        right: right-((numBalls-1)*digitWidth)
        top: upper
```

```
            bottom: upper+digitHeight.
aCanvas frameRectangle: rect color: Color black.
(pins at: 1) ifNotNil: [
    (pins at: 1) = 10 ifTrue: [
        aCanvas line: rect topLeft
            to: rect bottomRight color: Color black.
        aCanvas line: rect topRight
            to: rect bottomLeft color: Color black.
    ]
    ifFalse: [
        aCanvas
            drawString: (pins at: 1) printString
            at: (right-(numBalls*digitWidth)+3)@(upper+5)
    ]
].
rect := Rectangle
    left: rect left + digitWidth
    right: rect right+digitWidth
    top: rect top
    bottom: rect bottom.
aCanvas frameRectangle: rect color: Color black.
(pins at: 2) ifNotNil: [
    (pins at: 1) = 10 & ((pins at: 2) = 10) ifTrue: [
        aCanvas
            line: rect topLeft
            to: rect bottomRight
            color: Color black.
        aCanvas
            line: rect topRight
            to: rect bottomLeft
            color: Color black.
    ]
    ifFalse: [
        (pins at: 1) + (pins at: 2) = 10
            ifTrue: [
                aCanvas
                    line: rect topRight
                    to: rect bottomLeft
                    color: Color black.
            ]
            ifFalse: [ |digitPlace|
                digitPlace :=
                    (right-((numBalls-1)*digitWidth)+3) @
                    (upper+5).
                aCanvas
```

```
                        drawString: (pins at: 2) printString
                        at: digitPlace
                    ]
            ]
    ].
    numBalls = 3 ifTrue: [
        rect :=
            Rectangle
                left: rect left + digitWidth
                right: rect right+digitWidth
                top: rect top
                bottom: rect bottom.
        aCanvas frameRectangle: rect color: Color black.
    ].
    (numBalls = 3 and: [(pins at: 3) ~~ nil ])
        ifTrue: [
            (pins at: 3) = 10 &
            ((pins at: 1) + (pins at: 2) \\ 10 == 0) ifTrue: [
                aCanvas
                    line: rect topLeft
                    to: rect bottomRight
                    color: Color black.
                aCanvas
                    line: rect topRight
                    to: rect bottomLeft
                    color: Color black.
            ]
            ifFalse: [
                ((pins at: 1) = 10 and:
                [(pins at: 2) + (pins at: 3) = 10 ]) ifTrue: [
                    aCanvas
                        line: rect topRight
                        to: rect bottomLeft
                        color: Color black
                ]
                ifFalse: [
                    aCanvas
                        drawString: (pins at: 3) printString
                        at: (right-digitWidth+3)@(upper+5)
                ]
            ]
        ].
```

The above code is included here for completeness, but it does not raise any events that it does not itself respond to, and it does not illustrate any new concepts. We move now to a discussion of the BowlingScoreMorph class.

3.12.3 The BowlingScoreMorph Class

The `BowlingScoreMorph` class encapsulates a `BowlingScore` object and an array of ten `BowlingFrameMorph` objects. Its class description is as follows:

```
Morph subclass: #BowlingScoreMorph
    instanceVariableNames: 'score frameMorph fw fh textColor'
    classVariableNames: ''
    poolDictionaries: ''
    category: 'Morphic-Examples'
```

The instance variables are used in the fashion described in the following table.

TABLE 3.2 Instance variables in a `BowlingScoreMorph` object.

Instance variable	Usage
Score	The `BowlingScore` object used as a model.
frameMorph	An array of ten `BowlingFrameMorph` objects.
fw	Frame width.
fh	Frame height.
textColor	Black or red, depending on whether the morph has the keyboard focus.

The only class method is the instance creation method, as follows:

```
new: bowler
    ^super new initialize: bowler
```

Instance methods for initialization are as follows:

```
initialize: bowler
    | basePoint |
    super initialize.
    textColor := Color black.
    fw := BowlingFrameMorph width.
    fh := BowlingFrameMorph height.
    self bounds: (
        Rectangle left: fw right: 14*fw top: fw bottom: fh+fw
    ).
    basePoint :=
        (self bounds left + (3*fw) + 9) @ self bounds top.
```

```
score := BowlingScore new initialize: bowler.
self allocateFrames: basePoint.

allocateFrames: basePoint
    | bp |
    bp := basePoint.
    frameMorph := Array new: 10.
    1
        to: 9
        do: [:i |
            frameMorph
                at: i
                put: (BowlingFrameMorph new: 2 at: bp).
            bp := bp + ((frameMorph at: i) width - 1 @ 0)].
    frameMorph
        at: 10
        put: (BowlingFrameMorph new: 3 at: bp).
```

To control the appearance of the score morph, two business-class methods have been given their own versions there, namely **putBall:** and **putSpare**. Their definitions are…

```
putBall: pinCount
    | frame ball lastFrameScored |
    frame := score frame.
    ball := score ball.
    lastFrameScored := score lastFrameScored.
    (score putBall: pinCount)
        ifTrue: [(frameMorph at: frame)
                setPinCount: ball
                to: pinCount.
            self changed.
            score lastFrameScored ~= lastFrameScored
                ifTrue: [
                    lastFrameScored + 1
                        to: score lastFrameScored do: [:i |
                        (frameMorph at: i)
                            setScore:
                                (score scoreInFrame: i)
                        ]
                    ].
        ^ true].
    ^ false
```

```
putSpare
    | frame ball |
    frame := score frame.
    ball := score ball.
    frame < 10 & (ball ~= 2) ifTrue: [ ^false ].
    frame < 10 & (ball = 2) &
        ((score pinsAt: frame at: 1) = 10) ifTrue: [ ^false ].
    (ball = 2) & ((score pinsAt: frame at: 1) ~~ 10) ifTrue:
        [ ^ self putBall: 10 - (score pinsAt: frame at: 1) ].
    frame = 10 & (ball = 3) &
        (( score pinsAt: 10 at: 1) == 10) &
        ((score pinsAt: 10 at: 2) ~= 10)
    ifTrue: [
            ^ self putBall: 10 - (score pinsAt: frame at: 2)
        ].
    ^false
```

Following is an example of the problem we have with Smalltalk from an information hiding perspective, namely the inability to hide technical methods which the client programmer need not see. The method that follows will be called every time the morph is drawn (even though it actually need only be drawn when the bounding rectangle changes). This is also an illustration of the price we have paid for not using submorphs, because if our frames were submorphs, their positioning would be automatically managed for us.

```
positionFrames
    | basePoint |
    basePoint :=
        (self bounds left + (3*BowlingFrameMorph width) + 9)
        @ self bounds top.
    1
        to: 10
        do: [:i |
            (frameMorph at: i) moveTo: basePoint.
            basePoint := basePoint +
                ((frameMorph at: i) width - 1 @ 0)].
```

Because most of the work has already been done in the BowlingFrameMorph class, our drawing routine is now fairly simple:

```
drawOn: aCanvas
    aCanvas fillRectangle: self bounds color: Color white.
    aCanvas frameRectangle: self bounds color: Color black.
    self positionFrames.
```

```
1
    to: 10
    do: [:i | (frameMorph at: i)
        drawOn: aCanvas].
aCanvas drawString: score bowlerName
    at: self left + 10 @ (self bottom - 20)
    font: nil color: textColor
```

The **drawString:at:font:color:** method used here is given `nil` for a font, because we did not intend to change the default font. Our intent with the text color is that it should normally be black, but that clicking anywhere in the morph should both (a) change the text color to red, and (b) give the morph the keyboard focus. Because we must handle both keyboard and mouse events, then, we include the following event-handling methods:

```
handlesKeyboard: evt
    ^true


handlesMouseDown: evt
    ^true

mouseDown: evt
    textColor = Color black
        ifTrue: [textColor := Color red].
    evt hand newKeyboardFocus: self.
    self comeToFront.
    self changed
```

Because it is the hand that manages the focus, we needed to request that object to give the keyboard focus to the bowling score morph. The reason we can do this in such a simple fashion here is that every event object (parameter `evt` in the above code) has access to the hand via its **hand** instance method. So the job was accomplished elegantly as

```
evt hand newKeyboardFocus: self.
```

The following instance method determines the action performed when the mouse cursor leaves the bounding rectangle of the bowling score morph.

```
mouseLeave: evt
    textColor = Color red
        ifTrue: [textColor := Color black].
    evt hand newKeyboardFocus: nil.
```

As a superficial reading will reveal, the effect of the above is to change the text color to black and remove the keyboard focus from the morph.

Unfortunately, the `mouseLeave:` routine is not hard-wired into the morphic framework but is purely a product of the author's design. So how do we make sure it is actually called? We accomplish that by adding a single line (omitted above) to the `initialize` method, namely

```
self on: #mouseLeave send: #mouseLeave: to: self.
```

The `on:send:to:` method resides in the base class `Morph`, and keys on the type field of an event. When an event is raised, the morph identifies the type of the event object (a symbol), and reacts to the event type in a preprogrammed way. We have in our earlier examples been able to take advantage of this by simply overriding certain methods. In this case, however, the Morphic framework does not provide a specific method call for the `mouseLeave` event type. We must explicitly inform our morph that when a `mouseLeave` event occurs, it is to invoke the **mouseLeave:** method.

There is no override for `openInWorld`, so the base class version of that will be used. Everything needed to maintain the display, then, is in place after the command

```
lucyMorph := (BowlingScoreMorph new: 'Lucy') openInWorld.
```

The morph appears on the screen as in Figure 3.7.

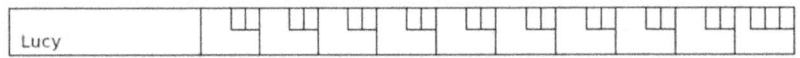

FIGURE 3.7 User's view of a `BowlingScoreMorph` object.

Everything is now programmed except our response to keyboard events. Our plan for handling the keyboard is to ignore all but thirteen keys: the digit keys 0–9, the x and X keys, the / key, and the backspace. Having returned `true` from `handlesKeyboard:`, and having given our morph the keyboard focus in reaction to the `mouseDown` event, we can be confident that the following method will be called in response to any keypress event, because `keyStroke:` is preprogrammed into the morphic framework in the same way as `mouseDown:`.

```
keyStroke: evt
    "React to user's keystroke.  If a digit,then store it at
```

```
    the currently relevant pin position.  If a backspace,
    then take back the last pin count.  If an x,score a
    strike.  If a slash,score a spare."
| char |
textColor = Color red ifTrue: [
    char := evt keyCharacter.
    (char < $0) not & (char > $9) not ifTrue: [
        | pincount |
        pincount := (char asInteger - $0 asInteger).
        self putBall: pincount
    ].
    char = Character backspace
        ifTrue: [ self handleBackSpace ].
    char = $x | (char = $X) ifTrue: [ self putBall: 10 ].
    char = $/ ifTrue: [ self putSpare ]
]
```

Most of the above response is clear after careful study. The only unfinished business is the `handleBackSpace` method referred to above. This routine is simply supposed to take back the last pin count, and would be very difficult to manage if it had not been for the inclusion in the business class `BowlingScore` of the `getPinCountList` method. As it is, with this tool at our disposal, all we need to do is fetch this list, destroy the old model, create a new one with the same bowler name, and reinstall all but the last pin count.

```
handleBackSpace
    | name pcl |
    pcl := score getPinCountList.
    name := score bowlerName.
    score := BowlingScore new initialize: name.
    self allocateFrames: 0 @ 0.
    self positionFrames.
    pcl size ~= 0
        ifTrue: [pcl removeLast].
            [pcl size ~= 0]
                whileTrue: [self putBall: pcl removeFirst].
            self changed
```

To recap, one interacts with the morph by clicking in it, then entering each pin count as a single key stroke, using x or X for ten pins, and / or the correct pin count for a spare. A backspace erases the last pin count, even if the game is over.

3.13 SUMMARY

Smalltalk remains as a unique design paradigm, like Lisp, Prolog, and APL. Its design was even more strikingly original in the days when it was the *only* object-oriented language. (In fact, there are still today enough substantial points of difference with other OOPLs that some Smalltalk adherents claim it is the only purely object-oriented language.) Let us summarize some of the salient features of the language.

Every data entity in Smalltalk is an object of some class type, and all classes descend from a common base type (`ProtoObject` in Squeak). An object can receive messages of one of three types: unary, binary, and keyword. Precedence is defined exactly by that order, with unary messages having the highest priority. Binary messages are calls on methods defined using operator symbols, and those methods, like all other methods, can be overridden in derived classes. Overrides produce polymorphic behavior by default, and that behavior cannot be suppressed except in a limited sense using the `super` reserved word. Names are not statically bound to a type, because the type resides with the named object, not the name itself, and complete type information is available at run-time for checking purposes. Declarations establish scope of a name only, not attributes. All names are run-time entities, and any name can be converted into a *symbol* for lookup purposes. Symbols which represent method names can be used to invoke that method using **perform:** and methods like it. Event handlers are objects, and the particular method invoked in a handler when an event occurs is denoted by a symbol and established in advance by the **on:send:to:** method or a similar method.

Smalltalk has little static structure, so many decisions must be put off until run-time. Type checking, existence checking, and range checking, for instance, must be done at run-time, and the type of the result of a method call may be different at different times during execution. The language's lack of structure makes it highly flexible, however. Its containers are heterogeneous, because the standard container classes assume nothing about the objects they contain. What other languages achieve by static structure can be achieved by run-time conventions, such as the convention that a class is abstract if the class method **new** has been overridden to terminate with an error if it is used to handle a message to that class.

The widely used "Model, View, Controller" design pattern originated in the Xerox PARC Smalltalk culture, and classes to support it are present in the Squeak implementation of Smalltalk. A simpler recursive design pattern called

Morphic is a salient feature of the current Squeak Smalltalk library and was used in this chapter to illustrate event-driven programming. In that model, the view object is called a morph and is populated by other objects, also called morphs and all descended from the base class `Morph`. The object which encapsulates the mouse cursor, called the *hand*, receives mouse and keyboard events and passes them along to their handler objects, which call specific methods in response to specific events, e.g., `mouseDown:` and `keyStroke:`. Standard graphics messages to draw lines and geometric figures and strings are sent to a drawing object called a *canvas*.

REVIEW QUESTIONS

1. Give a brief summary of the history of the Smalltalk language.
2. Explain what is meant by the statement that, in Smalltalk, "Everything is an object."
3. List and describe the three different types of Smalltalk messages.
4. Describe the precedence and associativity rules for Smalltalk. Why do these rules imply that keyword messages cannot be nested without the use of parentheses?
5. What are *symbols* in the Smalltalk language? What are they used for, and how can other types of expressions be transformed into symbols?
6. Why is the assignment `x := y` always legal in Smalltalk, provided *x* and *y* are in scope?
7. Describe the way in which Smalltalk partitions its name space.
8. What do we mean when we say that there is not a clear distinction between primitive types and library types in Smalltalk?
9. There is something surprisingly different about the result of the operation 5/2 and that of the operation 4/2. What is it?
10. What is different (i.e., unconventional) about Smalltalk numeric literals? Explain.
11. What does a `BlockContext` literal look like? What does a `BlockContext` object do when sent the **value** message?
12. What is the type of the object `nil`? What messages can it receive?
13. Describe the storage management strategy employed by Smalltalk.
14. What mechanisms govern flow of control in a Smalltalk program?

15. Describe what happens when the **ifTrue:** message is sent to a Boolean object in Smalltalk.

16. Are class variables and instance variables accessible to client code in Smalltalk? What does this mean with respect to the design of methods in Smalltalk classes?

17. Which methods are accessible to clients in Smalltalk? How is this policy different from OOPLs with which you have experience? What is the significance of this accessibility policy in software engineering terms?

18. What do we mean when we say that polymorphism is not optional in Smalltalk? How is this fact inescapable given the basic rules of Smalltalk semantics?

19. Explain what happens in a Smalltalk method when a message is sent to the pseudovariable super.

20. Explain why the following method will cause an infinite loop if the version of method *f* in the base class returns self.

    ```
    f
        super f f
    ```

21. When the message **at:** or the message **at:put:** is sent to an array object, in what class is the method reference resolved? What objects, then, can legally be sent one of these messages? What implications does this have for other classes which might want to include "subscripting" capabilities?

22. List and describe some of the container classes from the Squeak library.

23. Describe the Model, View, Controller (MVC) pattern.

24. Describe the Morphic pattern. How does it differ from MVC?

25. What is the *hand*? What is its type, and what information does it encapsulate? How does it figure into the Morphic event model?

26. Practically speaking, what two steps are necessary to configure a morph class to respond to the "mouse down" event?

27. Typically when we derive a new morph class we override **new**, **initialize**, and **openInWorld**.

    a. Which of these are instance methods and which are class methods?

    b. What is the purpose of overriding **new**, and when can that override be omitted?

    c. Why is **initialize** never called from class scope in the new class?

EXERCISES

1. Code the following functions in Smalltalk as `BlockContext` objects and assign them to variables named `f` and `g`, respectively:

   a. $f(x, y) = 3 + xy + y^2$

   b. $g(x) = \sqrt{1 + \sin x}$

2. Show how you would use the identifier associations you created in Exercise 1 to (a) evaluate the expression in part a at $x = 2.3$ and $y = 7.9$, and (b) evaluate the expression in part b at $x = 5\pi/7$. (Hint: browse class `Float` and you will find a class method which returns the value of π.)

3. Reformulate your answers to question 2 as **perform:** and/or **perform:with:** messages.

4. Translate the following pseudocode into Smalltalk code in two different ways: (1) using **ifTrue:ifFalse:** messages, and (2) using a **caseOf:** message.

   ```
   if r = s then r := r + 1
   else if r = t then r := t+2
   else if r = u then r := u+3
   else r := 0
   ```

5. Use a **whileTrue:** message to achieve the same effect as the following pseudocode:

   ```
   while a<b do
        a := 2*a
        b := b - epsilon
   end while
   ```

6. Use a **to:do:** message to achieve the same effect as the following pseudocode. Use an **at:** message for the subscripting operation.

   ```
   for i:=1 to n do x := x + a[i]
   ```

7. Write a new method called **moveDisksTo:from:using:** for class `Integer` that puts messages on the Transcript which are instructions on how to solve the Towers of Hanoi puzzle. When an integer `n` receives a message

   n **moveDisksTo:** 'target' **from:** 'source' **using:** 'temp'

   instructions should appear on the transcript for moving `n` disks from source to target using temp for temporary storage. If the value of *n* is 3, the output should appear on the transcript as follows:

```
Move a disk from source to target.
Move a disk from source to temp.
Move a disk from target to temp.
Move a disk from source to target.
Move a disk from temp to source.
Move a disk from temp to target.
Move a disk from source to target.
```

8. Give a Squeak class definition roughly equivalent to the following C++ class definition. What things do you have to leave out? Why? What do you have to add?

```
class MyClass {
private:
    float x, y;
    static int count;
public:

    ...
};
```

9. Give a method definition for a unary method called **cycle** in the class MyClass in question 8. The effect of calling **cycle** should be to add the value of x to that of y and then to increase count by 1. The value returned should be the resulting value of y.

10. Give two ways of instantiating a Point object representing the location in a morph's bounding rectangle whose x coordinate is 120 and whose y coordinate is 350.

11. Give at least three different ways of instantiating a Rectangle object whose base point is (200, 220), whose width is 200 pixels, and whose height is 150 pixels.

12. What sort of object is required in order to draw on a morph? Given such an object, named can, give a message or a sequence of messages which…

a. Draw a black line from pixel location (100, 20) to pixel location (400, 120).

b. Draw a green rectangle with a black border, having base position (50, 50) and corner point (150, 90).

c. Draw a yellow triangle with a red border. The border should be three pixels thick, and the vertices of the triangle should be at (40, 50), (140, 70), and (200, 100).

d. Draw the string 'Hello, World!' with base point (10, 10).

13. Give a message that a morph can be sent inside one of its methods, which...

    a. Sets its bounding rectangle to a size of 500 by 300 pixels and a base position of (200, 250).
    b. Sets its internal color to mauve.
    c. Sets its border color to black.
    d. Sets its border width to one pixel.

14. Write an override of the **openInWorld** method for a Morph subclass that sets the internal color to white and the border color to black, then sets up the bounding rectangle to have width 550, height 440, and upper left-hand corner (120, 120).

15. Implement the GreenSpotsMorph class as described in Section 3.11.1. Instantiate it and invoke its screen presence with the code GreenSpots-Morph **new openInWorld.**

    a. Try clicking in the window, then moving the window around and resizing it. What responses do you observe? How can you account for the odd behavior?
    b. Rewrite the code for GreenSpotsMorph so that it incorporates the changes in Section 3.11.2. Also, remove the drawing code from **mouseDown:** and replace it with the message self **changed**, so that all the drawing can be done by the **drawOn:** routine. Now try the same manipulations you tried in part a. Explain how the changes fixed the problem.

C++ *AND JAVA COMMON-ALITIES AND SIMILARITIES*

Although they are deceptively similar when examined superficially, a thorough and thoughtful analysis finds more differences than similarities between the C++ and Java languages. Nevertheless, it is useful to us to start our discussion of these major players in the field of programming language design by asking how it is that they are alike.

It is worth noting as we start to do this comparison that we are resolving to include *no* discussion of the newcomer C# (also a C-derived language) in this chapter. Much could be said about how its features compare to those of Java and C++, but those two languages are much older, more widely used, and more established, and so they have a greater claim to this discussion. This is not to mention the fact that comparing three languages side-by-side would be far too confusing! We will have much to say about C# in Chapter 8, "C# and the Common Language Infrastructure."

4.1 INTRODUCTION: THE C HERITAGE AND A DIVERGENCE OF GOALS

No one could have predicted the phenomenal success of C. Initially designed as a systems programming language for the UNIX operating system, C flew into prominence on the wings of that very successful system and remains very popular today because it shares the goals and priorities which were behind the production and propagation of UNIX. C, like UNIX, is designed to be portable, but it is also designed to make efficient use of its host machine. These apparently contradictory purposes come together to make the language highly appealing to the working programmer. C's popularity, then, arose from the ground up, through the enthusiastic acceptance of the programming community. It has outgrown its UNIX roots and now stands as the premiere procedural language for systems programming.

4.1.1 C and C++ Evolution and Backward Compatibility

The C language, however, was designed as a procedural language from the very beginning, and in the 1980s the idea of its being used successfully as a basis for an object-oriented language seemed as unlikely as the original acceptance and popularity of C itself. Precious few programmers in that decade would have considered it anything other than foolhardy to attempt to superimpose an object-oriented structure on C. But object-orientation was not the only late graft onto this improbable language design.

Code samples for this chapter are located on the companion CD-ROM.

For example, programmer-defined data types came into the C language as an add-in, via structured data objects very much like the data objects created with COBOL data descriptions. A declaration for such an object was introduced with the keyword `struct`. For example, to create a data object called `point` and having integer components `x` and `y`, the following syntax was used:

```
struct { int x, y; } point;
```

Here we see some basic trends in C syntax. First, set braces ('{' and '}') are used as delimiters for syntactic constructs, instead of the traditional *begin* and *end* used in most Algol-derived languages. The insistence on case sensitivity is important, too. Pascal, for instance, would have considered `point`, `Point`, and `POINT` all to be the same identifier. C, like UNIX, would treat them all differently. Factoring the type name out to the left in type declarations also differed from Pascal, and was instead modeled after the pattern employed by the Algol languages and FORTRAN. Finally, the semicolon is used as a terminator and is required after every statement, unless that statement is a block, or compound statement. (In Pascal, the semicolon is not syntactically part of the statement, but is used to separate statements in a block.)

Keep in mind that the above declaration defines an object, not a type. The object consists of two integers, named in COBOL-like fashion as `point.x` and `point.y`. Programmer-defined data types were in fact added to the language later, using so-called *structure tags*. A structure tag is added to the above declaration in the following line of C code, in which the identifier `Point` is being used as a structure tag:

```
struct Point { int x, y; } point;
```

Because the C language at that time required every declaration to begin with a reserved word, the easiest way to accommodate this addition to the language was to consider the type name to consist of both words; that is, the type name was `struct Point`, not merely `Point`. Thus, `point` is of type `struct Point`, as are `point2` and `point3` in the following declaration.

```
struct Point point2, point3;
```

Obviously, the declaration of the `struct Point` data type need not as a side effect also define an object, so the identifier `point` could be omitted to obtain the following:

```
struct Point { int x, y; };
```

Somewhat humorously, the semicolon at the end *cannot* be omitted, because if it is omitted the parser expects the next token to be a valid identifier, which it will interpret as the name of an object. This is the source of a time-wasting syntactic discontinuity in the language, because omitting the semicolon at the end is extremely easy to do and is catastrophic in its effect on the compiler's ability to match its understanding of the program's structure to the programmer's intent. When the class construct was added in C++, the mandatory ending semicolon was retained, compounding the problem but maintaining consistency. In that language, however, the requirement that the keyword `struct` be used as part of variable declarations was removed, so that the cleaner syntax indicated below can be used to declare variables.

```
Point point, point2, point3;
```

The above discussion points out one of several relics of questionable C syntax in the C++ language. The early versions of C++ retained the goal of backward-compatibility with C, to the extent that any valid C program could be compiled by a C++ compiler.

4.1.2 Java Abandons Compatibility

Java, on the other hand, kept only the general appearance of C. As in C and C++, all variables in Java are statically declared as to type, type names factor to the left in declarations, set braces are used as delimiters of blocks, and semicolons are statement terminators, not separators. Two commenting conventions are common to the two languages: the `//` sequence introduces a comment which ends at the end of the current line, and `/*` and `*/` are used as brackets for a comment which may extend over multiple lines.

Java does not allow the programmer to slip back into the old procedural style; Java Programs are necessarily object-oriented. Moreover, Java is a safer language in which to program and avoids a lot of awkwardness because it was never intended to be a superset of C. For example, Java class definitions do not end in semicolons.

NOTE *If we could summarize the C++ philosophy, we might say, "Power to the programmer!" or "Let the programmer beware!" In other words, C++ puts a lot of capabilities up for grabs which can be used for good or ill, with the assumption that the programmer has the sophistication to use those capabilities properly. On the other hand, the Java strategy is based on the assumption that the programmer is error-prone and will shoot himself in the foot if given the chance.*

In fact, Java abandoned backward compatibility with C from the beginning, changing syntax rules to make errors less likely and taking away features in C which are dangerous and/or error-prone. A short list of such features which are present in C++ but not in Java includes: (a) pointer variables and pointer arithmetic; (b) value semantics for structured data types; (c) liberal automatic conversions (coercions) between disparate types; and (d) programmer-controlled storage reclamation.

4.2 DECLARATIONS AND STATIC BINDINGS

Both C++ and Java have a distinct translation phase which produces low-level object files, with the difference being that C++ object files are not directly executable and require an extra link step. Because of their rather extensive translation phases, there is considerable static structure built into these languages in order to guide the actions of the translator. Because the programmer must accommodate and understand this structure, translation is part of the programmer's mental model of how to use these languages. The translation phase in both cases is appropriately called "compilation," although the two use a decidedly different strategy. C++, like C, compiles to native machine language code, while Java compiles to a standardized byte code which is machine independent. Both are statically typed languages, meaning that these languages use static scope rules and every program variable, whether a local variable, parameter, class variable, or instance variable, is associated with a type by a declaration.

This early binding strategy radically differentiates these languages from interpreted languages like Smalltalk, because when types are assigned using declarations, a variable is no longer a name only but has a type associated with it in every place where it appears. The Smalltalk language has no such type association, so when an expression such as x+y appears in a program, its evaluation requires a sequence of actions something like the following:

1. The object associated with x is dynamically discovered using the symbol x for a key in a table lookup.
2. The object's class is identified, using information stored in a symbol table or in the object itself.
3. The + operation is looked up in a table of instance methods for the class.
4. If there is no such operation, the program terminates with an error.
5. If the + operation was found in step 3, then the object associated with y is looked up and a pointer to it is found in a table.
6. The object found in step 1 is sent the + message with the object found in step 5 (y) as an argument. This causes the corresponding method to begin to execute.
7. During the execution of the + operation, if x and y are able to respond appropriately to all the messages sent to them, then all will go well. If not, the program will terminate with an error.
8. The result of the + operation will be an object, and if x+y is part of a larger expression then the result object will either receive the next message pending in the larger expression or will be used as an argument for another method in that expression.

Contrast that with the following sequence of actions performed by C++ in response to the same expression, separated into compile time actions and run-time actions.

Compile time:

1. The identifiers x and y are looked up in a table and their types are determined.

2. The types found in step 1 are used in a complex algorithm to determine which + operation to use, if any. There may in fact be a compiler error in case overload resolution fails here.

3. If necessary, code is generated to translate one or both of x and y into a different type, so that the operands of the + operation found in step 2 are of the appropriate type.

4. If the + operation is primitive, a single machine code instruction will probably suffice to invoke it. If not, then code is generated to perform the operation, either as inline code, as a procedure call, or as a method invocation.

5. Code may be generated to store the result of step 4 in a compiler-generated temporary variable, or it may be kept in a register. If x+y is part of a larger expression, then successive translations of other parts of that expression which refer to its result will refer to the register or to the location of the temporary.

Execution time:
6. The code generated in steps 1-5 above is executed, causing the sequence of steps below:

    a. Type conversions will be performed on one or both of x and y, as necessary.

    b. The + operation will be executed, either as a sequence of one or more primitive machine operations or as a machine level subroutine call.

    c. The result of the operation will be stored in a register or temporary location, and will then be available as an operand to succeeding machine instructions.

NOTE
Java would use a similar strategy to that of C++, except its "machine" is the Java Virtual Machine (JVM), not the native machine. The JVM is simulated by software, and is in fact a software interpreter for Java byte code.

Notice two things about this comparison. The first is that steps 1–5 for the compiled language are only performed once, at compile time. Steps 6a through 6c are the only steps executed at run-time. The second thing to notice is that the actions taken at run-time for the compiled language do not involve any type checking, existence checking, or table lookups.

The simple fact, then, is that type declarations allow for a more sophisticated translation phase, in which many of the attributes of the variables involved can be determined ahead of time. Let us say that in our translation we encounter a variable x being used in some executable expression in the program. In a statically typed language like C++ or Java, the reference to x is invalid if it is not preceded by a declaration of x giving a type for that variable. This early binding of x to a type is the key to a faster run-time, because there will be no need for run-time type checking, nor will there need to be a check at run-time to see if the operation being performed on or by x actually exists.

A major difference between C++ and Java is that the former permits uninitialized variables. In Java, even if no initialization is explicitly given for a variable, code will be generated to give it an initial value, in the following way. If the variable names a primitive numeric object, the initial value will be a form of zero appropriate to the type. If it names a `boolean` value, the initial value will be `false`. If it names a string or another first class object, the default initial value will be `null`.

4.3   FILES INVOLVED IN TRANSLATION

Another consequence of compilation and early bindings is that the programmer's mindset is not isolated from the file system. The result of compilation is stored in one or more object files, and the programmer must be aware of the location and type of the files, and the nature of their contents. Separate compilation is a characteristic of both languages, and so the programmer has multiple source files and multiple object files with which to deal. Nevertheless, the approach is radically different in the two languages. We begin with the C++ approach to separate compilation.

4.3.1 C++ Header Files, Source Files, and Object Files

A single compilation for the C++ language actually consists of two distinct phases. In the first phase, a simple text-processing translator called a *preprocessor* combines a single primary source file and a number of auxiliary files called "header files" into a *compilation unit*. In the second phase, the compilation unit is compiled into an object file. We begin this discussion by examining the difference between a source file and a header file.

The source file is the primary input into the C++ two-stage compilation process. A *header file* is pulled into that process by references in the source file and/or other header files. Both source files and header files can contain any valid C++ code, although the careful programmer will observe some voluntary constraints concerning the content of header files (more about that in the next chapter). A number of preprocessor instructions can also be included in these files. These instructions are very rudimentary and simple in their syntax, and each must appear on a line by itself. We will discuss only a few here, with simplified examples, and later we will give an example which integrates preprocessor commands into source and header files in a complete application.

A header file is brought into a compilation unit by the inclusion somewhere in the source file of the `#include` preprocessor statement. The form of the `#include` statement is

```
#include <file-name>
```

if the header file is a library file, and

```
#include "file-name"
```

if the header file is a programmer-supplied file.

The preprocessor can define its own variables, and the value of a preprocessor variable is always a text string. As the preprocessor constructs the compilation unit, it will make a pass through the source file and through all the included header files, and whenever it sees a reference to one of its own variables it will make a textual substitution of the value of that variable. For example, following the preprocessor statement

```
#define PI 3.141592654
```

wherever the token `PI` is encountered in the compilation unit, the text string `3.141592654` will be substituted for it.

The value of the preprocessor variable is taken to be everything on the line following the name of the variable, beginning with the first non-whitespace character and ending with the end of line. Consider the following example.

```
#define DUCK "a quacker"
```

In this case, the value substituted for `DUCK` will include the bracketing quotes. If we wish to get rid of this association later, we can use

```
#undef DUCK
```

To give DUCK an empty string value, we can use

```
#define DUCK
```

There is a *conditional compilation* facility which is heavily used in C and C++ source and header files, implemented using the #if and #endif preprocessor commands. For example,

```
#if DUCK == "Daffy"
    x = DUCK;
#endif
```

Here the line

```
    x = "Daffy";
```

will be inserted into the compilation unit if the value of the preprocessor variable DUCK is "Daffy", and if not the entire three-line sequence will be omitted. (Of course, *none* of the preprocessor commands will appear in the final result, i.e., in the compilation unit.) A very commonly used form of this conditional compilation feature is the #ifdef command, which is illustrated as follows:

```
#ifdef DUCK
    x = DUCK;
#endif
```

Here the line of code will be included, with the proper value substituted for DUCK, provided the preprocessor variable is defined at the time the #ifdef command is encountered.

It should be emphasized here that the preprocessor is a simple text substitution facility and has no knowledge of the C++ language other than a recognition of its tokens, which keeps it from going inside strings and comments and making substitutions. It does not know one type of token from another, however, and so will freely substitute its own variable values for C++ keywords if you ask it to do so. Some interesting and sophisticated things can be done with it, but a detailed discussion of the preprocessor is beyond the scope of this text.

Figure 4.1 pictures five header files, three of which are directly included in the source file and two of which are included by one of the header files. The preprocessor combines the header files and the source files into a compilation unit, which the compiler translates into a single object file.

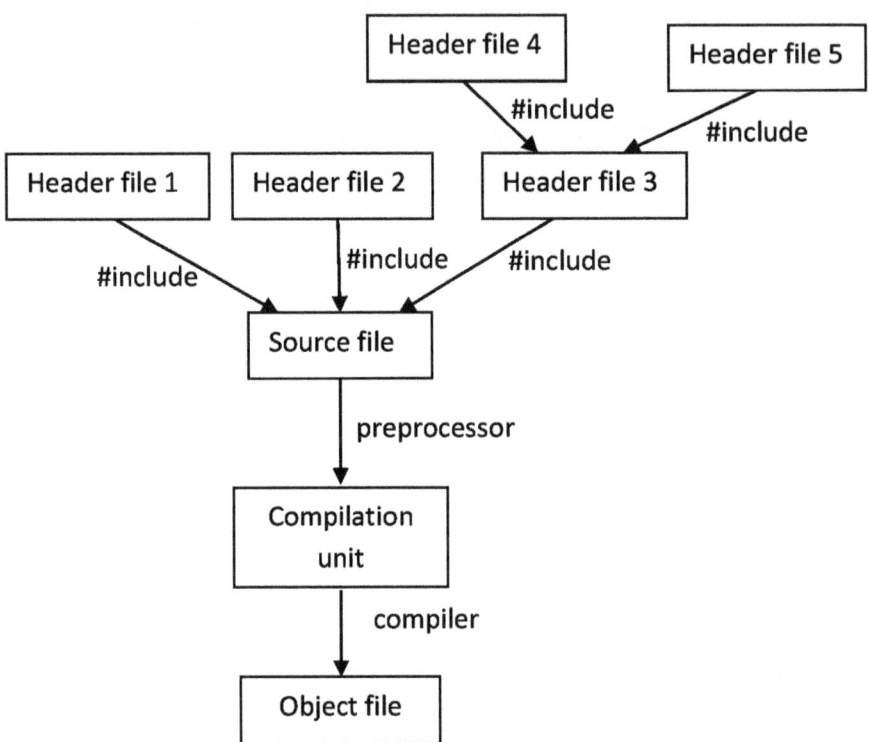

FIGURE 4.1 A C++ compile operation involving three directly included and two indirectly included header files.

The compiler, then, has no knowledge of source files and header files. The input to the compiler is the compilation unit produced by the preprocessor. Its output is an object file, which consists mostly of machine language code but is not in a form suitable for execution.

Why is the object file not suitable for execution? We begin to answer that question by noting that in large C++ applications it is advantageous to separate the source code into mutually dependent source files and separately compile them into multiple object files. This allows a programming team leader to use the file structure to assist him in grouping the conceptual units of the program in understandable ways. It also aids in assigning responsibilities, because a unit of code for which an individual or group of individuals is responsible can be defined for teamwork purposes as a set of source and header files. There is, of course, also a savings in compile time during the edit and test phase of software development if we do not have to compile the entire body of source code with every iteration of that phase.

The consequence of this division of labor is that yet another rudimentary translation step is needed, and that is the link step. A *linker* has the responsibility of transforming a set of one or more object files into an executable file. What makes it possible for the linker to do its job is that the compiler, when it encounters a reference to an object or procedure defined in a different compilation, makes a note in a table of (a) the name of the object or procedure, and (b) where the reference occurred in the object code. Also, the compiler makes a note of any declared objects and compiled procedures in the compilation unit which might be candidates for the resolution of external references. It will place in the object file a table of the relative locations of those objects and procedures within the compiled code. The central task of the linker is to create a storage map which includes all data and code needed at the start of execution, with space for the stack and the heap. The linker has all the information it needs to infer the size of this storage map and to place all the code and data from all of the object files within that storage map, because the linker is provided with the names and locations of those object files when it is invoked. As it places the individual machine instructions within this storage map, it must resolve any external references within each instruction by matching the name of the missing variable or procedure with one of the names stored in its tables and placing in the instruction the correct encoded version of the address of the referenced entity. The linker's operation is illustrated in Figure 4.2, in which four object files are shown being combined into one executable.

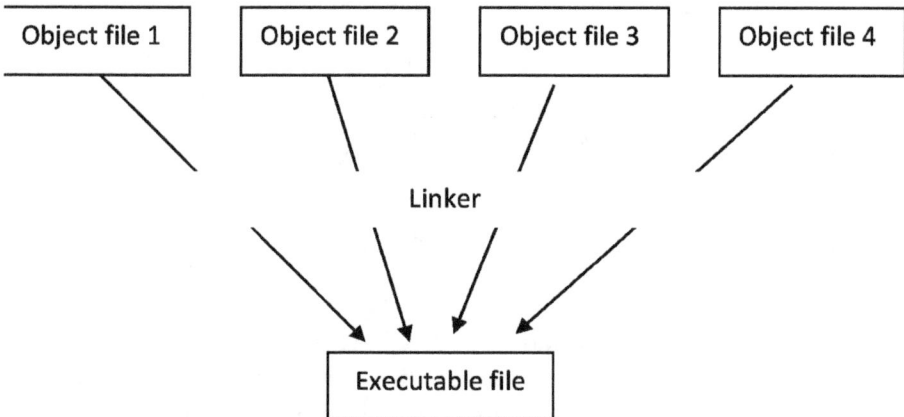

FIGURE 4.2 A link operation involving four separately compiled object files.

A consequence of this translation scheme is that the final result is a file the operating system recognizes as a native-code executable program. Note that the linker, like the preprocessor, need have no knowledge of C++. As a matter of fact, if the compiler conforms to the particular operating system's standard for object files there is no need for the language implementation to furnish a linker. The operating system's linker will link the files no matter what language was used to produce them.

This is an old and fairly cumbersome view of translation, but it is one that is largely shared by a number of languages which are considered compiled languages, including Fortran, C, and Ada. The result is a native code executable, which is the only option if maximum execution speed is desired.

4.3.2 Java Source Files, Class Files, and the JVM

Java, too, has a multiple source file strategy, but one that is almost exactly opposite to that of C++. Instead of producing one file per compilation, and consuming several files via include operations, Java can potentially produce a large number of different output files with each compilation. That is because of a very simple fact: Java compiles and stores one class at a time. If a source file defines five classes, then the act of compiling that source file produces five object files. Stored in each of those five files is the Java byte code version of one of those five classes. Figure 4.3 illustrates the situation.

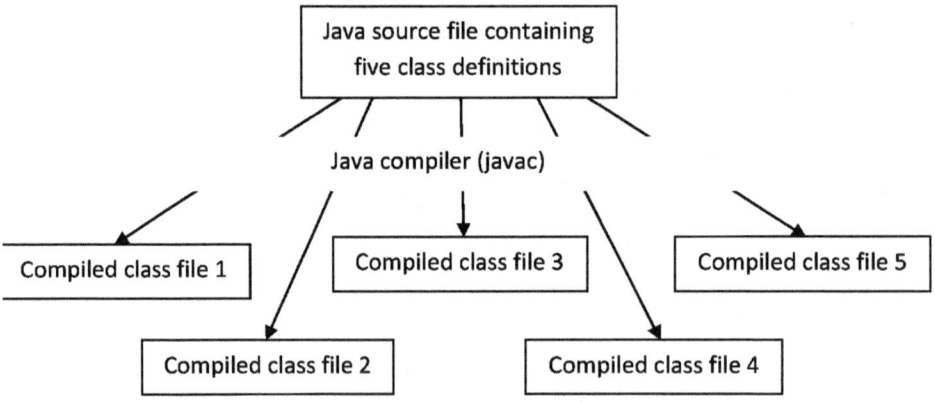

FIGURE 4.3 Compilation of a Java file containing five classes.

There is an important requirement here, which is that at most one of the five classes can be public, i.e., accessible to client programmers. (Here we are assuming there are no "inner classes" among the five—see Chapter 7, "Java and the Swing Library," for a discussion of Java inner classes.) Related to this is the fact that Java naming requirements extend to file names. In fact, if the name of the one public class is `Widget`, then the name of the source file must be `Widget.java`, using precisely that capitalization, and the compiled version of that class will be named `Widget.class` by the compiler. A similar naming convention is used for the compiled files corresponding to the nonpublic classes.

How are compiled classes used? After reading the last section, you might think that a link step is now needed to produce an executable file from multiple compiled class files. In fact, however, there is no link step. Any class which contains a properly constructed static *main* method may be directly executed by the JVM. As that method executes, additional compiled class files will be loaded as needed. What makes this work is that the only native code program being executed is the JVM itself, and the JVM knows the composition of a class file. The class file is constructed in such a way as to contain complete information concerning the locations and types of its data members, and how to access and execute each of the methods of the class.

Curiously, compiled class files are also used at compile time, in order to look up information concerning classes defined elsewhere, that is, not in the same source file. So not only is the JVM acquainted with the composition of a class file, but so is the Java compiler. In C++ terms, the compiled class file serves in all three roles: as a "header file," as an "object file," and as an "executable file."

4.4   SCOPE AND VISIBILITY OF NAMES

Recall from Chapter 1, "A Context-Sensitive Introduction," that a *declaration* is a statement that associates attributes with one or more identifiers. If the declaration gives full information concerning the statically ascertainable attributes of an identifier, it is said to be a *definition* for the entity named by that identifier. In this section, we investigate the question of the *scope* associated with a declaration or definition.

4.4.1 Static Scopes

In a language with static scope rules such as C++ or Java, the *scope* of a declaration is statically determined, meaning that it is defined as an extent of source code within which the declaration's bindings are valid. A *block scope*, for example, is defined in terms of the opening and closing braces of a block. Both C++ and Java use block scope, and inherit their rule for block scope from C. That rule is quite simple, and states that the scope of a declaration within a block extends forward from the declaration itself to the closing brace of the innermost block within which the declaration is enclosed.

Static scopes often overlap, and when they do they must overlap in a nested way. For example, blocks can appear as statements within an enclosing block. When there is such overlap, there is also potential for overlapping scopes, as for example when a data object named x is declared in both an inner and an enclosing outer block. We say that the *visibility*, not the scope, of the outer declaration is affected, as the outer declaration is eclipsed by the inner. In the example given, the name x will have the associations attached to it by the inner declaration only within the scope of that declaration. Everywhere else within the outer block its associations will come from the outer declaration.

4.4.2 Global Scope Rules and Java Packages

Global scope rules are at the opposite end of the spectrum from local, or block scope. They are rules which establish the ways in which identifiers can be given associations which are valid throughout an entire program. These differ dramatically between the two languages. C++ inherits a very liberal set of global scope rules from C, whereas in Java there are only a very few quite strict global scope rules.

Let us start with Java's rules concerning globally applied identifier associations. First of all, the *only* declaration which can be given a global scope in Java is a type definition. It is true that a package name is also global in some sense, but package names are file directory names and as such are not defined by the language but by the operating system. In Java, only public types can be made globally accessible in the sense that their names can be made visible in all the files which constitute a complete program, regardless of where those files are located. However, any class is accessible to classes in its "default package," which is the directory in which its compiled class appears.

Definition

A Java *package* is a collection of classes all defined in the same directory in a file system. The name of a package is the same as that of the directory in which it resides.

Access to public classes in other packages is obtained using an import statement. For example, the scope of any public class definition which is a part of package MathPackage can be extended throughout a source file in another package by including the statement

```
import MathPackage.*;
```

at the beginning of that source file. Any public class whose compiled class file appears in the `MathPackage` directory and which includes the statement

```
package MathPackage;
```

at the top of its source file is considered to be part of that package. There is more to the association of package names with directories in the file system than we are mentioning here, however, and becoming overly concerned with the exact correspondence is not necessary. Both the *Eclipse* and *NetBeans* IDEs manage the package/directory correspondence smoothly and transparently, and a complete description of that correspondence is not included here.

4.4.3 C++ Namespaces

The facility in the C++ language that roughly corresponds to the package is called a *namespace*. Like packages, namespaces can be spread out over multiple source files, but namespaces are not in any way related to file directories. Like a package, a namespace is an encapsulated set of declarations, but all declarations in a namespace are public by default. The notation for including a series of declarations in a namespace is similar to the notation for a class definition, and is outlined as follows:

```
namespace name {
    series of C++ declarations
}
```

Note the absence of the closing semicolon, which is not required for namespaces.

The namespace may be reopened in other compilation units and augmented with additional declarations, and the same syntax as above is used in all compilation units that provide declarations for the namespace. The relationship thus introduced between source files is symmetric, in that no source file can be said to "own" the namespace, but each compilation unit adds different information to it. Carrying this fact to its logical conclusion, the reader can correctly infer that his source files have the capability of adding new declarations to standard library namespaces such as *std*. Such modifications are a very bad idea, but in the C mindset good software engineering practices are supposed to be observed because of good citizenship, not because of rigorous requirements of the language or environment.

A programmer wishing to use portions of a namespace typically does two things. First, a preprocessor `#include` statement should be used for each header file containing a declaration from the namespace which will be needed by the current compilation unit. Second, one or more C++ using statements is typically coded for the purpose of allowing names from the namespace to be used without qualification. Thus, after issuing the statement

```
#include <iostream>
```

one can refer to the standard input stream object as std::cin. However, after the sequence

```
#include <iostream>
using std::cin;
```

the same object can be referred to as simply cin. A commonly employed, but risky, variant of the using statement is using namespace. Thus, if we code using namespace std; instead of the above using statement, then *all* the names in this compilation unit which are from the namespace std become useable without qualification. Of course, we now risk name collisions with other named entities in this compilation unit.

4.4.4 File Scope in C++

Rules for global associations in C++ are much more complicated than those for Java, and are tied up in the notion of "file scope," a concept again inherited from C. If a declaration is not a parameter declaration and is not entirely enclosed in a matched set of braces defining the beginning and end of a block, a class, or a struct, that declaration is said to have *file scope*. What this means is that the identifier associations established by the declaration, if not hidden by some more localized declaration, will be valid from the point in the file where the declaration appears until the end of the source file. Many entities in C++ can properly be given file scope, such as classes, structs, enumerations, constants, procedures, and named data objects. Only some of these can be promoted to the point where they have global status, however.

The C++ term which establishes whether or not a name is a candidate for global scope is the term *linkage*. A name that has *external* linkage can have its scope extended beyond the compilation unit in which its definition appears. Names of objects declared locally to a block *cannot* have external linkage.

An example of a name that *does* have external linkage is the name of a data object which is defined at file scope, or the name of a function (a pure procedure) whose definition appears at file scope. Let us take, for example, the declaration

```
int x;
```

given at file scope. This declaration is considered a complete definition for x in C++, even though no initialization is given. The fact that x has external linkage shows up in C++'s translation scheme in the requirement that x be included in the table of external symbols in the object file. This gives the linker the opportunity to complete a reference to x in a compilation unit different from that in which x was defined. However, because this is a strongly typed language, such a reference to x must be preceded by a declaration.

Suppose we wish to refer to the variable x in a compilation unit different from the one in which the above definition appears. Reproducing the same declaration in the new compilation unit would be an error (caught by the linker), because a variable cannot have two definitions. Instead, we introduce into the new compilation the declaration

```
extern int x;
```

which accomplishes two things: (1) it assigns a type to the symbol **x**; and (2) it informs the compiler that **x**'s definition appears in a different compilation unit. This allows the compiler to translate all references to x appropriately as to type, leaving **x**'s location information zeroed out in the compiled code but placing a pointer to each such reference in a table of unresolved references imbedded in the object file. The linker can then use the table of external symbols from the other object file to complete all references to **x** in the second object file.

4.4.5 Class Scope

Declarations which provide names for member functions and data members of C++ and Java classes have what we will refer to as *class scope*, meaning that any method definition in the class can contain a reference to the named entity. Of course, class methods (static member functions) may not contain unqualified references to instance variables or instance methods, but instance methods can make unqualified reference to class methods and class variables. Classes contained within classes are a special case, and the issue of whether an inner class can make reference to a named entity in the outer class is resolved differently in the two languages. (See Chapter 5, "Additional Concepts from the C++ Language," and Chapter 7, "Java and the Swing Library," for the C++ and Java views, respectively, of how inner class scopes interact with outer class scopes.)

4.4.6 Lifetimes of Variables

Although the scope of an identifier association is statically determined in both languages, the *lifetime* of a variable is always a dynamic issue. Normally in a language with static scope rules the lifetime of a variable coincides with its scope, in the sense that the variable comes into existence with the entry of execution into that scope and is destroyed when the scope is exited. For global variables, and indeed for all file-scope variables, this means that the variable's lifetime begins when the program begins execution and ends when execution ceases.

The lifetime of a block-scope variable normally begins when the block is entered, either by the normal sequential execution of commands or by an explicit call of the procedure whose body the block constitutes. The variable is then destroyed when the block is exited. An exception is a variable in C++ which is declared *static*. As explained in Section 1.3.8, the lifetime of a static local variable begins when its scope is first entered and extends throughout the remainder of the execution of the program. Thus, a procedure containing a static local variable "remembers" the value which that variable last had, every time the procedure is reentered. If the procedure is an instance method, each instance of the class to which the method belongs will of course have its own copy of the static local variable. Java does not allow static variables at block scope.

4.5   LOW-LEVEL OPERATIONS

Java does not try to define a radically different execution paradigm. The JVM has many of the same instructions one would expect to see in a standard von Neumann machine. Moreover, just as in C and C++, all the usual kinds of low-level data types one expects to see on such a machine are present, and the operations one would expect are also there. Most of these data types are even named the same as they are in C and C++: `char`, `short`, `int`, `long`, `float`, and `double` have similar meanings in all three languages. An important difference is that in C and C++ these types are typically associated with native data types on the underlying machine, for the sake of fast execution time. In Java, these data types are IEEE standards, and they are used whether or not the underlying machine supports them. The reason, of course, is platform independence.

> Definition
>
> A *platform* is a base upon which applications can be built. It is a specific (real or virtual) machine, along with a precisely defined set of support functions for communication with the outside world.

With minor exceptions, a Java program should compile and execute identically on any platform to which the Java compiler and the JVM have been ported. What's more, a compiled class file should be usable on any such machine without recompilation. A C++ program must be recompiled before it can run on a different machine, and may even need source code changes in order to meet its specifications, because differences in data types on different machines will affect precision and range. A C++ program which has been ported many times is usually amply supplemented with preprocessor variables controlling conditional compilation segments, directing the compiler to use different data types and different translation strategies depending on the target machine.

4.5.1 Translation of Expressions and Coercions

The strategy for translating expressions is similar in the two languages. The expression x+y translates to a (virtual or actual) machine addition operation if x and y are of the same numeric type, or if there is a corresponding mixed-type addition implemented on the machine. As in C++, Java's char type does double duty as a single-character data type and a numeric data type. However, C and C++ usually map this data type into a signed 8-bit machine data type, whereas Java uses an unsigned 16-bit value. (Java does have an 8-bit signed data type, however, which it calls byte.) In both languages, there is a promotion strategy where stored values of less precise types are translated to higher precision values if necessary to match the type of another operand in an arithmetic operation.

Automatic translation between numeric types also occurs when an argument in a function call does not match the type of the corresponding parameter, with compiler warnings issued when loss of precision might occur.

4.5.2 Basic Types, Arithmetic, and Bit-Level Operations

Besides the expected add (+), subtract (–), multiply (*), and divide (/) operations, some very low-level operations are included, in the C tradition. Both C++ and Java provide bit-level shifts, an 'and' operation, and an 'or' operation. Shift operations use the operators << and >>, the 'and' operator symbol is an ampersand (&), and the 'or' operator is the vertical line symbol (|). Besides & and |, both languages recognize a third bit-level operation called "exclusive or," which uses the caret operator symbol (^). All of these are overloaded operations which apply to a variety of numeric types and yield results of varying sizes and types.

Shifts need particular explanation because of their asymmetric effects. Both operands in a shift are integers, but the two play very different roles. The left-hand operand is a signed or unsigned integer data value, and the right-hand operand is a shift count. For example, the quantity represented by the expression 5<<3 is the quantity one would obtain by shifting the value 5, stored in binary, to the left by 3 bits. The resulting value is the same as the value 5×2^3, or 40. Special rules (and, in Java, a third operator symbol >>>) are needed to define when the expression makes sense and what it means, considering that the types involved may be signed or unsigned, and the value on the right may be large enough to overflow the storage unit being shifted, for which the size is strictly determined by the type of the left-hand operand.

There is another operation for which the meaning is very clear until we take into account the full range of values which may be used as operands. It is the remainder, or modulus, operation, for which both languages use the % operator. The meaning is usually explained by saying that x%y represents the remainder when x is divided by y. That explanation is perfectly satisfactory for most practical uses, but is open to interpretation when negative values are involved. Of course, the value on the right cannot be zero, but either of the two operands can be negative. The "Division Algorithm," an elementary theorem from number theory, would be a natural candidate for resolving unclear meanings, but in fact the implementation defies that convention. For example, for -35%3 the theorem would provide a quotient of -12 and a remainder of 1, whereas both C++ and Java return not 1 but -2 as the result of the expression. This is a potential source of human error, because modular arithmetic is an important tool for analysis, and the universal and very useful convention (upheld by the Division Algorithm) is that a remainder should always be nonnegative.

Both languages inherit from C the preincrement and predecrement (symbols ++ and --, respectively) operators and the post-increment and post-decrement versions of those same operators. New students of these languages continue to be surprised that these operators are included at all, because they seem so arbitrary and machine-like. Let us consider the incrementing of a single numeric variable x. In the preincrement form, ++x, the meaning is clear, which is to add one to the value of x and pass on to the next operation in turn the incremented value. As such, the expression has two effects, the side effect of storing a value and the effect of returning a value to be used in succeeding operations, but the value stored and the value returned are the same. The post-increment form, x++, is similar in that it has as its side effect the incrementing of the value of x. The difference is seen in the fact that the value returned is the old value of x, before the increment. So the effect of the following code segment is to store 1 in before and 2 in after.

```
x = 1;
before = x++; // Stores a 1
```

```
after = x;    // Stores a 2
```

In addition to the numeric types, there is a Boolean data type in both languages (called `boolean` in Java and `bool` in C++), and a type called `void`. The latter is a degenerate type in both languages, because no values of that type exist, and therefore it is illegal to declare a variable of type `void`. The major use of the `void` keyword is to indicate that a method of some class (or a procedure in C++) does not return a value, but in C++ it can also be used to declare a typeless pointer or reference.

4.5.3 Programmer-Defined Operators and Boolean Coercions

Many important differences in flavor between the two languages arise from the fact that programmer-defined overloading of operators is permitted in C++ but not in Java. Thus, the C++ programmer is more likely to associate the << and >> operators with input/output operations than shifts, because a large number of such uses are built into the C++ standard library. These I/O operations are used routinely in the language, whereas the use of the two operators as shifts is not as widespread a practice.

The comparison operators are identical in the two languages, namely >, <, >=, <=, ==, and !=. These all return Boolean values, either `true` or `false`. The logical operations 'and', 'or', and 'not' use symbols &&, | |, and !, respectively, again in both languages. The comparison operators, like the arithmetic operators, are heavily overloaded and employ type transfers routinely to attempt to construct a result which is likely to be what the programmer intended. The difference is that C++ also overloads the other operators by routinely transferring from numeric to Boolean types and vice versa, a thing that Java will not do.

In C++, the rules for transforming between Boolean and numeric values are simple. If a Boolean value is needed but the value supplied is numeric, the numeric value is transformed into the value `false` if it is zero, and into the value `true` if it is nonzero. If a numeric value is needed and the value supplied is Boolean, then `false` will be transformed into zero and `true` into one. No such rules exist in Java, which has erected a wall between the numeric types and its Boolean type, so that no type transfers occur in either direction.

For example, coding `-1 < x < 1` seems a natural thing to do, and one might expect that it would evaluate to `true` if x is a numeric variable whose value is zero. In fact, however, it cannot make sense unless the result of `1 < x` is a valid left-hand side for the < operator, a fact which causes Java to generate a compile-time error, but which in C++ triggers a type transfer. Because C++ transfers Boolean values to numeric values, and because `-1 < x` evaluates to `true`, that subexpression is evaluated as the value 1, and so the final value of the original expression is the value of 1 < 1, i.e., `false`, not `true` as expected. Of course, the programmer should have coded

```
-1 < x && x < 1
```

which evaluates to `true` without any type transfers in both languages.

4.5.4 The C++ void* Data Type

A seemingly perverse design decision for a strongly typed language is seen in the use of the data type `void*` as a legal variable type. The values of this type are essentially typeless machine addresses. This hints at a major difference in philosophy between the two languages, related to the fact that the `void*` data type is routinely used to defeat the type structure of the C++ language and is very dangerous because it can so easily be misused or used for malicious purposes.

In contrast, machine addresses are not part of the semantic domain of the Java language—one simply does not talk about them. Addresses as data cannot be achieved in the language and are not part of the Java mindset. Expert C++ programmers would argue, however, that it is precisely the ability of C++ to circumvent some of its rules when necessary that makes it well suited for a wide range of applications, including low-level systems programming. The `void*` data type, in particular, has a number of practical usage patterns which, if hidden behind a carefully designed interface, are effective, efficient, and perfectly safe.

4.5.5 Java Wrapper Classes

A collection of *wrapper classes* exists in Java for the purpose of providing more high-level functions associated with the primitive numeric types.

Definition
A *wrapper* is a high-level encapsulation of a set of one or more existing data types and operations, in which some of the operations in the encapsulated set are made available as part of a new interface, some are hidden, and some are repackaged to present a different appearance to the client.

Java's wrapper classes are all named in ways (`Integer`, `Float`, `Double`, etc.) that call to mind the corresponding primitive type, and all of them possess constructors which convert a primitive value into a first-class object. For example, 32 is a primitive value and `new Integer(32)` is a first-class object associated with that value. Arithmetic is not possible with wrapper-class objects, so that if x and y are of type `Integer`, not `int`, there is no addition operation defined for them. Instead, the code `x+y` invokes a facility called *unboxing*, and the message `intValue()` is sent to both sides of the + operator, resulting in an invocation of the `int` version of operator +. So the following code is correct but hides some details.

```
Integer x = 5, y = 6;
Integer z = x + y;
```

The two lines below explicitly represent what is going on behind the scenes…

```
Integer x = new Integer(5), y = new Integer(6);
Integer z = new Integer(x.intValue() + y.intValue());
```

The reason the Java wrapper classes exist is that sometimes it is convenient to have numbers behave like first-class objects (in Smalltalk fashion). Often more sophisticated operations must be performed, which machine-level integers are not capable of, such as converting between character string representations of a value and internal representations of those values. Also, the Java library container classes cannot store numbers but must store first-class objects; therefore, instead of a container for primitive numeric values the programmer creates a container storing the handles of the corresponding wrapper objects. C++ has no wrapper classes and addresses the above problems by: (a) allowing a given container to contain values of only one type, but that type may be a primitive type, a pointer type, or a class type; and (b) relying heavily on a sophisticated set of input/output operations (using overloads of the << and >> operators) which automatically convert between strings and primitive numeric values.

4.6   CONSOLE OUTPUT

For the sake of providing complete code examples in this chapter, we will discuss a procedure for producing output to the screen (or other standard output device) at this point. This is somewhat off-topic in a chapter on similarities and commonalities, because there is very little similarity between the approaches taken by the two languages. Both languages do, however, treat the standard output device as an object. Java accomplishes console output using `print()` and `println()` and similar messages to the object `System.out`, while C++ programmers typically use the operator << and the library object `cout` from namespace `std`. The Java compiler does not need an `import` statement, because it uses the `System` class

without being asked to do so, but C++ requires a preprocessor `#include` directive and a `using` statement, as follows:

```
#include <iostream>
using std::cout;
```

Let us use as an example a common debugging technique. Suppose `x` is an
`int` variable and we wish to produce on the console a labeled record of its current value at some point during program execution. The two languages handle
this in two totally different ways, as seen in the following code segments.
Java:

```
System.out.print("x = " + x);
```

C++:

```
cout << "x = " << x;
```

The key to C++'s comparatively simple syntax is that the `<<` operator is designed to make function composition clear and natural. There are actually two
overloaded versions of this operator being used in the example, and in fact there
are a large number of such operators in the C++ standard library, but all return
a reference to the left-hand operand (`cout` in the example) so that we can avoid
two separate statements.

The Java idiom above also avoids two separate statements, but in a totally different way. The `print()` and `println()` methods are also overloaded, but only
one form is being used in the example, the form that takes a `String` operand.
The three mechanisms that combine to make this idiom work are (a) autoboxing,
which creates a first-class `Integer` object from the primitive `int` value stored
at `x`, (b) a second built-in coercion which automatically calls the `toString()`
method of a first-class object when a string value is needed, and (c) string concatenation, invoked by the + operator in the example.

Definition
Autoboxing is Java terminology for the automatic encapsulation of a primitive value as an instance of a wrapper class, for the purpose of transforming that value into a suitable argument for some subsequent operation.

4.7   ARRAYS AND SUBSCRIPTING

Java and C++ use similar notations for array subscripting, but differ in their approaches to arrays. In Java, an array is a first-class object in the sense defined in Section 1.5, and can respond to messages. In C++, the array is a very low-level feature, inherited as-is from C. For example, consider the following declarations, in the two languages:

C++:

```
int a[10];
```

Java:

```
int a[] = new int[10];
```

A careful study of the declarations themselves will provide indications of many of the differences. The storage representation of C's array is an aggregate of ten integers, stored on the stack or in static memory, depending on where the declaration occurred. The data type is `int[10]` and is considered equivalent to the data type `int * const` (constant pointer to integer—this type is explained in Chapter 5, "Additional Concepts from the C++ Language"). Until it goes out of scope `a` will be consistently treated as another name for the address of the first integer in this array of ten. Java's array, however, is a handle referencing a heap object, the most salient feature of which is the same sort of aggregate of ten integers, but which also stores a `length` attribute and has a number of behaviors one expects of all first-class objects in Java.

A major restriction in C++ is that the array size must be a statically determined constant, whereas in Java it may be run-time computable. In both languages, the object, once allocated, is of fixed size. For example, the array object referred to as `a` above must remain an array of exactly ten integers. Because the C++ programmer cannot 'ask' the array `a` what its size is, then in order to use good abstraction practices and avoid explicitly coding **10** wherever the size is needed, he will usually place a named constant at the appropriate scope, with value **10**, then use that constant wherever the size of the array is needed. In Java, the notation `a.length` is all that is needed in any context where the array's size is required. Of course, `a.length` is itself immutable.

Although the object itself cannot change its size in either language, in Java it is a simple matter to reallocate a new object and associate the same name with the newly allocated object, as in the following:

```
a = new int[25];
```

The old object becomes garbage and is a candidate for reclamation by the garbage collector. Such reallocation of an array can be accomplished in C++ only through the use of pointer variables, a topic we will look at in more detail in the next chapter. In neither language can the base type of the array (int in the example) be changed.

The indexing, or "subscripting" operation uses square brackets to enclose an index expression in both languages, and is zero-based, so that in the example a[i] refers to the integer which is stored at an offset of "i times the size of an integer" past the beginning of the aggregate. The difference between Java and C++ is in the default run-time behavior of the subscripting operation itself. In C++, with no stored information existing at run-time concerning the size of the array, there is no opportunity for that operation to check the value of i before attempting to access the desired memory location, to make sure it does not go beyond the bounds of the allocated storage. In Java, there *is* such an opportunity, and in fact by default, the compiler will generate code if necessary to be sure that the value of i lies between 0 and a.length - 1, inclusively. Such run-time existence checking is not only impossible in C++, but is frowned on by the C culture as a drain on execution time.

Higher-dimensional arrays can be declared in both languages with notations like the following.

Java:

```
float b[][] = new float[20][30];
```

C++:

```
float b[20][30];
```

Java is more flexible, allowing arbitrary expressions for the dimension sizes. Java goes even further, however, because it allows the various rows or hyperplanes of a higher-dimensional array object to be of different sizes and shapes. An example of a Java code snippet that achieves this is as follows:

```
float b[][] = new float[2][];
b[0] = new float[3];  // First row has three elements
b[1] = new float[5];  // Second row has five elements
```

C++ can achieve the same flexibility using pointers and dynamic allocation (next chapter), but the programmer must then be responsible for carefully deallocating the storage when it is no longer needed. (This is not always easy, because neither the array b nor any of its "slices" is able to furnish size information at run-time.)

4.8 CONTROL FLOW

Facilities for controlling the flow of execution in both these languages are rather conventional, consisting of precedence and associativity rules on the expression level, various structured programming constructs on the statement level, and function composition. There are some significant differences between C++ and Java, however, which come to light when we examine the details.

4.8.1 Expression-Level Sequence Control

Both C++ and Java have a large number of operators, and the two lists are nearly identical. To control the order of evaluation in an expression, precedence rules and associativity rules are employed, in a very conventional way. However, some of the choices made are counter-intuitive. For example, bit-level operations, which because of their low-level interpretation seem closely related to arithmetic operations, are actually of a much lower precedence. In fact, the bit-level operators have lower precedence than any of the arithmetic or relational operators, and lower even than the shift operators. Thus, the innocent-looking expression

```
x & y == x | y
```

which seems to ask whether or not the 'and' of x and y is equal to the 'or' of x and y, actually performs y == x as its first operation. Parentheses are needed to enforce the desired order:

```
(x & y) == (x | y)
```

True to established conventions, multiplicative operators (*, /, and %) have higher precedence than additive operators (+ and –), and 'and' has higher precedence than 'or', both on the bit level and the logical level. Bitwise 'exclusive or' has a precedence greater than bitwise 'or' and less than bitwise 'and.'

Various forms of assignment are used in both languages, with the same syntax and meaning. Besides conventional assignment, which uses the = operator symbol, there are the assignments +=, –=, *=, /=, %=, >>=, <<=, &=, |=, and ^=. The meanings of all these are similarly defined. For example,

```
x += 3
```

has the same result as x = x + 3, and produces the same side effect.

Both languages consider all forms of assignment to be expression-level operations, with a right-to-left associativity. The value of an assignment operation is the value stored, but usually we execute such an operation for its side effect, not its value. When assignments are "chained" together, however, we are interested in both. Thus, the sequence of code

```
int x = 5, y = 1;
x += y += 2;
```

first performs the operation y += 2 and thereby stores 3 in variable y, and then performs the operation x += 3, storing 8 in variable x.

Assignment operators all share the same precedence level, which is the lowest of all operators save one in C++ and the very lowest precedence in Java, because Java has no comma operator. C++'s comma operator has the lowest precedence in that language. In C++, the expression

```
x , y
```

has as its value the value of y and ignores the value of x. Why have such an operator? Because the comma operator takes *evaluated* operands, which means the only really useful left-hand operand is one which has a side effect when evaluated, as in the following code:

```
x = 78, y = 12
```

The value of the above expression is 12, but the important thing is that values were stored in variables x and y. The above would be illegal as an expression in Java, which omits the comma operator and provides special statement forms for the situations in which the above pattern is useful.

NOTE

Both languages provide the ternary operation ?:, but naturally Java requires the first operand to be of type boolean. Assigning a type to the result of such an operation seems difficult, but there is a precedent to follow. For example, the expression

```
a > b ? 27 : 3.45
```

would appear to have either type `int` *or type* `double`, *depending on the result of the comparison. Such a situation would be perfectly tenable in Smalltalk, where the result of any expression is an object and every object can be, and routinely is, queried at run-time as to its type. But in a compiled language, the norm is to be able to determine the type of the expression using statically applied rules. In the above example, we take our cue from the* `+` *operation (or any other arithmetic operation, in either language), which when given as its two operands an* `int` *on one side and a* `double` *on the other would simply promote the* `int` *to a* `double` *before performing the operation. That is exactly what happens here, and the type of the expression is* `double` *in both languages. More complex rules apply where programmer-defined types are concerned, however.*

The function application (`operator()`) and subscripting (`operator[]`) operations have the same operator precedence as the postfix `++` and `--` operations, and as such share with those operations the most "tightly binding," or highest precedence, position among operators common to both languages. (This is true unless one counts the period as a "component selection" operator, in which case its precedence must be considered greater. C++ also has the pointer selection operator `->`, which has a higher precedence.) Of course, associativity for postfix unary operations must be "left to right" in order to make any sense syntactically. Prefix unary operations such as `-`, `++`, and `--` associate right to left for the same reason, and occupy the "next highest" precedence position after the postfix operations.

Function composition, when allowed to be both directly and indirectly recursive and when taken in concert with conditional execution, is a totally general sequence control mechanism. Both languages support recursion in this way, and so the programmer constructing an algorithm is often presented with a choice between a design which uses recursion and a design which uses statement-level sequence control, as described below.

4.8.2 Casts and Temporaries

Both languages allow the use of "casts." Casting consists of using a type name as an operator for the purpose of making type conversions, a practice which is used routinely in C, often for the purpose of defeating type security. C++ is much more permissive here, retaining all the power of the C casts, whereas Java limits casts to standard conversions between numeric types. The syntax which is permitted in both languages is to enclose the target type in parentheses and use it as a prefix operator, as in the following:

```
static const double pi = 3.14159264;
int y;
y = (int)(7*pi); // Casting double to int.
```

In C++, the parentheses around the type name may be omitted if the parameter of the cast is itself parenthesized. Oddly enough, C++ has deprecated these simple notations in favor of a very un-C-like set of four cast styles called static_cast, dynamic_cast, const_cast, and reinterpret_cast. The recommendation now is that the programmer should use

```
y = static_cast<int>(7*pi)
```

in the above code segment. The reason for these new notations is not to restrict the use of casts but to make them more "honest" in an attempt to make sure the programmer understands the purpose and effect of the cast.

The absolute power for defeating type security still remains in C++. For example, to reinterpret an int bit pattern as a float value one can use the notation

```
reinterpret_cast<float&>(integer variable)
```

C++ goes farther even than C in the use of casts, allowing the programmer to define his own meanings for them.

The result of a cast, like the result of any operation in an expression, is a *temporary*. A temporary is an unnamed variable, typically residing in a register or on the stack, which is used for the purpose of referring to an intermediate result in a computation. Storage for a temporary on the stack is allocated at block entry time and reclaimed at block exit time, just as for any local variable. Temporaries are usually taken for granted by the programmer, as the planning for their use is taken care of automatically by the compiler. On the other hand, there are situations in which the programmer deliberately creates a temporary for the purpose of sending it a message or for fashioning a particular type of parameter for a function call. Casts are an important part of this technique, as are conversion constructors, which have a very similar form. In fact, in C++ one form of the old cast syntax is identical to the syntax for calling a one-parameter constructor, namely *type_name(expression)*.

4.8.3 Statement-Level Sequence Control

Perhaps the most "barbaric" remnant of C which is retained by the C++ language is the labeled statement and the `goto` instruction. This facility is routinely omitted from students' instruction in the language, for the sake of promoting good software design practices. In fact, Java does not include `goto`'s, but with that one difference, C++ and Java have almost identical statement-level control flow features, which include all the structured programming patterns and some variants constructed in the same spirit.

We begin with the simple `if` statement. Syntax is the keyword `if`, followed by an expression in parentheses, followed by a statement. Let us consider an example.

```
if (a < b) c = d;
```

The meaning is clear. However, there is a major difference between the two languages here. In C++, any expression which can in any way be interpreted to yield a numeric result or a Boolean result is a valid candidate to appear in the parentheses following the `if`. In Java, the expression in that position *must* produce a Boolean result, or there is a syntax error. This restriction, along with others like it in Java, completely inoculates users of the Java language against the worst effects of one of the most common errors in the C++ language: mistakenly using the assignment operator = instead of the "test for equality" operator ==. Assuming a and b to be variables of some numeric type, in C++ the following statement is not incorrect and will produce at worst a warning from a C++ compiler.

```
if (a = b) c = d;
```

Of course, the programmer can use this "feature" of the language for his own purposes, but this pattern is far more likely to be the result of programmer error. When it occurs in this fashion, its result may be catastrophic in terms of the actual performance of the program, because contrary to the programmer's intent it will store a value in a, erasing the old value, and will execute the assignment `c = d` if and only if the value stored in a is nonzero. Depending on how the programmer has set the compiler flags, there may be a warning message here. But no compile-time or run-time *error* message will be generated as a direct result of the mistake. The same dangerous pattern could show up in some of the other C++ control structures.

Unlike the Pascal-derived languages, `else` is not an option on the `if` statement but rather a statement in its own right, which is required by a context-sensitive rule to follow immediately after some `if` statement. That `if` statement must be the one *immediately* preceding it, even if the one immediately preceding it is nested inside some other control structure. The statement subject to the `else` executes if and only if the result of the test in its accompanying `if` statement evaluated to `false`. This same approach is taken in both C++ and Java and, of course, it comes directly out of the C language.

To clarify this rule, consider the following example:

```
if (a < b)
    if (c < d)
        x = a;
else x = b;
```

The indentation here is either misleading and in poor style, or the programmer is in error, because the else goes with the inner, not the outer, *if*. To achieve the effect indicated by the indentation, we need a block, as follows:

```
if (a < b) {
    if (c < d)
        x = a;
}
else x = b;
```

Again, this nuance is shared by both languages.

The other conditional execution facility in these C-derived languages is the *switch* statement, which is usually used for the explicit purpose of choosing a single statement or block of statements to execute from a series of mutually exclusive choices, but which is actually a very primitive branching construct that is given an integral (whole number) value, then uses that value to select a branch location. A Java example illustrates the point:

```
switch (day) {
    case 12:
        System.out.println("\ttwelve drummers drumming,");
    case 11:
        System.out.println("\televen lords a-leaping,");
    case 10:
        System.out.println("\tten pipers piping,");
    case 9:
        System.out.println("\tnine ladies dancing,");
    case 8:
        System.out.println("\teight maids a-milking,");
```

```
    case 7:
        System.out.println("\tseven swans a-swimming,");
    case 6:
        System.out.println("\tsix geese a-laying,");
    case 5:
        System.out.println("\tfive golden rings,");
    case 4:
        System.out.println("\tfour calling birds,");
    case 3:
        System.out.println("\tthree French hens,");
    case 2:
        System.out.println("\ttwo turtle doves,");
    case 1:
        System.out.print(day>1?"\tand ":"\t");
        System.out.println("a partridge in a pear tree.");
}
```

Control flows from one case to the next unless there is another control transfer. Thus, in the case that day's value in the above code segment is 3, the console output will be the following text:

```
three French hens,
two turtle doves,
and a partridge in a pear tree.
```

Needless to say, the above behavior is very seldom what is desired. In most uses of this control structure, the programmer achieves mutually exclusive cases by placing a break after each case, as in the following:

```
String ordinal;
switch (cardinal) {
    case 1: ordinal = "first"; break;
    case 2: ordinal = "second"; break;
    case 3: ordinal = "third"; break;
    case 4: ordinal = "fourth"; break;
    case 5: ordinal = "fifth"; break;
    default: ordinal = "last";
}
```

Given that cardinal is an int with value 3, the above will store the string "third" in ordinal. Omitting the break statements would have caused "last" to be stored there. The switch performs a jump to the default label if the expression's value does not match any of the cases, so that if cardinal has the value 7, then again the string "last" will be stored at ordinal.

Looping constructs are nearly identical in the two languages, again with the proviso that conditions used for loop control are required to be of type `boolean` in Java. For example, the following loop computes the sum of the first twenty positive integers which are not multiples of three, and (in the proper context) works equally well in both languages.

```
int sum = 0, term = 1, count = 0;
while (count < 20) {
    if (term % 3 != 0) {
        sum += term;
        ++count;
    }
    ++term;
}
// The variable 'sum' now contains the desired computation.
```

A post-test `do...while` construct can be used in both languages, and again is inherited directly from C. A subtle difference exists, however, in the `for` constructs.

The following `for` loop, in a sense equivalent to the above `while` loop, also works in both languages, and has identical semantics in both cases. But the three variables declared in the initialization have a scope which is limited to the `for` statement itself, so that the most important variable in the computation, `sum`, is inaccessible to the statements placed after the loop.

```
for (int sum = 0, term = 1, count = 0; count < 20; ++term) {
    if (term % 3 != 0) {
        sum += term;
        ++count;
    }
}
// The variable 'sum' now no longer exists!
```

The solution to the problem, which again works in both languages, is to declare *sum* outside the loop. Let's suppose we declare all three variables outside the loop, as follows, to obtain the following code, which again works in both languages.

```
int sum, term, count;
for (sum = 0, term = 1, count = 0; count < 20; ++term) {
    if (term % 3 != 0) {
        sum += term;
```

```
        ++count;
    }
}
// The variable 'sum' now contains the desired computation.
```

What is different between Java and C++ is not the effect of the above computation, but its interpretation by the compiler. C++ considers all three portions of this particular `for` construct to be nothing more than arbitrary expressions, whereas Java has more stringent requirements, namely: (a) the initialization portion is a (possibly empty) list of expressions separated by commas, to be evaluated exactly once when the loop is first entered, in order from left to right strictly for their side effects; (b) the test portion (middle portion) is a `boolean` expression which is evaluated as a pretest and, each time it evaluates to `true`, causes the loop body to be executed again; and (c) the increment portion has exactly the same form and meaning as the initialization portion, except that it is to be executed *after* each execution of the loop body. The above rules are not necessary in the C++ language because that language has a comma operator and can consider the code

```
sum = 0, term = 1, count = 0
```

to constitute a valid expression. Curiously, then, C++ would accept the following code as just as valid, and it would produce the same result.

```
int sum, term, count;
for (sum = 0, term = 0, count = 0; ++term, count < 20;) {
    if (term % 3 != 0) {
        sum += term;
        ++count;
    }
}
// The variable 'sum' now contains the desired computation.
```

Java would, of course, reject the above as syntactically invalid because the pretest is not a Boolean expression. Java's syntactic precautions are taken here in order to avoid the comma operator, which can be error-prone, and to maintain the wall of separation between the type `boolean` and the numeric types.

Neither language is terribly dogmatic from a structured programming perspective, because one can easily violate the single-entry, single-exit requirement for looping under that discipline. Of course, in C++ a `goto` can destroy this pattern, but in either language the programmer can use the `break` and `continue` statements. When a `break` statement is used, it must be issued within either a `switch` construct or one of the looping constructs, and will cause an immediate transfer of control to the first statement after the inner-most such construct. When a `continue` statement is issued, it must be issued from within a loop body, and it will cause an immediate transfer of control to the test controlling the loop, whether it is a pretest or a posttest. In a `for` statement, the `continue` will bypass the increment step.

4.9   CLASS CONCEPTS

A Java class and a C++ class have similarities in form and meaning. For discussion purposes, let us construct two example classes in both languages, a `Point` class having the same properties as described above and another which might serve as a base class for geometric figures. The latter has a private data member `base` that is of the type `Point` and that designates the upper left-hand corner of the bounding rectangle of a figure.

C++ class descriptions:

```
class Point {
public:
     int x, y;
};

class BasedFigure {
     Point base;
public:
     BasedFigure(Point base): base(base) {}
     Point getBase() { return base; }
};
```

Java class descriptions:

```
public class Point {
     public int x, y;
}

public class BasedFigure {
     private Point base;
     public BasedFigure(Point base) {
          this.base = base;
     }
```

```
    public Point getBase() { return base; }
}
```

Note that because both Java classes are public, *the two class definitions will have to appear in two separate source files*. This is the last time we will mention this fact, but will in our examples consistently use public classes in our Java code in order to put those classes on par with those used in our C++ examples, because in that language classes that are not nested inside other classes or structs are public by default.

Not all initialization in Java occurs in constructors. Any class may include inline initializations which are independent of any constructor.

Definition

A Java *inline initialization* is a block of code inside a class that is not contained in any method of that class. If the block is preceded by the word `static`, then the initialization takes place before any instances of the class are created. If it is not preceded by that keyword, then the initialization takes place every time an instance of the class is created.

The following Java class has multiple constructors, but the class variable x receives an initial value of 5 and the instance variable *y* receives an initial value of 10 before any of those constructors is invoked.

```
public class MyClass {
    static int x;
    int y;
    static {
        x = 5;
    }
    {
        y = 10;
    }
    public MyClass(int a) {
        // More initialization
        . . .
    }
    public MyClass(int v, int w) {
        // More initialization
        . . .
    }
    . . .
}
```

4.9.1 Basic Syntax and Semantics

One major difference between the two languages is in the manner in which access privileges are granted to a client of a class. In C++, the default access is private access, so that in the example the data member `base` is private simply because no access specifier precedes it. In Java, in order to grant public or private access to a member, an explicit assignment of one of those attributes (keyword `public` or `private`) is needed in the declaration for each such member. In contrast, once the `public:` label has appeared in a C++ class definition, all members that follow are public until a label changing the access characteristics appears. Hence, another way of coding the C++ class above is as follows:

```
class BasedFigure {
public:
    BasedFigure(Point base): base(base) {}
    Point getBase() { return base; }
private:
    Point base;
};
```

The constructor in the C++ class illustrates the penchant which that language has for special-purpose syntax with somewhat technical semantics. It is possible in C++ to code the constructor in a similar way to that in which the Java constructor is coded, using the statement

```
this->base = base;
```

However, keep in mind that C++ uses value semantics, so that we cannot precisely duplicate the effect of the corresponding Java assignment without incorporating pointer variables and dynamic allocation and deallocation. We will discuss these semantic differences in the next section. At any rate, we have chosen not to make an assignment in the example but to use a particular form of the "initialization part" syntax, formed by placing a colon right after the closing parenthesis of a constructor's parameter list, and following it with a series of syntactic elements of the form *identifier(expression)*, separated by commas. Here *identifier* must be the name of a data member of the class, and *expression* is an expression evaluated as if it were part of the block of statements forming the body of the constructor. The value of the expression is computed when the constructor is called, and the result is stored in the data member, before the main body of the constructor begins executing. The curious effect in the example is that in the syntax *base(base)*, the *base* outside the parentheses refers to the data member of the class and the *base* inside the parentheses refers to the parameter of the constructor. (There are other uses for the initialization part, which will be discussed as they are needed.)

Again, keep in mind that in Java, in order to share the class with clients at all, it is necessary to apply the *public* attribute *to the class itself*. In C++, if the class declaration is available (typically via a header file) at compile time and its implementation is available at link time (as object code) or included in-line as part of the declaration, then the client may freely use it.

4.9.2 Value Semantics and Pointer Semantics

Examining the usage of the keyword `this` in the two languages, we note a major difference. In C++, the word denotes a pointer value, which is the *address* of the object. Addresses are valid data types in C++ and require either the -> pointer selection operator or an explicit use of the prefix asterisk operator in order to dereference them, so that the notation `*this` refers directly to the object, whereas in Java the object is simply referred to as `this`. Curiously enough, the storage representation for `this` in Java is essentially the same, i.e., a pointer, but since addresses are not valid data types in Java any usage of `this` or of any address value is automatically dereferenced as needed, i.e., is considered a reference to the object itself. This use of pointer semantics extends to all names of first-class objects in Java, which includes strings and arrays as well as class instances.

To further illustrate the value semantics of C++ as opposed to the pointer semantics of Java, consider the following two series of declarations:

C++ object instantiations:

```
Point p(35,96);
BasedFigure bf(p);
```

Java object instantiations:

```
Point p = new Point(35,96);
BasedFigure bf = new BasedFigure(p);
```

The Java notations are reminiscent of Simula and Smalltalk, where the `new` primitive indicates an allocation on the heap, with the name of the object denoting its *location* there. In contrast, the C++ declarations indicate an allocation either at the global scope or at block scope (depending on context), both of which carry with them the assumption that the identifier names the *value* of the allocated object. That value will be allocated as a block of bytes in the static or stack portion of the storage map, not on the heap. Java performs stack allocation here as well, but only for the *pointers* corresponding to p and to bf, which point to the value stored on the heap.

In both languages, the members of these objects are referred to using ordinary component selection notation, for example, using p.x and p.y to refer to the components of the Point object p. One should realize, however, that these notations in C++ compile directly to machine addresses or offsets on the stack, whereas Java uses an extra level of indirection to dereference p.

Heap space is automatically deallocated as necessary in Java by the run-time actions of a garbage collector. If one desires to use heap storage in C++, it can be done using pointer variables; however, C++ has no garbage collector and relies on explicit heap allocation and deallocation by the programmer. Such explicit heap operations should be carefully performed by a sophisticated programmer who understands the actions of both operations and has cultivated good habits for proper management of the heap. We will focus more on this topic in the next chapter.

The usual discussion of value semantics versus pointer semantics centers around examining what happens as a result of executing a simple assignment such as a = b. The short explanation is that in a language that uses pointer semantics the two names become associated with the same object, but in a language that uses value semantics a complete copy of b's value is made and placed in the storage referred to by the name a. This is true as far as it goes, but in the C++ language many issues can arise which make the above explanation incomplete. An obvious difficulty is that the assignment operator = may have been redefined by the programmer. In that case, it is impossible for the programmer to replace C++'s default value semantics with pointer semantics, but what it means to copy b's value into a can now be defined by the programmer.

> **NOTE**
>
> *One of the tasks routinely undertaken by the C++ programmer is to redefine the assignment operator so that it implements a deep, rather than a shallow, copy. This typically involves reconstructing one or more dynamically allocated data objects which are accessible via data members of b and insuring that the corresponding members of a have identical access to the reconstructed copies, a task which can be quite intricate.*

Another fine point in defining C++'s value semantics occurs when variables are initialized at the point of declaration, as in the following code:

```
Widget a = b;
```

Here it is tempting to the novice C++ programmer to assume that the assignment operator will be invoked, so that if the programmer has carefully defined assignment to implement the particular brand of value semantics he is attempting to achieve, then there is nothing to worry about here. In fact, the above is an initialization, not an assignment. Because of C++'s (rather complex) default initialization rules, in most cases the initialization will take place anyway, but only as a shallow copy. In order to get a deep copy here, the programmer must describe in code what is needed. However, we need to write not an assignment operator but a copy constructor, which is in fact what will be invoked by the above code.

4.9.3 Single Inheritance

Both languages permit the use of single inheritance, which provides for the establishment of a new class based on an already existing class. Java, however, permits only public inheritance, whereas C++ gives the programmer the choice of public, private, or protected inheritance. Consider the following example of public inheritance of a single base class, coded in each of the two languages in such a way as to produce equivalent data types.

C++ class description:

```
class Circle: public BasedFigure {
    double radius;
public:
    Circle(Point base, double radius):
        BasedFigure(base),radius(radius){
    }
    double getRadius() { return radius; }
};
```

Java class description:

```
public class Circle extends BasedFigure {
    private double radius;
    public Circle(Point base, double radius) {
        super(base);
        this.radius = radius;
    }
    public double getRadius() { return radius; }
}
```

Public inheritance makes the derived class a subtype of the base class, because all the public attributes and behaviors of the base class are also public in the derived class. That is precisely the case for both languages in the example above, and indeed the type `Circle`, as we have constructed it, is identical in the two languages; the only differences are differences in form, which we will examine now.

The major difference in form that has not already come to light is the difference in the two constructors. Again, the initialization part comes into play in the C++ code, but now it has a different interpretation, because the element `BasedFigure(base)` is clearly not an assignment to a data member of the class. The meaning is clear, however, because it obviously is meant to be an invocation of the base class constructor. The corresponding syntax in the Java class definition is **super**`(base)`, which must appear as the first statement in the body of the constructor. In both cases, the syntax mirrors a semantic requirement: that the portions of the object which belong to the base class must be initialized first, so that the code which follows may refer to those portions as needed in constructing the initial value of the derived class object.

Both languages allow multiple constructors. If there is a default constructor in the base class, it need not be explicitly invoked in the constructor for the derived class, but will be invoked implicitly, if necessary, before the statements in the derived class constructor are executed. If not, then one of the other constructors must be called explicitly, as we see in the example. Only one base class constructor will be called, however.

Generally, the use of the keyword **super** in Java is not so specialized as we see it here, but is similar to its use in Smalltalk. It refers to the current object, considered as an instance of the superclass. In Smalltalk, there is no need for a special form, because the initialization message is *voluntarily* sent to the base class version of the object, as a "good citizenship" expectation of the programmer. When Java and C++ were designed, they included the use of constructors and special forms because the designers perceived a necessity to *require* that base class initialization precede derived class initialization.

4.9.4 Abstract Classes vs. Concrete Classes

We say that a class is *abstract* if no instances can be created of that class type. In such a case, the class is designed for the express purpose of serving as a base class for other classes. A *concrete* class can have instances created of its type, as in the following instantiations of objects of type `Point`.

```
Point p(200, 150);  // C++ static or automatic allocation

Point p = new Point(200, 150); // Java allocation.
    // (Object will be garbage-collected.)

Point *p = new Point(200, 150); // C++ heap allocation.
    // (Requires an explicit delete operation.)
```

Both `Point` and `BasedFigure` as introduced above are concrete classes. By rights, however, one could argue that the latter class should not be concrete, because it is intended only as a base class for geometric figures drawn on the screen. In Java, the only thing needed to convert it to an abstract class is to use the keyword *abstract* as an attribute of the class in the first line of the definition, as follows:

```
abstract class BasedFigure {
    // First line of a Java abstract class
```

No such syntax exists in C++, however. In C++, the compiler must work a little harder to determine whether a class is abstract or not; a class is abstract if and only if one of its member functions is a *pure virtual function*. So, in the case of our `BasedFigure` data type, we must either make one of its member functions pure virtual or introduce a new member function. Let us take the latter approach and introduce a `getBounds()` member function, intended to return to the caller the bounding rectangle for a based figure. In order to do this, we must first define the `Rectangle` data type. While we are at it, we will give `Point` a constructor, to make our life a little easier.

```
class Point {
public:
    int x, y;
    Point(int x, int y): x(x), y(y) {}
};

class Rectangle {
    Point base, corner;
public:
    Rectangle(Point base, Point corner):
        base(base), corner(corner) {}
    Point getBase() { return base; }
        // The 'base' is the upper left-hand corner.
```

```
        Point getCorner() { return corner; }
            // The 'corner' is the lower right-hand corner.
    };

    class BasedFigure {
    public:
        BasedFigure(Point base): base(base) {}
        Point getBase() { return base; }
        virtual Rectangle getBounds() = 0;
    private:
        Point base;
    };
```

Note the syntax of a pure virtual function, as seen in the line of code

```
        virtual Rectangle getBounds() = 0;
```

Two things are necessary: (1) the keyword `virtual` announces that overrides of this function in derived classes will have polymorphic behavior, and (2) the function must not be given a body, and instead must end with the odd notation above that appears to initialize the function to zero. These notations announce that the body will not be furnished in this class and must be supplied as an override in any concrete class which is derived from this class.

In Java, such a function is called an *abstract* function. As we indicated above, a Java class does not have to have abstract functions in order to be declared abstract, but of course, only an abstract class can contain abstract functions. Following is the Java equivalent of the above code:

```
    public class Point {
        public int x, y;
        public Point(int x, int y) {this.x = x; this.y = y; }
    }

    public class Rectangle {
        private Point base, corner;
        public Rectangle(Point base, Point corner) {
            this.base = base;
            this.corner = corner;
        }
        public Point getBase() { return base; }
        public Point getCorner() { return corner; }
    }
```

```java
public abstract class BasedFigure {
    public BasedFigure(Point base) { this.base = base; }
    public Point getBase() { return base; }
    abstract public Rectangle getBounds();
    private Point base;
}
```

When we derive a class from an abstract class, we do not necessarily have to furnish implementations of all its abstract member functions. If we do not, however, the result is another abstract class. Following are updated definitions in both languages of our concrete `Circle` class derived from the abstract class `BasedFigure`.

Java definition:

```java
public class Circle extends BasedFigure {
    private double radius;
    public Circle(Point base, double radius) {
        super(base);
        this.radius = radius;
    }
    public double getRadius() { return radius; }
    public Rectangle getBounds() {
        return new Rectangle(
            getBase(),
            new Point(
                getBase().x + (int) (2 * radius + 0.5),
                getBase().y + (int) (2 * radius + 0.5)
            )
        );
    }
}
```

C++ definition:

```cpp
class Circle: public BasedFigure {
    double radius;
public:
    Circle(Point base, double radius):
        BasedFigure(base),radius(radius){}
    double getRadius() { return radius; }
    virtual Rectangle getBounds() {
        return Rectangle(
            getBase(),
```

```
        Point(
            getBase().x + (int) (2 * radius + 0.5),
            getBase().y + (int) (2 * radius + 0.5)
        )
    );
}
};
```

Note that the attribute `virtual` seen in the base class on the `getBounds()` method in the C++ version is still applied in the derived class, but no indication appears in the Java version to imply that the `getBounds()` member function is different in any way from any other member function. In fact, such explicit use of `virtual` in the C++ code is not needed, because an override of a virtual function is implicitly virtual. It is considered good practice to include it, however, as an additional means of informing the client programmer that this particular behavior is polymorphic.

In the definitions above, we see a difference between the two languages, a difference which we have already stated but which is dramatically illustrated in the two different syntaxes. In both cases, constructors are used to create temporaries for two different purposes, namely of (1) returning a `Rectangle` object in response to a `getBounds()` call and of (2) fashioning a `Point` parameter to supply as the second argument in the `Rectangle` constructor call. The obvious difference is in the use of the `new` operator for these purposes in Java, whereas no such operator is needed in C++. The `new` operator, when it is used in both languages, denotes a dynamic allocation on the heap. Because of automatic dereferencing in Java, this pointer value is the proper value to use as a temporary. Because no such dereferencing occurs in C++, the `new` operator is inappropriate and will not cause the appropriate type of operand to be generated. The effect of the C++ code as written is to construct the temporaries on the stack as complete values, not as pointers. Both values will be copied to other locations, and the temporaries on the stack frame will be reclaimed at block exit. The Java temporaries will also be reclaimed at block exit, but in that case the temporaries are just pointers, and those pointers will be copied to other locations, so that the actual `Point` and `Rectangle` objects, residing as they do on the heap, will not be reclaimed. Only when no access paths remain will the objects themselves be candidates for reclamation by the Java garbage collector.

4.9.5 Overrides and Polymorphism

Why is it considered important in C++ to provide individual notification of the `virtual` attribute for member functions, when there is no similar requirement in Java? The reason is that, like Smalltalk, Java makes no distinction: all overrides exhibit polymorphism. Let us examine the mechanisms that are at work in the two languages to enforce polymorphism, and the reason for the difference should then be clear.

Consider the method call a.f(), where a is a variable or parameter declared to be of type A and f is an instance method of class A. In Java, the run-time representation of the object a is a pointer to an object on the heap, and the reference to method f is routed through that pointer. Hence, it is the object, not a statically assigned type, that is responsible for overseeing the execution of the method. So in Java polymorphism occurs very naturally—the object itself only has access to the method that its own class implements, and that is the method which will be invoked. But in C++, the expression a.f() would not normally be compiled as a run-time lookup. The compiler has access to a complete specification of the interface to class A, or it would not have been able to successfully compile the program. If a is a declared object and not a reference, or if the compiler has *not* been informed by A's interface specification that the method f is virtual, then it will bind the call to the particular implementation of f defined by class A (denoted A::f()). This binding will either occur at compile time, in case a complete definition of A::f() is present in the compilation unit, or at link time, when the machine-level function call is actually bound to a particular offset at which the machine-language version of the method A::f() is to be stored. There is no room in this scheme for polymorphism, because it is the declared type A, not the object a, that determines which function is called. This is true even if A is merely a base type and the actual type of the object named a is that of some class derived from A.

Virtual functions are an exception to this normal translation strategy of C++. If the method *f* is virtual and *a* is a reference, then the expression a.f() translates in a different manner (as does the expression p->f(), where p is a pointer). Whenever at least one of the methods in class A is a virtual function, then one additional piece of overhead is added to the run-time representation of a: the virtual function pointer. This pointer points to the virtual function *table*, which is common to all objects of a's actual class (which will be A or some class derived from A). Therefore, if f is the third virtual function in class A, then the expression a.f() gets translated as a call on the machine language routine stored at the address contained in the third location in the virtual function table, where that table itself is located wherever the virtual function pointer in object a is pointing. This works because the inheritance pattern assures us that the third virtual function (or an override of that function) in class A is also the third virtual function in any class derived from A.

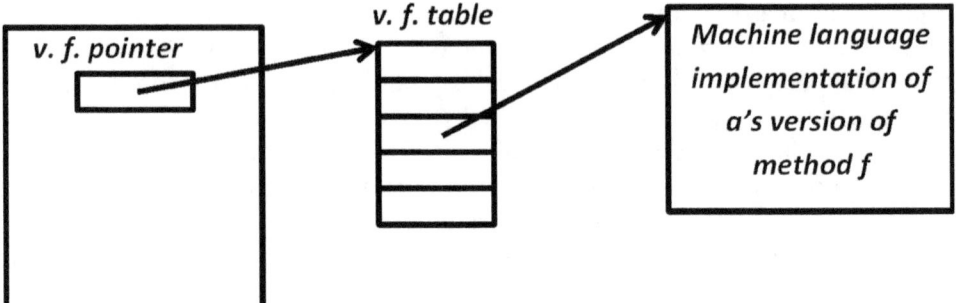

FIGURE 4.4 The virtual function table associated with object *a*.

4.9.6 Run-Time Type Checking and Casting

Both languages allow a certain amount of run-time type checking, but C++ is much less likely to tolerate such overhead. The only types in C++ which keep type information around at run-time are polymorphic types, i.e., classes that have virtual functions. The information itself has a natural home in that case, as another component to the directed graph that begins at the virtual function table. By way of contrast, Java maintains run-time type information for all classes.

Perhaps the most common operation which requires run-time type checking is *down-casting*. If object `obj` has been declared to be of type `A`, and its actual type `B` is a derived type of `A`, then a function `f` on `B`'s public interface may be called in Java using a cast, as follows:

```
((B)obj).f()
```

Such a cast is called a *down-cast*. The same syntax succeeds in C++ (if class A contains a virtual function), but the current C++ standard offers a more "honest" set of casts which provide more of an indication of their manner of implementation. In the new notation, the above would be coded as…

```
dynamic_cast(obj).f();
```

Both languages would check to see that the object `obj` really has type `B` before performing the cast and allowing the operation.

All Java casts are checked, either statically or dynamically. On the other hand, C++ retains as part of its C legacy the ability to cast any type to any other type in a totally unrestricted manner. The `reinterpret_cast` seen earlier can be used for this purpose.

4.9.7 Named Constants

Sophisticated capabilities for creating and scoping named constants are an essential part of any programming language which claims to promote good abstraction. In compiled languages, this is usually accomplished via static declarations. For example, consider the simple class A defined below, with class-scope constant c.

C++:

```
class A {
public:
    static const int c = 30;
};
```

Java:

```
public class A {
    public static final int c = 30;
}
```

In either language, if class A is in scope, then the class constant c can be freely referenced. In C++, this reference appears as A::c, whereas in Java it is A.c. The use of the keyword final in Java instead of const in this context is curious. The final keyword has other, only vaguely related, uses. Like C++, Java tends to overload keywords to mean different things in different contexts, but C++'s use of the keyword const is more limited than Java's use of final, as we will see in the following chapters.

A difference exists between the two languages concerning the way in which some of these class constants must be declared. The syntax seen above for C++ is only valid for integral types, so that the following code is invalid:

```
class A {
public:
    static const float c = 30.0f; // Invalid.  'float' is not
        // an integral type.
};
```

In C++, a nonintegral class constant must be allocated separately, preferably in a compilation unit containing only implementation code for class A and other classes related to it, not with client code. So, for example, we might achieve the effect desired above with the following two C++ files.

File 'A.h':

```
class A {
public:
    static const float c;
};
```

File 'A.cpp':

```
#include "A.h"
const float A::c = 30.0;   // Keyword 'static' not used here.
```

Both languages also have the capability to declare *instance constants*, i.e., constants that are bound to their values at instance creation time. For example, consider the following variation on the above declarations:

C++:

```
class A {
public:
    const int c;
    A(int x): c(x) {}
};
```

Java:

```
public class A {
    public final int c;
    public A(int x) { c = x; }
}
```

In both cases, the data member c is constant for the lifetime of any particular instance of class A, but that constant value may differ from instance to instance of the class.

Of course, both languages allow the creation of block-scope constants, and C++ is not so restrictive there, having very similar rules to those of Java. For example, the following two C++ declarations could legitimately appear in any block where x and y are constants or variables which are accessible in the current scope without qualification and have appropriate types.

```
const double pi = 3.141592654;
const int c = 3*x + y;
```

A similar statement could be made for Java, but in that language we would substitute the keyword `final` for `const`.

The above definitions for `pi` and `c` could occur *at file scope* in C++, provided `x` and `y` were also at file scope and had been bound statically to specific values previously. Of course, file scope does not exist for variables or constants in Java.

Another way of creating constants is with *enumerations*. The following code, in either language, establishes a series of ten named constants:

```
enum DigitType {
    ZERO, ONE, TWO, THREE, FOUR, FIVE, SIX, SEVEN, EIGHT, NINE
};
```

In this syntax, allowed by both languages, the values are not explicitly assigned but are always implicitly assigned as 0, 1, 2, etc. The above syntax declares a data type with a universe of ten values, and establishes names for those values. In the example, we have chosen names that match the actual values associated with them (e.g., `FIVE` has the value 5). In C++, the names can stand without qualification, whereas in Java they are referred to as `DigitType.ZERO`, `DigitType.ONE`, etc. Java has taken a much different direction with its enumerated types, which will be described more fully in Chapter 7.

Enumerations are not a good facility for naming constants for general use in Java, because the data types so created are not compatible with, and cannot be cast to, primitive types such as `int`. As is the case with the `boolean` data type, there is a "wall" between enumerated types and other primitive types. Knowing that the value associated with `ZERO` is 0 does not mean that the constant `ZERO` can be substituted in any context for that literal. The opposite is true in C++, where the name `DigitType`, after the above statement, will essentially be associated with the subrange 0–9 of the integers and its constants will be totally compatible with the integral data types. The type name is optional in C++, and individual assignments of values are allowed, as in the following:

```
enum { MIN_ITEMS = 10, MAX_ITEMS = 50 };
```

NOTE

The enum notation in C++ is so compact and handy that it is often used instead of the const declarations described previously. Keep in mind an important difference, however. Enumeration constants name values, not storage locations. This means they cannot be used in situations which require an associated address (an l-value, in C terms; see the following chapter). Having no storage assigned can obviously be of value if one is trying to conserve space, however, and this facility is the only facility in C++ that will allow the programmer to introduce named constants that are tied to a specific scope and that are not associated with a storage location.

Some programmers in C++ use preprocessor variables as named constants. This can be insidious, because there is no way to limit the scope of such a constant: the preprocessor does not "understand" C++; it simply goes blindly through the source file substituting one string for another.

4.10   EXCEPTION HANDLING

Facilities for synchronously responding to exceptional conditions in the two languages are quite similar. A typical scenario proceeds as follows:

1. An exceptional condition is tested for (for example, a divisor is zero in an upcoming division operation or a subscript will be out of range) and found to be true.

2. A `throw` command is executed, typically throwing an object of a type which is a specialized version of a library exception class.

3. If the `throw` is contained within a `try` block, an attempt is made to match the type of the thrown object with that of a parameter in a series of `catch` blocks which follows the `try` block.

4. If a match is found, it will be the *first* `catch` block in the series which is successfully matched with the thrown object. That `catch` block is executed, with the thrown object being bound to the `catch` parameter. During the execution of the `catch` block, another `throw` may occur and will be handled in the same way as the original `throw`, i.e., starting with step 2 above.

5. If no match is found, or if the `throw` occurred outside the context of any `try` block, the stack will be unwound (the current stack frame will be deleted), and execution will proceed as if the same `throw` operation were executed at the point of call in the calling context (if the original block was entered via procedure call) or in place of the current block (if the original block was entered via normal sequential flow through the

program). The thrown object must be preserved during this process, so it cannot reside in the original stack frame.

6. This process continues until a handler is found for the `throw`, or until the bottom stack frame is unwound, at which point a language run-time default handler will execute, typically issuing an "unhandled exception" error message and ending the program.

In C++, any data value may be thrown, whether a primitive value or a first-class object. But in Java only handles may be thrown, and those must point to objects which are instances of a class derived from the class `Throwable`. The Java documentation encourages programmers, however, to derive all exception classes from the subclass `Exception`. The software engineering mindset behind this design is that it is desirable to have all thrown objects inherit from a common base class so that a default handler may be established. In the following Java example, an `Exception` object is thrown and caught under certain conditions.

```java
try {
    if (x > y) return Math.sqrt(x - y);
    else throw
        new Exception("x's value must be greater than y's");
}
catch (Exception e) {
    System.out.println(e.getMessage());
}
```

Note that `Exception` objects may be tailored "on the fly" by passing a string in the constructor, and that string can be retrieved using the `getMessage()` instance method.

In C++, there is also a library class, called `exception`, which programmers are encouraged to use as a base class for exception classes. There is also special syntax for a default `catch` handler which, if used, must be the last in the series of handlers. In such a handler, the notation . . . is used in place of a parameter. Following is an example:

```cpp
try {
    if (x > y) return sqrt(x - y);
    else if (x == y) throw 0;
    else throw exception(
        "Can't extract square root of a negative number"
    );
```

```
    }
    catch(exception e) {
        cout << e.what() << endl;
    }
    catch(...) {
        cout << "Error" << endl;
    }
```

Note concerning the C++ example that member function `what()` serves the same purpose as `getMessage()` in the Java example. Note also the absence of `new`, because we are throwing values, not pointers.

In Java, any method that throws an exception (other than a `RuntimeException`) that it does not catch must declare the fact in its interface. Syntax for this is demonstrated by the following code segment:

```
    public int f(int i)
            throws OutOfBoundsException, ZeroDivideException {
        if (i < 0 || i > max) throw new OutOfBoundsException();
        if (a[i] == 0) throw new ZeroDivideException();
        return x / a[i];
    }
```

C++ has a similar notation, but the nature of separate compilation in that language makes impractical the notion that a complete compile-time check can be undertaken of this list of possible exception types. Some such checking is possible, but not all compilers undertake to perform this check, and the exception specification syntax `throw(exception-list)` is sometimes treated as little more than a comment. Note that the keyword here is `throw`, not `throws`, and the list of exception types must be enclosed in parentheses. Following is the C++ syntax for the above code segment:

```
    int f(int i)
            throw(OutOfBoundsException, ZeroDivideException) {
        if (i < 0 || i > max) throw OutOfBoundsException();
        if (a[i] == 0) throw ZeroDivideException();
        return x / a[i];
    }
```

The following Java class implements a quadratic polynomial, throwing and catching exceptions as needed. Note the use of the `throw` statement inside the constructor, which, if executed, causes the block from which the constructor was called to be exited (after the execution of an exception handler, if such a handler is present). This is as natural a way to abort the construction attempt as one can hope to achieve.

```java
public class QuadraticPolynomial {
    double a, b, c;
    public QuadraticPolynomial(double a, double b, double c)
throws Exception {
        this.a = a; this.b = b; this.c = c;
        if (a == 0)
            throw new Exception("Not a quadratic");
    }
    public double discriminant() {
        return b * b - 4 * a * c;
    }
    public int rootCount() {
        double disc = discriminant();
        if (disc < 0)
            return 0;
        else if (disc == 0)
            return 1;
        else
            return 2;
    }
    public double valueAt(double x) {
        return (a * x + b) * x + c;
    }
    public double getRoot(int i) throws Exception {
        // i should be passed as either 1 or 2.
        if (i < 1 || i > 2) {
            throw new Exception("Improper root number");
        }
        try {
            int n = rootCount();
            if (n < i)
                throw new Exception("Root does not exist");
            else if (i == 1)
             return (-b - Math.sqrt(discriminant())) / (2 * a);
            else
             return (-b + Math.sqrt(discriminant())) / (2 * a);
        }
        catch (Exception e) {
            System.out.println(e.getMessage());
            throw e;
        }
```

```
        }
    }
```

The construction of the C++ equivalent to the above is straightforward and is left as an exercise to the reader. There is one exception-handling feature in C++ which has no exact equivalent in Java, however. From within a `catch` block, the `throw` statement may be issued without an operand, so that the `throw e` statement at the end of the above example could be coded simply as `throw`. The effect of this command is to throw exactly the same object as was caught by the handler. The reason this is a significant difference is that in the C++ language it is the *value* of the object which is "thrown," and not just a pointer. If the parameter were of a base class type and the object caught was of a derived type with additional attributes, the `throw e` form would throw only a "sliced" base class version of the caught object, whereas `throw` would throw the derived class object.

The matching of a thrown object to a corresponding `catch` parameter is very strict in both languages. C++, which has the more permissive policy regarding what objects may be thrown, must necessarily have the more complicated rules for such matching. The thrown object's type must be either exactly the same as that of the parameter, or it must be of a type derived by inheritance from that of the parameter, directly or indirectly, or both must be pointers or references. If the two are pointers or references, then the same rules as described above apply to the base types of the objects. They must be exactly the same, or the type of the object pointed to by the thrown pointer must be of a type derived from the type pointed to by the parameter. Of course, the ... pattern matches any thrown object. Java simply requires an exact match or the inheritance relationship referred to above.

In both cases, the search for a handler corresponding to a thrown object must proceed sequentially from first to last, and the first match determines which handler executes. For this reason a handler for a derived class parameter should always precede a handler for any of its base classes, because placing them in the other order produces unreachable code. The Java compiler, in fact, flags the latter placement as an error. The C++ compiler, on the other hand, will produce at most a warning message.

An option open to the Java programmer is the `finally` block. If such a block is included, it must follow all `catch` handlers. It has no parameter list; it is simply a block of statements, preceded by the keyword `finally`, which is executed after the `try` block and the applicable `catch` block (if any) are executed. If it is present, the `finally` block may not be skipped, even if one of the `catch` blocks throws another exception.

<table>
<tr><td>**NOTE**</td><td>*It should be noted that this exception handling facility is rich in run-time searching and type-checking actions, and as such it is decidedly less efficient than the normal mechanisms of these languages. This extra overhead is especially ugly to the knowledgeable C++ programmer, who often has chosen the language for its run-time efficiency. To the novice programmer unacquainted with the cost of these mechanisms it is a performance trap, because exceptions can be used for normal processing activities in creative ways, but this creativity will perhaps be far more costly than the programmer realizes.*</td></tr>
</table>

4.11   LIBRARY COMMONALITIES

The standard C++ and Java library container classes have much in common. Both are intended to be as general as possible within the limits of practicality, and the major classes of containers are present in both libraries. There are radical differences between the two, nevertheless. The most obvious of these differences is that only first-class objects are candidates for membership in a Java container, whereas C++ containers can house both primitive and first-class objects. However, Java containers are more heterogeneous, in a sense.

4.11.1 Heterogeneity and Genericity

Java containers instantiated from the older library container classes assume nothing more about their resident elements except that they are all of type `Object`. That requirement is not much of a restriction, because all first-class objects in Java are of types descended from the `Object` base class. To put it another way, if a Java class is not specifically assigned a base class in its definition, the Java compiler automatically assigns `Object` as its base class. So, for example, the `Vector` class is flexible enough to allow the following usage pattern, where `MyClass` is some programmer-defined class having a default constructor.

```
Vector v = new Vector();
v.add(new Integer(5));
v.add(new Double(7.89);
v.add(new MyClass());
```

<table>
<tr><td>**NOTE**</td><td>*In order to use the Vector class in the fashion indicated, the programmer must include the import java.util.Vector; statement at the beginning of the source file containing this code segment.*</td></tr>
</table>

Heterogeneity often comes at the price of run-time type checking and casting operations, however, because the more specific properties of an object are not available as methods of the `Object` class. For example, in order to do arithmetic with the items in the Java vector above we must cast to the appropriate numeric types, as in the following code:

```
// Store the sum of the first two elements of v in 'sum'.
Double sum = new Double(
      ((Integer)v.get(0)).intValue() + ((Double)v.get(1)).dou-
bleValue()
   );
```

Of course, even to code the above with confidence we must know beforehand that the first element of the vector is of type `Integer` and the second is of type `Double`.

This "heterogeneous vector" usage pattern is not present in C++ because it is not highly valued in the C and C++ culture. What's more, the C++ programmer argues, this heterogeneity arises from a convention, not from anything inherent in the design of the `Vector` class itself. In fact, all such vectors are simply vectors consisting of elements of type `Object`, a pattern easily duplicated in C++. What C++ lacks is simply the requirement that all first-class objects inherit from a common base class.

The corresponding `vector` class in the standard C++ library is a template, so that every instantiation of a `vector` object must be associated with a type of member, as in the following code:

```
vector<int> v;
v.push_back(34);
v.push_back(78);
v.push_back(-13);
```

NOTE *In order to use the template vector in the above fashion, the programmer must place the preprocessor statement #include <vector> at file scope and the C++ statement using std::vector; in any containing scope preceding this code segment.*

The binding of the container `v` to a specific primitive type in the above example makes heterogeneity impossible, but achieves a complementary aim which is more attractive to the programmer concerned with execution time efficiency. Namely, the container so constructed has the property that elements retrieved from it are associated at compile time with type `int`, so that no run-time checking or casting is required, neither as elements are placed into the container nor as they are retrieved and used.

Newer forms of the Java container classes also allow container objects to be defined in a type-specific way, as seen in the following code segment:

```
Vector<Integer> v = new Vector<Integer>;
v.add(new Integer(34));
v.add(new Integer(78));
v.add(new Integer(-13));
```

Relying on autoboxing to do the conversion to wrapper objects, we can actually code the above without the explicit calls on the `Integer` constructor (e.g., `v.add(34)` compiles and executes perfectly well). We will do this in the following code, but the reader should keep in mind that these constructors are being implicitly called anyway, so that the above code is more "honest."

NOTE

Again, we are losing heterogeneity here but gaining a more run-time-efficient usage pattern. Note, however, that we must use the "wrapper class" Integer, not int, because primitive types do not inherit from Object and the requirement that all Java library containers consist of first-class objects has not been removed with the introduction of the newer forms.

The newer Java container classes, which use a notation very much like C++ templates, are called *generic* container classes. There is a certain amount of irony in this terminology, because the term "generic" is usually understood to mean the opposite of "type-specific." What is actually true about the Java generic container classes, as opposed to the original container classes by the same names, is that the classes are indeed generic, in almost the same sense as the (roughly) corresponding C++ standard library class templates are generic. By this we mean that for each such Java generic container class a single source code definition permits the instantiation of many different types of container objects. This was not so concerning the original Java container classes, which could only instantiate one type of object each. However, for the older "non-generic" classes it is the *container objects themselves* which are "generic," as seen by our original Java *Vector* example, in the sense that such a container object can house anything that a container object instantiated from the corresponding generic class could house. The ironic fact, then, is that the new generic classes were created to permit the instantiation of *type-specific* container objects!

What is gained, therefore, by the use of the Java generic container classes, is not greater generality but rather a very C-like goal: greater run-time efficiency through the use of compile-time checks. The old `Vector` class, for example, is every bit as general in its application as the new generic class by the same name. However, its use must be accompanied by a systematic series of casts (with accompanying run-time type checks), in order to gain access to the public attributes and behaviors of the stored objects that go beyond the limited capabilities of the `Object` base class. Such checks are unnecessary with the most common uses of container objects instantiated with the new generic classes.

The techniques for construction of Java generic classes and C++ class templates will be discussed in the respective chapters on those two languages. For now, we will restrict our attention to the library container classes. In our Java examples, we will use the generic classes, bearing in mind that they do almost completely supersede the old classes. For example, `Vector` and `Vector<Object>` are alike in nearly every way. They are *not* compatible as types, however.

4.11.2 The Vector Classes—Direct Access and Adjustable Size

As implemented in both the Java and the C++ standard libraries, vectors share the following properties: (1) There are a number of constructors, including a default constructor which constructs an empty vector; (2) New elements can be added onto the end of a vector (`add()` or `addElement()` in Java, `push_back()` in C++, as seen in the previous section); (3) Direct access is provided to any element of the vector using a zero-based index, just as with arrays; and (4) the current size of the vector is available at any time using the `size()` method call (same method name in both languages). Other capabilities are provided, of course, but these are the most commonly used, and they are the operations which are optimized for this container.

A major difference between vectors as implemented in the two languages is the approach to direct access. Two facilities are provided in the C++ `vector` class template, the subscripting `operator []` and the `at()` method. Using the subscript operator provides unchecked access to elements, for situations in which performance is the major goal. Thus, `v[i]` supplies the element at position `i` in the vector `v`, if such an element exists, but what it supplies if `i` is out of range is undefined. The `at()` member function provides checked access, so that `v.at(i)` returns the same result as `v[i]` if the ith element exists but throws an exception of type `out_of_range` if `i` is not between 0 and `v.size() - 1`, inclusively. The `get()` method in the Java version of this container class (the generic class `Vector<>`) provides checked access, and makes exactly the same range check as C++'s `at()` method, throwing an `ArrayIndexOutOfBoundsException` object if the check fails. Java does not supply an unchecked version of this method.

C++ does not need a direct-access "write" operation for elements of vectors, because the expressions `v[i]` and `v.at(i)` evaluate as references (see the next chapter), so that the following code stores 10 at the first location and 20 at the second in vector `v`.

```
v[0] = 10;
v.at(1) = 20;
```

The Java write method is `set()`, so that the Java equivalent to the above is as follows:

```
v.set(0,10);
v.set(1,20);
```

Not all vectors need to grow dynamically, beginning in an empty state. In C++, if the vector's initial size is known or can be computed, the vector can be supplied with that size at construction time. For example, if the size is `n`, then a vector `wVec` of `n` objects of type `Widget`, let's say, can be constructed in C++ as follows:

```
vector<Widget> wVec(n);
```

The catch here is that if `Widget` is a class, then it must have a default constructor. Execution of the above statement produces a vector of `n` default-constructed `Widget` objects.

The Java constructor illustrated by the following code is *not* equivalent:

```
Vector<Widget> wVec = new Vector<Widget>(n);
```

This construction is misleading to the C++ programmer because it still constructs an empty vector. Here `n` is used as an initial *capacity*, which is only a physical size. The logical size is still zero, but `n` contiguous unused locations will be allocated for future use. The Java code sequence we need here is as follows:

```
Vector<Widget> wVec = new Vector<Widget>();
wVec.setSize(n);  // Change logical size from 0 to n.
```

The Java and C++ examples are still not equivalent, however. Again, remember the difference between value semantics and pointer semantics. Instead of creating a vector of n default-constructed items, the code above produces a vector of n null handles. To over-write these with handles for default-constructed widgets takes a traversal such as the following:

```
for (int i=0; i < wVec.size(); ++i) wVec.set(i, new Widget());
```

4.11.3 Iterators—Traversing a Container

Every container object exists to manage a set of values of some type, whether primitive values or structured values. These values are related to each other in logical ways defined by their own properties and in structural ways defined by the container itself. An *iterator* is an object that provides one-at-a-time access to the values in a container. By providing such access, the iterator defines an order on the elements of the container, an order which may be defined in different ways for different types of container, based on the relationships mentioned above. For example, suppose we have a vector v whose elements are of type int (C++) or Integer (Java). The code segments below each make a pass through the vector, displaying each value on a separate line of the console.

Java:

```
import java.util.Vector;
import java.util.Iterator;
...
    Iterator<Integer> i = v.iterator();
     while (i.hasNext())
        System.out.println(i.next());
```

C++:

```
#include <vector>
using std::vector;
...
    vector<int>::iterator i = v.begin();
     while (i != v.end())
        cout << *i++ << endl;
```

Here again we see a fundamental difference in approach between the two languages. In Java, the name Iterator is associated with an *interface*, not a class. An interface is something like an abstract class, in that it presents to the client programmer a collection of methods, each of which must be provided by any class which claims to "implement" the interface. By calling the `iterator()` method of the vector `v`, we are asking `v` to create an object of a type that implements the `Iterator` interface and to return a handle to that object as a result of the call. This iterator object has access to the internal representation of the vector, and successive calls on its `next()` method produce the elements of the vector in the order in which they are stored. The iterator has finished its traversal of the vector when `hasNext()` returns `false`.

In C++, each container class created from a library container template has its own internal iterator class. We can read the notation `vector<int>::iterator` as "the `iterator` class belonging to the `vector<int>` class." This iterator has similar properties to those described above for Java iterator objects. In this case, however, the highly operator-oriented C++ language gives this code a very different look from the Java version. The `begin()` and `end()` methods of `vector<int>` return iterators positioned, respectively, at the first element of the vector and at the end position in the vector (at which no element is stored). The iterator returned by `v.begin()` provides the initial value of the iterator which will do the traversal, and the `operator !=`, overloaded to apply to iterators, compares that value with `v.end()` on every iteration of the loop. The prefix `*` operator is also overloaded with a library-defined meaning, and returns the specific element at which the iterator is currently positioned. Finally, the overloaded postfix `++` operator performs in classic C++ fashion, first returning the current value of the iterator object and then advancing the iterator to the next item in turn. Precedence is given to the postfix operator, so that the iterator is incremented before the `*` operator is applied, but because of the odd behavior of the postfix `++` operator, `*i++` returns the item at the location `i` designated *before* the increment.

NOTE

The °i++ pattern is a classic C pattern which is roundly denounced in some quarters as cryptic, and just as staunchly defended in others as being compact, efficient, and not lacking in clarity for anyone but the novice programmer. This is reminiscent of the debate in the old COBOL language over whether or not to allow operators at all, because some found them to be cryptic.

It is instructive to note that the above C++ code can be reformulated as a `for` loop that looks very much like a pass through an array:

```
for (vector<int>::iterator i = v.begin(); i != v.end(); ++i)
    cout << *i << endl;
```

In both languages, we now have a way to traverse a vector without using the direct-access characteristics of that vector. This is important for run-time efficiency because, strictly speaking, direct-access requires the computation of an address from scratch, whereas advancing an iterator means simply adding a fixed amount to an already computed address. But keep in mind that a good optimizing compiler can sometimes analyze the parameters of a loop in which direct-access operations are used and avoid the address computation, even in situations where direct-access operations such as subscripting and the `at()` and `elementAt()` methods are being used. Loops that are as conventional as the above also may sometimes be translated in such a fashion that subscript range checks are eliminated, because the above patterns are guaranteed not to produce range errors.

When the container's values are structured objects, the iterator can be used in either language to access its components. However, the mechanisms are quite different. For example, if `i` is an iterator into a container of `Point` objects, the notation `i->x` accesses the x component in C++, whereas the notation in Java is the more obvious `i.next().x`. C++'s prejudice in favor of operators shows up here; however, the primitive-looking `->` operator is not actually a C++ built-in operator but a library-defined overload of the operator.

Iterators such as those described above, if obtained for the purpose of traversing a vector, will always produce the values in the expected order, starting with the element at position 0. (C++ provides a `reverse_iterator`, however, which traverses the vector from end to beginning.) Other container classes may produce an order that is not directly related to physical position, as we shall see.

4.11.4 The List Classes—Efficient Insertions and Deletions

Vector classes in both languages allow insertions in the middle of a vector, but such insertions are costly in terms of execution time because space for the elements of a vector is allocated contiguously, and in order to do an insertion anywhere other than at the end it is necessary to move some (perhaps many) of the other elements from where they currently reside to higher memory locations. In the same way, elements can be removed from the collection, but in the vector storage scheme deletion from early positions in a large collection may cause a lot of data movement. So for some situations, in which a collection of data will require many insertions and deletions at random locations, the programmer may feel it more appropriate to use a list, rather than a vector. Some variant of linked list is typically used for the implementation of such a class, so that insertions and deletions may occur anywhere with no (or very few) elements being moved from their current locations.

The Java linked list class is named `LinkedList`, and resides in package `java.util`. It implements the `List` interface, which contains all the operations in which we are primarily interested in this section. The corresponding C++ standard library container is `list`.

We will start our discussion of list operations by discussing those which we have already seen in the context of vectors. For example, appending an item to the end of a list is done in the same way as for vectors, so that each of the following code sequences produces a list whose first element is 34.78 and whose second element is 89.04:

Java:

```
import java.util.LinkedList;
...
    LinkedList<Double> myList = new LinkedList<Double>();
    myList.add(34.78);  // Note autoboxing.
    myList.add(89.04);  //  "           "
```

C++:

```
#include <list>
using std::list;
...
    list<double> myList;
    myList.push_back(34.78);
    myList.push_back(89.04);
```

Direct access is not provided in the C++ version of this container, presumably because to do so would be misleading to the programmer, who demands that library operations in that language be efficient. Efficient direct access is not possible in a linked list, because in general to find the `i`th location requires a loop which starts at the beginning of the list and performs a partial traversal, incrementing a count with each iteration of the loop. In spite of this inefficiency, however, Java does provide direct access using the `get()` and `set()` operations. For example, the following Java code swaps the `i`th and `i+1`-st elements of the list `myList`.

```
// The following swap can be TERRIBLY inefficient!
Double temp = myList.get(i);
myList.set(i,myList.get(i+1));
myList.set(i+1,temp);
```

Java and C++ lists are also quite dissimilar in the way in which they insert elements into the middle of a list. Java provides an overloaded version of the `add()` method, with two operands. For example, to insert `-29.86` as the 2nd element (element 1) of the above list we would execute the command below.

```
myList.add(1,-29.86); // Inserts -29.86 between the first two
       // elements of myList, increasing the size of myList by 1.
```

Again because of the inherent inefficiency of referring to list locations by an index number, C++ does not allow this type of insertion but insists that insertion operations designate the insertion point using an iterator. Thus, if `j` is an iterator positioned somewhere in the list `myList`, the following code very efficiently inserts the value `-29.86` at that position, moving everything at or after that position forward in the sequence by one.

```
myList.insert(j,-29.86);
```

The reason this operation is more efficient is because however `j`'s value is stored, it contains information (either an address or an offset) from which the precise location of a particular list element can be obtained. No loop is necessary because *j* has access to private information encapsulated within `myList` which communicates to that list object exactly where the insertion is to occur. (Of course, a loop may very well have been used in order to position `j` to its current location in the list.)

Other insert operations involving iterators are allowed in C++. For example, we can use the following code to insert all elements in the sequence determined by iterators `iter1` and `iter2` at the position indicated by iterator *j*.

```
myList.insert(j,iter1,iter2);
```

Here `iter1` and `iter2` must be iterators associated with the same container, `iter2` must be positioned at or beyond `iter1`, and the type of element in the container must be `double`. The sequence includes all elements beginning at the position designated by `iter1` up to but not including that designated by `iter2`.

The Java `LinkedList` class provides a `listIterator()` method that returns an object implementing the `ListIterator` interface, which allows the efficient insertion of items into a list. Such insertions are messages not to the list but to the iterator. Thus, in Java we could use the sequence

```
ListIterator<Double> j = myList.listIterator();
```

```
... // Position j to the desired location.
j.add(-29.86);
```

Removal of an element can be accomplished in Java using either a message to the list object or to an iterator positioned inside the object. For example, the following code removes the third element of `myList`.

```
myList.remove(2); // Remove list element at index position 2.
```

As with `get()` and `set()`, the `remove()` method throws an `IndexOutOf-BoundsException` if the index position does not exist in the list.

Alternatively, the same objective is accomplished with the following:

```
Iterator<Double> i = myList.iterator();
i.next();
i.next();
i.next();
i.remove();
```

Note that `next()` is called three times, because `i.remove()` removes the *previous* element, not the current element, designated by `i`. Sending the `remove()` message to a newly instantiated iterator before executing the `next()` operation is an error and causes an `IllegalStateException`.

NOTE

The remove() method of a C++ list may look deceptively similar to the method by that name in Java's List, but it does not behave in the same manner. Instead of removing elements at a particular location in the list, it removes all elements having the same value as the operand.

Removal of an arbitrary element or sequence of elements *by location* in a C++ list is accomplished using iterators and the `erase()` member function of the *list* class template. For example, if `j` is an iterator positioned somewhere in `myList`, the statement

```
myList.erase(j);
```

removes the item referred to by `j` from the list. If `iter1` and `iter2` are iterators positioned within `myList`, then

```
myList.erase(iter1, iter2);
```

will remove all elements between `iter1` and `iter2`, including `*iter1` but not including `*iter2` (hence `*iter2` need not exist at all, and will not if `iter2` is equal to `myList.end()`).

Operations which search for a particular value within a list are available in both languages as well. Java provides that functionality via the `indexOf()` member function of the `List` interface, whereas in C++ the programmer must include the `<algorithm>` header file (`#include <algorithm>`) and use the file-scope function template `find()` (using `std::find`). The `find()` function operates on ranges defined by iterators, and is unaware of the structure of the underlying container. Naturally, Java returns an integer index and C++ returns an iterator, as in the following code sequences.

Java:

```
int i = myList.indexOf(89);
```

C++:

```
list<int>::iterator j =
    find(myList.begin(), myList.end(), 89);
```

If the Java search fails, the `indexOf()` method will return -1. If the C++ search fails, then the `find` function returns `myList.end()`. Both the Java search and the C++ search seek a particular *value*, not a handle. The Java search uses the `equals()` member function of the element class (`Integer` in this case), so that it finds the first element `e` of the list for which `e.equals(89)` is true. C++ uses value semantics by default, and hence no operators are needed other than the primitive comparison operators of type `int`. If, on the other hand, a programmer-defined type is used as the element type of a list, overloads will need to be defined for some of those comparison operators.

4.11.5 Sets and Maps—Efficiently Searchable Trees

Searching a list is inherently inefficient, because such a search must of necessity be sequential. Both the Java and C++ libraries possess generic container classes which are implemented using some variety of "balanced" binary search tree which offers comparatively efficient access to elements based on the value of a key. If the only values stored in the tree are keys, we call the container a *set*. If each key is paired with a value providing accompanying information, the container is called a *map*. The classes concerned are `TreeSet` and `TreeMap` in Java, and simply `set` and `map` in C++. We will start with the set types.

Each of the following code excerpts creates a set *s* of integers and inserts into it all the values stored in the array *values*.

C++:

```
#include <set>
using std::set;
...
    int values[] = {57, 39, 23, 17, 88, 97, 48, 63, 29};
    set<int> s;
    for (int i=0; i<sizeof(values)/sizeof(int); ++i)
        s.insert(values[i]);
```

Java:

```
import java.util.TreeSet;
...
    int values[] = {57, 39, 23, 17, 88, 97, 48, 63, 29};
    TreeSet<Integer> s = new TreeSet<Integer>();
    for (int i=0; i<values.length; ++i)
        s.add(values[i]);
```

Note the high degree of similarity between these code segments. In spite of this similarity, there are some significant semantic differences, which we enumerate here even though some of the points we make are made for the sake of review. First, although the code for creating the array values is identical, the C++ array is a value stored on the stack, whereas Java stores only a pointer on the stack while storing the actual array on the heap. When the pointer goes out of scope it will be popped off the stack and the array will be a candidate for garbage collection. Similar things are true of the Java and C++ versions of the set s, but there are more syntactic hints to that effect in that case.

NOTE

Note also that the number of elements in the array is computed in both cases, but with C++ the low-level sizeof operator is used, an operator which must be statically evaluated and returns the size in bytes of the array. To obtain the element count we must divide by sizeof(int). No equivalent exists in C++ to the length attribute we are using to determine the logical size of the Java version of the values array.

In terms of the actual insertion operation, there will be very little difference in its conduct. The `insert()` member function of the C++ `set` class and the `add()` member function of Java's `TreeSet` class should behave in very similar fashion, as binary search tree insertion operations. Tree balancing algorithms which sometimes come into play during such insertions may differ between particular implementations of C++ and Java, but they also may differ between different implementations of the library when the language is the same.

An iterator making a pass through this set of values will encounter them in numerical order, not in the order in which they were inserted. Thus, the Java code sequence

```
Iterator<Integer> i = s.iterator();
while (i.hasNext()) System.out.println(i.next());
```

and the C++ code sequence

```
set<int>::iterator i = s.begin();
while (i != s.end()) cout << *i++ << endl;
```

will both produce the output

```
17
23
29
39
48
57
63
88
97
```

Test for membership is conducted by the member function `contains()` of the Java `TreeSet` and by the member function `find()` in C++'s `set`. The value returned is different, however. The call `s.contains()` returns a `boolean` result, whereas `s.find()` returns an iterator positioned at the found element or `s.end()` if the element is not found. The following code executes function `f()` if the value `28` is found in the set `s` and function `g()` if that value is not in the set.

Java:

```
if (s.contains(28)) f(); else g();
```

C++:

```
if (s.find(28)!=s.end()) f(); else g();
```

Because a search involves a series of comparisons which test for order relationships, both languages provide ways for the programmer to define or redefine those relationships to induce new orderings on the data. In Java, the programmer can create a class which implements the `Comparator` interface and can then pass an object of that type as an argument to the `TreeSet` constructor. The only methods needed by such a class are the `compare()` method and the `equals()` method. (Usually the `equals()` method is not redefined for comparators, because it already exists in the base class `Object`.) A new ordering relationship is defined using the `compare()` method as follows. For two objects `obj1` and `obj2`, of type `Object`, the comparator object `c` is sent the message `c.compare(obj1,obj2)`, and returns an `int`. The integer returned should be either `-1`, `0`, or `1`, indicating whether this comparator wishes `obj1` to precede, to be equal to, or to follow `obj2` in the new order. Thus, a comparator class that sorts `Integer` objects in descending order can be defined as follows:

```
public class DescendingIntegerComparator
        implements Comparator {
    public int compare(Object o1, Object o2) {
        int i1 = (Integer)o1,
            i2 = (Integer)o2;
        if (i1 > i2) return -1;
        else if (i1 == i2) return 0;
        else return 1;
    }
}
```

Now if we build our `TreeSet` as follows, it will keep the set organized from largest to smallest value and our output loop above will display them in that order.

```
TreeSet<Integer> s = new TreeSet<Integer>(
    new DescendingIntegerComparator()
);
```

NOTE

In C++, the programmer can achieve this effect by redefining operator < for the type of objects stored in the container, an impossible feat for primitive type int, because the integer comparison operators are primitive and cannot be over-ridden. For programmer-defined element types, of course, it is a simple matter to define a < operator. There are other ways in C++ to accomplish this "reordering," but they involve using template parameters in a way we are not at present prepared to discuss.

It should be remarked here that much of the functionality of the Java generic class `TreeSet` comes from the fact that it implements the `Set` interface. In particular, the methods `add()`, `contains()`, and `iterator()` are part of that interface.

In all cases (in both languages and in all approaches to redefining order), the ordering imposed by the programmer must be *total*, meaning that not only must it be a partial ordering (reflexive, antisymmetric, and transitive) but any two values of the given type must be comparable. For example, the subset ordering on sets is *not* total. If we look at the two sets {1, 2} and {2, 3} we see that they are not comparable relative to that ordering (neither is a subset of the other). Thus, if we want a "set of sets" we must use some other idea of order in order to make the pattern fit.

Maps are very similar in their characteristics to sets. A map is also stored as a binary search tree, but the nodes of the tree store both keys and values. In C++, a tree node is always an item of a type produced from the class template `pair`. For example, if we precede it at file scope with `#include <map>` and `using std::map;` the statement

```
map<int,double> m;
```

creates a map `m` that stores objects of the type `pair<int,double>`. Each element `e` stored in the map `m` has a key component `e.first` of type `int` and a value component `e.second` of type `double`.

In the same way, after placing `import java.util.TreeMap;` at the beginning of the source file, we can code the following to produce a `TreeMap` having properties similar to the above C++ map.

```
TreeMap<Integer,Double> m = new TreeMap<Integer,Double>();
```

Each (key, value) pair inserted in this map will be of a type which conforms to the interface `Map.Entry<Integer,Double>`.

Inserting (key, value) pairs in the C++ map `m` is accomplished using the subscript operator, as follows:

```
m[297] = 3.17798;
m[-78] = 0.04527;
```

Similar work is accomplished in Java by sending the following `put()` messages:

```
m.put(297,3.17798);
m.put(-78,0.04527);
```

Fetching the value corresponding to a given key is now pretty obvious. The subscript operation by itself clearly suffices in C++, so that after the above assignments the value of m[297] is 3.17798.

NOTE   *The C++ programmer seeing this notation for the first time must overcome the impression that m is a large array. In fact, if it is developed in the way described here, it is a binary search tree storing only two (key, value) pairs.*

Just as obviously, in the Java version m.get(297) fetches a Double object whose encapsulated double value is 3.17798.

The following code iterates through the C++ map and displays the pairs one to a line:

```
map<int,double>::iterator i = m.begin();
while (i != m.end()) {
    pair<int,double> p = *i++;
    cout << "Key:  " << p.first
        << ", Value:  " << p.second << endl;
}
```

In Java, no iterator exists for the class. In order to produce the above output we can first extract the set of (key, value) pairs, and then obtain an iterator for that set, as follows. (We must import interfaces Java.util.Map and Java.util.Iterator.)

```
Iterator<Map.Entry<Integer,Double>> i = m.entrySet().iterator();
while (i.hasNext()) {
    Map.Entry<Integer,Double> pair = i.next();
    System.out.println(
        "Key:  " + pair.getKey() + ", Value:  " + pair.getValue()
    );
}
```

Alternatively, to produce the above output in Java we can (a) extract the set of keys, (b) extract the collection of values, and (c) iterate through the two in parallel. Here is the Java code which implements that strategy:

```
Set<Integer> k = m.keySet();
Collection<Double> v = m.values();
Iterator<Integer> i = k.iterator();
Iterator<Double> j = v.iterator();
while (i.hasNext())
    System.out.println(
        "Key:   " + i.next() + ", Value:   " + j.next()
    );
}
```

In the above code sequence, `Collection`, like `Set`, is an interface. The `TreeMap` object `m` manufactures an object which implements the `Set` interface (probably a `TreeSet` object) and returns that object in response to the call on its `keySet()` method. Similarly, in response to the call on `m`'s `values()` method an object is created and returned which implements the `Collection` interface.

4.12   SUMMARY

C++ code and Java code look very much alike at first glance, and many of their capabilities are genuinely identical. However, underlying the two languages are radically different semantic models. The use of value semantics permeates C++'s design, whereas Java's use of value semantics is severely restricted. This one difference has enormous repercussions almost everywhere one looks. A related issue is C++'s reliance on operator overloading, which is not just permitted but required in order to take advantage of some of the capabilities of the library classes. Java, on the other hand, not only does not allow programmer-defined operator overloading but usually does not provide any operators with its nonprimitive types, the one exception being the use of the + operator to denote concatenation of strings.

C++ is a multi-paradigm language, permitting several styles of programming, most notably procedural and object-oriented. On the other hand, Java was designed to be an almost purely object-oriented language from the beginning, the major exception being the inclusion of primitive values which are not first-class objects.

Giving the programmer explicit control of memory management gives C++ a deserved reputation as a "dangerous" language. On the other hand, Java's reliance on garbage collection, a necessity because of its dependence on pointer semantics, makes it impossible to know exactly when an object will be reclaimed.

Both languages rely heavily on separate compilation, but the two take extremely different views of that mechanism. On the one hand, the division of source code into separate files is a design decision by the C++ programmer that can be made in many ways, and that decision is only very loosely constrained by the structure of the program. On the other hand, the Java programmer is faced with the fact that the mapping of a class or package to certain files and directories is language-defined.

The older C++ compilation model produces native machine code which, when linked by an operating-system-specific linker, produces files which are recognized by the operating system as executable files. On the other hand, Java compiled object files are standardized across machines and independent of any specific machine. These object files are meant to be read and understood only by (1) the Java compiler, which imports needed classes and their attributes from object files produced in previous compilations, and (2) the Java Virtual Machine, which reads and executes the object files directly. There is only one phase to the compilation of a Java source file, whereas C++ incorporates three separate translation phases: preprocess, compile, and link.

Variables are fully declared as to type in both languages, and both languages use similar static scope rules. The major difference is the use of file scope in C++ and the use of the linker to complete references to any of a number of entities which have run-time representations. Entities that are candidates for "global" scope in C++ include types, procedures, and ordinary variables declared at file scope. In Java, the only globally accessible names are names of packages and types.

Having type associations for all names used in a computation makes it unnecessary in many cases to employ run-time type checking, the major exception being in circumstances when a name is "down-casted" to a derived class type. Run-time type transfers, both explicit and implicit, are abundantly used in both languages for the sake of matching argument type to parameter type. Casting is always statically checked in Java, and may also require a run-time check, whereas C++ retains some casting operations which are completely unchecked.

The two languages employ almost identical sequence control mechanisms, relying on the same basic set of operators for numeric and Boolean quantities, with a few exceptions, and inheriting their statement-level mechanisms from the C language. Very similar operator precedence and associativity rules are used at the expression level. Java modifies the C sequence control semantics subtly, removing automatic coercions between numeric and Boolean types, restricting tests to Boolean expressions, and omitting labeled statements and "goto"s. Both languages employ the `break` and `continue` "limited goto" forms.

Rules governing the formation of classes and single inheritance are similar, with most syntactic differences being minor. An interesting syntactic construct in C++ not seen in Java is the "initialization part," which is inserted between the parameter list and body of the constructor and which uses a sequence of elements very similar in form but with a variety of different meanings. Likewise, Java puts a different twist on initialization of a class by allowing inline initializations for class and instance variables which are invoked before any constructor.

Run-time polymorphism is a property automatically bestowed by Java on any method of a class which is overridden in a derived class. Polymorphic behavior in C++ does not occur by default but must be requested by declaring the method virtual in the base class. Virtual function calls involve run-time overhead taken for granted in Java but uncharacteristic in C++, which usually resolves method references statically or at link time.

Exception handling is very similar in the two languages and involves encapsulating code segments which may possibly throw exceptions in a `try` block, which is followed by one or more handlers represented as `catch` blocks. Value semantics make C++'s mechanisms more complex here. Rules for matching thrown objects or handles to corresponding catch parameter types are also more complex in C++, for the same reason. Both languages use stack unwinding and a sort of backwards procedure call mechanism, involving heavy use of run-time decision making by the language implementation.

The Java and C++ standard library container classes have many commonalities and many differences. Both implement vectors, lists, sets, and maps, and each has a number of variants of these essential data structuring patterns. True to form, Java stores only handles to first-class objects in its containers, while C++ stores values. Both languages have container-specific iterator classes, but they differ in their approaches to iterators.

REVIEW QUESTIONS

1. As C-based languages, there are some similarities between Java and C++. What are some of those similarities?

2. Describe the difference in philosophy between the design of C++ and that of Java. Which is most closely allied with C? Explain.

3. Describe two infamous syntactic discontinuities in the C language, and describe Java's approach to eliminating those discontinuities.

4. Describe the actions taken by the Smalltalk interpreter in evaluating the expression x+y, and the actions taken by a compiled language with strong typing in translating and executing the same expression.

5. Although both languages execute on software-simulated machines, Java has a radically different run-time model from that of Smalltalk. What drives that difference? How is it manifested in terms of performance?

6. Explain the difference between the compilation of a C++ program and the compilation of a Java program.

7. Explain the advantages and disadvantages of early bindings and late bindings, in general. Give examples.

8. Explain the Java compilation and execution model, and describe specifically how source files relate to class files. How are class files used at compile time? At execution time? Is a class file more like an executable file or a source file, or does it have elements of both? Explain.

9. What names can have global bindings in Java? How are those bindings resolved by the compiler?

10. Explain the concept of a Java package. In what ways is it different from a C++ namespace?

11. How are class members distinguished from instance members in Java? Is that different from the way they are distinguished in C++? Explain.

12. (a) Discuss primitive types in Java. How are they defined? Does the way in which a Java value of a particular primitive type is stored on one machine differ from the way it is stored on another machine? Why or why not? (b) Answer the same question for C++.

13. Some say that the situation with Java is not so much that it is platform-independent but that it *is* a platform. What is meant by that statement? Why would we not say the same for C++?

14. Which assignment operations in Java are explained using pointer semantics, and which are explained using value semantics?

15. Recall the definition of the term *coercion*. Describe some coercions that are routinely done in Java, and describe some that are done in C but not in Java.

16. (a) Describe the Java numeric wrapper classes. What is their purpose, and why are they necessary? Give two examples. (b) Why are such classes not used in C++?

17. Define the term "autoboxing," describe its purpose, and give an example of its use. What mechanism from C++ does it resemble?

18. (a) Give a detailed description of the actions which take place "behind the scenes" in evaluating the operand of the call `System.out.println("x = " + x);` (b) How would you code the same console output operation in C++, and what mechanisms underly it?

19. (a) Are C++ arrays statically bound to a declared size? Why or why not? (b) Answer the same question for Java. (c) Comment on the statement, "The length attribute of a Java array is immutable" relative to your answer in (b).

20. What do we mean when we say that Java arrays are first-class objects? Can the same be said for C++ arrays? Why or why not?

21. What is the fundamental difference between the way Java translates the subscripted variable reference `a[i]` and the way C++ translates a similar reference involving a primitive array `a`?

22. (a) What do we mean when we say that two-dimensional Java arrays can be allocated as "ragged arrays"? Give a simple example. (b) Is there an obvious analog to this idea in C++? Why or why not?

23. In both Java and C++, what is the type of the expression `a>b?1:0.1`? Does this seem a reasonable resolution of the issue of mixed types within a `?:` operation? Why or why not?

24. Why do first-class Java temporaries generated by constructor calls need the *new* operation, whereas in C++ they would not? Explain.

25. The Java `for` statement has a similar appearance to that of a C++ `for` statement, but their rules of formation are quite different. What gives rise to this difference, and what are its implications? Give an example of a C++ `for` statement which would be illegal in Java.

26. Describe Java inline initializations, both class and instance initializations. How do they relate to constructors?

27. Compare Java inline initializations to the initialization of a Simula 67 class.

28. Given that `MyClass` is a programmer-defined class with a constructor requiring an integer parameter, the following C++ code instantiates an object `m` of that class.

```
MyClass m(25);
```

29. Give a line of Java code that performs the same instantiation, and describe the difference in implementation between the two languages.

30. A Java constructor has no "initialization part" for handling the call of base class constructors and the initialization of instance data. How are these necessary duties managed in Java?

31. How does an abstract class in Java differ in form from an abstract class in C++? How do we derive a concrete class from an abstract class?

32. Is the Java model for polymorphism closer to that of Smalltalk or that of C++? Explain.

33. Describe with an example the syntax for declaring and initializing a class constant in Java. Do the same for declaring and initializing an instance constant. Do the same for a block-scope constant.

34. How do Java enumerated types differ from C++ enumerated types? Describe all the differences you can discover.

35. Describe the restrictions on Java exception handling, and how exception handling in Java differs from exception handling in C++.

36. Describe the difference between the way exception specifications are handled in C++ and in Java. When must a Java function include an exception specification?

37. Describe how a *finally* block is used in Java. Is there a corresponding feature in C++? If so, what is it? If not, comment on why you think the omission is important or unimportant.

38. Explain what we mean when we say that the old-style Java container classes were *heterogeneous*. Illustrate with code examples.

39. What is the "down-side" to Java heterogeneity in terms of run-time costs?

40. In what sense are the Java "generic" containers truly generic, and in what sense are they not so? What is the main advantage of the generic container classes? Is that advantage different from the advantage gained by C++ container templates?

41. How are the types `Vector`, `Vector<Object>`, and `Vector<Integer>` related to each other in terms of compatibility in assignments, tests for equality, and parameter passing? What reasoning underlies the rules regarding such relationships?

42. Both C++ and Java offer vector classes that provide direct access to their elements using a zero-based index. How do the two languages differ in the way they provide that functionality?

43. (a) How does a C++ vector differ from a C++ array? (b) Answer the same question for Java vectors and arrays. (c) In what language is the difference most dramatic, and why?

44. Discuss in detail the difference between Java's iterators for its container classes and those provided by C++.

45. (a) Describe some of the operations available with Java's `LinkedList` class. (b) Answer the same question for the C++ `list<>` template.

46. Direct-access operations based on ordinal position (0-th element, 1-st element, etc.) are included in Java's `LinkedList<>` but not in the C++ `list<>` class. Why does C++ not provide these, and how is that consistent with the C++ philosophy?

47. Describe the form and meaning of the `compare()` method in interface `Comparator`. For what purpose are comparators used?

EXERCISES

1. Write a complete definition for a java console-output "Hello, world!" program, and then write the corresponding program in C++. Comment on each difference between the two programs.

2. Java has two styles of inline initialization blocks. Describe each and comment on how similar initializations could be undertaken in C++, a language which does not incorporate inline initialization in the same way. Give code examples.

3. (a) Write a small segment of C++ code intended to perform some straightforward task (such as a simple pass through an array), with the objective of making the code as readable and maintainable as possible. Then (b) rewrite that code using whatever "tricks" the language makes available to you, with the objective of making the code as succinct (but not necessarily understandable) as possible.

4. Do problem 3 using Java. Is it more difficult or less difficult to achieve the second stated objective in Java, as opposed to C++? Say why you answered as you did.

5. Given that `MyClass` is a class with a default constructor and n is a variable of type `int` containing a positive integer, provide Java code to instantiate a vector containing n default-constructed `MyClass` objects. Do the same

for C++, and comment on the reason for the difference in appearance between the two code segments.

6. Rewrite the Java `QuadraticPolynomial` class from this chapter in C++. What are the most significant differences between the Java and C++ versions?

7. (a) What are the limitations for invoking base class behaviors for an overridden method in Java? In other words, if an object `obj` has behavior `f()`, and its base class has that same behavior, under what circumstances can the base class behavior be invoked, and what is the syntax for doing so? (b) Answer the same question for C++.

8. Give a Java line of code equivalent (as much as possible) to the C++ declaration

   ```
   set<int> s;
   ```

   Explain the difference between the run-time actions occurring in each case.

9. (a) Given that `s` is a Java container of type `TreeSet<Integer>`, provide some lines of code that traverse the container and display all its elements, one to a line. (b) Do the same for a C++ container of type `set<int>`. (c) In what order will the values be displayed, in both cases?

10. (a) Again, suppose `s` is a container of type `TreeSet<Integer>`. Write a line of code that assigns the value `true` to Boolean variable `foundIt` if the value `837` is in `s` and assigns the value `false` to `foundIt` otherwise. (b) Answer the same question for a container of type `set<int>`.

11. Java's `indexOf` method and C++'s `find` function, used with their respective linked list containers, have differences in interface and in efficiency. Write in each language a segment of code that uses these facilities to find and remove the first occurrence of the value 3479 from a list of integers, and comment on the relative efficiency and readability of the two code segments.

12. Write a complete program in Java with a main class which reads an integer n from the keyboard, then reads n different integer values into a `Tree-Set` object. It then passes that object to a static procedure named `median` which returns the median value of the set. Now comment on what would change about your program if you could instead use a `TreeSet<Integer>` object to store the values.

13. What part of question 12 would be irrelevant if it were asked about the C++ language and the `set<>` template? Why? Write in C++ the program you wrote for question 12.

14. (a) Write Java code to build a `TreeMap<String,String>` object called `manAndWife` and place in it three pairs using first names of married couples you know. (b) Do the same for a C++ container of type `map<int,int>`.

15. Referring to the collection `manAndWife` mentioned above, write Java code which uses an iterator and pairs of type `Map.Entry<String,String>` to fetch from that collection all the pairs where the first letter of the man's name begins with 'P' and write them in alphabetical order (based on the man's name) to `System.out`.

16. Write a similar piece of code to the above, but this time use the `values()` and `keyset()` methods of class `TreeMap<String,String>` and iterate through the two container objects extracted by those methods using two iterators advancing synchronously.

17. Compare the Java and C++ strategies with respect to how the programmer is enabled to go against the "natural order" when objects are stored in ordered containers. As an example, write code illustrating how the `manAndWife` container object from the preceding problems can be altered so that the items are stored in *descending* order of the man's first name. Write that code for (a) Java and (b) C++.

CHAPTER 5

ADDITIONAL CONCEPTS FROM THE C++ LANGUAGE

In this chapter, we discuss capabilities of C++ that are radically different from those of Java and hence are not mentioned in the previous chapter. As we further develop our knowledge of this very large and complex language, the amazing harmony that is displayed by its huge set of interacting features and mechanisms will become apparent, and we will begin to see that, although there are some seemingly arbitrary restrictions imposed here and there, the programmer is able to operate in a vast and unrestrained environment, and that the overall effect turns out to be quite consistent and intelligible. Throughout the language there is a predominant motivation to enable the programmer and to assume he can handle whatever dangers and complexities the language design presents.

As we begin to explore the issues that separate C++ and Java, the issue of orthogonality of design is important. A language's design is *orthogonal* if its features have been independently designed and do not conflict, and if there are no restrictions on what features can be used in combination with each other. Although only the simplest of programming languages could be said to be completely orthogonal, C++ does score rather high on this scale because its features are not encapsulated in such a way that they can only be used in selected circumstances. Each feature distributes over all the others in all reasonable ways. Since there will from time to time be "unreasonable" combinations, specific rules sometimes must be applied to clarify meanings and avoid contradictions and ambiguities. Many of the most difficult issues arise from one design decision: the decision to allow addresses as data.

ON THE DVD

Code samples for this chapter are located on the companion CD-ROM.

5.1   L-VALUES, POINTERS, AND REFERENCES

Being a systems programming language, it was important that C incorporate some machine-level concepts. One of the most important of those concepts was the idea of a machine address, because the operations of fetching and storing data from and into specific locations in memory constitute a large part of any low-level routine. A vague idea of machine addresses is in some sense a part of any programmer's mental model of what should be going on when a program executes, but the language of C and C++ documentation sharpens the concept. C terminology, passed down to C++, links addresses to variables explicitly and invents a term for the address attribute, calling the address of a variable its l-value. This concept is the jumping-off place for giving addresses a much more visible role and status in this language than in any of the other object-oriented languages.

5.1.1   L-Values and R-Values

The terms *l-value* and *r-value* were originally used to differentiate the attributes needed of variables on the left-hand side of an assignment statement versus those needed on the right-hand side. One considers that on the right-hand side of an assignment there is a computation taking place, and the important contribution of a variable in that computation is the value stored at its address, not its address per se. On the left-hand side, it is the *address* of the variable that is the input to the assignment operation, because the purpose of that variable in that setting is to provide a place to put the computed value.

When the term "l-value" was introduced, it naturally divided all expressions in a program into two categories—those which had l-values and those which did not. Single variables and subscripted variables have l-values, of course, because they can legitimately appear on the left-hand side of an assignment. Literals are not given an l-value, nor are sub-expressions yielding only a temporary computed value, because the ultimate repository for the result of the computation may be a machine register with no memory address. But since named, stored constants actually have addresses, we say that these names when used in an expression have l-values even though they may not legitimately appear on the left-hand side of an assignment statement.

The above discussion seems odd to those not versed in C terminology, because even though these invented terms could be applied in most languages there is no need to do so there, because addresses in those languages do not figure heavily into the programmer's mental model. But C needed these terms in order to clarify some central questions which naturally arose when they elevated addresses to data type status.

5.1.2 Pointers

C incorporated the idea of *pointer* data types and variables, and C++ has retained them in their original form. Depending on the implementation and on the target machine, a pointer variable either directly stores a machine address or it stores information by which a machine address can be quickly computed at run-time. The actual content of the variable is usually not important to the programmer— the important thing is that it provides a link to some area of memory, usually the home of some data object of a specific type, because pointer variables are tied in their declarations to a base type. The following C++ declaration instantiates a data object p whose values are pointers to primitive data objects of type `double`.

```
double *p; // p is of type "pointer to double"
```

Depending on where the above declaration appears, it may or may not be initialized. If it is global or a static local variable, then its value will be initialized to a "null pointer," which in all probability means that a zero will be stored there. If it is local, then it will probably not be initialized, and so it will contain a random value which, if used, could cause the program to behave unpredictably. For this reason the programmer is well advised to include an initializer, as shown for the variable `q` in the example below.

Although the type of `p` above is called `double *`, it is not permissible to factor out the asterisk with the type name; rather, each pointer variable must be supplied with its own asterisk. The following declares pointers `p` and `q` and an ordinary `double` variable `x`:

```
double *p, *q = 0, x; // *p, *q, and x are doubles.
```

Here the pointer `q` is initialized to the null pointer, whether the machine in question actually uses a bit pattern of all zeros to represent a null pointer or not.

Along with the pointer data type come two important prefix operators, `&` (ampersand) and `*` (asterisk), which can be read "address of" and "the object stored at," respectively. The asterisk operator is sometimes called a "dereferencing" operator, because it replaces a pointer by the object to which it is pointing.

The primitive ampersand and asterisk operators are nearly "inverses" of each other, but not quite. Consider the declaration above for `p`, `q`, and `x`. After the assignment

```
p = &x;
```

the expression `*p` is now in every way an alias of `x`, meaning that it has an l-value and an r-value and both attributes are the same as those of `x` itself. In fact, we can make the categorical statement about the primitive operators `*` and `&` that *any* valid expression that begins with `*` has an l-value, and there is *never* any reason to start an expression with the sequence `*&`, because when applied in that direction, the two operators "cancel." (All bets are off when the programmer redefines these operators, of course!)

Now consider the expression `&x` by itself. It has an r-value, and in fact, its r-value is the l-value of `x`. Does it have an l-value? Of course not, no more than the expression `-x`. In fact, `x`'s address as computed by the expression `&x` need not be stored in a program variable, nor even necessarily in a memory location—the "temporary" where the computed value `&x` resides could just as well be a CPU register. In fact, we can now make another categorical statement concerning the prefix `&` operator, and that is that *no* expression beginning with that operator has an l-value, unless the programmer has redefined the operator and given it another meaning. For this reason, the expression `&*p` is not quite the same as `p`. It has the same r-value as `p`, but it has no l-value.

If `p` is a pointer to an object which has structure, such as a struct or a class, then we can obtain access to the various named components of that structure using the pointer selection operator, which is a hyphen followed by a greater-than symbol. Thus, if `p` is a pointer to a class having public data member `x`, then `p->x` refers to the `x` component of the object to which `p` is pointing. In the same way, if `f` is a parameterless member function of the class, then the notation `p->f()` invokes the behavior associated with the method `f`. This is clearly preferable to the alternative awkward-looking notation `(*p).f()`.

5.1.3 References

A *reference* is nothing more than a pointer that is automatically dereferenced. We have seen them before in disguise, because every name of a first-class object in Java is exactly that: a reference. Although such names in Java do in fact denote pointers to objects stored on the heap, there is no explicit dereferencing operation like the C++ prefix `*` in Java. In any context, the compiler decides for itself whether or not the pointer needs dereferencing and acts accordingly.

Reference parameters have their own rules, discussed in Section 5.4.1, but the programmer may declare any variable to be a reference. Unlike the declaration of a pointer variable, where an initializer is optional, a declaration for a reference variable *must* guarantee that the reference is initialized before it is used, and once initialized a reference's r-value (that is, the address with which it is associated) may never change. A reference declaration uses the ampersand as a modification to the type, in the same way that a pointer declaration uses the asterisk. The expression used as an initializer must have an l-value, and must have a type that matches the type of the reference. The r-value of the reference is initialized to be the l-value of the initializer. Thus, the declaration

```
double &y = x;
```

essentially declares `y` to be an alias for `x`. Instance variables, i.e., data members of a class or struct, that are references must be initialized in the initialization part of every constructor, and there must be at least one explicitly defined constructor for any class or struct which contains a reference member.

Pointers, arrays, and references mix with base types and the `const` attribute in a dizzying variety of possible types. When we read a declaration, we must always remember to read from the identifier being declared outwards, using precedence to guide our understanding of the type. We read `*` as "pointer," `&` as "reference," and `[]` as "array." Thus, the declaration

```
int * const p;
```

is for a constant pointer to an integer, whereas

```
const int *p;
```

declares a pointer to an integer constant. When parentheses are used following an identifier, they designate a function declaration and can be thought of as having the same precedence as the function application operator `()`. When used in any other context parentheses are simply meant to guide our reading of the type, as follows.

```
char *f(int []); // f is a function taking an integer array as
    // a parameter and returning a pointer to a character.
char (*f)(int []); // f is a pointer to a function taking an
    // integer array as a parameter and returning a character.
```

The only difference between the two declarations above is the presence or absence of the parentheses around `*f`. Without the parentheses, we can use the fact that the postfix `()` operator has higher precedence than the prefix `*` operator to conclude that `f` is not a pointer but a function. The parentheses around `*f` in the second declaration clearly tell us to think of `f` as a pointer.

5.1.4 Pointers to Members

We mentioned earlier in the text the concept of a callback table, being a table of addresses to which control should branch in response to different events. This technique for event-handling is very low-level, and is typically seen in assembly language and in procedural languages with a strong machine-oriented flavor, like C. A file-scope function is fully specified by its call/return interface and its address in memory. This is not so with instance methods. An instance method needs both a code pointer and a data pointer to precisely specify an invocation, and so the callback table idea needs modification in an object-oriented setting in order to serve as an implementation technique for event handling.

We have just seen that C and C++ allow "pointers to functions" as data types, so that if we wish to use file-scope functions or static class functions as event handlers then it is quite easy to specify a callback table in the C++ language. Thus, with just the operating system's message handling support the programmer, or the library in our case, could supply an event-handling model written in C++ and using old-style procedural event handlers. Suppose, however, we want our library to be truly object-oriented in its approach to event handling, so that methods of classes are our event handlers. The data pointer is easy, because object addresses are *bona fide* data types. How do we add to this the code pointer, i.e., the pointer to the method? Does such a thing exist? As anyone who has picked up on the design philosophy of C++ could now predict, the answer is yes.

In C++, we can declare pointers not only to methods, but to data members, of a class. For this we use the feature called "pointers to members." We will begin by illustrating the idea of a pointer to an integer data member. The declaration

```
int MyClass::*p;
```

declares `p` to be a "pointer to a member of `MyClass` of type `int`." Again, we read the declaration from the identifier outward, following precedence rules. How can we use such a declaration? Suppose `MyClass` is declared as follows:

```
struct MyClass {
    int x, y, z;
```

```
    void add() { z = x + y; }
    void subtract() { z = x - y; }
    void multiply() { z = x * y; }
    void divide() { if (y != 0) z = x/y; }
};
```

Then, we can store the "address" of `MyClass::y` in `p` with the statement below:

```
p = &MyClass::y;
```

This seems a very curious thing to do, because `y` is an instance variable, i.e., a nonstatic data member, and therefore has no existence apart from any object in which it is included. In fact, there might at any time be hundreds of `MyClass` objects, and therefore hundreds of different copies of `y`. So how can we place in `p` "the" address of `y`? The answer lies in the simple observation that in every copy of a `MyClass` object the relative location of `y` will be the same. Any such object will occupy `3*sizeof(int)` bytes (ignoring any run-time overhead items), and the value of `y` will be stored as the second `int` object. Although the compiler writer may choose to deviate, normally on a machine in which `int` values occupy four bytes, `x` will be stored at an offset of 0, `y` will be stored at an offset of 4, and `z` will be stored at an offset of 8. The relative offset at which all `y`'s are stored is the only reasonable candidate for what we mean by the "address" of `MyClass::y`. We expect, then, that usually the value stored in `p` by the above assignment statement will be 4.

How can we use a "pointer to member" to gain access to a particular location within an object? In order to do this, we introduce two totally new operators, "dot-star" (`.*`) and "arrow-star" (`>*`). If `m` is a `MyClass` object, and `q` is a pointer to a `MyClass` object, and if `p` is defined as above and has been given the value indicated above, then the notation

```
m.*p
```

refers to (has the same l-value and the same r-value as) `m.y`, and the notation

```
q->*p
```

refers to `q->y`.

Now let us suppose that identifier `fp` refers to a "member function pointer" which could refer to one of the methods of `MyClass`. Because all four methods take no parameters and return `void`, then we would need to define `fp` as follows:

```
void MyClass::(*fp)();
```

The pointer `fp` could point to any of the four methods. For example, the assignment

```
fp = &MyClass::add;
```

will cause `fp` to "point to" the `add()` method. We can now use the dot-star operator or the arrow-star operator to invoke the function on the end of a "pointer to a method." Thus, the notation `(m.*fp)()` invokes the `add()` method of object `m`, and `(q->*fp)()` invokes the `add()` method of object `*q`.

> **NOTE**
>
> *Note that pointers to member functions will not be stored as offsets from the base address of an object, because multiple copies of member functions are not needed nor used. These will be true addresses, the addresses in memory where the translated forms of those member functions will reside. Clearly the compiler must provide such a translated form for any member function whose "address" is referred to as in the above assignment. Inline translation is not sufficient once such an address has been requested.*

With the above facilities it becomes practical to define callback tables that are arrays of pointers to methods, an approach which is in fact employed in the MFC library. This scheme will employ a different callback table for each class whose objects are capable of responding to events, so that the "object" portion of the (object, method) pair has been factored out and is common to all the pointers in the table. Only one table is necessary for the class, and different objects using that table will use the same pointers but will furnish their own addresses as data pointers.

5.2 STORAGE MANAGEMENT AND CLASS DESTRUCTORS

If your language is Java, storage management is simple. In Java, locally declared objects are small, being either primitive values or handles, and are allocated on the stack. Stack frames do not get large, and stack storage management is standard. Static storage is used only for class definitions, which store only instance methods, class methods, class variables, and some overhead items (run-time type information, for example). An instantiation of a class, a contiguous block consisting of instance variables and a run-time descriptor, is stored on the heap and allocated with an explicit *new* operation. For the Java programmer, however, transitioning to C++ introduces complications.

In C++, where first-class objects are represented by values, not handles (pointers), locally declared objects reside on the stack by default. This is no more complicated than storing smaller items on the stack, but the programmer may sometimes have to take specific measures to avoid stack frames that are too large, since stack space is usually more limited in size than heap space. Heap storage management is complicated by the fact that the typical C++ environment has no garbage collection facility and instead leaves it up to the programmer to decide when to free objects which were allocated on the heap.

Let us begin to illustrate some heap storage management considerations by assuming we have a class `MyClass`, which has a default constructor, and a pointer `p` which has been declared to be of type `MyClass *`. The syntax for allocating a `MyClass` object on the heap and storing a pointer to that object in `p` is almost identical to that used in Java, and appears as follows:

```
p = new MyClass;
```

There is only one slight difference between the C++ and Java versions of this statement, and that is that in order to invoke the default constructor the Java version would require an empty set of parentheses after `MyClass`.

Another difference from Java's approach to heap allocation is that in C++ primitive data objects can be allocated on the heap, another example of the C philosophy that the programmer should not be constrained by artificial rules. Thus, the following code is perfectly legitimate:

```
double *p = new double;
*p = 23.485;
```

Release of heap storage is accomplished with the `delete` primitive, for which there is no equivalent in Java. For example, the storage allocated above (let's say eight bytes, a likely figure) can be freed with the statement:

```
delete p;
```

This causes the run-time routines associated with the heap to reorganize the storage nodes in the heap in such a fashion as to make those eight bytes available for reallocation.

A *very* important point here is that the `delete` operation receives the pointer in `p` by value, which means that it cannot change `p` itself but only the heap area that `p` is pointing to. So after the reorganization called for in the execution of the `delete` operation, the pointer in `p` is still the same. This means `p` *is now pointing to internal heap space, not to user space*. That space may contain pointers, counts, or other heap overhead items which should not be manipulated by user code. The value in `p` has become a dangling pointer, and `*p` is a dangling reference. At this point in time, executing a statement which changes `*p`, such as

```
*p += 1;
```

is a programmer error and could cause catastrophic effects by modifying one or more key overhead items in some heap node. If such modification occurs, we say that the heap has become *corrupted*. The most devastating effects of heap corruption are seen when, as is very likely, no run-time error occurs at the point where the actual corruption of the heap took place, but rather the effects of heap corruption show up at some indeterminate future time. The exact nature of those effects is hard to predict. Depending on the machine, the operating system, and the language run-time, and even depending on variable characteristics of the system state when the program began execution, any of the following are possible: (1) the program could complete its run without any visible error, (2) the program could exit with an exceptional condition, (3) the program could appear to execute without errors but with wrong results, or (4) actual damage could occur to key internals of the operating system image, forcing a reboot.

NOTE
Finding a heap error is extremely difficult, since the evidence of the error may only surface when we are "miles away" from the actual place where the error occurred. If a "debug mode" compilation is available, the programmer is well advised to use it during testing and thereby take advantage of special debug mode versions of the heap management routines which carefully monitor heap activity.

In order to automate to some extent the process of removing objects allocated on the heap and to make errors less likely, C++ allows the programmer to incorporate a *destructor* into classes and structs. A destructor is a member function which is automatically called just before the space occupied by an object is reclaimed, whether that space is reclaimed at block exit, at program termination, or in response to a `delete` operation. The most valuable use to be made of such a routine is to delete any additional storage that has been dynamically allocated as a result of actions taken by the member functions of the class during the lifetime of the object.

For example, suppose a program defines a structure of type `Huge` with large space requirements and there is a reason to avoid placing such objects on the stack. Also suppose procedure `f()` needs to make and use such an object in order to accomplish its mission. A pattern which accomplishes this is given below:

```
void f() {
    Huge *hp = new Huge;
    // Ensuing code refers to members m of the structure using the
    // notation hp->m.
    ...
    delete hp;
}
```

The code above is perfectly sound, but puts the burden on the programmer to explicitly delete the object from the heap. The pointer on the stack will be reclaimed using standard stack management, but without the `delete` operation the object on the heap would remain as garbage until the program finished execution (or longer if the language run-time uses the operating system's heap and the latter is sufficiently unsophisticated).

We wish to point out a better usage pattern which employs destructors, so let us get more specific with our example. Suppose the structure `Huge` has two public member functions, say `g()` and `h()`. We can automate the creation and destruction of heap storage by encapsulating the `Huge` pointer in a class and duplicating its interface, providing a constructor and destructor for the class that automatically manage the allocation and deallocation of heap storage. The syntax for declaring a destructor, as seen in the example below, consists of a tilde character (~) followed by the class name, followed by empty parentheses (destructors do not have parameters). As with any member function, the programmer has the option of coding the declaration inline or putting in a prototype and providing the definition in a separate source file. Here the destructor is simple, and we define it inline.

```
class HugeClass {
    Huge *hp;
```

```
public:
    HugeClass(): hp(new Huge) {} // Default constructor
    ~HugeClass() { delete hp; }  // Destructor
    int g(int x) { return hp->g(x); }
    double h(double y) { return hp->h(y); }
};
```

Now we can write the function `f()` above as follows:

```
void f() {
    HugeClass h;
    // Ensuing code calls member functions g and h using
// notations h.g() and h.h().
...
}
```

Note that we have been able to dispense with the explicit calls on `new` and `delete` in client code, because the constructor for `HugeClass` will automatically allocate the space at block entry and the destructor will automatically delete it at block exit. Note also we have still accomplished our original objective of saving stack space.

One additional storage class bears mentioning. The `static` attribute applied to a block-scope variable causes that variable to have a separate existence which does not depend on whether or not a thread is currently executing in the function. For example, the following is a very simple (and very poor) random number generator:

```
double random() {
    // Returns a random fraction between zero and one
    static double seed = 0.198476352873321098;
    static int multiplier = 762981;
    seed *= multiplier;
    seed = seed - floor(seed); // Throws away all but the frac-
tional
        // part of seed.
    return seed;
}
```

In the above example, the items named `seed` and `multiplier` are `static` local variables which come into existence and are initialized the first time the function `random()` is called and are not destroyed until the program finishes execution. Thus, they do not participate in stack unwinding, and from call to call they retain the same l-values. Their r-values vary as usual, but their r-values at the beginning of each call are the same as they were at the last return. Hence, `random()` returns a different randomly generated fraction each time it is called.

5.3 ARRAYS, STRINGS, AND POINTER ARITHMETIC

There is an interesting equivalence between arrays and pointers in C++, based on the identification of an array name with the address of its first element. For example, the parameter types `int * const` and `int[]` are equivalent, and the name of an array with the same base type can be used as an initializer for a pointer, as follows:

```
int primes[] = {2, 3, 5, 7, 11, 13, 17, 19, 23, 29};
int * p = primes;
```

Because subscripted variables have l-values, the following makes sense as well:

```
p = &primes[3];   // p points at the element containing 7.
```

Pointers can be subscripted as if they were arrays. After the assignment `p = primes` the expressions `p[i]` and `primes[i]` have both the same l-value and the same r-value, and after the assignment `p = &primes[2]` the expression `p[i]` has the same l-value and r-value as `primes[i+2]`.

Pointers can be incremented (or decremented) and repositioned by adding or subtracting integer values. The key here is that in general for an integer `i`, `*(p+i)` is identical in its l-value and r-value to `p[i]`. Thus, although we think of pointer values as memory addresses we do not interpret `p+1` as pointing one byte beyond where `p` is pointing, but rather one `int` beyond where `p` is pointing. As another example, for some programmer-defined data type `Widget`, if `q` is of type `Widget *`, then `q[i]` and `*(q + i)` both designate the `Widget` object located at a displacement of `i*sizeof(Widget)` bytes beyond the address stored in `q`. In the same way, `*(q - i)` designates the object located `i*sizeof(Widget)` bytes *before* that address.

Pointer arithmetic also extends to subtraction of two pointer values having the same base type, but that subtraction has no reliable meaning unless both pointers are pointing into the same contiguously allocated block of data objects, where those objects have the same type as the base type of the pointers. Thus, after the assignments `p = primes` and `q = &primes[5]`, the computation `q - p` yields the value 5.

In Chapter 4, "C++ and Java Commonalities and Similarities," we noted that arrays in C++ must be declared with statically determined bounds. No such restriction exists, however, with heap allocation. There is a variant of the `new` operator that allows the programmer to dynamically allocate `n` objects in a contiguous block, so that the allocated block can be treated as an array. The value returned by this `new` operator is the address of the first object in the dynamically allocated array, so that if we place the return value in a pointer then the pointer can be subscripted to gain access to the other objects. For example, to allocate `n` integers and store the address of the first such integer in pointer variable `q`, we use the instruction

```
int * q = new int[n];
```

where `n` can be run-time variable. The expression `q[i]` makes sense now if `i` is between 0 and `n - 1` inclusively, and designates the `i`th element of the array. The space allocated by this alternative form of the `new` operator must be freed in a slightly different way, as follows:

```
delete [] q;
```

Any primitive type, but also any class or struct which has a default constructor, is a candidate for this style of dynamic allocation.

NOTE

If class A has constructors and does not have a default constructor, there is no syntax which allows us to create an array of objects of type A. The practical solution is usually to dynamically allocate an array of pointers to such objects, and then iterate through the array to individually allocate the objects on the heap, using an appropriate constructor.

Recall that character strings in Java are first-class objects and are built into the language. In contrast, the "built-in" C++ character string types are simple character arrays and character pointers. The library routines for manipulating such strings are inherited from C and all take operands of type `char *` or `const char *`. A C-style string is therefore not a first-class object. It is nothing more than a sequence of characters in consecutive memory locations, ending with a null character (character code 0). There is no structure even to support the null-termination requirement; it is just a convention and an assumption used by the library routines, all of which have built-in tests for the terminating null character. This is the source of perhaps the most notorious insecurity in history. If the library routines do not find the null character, they simply keep iterating. If the null character is not where it is supposed to be, then arbitrarily large areas of memory may be overwritten by these algorithms. All these routines are deprecated today, but they are still in use and much legacy code depends on them. Fail-safe techniques have always existed for using these library routines, but programmers typically have made their decisions using the C mind-set, which is that execution time should be kept short and that extra tests and precautions are time consuming.

The following example illustrates the technical nature of working with native strings. Note how easy it would be to omit the trailing `'\0'` (last line of the `decorate` routine), or to provide too little space in the receiving buffer field. Such an error would not be caught with the compile, and would be difficult to find in a debugging session.

```cpp
#include <cstring>
#include <iostream>
using std::cout;
using std::endl;

void decorate(char decoration, int count,
              const char * original, char *altered) {
    int spaceNeeded = strlen(original) + 2*count;
    int i;
    for (i=0; i<count; ++i) altered[i] = decoration;
    for (i=i; i<count+strlen(original); ++i)
        altered[i] = original[i-count];
    // We could replace the above loop by
    //      strcpy(&altered[i], original);
    for (i=i; i<spaceNeeded; ++i) altered[i] = decoration;
    altered[i] = '\0';
}

int main() {
    char message[] = "Happy Birthday!";
    const int asteriskCount = 5;
    char buffer[sizeof(message)+2*asteriskCount+1];
    decorate('*', asteriskCount, message, buffer);
    cout << buffer << endl;
```

```
    return 0;
}
```

Happily, there is a very nice `string` data type in the C++ standard library. Like the Java `String` type, it uses an infix `+` operator for concatenation, and tests for equality and inequality use the `==` and `!=` operators. (Comparing two `char *` operands using the `==` operator will yield a `true` result only if the pointers are pointing to exactly the same location!) Similarly, the `<`, `<=`, `>`, and `>=` operators all compare strings using lexicographic, or dictionary, order. A `char *` or `const char *` argument can be used as input to a `string` constructor, so native string literals are assignment-compatible with the library `string` type.

The following example is equivalent to the above and illustrates the use of the `string` type:

```cpp
#include <string>
#include <iostream>
using std::cout;
using std::endl;
using std::string;

string decorate(char decoration, int copies,
                string original) {
    string decorator = "";
    for (int i=0; i<copies; ++i) decorator += decoration;
    return decorator + decoration + decorator;
}

int main() {
    cout << decorate('*',5,"Happy Birthday!") << endl;
    return 0;
}
```

Note the seamless mixing of the primitive types `char` and `const char *` (the type of a native C++ string literal) with the library type; this mixing is enabled by the `string` conversion constructors and the various overloads of the `+` operator. The `string` data type is nicely integrated into the standard library and is compatible with its containers and iterators. As indicated by the example, there are also overloaded `>>` and `<<` operators, so that strings can be streamed in and out easily and naturally. (See Section 5.5.)

5.4 PARAMETER TRANSMISSION MODES AND MUTABILITY

Parameter transmission in Java is exclusively by value, but sometimes the value transmitted is a handle, or an address, and this address is automatically dereferenced when necessary. In Java, there is no way to cause a variable's value to change by using that variable as an argument in a method call, because neither the variable's location, nor the identifier which names the variable, nor any particular run-time representation of the identifier, is actually transmitted to the method.

But in C++ there is, in a sense, a run-time representation of an identifier used as the name of a data object, namely the l-value of the name. With its capability to directly refer to the address of a variable, C++ allows methods and procedures to actually change a variable's value as a side effect of a method call. Thus, in Java a request for object `a` to change the value of `x`, coded as `a.change(x)`, could not actually produce any change in `x`'s value. In the case that `x`'s value is a handle, the call may produce internal changes in the object `x` refers to, but could not cause `x` to refer to a different object. If `x`'s value is primitive, it will necessarily remain totally unchanged by the call. In C++, however, it is quite easy and natural to code `change()` so that it completely changes `x`'s value. All that is necessary is that the method `change` have as its parameter a reference variable of the same base type as `x`. We call this implementation technique "parameter transmission *by reference*." It actually works the same way as an initialization of a reference variable, because the semantics of parameter transmission in C++ are defined to be exactly those of initialization.

5.4.1 Reference Parameters

Let us use as an example a routine for swapping the values of two integer variables passed as parameters. In C++, this could be coded as follows:

```
void swap(int &x, int &y) {
    int temp = x;
    x = y;
    y = temp;
}
```

Note that the two parameters `x` and `y` are coded as references, but because they are parameters their initialization occurs at the point of call. Therefore when the programmer codes `swap(r, s)` the l-values of `r` and `s` are transmitted, respectively, to `x` and `y` as their initializers. When the routine returns, `r`'s value has become that of s and vice versa. Such a swap routine cannot be written in Java.

Remembering that reference parameters are actually restricted pointers which are automatically dereferenced, we should not be surprised to hear that there is another way of accomplishing the goal of changing a variable's value as a side effect of a method or procedure call. That method uses pointers and explicitly coded * and & operators, as illustrated in the alternative version of the swap routine that follows:

```
void swap(int *x, int *y) {
    int temp = *x;
    *x = *y;
    *y = temp;
}
```

To produce the same effect as above, however, the call should be coded as swap(&r, &s).

Reference parameters can also be given the const attribute, and in that case the called routine is forbidden to use the parameter in any context where its value could be changed. This is useful when large objects are to be transmitted but should not be changed by the call. Normally an object transmitted as an argument is transmitted by value, meaning the parameter's value resides on the receiving routine's stack frame and is initially a copy of the corresponding argument's value. However, because the value transmitted is only a copy, no side effects can be caused in the calling routine by changing the parameter's value. To achieve this effect of protecting the calling routine's copy of the argument, while using no more space on the stack than that required for storing a pointer, we can use *call by constant reference*. An example follows, where Huge is a type whose values occupy a lot of memory:

```
void f(const Huge &h) { etc. etc. }  // Call by constant
    // reference saves stack space.
```

It turns out that call by constant reference is an essential parameter transmission mode for even more important reasons. A copy constructor for a C++ class must receive as its only parameter an already-constructed value of that type. But if the constructor's parameter is passed by value, then *the mechanism of parameter transmission is itself a copy construction and will invoke the copy constructor*. This then amounts to a never-ending recursive call, which would ultimately overflow the stack and end the program. Thus, the following class definition is in error:

```
class MyClass {
    int x;
public:
    MyClass(int x=0): x(x) {}
    MyClass(MyClass m): x(m.x) {} // ERROR. Infinite
        // recursion. Should be MyClass(const MyClass &m) etc.
};
```

We begin now to see the proliferation of multiple mechanisms in C++ which accomplish the same or nearly the same objective. Whether to use call by value or call by constant reference is a design decision on the part of the programmer, and it is only one of many such language-enabled design decisions the C++ programmer must make with even small- to medium-scale programs. It is this huge design space, within which a given decision may have a subtle effect which only shows up later in the project, perhaps when it is too late to reverse the decision, which makes C++ a feared, and at the same time much respected, language.

5.4.2 Mutability and const Functions

We say that an object is *mutable* if sending a message to it can change its value, or its internal state. Clearly parameters transmitted by constant reference should not be mutable, nor should any variable with the const attribute, and the compiler will not allow such a parameter or variable to appear as the left-hand operand of an assignment, nor will it allow it to be transmitted in turn to any function except by value or by constant reference. But since sending it a message can change its value, does that mean that no messages can be sent to it? Not exactly, but it is in fact only allowed by the compiler to receive certain messages, namely those that have been declared const. Consider the following example:

```
class MyClass {
public:
    ...
    void change();
    void dontChange() const;
    ...
};

void f(const MyClass & m) {
    m.dontChange();  // Perfectly legal.
    m.change(); // Generates a compiler error.
};
```

In the example, the first line of *f*'s function body is legal because member function `dontChange()` has been declared `const`. However, member function `change()` cannot legally be sent as a message, so the second line will prevent the code from being compiled. This is true even if `change()` does not in fact change the internal state of a `MyClass` object. The compiler will not examine the internals of a member function and try to determine whether or not it should be declared `const`. It must rely on the programmer to do that declaration explicitly, partly because the actual definition of the member function may not even be accessible in the current compilation.

The compiler *will* check the internals of a method once it has been declared `const`, however. Its check will be performed as if `*this` had been transmitted to the method by constant reference. Normally no data member of the class can be changed (there is an exception given below) by any code in the definition, meaning no such data member can appear on the left-hand side of an assignment, nor can it be used as an argument unless the call is by value or constant reference, nor can it be sent any non-const messages.

There are exceptions to the rule against changing data members of a class in a **const** member function of that class. One of those is when the member in question is declared **mutable**. Thus, the declaration

```
mutable int x;
```

states that member `x` can be changed by any member function, including `const` member functions. Another exception which can be made on-the-fly is to use a `const` cast. While execution is inside a `const` member function, an `int` instance variable `x` is actually considered to be of type `const int`. If we wanted to change its value, say by adding 1, we could use the (rather cumbersome) notation

```
const_cast<int &> x = x + 1;
```

5.5 TYPE COERCIONS, PARAMETER MATCHING, AND OVERLOAD RESOLUTION

In transmission by value, conversion to and from various numeric data types is routine. For example, `sqrt(32)` is a perfectly legitimate expression, even though the library `sqrt` routine takes a `double` parameter and 32 is an `int` literal. The compiler will simply make the change itself and transmit a `double` version of the value

32. If an `int` variable is transmitted instead of a literal, the compiler will generate code to compute the corresponding `double` representation before generating the code for the call, and will transmit this computed value. This mechanism is extended beyond standard types, to include conversion constructors and programmer-defined type conversion operators. For example, if `MyClass` is a class with an `operator double()` method, and *m* is a `MyClass` object, then `sqrt(m)` makes sense and will implicitly invoke the programmer-defined `double` operator. In other words, it will be translated as if the programmer had coded `sqrt((double) m)`. (Recall that such an implicit type conversion is called a *coercion*.)

In the same way, if `f` is a function which has a parameter of type `A`, and `b` is an object of type `B`, then `f(b)` makes sense if `A` has a conversion constructor with a parameter of type `B`, and the expression will be translated as if it were coded `f(A(b))`. This shows up one of those areas in which the multiple alternative mechanisms in C++ can come into conflict. If it is both true that (1) `A` has a conversion constructor with a parameter of type `B` and (2) `B` has a conversion operator which converts `B` values into `A` values, then the expression `f(b)` cannot be translated—there is a conflict.

Except for an old and seldom used C parameter matching mechanism that we do not discuss in this text, programmer-defined conversions are the least favorite ways for the compiler to match argument with parameter. The compiler prefers an exact type match, and if there is an overload with an exact match it will use it over one which requires any type of conversion. Language-defined conversions such as `int` to `double` or vice versa are called *standard* conversions and are preferred over user-defined conversions.

If a function `f` has *m* overloaded forms with *n* parameters, where *m* and *n* are each greater than or equal to 1, then a call to that function may fail, not because there is no suitable match but because there are too many matches. The process of matching a call to a particular version of an overloaded function is called *overload resolution*, and the call on `f` succeeds only if the compiler can find a particular overload which (1) has as good a match to the corresponding argument in the call as any of the other overloads in each of the *n* parameter positions, and (2) has the best match in at least one of the parameter positions. If no such overload can be found, then overload resolution fails and the compiler generates an error message. (The algorithm for conducting this overload resolution process is exactly the algorithm for testing for the existence of, and finding, a maximum element in a partially ordered set.)

Let us consider an example using file-scope procedures. The following is an interpolation function useful in graphics displays for computing new pixel locations when an object is resized.

Version 1:

```
inline int map(int x, int a, int b, int c, int d) {
    // Transform an integer value x between bounds a and b into a
    // corresponding integer value between bounds c and d.
    return static_cast<int>(((x-a)/(float)(b-a) * (d-c)) + c);
}
```

The function does its division and its multiplication in floating point, and casts the final result back to int. On the other hand, the function below is useful for transforming a computed model value into a pixel coordinate value.
Version 2:

```
inline int map(double x, double a, double b, int c, int d) {
    // Transform a double value x between bounds a and b into a
    // corresponding integer value between bounds c and d.
    return static_cast<int>(((x-a)/(b-a) * (d-c)) + 0.5) + c;
}
```

Consider what happens with each of the following calls:
Call number 1:

```
map(32, 200, 500, 0, 1023)
```

Call number 2:

```
map(35, 197.8, 333.7, 0, 1023)
```

Call number 1 is an exact match with the first version of map, because all five arguments are of type int. This is the best possible situation and will produce a call on that version of the routine. On the other hand, call number 2 does not produce an exact match for either of the two versions of map, and causes difficulties when overload resolution is attempted. The first argument (35) does not match its parameter in version 2, but does match in version 1, a fact that leaves only version 1 in the running. On the other hand, the second argument (197.8) does not match its parameter in version 1, but provides an exact match for version 2. Neither of the two versions satisfies the requirements for overload resolution, so a compiler error results.
Now consider a third call.
Call number 3:

```
map(2, 0, 10, 1.5, 3)
```

Again, the arguments do not match the parameters exactly for either of the two versions, but in this case overload resolution succeeds. Version 1 provides as good a match as version 2 in all five parameter positions, and provides a strictly better match in position 1 (or position 2 or 3, but one position is sufficient). So version 1 of the routine will be called.

5.6   STREAM INPUT AND OUTPUT

We are finally in a position to discuss console input in C++, which is a feature of the language far easier to use than to explain. Console input and output are a special case of *stream* input and output, a mechanism which resides in the `ios_base` base class and its descendants, including `istream` and `ostream`, and whose salient features revolve around the stream insertion operator `<<` (which we discussed in the last chapter in the context of console output) and the stream extraction operator `>>`.

5.6.1 Console Input

We have delayed discussing operator `>>` to this point because of its extreme difference from any input mechanisms in Java. All the library overloads of operator `>>` and all conventionally constructed user-defined overloads of it must define it in such a way that its second operand is passed *by reference*. For example, the standard console input object, called `cin`, can be requested to obtain from the standard input device (typically the keyboard) a value for variable `x` by coding the statement

```
cin >> x;
```

This statement works by side effect, namely the effect of storing in `x` a value obtained by translating some substring of a buffer (which will contain characters determined by the user's sequence of keystrokes) into some internal value. The particular version of operator `>>` invoked by this statement will be determined by overload resolution.

Like the stream insertion operator `<<`, operator `>>` has left to right associativity and conventionally returns as its result a reference to the left-hand operand. The expression

```
cin >> x >> y;
```

evaluates by first obtaining a value for x from standard input, thereby causing changes in both x and cin, because cin's buffering mechanisms will advance the input pointer and possibly fill a new buffer. The changed object cin is then returned as a result of the first invocation of >>, and used as input to the second invocation.

Each data type has its own defined response to the streaming operators. For all primitive numeric types, including int and double, stream insertion outputs a single numeric literal with no imbedded white space, and that same string could be read back into a variable of the appropriate type if the output file were used as input. Stream extraction for numeric types starts at the current input pointer and discards all leading white space characters such as spaces, tabs, and end-of-line characters. When a stream extraction algorithm for a numeric type encounters a non-whitespace character, it tries to interpret the ensuing string of non-whitespace characters as a numeric literal capable of translation into a type which can be converted and stored in the target variable. Special rules apply that are specific to type. For example, this process will read an int literal into a double variable, but if the input is a double literal and the target is an int variable, then the reading process will cease at the decimal point, leaving that character and the characters in the fractional part of the literal to be input by succeeding operations on the stream.

NOTE

Stream I/O is predicated on the assumption that clients interested in integrating new types into this I/O framework will write their own overloaded versions of the operators >> and <<. These overloads are typically file-scope procedures both of whose parameters are reference parameters. The left-hand operand for a new overload of << should be a reference with base type ostream, and the inheritance mechanism takes over to make the operation apply to all derived classes, so that the same operator can be used for file output streaming or streaming to the console. Generally speaking, the programmer is expected to design the two operators in such a way that values inserted into a stream with << can be read back into memory with the corresponding >> operator.

For objects of type string, the stream extraction operator >> executes similarly to the above-described behavior for numeric types, meaning that it will not input white space but will search for, and find, the next-occurring largest consecutive sequence of non-whitespace characters and place that sequence into the argument string variable. This of course means that when the programmer desires to input a string which includes whitespace, the operator is not a viable option. In that case, the programmer typically resorts to `getline()`, a file-scope function template in namespace `std` whose definition is pulled in with `#include <string>`. The action of `getline()` is simply to start at the current input pointer and place the ensuing characters (whitespace or not) in order into the string, stopping short of including the end-of-line character. For example, for a variable `s` of type `string` the call `getline(cin, s)` places the remainder of the current line of input from the keyboard in `s`.

5.6.2 File I/O Using Streams

We mention briefly here the procedure for using streams to perform file I/O. Not much needs to be said, since all of what was mentioned in the previous section about console I/O also applies to file I/O. The input file stream class, `ifstream`, inherits from `istream` and therefore can be manipulated using operator `>>` and the `getline()` string input function. To instantiate an `ifstream` object `fin` able to read from file *c:\documents\indata.txt*, we use the declaration

```
ifstream fin("c:\\documents\\indata.txt");
```

If we wish now to place all of the "words" (i.e., maximal substrings containing no whitespace) from the file into a set of strings, omitting whitespace, we could use the following loop:

```
string word;
set<string> words;
while (fin >> word) words.insert(word);
fin.close();
```

Notice the expression `fin >> word`, which is an odd combination of input and test. Since it is used as the test condition in a `while` statement, the reader will correctly infer that there is a way to express its result as a Boolean value. In fact, however, we know that it returns an `istream` object, namely `fin` itself. How are we to think of that as a Boolean? There is, in fact, no `operator bool` in the public interface of `istream` or `ifstream`. However, there is an `operator void*`. This operator returns a non-zero pointer value (the location of the stream object itself) while the stream is functional and not positioned at the end of file. However, it returns zero if the stream is positioned at the end of the file, which is why the above `while` loop performs as desired. This mechanism is available because C++'s system of implied casts from numeric types to Boolean extends in a similar way to pointers; specifically, a non-zero pointer used in a context where a Boolean is required is considered true, and a null pointer is considered false.

If the last line of the above code segment seems too cryptic, the following loop is equivalent:

```
fin >> word;
while (!fin.eof() && !fin.fail()) {
    words.insert(word);
    fin >> word;
}
fin.close();
```

Output files behave in a similar way to the above. The instantiation of a stream for an output text file can be done in precisely the same way as that for the input file above, except the type is ofstream, so that

```
ofstream fout("c:\\documents\\outdata.txt");
```

prepares us to use stream fout to write to the given file. If the file did not exist before this instantiation, it would be created. If it did exist, its contents would be destroyed, so that in any case the declaration as given produces an empty file. (Of course, there are versions of the constructor which configure the stream to append to the end of an existing file as well.) Thus, if we wish to write to this stream all the strings from the set words which have eight or more characters, one to a line, we could do so with the following *for* statement.

```
for (set<string>::iterator i = words.begin();
                    i != words.end(); ++i))
    if (i->size() >= 8) fout << *i << endl;
```

Closing a file associated with a stream can be accomplished with the close() message, but the file will automatically be closed when the stream is destroyed.

5.6.3 String Streams

A text file is a named sequence of characters, and as such is conceptually identical a string. In fact, using the Standard Library facilities of C++ we can treat a string like a stream. String streams can be instantiated to perform input operations which parse strings containing numeric literals and/or other substrings with specific meaning to an application. Conversely, output operations on string streams convert internal data into string representations. There are in fact two sets of such stream classes, one set targeted for character arrays and a more recent set of classes built around the `string` data type. We will concentrate on the latter, because it is safer and easier to use. In fact, the only new class with which we will need to familiarize ourselves is the `stringstream` class, which serves as well for input as for output.

When instantiating a `stringstream` object for output, we need no constructor parameters. We simply declare the object and begin streaming to it. All the overloaded versions of operator `<<` which have been defined for class `ostream` apply, because `stringstream` is a derived class of `ostream`. Even programmer-defined streaming operators apply, assuming they use `ostream` as the left-hand parameter type. For example, the following code places literals representing all the integers in an array of ten in a string stream, separated by spaces, then extracts a string containing this external representation of the array. (The class `stringstream` can be defined in a given compilation by including <sstream>, and made visible without qualification with the statement `using std::stringstream;`.)

```
int a[10];
... // Compute and store values in a[0], a[1], ..., a[9].
stringstream strout;
for (int i=0; i<10; ++i) strout << a[i] << ' ';
string aRep = strout.str();
// We can now use the string 'aRep' to show the contents of
// the array a to the user, or subject it to further string
// manipulation.
```

The above is a particularly important technique, because strings are the "common currency" of user interfaces. In MFC, in particular, the common pattern for displaying data textually is to first convert it to text and then place that text in the correct location in a window.

When instantiating a `stringstream` for input, we give the constructor a single parameter, the string from which the stream object is to read. The following code sequence illustrates:

```
string inputstring = "cost 112.98 size 8 quantity 7";
map<string,double> value;
stringstream strin(inputstring);
string name;
while (strin >> name) {
    double val;
```

```
        strin >> val;
        value[name] = val;
    }
```

The above stores `value["cost"]` as 112.98, `value["size"]` as 8, and `value["quantity"]` as 7.

5.7   FILE-SCOPE VARIABLES AND PROCEDURE DEFINITIONS

Although this text concentrates on object-oriented languages and features, there are certain aspects of C++ which are not object-oriented but nonetheless need to be discussed in order to provide the reader with a pragmatic knowledge of how to use the language. For example, it is impossible to construct a C++ program without at least one file-scope procedure, namely the `main()` function. The `main()` function is normally where execution begins in every C++ program, and it is not part of any class or namespace but is simply a procedure name with external linkage which the linker must find, or it will generate an error and the link step will fail. The value returned by the `main()` function is an integer return code, the interpretation of which is operating-system dependent. This return code is the program's report to the operating system on the success or failure of the run, and a normal run without errors is usually reported by returning a zero. (Some operating systems and programming environments have other naming conventions and special-purpose attributes for informing the linker concerning which procedure is to be the entry point to a computation.) C++ programmers often freely mix file-scope procedures (in addition to the `main()` function) into their programs, even when those programs are largely object-oriented in their design.

Besides procedures coded at file scope, it is common practice for programmers to use global variables, i.e., variables with external linkage whose definitions are not encapsulated inside a larger structure and are visible throughout large portions of a compilation unit. As we discussed in the previous chapter, such variables can even be made visible across multiple compilation units. Following is a simple complete application with no object-oriented features which implements an "Animal, Vegetable, or Mineral?" game, keeping its questions in a general tree. In this case, the tree type is called `Category` and encapsulates (1) a category name, (2) a yes or no question by which the category can be identified, and (3) a list of subcategories (each of which is also of type `Category`). If the list of subcategories is empty, the `Category` object is a leaf node in the tree. The root of the tree has empty string values for the category name and the identifying question, and the `initializeTop()` routine installs the three subcategories "Animal," "Vegetable," and "Mineral."

```cpp
#include <iostream>
using std::cin;
using std::cout;
using std::endl;
#include <string>
using std::string;
#include <list>
using std::list;

struct Category{
    Category(string name="", string yesOrNoQuestion=""):
        name(name), yesOrNoQuestion(yesOrNoQuestion) {}
    string name;
    string yesOrNoQuestion;
    list <Category> subcategories;
};

Category top;

void initializeTop() {
    top.subcategories.push_back(Category(
        "Animal","Is it an animal?"));
    top.subcategories.push_back(Category(
        "Vegetable","Is it a vegetable?"));
    top.subcategories.push_back(Category(
        "Mineral","Is it a mineral?"));
}

bool answerIsYes() {
    string yesno;
    cin >> yesno;
    return yesno[0] == 'Y' || yesno[0] == 'y';
}

void getStringFromUser(string prompt, string &answer) {
    bool userIsSure = false;
    while (!userIsSure) {
        answer = "";
        cout << prompt << endl;
        while (answer == "") {
            getline(cin,answer);
        }
```

```
            cout << "Your answer is \"" << answer << "\"."
                << endl;
            cout << "Are you sure this is what you want? (y/n) ";
            userIsSure = answerIsYes();
        }
    }

    void addNewSubcategory(Category &category) {
        string namePrompt =
            "Please enter the name of a new subcategory of " +
            category.name + ".";
        Category newSubcategory;
        getStringFromUser(namePrompt, newSubcategory.name);
        string questionPrompt =
            string("Please enter a yes or no question by which") +
            " we can identify a " + newSubcategory.name + ".";
        getStringFromUser(
            questionPrompt, newSubcategory.yesOrNoQuestion);
        category.subcategories.push_back(newSubcategory);
    }

    void converseWithUser(Category &category,
                          list<Category>::iterator nextTry) {
        if (nextTry == category.subcategories.begin() &&
            category.name != "")
            cout << "The answer is '" << category.name << "'."
                << endl;
        if (nextTry != category.subcategories.end()) {
            cout << nextTry->yesOrNoQuestion << " (y/n) ";
            if (answerIsYes())
                converseWithUser(
                    *nextTry, nextTry->subcategories.begin());
            else converseWithUser(category, ++nextTry);
        }
        else if (category.name != "") {
            cout << "Would you like to further identify the "
                << "type of " << category.name << "? (y/n) ";
            if (answerIsYes()) addNewSubcategory(category);
        }
        else
            cout << "You must choose animal, vegetable, or "
                << "mineral!" << endl;
    }

    int main() {
```

```
        initializeTop();
        bool userStillPlaying = true;
        while (userStillPlaying) {
            converseWithUser(top,top.subcategories.begin());
            cout << "Try another game? (y/n) ";
            userStillPlaying = answerIsYes();
        }
        return 0;
    }
```

The recursive routine `converseWithUser()` guides the user through a root-to-leaf descent into the classification tree beginning at the top node (identified by the global variable `top`), using a subtree (of type `Category`) and an iterator positioned within the list of subcategories in the subtree's root to mark its place in the tree. With every top-level invocation of `converseWithUser()` the user is given the opportunity to add a new node to the tree, either (1) after a successful search, in which case the user may convert a leaf node into an internal node by introducing subcategories or (2) after an unsuccessful search, by adding a new subcategory (new leaf) to a list of categories. Before invoking `converseWithUser()`, it is expected that the programmer will call the `initializeTop()` routine.

The experienced object-oriented programmer no doubt will see a problem with this design, relying as it does on a global variable and on good citizenship by the programmer, in that he is expected to explicitly call the initialization function. But it has its good points, one of which is its simplicity and readability. We will, however, introduce an object-oriented version in succeeding sections.

5.8   INLINE IMPLEMENTATION VS. SEPARATE COMPILATION

The normal method used by compilers for translating procedures, whether at file scope or class scope, is to construct a machine language subroutine which is the equivalent of the procedure coded by the programmer in the source language. That subroutine will have a specific memory address and will use a calling convention, specific to the language, which specifies the format of the stack frame that is built during the process of executing a low-level call. All machines have call instructions, which typically will perform at least the following two actions: (1) save the address of the instruction after the call as the return address, placing it either in a register or on the stack; and (2) transfer control to the first instruction of the machine language subroutine. Duties for building and maintaining the stack frame in the proper format are split up between the calling routine and the called routine, as are the duties for properly removing the stack frame upon return from the call. Thus, the high-level method call or procedure call translates to a low-level call with accompanying "housekeeping" instructions. This is the standard mechanism, but it is not always the best mechanism.

The C++ programmer may request that the compiler do an inline translation of any procedure, whether a file-scope function, a class method, or an instance method. For file-scope procedures the request is made by using the explicit `inline` attribute, as follows:

```
inline bool answerIsYes() {
    string yesno;
    cin >> yesno;
    return yesno[0] == 'Y' || yesno[0] == 'y';
}
```

Inline translation means the compiler does not produce a machine language equivalent of the function, but instead saves a tokenized version of the source definition in a buffer and uses it as a pattern for translating calls on the function, so that each call is replaced by its own modified version of the function definition. Thus, calls are more efficient in their use of execution time, because no new stack frame is built as a result of the call and there are no transfers of control. However, the footprint of the code used to translate the call will likely be larger, so if the function definition is large and there is a sufficiently large number of calls on a routine which is translated inline then the size of the object code can be significantly increased.

For methods of classes the programmer does not need to use the `inline` attribute to request inline translation. All the programmer need do is code the method as he would code a Java method, and that is by placing all the code constituting the method definition physically inside the class definition.

The final decision whether the translation of a method or procedure is actually done inline or not belongs not to the programmer, but to the compiler. If the programmer requests inline translation, but the compiler sees that the routine for some reason needs to reside at a well-defined memory address at run-time, then the compiler will ignore the request and do a conventional translation.

The only real alternative to inline translation is separate compilation. See Section 5.10 for the pragmatics of how to successfully set up separately compiled functions and methods.

5.9 OPERATOR OVERLOADING

The C++ overloading conventions extend smoothly to programmer-defined operators. After all, an operator is just a function, as this file-scope definition for an addition operator on objects of type `Point` demonstrates.

```
Point operator + (Point a, Point b) {
    return Point(a.x+b.x, a.y+b.y);
}
```

After the above definition has been made, then we can code the following:

```
Point p(3,4), q(-5,6);
p = p+q; // Invokes operator+(). Now p.x is -2 and p.y is 10.
```

The notation `p+q` is short for `operator+(p,q)`, and in fact one could code the latter instead. But doing so would defeat the purpose of operator overloading, which is incorporated into the language because operator notation is considered not only brief but extremely clear by those who are accustomed to using it. (That this point of view is not universal may not be obvious, but in fact there is at least one high-level language, namely COBOL, for which a heated and vigorous opposition was mounted *against* the inclusion of operators [Sammet81]. Thankfully the effort failed.)

Can an operator be designed as a method, and not as a file-scope function? Of course it can, as the following reworking of the `Point` class demonstrates:

```
class Point {
public:
    int x, y;
    Point(int x=0, int y=0): x(x), y(y) {}
    Point operator+(Point p) {
        return Point(x+p.x, y+p.y);
    }
};
```

Here we see `operator+` incorporated into the definition of the `Point` class as a method, or member function. The alternative notation for `p+q` in this case is `p.operator+(q)`, an expression that works but should never be seen in well-written code.

It should now occur to the perceptive reader that the language has yet again presented the programmer with a choice between two extremely similar alternatives, namely whether to define an operator overload as a member function or as a file-scope function. Choosing one approach over the other may have subtle repercussions in the future as the programmer's project progresses. The interesting thing here is that to the client programmer there is no difference—the sum of two points `p` and `q` is coded `p+q` independently of this choice.

File-scope operator definitions are the only option, of course, when the programmer wishes to define an operator whose left-hand operand is of a primitive type or of a type which cannot be altered by the programmer. An example is I/O streaming, as in the following code segment defining `operator <<` and `operator >>` for `Point` objects:

```
istream & operator >> (istream &in, Point &p) {
    char lparen, comma, rparen;
    in >> lparen;
    if (lparen != '(') in.setstate(std::ios_base::failbit);
    in >> p.x;
    in >> comma;
    if (comma != ',') in.setstate(std::ios_base::failbit);
    in >> p.y;
    in >> rparen;
    if (rparen != ')') in.setstate(std::ios_base::failbit);
    return in;
}

ostream & operator << (ostream &out, Point p) {
    out << '(' << p.x << ", " << p.y << ')';
    return out;
}
```

NOTE

The above code follows the convention that an input stream which encounters invalid input should not throw an exception but should set the "fail bit," and that the client programmer should regularly check the fail bit using the fail() method of ios_base. If the user does not enclose a Point value input from the keyboard in parentheses and separate the two coordinates with a comma, .then the stream will fail. Thus, if a client programmer issues a call to operator >> for a Point object p, then he is expected to test the fail bit and react, as in the following code.

```
Point p;
cin >> p;
if (cin.fail()) {
```

```
        cin.clear();
        ... // Now fix the mess.
    }
    else // etc. etc.
```

A stream which has had its fail bit set will be inoperative until that bit is cleared, say with the `clear()` method, as seen above. For an input stream, what we mean by inoperative is that it will still allow calls on its methods, but it will not advance the input pointer nor fill input buffers, nor will it produce any changes in the operands of a streaming operation.

It is instructive in several ways now to look at how one might overload the prefix and postfix increment operators for the `Point` data type. Suppose we wanted `++p` or `p++` to cause (as a side effect) both the `x` and the `y` coordinates of `p` to be incremented by one. If we want to be consistent with all the other overloaded meanings of these operators, then we wish the pre-increment expression to return the changed value and the post-increment expression to return the old value. This means we need two separate definitions. But is it possible to overload both operators, since both should under any reasonable set of expectations be referred to as `operator++`? And wouldn't both have the same interface?

The designers of C++ were faced with a hard choice here. There is no clear and natural way to allow the programmer to define both operators. But again the philosophy of the language is to give the programmer as many options as can be considered reasonably possible. The designers thus decided on a syntactic rule that is neither clear nor natural. The trick is that if `operator++` is coded in the natural way, with one operand in its file-scope procedure form or zero operands in its instance method form, then it will be considered a definition of the prefix operator, but if it is given an extra (unused) operand of type `int`, then it will be considered a definition of the postfix operator. Here are the two operators coded inline as instance methods:

```
class Point {
    ...
public:
    ...
    Point & operator ++ () {  // Prefix increment
        ++x;
        ++y;
        return *this;
    }
```

```
Point operator++(int) { // Postfix increment. Notice the
    // unused parameter.
    Point p(x,y);
    ++x;
    ++y;
    return p;
}
...
};
```

Note that the prefix increment returns a reference, but returning a reference from the postfix operator makes no sense as the natural l-value to return is that of the left-hand operand, which has the wrong r-value for the postfix expression. Now consider the following client code:

```
Point p(19,-7), q;
q = p++;
cout << "Value of p before incrementing is " << q << "." << endl;
p = q;
cout << "Value of p after incrementing is " << ++p << endl;
```

Output appears as follows, and indeed the operators perform as advertised.

```
Value of p before incrementing is (19, -7).
Value of p after incrementing is (20, -6)
```

The programmer is not allowed to use operator overloading to redefine an existing meaning for an operator (unless, of course, it is defined as an override in a derived class). This is true for built-in data types as well as programmer-defined data types. For example (thankfully), the programmer cannot redefine what it means to add two integers. (Recall that in Smalltalk even this seeming travesty is permitted!) A related rule is that at least one of the types in an operator definition must be programmer-defined.

5.10 MORE ON C++ HEADER FILES AND SOURCE FILES

A C++ header file is meant to carry information useful to the compiler during the translation of a single compilation unit, but it should not contain code that translates directly into named object file entities, whether stored procedures or stored data. This is because a program typically consists of multiple object files linked into one executable. These object files are the result of compiling multiple compilation units, and it is quite likely that more than one such compilation unit "includes" the same header file. If that header contains an item which defines an association for a name that has a run-time representation and is capable of being linked to references in other compilation units, then one risks having multiple copies of the defined entity around at link time, thus causing a link error. The header file below makes two such mistakes:

```
#include <cmath>

class A {
    static int count;
    int n;
public:
    A(int n): n(n) {
        count += 1;
    }
    int f();
};

int A::count = 0;
int A::f() { return rand() % n; }
```

In the class definition above, the class variable `count` is separately defined and initialized, as is the member function `f()`. If those separate definitions appear in the same file with the class definition, i.e., if all the code at right appears in the same header file, say *A.h*, then in any application that uses class `A` that header file cannot be included in more than one of the compilation units which will eventually be linked to form the executable. Supposing that class `A` were being developed for general use, the designer could not reasonably make such a restriction on client programmers. Hence, the two pieces of code must be separated, as follows:

File *A.h*:

```
#ifndef __A_H
#define __A_H

#include <cmath>

class A {
    static int count;
    int n;
```

```
    public:
        A(int n): n(n) {
            count += 1;
}
        int f();
    };

    #endif
```

File *A.cpp*:

```
    #include "A.h"

    int A::count = 0;
    int A::f() { return rand() % n; }
```

The reason this technique works is simple. Because *A.cpp* is a source file, it requires its own compilation step. Assuming its two definitions do not appear in any other source files in the linkage, a natural assumption, there can be no multiple definition errors at link time.

___

NOTE

The header file A.h uses what are called "preprocessor guards." The set of three preprocessor instructions #ifdef __A_H, #define __A_H, and #endif in the above code constitute a guard mechanism which avoids including the same header file twice in one compilation unit. This seems like an awkward device, but it is an essential technique for organizing source code when the relationship between source files and headers files defined by #include becomes complex, as it usually does. The mechanism is simple, and is based on the fact that the preprocessor has one symbol table which it uses for the construction of the compilation unit, and any symbol that has been defined at any time during preprocessing will be defined until it is explicitly "undefined" using #undef or until the compilation unit is complete and compilation begins. The first instruction asks whether symbol __A_H has been defined. This symbol, constructed by capitalizing the file name, replacing the period with an underline, and prefixing it with two additional underlines, is quite unlikely to have been defined during preprocessing by any other mechanism than executing an #include "A.h". Therefore, if it is defined, this constitutes the second *attempt to include the same file within this compilation unit. In that case, all code encountered after the #ifndef and before the #endif will not be included and no multiple definition errors will result during compilation.*

This transformation of a file name to a preprocessor symbol is typical of such conventions, but it is by no means the only such convention. The essential thing for such a transformation is that (a) it is a one-to-one transformation, so that two different file names will result in two different symbols, and (b) it produces a symbol unusual enough so that no other mechanism is likely to produce it.

To further illustrate these source file construction techniques, let us rewrite the "Animal, Vegetable, Mineral" game application from Section 5.7 in a more object-oriented fashion. We will place the source code in three files, named *main.cpp*, *AVMGame.h*, and *AVMGame.cpp*.

File *main.cpp*:

```cpp
#include "AVMGame.h"
#include <iostream>
using std::cout;

int main() {
    AVMGame game;
    bool userStillPlaying = true;
    while (userStillPlaying) {
        game.converseWithUser();
        cout << "Try another game? (y/n) ";
        userStillPlaying = GameUtilities::answerIsYes();
    }
    return 0;
}
```

File *AVMGame.h*:

```cpp
#ifndef __AVMGAME_H
#define __AVMGAME_H

#include <iostream>
using std::cin;
#include <string>
using std::string;
#include <list>
```

```cpp
using std::list;

struct Category {
    Category(string name="", string yesOrNoQuestion=""):
        name(name), yesOrNoQuestion(yesOrNoQuestion) {}
    string name;
    string yesOrNoQuestion;
    list<Category> subcategories;
};

class AVMGame: public Category {
private:
    void initialize();
    void addNewSubcategory(Category &category);
    void converseWithUser(Category &category,
                          list<Category>::iterator nextTry);
public:
    AVMGame() { initialize(); }
    void converseWithUser() {
        converseWithUser(*this,subcategories.begin());
    }
};

class GameUtilities {
public:
    static bool answerIsYes() {
  string yesno;
  cin >> yesno;
        return yesno[0] == 'Y' || yesno[0] == 'y';
    }
     static void getStringFromUser(string prompt, string &an-
swer);
    };

    #endif
```

File *AVMGame.cpp*:

```cpp
#include "AVMGame.h"
#include <iostream>
using std::cin;
using std::cout;
using std::endl;
#include <string>
using std::string;
```

```cpp
#include <list>
using std::list;

void AVMGame::initialize() {
    subcategories.push_back(
        Category("Animal","Is it an animal?"));
    subcategories.push_back(
        Category("Vegetable","Is it a vegetable?"));
    subcategories.push_back(
        Category("Mineral","Is it a mineral?"));
}

void AVMGame::addNewSubcategory(Category &category) {
    string namePrompt =
        "Please enter the name of a new subcategory of " +
        category.name + ".";
    Category newSubcategory;
    GameUtilities::getStringFromUser(
        namePrompt, newSubcategory.name);
    string questionPrompt = String("") +
        "Please enter a yes or no question by which we can " +
        "identify a " + newSubcategory.name + ".";
    GameUtilities::getStringFromUser(
        questionPrompt, newSubcategory.yesOrNoQuestion);
    category.subcategories.push_back(newSubcategory);
}

void AVMGame::converseWithUser(Category &category,
                    list<Category>::iterator nextTry) {
    if (nextTry == category.subcategories.begin() &&
        category.name != "")
        cout << "The answer is '" << category.name << "'."
            << endl;
    if (nextTry != category.subcategories.end()) {
        cout << nextTry->yesOrNoQuestion << " (y/n) ";
        if (GameUtilities::answerIsYes())
            converseWithUser(
                *nextTry, nextTry->subcategories.begin());
        else converseWithUser(category, ++nextTry);
    }
    else if (category.name != "") {
        cout << "Would you like to further identify the "
            << "type of " << category.name << "? (y/n) ";
        if (GameUtilities::answerIsYes())
            addNewSubcategory(category);
```

```
        }
    else
        cout << "You must choose animal, vegetable, or "
            << "mineral!" << endl;
    }

    void GameUtilities::getStringFromUser(string prompt,
                                          string &answer) {
        bool userIsSure = false;
        while (!userIsSure) {
            answer = "";
            cout << prompt << endl;
            while (answer == "") getline(cin,answer);
            cout << "Your answer is \"" << answer << "\"." << endl;
            cout << "Are you sure this is what you want? (y/n) ";
            if (answerIsYes()) userIsSure = true;
        }
    }
```

Note that here it was not necessary to call a separate routine to perform initializations; the initializations were performed as a matter of course by the constructor, as a side effect of instantiating the game. All the needed functionality is encapsulated in the game object, so that the only global associations are type names. The design is much improved for this reason, and also for the reason that the published client interface is now much clearer.

5.11   C++ ACCESS CONTROL AND INHERITANCE PATTERNS

There are a few important points to observe about the example in the previous section. The first is that Category is a struct, yet is used as the "base class" for AVMGame, a class. In fact, the struct and class constructs both participate equally in inheritance relationships, so that a struct can inherit from a class and vice versa. The only difference between them is their default access characteristics. All items in a struct are public by default, and all items in a class are private by default. Explicit access specifiers can be used to override these defaults, however. Thus, the following code is equivalent to the struct defined above.

```
    class Category {
    public:
```

```
        Category(string name="", string yesOrNoQuestion=""):
            name(name), yesOrNoQuestion(yesOrNoQuestion) {}
        string name;
        string yesOrNoQuestion;
        list<Category> subcategories;
    };
```

Access control, like many other aspects of this language, permits a great deal of fine-tuning by the programmer, a process that gets complicated when multiple inheritance is added to the mix.

5.11.1 Protected Access and Friends

Somewhere between `public` and `private` in its restrictiveness is the `protected` access specifier. Items with `protected` access can be referenced in derived classes but not in client code. The ramifications of using protected access turn out to be trickier in practice than one might imagine. For example, we might reason in the above program that the client programmer has no need to access the members of `Category` at all, and hence in place of `public` we might try to substitute `protected` in the above code, so that only derived classes have access to the members of `Category`. This strategy doesn't take into account a very important point, which is that *code within instance methods of derived classes can only refer to the protected members of objects of the specific derived class*. That code may not make reference to protected members of objects of the base class type or of other class types derived from it. This means that if we declare that the members of `Category` are `protected`, for example, then the instance method `AVMGame::addNewSubcategory()` can no longer legally make reference to the data items `category.name`, `newSubcategory.name`, `category.subcategories`, etc., because all those are members of objects of type `Category`, not of type `AVMGame`! Not only that, but the `AVMGame::initialize()` method cannot even use the constructor `Category()` to construct the three essential animal, vegetable, and mineral nodes of the game tree! The use of tightly restricted access control needs careful thought, then, to make sure that (1) client programmers of the class receive exactly that level of access needed in order to attain their objectives and (2) any reasonable set of objectives by client programmers is accommodated.

One way to permit access to private and protected members by entities which are not at class scope is to declare them as *friends* of the class. Thus, a function which receives an object of that class as a parameter, or has access via an enclosing scope to such an object, may make reference to nonpublic members if there is a friend declaration for the function within the class definition itself. Static and nonstatic member functions, and even file-scope functions, may be given friend status. The syntax for a friend declaration for function *f*, giving it access to the nonpublic members of class `MyClass`, consists of a prototype for the function preceded by the keyword `friend`.

Entire classes may be given friend status in a similar way. Thus, the following pattern is for declaring file-scope function `f()`, member function `g()` of class `HerClass`, and class `HisClass` to be friends of `MyClass`.

It does not matter whether the friend declarations come in a public, private, or protected portion of the class.

5.11.2 Protected and Private Inheritance

C++ extends its fine-grained approach to access control by introducing two additional types of inheritance, namely private inheritance and protected inheritance. We could utilize protected inheritance in the above example by replacing `public` by `protected` in the definition of `AVMGame`, as follows:

```
class AVMGame: protected Category { etc, etc. };
```

This strategy works, and achieves some of what we were after in our discussion about making the members of `Category` protected. With protected inheritance, the public members of the base class become protected in the derived class. This means that clients can instantiate a `Category` object and make references to any of its members, but clients who instantiate an `AVMGame` object have no access to its base class members without using type-defeating reinterpret casts.

Protected inheritance means that methods in classes derived from `AVMGame` have access to the members of `Category`, but `private` inheritance closes that door, effectively redefining the interface to `AVMGame` for all programmers who use that class, by sealing away any possibility of directly using the base class members. Again, this strategy can be defeated by the client programmer using the cast `reinterpret_cast<Category&>()`. Interestingly enough, a similar static or dynamic upcast would be illegal.

An important language-theoretic issue raised in Chapter 1, "A Context-Sensitive Introduction," must be revisited here, namely the difference between inheritance and subtyping. In Smalltalk and in Java, derived classes are always subtypes of the base class. But if in C++ we create a new type using private or protected inheritance, then we are not creating a subtype. An object of such a derived type cannot be used as an argument to be passed to a corresponding parameter of the base class type, since doing so could give access rights to attributes and behaviors of the passed object in the called routine which are not granted in the caller.

5.11.3 Multiple Inheritance

Up to this point in the text we have seen only single inheritance, in which no class has more than one direct base class. But there are situations that naturally call for two or more base classes. For example, suppose we are developing a system of classes for controlling a set of interacting manufacturing processes. Each process is represented by a model class that keeps essential information regarding the current state of the process. Each model class has a set of inputs and a set of outputs, where the inputs are outputs from some other manufacturing process. (A process with no inputs is assumed to be a stream of pre-fabricated parts or raw materials.) Some processes are automated to the extent that they are accompanied by controller objects that (1) operate by reading a set of sensors to determine the current state of the process, and (2) respond to the current state of the process by modifying a set of effectors, each of which has a direct or indirect effect on the process. The passing of control information between controller and process is modeled in software by the transmission of messages between a controller object and a process model object. Also, the physical interaction between processes is modeled in the same way, by the transmission of messages between different processes. The objects which model the processes all descend from a base class called `Process`, but some are also capable of being controlled by objects descended from a class called `Controller`. Any object capable of being controlled will be of a type which descends from the base class `Controllable`.

```cpp
class Process {
// This is the base class for models of manufacturing
// processes.
public:
    virtual Process(int numInputs, int numOutputs) = 0;
    virtual int getInput(int i) = 0;  // This will obtain its
        // value by sending the getOutput() message to obtain
        // the appropriate output from some connected process.
    virtual int getOutput(int i) = 0;
        // This typically returns a value stored from the
        // previous call on cycle().
    virtual void cycle() = 0; // Check all inputs, then use a
        // mathematical transformation to obtain the
        // appropriate outputs.  Store these outputs in
        // anticipation of calls on getOutput().
```

```
};

class Controllable {
// This is the base class for all models of controllable
// objects.
public:
    virtual int getSensorReading(int i) = 0; // Used by a
     // controller to determine the current reading of a
     // sensor.
    virtual int getDesiredReading(int i) = 0; // Used by a
     // controller to determine the desired reading of a
     // sensor.
    virtual void putEffectorOutput(int i, int value) = 0;
     // Used by a controller to make adjustments to the
     // internal state of the object.
};

class ControllableProcess: public Process,
                           public Controllable {
     vector<Controller *> controllers;
public:
     void attachController(Controller * controller) {
      controllers.push_back(controller);
     }
     virtual void cycle() {
        Process::cycle(); // Simulate the execution of one
            //cycle in the life of the process.
            for (vector<Controller*>::iterator i =
                controllers.begin(); i != controllers.end;
                ++i)
               i->cycle(); // Allow each attached controller
                   // to perform any needed modifications to
                   // the process.
     }
};
```

The details here are deliberately sketchy, but it doesn't take much imagination to see the convenience of a class like `ControllableProcess`, which has all the capabilities of a process and is also controllable.

So the "multiple inheritance" feature of C++ apparently gives it somewhat of an advantage in modeling certain relationships. What are the difficulties here which may have prevented other languages from adopting this more general view of inheritance? An obvious difficulty is name collisions that occur when the same name is used in each of the two base classes, but this difficulty can be overcome with the class scope override notation. To illustrate, consider the case where there are two base classes A and B, each with a public or protected member function named f. Then the two versions of f will both be visible in the derived class, and can be referred to as A::f and B::f.

A certain awkwardness arises in the initialization of an object instantiated from a type with two base classes. To illustrate, let us construct an example:

```
class A {
    int x;
public:
    A(int x): x(x) {}
};

class B {
    int y;
public:
    B(int y): y(y) {}
};

class C: public A, public B {
public:
    C(int x, int y): B(y), A(x) {}
};
```

Here class C has two base classes, A and B. When an object of type C is instantiated, the instantiation must call the constructor, as in the following client code:

```
C c(25,49);
```

This will entail a call on the constructor for A and a call on the constructor for B, as indicated by the initialization part of C's constructor. The implication of the order of base class constructor calls in that initialization part is that the latter will execute first. However, this is not the case. Instead, the order of initialization is determined by the first line of the class definition, which we reproduce here:

```
class C: public A, public B {
```

Note that the base class A is mentioned first. The order given here determines the appearance of the storage map for objects of type C, as well as the order of initialization. Thus, objects of type C will be stored with the x component occurring in the low memory position and the y component in the high memory position, and x will be initialized before y. The problem here is, of course, that this order of initialization seems to go against the express wishes of the programmer in the following line of code:

```
C(int x, int y): B(y), A(x) {}
```

None of this code is considered to be in error. On the contrary, the compiler simply does what it is required to do by the language, making the call A(x) *before* the call B(y). It is quite likely, however, that the programmer assumed that he would be enforcing the opposite order.

The hope is that the knowledgeable programmer will not make this mistake, since the rules of the language are quite explicit. But this is just another of those situations that develop when one uses a complex language with many interacting features. The two mechanisms of base class initialization and multiple inheritance are independent, but here a situation has arisen in which they interact. So a rule must be established to govern this interaction. Again and again we see the necessity for such rules in C++, so much so that this book cannot claim to cover all the fine points. Regarding the situation under discussion, we begin to see why most languages avoid multiple inheritance. But we have not yet seen all the reasons.

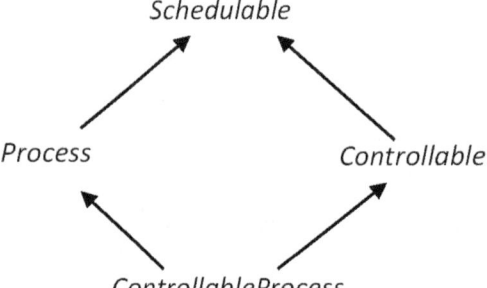

FIGURE 5.1 Four classes forming a diamond-shaped inheritance hierarchy

Simple-seeming decisions in language design, like the decision to permit multiple inheritance, often have complex consequences. Let us return to the ControllableProcess class, which had two base classes Process and Controllable. Suppose that the factory floor is modeled in such a way that all entities with active roles in the simulation are scheduled for execution from a master queue and must all descend from an ultimate base class called Schedulable. In this case, we have the inheritance diagram in Figure 5.1, where ControllableProcess now inherits *twice* from the indirect base class Schedulable. Suppose also that class `Schedulable` has an instance variable called `lastScheduled` which contains a time stamp of the last execution of the `cycle()` method of its containing instance. As indicated in Figure 5.1, the memory map for a `ControllableProcess` object will contain a copy of a `Process` object and a copy of a `Controllable` object, and the order of appearance in the memory map of these two objects will depend on the source code. The first two lines of the definition of `ControllableProcess` appear as follows:

```
class ControllableProcess: public Process,
                           public Controllable {
```

Thus, the memory map will store the `Process` object before the `Controllable` object. But if both those classes inherit from `Schedulable`, then each of those objects will incorporate its own copy of a `Schedulable` object, so that the memory map now appears as in the block diagram of Figure 5.2.

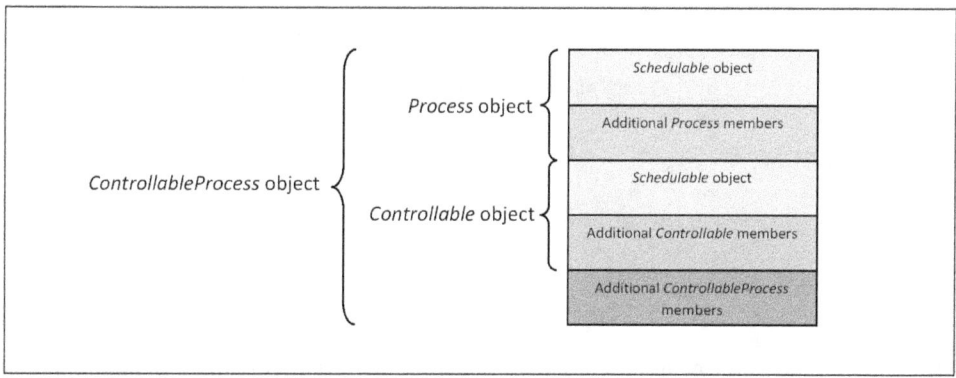

FIGURE 5.2 Storage map for a `ControllableProcess` object

One consequence of this arrangement is that every `ControllableProcess` object will have two copies of the data member `lastScheduled`. These two copies can be distinguished using class scope overrides, as `Process::lastScheduled` and `Controllable::lastScheduled`, but that is not the point. Whatever object is responsible for updating the `lastScheduled` data member will probably not know that there are two copies, because it will most likely only have access to the object through a `Schedulable` pointer or reference. Knowing the storage map, we can easily infer that the copy which is updated will be `Process::lastScheduled`, so programmers working deeper in the inheritance hierarchy will need to know to avoid referencing `Controllable::lastScheduled` in favor of the former. A helpful technique would be to insert the statement

```
using Process::lastScheduled;
```

inside the `ControllableProcess` definition, which once and for all disambiguates the identifier `lastScheduled`. Some programmers would, understandably, balk at having to know all these details in order to properly interpret the run-time interactions between objects. Yet that is, and must be, the C++ mindset.

If we grant that having two copies of a data member is a bad thing, then we must ask the question whether the language provides a reasonable way to avoid that occurrence. Given what we know about the C++ design philosophy that emphasizes putting as many options into the programmer's hands as is reasonably possible, our guess would be "yes," and that is indeed the correct answer. Let's suppose our objective is to have a storage map like that pictured in Figure 5.3, as opposed to Figure 5.2.

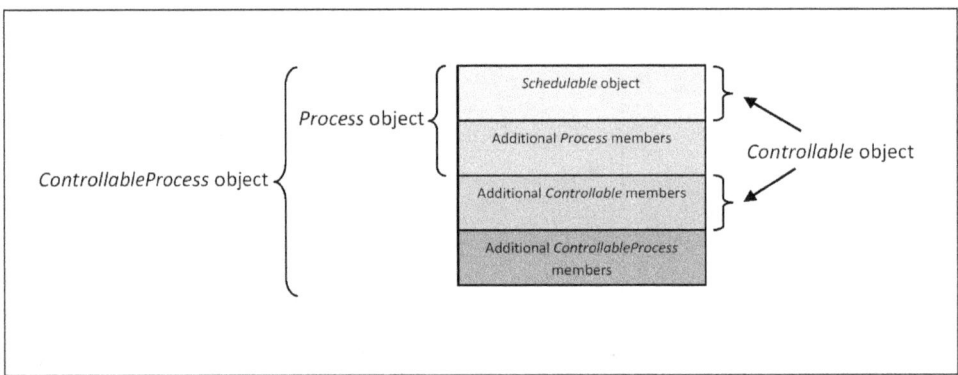

FIGURE 5.3 Alternative storage map for a `ControllableProcess` object

We can achieve this effect by using *virtual inheritance*. In this scheme, we must warn the compiler in advance that the storage for a `Controllable` object or a `Process` object might not be contiguous, using the notation below:

```
class Controllable: virtual public Schedulable { etc. etc. }

class Process: virtual public Schedulable { etc. etc. }
```

What does this do to the mechanisms for locating instance variables within an object? Normally, a reference to an instance variable in a class is resolved statically by the compiler, as an offset from the beginning of the instance's memory map. That scheme obviously does not work here. Instead, references to some data members in such classes may need to invoke run-time actions.

So the programmer is, yet again, forced with a design decision: retain the redundant copy of the base class and thereby retain the expected level of efficiency of references to data members, or get rid of the redundant copy and suffer some run-time overhead.

5.12   SLICING

When we combine, as C++ does, the mechanisms of call by value and value semantics, we are forced to routinely make copies of the values of objects which are transmitted as arguments to value parameters. (This is one area where Java actually seems to be more efficient than C++, because it *never* makes copies of large objects without being explicitly asked to do so using the `clone()` method.) The issue we wish to consider here is what happens when the receiving parameter is not of the same type as the passed argument, but rather is of a direct or indirect base class type for that argument. Because the parameter is treated as a local variable, and because the method or procedure is statically compiled with no knowledge of run-time events, there is no room for the storing of derived-class instance variables, nor is it safe to invoke derived-class behaviors, because those behaviors might try to gain access to nonexistent data members. So the compiler generates code to fashion a new value for the receiving parameter, a value having only the attributes of the base class. If the receiving parameter's class is a virtual base class, its virtual function pointer will point to the virtual function table for the base class (the class of the receiving parameter), not the derived class, making it impossible for the parameter object to respond to messages by attempting to invoke derived-class behaviors.

In the situation described above, we say that the passed argument has been *sliced,* or that the parameter has not received the entire object but only a base-class *slice* of the argument. This slicing occurs with method calls and procedure calls which have base-class parameters, but it will also occur when a `catch` block receives its argument by value. Slicing does *not* occur, however, when a pointer or reference is transmitted. If a pointer to a derived class object is transmitted, or if the object is transmitted by reference, then the object will still retain all its attributes and behaviors. Some of those attributes and/or behaviors may be inaccessible via the base class parameter, however, unless the programmer forces the issue using explicit casts.

Some curious things occur with `catch` parameters. If the `catch` parameter is a reference parameter, then of course there is no slicing. But suppose that the object whose reference was thrown was local to a stack frame which was "unwound" as a result of the throw. What storage is being referred to, because the environment in which the thrown object resided has been destroyed? Clearly, the exception-handling mechanism must make some unique arrangements, storing a copy of the thrown object either on the heap or on the catch block's stack frame, and transmitting a reference to the copy. But another odd consideration arises here, whether the catch parameter is a value parameter or a reference parameter. Let's suppose the object caught by the catch block is called by the parameter name e. If inside the catch block another throw occurs, passing that object backwards down the calling chain to an earlier catch block, then it may matter whether we do so using the statement

```
throw e;
```

or simply

```
throw;
```

If e is a reference parameter, then the two statements achieve the same result. However, if e is a value parameter, then throw e makes the slicing permanent, whereas throw is required by the language to throw exactly the object which was caught, and must therefore somehow "undo" the slicing. Again the programmer is presented with a subtle and powerful choice, and the compiler writer is left with a difficult implementation task.

5.13   DOWNCASTING, CROSSCASTING, AND RUN-TIME TYPE INFORMATION

The incorporation of run-time type information (RTTI) into C++ was a big departure from the C tradition. The notion that one should be able to ask an object what type it is at run-time never appears in C. Generally speaking, run-time type descriptors are not a common thing among compiled languages, Java being a notable exception. C++ does not normally give us that capability either, because there is no obvious place to keep the information and C++ programmers tend to resent overhead. However, if an object belongs to a class which is virtual, meaning that it or one of its base classes uses virtual inheritance or incorporates a virtual function, then run-time type information is incorporated into structures accessible via the virtual function table for the class.

The programmer takes advantage of the presence of RTTI when he uses `dynamic_cast` to *downcast* or *crosscast* a pointer. For example, suppose `B` is a class and `D` is a class derived from `B`, and suppose `p` is a pointer of type `B*`. Then the downcast expression `dynamic_cast<D*>(p)` can only be evaluated if (1) `B` is a virtual class, and (2) the object `p` is pointing to is of type `D` or a type descended from it. In uncharacteristic fashion, C++ uses a run-time check to verify that the cast is valid, a run-time check that would be impossible if the types involved did not incorporate RTTI.

The issue of crosscasting can only arise in languages permitting multiple inheritance. For an example of successful crosscasting in C++ we can use the hierarchy consisting of the classes `Schedulable`, `Process`, `Controllable`, and `ControllableProcess` described in Section 5.11. Suppose `p` is a pointer of type `Controllable*`. Then the cast `dynamic_cast<Process*>(p)` succeeds and returns a `Process*` pointer provided the object `p` is pointing to is actually a `ControllableProcess` object and therefore also a `Process` object.

In order to make a run-time decision based on RTTI, we can use the `typeid` operator. This operator is used in a manner similar to `sizeof`, but instead of returning a simple integer it returns an object of type `type_info`. If we apply the `typeid` operator to an object which is not of a polymorphic type, then it will be evaluated statically, but if we apply it to a polymorphic type it will perform run-time actions to access the type information available by following the virtual function pointer. The operators `==` and `!=` are overloaded for `type_info` objects, so that code like the following makes sense:

```
if (typeid(*p) == typeid(*q)) {
    // Perform these actions if the types of objects pointed
    // to by p and q are identical
    ...
}
else {
    // Perform these actions if *p and *q are different types
    // of object.
}
```

Here the programmer must make a software-engineering judgment; the explicit testing of types, as seen in the above code segment, is often poor style and can be unnecessary if polymorphism is available as an alternative mechanism. If there is a choice, polymorphism should always be chosen over the explicit accessing of type information.

5.14 MACROS AND FUNCTION TEMPLATES

A *macro* is a text-substitution pattern employed by the preprocessor, a pattern established by using a more complex form of the `#define` preprocessor command. The macro facility is a legacy capability from C, and its mechanisms are relatively primitive. As we have stated before, the preprocessor does not know C or C++, but understands only its own commands, and has as its mission the transformation of a source file and a collection of header files into a compilation unit. Macros make that transformation a little more sophisticated.

For example, suppose we wish to establish a pattern called `max` for the selection of the larger of two values. We could do so with the following preprocessor directive:

```
#define max(a,b) a>b?a:b
```

Because this definition is made on a level which is totally ignorant of C++ scope rules, we have now established a pattern which can be used *anywhere* in the compilation unit after the appearance of this directive (unless an `#undef` `max` statement or a redefinition of the preprocessor variable `max` is encountered). So in any subsequent line of code encountered by the preprocessor, the expression `max(32,y)` will be transformed, and will appear in the final compilation unit as `32>y?32:y`. This looks like a useful macro, but as presented above it does not account for C++ precedence and associativity rules. For example, the expression `max(r,s)+12` will be transformed into `r>s?r:s+12`, clearly not what was intended. All that is necessary to fix the problem is to use some extra parentheses, as follows:

```
#define max(x,y) ((x)>(y)?(x):(y))
```

Multi-line macros may be constructed by using the continuation character, a backslash, at the end of each line which is not complete. An example follows:

```
#define swap(type,x,y) { \
    type temp = x;        \
    x = y;                \
    y = temp;             \
}
```

The above discussion does not begin to explore the full power of macros, but we do not wish to explore any further in that direction because it would distract us from the goal of understanding the design and implementation of C++ proper. In fact, the macro substitution facility is both cryptic and dangerous, and should be avoided in most cases. Instead, the use of *function templates* is encouraged.

The power of the macro substitution facility comes from its generality. For example, if `sum1` and `sum2` are integer variables, then `swap(int, sum1, sum2)` will swap their values, whereas if `term` is a double-precision array and `i` and `j` are integer variables containing values which are valid subscripts in `term`, then `swap(double, term[i], term[j])` will swap its `i`th and `j`th values. But we can achieve the same generality with a programmer-defined *function template*, as follows:

```
template<class Type>
void swap(Type &x, Type &y) {
    Type temp = x;
    x = y;
    y = temp;
}
```

Now anywhere within the scope of this definition one can code `swap<int>(sum1, sum2)` or `swap<double>(term[i], term[j])` to achieve the results mentioned in the examples above. But more than that, since the template facility is implemented by the compiler and not the preprocessor, the types of the operands can be determined from the symbol table and the expressions above can actually be coded simply as `swap(sum1, sum2)` and `swap(term[i], term[j])`.

Note here the use of two levels of parameterization. The template itself is parameterized over `Type`, and once `Type` is bound to the necessary type then `x` and `y` can be bound to variables of that type. What exactly is being done in order to bind the type? When the compiler encounters the definition of a macro, it saves the definition in tokenized form in an internal buffer. If the name of the function is never referenced, the definition is never used and is discarded at the end of compilation. On the other hand, if a particular version of the `swap` function is referenced, then the compiler generates code for it as needed. That code may be generated in the conventional way, as a stored machine language subroutine, or it may be generated as an inline function definition, whichever the compiler deems necessary. The call `swap(sum1, sum2)` may be translated inline, because there is no explicit reference to the address in memory of a swap routine. On the other hand, the following code demands a separate compilation of the integer swap routine into an actual machine-language subprogram, because an address is demanded by the assignment:

```
void (*fp)(int &, int &);  // fp is a pointer to a function
    // which takes two integer parameters by reference and
    // returns void.
fp = swap<int>;  // Use the template to generate an integer
    // swap routine, then place the address of that routine
    // in the pointer variable fp.
```

The keyword `class` before a template parameter indicates the parameter is a type. That type does not have to be a class type, as indicated by the above examples, in which `int` and `double` were used to substitute for the parameter `Type`. Nontype parameters can be used, but some restrictions apply. For example, a nontype parameter cannot be a class or floating point type, and an argument supplied to it may not have an l-value. In fact, the value supplied to a nontype parameter must be a compile-time evaluable expression. For example, the following simple random number generator has a single integer template parameter which supplies its initial seed:

```
template < int seedStart >
int randm() {
    const int modulus = 1<<16, multiplier = 23477,
            term = 17712;
    static int seed = seedStart;
    seed = (seed * multiplier + term) % modulus;
    return seed;
}
```

The following code now gives us four "different" random number generators:

```
// Each of the following function pointers invokes a
// function which starts the random number sequence at a
// different initial seed value.
int (*ran0)() = randm<62002>;
int (*ran1)() = randm<23917>;
int (*ran2)() = randm<27225>;
int (*ran3)() = randm<42285>;
```

The C++ convention for calling functions on the ends of pointers is that the pointer is automatically dereferenced if used with the function call (postfix parentheses operator) syntax, so that the expression `ran2()`, for example, invokes the particular version of the random number generator for which the initial seed is 27225.

5.15 CLASS TEMPLATES AND MEMBER FUNCTION TEMPLATES

Generic file-scope procedures, or functions, can be described using function templates. Similar notations can be used to describe generic classes and generic methods, or member functions. For example, the following class template is for generating arrays of a fixed size, with optional subscript range checking via an `at()` member function:

```
template<class BaseType, int size = 100>
class Array {
    BaseType member[size];
public:
    class OutOfRangeException: public exception {};
    BaseType & operator [] (int i) { return member[i]; }
    BaseType & at(int i) {
        if (i < 0 || i > size) throw OutOfRangeException();
        return member[i];
    }
};
```

Notice the default value of 100 on the size of the array. Default values like this are only permitted for nontype parameters of class templates, and may not be used for function templates and method templates. The following client code demonstrates the flexibility of the `Array` template by instantiating objects `a`, `b`, and `c` of three different types. The types themselves (i.e., `Array<int,500>`, `Array<double>`, etc.) are called *template classes*, because they are classes formed from a template.

```
Array<int,500> a;  // An array of 500 integers.
Array<double> b;  // An array of 100 doubles.
Array<Array<int,10>, 10> c; // A 10 by 10 array of integers.
```

Unlike raw C++ arrays, the template classes used above will accept any numeric type as a subscript because the language routinely converts between numeric types at the argument-to-parameter interface. Thus, `a[34.56]` and `a.at(34.56)` are both valid and mean the same thing as `a[34]` and `a.at(34)`, respectively, because the conversion to an integral type from a floating point type requires that the fractional part be dropped. The following version of the class employs *member function templates* which round up if the subscript is of type `float` or `double` and the fractional part is 0.5 or greater.

```
template<class BaseType, int size = 100>
class Array {
    BaseType member[size];
public:
    class OutOfRangeException: public exception {};
     template<class NumericType>
    BaseType & operator [] (NumericType i) {
        int j = i;
        if (typeid(NumericType) == typeid(float) ||
            typeid(NumericType) == typeid(double))
            j = (int)(i+0.5);
          return member[j];
    }
     template<class NumericType>
    BaseType & at(NumericType i) {
        int j = i;
        if (typeid(NumericType) == typeid(float) ||
            typeid(NumericType) == typeid(double))
            j = (int)(i+0.5);
        if (j < 0 || j > size) throw OutOfRangeException();
        return member[j];
    }
};
```

With the new definition, the reference `a[34.56]` will be the same as `a[35]`.

Notice the use of an internal exception class. To take advantage of checked subscripting, we can use `try` and `catch` blocks like the following:

```
try {
    Array<double, 1000> x;
    int i;
    ... // Initialize i and the 1000 values of the array x.
    cout << "x[i] = " << x.at(i);  // Any call of the at()
        // method may throw an exception.
    ... // Further processing which may throw exceptions.
}
catch (Array<double,1000>::OutOfRangeException) {
    cout << "Subscript out of range" << endl;
}
catch(exception e) {
    cout << e.what() << endl;
}
catch(...)  {
    cout << "Exception of unspecified type occurred" << endl;
}
```

5.16   HASH TABLES IN C++

Hash tables are included in the C++ 11 standard, as class templates `unordered_set<>` and `unordered_map<>`. In their simplest form they make use by default of a class template called `hash<>`, the instantiations of which are function objects (see review question 28 in this chapter) that compute hash values based on casting to type `size_t`. All primitive types can be cast to `size_t`, and are therefore hashable, and many other library types, including `string`, are hashable. The following code segment illustrates the use of `unordered_map<>` to store hourly wages for a group of employees:

```
#include <unordered_map>
using std::unordered_map;
...
    unordered_map<string,double> payRate;
    payRate["Louise"] = 15.67;
    payRate["Ted"] = 12.89;
    payRate["Helen"] = 11.78;
    payRate["Marvin"] = 12.50;
    unordered_map<string,double>::iterator i;
    for (i=payRate.begin(); i!=payRate.end(); ++i)
            cout << i->first << " earns "
                << i->second << " an hour.\n";
```

Output from the program as compiled in Visual C++ is as follows:

```
Ted earns 12.89 an hour.
Louise earns 15.67 an hour.
Helen earns 11.78 an hour.
Marvin earns 12.5 an hour.
```

The simplest way to make a programmer-defined type hashable is to provide definitions for `operator ==` and `operator size_t`. An example follows, in which the class `Point` is given overloads for these two operators:

```
class Point {
public:
    int x, y;
    Point(int x=0, int y=0): x(x), y(y) {}
    bool operator == (const Point p) const {
        return x == p.x && y == p.y;
    }
```

```
    operator size_t() const {
        return (size_t)(x ^ y);
            // xor is the best operation for hashing
    }
};
```

Now the `Point` type is hashable. The succeeding code uses an `unordered_set<Point>` collection to collect all the points with integer coordinates within a specific radius of a particular point.

```
void findPointsWithinRadius(Point center, int radius,
                              unordered_set<Point> &points) {
    points.clear();
    int max = radius*radius;
    for (int x = center.x - radius;
         x <= center.x + radius; ++x) {
        int xDist = center.x - x;
        for (int y = center.y - radius;
             y <= center.y + radius; ++y) {
            int yDist = center.y - y;
            if (xDist*xDist + yDist*yDist <= max)
            points.insert(Point(x,y));
        }
    }
}
```

If the output streaming operator for type `Point` is defined as we defined it earlier, the following code outputs all the points with integer coordinates within a radius of two of the origin:

```
void outputPointsInDisk(Point center, int radius) {
    unordered_set<Point> points;
    findPointsWithinRadius(center,radius,points);
    bool first = true;
    for (unordered_set<Point>::iterator i = points.begin();
         i != points.end(); ++i) {
        if (!first) cout << ", ";
        first = false;
        cout << *i;
    }
    cout << endl;
}
```

```
int main() {
    outputPointsInDisk(Point(),2);
    return 0;
}
```

Output from Visual C++ is as follows. Note the characteristic randomness of the hash table storage order:

```
(1, -1), (-2, 0), (-1, 1), (0, -2), (1, 1), (-1, -1), (0, 0),
(-1, 0), (0, -1), (1, 0), (0, 1), (2, 0), (0, 2)
```

5.17 SUMMARY

The C++ language incorporates a number of concepts not encountered in Java nor in most other object-oriented languages, and one of the most controversial of these is the concept of addresses as data. An address stored as data is called a *pointer*, and although in C++ pointers must be tied to a base type, that base type can be `void`, so that pure address variables can be created, capable of referring to any location in or outside of the application's address space. Moreover, a `reinterpret_cast` can be used to make any pointer compatible with any other, an action which can totally defeat the type safety of the language. C++ allows *any* data or program object to be referred to by a pointer. *Reference* types are like pointers, with three important differences. First, a reference must be initialized when it is instantiated. Second, a reference may not be changed during its lifetime, meaning that it cannot be made to refer to a different memory location. Finally, reference variables are automatically dereferenced when they appear in expressions, whereas pointers must be eplicitly dereferenced with the prefix asterisk (*) operator or using pointer selection (->) notation.

A C++ expression is said to have an *l-value* if it has an associated address which can be extracted using the prefix ampersand (&) operator. Only an expression with an l-value may appear as the left-hand operand of an assignment operator. When a reference is used as a parameter, the corresponding argument must have an l-value, and the receiving routine gets access to that l-value and can therefore change the value assigned to the argument in the calling routine. This becomes a side effect, but a side effect that is at least partially implied in the function's interface by the parameter type. Notations and conventions are also employed for extending the concept of "address" to data members and member functions of a class.

C++ is a *multi-paradigm* language, supporting object-oriented programming, but also supporting procedural programming with file-scope procedures and variables. These file-scope entities have or can be granted global accessibility throughout a program. A consequence of the existence of file-scope run-time entities is that side effects can occur when a method or member function is called, due to the modification of file-scope variables. This type of side effect cannot be inferred from examining the function's interface. Procedural elements and object-oriented elements are often freely mixed together in the design of a C++ program.

Storage management in a C++ program tends to rely more heavily on the stack than the heap, because the language incorporates *value semantics*. The value of a file-scope variable or a static local variable, even a variable of class type, resides in static storage, and space for it is typically allocated at program load time. Any other variable declared locally denotes a value stored on the stack, a fact which contrasts to Java's behavior in which, for first-class objects, only a pointer is stored on the stack, while the object itself must always be constructed on the heap. Heap storage management in C++ must involve a pointer or reference variable, and provides the ability both to allocate and to deallocate objects on the heap. Considering the language's libertarian approach to pointer variables, the deallocation of an object with the `delete` operator can be dangerous if not done properly. More specifically, such deallocation may leave a pointer variable in a state where it is referring to storage that no longer belongs to the application, a situation often referred to as a *dangling pointer*, or *dangling reference*. The complementary problem of *garbage* may occur, in which there is space allocated from the heap to which there is no access path from the program. Although garbage is routinely created in Java, that language assumes that garbage collection is taking place, and indeed all Java virtual machines must incorporate a garbage collector. No such assumption is made in the C++ language. To help the programmer plan for the orderly creation and destruction of heap objects, C++ provides the capability to define a *destructor* for each class, a member function with distinctive syntax which typically has the responsibility of explicitly deleting any heap storage which may still be claimed by the object at the time it is destroyed.

The name of an array in C++ denotes the address of its first element, and for that reason an array name with no subscripts has no l-value. Such a name may, however, be used as an r-value for the purpose of storing that address in a pointer variable. After such a store, the pointer variable may be subscripted, and doing so yields an expression having precisely the same l-value and r-value as if the array name itself had been used. Adding an integer value `i` to a pointer having base type `Type` yields an expression with no l-value, whose r-value is that of the original pointer plus `i*sizeof(Type)`. Subtracting two pointers with base type `Type` makes sense if both are positioned within the same contiguously allocated collection of objects of that type, and yields the number `i`, provided the actual numerical difference between the two addresses is `i*sizeof(Type)`.

The native string type in C++ is a null-terminated character array. Library functions which manipulate it may be dangerous if used without caution. The `string` data type from the standard library is powerful, efficient, and safe, and is in most situations to be preferred.

Member functions of a class may be declared to be `const` functions, meaning that the only data members they change are those explicitly declared `mutable`. Such `const` functions represent the only messages which can legally be sent to a `const` object or a `const` parameter.

At the function call interface, arguments of a built-in type that are sent to value parameters are routinely coerced into the corresponding parameter type when that is a reasonable thing to do. This mechanism is extended in C++ to incorporate rules for using programmer-defined conversion operators and conversion constructors to perform these type changes. This approach to parameter passing combines with the capability to overload functions to produce a fairly complex situation when more than one method or file-scope function has the ability to respond to a given call. Rules for resolving a call in the presence of overloads are precise but fairly complex, and may result in an ambiguity which prevents correct compilation. When inheritance mixes with value semantics at the argument/parameter interface, the issue of *slicing* must be resolved. More specifically, when the argument is of a type derived from that of the parameter, and when that parameter is a value parameter, then the derived class portions of the argument must be removed and any polymorphic behavior resulting from the derivation must be prevented.

Most operators in C++ may be overloaded to provide programmer-defined meanings, but this mechanism cannot be used to redefine any meanings of operators when applied to built-in types. The *stream* I/O facilities in C++ use the highly overloaded operators `>>` and `<<`, and these operators are routinely overloaded by programmers to incorporate the streaming of objects of programmer-defined types to and from files or other I/O entities. Strings can be converted to and from a certain class of streams called *string streams*, and the latter are a commonly used tool for conversion of stored values to and from literals or other string representations.

The distribution of code between header files and source files presents a design issue, especially since there are few constraints. One important constraint, however, is that there be no statements included in header files which give a complete definition to any entities that will be visible to the linker, since doing so risks multiple definitions which will be rejected in the link step. Functions that are implemented *inline*, whether file-scope or member functions, are exempt because they do not have representations in the memory map of the program as separately compiled entities.

The designations `public`, `private`, and `protected` may be applied in several places. When used as labels in a class definition they specify access rights for client programmers, who are given unrestricted access only to public entities and have access to protected entities only from class scope in derived classes. However, *protected inheritance* makes members which were public in the base class protected in the derived class, so that client code which is not inside a derived class has no access to those. Finally, *private inheritance* completely hides the entire public interface of the base class from the client. Using protected or private inheritance prevents derived classes from behaving as subtypes.

Multiple inheritance allows one class to have more than one direct base class, and the decision to allow this mechanism gives an already complicated language another very interesting set of complicated issues, all of which are resolved in a pragmatic way that can result in oddities such as objects which are not stored contiguously. The mechanism which leads to noncontiguious storage allocation is called *virtual inheritance*.

Classes and structs which use virtual inheritance or contain virtual member functions will automatically incorporate *run-time type identification*, and can legitimately be involved in `dynamic_cast` operations. This allows for checked *downcasting* of pointers to polymorphic types, and for checked *crosscasting* when both polymorphism and multiple inheritance are involved.

C++ supports *generic programming*, in the form of function, class, and method *templates*. Templates are parameterized source code, similar to macros but more sophisticated and managed by the compiler rather than the preprocessor. Template *type parameters* may serve as stand-ins for any type, whether built-in or programmer-defined, and *non-type parameters* provide an effective way of introducing constants which help to define the configuration and behavior of objects and procedures created from templates.

Hash tables are a very recent addition (C++ '11) to the C++ language, and they are incorporated into C++ in a quite different way from that in which they are incorporated into Java. Since C++ containers store values, not references, the design allows for the instantiation of either an `unordered_set<>` or an `unordered_map<>` collection, where the key type can be any primitive type. Many library types can also be keys in a hash table, as can any programmer-defined type with the right behaviors. Specifically, any type which supplies an `operator ==` definition and an `operator size_t` definition qualifies as a key for a hash table.

REVIEW QUESTIONS

1. Describe the differences between the C++ and Java design philosophies.

2. Explain why the term l-value, or a term like it, is not found in most languages, given that its use is so prominent in C and C++ documentation.

3. Compare the Java component selection notation `a.x` with the C++ notations `a.x` and `p>x`. Which of the latter two notations more closely matches in its semantics the Java notation? Why?

4. Explain the concept of a "pointer to a member." How are the "dot-star" and "arrow-star" operators used, and how are the "address of" operator `&` and the class-scope override notations used, to store and manipulate pointers. Give examples.

5. What is the run-time representation of a pointer to an instance variable (data member) of an object? What is the run-time representation of a pointer to a member function (instance method)? Why are the two representations different?

6. How can pointers to members be used to construct an object-oriented version of the callback table for event handling?

7. In a certain sense, there is no difference in the meaning of the value returned by the `new` operator in Java and C++. The differences are in (a) where one places that value and (b) how it is used in succeeding expressions. Explain these differences.

8. Explain the meaning of the `delete` operator. Why is there no operation in Java which is equivalent to it?

9. Explain the meaning and functioning of class destructors in C++. What usually takes place when a destructor is executed? Why is there no equivalent in Java?

10. Explain why dangling pointers are such a common problem in C++, and explain why they are among the most catastrophic errors a programmer can commit. Describe what is meant by a corrupted heap.

11. Explain the meaning and usefulness of static local variables in C++.

12. Given that `p` and `q` are pointer variables and `i` is an `int` variable, explain carefully the meaning of (a) the expressions `p+i` and `p-i` and (b) the expression `p-q`. Are there situations in which any of these expressions would cause a compiler error? A run-time error? Explain.

13. Explain when the prefix `*` operator is valid when applied to the results to the expressions `p+i`, `pi`, and `p-q` mentioned in Exercise 12.

14. The C++ literal `"I am a string"`, because of backward compatibility with C and because of a continuing desire to keep the language efficient, is not a first-class object but instead has the primitive type `const char *`. It is, however, compatible in a very flexible way with variables of the library `string` data type. In fact, both lines of code below are valid and achieve the effect which is obviously desired.

    ```
    string s = "I am a string";
    s += ", but my type is primitive";
    ```

    What mechanisms make this code work? Give a detailed answer.

15. Explain carefully in your own words why the argument in a call to a "copy constructor" should always be passed by constant reference.

16. What does it mean when we declare a data member of a class to be `mutable`? Explain carefully.

17. Describe carefully the meaning of, and the actions performed in executing, the statement

    ```
    cin >> x >> y;
    ```

    where `x` and `y` are `int` variables. Describe in detail.

18. Describe how and why the expression `fin >> x`, where `x` is a variable and `fin` is a stream, can be used as a testable condition, and give the meaning of that condition.

19. In what way is a C++ stream like a string? What do we mean when we say we can treat strings as streams? Describe how a programmer-defined output operation, once defined properly, is made available for multiple purposes, including the conversion to string form.

20. Why are string streams useful for building GUIs?

21. A Java program has as its entry point a static method named `main()`, residing in the one public class which was initially loaded. Discuss the initial referencing environment for such a program, and compare it with the initial referencing environment of a C++ program.

22. At one time all libraries were procedural libraries, meaning that they were composed of file-scope functions. Discuss the advantages and disadvantages of procedural libraries, as opposed to class libraries. (Hints: (a) Consider the effects of a named and encapsulated "state." Would messages to an object encapsulating such a state need the same kinds of argument lists as calls to a file-scope procedure? (b) Consider the application area. Does a library for event-driven programming have the same kinds of needs as a library for numerical analysis?)

23. Summarize the C++ approach to inline translation. Which procedures (file-scope functions, member functions, and/or static member functions) can be implemented using inline translation? In each case, how is inline translation requested? Is the compiler bound to use the inline translation strategy when requested to do so?

24. Describe why programmer-defined operators can be a hindrance to readability. Are these problems specific to programmer-defined operators, or can poor usage of the function and method definition features in general cause these same problems? State your opinions on this issue. Suggest some program design guidelines for C++ programmers which may help to insure that the introduction of a programmer-defined operator does not hinder program readability.

25. We described two ways in which the + operator can be overloaded so that it is defined for coordinate-wise addition of two `Point` objects, namely (1) as a file-scope function, and (2) as an instance method of the `Point` class. A possible third way would be to define operator + as a static member function (class method) of class `Point`. Does C++ allow this? Give what you would consider to be the natural syntax for this third strategy, then try it with your favorite C++ compiler. Does the code compile? If so, give a sample program which uses the operator in that form. If not, speculate on why C++ might have excluded this possibility.

26. The following program appears at first glance to be the standard "Hello, world" program in C++.

    ```
    #include "iostream.h"
    int main() { cout << "Hello, world!\n"; }
    ```

    What is wrong with the program? In other words, why is it not the program it appears to be?

27. Describe how, by supplying a custom *iostream.h* file and by linking to other object files, this program can be made to do *anything* the programmer desires.

28. Research the C++ idea of "function objects," i.e., objects of a user-defined class type in which `operator ()` is redefined. In what way are they used? What potential do you see in their use?

29. From the client programmer's point of view, a numerical data type constructed using operators can look very much like a built-in data type. For example, a "rational" data type, a "complex" data type, or perhaps an indefinite-precision integer type, can be constructed and given a full set of operators. What are the limitations on this viewpoint? Are there any? In other words, what "hints" inform the client that the data type is not native, but library-supplied?

30. Comment on the issue of derived classes which are not subtypes. How can this be done in C++? Can it be done in any other languages you know? If so, how?

31. The initialization order of multiple direct base classes is another example of what we have called a *syntactic discontinuity*, i.e., a case where a slight change in the syntax of a working program produces a program almost identical in appearance but radically different in meaning. Construct an example and explain the code change and the resulting change in meaning.

32. Suppose you are leading a team of programmers in a design effort using the C++ language. What limitations would you put on the use of multiple inheritance so that your programmers could use it yet avoid the ambiguities and syntactic discontinuities, as well as the inefficiencies, that we have discussed? If you are a Java programmer, use your acquaintance with that language to guide your responses.

33. Explain the concept of slicing. Does slicing occur with reference parameters? With pointer parameters? Describe the situations in which slicing occurs.

34. Suppose a catch block has parameter `e`. When does the effect of the statement `throw e` differ from that of `throw`, when issued from within the catch block? Explain.

35. Explain why explicit testing of types is considered by some to be a poor software engineering practice. Give an example where polymorphism would be a better mechanism on which to rely.

36. Explain the difference between macros and templates. Which is safer, and why?

EXERCISES

1. Assuming `x` and `y` are `int` variables, `p` is a pointer variable, and `a` is an `int` array, which of the following C++ expressions do, and which do not, have l-values?

   (a) `x`
   (b) `a[0]`
   (c) `*&x`
   (d) `&a[0]`
   (e) `a+1`
   (f) `*(a+1)`
   (g) `x+y`
   (h) `*p`
   (i) `&*p`

2. Translate each of the following declarations into its English-language description. For example, the declaration

   ```
   int *x;
   ```

   translates as "x is a pointer to an integer."

   (a) `int a[10];`
   (b) `float &y = z;`
   (c) `void (*p)(int []);`
   (d) `char *p[20];`
   (e) `const float *f(int);`
   (f) `const int * const p;`
   (g) `char (*p)[];`
   (h) `int (*g)(float, float);`
   (i) `int f(void *());`

3. Consider the following Java code snippet, creating a "ragged array."

   ```
   float b[][] = new float[2][];
   b[0] = new float[3];   // First row has three elements
   b[1] = new float[5];   // Second row has five elements
   ```

   How would you write an equivalent code sequence using C++ heap allocation, so that the notation `b[i][j]` (for allowable values of `i` and `j`) has a similar meaning.

4. In the above example, Java needs no explicit deallocation but relies on garbage collection. However, C++ needs explicit deallocation. Write the C++ deallocation code.

5. The code below is valid, but could yield two different results in two different implementations of C or C++, or it could execute differently using different compiler settings. Why do you think this is the case? Give a detailed answer.

```
const char *s = "I am a string";
const char *t = "I am a string";
if (s == t) cout << "Same"; else cout << "Different";
```

6. In C++, we could code a "square" routine for an `int` variable so that it could be called either as `x = square(x)` or simply as `square(x)`. In Java, only one of these alternatives is feasible. Which is it, and why? Code both C++ routines.

7. Code the squaring routine above so that it can be called as `square(&x)`.

8. Describe the differences between the following member function declarations:

```
void f(MyClass &x) const;
void f(const MyClass &x);
void f(const MyClass &x) const;
const MyClass * f();
```

9. Consider the C++ code below, which will not compile:

```
#include <iostream>
using std::cout;
using std::endl;

class C2;

class C1 {
    int x;
public:
    C1(int x = 0): x(x) {}
    C1(const C2 &c);
    int f(C1 c) const { return c.x * x + x/c.x; }
    operator int() const { return x; }
};

class C2 {
    int x;
```

```
public:
    C2(int x = 0): x(x) {}
    operator int() const { return x; }
    operator C1() { return C1(2*x); }
};

C1::C1(const C2 &c) {
    x = (int)c/2;
}

int main() {
    C1 c1(4);
    C2 c2(6);
    cout << c1.f(c2) << endl;
    return 0;
}
```

(a) Why will the code not compile? Be specific.

(b) Identify two member functions for which the removal of either would allow the code to compile.

(c) Identify the number output in each case for part (b).

10. Consider the following class, which has three overloads of static member function *f*.

```
class C {
public:
    /* (a) */ static void f(int, int, double);
    /* (b) */ static void f(double, int, int);
    /* (c) */ static void f(int, double, int);
};
```

Will the call `C::f(5,1.7,4)` compile? If not, why not? If so, which member function will be called?

11. In the previous question, will the call `C::f(5,1.7,4.0)` compile? If not, why not? If so, which member function will be called?

12. Write a purely procedural C++ program for playing a simple game. Keep it simple; the purpose is to acquaint yourself with the procedural style, not to write a comprehensive application.

13. Write a C++ console program which reads a text file called *textin.txt* and echoes to the console the first "word" on each line. Each word is to be echoed on a line by itself, and if a line of input is empty then a blank line is to be echoed. A word is defined as a string of non-whitespace charac-

ters flanked on the right and left either by whitespace, by the beginning of a line, or by the end of a line. You may assume that every line of text is a complete line, i.e., is followed by the end-of-line character or character sequence.

14. In C++, we can redefine the assignment operator (`operator =`) for a given class type to mean whatever we wish. Such redefinitions must be instance methods of that particular class. Give a definition for a `Point` assignment operator, being careful to keep all the expected properties of that operator.

15. The `set<>` and `map<>` class templates from the C++ standard libraries use `operator <` to guide the way in which they insert, find, and delete items. The documentation clearly states that `operator <` must define a *total order* on the values of a type. This means that any two values x and y of that type which are different from each other must relate to each other so that either $x < y$ or $y < x$. Find two different ways of defining `operator <` on the `Point` class, one that defines a total order and one that does not. Experiment with using the type `set<Point>` or `map<Point>` in both cases. Report your findings.

16. Define a class `IntArray` implementing a dynamic array of integers, which has only a default constructor and allocates additional space as needed. The destructor should free all space allocated during the lifetime of the object. The instance method `size()` should be provided, returning the current size of the array. The instance methods `operator []` and `operator =` should be defined, and the return value from both of these should be a *reference*, in the first case to the specific integer being accessed, and in the second to the object receiving the message. A reference to a nonexistent element should cause enough additional space to be allocated so that the reference is valid. All locations not explicitly assigned a value should have the value zero. Assignment should cause the construction of a complete, separate copy of the value of the right-hand side, so that after the following code is executed the values of `a`, `b`, and `c` should be identical and no aliases should be created:

```
IntArray a, b, c;
a[5] = 77;
a[7] = 99;   // a's content is now the sequence
             // 0, 0, 0, 0, 0, 77, 0, 99.
c = b = a;   // a's, b's, and c's contents are the same.
```

17. Define `operator == ` and operators `<`, `>`, `<=`, `>=`, and `!=` for the class `IntArray` in the previous exercise. For the ordering operations, use lexicographic order with the first key being the one with subscript zero (i.e., `a < b` if `a[0] < b[0]`, and if `a[0]` is equal to `b[0]` we apply the same principle recursively to subscripts 1 and following). If the two operands are of different lengths, extend (logically) the shorter operand with zeros in the higher-order positions. Two arrays should be considered equal if and only if they have exactly the same elements up to and including the last non-zero element, so that trailing zeros are ignored. Do not exclude the possibility of negative entries. For example, (8, -7, 0) should be considered less than (8).

18. Consider the following code. What should be output when an object of type `C` is instantiated, assuming `cout` has been made accessible in the usual way?

```cpp
class A {
public:
    A() {cout << "A";}
};

class B {
public:
    B() {cout << "B";}
};

class C: public A, public B {
public:
    C(): B(), A() {cout << "C\n";}
};
```

19. Consider the following code, in which `A` is an indirect base class of `D` in two different ways:

```cpp
class A {
public:
    A(char c='D') {cout << c << "'s A ";}
};

class B: public A {
public:
    B(): A('B') {cout << "B ";}
};

class C: public A {
public:
```

```
        C(): A('C') {cout << "C ";}
    };

    class D: public B, C {
    public:
        D() { cout << "D\n";}
    };
```

(a) What is output as a side effect of instantiating a D object? Explain how the output occurs.

(b) Now make each of B and C use virtual inheritance from A. What is output now? Explain.

20. Write a C++ function template which takes an array as an operand and "adds" all its members, returning the sum.

21. Write a C++ class template for a rational type; in other words, write a class template for a type with a "whole number" numerator and denominator, which incorporates operators for addition, subtraction, multiplication, and division, as well as getNumerator() and getDenominator() access functions. Write your template so that it works with any integral data type. (Hint—keep the denominator positive. If the rational is negative, give it a negative numerator.)

22. The C++ standard requires that an implementation furnish a way to "separately compile" a template. What difficulties do you see for the compiler-writer in implementing this capability?

REFERENCES

[Sammet81] Sammet, Jean E. "The Early History of COBOL". In *History of Programming Languages.*, ed. Richard L. Wexelblat. Prentice-Hall, 1981.

CHAPTER 6

VISUAL STUDIO AND THE MICROSOFT FOUNDATION CLASSES

Microsoft Visual Studio® is similar to other integrated development environments (IDEs). Its facilities for the support of C++ programming include a source editor, a compiler (and preprocessor), a linker, and a debugger, all integrated into one windowed application, along with tools for organizing projects involving multiple source files. This text will not attempt to provide a detailed description of how to use it, but will make reference to various capabilities of the IDE as they are needed. We will begin with a brief discussion of Windows messages, followed by an overview of the Microsoft Foundation Classes® (MFC) and the single document interface (SDI). SDI is a style of application supported by Visual Studio and is the only style of native Win32 application we discuss in this text.

NOTE

Another option for C++ developers on the Microsoft Windows® platform is the .NET ("dot-net") library, also fully supported by Visual Studio. The .NET framework is covered by this text, but in the context of the C# language (see Chapter 8, "C# and the Common Language Infrastructure"). It is possible to use both MFC and the .NET features for C++ in the same program, but the two worlds culturally tend to be quite separate. The programmer should realize that there are many similar features included in the standard library, MFC, and .NET, and that sometimes the features available in one of those libraries incorporate design choices that are alien to the other libraries. For example, .NET manages heap space automatically, so the classes are so-called "managed classes," whereas space for MFC and standard library classes is not managed in the same sense.

6.1 WIN32 MESSAGES AND THE MESSAGE LOOP

All Win32 event-driven programs have essentially the same main program, which follows a very simple algorithm similar to the following:

```
Allocate resources and perform other initializations
Executing = true
While Executing do:
    While there are no messages on the message queue do:
        Perform idle processing
    Remove a message from the message queue
    If the message is to terminate the application then
        Executing = false
    Else call an event handler to respond to the message
End while
Free resources and perform other termination duties
```

The message queue for a process is maintained using operating system support. The message type is identified with a small integer type code, the specific values of which are assigned preprocessor names in header file *winuser.h*. For example, the message sent to repaint a window has message code 15, but that code is referred to in windows programs as WM_PAINT.

C programs respond to events using a callback function, identified by a pointer stored in a callback table. The message type is used to select the specific function. This raw mechanism is hidden by the Visual Studio code generators for MFC programs, which use macros and method naming conventions to make the correspondence between events and their handlers more natural, and to make the process of setting up an event handler less repetitive.

Code samples for this chapter are located on the companion CD-ROM.

6.2 THE MFC LIBRARY AND THE DOCUMENT/VIEW ARCHITECTURE

The application programming interface (API) for Microsoft's Win32 series of operating systems is not object-oriented, but is in fact a collection of thousands of C-language functions. Nevertheless, there is a distinct object-oriented influence seen in its design. Many of the API calls do in fact create "objects," which outlive the function invocation that created them. These objects have an internal state that varies over time in response to other API calls. Once an object has been created, it can be identified by an operating-system-maintained "handle." Other API calls that wish to inspect or change the internal state of the object can do so by supplying the handle as one of the parameters of the call. A typical "lifetime" of such a Win32 object proceeds as follows:

1. The object is "instantiated" with a call on a particular "create" function, such as `CreateWindow()`. That call returns a handle which is the operating system's identification for the object.

2. The object is manipulated via a series of API calls which reference the object's handle.

3. The object is "destroyed" using a targeted function such as `DestroyWindow()`. This call releases the resources claimed by the object.

4. The handle is returned to the OS for reuse using the `CloseHandle()` function call.

The MFC library tries to capitalize on the presence of these rudimentary Win32 "objects," by partitioning a large portion of the Win32 API functionality into classes, some of which encapsulate Win32 handles. The MFC classes are sometimes called "wrapper classes," because they provide an explicit object-oriented programming interface to an already-existing set of operating system-defined objects. Indeed, MFC is remarkable in its restraint, concentrating on repackaging existing functionality instead of attempting to impose any design paradigms of its own.

NOTE *The original name for MFC was "Application Framework eXtensions," abbreviated AFX. The initial concept for AFX was more ambitious than the current MFC design, and imposed a more elaborate windowing paradigm. Ultimately the direction changed, as the design team realized too much run-time overhead was being generated.*

> *The C++ community, they realized, is steeped in the cultural tradition of C, which values run-time efficiency and would not strongly support a complex run-time environment. Many features of MFC do, however, date back to that earlier design, and still retain the AFX prefix.*

Visual Studio provides resources for, and can generate skeleton code for, a number of application types. We are primarily interested in presenting MFC's facilities for event handling, so we will concentrate on one particular application style called the single document interface (SDI). SDI is the simpler form of the document/view architecture which is supported by Visual Studio, and is a variant of the Smalltalk MVC, or model/view/controller, pattern. In the SDI, there are four required classes: an application class, a frame window class, a document class, and a view class. These classes could be constructed by hand, but the process of maintaining hand-constructed MFC code is laborious, repetitive, and unnecessary. The act of creating a new "MFC application" project will cause the IDE to invoke a wizard to generate skeleton code, and it will cause wizards for adding and deleting event handlers to become accessible. The reader is well-advised to use those wizards. To hand code an MFC project from scratch is to commit to a painstaking and error-prone editing regimen which must be conducted every time a new event handler is added. The most compelling argument for avoiding wizards is that wizard code and programmer-supplied code become hopelessly intermingled, and we shall meticulously avoid this trap.

All MFC class names, whether names of library classes or names of wizard-generated classes, begin with the letter C. The base classes for the four wizard-generated SDI classes are `CWinApp`, `CDocument`, `CFrameWnd`, and `CView`. Except for the frame window class, which is always named `CMainFrame`, the classes the wizard derives from these base classes will be named in such a way as to incorporate the project name. For example, for a project named `Hello`, the four classes are `CHelloApp`, `CHelloDoc`, `CMainFrame`, and `CHelloView`. Let us enumerate the responsibilities of these four classes.

The application class is where execution begins. Recall that C++ is a mixed-paradigm language, and procedural elements mix freely with object-oriented elements in a typical C++ program. A Win32 program is no different, and in fact the "main program" for every MFC application is a file-scope procedure defined by the library. Why then do we say that execution begins in the application class? Because exactly one application object must be instantiated at file scope in one of the source files of the project (the application source file), and since it is a static object its constructor will be called before the main program begins execution. This constructor will probably do nothing more than pass control back to the base class constructor `CWinApp()`, which performs a long list of necessary initializations of data members in the application class. We will make no modifications to the wizard-generated application class in the projects we create in this text.

The frame window class encapsulates, among other things, a handle for the single operating system-defined (top-level) frame window which is created in the application class's `InitInstance()` method. The frame window is supplied with a menu which can be edited, and to which event handlers can be attached. The drawing of the frame window is only partially under the programmer's control, as the border, title bar, status bar, and menu representations must conform to a particular "look and feel." We will not modify the frame window code, and when we attach event handlers to menu items, we will take pains to insure that those handlers do not reside in the frame window class.

The document class is the "model class," or business class. Conceptually, the document class for an SDI project should be a "singleton" class, in the sense that it should be designed under the assumption that exactly one object of the class will be instantiated with each run of the program. We will make modifications to the wizard-generated document class only if our application makes changes to persistent data, because it is in the document class that the functionality for saving objects to a file, and restoring objects from a file, resides.

The view class is where we will be doing most of our work. In the classic MVC pattern, this is where we would craft some textual or graphical representation of the internal state of the document object for external viewing purposes. The view class constructs its display in the "client area," i.e., the interior portion of the window, the portion typically appearing in a skeleton application as a white rectangle forming the interior portion of the window. The client area is framed by the border, title bar, menu, and status bar, all of which are maintained by the frame window class. For most of our example projects, we will be inserting all our business logic and display logic, as well as all our event handlers, into the view class. We will do so very carefully, however, in order to keep our hand-constructed code separate from the wizard-generated code as much as possible.

Objects of the `CView` class and the `CFrameWnd` class are all "windows," and these two classes derive from a common window class called `CWnd`. Much of the functionality of window objects resides in `CWnd`. For example, the `CWnd::GetClientRect()` function is used to determine the extent of the client area. It requires one pointer parameter, of type `CRect *`. Thus, inside the scope of any window class we can use the following code snippet.

```
CRect R;
GetClientRect(&R);
```

The result of the call will be to place in `R.left`, `R.right`, `R.top`, and `R.bottom` the pixel coordinates that define the extent of the client area. Default behavior of these windows is to use relative pixel coordinates, so that usually `R.left` and `R.top` are set to zero.

6.3 USING THE CODE GENERATORS TO DEVELOP AN MFC APPLICATION

C++ makes it fairly easy to maintain the integrity of hand-written code in an MFC application, using a combination of include files (header files), separate compilation, multiple inheritance, polymorphism, and cross-casting. To illustrate the technique, we will show how to generate a very simple application, one that simply draws a circle of radius 100 pixels in the upper left-hand corner of the client area of a window. Nearly all of our own code is contained in the following hand-constructed header file, but in fact the `#include` statement at the top pulls in thousands of lines of library code, most of which are not needed and will not be compiled into any kind of run-time representation.

File *HCCircle100.h*:

```
#include "stdafx.h"

class HCCircle100 {
public:
    void onDraw(CDC *pDC) {
        pDC->Ellipse(0,0,200,200);
    }
};
```

Throughout this chapter, we will consistently name classes and files that have been constructed by hand for an MFC project beginning with the prefix HC, for "hand-coded." For event handlers we will use a naming convention whereby the hand-coded routine is identical in name to the wizard-generated routine except that the first character of the name is lower-case. (Hence we use `onDraw()` instead of `OnDraw()`.) The programmer who is aware of these conventions can determine how to reconstruct the wizard code needed to support the hand-coded files just by inspecting the contents of those files. The programmer finishes the coordination by inserting the proper hooks into the wizard code to bring into play his hand-coded routines.

To begin constructing the application, the programmer adds a new project. In Visual Studio 2010, this can be done with the menu choices *File...Add...New Project*. The project type should be selected first as *C++*, then as *MFC*. Another pane in the resulting dialog box should now allow the programmer to choose the installed template *MFC Application*. An edit box should also be present which allows the programmer to enter the name of the application, which we will enter as *Circle100*.

At this point, clicking on the OK button brings up the MFC application wizard. If the wizard's defaults are taken now, the resulting application will be a multiple document interface (MDI) application, which is over-engineered for our purposes. Instead, we click on *Application Type* and select *Single document* and *MFC Standard*. To simplify the appearance of the window, we also click on *User Interface Features* and select *Use a Classic Menu*. Clicking on the *Finish* button completes the wizard and generates the skeleton code. We will use this same procedure to generate all the MFC projects we construct in this text.

There should be a tabbed pane to one side of the edit pane in the Visual Studio window, which has a *Solution Explorer* tab, and that tab should be on top at this point in time. Within this solution explorer window, there should be the names of a large collection of files which have been generated by the wizard. Together, these files constitute the source code for the four SDI classes, as well as some scripting code which defines certain resources needed by the project. (For example, one resource generated by the above project is a menu with default content, to be added to the frame window.)

Two of the files in the Solution Explorer contain the code for the view class, which we desire to modify in order to incorporate our snippet of code above. These files are named *Circle100View.h* and *Circle100View.cpp*. Before we modify these files, however, we need to add the *HCCircle100* class above to the project by including header file *HCCircle100.h*. This can be done by right-clicking on *Header files* under the *Circle100* project "subdirectory" and selecting *Add... New Item...* from the resulting pop-up window. The type *Header File* should be selected, and the name *HCCircle100.h* should be typed into the *Name:* edit box, and the *Add* button pressed. This will place the empty header file in the appropriate directory and open an edit window. The programmer then enters the above source code and saves the result.

Incorporating the code in the header file into the application's view class is now accomplished by doing three things. First, the generated view class's header file should be modified to include the hand-coded header file. Second, in that same header file the generated class (*CCircle100View* in the example) should be modified so that it inherits not only from *CView*, but also from *HC-Circle100*. Third, the source file for the view class (*Circle100View.cpp* in the example) should be modified so that the function `CCircle100View::OnDraw()` calls the corresponding `onDraw()` function in the hand-coded class. In order to do this, the programmer must remove the comment brackets around the `pDC` parameter name in `OnDraw()` and insert the call `onDraw(pDC);` at the very end of the function.

To reiterate, let us look at the "before and after" appearance of the source code. First let us look at the header file *Circle100View.h*. Before the change, the first line of the `CCircle100View` class definition looks as follows:

```
class CCircle100View : public CView
```

This line of code should be replaced by the following lines:

```
#include "HCCircle100.h"
class CCircle100View : public CView, public HCCircle100
```

Also, before the editing changes the appearance of the `OnDraw()` member function in the file *Circle100View.cpp* was as follows:

```
void CCircle100View::OnDraw(CDC* /*pDC*/ )
{
    CCircle100Doc* pDoc = GetDocument();
    ASSERT_VALID(pDoc);
    if (!pDoc)
        return;
    // TODO: add draw code for native data here
}
```

After the change we have the following:

```
void CCircle100View::OnDraw(CDC* pDC)
{
    CCircle100Doc* pDoc = GetDocument();
    ASSERT_VALID(pDoc);
```

```
    if (!pDoc)
        return;
    // TODO: add draw code for native data here
    onDraw(pDC);
}
```

With these changes the project compiles, and performs as expected.

6.4 DEVICE CONTEXTS, GRAPHICS, AND MAINTAINING THE VIEW WINDOW

The OnDraw() member function of a generated view class is not, strictly speaking, an event handler, but it is called from one. The event that causes it to be invoked is the paint event, called WM_PAINT in the Win32 header files, a name which gets translated by the preprocessor into an integer code which will be used at run-time to identify the message type. The CView method that handles this event is called OnPaint(), and it responds by constructing a device context object and passing a pointer to it to the OnDraw() routine. The latter routine is virtual, so the call causes either the wizard-generated view class's routine of that name, or an override in a derived class if one exists, to be invoked.

The WM_PAINT event is generated whenever a window needs to be redrawn. This happens when the window is minimized then restored, when it is resized, and when it is "invalidated" synchronously by application-specific actions. The OnDraw() method in the view class is typically designed to redraw the entire window from scratch using the device context object pointed to by its one parameter. It should not be called from client code, but rather should be indirectly invoked by raising the WM_PAINT event. The client which has a pointer pWnd to the view object can indirectly cause the event to be raised by invalidating the window with the call

```
    pWnd->Invalidate();
```

which sets a flag in the corresponding operating system-defined window; this lets the operating system know to raise a WM_PAINT event for the window. But before we talk any more about events and how to cause and react to them, let us investigate the device context class and see what its objects are capable of doing for us.

The base device context class is CDC, and its two derived classes are CPaintDC and CClientDC. Typically, we use the former if responding to a paint event and the latter if we are drawing only a portion of the client area. The important functionality resides in the base class, however, which encapsulates a large assortment of tools for drawing. Among other things, the device context keeps pointers to a pen object (type `CPen`) for drawing lines, a brush object (type `CBrush`) for filling regions, and a bitmap object (type `CBitmap`). Any of these pointers can be changed using the overloaded `SelectObject` methods. Most of the drawing primitives make no reference to color, because for most purposes the colors used will be determined by the pen and the brush. The default pen is black, and the default brush is white.

An important MFC data type we will be making use of in our examples is the class `CPoint`, with components `x` and `y`, which are non-negative integers designating a pixel location (x, y). If we let `p1` and `p2` be `CPoint` objects, `pDC` a pointer to a `CDC` object (type `CDC *`), and `x1`, `y1`, `x2`, and `y2` non-negative integers used as pixel coordinate values, we can get a good feel for how device contexts are used by studying the following calls, which illustrate some of the basic graphics primitives.

```
// Draw a line from (x1, y1) to (x2, y2)
pDC->MoveTo(x1,y1);  // Or pDC->MoveTo(p1);
pDC->LineTo(x2,y2);  //    pDC->LineTo(p2);
                     // to draw a line from p1 to p2.

// Draw a rectangle with one corner at (x1, y1) and the
// diagonally opposite corner at (x2, y2).
pDC->Rectangle(x1,y1,x2,y2);

// Draw an ellipse inscribed in that same rectangle.
pDC->Ellipse(x1,y1,x2,y2);

// Draw a triangle with vertices at (30, 50), (80, 100),
// and (300,100).
CPoint points[] = {CPoint(30,50),CPoint(80,100),
                   CPoint(300,100)};
pDC->Polygon(points,3);

// Display the message 'Hello, World!' on the screen,
// inside a bounding rectangle with upper left-hand corner
// at (x1, y1) and size determined by the current font.
pDC->TextOut(x1, y1, _T("Hello, World!"));
```

The `_T()` macro used in the last example makes our code more portable, because it is defined in the header file *tchar.h* in such a way as to modify the type of the character string literal if the Unicode character set is being used. Using this macro consistently makes it possible to switch from ASCII to Unicode and back by changing a compiler setting.

6.5   COLORS, PENS, AND BRUSHES

A color in the Windows API is an unsigned long integer. A `typedef` declaration in *WinDef.h* establishes the identifier `COLORREF` as a synonym for `DWORD`, which is in turn currently defined in the same file to be `unsigned long`. The most convenient way to build a `COLORREF` value is with the `RGB()` macro, defined in *WinGDI.h* with three operands, each of which should be in the range 0 to 255. As expected, `RGB(0,0,0)` is black and `RGB(255,255,255)` is white. The first parameter is the red level, the second the green level, and the third is the blue level. The three values are packed into the low-order 24 bits of the 32-bit integer. (The high-order eight bits hold a transparency level, which we will ignore.)

When lines are drawn, either with `CDC::LineTo()` or as the boundary of a geometric figure, they are drawn with a pen. The default pen is a black pen which draws a solid line, one pixel wide. Other types of pens can be created with the `CPen()` constructor, which takes three parameters. The first parameter is a pen style: zero is solid, and is given the preprocessor name `PS_SOLID` in header file *WinGDI.h*. Values greater than zero yield different "dashed" styles, and have preprocessor names like `PS_DASH`, `PS_DOT`, and `PS_DASH_DOT`. (But when the pen width is more than one pixel, all lines are drawn as `PS_SOLID`.) The second parameter is the width in pixels, and the third is a `COLORREF` parameter giving the color of the pen strokes. Thus, the following code instantiates a pen able to write green lines three pixels thick:

```
CPen thickGreenPen(PS_SOLID,3,RGB(0,255,0));
```

When geometric figures are drawn, say with `CDC::Rectangle()`, `CDC::Ellipse()`, or `CDC::Polygon()`, they are automatically filled using the device context's current brush tool, of type `CBrush`. The default brush is a white brush, but again the constructor allows us to build brushes of different colors. For example,

```
CBrush yellowBrush(RGB(255,255,0));
```

constructs a yellow brush.

The brush and pen which are created along with the device context, its default brush and pen, must always be restored to it. We can temporarily switch it to another brush or pen of our own making, but when we have done our drawing we must give back to the device context the brush and/or pen it had originally. The CDC methods we use to change these tools are both named SelectObject(). Each receives a *pointer* to the new pen or brush, and returns to the caller as its value a pointer to the tool of that type which it had been using before the call. It is up to the caller to save this pointer in a variable and use it to restore the old pen or brush at the right time. A typical scenario is played out in the code below, where dc is a device context object:

```
CBrush *oldBrush = dc.SelectObject(&yellowBrush);
// Now do the necessary drawing, in which all regions will
// be filled with yellow.
...
dc.SelectObject(oldBrush);   // Restore the old brush.
```

Similar protocol needs to be followed in order to draw with a different pen.

6.6   USING THE VISUAL STUDIO "PROPERTIES" WINDOW

The central activity in MFC programming, as it is in any event-driven environment, is the establishment of events and the writing of handlers for those events. That process is greatly enhanced in the Visual Studio IDE by the provision of wizards for the construction of event handlers; those wizards are invoked from the properties window.

We will illustrate the use of the properties window by writing a small application, involving the drawing of ellipses in response to mouse events. This example illustrates the "click and drag" technique—the drawing of an ellipse begins with the WM_LBUTTONDOWN event, is updated using the WM_MOUSEMOVE event, and ends with the WM_LBUTTONUP event. Drivers for those events are named in a standard fashion, as we shall see. In segments below, we give the entire source code, in file *HCEllipses.h*, for the hand-coded class. The recommendation is that this hand-coded file be constructed before any wizard code is generated. After we generate the wizard files, we will incorporate our own code into the wizard's view class using the same technique discussed above, but we will add event handlers to that class which use our own methods.

The file begins with the inclusion of the *stdafx.h* header file, as always. No using statements are needed for the named entities in that header file, because none of the types we will use from that include are hidden inside namespaces. Because we will be keeping track of the ellipses in the window using a list, we also include the `list` header file, and the corresponding `using` statement. Because each ellipse is to be characterized by a pair of `CPoint` objects, we include the `map` header file and establish `pair` as a name to be used without qualification.

```cpp
#include "stdafx.h"
#include <list>
using std::list;
#include <map>
using std::pair;
```

The private portion of the hand-coded class is given below. We begin by using a `typedef` to define the `PointPair` type as a pair of `CPoint` objects, then we define `pointPairs` to be a list of such pairs. The boolean variable `dragging` is intended to be true from the occurrence of a `WM_LBUTTONDOWN` event until the occurrence of a corresponding `WM_LBUTTONUP` event. While `dragging` is true, object `currentPointPair` is dynamically changing in response to occurrences of `WM_MOUSEMOVE`. The two utility routines `drawEllipse()` and `eraseEllipse()` will be called multiple times as the ellipse defined by `currentPointPair` changes. That ellipse is always drawn using a dashed line for the perimeter, so during that process the default argument of `PS_SOLID` for the third parameter of `drawEllipse()` will be overridden with the value `PS_DASH`.

```cpp
class HCEllipses {
private:
    typedef pair<CPoint,CPoint> PointPair;
    list<PointPair> pointPairs;
    PointPair currentPointPair;
    void drawEllipse(CDC *pDC, PointPair p, COLORREF color = 0,
                     int style = PS_SOLID) {
        CPen pen(style,1,color);
        CPen *oldPen = pDC->SelectObject(&pen);
        pDC->Ellipse(p.first.x, p.first.y, p.second.x,
                     p.second.y);
        pDC->SelectObject(oldPen);
    }
    void eraseEllipse(CDC *pDC, PointPair p) {
        drawEllipse(pDC,p,RGB(255,255,255));
    }
    bool dragging;
```

The remainder of the class definition is given below. The constructor does nothing but set `dragging` to `false`, so that the user must push the left mouse button to initiate the drawing of an ellipse. The `onDraw()` routine, which we will cause to be called whenever a `WM_PAINT` event occurs, uses an iterator to sequence through the pairs in `pointPairs` and draw all the ellipses which have been generated by past user actions. The `onLButtonDown()` method, which we will cause to be called whenever `WM_LBUTTONDOWN` occurs, sets `dragging` to `true` and alters the value of `currentPointPair` so that both points are identical to the point indicated by the mouse cursor at the time of the event. This begins the drawing of an ellipse. The `onMouseMove()` function is to be called whenever `WM_MOUSEMOVE` occurs, and does nothing unless `dragging` is set to `true`. When that is the case, it acts by first erasing the ellipse defined by `currentPointPair`, then moving `currentPointPair.second` to the place currently indicated by the mouse cursor, then drawing the new ellipse with a dashed border. Finally, `onLButtonUp()` makes a final adjustment to the value of `currentPointPair.second`, adds the value of `currentPointPair` to the list `pointPairs`, and redraws all the ellipses in the list from scratch by sending the message `Invalidate()` to the view window. Importantly, `dragging` is then set to `false` so that the dashed ellipse the user is seeing becomes a solid ellipse and the drawing process ceases.

```
public:
    HCEllipses(): dragging(false){}
    void onDraw(CDC *pDC) {
        for (list<PointPair>::iterator i = pointPairs.begin();
            i != pointPairs.end(); ++i)
            drawEllipse(pDC,*i);
    }
    void onLButtonDown(CPoint p) {
        dragging = true;
        currentPointPair.first = currentPointPair.second = p;
    }
    void onMouseMove(CPoint p, CWnd *pWnd) {
        if (dragging) {
            CClientDC dc(pWnd);
            eraseEllipse(&dc, currentPointPair);
            currentPointPair.second = p;
            drawEllipse(&dc, currentPointPair, 0, PS_DASH);
        }
    }
    void onLButtonUp(CPoint p, CWnd *pWnd) {
        if (dragging) {
```

```
                currentPointPair.second = p;
                pointPairs.push_back(currentPointPair);
                pWnd->Invalidate();
                dragging = false;
            }
        }
    };
```

With the code above residing in file *HCEllipses.h*, we can generate a new MFC project called *Ellipses* using the procedure established in Section 6.3. This requires the following steps:

1 Create a new MFC project:
   a. Make it a single document project.
   b. Click on *User Interface Features* and select *Use a Classic Menu*.
   c. Name the project *Ellipses*.
2. Insert hooks into *EllipsesView.h*:
   a. #**include** HCEllipses.h
   b. **class** CEllipses: **public** CView, **public** HCEllipses

We could also hook into the OnDraw() function manually, as described in 6.3, but here we wish to put the emphasis on the event handler wizards. In order to do this, we need to bring up the *Properties* window (*not* the *Property Manager* window) for the wizard-generated view class. In the main menu select *View... Other Windows...Properties Window*. This will bring up a properties window, but when it first comes up it may be displaying the properties from some other class. Your *EllipsesView.h* file should be on top in your edit window. Place the mouse cursor on the line indicated by 2b above, i.e., the first line of the class definition, and left-click. The pane in Figure 6.1 should appear in the properties window. However, it is the three icons indicated in the figure that are of most interest to us.

Each of these is a hot button, and pressing one of them changes the appearance of the properties window. Each also allows the user to invoke wizards to generate code to either respond to an event or to override a virtual function in the base CView or CWnd classes. The lightning bolt is for library- or programmer-defined events, the middle icon is for Microsoft Windows operating system events, and the green box is for overrides of existing methods.

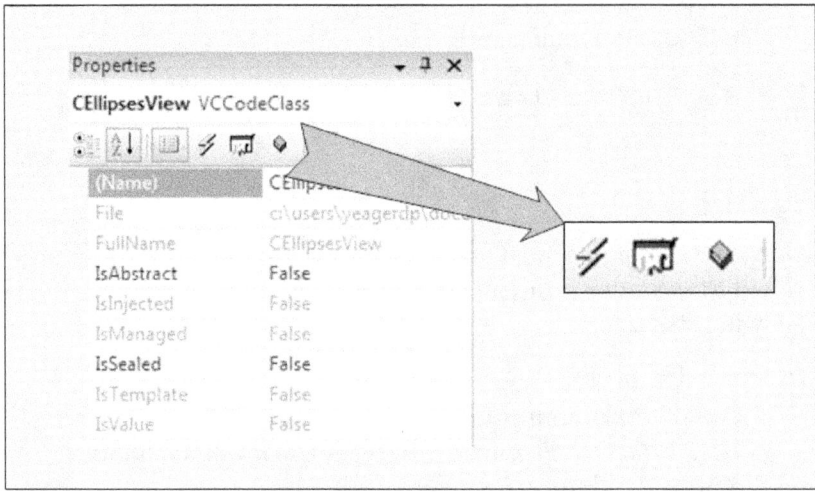

FIGURE 6.1 The Properties window for class `CEllipsesView` with relevant code-generation icons indicated

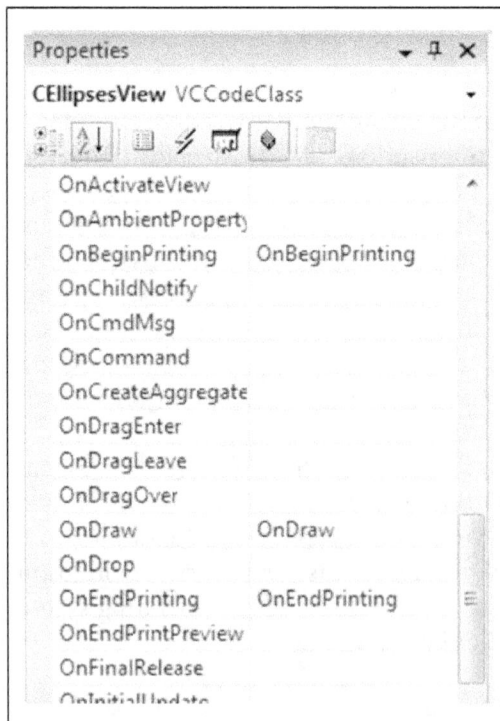

FIGURE 6.2 The Properties window showing overrides

Let us begin with an override, by clicking on the green box icon. The properties window changes, revealing two columns of virtual function names, as seen in Figure 6.2. The left-hand column consists of functions defined in one of the base classes. Most of the right-hand entries are blank, indicating that the wizard has provided no overrides for those functions. The `OnDraw` entry in particular, however, does have an override in the wizard-generated code. Clicking on that line of the table activates a drop-down list, which can be used to bring up two choices. The first choice is to delete the wizard's override, not a good idea. The second choice is the one we will make, to edit the override. Clicking here does not generate code, but does bring up the implementation code for the wizard's view class, offering us a chance to insert our own code. This just brings us to where we were in Section 6.3, and as before we un-comment the parameter name `pDC` and insert `onDraw(pDC);` as the last line of the routine.

At this time, we discover that the properties window changes as we negotiate edit windows. Specifically, at any given time, it attempts to show us the properties of the class or method currently being displayed in the edit window. In our case, the properties window is now showing us the properties of the `CEllipsesView::OnDraw()` method. We wish to get back to the properties of the `CEllipsesView` class. There are two quick ways to do this. We could (a) select the *EllipsesView.h* tab at the top of the IDE's edit pane, or we could simply (b) press Ctrl-Tab to return to the last file we were editing.

Once back to the `CEllipsesView` properties window, we can click on the *Messages* icon to bring up all the Windows messages the wizard code either does or can respond to. In fact, the view class is not at this time reacting to any messages, so the right-hand column is completely blank. We scroll down to `WM_LBUTTONDOWN`, click there, drop down the list, and select *<Add> OnLButton-Down*. The wizard then does the following three things:

1. Generates the prototype

   ```
   afx_msg void OnLButtonDown(UINT nFlags, CPoint point);
   ```

   inside the class definition in *EllipsesView.h*.
2. Generates the macro call

   ```
   ON_WM_LBUTTONDOWN()
   ```

   inside the message map (defined using macros) in file *EllipsesView.cpp*.
3. Generates skeleton code for the `OnLButtonDown()` member function in *EllipsesView.cpp*.

The message map is essentially a callback table using "pointers to members." Its actual structure, however, is completely obscured by the heavy use of macros, and viewing this table constructed with macros gives the uninitiated reader the confusing (and false) impression that non-C++ code has been inserted into a C++ source file. We will not "look under the hood" here, but just note that the table contains an entry for every event that this particular object will respond to. At this time, our main concern is that the code we designed gets executed at the right time. Accordingly, we insert the line of code

```
onLButtonDown(point);
```

as the last line of the function `CEllipsesView::OnLButtonDown()`. Because `CEllipsesView` inherits from our class `HCEllipses`, this causes our code to be invoked every time `WM_LBUTTONDOWN` occurs.

Similar actions are required to establish event handlers for `WM_MOUSEMOVE` and `WM_LBUTTONUP`. Those functions require an extra `CWnd *` parameter, however, so our added lines of code in those two cases are

```
onMouseMove(point,this);
```

And

```
onLButtonUp(point,this);
```

respectively. After these event handlers have been established, the project should perform as described.

6.7 TIMERS AND ANIMATIONS

In this section, we will start from scratch with a new application which generates random moving circles, using a timer to achieve animation. We will develop an inheritance hierarchy of circle types, starting with the following class definition, stored in file *circle.h*.

```
#ifndef __CIRCLE_H
#define __CIRCLE_H

#include "stdafx.h"
#include <cmath>
```

```
    class Circle {
    public:
        friend bool touching(const Circle &c1, const Circle &c2);
        // Two circles are touching if the distance from one's
        // center to that of the other is less than or equal to
        // the sum of their radii.
        Circle(double radius=1, double centerX = 0, double centerY
= 0)
            :radius(radius), centerX(centerX), centerY(centerY) {
            if (radius < 1) this->radius = 1;
        }
        // Some access functions.
        double getArea() const { return pi*radius*radius; }
        double getRadius() const { return radius; }
        double getX() const { return centerX; }
        double getY() const { return centerY; }
        Circle operator + (Circle c) {
            double sumAreas = getArea() + c.getArea();
            double newRadius = sqrt(sumAreas/pi);
            double newCenterX =
                (centerX*getArea()+c.centerX*c.getArea())/sumAreas;
            double newCenterY =
                (centerY*getArea()+c.centerY*c.getArea())/sumAreas;
            return Circle(newRadius, newCenterX, newCenterY);
        }
        void randomizeRadius(int radiusLowerLimit,
                             int radiusUpperLimit) {
            radius = rand()
                    % (radiusUpperLimit - radiusLowerLimit + 1)
                    + radiusLowerLimit;
        }
        void randomizeCenter(int xLower, int xUpper,
                             int yLower, int yUpper) {
            centerX = rand() % (xUpper - xLower + 1) + xLower;
            centerY = rand() % (yUpper - yLower + 1) + yLower;
        }
        virtual void draw(CDC &dc);  // Draw the circle.
        virtual void erase(CDC &dc); // Erase the circle.
        static const double pi;
    protected:
        double radius;
        double centerX, centerY;
    };

    #endif
```

The above `Circle` data type seems simple and straightforward, except for the addition operation, which is meant to mimic in two dimensions what happens when three-dimensional bubbles collide. The sum of two circles will only be computed when those circles are "touching," as defined by the Boolean friend function `touching()`, and will be a larger circle with an area equal to the combined areas of the two operand circles. The center of the circle representing this 'sum' is positioned on the line segment joining the centers of the original two circles, and its coordinates are a weighted average of the coordinates of the two circles, where the area of a circle is its weight. Thus two colliding circles will appear to "jump" together, the smaller of the two jumping the most.

The implementation file *circle.cpp* appears as follows:

```
#include "stdafx.h"   // Need this to use precompiled headers.
#include "circle.h"

bool touching(const Circle &c1, const Circle &c2) {
    double distance = sqrt(
        pow(c1.centerX - c2.centerX, 2) +
        pow(c1.centerY - c2.centerY, 2)
    );
    return distance <= c1.radius + c2.radius;
}

void Circle::draw(CDC &dc) {
    dc.Ellipse(
        int(centerX-radius+0.5), int(centerY-radius+0.5),
        int(centerX+radius+0.5), int(centerY+radius+0.5));
}

void Circle::erase(CDC &dc) {
    CPen whitePen(0,1,RGB(255,255,255));
    CPen * oldPenPtr = dc.SelectObject(&whitePen);
    draw(dc);
    dc.SelectObject(oldPenPtr);
}

const double Circle::pi = 4*atan(1.0);
```

The circle class as constructed incorporates no movement and no color. To make the program more interesting, before we construct our MFC project we wish to define a derived class called `MovingCircle`. The new class adds some animation attributes, namely `deltaX`, `deltaY`, and `framesPerSecond`, and some color attributes, namely `redlevel`, `greenlevel`, and `bluelevel`. Its definition is given in the file *MovingCircle.h*, reproduced below:

```
#ifndef __MOVINGCIRCLE_H
#define __MOVINGCIRCLE_H

#include "Circle.h"

class MovingCircle: public Circle {
public:
    enum { MAXFRAMESPERSECOND = 100 };
    MovingCircle(double radius=1, double centerX = 0,
                 double centerY = 0, double deltaX = 1,
                 double deltaY = 1, int framesPerSecond = 20)
        :Circle(radius, centerX, centerY), deltaX(deltaX),
         deltaY(deltaY), framesPerSecond(framesPerSecond) {}
    MovingCircle operator + (const MovingCircle &mc) {
        MovingCircle result;
        (Circle &) result = (Circle&)(*this) + mc;
        double sumAreas = getArea() + mc.getArea();
        result.deltaX =
            (deltaX*getArea()+mc.deltaX*mc.getArea())
                / sumAreas;
        result.deltaY =
            (deltaY*getArea()+mc.deltaY*mc.getArea())
                / sumAreas;
        result.redlevel =
            int((redlevel*getArea()+mc.redlevel*mc.getArea())
                / sumAreas + 0.5);
        result.greenlevel =
            int((greenlevel*getArea()+
                mc.greenlevel*mc.getArea())/sumAreas + 0.5);
        result.bluelevel =
            int((bluelevel*getArea()+
                mc.bluelevel*mc.getArea())/sumAreas + 0.5);
        return result;
    }
    // Access functions.
    double getDeltaX() const { return deltaX; }
    double getDeltaY() const { return deltaY; }
    void putFramesPerSecond(int count) {
        if (count <= 0) count = 1;
        if (count > MAXFRAMESPERSECOND)
            count = MAXFRAMESPERSECOND;
        framesPerSecond = count;
```

```
        }
    MovingCircle operator++() {
        // Pre-increment.  Take the circle through one time
        // unit of its life.
        centerX += deltaX/framesPerSecond;
        centerY += deltaY/framesPerSecond;
        return *this;
    }
    void randomizeDirection(int maxDelta) {
        deltaX = rand()%(2*maxDelta+1) - maxDelta;
        deltaY = rand()%(2*maxDelta+1) - maxDelta;
    }
    void randomizeColor() {
        redlevel = rand()%256;
        greenlevel = rand()%256;
        bluelevel = rand()%256;
    }
    void draw(CDC &dc) {
        CBrush brush(RGB(redlevel,greenlevel,bluelevel));
        CBrush * oldBrush = dc.SelectObject(&brush);
        Circle::draw(dc);
        dc.SelectObject(oldBrush);
    }
private:
    double deltaX, deltaY;  // Number of pixels traversed
                            // in one second
    int redlevel, greenlevel, bluelevel;
    int framesPerSecond;
};

#endif
```

Notice in particular the `operator+` function, which begins with the two lines

```
    MovingCircle result;
    (Circle &) result = (Circle&)(*this) + mc;
```

Here we see the calling of the base class `Circle::operator+()` function to perform the addition for the base class portions of the object, accomplished by casting `*this` to type `Circle&` to obtain the left-hand operand. Another cast is needed on the left-hand side of the assignment operator to store the resulting value in the base class portions of the `MovingCircle` object `result`.

The remainder of `operator+` is constructed much as it was in the base class, using area as a weight for weighted averages. The speed in the x direction is affected more by the larger of the two circles than by the smaller, and the same is true for the speed in the y direction. Color must be separately mixed to have the desired realistic effect, so that weighted averages are taken independently for red, green, and blue.

The `operator++` method is supplied for the purpose of moving the circle to where it should appear in the next frame, where frames are coming at the rate given by the data member `framesPerSecond`.

The `draw()` function creates a brush from the `redlevel`, `greenlevel`, and `bluelevel` data members, gives the device context the address of the newly created brush, calls the base class `draw()` routine, then gives the old brush back to the device context. Some access functions and randomization functions complete the class.

The hand-coded class to be grafted into our MFC project's wizard code must do several things. It must maintain a list of `MovingCircle` objects, it must establish a regular schedule of `WM_TIMER` events to respond to, and it must respond to each timer event as follows:

1. It must cause the circles to move the appropriate amount by calling `operator++` for each circle.

2. It must check for circles which are "touching." Whenever it finds two that are touching, it should combine the two using `operator+`, remove one of the two from the list, and replace the other with the sum. It should continue doing this until no two circles are touching.

3. It must invalidate the window, causing it to be repainted from scratch with a call to `onDraw()`.

Let us examine the file *HCMovingCircles.h* in installments. The first installment contains the preprocessor guards and includes, as well, the private data members.

```
#ifndef __HCMOVINGCIRCLES_H
#define __HCMOVINGCIRCLES_H

#include "stdafx.h"
#include "MovingCircle.h"
#include <ctime>

#include <list>
using std::list;

class HCMovingCircles {
    list<MovingCircle> circles;
```

```
enum {FRAMETIMER = 555, FRAMESPERSECOND = 30, COUNT = 40,
      MINRADIUS = 10, MAXRADIUS = 30, MAXSPEED = 50};
CWnd *pWnd;
```

The central data structure is again a list, this time a list called `circles` consisting of `MovingCircle` objects. It will start out with `COUNT` objects, and will diminish in size as circles collide and merge. All of the other constants' meanings are self-evident, except for one. The constant `FRAMETIMER` is given the value 555, but not because that number has any inherent meaning. In fact, the choice of 555 is quite arbitrary; this number is simply a run-time identifier for the timer event we will be responding to, and our response each time that event occurs will be to perform the three actions listed above. The windows message identifier `WM_TIMER` would be enough by itself if each application had need of no more than one timer, but it is easy to see that such a restriction would be unreasonable. For example, we could add a `REGENERATETIMER` and give it another value, say 556. In response to that timer, we might want to destroy all the current circles and generate a new population.

We now must deal with the issue of a two-stage window creation. The constructor is called to initialize the view object incident to its creation, as usual. However, the actual `CWnd` window object will not be constructed until after the object of our hand-coded class type has already been constructed. So if we wish to keep a pointer to the window, we must wait until later to initialize that pointer. Also, if we wish to issue commands to that window we must wait until it is ready to respond. Hence, we must put off some of our initialization until the wizard-generated `OnInitialUpdate()` override has been called. In our case, we choose to do ALL our initialization in our own `onInitialUpdate()`, which we will call from the corresponding method in the wizard view class.

```
public:
    void onInitialUpdate(CWnd *pWnd) {
        HCMovingCircles::pWnd = pWnd;
        CRect R;
        pWnd->GetClientRect(&R);
        srand(int(time(0)));
        for (int i=0; i<COUNT; ++i) {
            MovingCircle c;
            c.randomizeRadius(MINRADIUS,MAXRADIUS);
            c.randomizeCenter(R.left,R.right,R.top,R.bottom);
            c.randomizeDirection(MAXSPEED);
            c.randomizeColor();
```

```
            c.putFramesPerSecond(FRAMESPERSECOND);
            circles.push_back(c);
        }
        pWnd->SetTimer(FRAMETIMER,1000/FRAMESPERSECOND,0);
    }
```

The initialization consists of saving the pointer to the window to a class-scope variable, asking that window for the limits of the client rectangle, setting a random number seed to the time of day, generating the list of randomized circles, and initializing the timer. Note that two key initializations, namely identifying the client rectangle and initializating the timer, depend on an already instantiated and fully functional view window. These kinds of initializations should always be done incident to a call on the virtual function `CView::OnInitialUpdate()`. The timer initialization on the next-to-last line supplies three parameters: the event identifier, the timer interval in milliseconds, and the address of a callback function, which we have coded 0. In the absence of the callback function address, the view object will call its `OnTimer()` function in response to the `WM_TIMER` event, and that function will in turn call the function we supply below:

```
void onTimer() {
    for (list<MovingCircle>::iterator i=circles.begin();
        i!=circles.end(); ++i)
        ++*i;
    bool changes = true;
    while (changes) {
        changes = false;
        list<MovingCircle>::iterator iCircleToErase;
        for (list<MovingCircle>::iterator i=circles.begin();
            !changes && i!=circles.end(); ++i)
            for (list<MovingCircle>::iterator j = i;
                !changes && ++j != circles.end(); ) {
                if (touching(*i, *j)) {
                    *i = *i + *j;
                    iCircleToErase = j;
                    changes = true;
                }
            }
        if (changes) circles.erase(iCircleToErase);
    }
    pWnd->Invalidate();
}
```

As discussed above, the code proceeds by iterating through the list of circles and incrementing each, then entering a `while` loop which iterates through the list multiple times looking for touching circles and combining them. It ends with an `Invalidate()` call to the window. The `while` loop must be carefully constructed, because a list should not be changed while there are active iterators inside it. Therefore the `erase()` function is actually called outside the nested loop in which iterators `i` and `j` are active. The nested loop is reentered again and again by the outer loop until there are no more changes.

The `WM_DESTROY` message is sent when the view window is destroyed. We respond by killing the timer. The `onDestroy()` method below accomplishes that task, and finally the `onDraw()` routine iterates through the list of circles asking each to draw itself:

```
    void onDestroy() {
        pWnd->KillTimer(FRAMETIMER);
    }
    void onDraw(CDC *pDC) {
        for (list<MovingCircle>::iterator i=circles.begin();
            i!=circles.end(); ++i) i->draw(*pDC);
    }
};
```

#endif

The combining of the above hand-coded class with wizard code is done in a manner similar to the previous example. The event handler and override modifications to the wizard code are summarized below. Don't forget to include *HCMovingCircle.h* at the top of the view class header file and have that class doubly inherit from `CView` and `HCMovingCircle`. Again, work from the properties window of the wizard-generated view class.

1. Choose the `OnInitialUpdate` override, add the wizard version of that routine to the view class, and add the call `onInitialUpdate(this)` at the end of it.

2. Choose the `OnDraw` override, then edit the code by un-commenting `pDC` and adding `onDraw(pDC)` at the end.

3. Choose the `WM_TIMER` windows message, add event handler `OnTimer()`, then add the call `onTimer()` at the place indicated by the comment.

4. Choose the `WM_DESTROY` windows message, add event handler `OnDestroy()`, then add the call `onDestroy()` at the end.

Something that happens for free with this project is that the *file…new* menu choice will cause more moving circles to be added to the list. This is because the application object's `OnFileNew()` member function, the default event handler for the menu choice, will always call `OnInitalUpdate()` for all its views. This is interesting, but since the circles tend to move away to infinity, it might be better to also have *file...new* move through the list and delete all circles which are completely outside the client rectangle before calling `onInititialUpdate()`. We can do this by (a) adding an `onFileNew()` method to our hand-coded class, and (b) placing an event handler for *file...new* in our view class. Our new method should be coded as follows:

```
void onFileNew() {
  CRect R;
  pWnd->GetClientRect(&R);
    bool changes = true;
    while (changes) {
        changes = false;
        list<MovingCircle>::iterator iCircleToErase;
        for (list<MovingCircle>::iterator i=circles.begin();
            !changes && i!=circles.end(); ++i)
            int leftCircleEdge = i->getX() - i->getRadius(),
                rightCircleEdge = i->getX() + i->getRadius(),
                topCircleEdge = i->getY() - i->getRadius(),
                bottomCircleEdge = i->getY() + i->getRadius();
        if (R.left > rightCircleEdge ||
            R.right < leftCircleEdge ||
            R.top > bottomCircleEdge ||
            R.bottom < topCircleEdge) {
            iCircleToErase = i;
            changes = true;
        }
    }
        if (changes) circles.erase(iCircleToErase);
    }
}
```

Now we add the handler for the menu choice by using the "lightning bolt" button of the properties window for the view class, which then lists IDs of programmer-defined events. This menu event corresponds to the identifier ID_FILE_NEW. Clicking on the + sign beside this identifier drops down a list with two choices, each of which corresponds to a macro for establishing event handlers. We choose COMMAND, then on the right in the blank area we choose *<Add> OnFileNew*. This generates an ON_COMMAND() macro call in our message map, adds the appropriate prototype to the view class's header file, then adds the handler for the event to the view class source file. The handler is empty until we add our own code, consisting of the two calls to our own routines.

```
void CMovingCirclesView::OnFileNew()
{
    // TODO: Add your command handler code here
    onFileNew();
    onInitialUpdate(this);
}
```

By adding this handler, we have usurped the application class's responsibility and made the view class responsible for reacting to the menu choice.

6.8   A PERSISTENT AND TRAVERSABLE AVM GAME CLASS

Our technique of tying all our code to the view class served the purpose of getting us into MFC projects quickly. However, in order to use the single document interface in the way it was intended to be used, we need to involve the document class. To be consistent with the techniques we have developed, we will do this by writing both a hand-coded view class and a hand-coded document class. The document class, however, is like the "model" in the Smalltalk MVC pattern, meaning it is a "strictly business" class and need not have any knowledge of MFC whatsoever. It does not need, then, to define any event handlers and will not need to conform to our naming patterns. It need only provide enough access to its internal state in its public interface to allow a view class to represent that state in the client rectangle.

The example we will work through in this context is based on the AVMGame class found in Section 5.10. We will use the same basic structure, but we must design a game class whose state between method calls is more incremental. Recall that each AVMGame is at its core a Category, which is a self-referencing data structure. Specifically, one of the data members of Category is a list of objects, each of which is also of type Category. In fact, the game data structure is a tree, specifically a tree of (name, question) pairs. In the console version of the project, we employed a single converseWithUser() method to traverse the tree and discover the object of which the user was thinking. We need now to break that traversal down into a series of methods which allow the conversation with the user to be displayed as a series of snapshots of the game's internal state. Thus, we must traverse the category tree one step at a time, saving our place as we go.

To help keep track of our location in the tree, we will store in each `Category` object an integer attribute called `childNumber`, so that we do not need to know the identity of the parent to know where we are in the sequence of children.

The reason we need to store a sequence number is tied up in the fact that we are going to have to settle on an external representation of our game data. That representation is illustrated in the following data file:

```
1 "Animal" "Is it an animal?"
1.1 "Dog" "Is it a dog?"
1.1.1 "Poodle" "Is it a poodle?"
1.1.2 "Collie" "Does it have long hair and look like Lassie?"
1.2 "Cat" "Is it a cat?"
1.2.1 "Long-haired Cat" "Is it a long-haired cat?"
1.2.1.1 "Persian" "Is it a Persian?"
1.2.2 "Short-haired Cat" "Is it a short-haired cat?"
1.2.2.1 "Siamese" "Is it Siamese?"
2 "Vegetable" "Is it a vegetable?"
2.1 "Cabbage" "Is it a cabbage?"
2.2 "Green bean" "Is it a green bean?"
2.2.1 "Half Runner" "Does it have stringy pods?"
2.2.2 "Kentucky Wonder" "Are the pods wide and fleshy?"
3 "Mineral" "Is it a mineral?"
3.1 "Coal" "Is it black and dirty and does it burn?"
3.2 "Plastic" "Is it plastic?"
3.3 "Iron" "Is it made of iron?"
3.4 "Man-made Object" "Is it a man-made object?"
3.4.1 "Automobile" "Is it an automobile?"
```

One may argue about the ability of the tree indicated here to correctly identify all of the objects incorporated into it, but the structure of the tree is fairly self-evident. A root-to-leaf traversal is indicated by appending a new sequence number with every 'yes' answer to the user's questions. Thus, an identification of a Siamese cat would traverse the tree in the following order:

```
1 "Animal" "Is it an animal?"
1.2 "Cat" "Is it a cat?"
1.2.2 "Short-haired Cat" "Is it a short-haired cat?"
1.2.2.1 "Siamese" "Is it Siamese?"
```

The user should never see the tree coordinates. They are there to allow the tree to be precisely reconstructed from a text file representation.

We will begin our project by constructing a new header file for the "animal, vegetable, mineral" game, in which we make some changes to class `Category` and introduce a new game class called `TraversableAVMGame`. The changes center on (a) building in more fine-grained state information and (b) saving and restoring the game using streams. The first segment of the header file begins with the preprocessor guards and ends with the new definition of `Category`.

```
#ifndef __TRAVERSABLEAVMGAME_H
#define __TRAVERSABLEAVMGAME_H

#include "stdafx.h"

#include <string>
using std::string;
#include <list>
using std::list;
#include <iostream>
using std::ostream;
using std::istream;

struct Category {
    Category(string name="", string yesOrNoQuestion="",
        int childNumber = 0): name(name),
        yesOrNoQuestion(yesOrNoQuestion),
        childNumber(childNumber){
    }
    string name;
    string yesOrNoQuestion;
    int childNumber;
    list<Category> subcategories;
    void writeTo(ostream &out, list<int> prefix);
    bool install(list<int> coordinates, Category category);
};
```

Besides adding the `childNumber` attribute, we have removed the old `getNewSubcategoryFromUser()` function and added two new member functions `writeTo()` and `install()`. Although their names are dissimilar, these latter two functions provide complementary services, the first for output operations and the second for input. Both are recursive utility functions which associate the `Category` object with a set of coordinates derived from a `list<int>` parameter and the `childNumber` attribute, and both are called from class scope in the derived class `TraversableAVMGame`, whose definition ends the header file *TraversableAVMGame.h*. We will begin that definition now by listing the class header and its private members.

```
class TraversableAVMGame: protected Category {
    struct PlaceMarker {
        Category * category;
        list<Category>::iterator nextSubcategory;
    };
    PlaceMarker place;
    stack<PlaceMarker> history;
```

There is much that is new here. The `PlaceMarker` type and the data member `place` are used to facilitate the incremental traversal of the category tree. The component `place.category` points to the current node, and the currently selected child of that node is indicated by the iterator `place.nextSubcategory`. The stack `history` will be used to record the path by which a given traversal has reached its current place in the tree, so that backtracking is possible.

Listed below are the public members of the class, with inline definitions given for all but the I/O routines. As before, the constructor calls the `initialize()` routine, which will install the three top categories named "Animal", "Vegetable", and "Mineral". The test `atSubtreeEnd()` informs the client whether the current location in the tree has reached the end of a list of child nodes, and `atEnd()` returns true if there are no nodes remaining in the tree. A series of 'get' access functions follows, and then the traversal operations `accept()`, `reject()`, and `reset()`. The `accept()` method descends deeper into the tree, `reject()` rejects the current subcategory and advances to the preorder successor, and `reset()` sets the tree location back to the root, emptying the stack in the process.

The fact that `reset()` is declared to be a virtual function has nothing to do with the most obvious reason for declaring a function virtual. There are no derived classes of this class, and if there were it would probably not be necessary to override this function. This function has been arbitrarily chosen to be declared virtual for the sole purpose of imbedding run-time type information into the class. This is important because the inheritance relationships which will be present between this class, the `CDocument` class, and the wizard-generated document class will force a cross-cast operation, which can only be a `dynamic_cast` and must therefore be run-time checked.

```
public:
    void initialize();
    TraversableAVMGame() { initialize(); }
    bool atSubtreeEnd() {
        return place.nextSubcategory ==
            place.category->subcategories.end();
```

```
        }
    bool atEnd() {
        return atSubtreeEnd() && place.category == this;
    }
    string getName() {
        return place.category->name;
    }
    string getQuestion() {
        return place.category->yesOrNoQuestion;
    }
    string getNextName() {
        return place.nextSubcategory->name;
    }
    string getNextQuestion() {
        return place.nextSubcategory->yesOrNoQuestion;
    }
    void accept() {
        if (!atSubtreeEnd()) {
            history.push(place);
            place.category = &*place.nextSubcategory;
            place.nextSubcategory =
                place.category->subcategories.begin();
        }
    }
    void reject() {
        if (!atSubtreeEnd()) place.nextSubcategory++;
        else {
            while (atSubtreeEnd() && !history.empty()
                    && !atEnd()) {
                place = history.top();
                history.pop();
            }
        }
    }
    virtual void reset() {
        // Must have a virtual function in order to do a
        // dynamic cast.
        place.category = this;
        place.nextSubcategory = subcategories.begin();
        while (!history.empty()) history.pop();
    }
    void readFrom(istream &in);
    void writeTo(ostream &out);
};

istream & operator >> (
```

```
        istream &in, TraversableAVMGame & game);
    ostream & operator << (
        ostream &out, TraversableAVMGame & game);
```

#endif

The `readFrom()` and `writeTo()` functions, and the stream I/O operators, will save the game tree to a file in the form indicated above. The implementation file *TraversableAVMTree.cpp* contains those definitions, along with the required method definitions from the base class `Category`. The file begins with the `include` and `using` statements, followed by an altered `initialize()` routine which must now initialize the two components of `place` in order to start the game at the first subcategory of the root, namely "`Animal`".

```
#include "stdafx.h"
#include "TraversableAVMGame.h"
#include <iostream>
using std::endl;
#include <string>
using std::string;
#include <list>
using std::list;
#include <fstream>
using std::ofstream;
using std::ifstream;
#include <exception>
using std::exception;

void TraversableAVMGame::initialize() {
    subcategories.clear();
    subcategories.push_back(Category(
        "Animal","Is it an animal?",1));
    subcategories.push_back(Category(
        "Vegetable","Is it a vegetable?",2));
    subcategories.push_back(Category(
        "Mineral","Is it a mineral?",3));
    place.category = this;
    place.nextSubcategory = subcategories.begin();
}
```

A utility routine follows, written at file scope. It is a stream insertion operator for writing a list of integers to a stream, inserting periods between each pair of two consecutive integers. This will be used to output the coordinates of a node of the tree.

```
ostream & operator << (ostream &out, list<int> coordinates) {
    bool first = true;
    while (coordinates.size() > 0) {
        if (!first) out << '.';
        first = false;
        out << coordinates.front();
        coordinates.pop_front();
    }
    return out;
}
```

The rest of the output methods follow. First, we look at the code for writing a Category object to a file. Note that it is a recursive utility routine with an auxiliary parameter, a list of integers called prefix. It is called three times from the top level, each time with an empty prefix list, in order to write out the three subtrees corresponding to categories Animal, Vegetable, and Mineral. Each recursive descent extends prefix by adding that particular node's childNumber component to the back of the list.

```
void Category::writeTo(ostream &out, list<int> prefix) {
    if (!prefix.empty()) out << prefix << '.';
    out << childNumber << " \"" << name << "\" \""
        << yesOrNoQuestion << "\"" << endl;
    prefix.push_back(childNumber);
    for (list<Category>::iterator i = subcategories.begin();
         i != subcategories.end(); ++i)
        i->writeTo(out,prefix);
}

void TraversableAVMGame::writeTo(ostream &out) {
    list<int> prefix;
    for (list<Category>::iterator i = subcategories.begin();
         i != subcategories.end(); ++i)
        i->writeTo(out,prefix);
}

ostream & operator << (ostream &out,
                       TraversableAVMGame & game) {
    game.writeTo(out);
    return out;
}
```

The last routine, the stream insertion operator, simply calls the `writeTo()` method of its `game` operand. The functions performed by that method could not have been performed by the stream operator itself because of protected inheritance.

The next two functions included below are file-scope utility functions. The first is used to find a quoted string in a file, strip the quotes from it, and place it in a `string` reference parameter. The second extracts a list of integers from a stream in such a way as to complement the stream insertion operator discussed above for lists of integers.

```
void getQuotedString(istream &in, string &s) {
    s = "";
    char discard = ' ';
    while (discard != '"' && in >> discard);
    char c = ' ';
    while (c != '"' && !in.fail()) {
        in.get(c);
        if (c != '"') s += c;
    }
}

istream & operator >> (istream &in, list<int> &L) {
    int number;
    L.clear();
    in >> number;
    L.push_back(number);
    while (in.peek() == '.') {
        in.get();
        in >> number;
        L.push_back(number);
    }
    return in;
}
```

The `install()` method of class `Category` is the final piece of the input puzzle, and allows us to place a new category in the right location in the tree based on a list of integer coordinates. It is recursive and generally acts by descending one level into the tree, removing the front coordinate, and calling itself. In the base case where the `coordinates` parameter is empty, the function uses the child number of the category to check the validity of the addition, then if there is no problem it installs this category as the last in the list of subcategories.

```
bool Category::install(list<int> coordinates,
                       Category category) {
    if (coordinates.empty()) {
        if (category.childNumber != subcategories.size()+1)
            return false;
        subcategories.push_back(category);
    }
    else {
        list<Category>::iterator i = subcategories.begin();
        while (i->childNumber != coordinates.front()) ++i;
        coordinates.pop_front();
        i->install(coordinates, category);
    }
    return true;
}
```

The stream extraction operator for reading a `TraversableAVMGame` object must first call the `readFrom()` method below, because access to the `Category` base class is denied to the file-scope operator. The `readFrom()` routine sequences through the stream, using the above utility functions again and again to first read a coordinates list, then two quoted strings (name and question). For each such combination, the last coordinate is stripped off for a child number, then the category is instantiated and placed in the tree with the `install()` method.

```
void TraversableAVMGame::readFrom(istream & in) {
    subcategories.clear();
    list<int> coordinates;
    while (in >> coordinates) {
        string name, question;
        getQuotedString(in, name);
        getQuotedString(in, question);
        int childNumber = coordinates.back();
        coordinates.pop_back();
        Category subCategory(name,question,childNumber);
        if (!install(coordinates,subCategory))
            throw exception("Invalid coordinates");
    }
}

istream & operator >> (istream &in,
                       TraversableAVMGame & game) {
    game.readFrom(in);
    game.reset();
    return in;
```

```
}
```

Finally, note that upon reading the new category tree from the file, the stream extraction operator resets the game so that the interrogation of the user can start at the beginning.

6.9   AN AVM GAME APPLICATION USING THE DOCUMENT CLASS

At this point, it is appropriate to discuss the CArchive class, used by MFC instead of a stream for storing binary data to a file or recalling such data. Like the istream and ostream classes from the standard library, CArchive incorporates a large number of overloads of the operators << and >>. Its purpose, however, is to store data in its raw form, a binary form not intended for viewing on-screen. For example, if ar is a CArchive object and x is an int variable, then the expression ar << x simply transfers the bits of x's memory representation to disk, and ar >> x fetches a binary integer from disk and stores it at x.

We wish to make the *File...Save* and *File...Open* menu choices of our project operational. We could do this by attaching our own handlers to the programmer-defined events ID_FILE_SAVE and ID_FILE_OPEN, but at this time the easiest thing to do is to use the default handlers already in place in the CDocument class. This is especially convenient because both call the Serialize() virtual member function, which we can override in our wizard-generated document class. Serialize() has a very simple form, as we will see, and relies on the operators above. We will have a small problem to solve, however, because all our I/O operations above read and write text, not binary.

It is now time for us to look at the hand-coded view class *HCAVMView*, beginning with the initial part of header file *HCAVM.h*, which we will cut off for now after the private portions of the class.

```
#ifndef __HCAVM_H
#define __HCAVM_H

#include "stdafx.h"
#include "TraversableAVMGame.h"
#include <fstream>
using std::ofstream;

class HCAVMView {
```

```
enum {NAME_X = 10, NAME_Y = 10, QUESTION_X = 10,
      QUESTION_Y = NAME_Y+20, YESLABEL_X = 50,
      YESLABEL_Y = QUESTION_Y+20,
      NOLABEL_X = 120, NOLABEL_Y = YESLABEL_Y,
      YESBOX_X = YESLABEL_X+30, YESBOX_Y = YESLABEL_Y,
      NOBOX_X = NOLABEL_X+30, NOBOX_Y = NOLABEL_Y,
      BOXWIDTH = 15, BOXHEIGHT = 15};
enum {
      QUESTIONING, OFFERING_NEW_GAME, GAME_OVER
} state;
CRect YesBox, NoBox;
bool inRectangle(CPoint p, CRect r) {
    return p.x >= r.left && p.x <= r.right
        && p.y >= r.top && p.y <= r.bottom;
}
void displayYesNo(CDC *pDC) {
    pDC->TextOut(YESLABEL_X, YESLABEL_Y, _T("Yes"));
    pDC->TextOut(NOLABEL_X, NOLABEL_Y, _T("No"));
    pDC->Rectangle(&YesBox);
    pDC->Rectangle(&NoBox);
}
CWnd *pWnd;
TraversableAVMGame *pGame;
```

The first list of enumeration constants simply establishes row and column alignments for various aspects of the screen display. The display will be entirely text except for two small squares which the user can click on to indicate a yes or no answer to the current question. A snapshot of the interrogation appears in Figure 6.3.

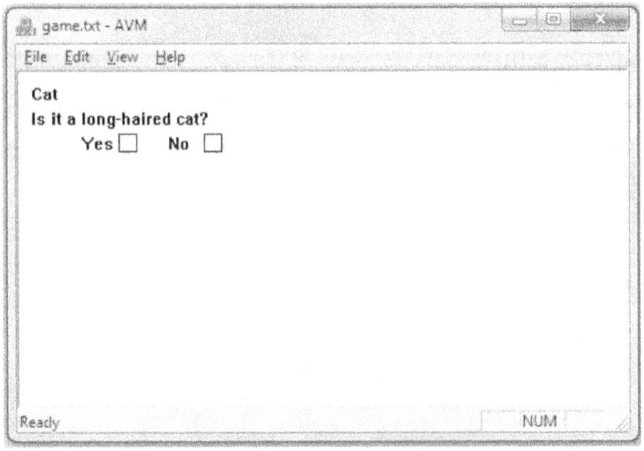

FIGURE 6.3 Playing "Animal, Vegetable, Mineral"

The next set of enumeration constants is given incidental to the declaration of data member `state`, and establishes numeric codes for the three states of the game, namely `QUESTIONING`, `OFFERING_NEW_GAME`, and `GAME_OVER`. How the window responds to a mouse click depends on which state it is in. We will add an additional state in the next section.

The `CRect` objects `YesBox` and `NoBox` are the internal representations of the two squares in the view window. The `inRectangle()` routine answers the question whether a given point is in a given rectangle, a service we will obviously need, and `displayYesNo()` adds the two boxes and their labels 'Yes' and 'No' to the display. The two pointers `pWnd` and `pGame` point to the wizard-generated view object and to the game object, respectively, and will be initialized in `onInitialUpdate()`. (Note that `onInitialUpdate()` will receive a `CDocument` pointer as its second parameter and will use a dynamic cross-cast to convert that pointer to type `TraversableAVMGame*`.)

The public portions of the class are given below, beginning with a constructor that initializes `YesBox` and `NoBox`, then initializes `state` to `QUESTIONING`. The `onDraw()` routine follows that, and produces a different display depending on the value of `state`. But `onDraw()` automatically assumes the game is just beginning if the object `pGame` is not positioned at the end, and in that case, it forces `state` to the value `QUESTIONING`.

```
public:
    HCAVMView():YesBox(YESBOX_X, YESBOX_Y, YESBOX_X+BOXWIDTH,
                       YESBOX_Y+BOXHEIGHT),
               NoBox(NOBOX_X, NOBOX_Y, NOBOX_X+BOXWIDTH,
                       NOBOX_Y+BOXHEIGHT),
               state(QUESTIONING) {}
    void onInitialUpdate(CWnd *pWnd, CDocument *pDoc) {
        pGame = dynamic_cast<TraversableAVMGame*>(pDoc);
        HCAVMView::pWnd = pWnd;
    }
    void onDraw(CDC *pDC) {
        if (pGame->getName() == "" && !pGame->atEnd())
            state = QUESTIONING;
        switch(state) {
        case OFFERING_NEW_GAME:
            pDC->TextOut(NAME_X, NAME_Y,
                         CString(pGame->getName().c_str()));
            pDC->TextOut(QUESTION_X, QUESTION_Y,
                         _T("Would you like to play again?"));
            displayYesNo(pDC);
            break;
```

```
        case GAME_OVER:
            pDC->TextOut(NAME_X, NAME_Y, _T("Game over"));
            break;
        case QUESTIONING:
            pDC->TextOut(NAME_X, NAME_Y,
                        CString(pGame->getName().c_str()));
            pDC->TextOut(QUESTION_X, QUESTION_Y,
                CString(pGame->getNextQuestion().c_str()));
            displayYesNo(pDC);
            break;
        }
    }
    void onLButtonDown(CPoint p) {
        switch(state) {
        case QUESTIONING:
            if (inRectangle(p,YesBox)) pGame->accept();
            else if (inRectangle(p,NoBox)) pGame->reject();
            if (pGame->atEnd()) state = GAME_OVER;
            else if (pGame->atSubtreeEnd())
                state = OFFERING_NEW_GAME;
            break;
        case OFFERING_NEW_GAME:
            if (inRectangle(p,YesBox)) {
                pGame->reset();
                state = QUESTIONING;
            }
            else if (inRectangle(p,NoBox)) state = GAME_OVER;
        }
        pWnd->Invalidate();
    }
    void onFileNew() {
        pGame->initialize();
        pGame->reset();
        CDocument *pDoc = dynamic_cast<CDocument *> (pGame);
        CString pathName = pDoc->GetPathName();
        int i = pathName.GetLength();
        while (i > 0 && pathName[--i] != '\\');
        pathName.Delete(i+1,pathName.GetLength()-i-1);
        pathName.Append(_T("Untitled"));
        ofstream(pathName).close();
        pDoc->SetPathName(pathName);
        pDoc->SetTitle(_T("Untitled"));
        pWnd->Invalidate();
    }
};
```

The last two routines are the event handlers `onLButtonDown()` and `onFile-New()`. The former, like `onDraw()`, is a switch on the value of `state`, except that the response here is to oversee the transition from state to state, using the current state and the condition of `*pGame` to guide the transitions. The `onFile-New()` function empties the tree except for the three top-level categories and repositions the game to the beginning, by calling the `initialize()` function. It also sets the name of the file associated with the document back to *Untitled*, so that an inadvertant save will not wipe out the contents of the last data file used. Doing this is a little technical and requires some manipulation of the MFC `CString` string data type, as well as some additional communication with the document object, namely calls on the `GetPathName()`, `SetPathName()`, and `SetTitle()` methods. A careful inspection of the code by the reader should illuminate the details.

The last few lines of the header file *HCAVM.h* are as follows:

```
CArchive & operator << (CArchive & ar,
                        TraversableAVMGame & game);
CArchive & operator >> (CArchive & ar,
                        TraversableAVMGame & game);

#endif
```

These declare the operators for saving and restoring a game to or from an archive. We complete their definitions in the *HCAVM.cpp* file, as follows:

```
#include "stdafx.h"
#include "HCAVM.h"
#include <string>
using std::string;
#include <sstream>
using std::ostream;
using std::ends;
using std::stringstream;

CArchive & operator << (CArchive & ar,
                        TraversableAVMGame & game) {
    stringstream strout;
    strout << game << ends;
    string gameString = strout.str();
    const char *cp = gameString.c_str();
    while (*cp != '\0') ar << *cp++;
    ar << '\0';
```

```
        return ar;
    }

    CArchive & operator >> (CArchive & ar,
                            TraversableAVMGame & game) {
        string instring;
        char c;
        ar >> c;
        while (c != '\0') {
            instring += c;
            ar >> c;
        }
        stringstream strin(instring);
        strin >> game;
        game.reset();
        CDocument *pDoc = dynamic_cast<CDocument*>(&game);
        pDoc->SetModifiedFlag();
        return ar;
    }
```

These are somewhat technical, because CArchive's operators >> and << have no overloads for the string type, and so we must read and write single characters. Accordingly, in the output routine we begin by using the previously defined text-oriented streaming operators to stream the game to a string. Then we use the c_str() method of class string to obtain a char * pointer into that string, which we advance through the string, streaming one character at a time to the archive. We finish by writing a null character ('\0') to the archive as a trailer.

The input routine reconstructs a string in the converse way, by beginning with an empty string and appending each character read by the archive to the end of that string. It then instantiates a stringstream from the string thus read, and uses that stream and the istream version of operator >> to stream the data into the game object. Finally, the view class must be notified that a new file has been loaded, so that it can redraw the view. This is done in a roundabout manner by calling the SetModifiedFlag() function of CDocument.

Note that in order to obtain the document pointer above we performed a dynamic cast of the address of the game object. This will work because of two things. First, we made sure our game class was virtual by artificially declaring one of its member functions virtual. Second, we plan to modify the wizard-generated document class so that it inherits not only from CDocument but also from our TraversableAVMGame class. Because much of what is needed to create the project is similar to what we have already done, we will succinctly list the steps needed to construct it:

1. Create a single document interface project named *AVM*. Place all the source files from this section and the previous section in the project directory.

2. Cause the view class header file to include *HCAVM.h* and cause the class itself to inherit from both `CView` and `HCAVMView`.

3. Cause the document class header file to include *HCAVM.h* and cause the class itself to inherit from both `CDocument` and `TraversableAVMGame`.

4. Add the source files *TraversableAVMGame.cpp* and *HCAVM.cpp* to the project.

5. In the view class,

   a. Edit the `OnDraw()` override to make it call `onDraw()`.

   b. Add an override for `OnInitialUpdate()`. Add the following line of code to the bottom of the override:

   ```
   onInitialUpdate(this,GetDocument());
   ```

   c. Add the `OnLButtonDown()` handler to the view class for the windows message `WM_LBUTTONDOWN`. Modify it by adding the line

   ```
   onLButtonDown(point);
   ```

   at the bottom.

   d. Add the `COMMAND` handler `OnFileNew()` for programmer-defined event `ID_FILE_NEW`. Have it call `onFileNew()`.

   e. In the document class, edit the `Serialize()` override so that it appears as follows:

   ```
   void CAVM2Doc::Serialize(CArchive& ar)
   {
       if (ar.IsStoring())
       {
           // TODO: add storing code here
           ar << *this;
       }
       else
       {
           // TODO: add loading code here
           ar >> *this;
       }
   }
   ```

   This brings into play all the I/O routines we have so carefully constructed.

The project should now compile and link, and execute as expected. The user is now capable of doing everything he was able to do with the original console-based *AVMGame* application, except add to the tree on the fly. The tree can be expanded offline by editing the stored file, however. For example, adding the line

```
2.2.3 "Blue Lake" "Are the pods stringless?"
```

to the data file in Section 6.8 successfully adds "Blue Lake" beans to the list of green beans, as long as the addition to the file is made *after* entry 2.2.2. Siblings in the tree must be added in the correct order, and cannot be added before their parents.

6.10 DESIGNING AND USING A DIALOG BOX

Recall that our console-based "Animal, Vegetable, Mineral" game had no problem modifying the tree on the fly. In fact, if we were to develop a new console project using the `TraversableAVMGame` class and its streaming operators, we could make it much more functional than the MFC project we have spent so much time developing, because we could easily add the file save and restore feature. On the other hand, the look and feel we have developed, although quite simple in design, is clearly superior to the console project. All that we lack to make it fully functional are the following capabilities, to be initiated after the user has exhausted all the possibilities currently stored in the tree for more precisely specifying the item:

1. Ask the user whether he wishes to further specify the item.
2. If the answer is yes, then:
   a. Prompt the user for:
      i. A new subcategory name.
      ii. A new identifying yes/no question.
   b. Add the new subcategory to the tree.

Because requirement number 1 is a yes or no question, we can use the framework we have already developed to implement it. For the rest, we need a dialog box.

The best way to design a dialog box is to use the Visual Studio resource editor. Drawing and assigning names to the various components of the dialog box is very much expedited using that tool. On the other hand, the programming of events needs careful thought. We will begin with a discussion of the "drag and drop" dialog construction, then present a hand-coded dialog class which represents the active content, and finally we will discuss how to tie the two together and incorporate this functionality into the larger project.

Returning to the AVM project, we bring up the Solution Explorer, right-click on the AVM project, and select *Add...Resource* from the resulting pop-up menu. An "Add Resource" window appears, whereupon we select *Dialog* and click the *New* button. A blank dialog appears in the edit window, containing nothing but an *OK* and a *CANCEL* button. There should also appear at this time a Dialog Editor toolbox, containing a large assortment of drag and drop components. Although many of these are quite useful in a large number of settings, in the interest of brevity we shall confine ourselves in this text to the existing buttons and the "Static Text" and "Edit Control" components. Specifically, we need three static text controls containing the labels "Category:," "New Subcategory:," and "Identifying Question:," and we will draw an edit control below each of the latter two to compose a dialog box. Configuring the dialog to give it the appearance depicted in Figure 6.4 involves first using the proper drawing tool (static text or edit control) to place the object where it belongs, then right-clicking on it and selecting *Properties*. For the static controls, we edit the *Caption* property, which has the intial value 'static.' We replace that string with the label we wish to appear in the dialog, for example, 'Category:' for the top control. We also wish to change the *ID* property of the top control from `IDC_STATIC` to `IDC_CATEGO-RY_LABEL`, so that we can properly identify this particular static control, because its value will change at run-time. For similar reasons, we change the `ID` properties of the two edit boxes to `IDC_EDIT_SUBCATEGORY` and `IDC_EDIT_QUESTION`. Finally, clicking on the title bar of our dialog box brings up the properties of the dialog itself, and we can then change its *Caption* property to 'New Subcategory Dialog' and its ID property to `IDD_NEW_SUBCATEGORY_DIALOG`.

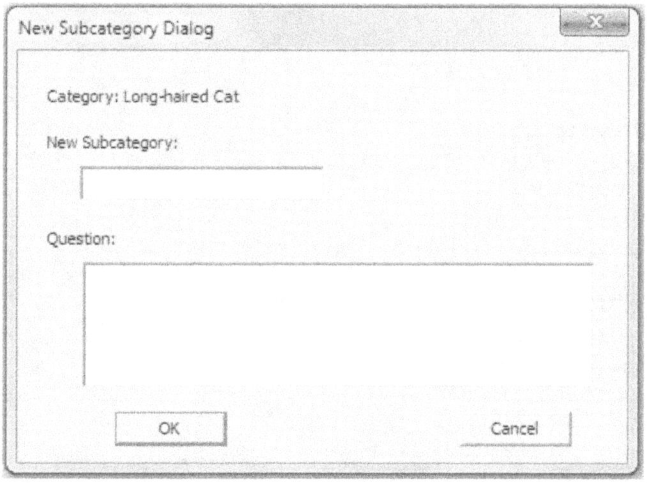

FIGURE 6.4 The *New Subcategory* dialog box

In order to give this dialog box a representation in our program as a class, we right-click on the title bar again of the dialog box resource we are editing, and select *Add Class....* This brings up the MFC Class Wizard for the purpose of building a class around the dialog box. We name the new class CNewSubcategoryDialog, make sure its base class is CDialog, then click on *Finish*, taking the defaults for all other choices. We now have two new source files in our project, the header file *NewSubcategoryDialog.h* and the source file *NewSubcategoryDialog.cpp*.

At this time, we will make a simplifying assumption in order not to make our code too technical. We have been using the STL string data type throughout, and extracting a C-style string from it using the c_str() message, so we are tied to an 8-bit character data type. In order to make the above code work, we will have to abandon any attempt to keep things general enough to accommodate multi-byte character types. Accordingly, we need to change the properties of this project.

The default project built by the wizard uses the Unicode character set for its resources such as text boxes and static controls. We will change that as follows: (1) In the Solution Explorer, right-click on the project name, and select 'Properties.' (2) Notice on the right under the "Character set" property, the value selected is "Use Unicode character set." Clicking on that reveals that this is a drop-down box. (3) Drop it down, and select "Not set." This will make our string data type compatible with the drag and drop controls.

We will ignore the wizard-generated files for the present and add additional lines to our hand-coded file, in order to define a separate hand-coded class, HCNewSubcategoryDialog. The following code should be added to file *HCAVM.h* at the end of the file, but *before* the final #endif.

```
#include "Resource.h"

class HCNewSubcategoryDialog {
    CStatic* pCategoryLabel;
    CEdit* pSubcategoryName;
    CEdit* pQuestion;
    string subcategoryName, question, categoryName;
public:
    enum {NAMESIZELIMIT=80, QUESTIONSIZELIMIT=200};
    HCNewSubcategoryDialog(string categoryName)
        :categoryName(categoryName){}
    void onInitDialog(CWnd *pWnd) {
        pCategoryLabel =
            (CStatic *) (pWnd->GetDlgItem(IDC_CATEGORY_LABEL));
        pSubcategoryName =
```

```
            (CEdit*)(pWnd->GetDlgItem(IDC_EDIT_SUBCATEGORY)));
          pQuestion = (CEdit*)(pWnd->GetDlgItem(IDC_EDIT_QUES-
TION)));
        pCategoryLabel->SetWindowText(
            ("Category: " + categoryName).c_str());
    }
    string getSubcategory() { return subcategoryName; }
    string getQuestion() { return question; }
    void onDestroy() {
        char buffer[QUESTIONSIZELIMIT+1];
        pSubcategoryName->GetWindowText(
            (LPTSTR)buffer,NAMESIZELIMIT);
        subcategoryName = buffer;
        pQuestion->GetWindowText(
            (LPTSTR)buffer,QUESTIONSIZELIMIT);
        question = buffer;
    }
};
```

The file begins with an include statement for a file called *Resource.h*. This file contains actual numeric values assigned by the resource editor to the IDs for the controls in our dialog box, as well as other numeric constants generated by the project construction wizard. When we open this file we see that the IDs we named, for example `IDC_EDIT_SUBCATEGORY`, get translated into numeric constants and associated with the names we assigned them using `#define` preprocessor statements.

The constructor for our hand-coded dialog box class is furnished with the name of the category we are subdividing, so that the user can be made aware of where he is in the tree as he is editing. The category name is saved to file scope, and is then used in `onInitDialog()` to change the contents of the static control `IDC_CATEGORY_LABEL`. The reader should at this time have guessed from the naming pattern that `onInitDialog()` is intended to be called from a wizard-generated override of the virtual function `OnInitDialog()`. Similarly, the name `onDestroy()` telegraphs the fact that this routine as well is intended to be called from an event handler. Specifically, `onDestroy()` will be called from the handler `OnDestroy()`, which the wizard will generate at our request. All that remain are the two self-explanatory access functions.

Some explanation is warranted for the contents of `onInitDialog()`. The three pointers `pCategoryLabel`, `pSubcategoryName`, and `pQuestion` are pointers to windows controls, which we indirectly constructed in the resource editor. These controls were described with text using a resource description language which the reader can readily view by opening the file *AVM.rc*, found in the Solution Explorer under the heading "Resource Files." In order to view the actual resource descriptions it should be opened with a right-click and a choice of the menu item "View Code." An inspection of this file reveals that not only our dialog box but the menu attached to the frame window, all the menu choices, some "accelerator keys," an "about" dialog, and every control inside our dialog box, are described using this resource description language.

The resources we wish to "talk to," i.e., the *Category* label and the two edit boxes, are identified in the resource file and in the header file by their IDs, but inside `onInitDialog()` we put MFC class wrappers around them, allowing us to talk to them by sending them messages in the form of member function calls. By the time `onInitDialog()` is called these controls already exist as Windows objects, but for each such object calling `GetDlgItem()` and passing the control's ID causes the dialog window to manufacture an object of the appropriate MFC class type as a wrapper around it. `GetDlgItem()` is generic, receiving an integer parameter and returning a `CWnd *` pointer, which is consistent because all the MFC control classes (`CStatic`, `CEdit`, etc.) are windows and derive directly or indirectly from `CWnd`.

The `WM_DESTROY` message will be sent to the dialog box when it is removed from the screen, either by clicking on one of the *OK* and *Cancel* buttons or by clicking on the "x" close control on the main frame window. At that time, the user's editing will be over, and it is important to fetch the text from the two edit controls and place it at class scope where it can be accessed by the client. For this reason, in the `onDestroy()` function, we use a raw C array called `buffer` and the `GetWindowText()` function. A rather arbitrary limit of 80 characters for the subcategory name and 200 characters for the accompanying question are used in the above code, and these numbers are used as limits inside `GetWindow-Text()`, a necessary precaution with these low-level tools.

The technique for melding the wizard-generated dialog class with the hand-coded class is similar to techniques we have already used. Inside *NewSubcategoryDialog.h*, the wizard's header file, we place the statement

```
#include "HCAVM.h"
```

and we make the wizard's class inherit doubly from `CDialog` and from our own class, as follows:

```
class CNewSubcategoryDialog : public CDialog,
                             public HCNewSubcategoryDialog
```

Now with the text cursor in the class name `CNewSubcategoryDialog` in the above line of code, we click on the "Properties" tab (or if for some reason there is no such tab use *View…Other Windows…Properties Window*). Use this properties window to tie into our `onInitDialog()` and `onDestroy()` functions in the same manner as we have done before. The `OnInitDialog()` function will not be present in the right-hand column of the "Overrides" (green box icon), so the reader will need to choose *<Add> OnInitDialog* from the drop-down menu which appears when the mouse is clicked on that line of the table. The line

```
onInitDialog(this);
```

should be added at the end of that routine. Similarly, under the "Messages" category we find `WM_DESTROY` and add the `OnDestroy()` message handler, adding the line

```
onDestroy();
```

at the bottom of that routine.

All of the above is intended to give us the *capability* of invoking a dialog box. In order to actually use it, we need to change our main view class's response to events. In fact, we need to increase by one the number of states the view class supports. We will call the new state `ASKING_FOR_SUBCATEGORY`, and we will enter it when a yes or no answer to one of the questions posed to the user results in our game tree being positioned at the end of a list of subcategories but not at the end of the game (in other words, results in `pGame->atSubtreeEnd()` being true while `pGame>atEnd()` is false).

The response of the `onDraw()` method when it sees that the state is `ASKING_FOR_SUBCATEGORY` is similar to its response in states `QUESTIONING` and `OFFERING_NEW_GAME`. It will display a question tailored for the current position in the tree, such as "Would you like to further specify the type of Poodle?," and display the yes and no boxes. It is in the `onLButtonDown()` routine that our dialog box comes into play.

Below are listed the necessary modifications to the description of class `HCAVMView` in file *HCAVM.h*.

1. Add the enumeration constant `ASKING_FOR_NEWSUBCATEGORY` to the list of states.

2. Add the following case to the `switch` statement in `onDraw()`.

```
case ASKING_FOR_SUBCATEGORY:
    pDC->TextOut(NAME_X, NAME_Y,
```

```
                        CString(pGame->getName().c_str())));
              string question =
                 "Would you like to further specify the type of ";
              question += pGame->getName() += "?";
              pDC->TextOut(QUESTION_X, QUESTION_Y,
                           CString(question.c_str())));
              displayYesNo(pDC);
              break;
```

3. Remove the definition of `onLButtonDown()` and code it as a prototype, as follows:

```
         void onLButtonDown(CPoint p);
```

Note now that `onLButtonDown()` is no longer coded inline. This is not an arbitrary decision, but a forced one. In any file where an object of type `CNew-SubcategoryDialog` is instantiated, an include will have to be given for the file *NewSubcategoryDialog.h*. But if we put such an include in our hand-coded header file we will introduce a circular relationship between the included files, because *NewSubcategoryDialog.h* also includes *HCAVM.h*. But now the (necessary) presence of preprocessor guards makes it impossible for the definition of the wizard dialog class to be encountered before it is used. Our response is to separately compile the definition of `onLButtonDown()` by placing it in the source file instead of the header file.

So we will place the method `onLButtonDown()` in file *HCAVM.cpp*. In that method, if the state is `ASKING_FOR_SUBCATEGORY`, our response will be to bring up the dialog box we have just constructed. This works perfectly well when we separately define the method in *HCAVM.cpp*, because then the storage map and the interface to the hand-coded and the wizard-generated dialog classes will have been completely defined before the method definition is encountered. Below is the code for the method:

```
   void HCAVMView::onLButtonDown(CPoint p) {
       switch(state) {
       case QUESTIONING:
           if (inRectangle(p,YesBox)) pGame->accept();
           else if (inRectangle(p,NoBox)) pGame->reject();
           if (pGame->atEnd()) state = GAME_OVER;
           else if (pGame->atSubtreeEnd())
               state = ASKING_FOR_SUBCATEGORY;
           break;
       case ASKING_FOR_SUBCATEGORY:
```

```
   if (inRectangle(p,YesBox)){
       CNewSubcategoryDialog dlg(0,pGame->getName());
       int rv = dlg.DoModal();
       if (rv == IDOK) {
           string subcategoryName = dlg.getSubcategory();
           string question = dlg.getQuestion();
           pGame->addSubcategory(
               subcategoryName,question);
       }
       state = OFFERING_NEW_GAME;
   }
   else if (inRectangle(p,NoBox))
       state = OFFERING_NEW_GAME;
   break;
case OFFERING_NEW_GAME:
   if (inRectangle(p,YesBox)) {
       pGame->reset();
       state = QUESTIONING;
   }
   else if (inRectangle(p,NoBox)) state = GAME_OVER;
   }
   pWnd->Invalidate();
}
```

The first change we see is in case `QUESTIONING`, where we transition to state `ASKING_FOR_SUBCATEGORY` when `pGame->atSubtreeEnd()` is true. The more substantial code change is inside case `ASKING_FOR_SUBCATEGORY` itself. Let us duplicate below for discussion purposes the code segment which instantiates, displays, and reacts to the dialog box:

```
CNewSubcategoryDialog dlg(0,pGame->getName());
int rv = dlg.DoModal();
if (rv == IDOK) {
    string subcategoryName = dlg.getSubcategory();
    string question = dlg.getQuestion();
    pGame->addSubcategory(subcategoryName,question);
}
state = OFFERING_NEW_GAME;
```

The first operand of the dialog constructor is transmitted as the address of the "parent window." The parent/child relationship between windows is maintained by the operating system, but we do not need to specify such a relationship here so we code this pointer null by passing a zero to it. The second operand we pass to the constructor is the name of the category we are subdividing. This first line of code produces a dialog object `dlg` of the wizard-generated type, which contains all the information we edited into it with the resource editor and the source code editor. But just instantiating the dialog object does not make it visible on the screen, and does not make it interact with the user. Those things are accomplished with the `CDialog` member function `DoModal()`. When we execute `dlg.DoModal()`, the dialog box appears and has the focus, and at this time the user can interact freely with the dialog controls. The view window loses the keyboard and mouse focus and will not regain them until the user specifically removes the dialog window from the screen. When the user clicks on *OK* or *Cancel*, or on the system's 'close' icon, then `DoModal()` exits, a `WM_DESTROY` message is sent to the dialog object, causing `onDestroy()` to execute, and the dialog box disappears. If the *OK* button was pressed, then `DoModal()` will return the integer value `IDOK`, which causes the new subcategory to be generated based on the information stored in the hand-coded dialog class. Regardless of whether or not a new subcategory was added, the state transitions to `OFFERING_NEW_GAME`.

There is an item of unfinished business. The second parameter of the wizard dialog class's constructor, the category name, is not present in the wizard-generated code, so we need to change that code by hand in two places. In the header file *CNewSubcategoryDialog.h*, we change the prototype of the constructor so that it looks like the following:

```
CNewSubcategoryDialog(CWnd* pParent = 0,
                      string categoryName="");
```

Note that we are forced to give the second parameter a default argument, because the first parameter has a default argument.

The second change we must make to the wizard code is in the definition of the constructor. It should be changed so that it appears as follows:

```
CNewSubcategoryDialog::CNewSubcategoryDialog(
    CWnd* pParent /*=0*/,
    string categoryName)
    : CDialog(CNewSubcategoryDialog::IDD, pParent),
      HCNewSubcategoryDialog(categoryName)
{
}
```

In other words, the second parameter must be added and the call on the hand-coded class's constructor must be added to the initialization part.

This completes the project, which should compile, link, and execute correctly at this time.

6.11   SNAPSHOTS, BIT BLOCK TRANSFERS, AND ACCELERATOR KEYS

Besides the pen and the brush, there is another important resource the device context keeps track of, namely the bitmap. This is the memory which is associated with the device context, and issuing drawing messages to the device context is essentially nothing more than changing the contents of this block of memory. If that memory is mapped by hardware to the display, then we will see the results of the drawing commands as they are executed. If not, then the drawing will be done "off-screen," and we can at some later time move the results to the visible display. Drawing off-screen is a common technique in cases where generating a display is computation-intensive or in cases where a display is built up over time. This section discusses techniques for drawing off-screen and for transferring the off-screen image to the visible display. Similar techniques, we will note, are used to transfer on-screen images to memory blocks, an operation called a "screen grab." We will use our "Moving Circles" project to illustrate the latter technique. Specifically, we will modify the program so that the letter 's' is a "hot key" which brings up a pop-up window containing a freeze-frame of the display.

We begin with a discussion of bitmaps and their interaction with device contexts. The MFC class for a bitmap is `CBitmap`, and like a window one normally uses a two-stage creation for these objects. The default constructor creates a bitmap, but does not associate any particular size with it. The best way to size a bitmap is to use a pointer to an available device context as an argument to the `CBitmap::CreateCompatibleBitmap()` method, thus completing the two-stage creation begun with the default constructor. To illustrate, if we have a pointer `pWnd` to a `CWnd` object, the best way to build a bitmap object `bmp` having just enough memory to paint the client area of the window is to execute the following statements.

```
CBitmap bmp;
CClientDC dc(pWnd);
CRect R;
pWnd->GetClientRect(&R);
bmp.CreateCompatibleBitmap(&dc,R.Width(),R.Height());
```

However, the above does not actually place any drawing information in the window. If we were to move the above bitmap to the display it probably would be completely black, indicating that the memory was zeroed out. We may write to this bitmap by associating with it a *memory device context*. Creating a memory device context is similar in form to creating a bitmap, and again it is a two-stage process. Begin by using the default constructor for CDC, and then call CDC::CreateCompatibleDC(). The following code is intended as a follow-up to the above, in which the existing object dc is used as a pattern for creating our memory device context memDC.

```
CDC memDC;
memDC.CreateCompatibleDC(&dc);
```

Now both the bitmap and the memory device context exist, but they do not know about each other. To give the bitmap to the memory device context as a resource, we call yet another overloaded form of SelectObject(), being sure to save the address of the old bitmap which was associated with memDC when it was created.

```
CBitmap *oldBitmap = memDC.SelectObject(&bmp);
```

Now any drawing we do using the device context memDC will be done to the bitmap bmp. (Again, before the object memDC is destroyed we should restore to it its old bitmap, using CDC::SelectObject() in the usual way.)

Before we begin drawing using our memory device context, we may want to flood the background with white. This can be done with the "Pattern block transfer" operation, i.e., with CDC::PatBlt(). The precise statement we need for the example is the following:

```
memDC.PatBlt(0,0,R.Width(),R.Height(),WHITENESS);
```

The first two parameters are the x and y coordinates of the top left corner of the rectangle we are filling with white, and the next two are the width and height of that rectangle. The constant WHITENESS is an integer code implemented as a preprocessor constant, defined in *WinGDI.h*. The example floods the entire bitmap with white.

Once we have finished with all our off-screen drawing, how do we get the drawing to appear in a particular client rectangle of a screen window? We typically do that with either CDC::BitBlt() ("bit block transfer") or CDC::StretchBlt()

("stretch block transfer"). The first operation does not sound at all like a graphics primitive, and in fact it is not. It is just a copy operation from one memory location to another, involving two rather large areas of memory which are identical in size. The indicated portion of the bitmap attached to the device context receiving the `BitBlt()` call is changed in some manner using the contents of the corresponding portions of the bitmap coded as the fifth parameter. For example, if we had finished all our writing to `memDC` and wished to display the results on device context `dc`, we could do so as follows:

```
dc.BitBlt(0,0,R.Width(),R.Height(),&memDC,0,0,SRCCOPY);
```

Again, `SRCCOPY` is a preprocessor constant defined in *WinGDI.h*, a file that will automatically be pulled in with the normal include statements of an MFC project. `SRCCOPY` is an integer code that informs `BitBlt()` that no transformations are needed in the copy operation, and that the destination portions of the bitmap are to be simply overwritten. There are other important choices for this parameter, such as `SRCPAINT`, `SRCINVERT`, and `NOTSRCCOPY`, all of which involve bit-level operations to be done with all the bits of all the pairs of corresponding pixels. `SRCCOPY` is the most commonly used, and the only one which suits our purposes here.

We do a "Stretch BLT," when we have two client rectangles which may be of different sizes, but we want the destination bitmap to receive an expanded or compressed image equivalent to the source bitmap. Its interface is similar to that for `BitBlt()`, except that it needs to specify the complete source rectangle, not just the upper left-hand corner. The statement

```
dc.StretchBlt(0,0,R.Width(),R.Height(),&memDC,0,0,
              R.Width(),R.Height(),SRCCOPY);
```

would be equivalent to the above call on `BitBlt()`. As another example, the call

```
dc.StretchBlt(0,0,R.Width(),R.Height(),&memDC,0,0,
              200,150,SRCCOPY);
```

would take a 200-pixel by 150-pixel rectangle and either expand or compress it to fill the bitmap associated with device context `dc`.

Let us develop a "snapshot" capability for the "Moving Circles" project from Section 6.7. We will do this by (1) installing the key 's' as a "hot key" (or *accel-*

erator, as MFC refers to it), (2) associating our accelerator with a handler in the view class which we will call `OnSnapshot()`, (3) adding to class `HCMovingCircles` a corresponding `onSnapshot()` routine, and (4) tying the two together in the usual way. But before we do this we will need a new class for the snapshot window itself, which is to be a pop-up window that appears on the screen when the key 's' is pressed.

The quickest and easiest way for us to design a pop-up window is to add it to the project as a dialog resource. Accordingly, we go to the Solution Explorer, right-click on the "Moving Circles" project, and select *Add...Resource....* We then select *Dialog* and press the *New* button. The dialog editor appears, as in the last section, and we begin to design our pop-up window.

The first thing we do is to delete the *OK* and *Cancel* buttons, as we are only going to interact with this window by resizing, moving, minimizing, maximizing, and finally, destroying it. To get rid of the two buttons, we simply click on each in turn and press the delete key. We then resize the dialog window to whatever size we wish to be its initial size when it appears on the screen. The only remaining thing to do is to set its properties in whatever way we wish. Table 6.1 is a list of properties and the values we will give them.

TABLE 6.1 Properties of the screen shot pop-up.

Property	**Value**
Border	Resizing
Caption	Snapshot
Client Edge	True
ID	IDD_Snapshot
Maximize Box	True
Minimize Box	True

Again, if the properties window is not visible, we can bring it up by right-clicking on the title bar of the dialog we are editing and selecting *Properties* from the resulting menu. We take the default on all the properties except those listed in the table.

When we have finished setting all the properties, we must establish a class to associate with the pop-up window. Accordingly, we right-click on the title bar of our dialog in the resource editor, and select *Add Class....* In the resulting window, we fill in `CSnapshotWnd` as the name of the new class and use `CDialog` as its base class. We press *Finish*, taking the default for all other choices. Now we bring up the Solution Explorer, double-click on the file *SnapshotWnd.h*, and make our customary changes to incorporate a corresponding hand-coded class HCSnapshotWnd, the details of which we will describe shortly. We also add to the *SnapshotWnd.h* file an include statement for *Resource.h*. The affected areas of the file should now appear as follows:

```
#include "HCMovingCircles.h"
#include "Resource.h"

class CSnapshotWnd : public CDialog, public HCSnapshotWnd
```

Before incorporating a hand-coded file for this "dialog" into the project, we add a new parameter to the CSnapshotWnd constructor, altering the wizard-generated files *SnapshotWnd.h* and *SnapshotWnd.cpp* so that CSnapshotWnd::CSnapshotWnd() has a second parameter of type CBitmap *, with a default value of NULL.

We finish off this class by adding the following lines to file *HCMovingCircles.h*.

```
class HCSnapshotWnd {
    CWnd *pParent;
    CBitmap *bmp;
public:
    HCSnapshotWnd(CWnd *pParent, CBitmap *bmp):
        pParent(pParent), bmp(bmp){}
    virtual void onPaint() {
        CRect R, SnapR;
        pParent->GetClientRect(&R);
        CWnd *pWnd = dynamic_cast<CWnd*>(this);
        pWnd->GetClientRect(&SnapR);
        CDC memDC;
        CClientDC parentDC(pParent);
        memDC.CreateCompatibleDC(&parentDC);
        memDC.SelectObject(bmp);
        CClientDC dc(pWnd);
        dc.StretchBlt(SnapR.left,SnapR.top,SnapR.Width(),
            SnapR.Height(),&memDC,0,0,R.Width(),R.Height(),
            SRCCOPY);
    }
    void onDestroy() {
        delete bmp;
    }
};
```

Once we have done this, we can add a call on our hand-coded class constructor to the initialization part of class `CSnapshotWnd`. Here the hand-coded snapshot window class receives the same parameters as the derived class; the bitmap it receives is one which is created by the view class on the heap but which it will be the pop-up window's responsibility to delete. That bitmap will already have been loaded by the view class with the snapshot data. Here our only responsibilities (as fulfilled in the above code) are to (1) write an `onPaint()` routine to use that data to construct the client display in the pop-up, and (2) provide an `onDestroy()` routine to delete the bitmap when the pop-up window is destroyed. Note that we need a pointer to the pop-up window, but we did not get it in the above code in the same way we received the `pWnd` pointer to the dialog object in the preceding section. We did not provide an `onInitDialog()` method. If we had, there would have been nothing for it to do but pass on a pointer to the *CDialog* object, destined to be stored in the hand-coded class as the pointer `pWnd`. In the above code segment, we have instead used run-time type identification and the `dynamic_cast` function template. Again, in order to incorporate RTTI, we needed a virtual function, so `onPaint()` has been declared virtual. The details of how to use the bitmap to construct the display are technical, but in light of the discussion at the beginning of this section they should not be unexpected—the code should be understandable with careful study.

We can now proceed to the establishment of the accelerator key. In the *Resource View* pane, expand the *Accelerator* category, then double-click on `IDR_MAINFRAME`. This will bring up an editor for modifying, deleting, and creating hot keys. Several hot keys come "for free" with an SDI project, and they are listed already in the table. We wish to add one more. Accordingly, we click once on the long white rectangle just below the last non-blank entry in the table. This fills out that row with some default values. We edit the first value and change it to `ID_SNAPSHOT`. Then we right-click on the row we just created and select "Next Key Typed." We press the 's' key, thereby completing this row of the table and making 's' an accelerator key.

To establish a handler for the event that the "s" key is pressed, right-click on the row we just added and select *Add Event Handler…*. Choose message type *COMMAND*, and in the class list choose `CMovingCirclesView`. In the edit box under *Function handler name*, enter *OnSnapshot*. Then click on *Add and Edit*, and all the necessary changes will occur in the wizard files. The source editor will show file *MovingCirclesView.cpp*, and the text cursor will be positioned inside the body of the newly added handler. Simply insert a call on `onSnapshot()` at the bottom, resulting in the following code:

```
void CMovingCirclesView::OnSnapshot()
{
    // TODO: Add your command handler code here
    onSnapshot();
}
```

The only change which needs to be made in file *HCMovingCircles.h* is the single line

```
void onSnapshot();
```

in the public part of the class definition for HCMovingCircles, declaring the new method in the hand-coded view class. But now we must actually provide the code for the onSnapshot() routine, and it must be placed in a separately compiled file because it makes reference to the wizard-generated pop-up window class. Accordingly, we create file *HCMovingCircles.cpp* and place in it precisely the following lines:

```
#include "stdafx.h"
#include "HCMovingCircles.h"
#include "SnapshotWnd.h"
#include "Resource.h"

void HCMovingCircles::onSnapshot() {
    CRect R;
    pWnd->GetClientRect(&R);
    CClientDC dc(pWnd);
    CDC memDC;
    CBitmap *bmp = new CBitmap();
    bmp->CreateCompatibleBitmap(&dc,R.Width(),R.Height());
    memDC.CreateCompatibleDC(&dc);
    CBitmap *oldBitmap = memDC.SelectObject(bmp);
    memDC.BitBlt(0,0,R.Width(),R.Height(),&dc,R.left,R.top,
                 SRCCOPY);
    memDC.SelectObject(oldBitmap);
    CSnapshotWnd snapWnd(pWnd,bmp);
    snapWnd.DoModal();
}
```

The handler for the accelerator key was the only event handler we needed in the view class. We need event handlers for WM_PAINT and WM_DESTROY in the pop-up window class, as is evident from the presence of the routines onPaint()

and `onDestroy()` in the definition above for the corresponding hand-coded class. These are easily furnished via the properties window for class `CSnapshotWnd`, and should appear as follows when the reader has correctly generated and edited them.

```
void CSnapshotWnd::OnPaint()
{
    // CPaintDC dc(this); // device context for painting
    // TODO: Add your message handler code here
    // Do not call CDialog::OnPaint() for painting messages
    onPaint();
}

void CSnapshotWnd::OnDestroy()
{
    __super::OnDestroy();

    // TODO: Add your message handler code here
    onDestroy();
}
```

In the `OnPaint()` method, we have commented out the instantiation of the `CPaintDC` device context, in favor of a client device context. These objects have subtly different ways of interacting with the display. The reader may want to try un-commenting and using the paint device context to see how its manner of managing the display differs from that of the client device context on his machine. The initial appearance of the snapshot window will be the same in either case, but in resizing or maximizing the window the operating system may try to economize concerning which portions of the client area it actually draws in response to the call on `StretchBlt()`, and the different effects can be interesting.

6.12 SUMMARY

MFC has been designed as a library in a manner similar to the way in which C++ was designed as a language, which is to get in the way of the platform on which it is running as little as possible. Because the Windows family of operating systems has a distinctly object-based flavor in spite of its procedural API, the essential pattern for the design of MFC was already strongly suggested. Although deliberately restrained in its design, the library is still quite large. In order to keep our attention focused on a manageable subset, in this chapter we have looked at a specific MFC project type, similar to Smalltalk projects constructed around the MVC pattern, called the Single Document Interface, or SDI. Our discussion has centered around the four classes in an SDI project.

The four classes in an SDI project are the application class, the frame window class, the document class, and the view class. The MFC base classes for the four are `CWinApp`, `CFrameWnd`, `CDocument`, and `CView`, respectively. Except for customization of the menu attached to the frame window, most of the variation from project to project is to be found in the document class and the view class. In the SDI pattern, all four classes are effectively singletons, and in particular exactly one object of the application class will be instantiated, at file scope, in the application source file. Its constructor will do some essential initializations before the main program begins execution. The main program is in fact a library routine which ultimately gives control over to a message loop, so that the programmer achieves his aims chiefly by writing event handlers.

Both the creation of the four classes for an SDI project and the addition of event handlers are managed by Visual Studio's code generation wizards. The event handler wizard also generates overrides for specific virtual functions in the base classes, such as `OnDraw()` and `OnInitialUpdate()`, which are not event handlers but are called from event handlers. Besides overrides, this wizard generates code for two types of event handlers, namely those which respond to Windows messages and those which respond to programmer-defined events.

To maintain the integrity of his original solutions, the programmer is advised to modify the wizard-generated code as little as possible, and to keep most of his work in separate hand-coded files. This practice not only helps to protect the programmer's creative rights, but also aids in portability and maintenance. A simple way to manage some types of small-to-medium-sized SDI projects is to place all event handlers in the wizard-generated view class and to insert a single call in each such handler to a corresponding method in one of the user's hand-coded classes. A practice which aids this approach is to have the wizard-generated view class inherit doubly from its MFC base class, `CView`, and the programmer's hand-coded class. Some simple naming conventions can be used to make the correspondence between view class and hand-coded class, and between wizard-generated handler and programmer-defined handler, quite clear and obvious, to the extent that the regeneration from scratch of the entire project based on clues in the hand-coded files is straightforward.

As in the MVC pattern, a view object is intended to be a "window" into the state of a model object, here called a document. The central task of the SDI view object is to construct a representation of the current state of the document, and to maintain that representation in response to the windows paint message `WM_PAINT` and other events. The programmer's response to the paint message is supplied in this chapter by overriding the `OnDraw()` function in the wizard-generated view class. The view window is drawn upon using a *device context*, which encapsulates a number of drawing tools including a bitmap, a pen, and a brush. All the standard drawing operations can be accomplished with a device context, which "owns" from its instantiation default tools which can be swapped for more specifically targeted tools created by the programmer. That swapping is done using the overloaded `SelectObject()` method of the base device context class `CDC`. It is generally unsafe to fail to restore the default tool before the device context object is destroyed.

Animation and other periodic effects can be achieved by requesting the view window to generate `WM_TIMER` messages at regular intervals. The `CWnd` methods concerned are `StartTimer()` and `KillTimer()`. Both are provided with an integer ID to identify which sequence of timer interrupts has caused a specific timer message. The ID is furnished to the `OnTimer()` event handler, which can use it to determine which repeated action to perform. In the pattern described above, a convenient place to call `StartTimer()` is in the `onInitialUpdate()` method called from the corresponding override in the view class, and the `onDestroy()` method, called by the wizard-generated handler for `WM_DESTROY`, should usually call `KillTimer()`.

The most convenient way to achieve persistence in the SDI pattern is to bring the document class into play. Any class can be used as a "model" class in the MVC sense, and can be made conveniently accessible by making it an additional base class (in addition to `CDocument`) for the wizard-generated document class. An override of the virtual function `Serialize()` in that class can be made to save and restore the "document" using the `CArchive` class, a stream-like binary file manipulation class containing overloads of the stream insertion and stream extraction operators for all built-in C++ types.

Character string input in an MFC project is best done by means of tailored dialog classes, which can be generated by an MFC wizard based on a dialog resource created by the resource editor using "drag and drop" tools. Many such tools are available, but this text has confined itself to static text controls and edit controls. A dialog box can be brought up in modal fashion by instantiating a dialog object of the appropriate class and sending it the `DoModal()` message. Most dialog initialization takes place inside the dialog class in the `OnInitDialog()` override, which has as its major task the association of each of the controls in the dialog box with a dialog class member, usually a pointer with an MFC control type, such as `CEdit`, as its base type. These objects are not owned by the dialog class and should not be deleted by it. Most of the activity of the dialog box in response to user actions is preprogrammed into the controls themselves, but it is important that the programmer in his hand-coded dialog class supply an `onDestroy()` method which copies the important data from the controls themselves to class scope. Again, the recommendation here is that there be a hand-coded dialog class which is used as a second base class for the wizard-generated dialog class. The latter class should be given a handler for the windows `WM_DESTROY` event, and that handler should call `onDestroy()`. Access functions can then be provided which can be used to quiz the dialog object about its internal state after it returns from the call on `DoModal()`.

Off-screen drawing is often a good idea, and is accomplished using a memory bitmap. Like many objects in MFC, memory bitmaps require a two-stage creation process, using the default constructor first, then a call on `CBitmap::CreateCompatibleBitmap()`. A memory device context can then be constructed using a very similar protocol, and the device context's `SelectObject()` method can then be used to associate the memory bitmap with the memory device context. Any drawing done to this device context will be off-screen, but can be moved on-screen using `CDC::BitBlt()` or `CDC::StretchBlt()`.

REVIEW QUESTIONS

1. The Win32 API is not object-oriented, but object-based. Explain what this means.
2. Why are the MFC classes called "wrapper classes"?
3. What is contained in the preprocessor file *winuser.h*?
4. Explain the SDI application style.
5. What are the names of the base classes for the four wizard-generated classes in an SDI application? What role does each play?
6. Where is the "main program" in an SDI application? Why does it *not* begin executing before any other code?
7. Where (i.e., in which named program unit) does the top-level window in an SDI application get created, as a Win32 object?
8. The document class in an SDI application is effectively a singleton. What do we mean by that? In the multiple document interface (MDI) style it is not a singleton. Many popular Win32 applications, such as Visual Studio,

use the MDI. Why is the document class not a singleton in an MDI application?

9. What is the purpose of the view class? What is the common indirect base class for the view class and the frame window class (i.e., the base class for all windows)?

10. For an SDI application entitled *PointOfSale*, what are the names of the four wizard-generated classes for the application?

11. What method call, issued inside a method of a CWnd-derived class, places in the CRect object R the attributes of the current client rectangle?

12. Describe the event that is associated with the event type WM_PAINT. What method in CView responds the WM_PAINT event? Why do we not modify that method when we create an SDI application?

13. What is a device context used for? What is the base class for device contexts in MFC?

14. What are the two derived classes of CDC in the MFC library? What is each used for?

15. Why do the drawing methods of CDC make no mention of color?

16. Any device context encapsulates three resources. What are they, and how can we "switch" the default resource for a new one? Give an example. What must we always do when we perform such a switch, before destroying the device context object?

17. What three events were used in the drawing of ellipses in the *HCEllipses.h* file, and how were they used? In other words, what happened with each event? (Note that all "click and drag" operations follow a similar protocol.)

18. The three classifications for Visual Studio wizard-generated code are called "events," "messages," and "overrides." Describe the difference between these three.

19. What does OnDraw() do? Why is it not an event handler?

20. Explain why it is often true that not all the initialization in a hand-coded view file, as described in this chapter, can be done inside the constructor. Where must it be done, if it cannot be done in the constructor, and why?

21. In the moving circles application, why was it not possible to merge two circles immediately when they were found to be "touching"? Explain.

22. When is it not feasible to write an SDI application by placing all the code in the view class? Explain.

23. Explain, in the "animal, vegetable, mineral" game application, why the use of a graphical user interface required a radical change in the way user interaction was controlled, over the earlier console-based version.

24. Explain, in the "animal, vegetable, mineral" game application, why it made sense to make `TraversableAVMGame` class use protected inheritance. Could we now use a `TraversableAVMGame` object as an argument for a `Category` parameter in a method call? Do you think this is good design? Why or why not?

25. Explain, in the "animal, vegetable, mineral" game application, why the `reset()` function was declared to be virtual.

26. How does `CArchive` differ from a stream? Once you have overloaded `<<` and `>>` operations for a class, what code modifications are necessary to tie save and restore operations to the corresponding menu items?

27. Explain the operation of `CWnd::GetDlgItem()`.

28. What happends when we send the `DoModal()` message to a dialog object? What values can be returned from this call, and when is each returned? Explain.

29. What should the event handler for a dialog box do upon receiving the message `WM_DESTROY`?

30. Explain how a bitmap can be constructed of a size compatible with a given device context object `dc`, and describe how the bitmap can be filled with white pixels.

31. What do we call an operation which copies the contents of the bitmap associated with device context `dc1` to that associated with device context `dc2`? What two types of this operation are there, in what class do these functions reside, and what does each do?

EXERCISES

1. Look closely at the Win32 message loop algorithm in Section 6.1. Why is it not strictly true that the only work done in such an algorithm is done by event handlers? What do we call this "other kind" of work, and what work do you imagine might be done there? Can this type of processing be integrated into an MFC project?

2. Explain how the client programmer who starts with properly constructed hand-generated code can be sufficiently guided by a set of naming conventions to properly set up and modify wizard-generated code to implement the custom SDI application intended by the original programmer.

3. Use the procedure you detailed in Exercise 2 to create an application around the following header file. What does the application do? Describe all the behaviors of the application carefully, and explain why they occur.

```
#ifndef __HCMAPPER_H
#define __HCMAPPER_H

#include "stdafx.h"
#include <vector>
using std::vector;
#include <cmath>

class HCMapper {
    enum {DIAMETER = 15};
    vector<CString> cities;
public:
    HCMapper() {
        cities.push_back(_T("Kings Landing"));
        cities.push_back(_T("Paris"));
        cities.push_back(_T("Tates Creek"));
        cities.push_back(_T("Hog Wallow"));
        cities.push_back(_T("NorthPort"));
    }
    void onDraw(CDC *pDC, CView *pWnd) {
        CRect R;
        pWnd->GetClientRect(&R);
        CBrush BB(RGB(0,0,0));
        CBrush *oldBrush = pDC->SelectObject(&BB);
        for (int i=0; i<cities.size(); ++i) {
            int x = R.left + rand()/(double)(RAND_MAX+1) *
                            (R.right - R.left);
            int y = R.top + rand()/(double)(RAND_MAX+1) *
                            (R.bottom - R.top);
            pDC->Ellipse(x,y,x+DIAMETER,y+DIAMETER);
            pDC->TextOut(x+DIAMETER,y+DIAMETER,cities[i]);
        }
        pDC->SelectObject(oldBrush);
    }
};

#endif
```

4. Modify the "Mapper" program in Exercise 3 so that the randomness involved in the drawing of the view occurs only once—when the application is started. The display should remain the same when the window is resized or minimized and restored.

5. Explain why value semantics are important in the sequence below, taken from the AVM application:

```
history.push(place);
place.category = &*place.nextSubcategory;
```

6. An alternative to the "modal" style of dialog box interaction discussed in this chapter is the "modeless" style, in which bringing up the dialog box does not freeze the parent window. In modeless interaction, either or both windows can respond to events. Investigate how a modeless dialog box can be created and used in an MFC application.

7. Using the naming conventions advocated in this chapter, create a hand-coded "include file" for an application that maintains a complete graph by drawing a small red spot with a black border, radius ten pixels, at the location of each mouse click, storing the location of each such spot in a list and keeping every spot connected by one-pixel-wide black lines to every other spot.

8. Alter the hand-coded file you created in Exercise 7 in order to respond to "click and drag" operations, so that the user can move the red spots around on the screen. The lines should remain on the screen, but should move along with the spots so that the complete graph is always correctly drawn.

7

JAVA AND THE SWING LIBRARY

The Java language stands apart from C++ by virtue of its emphasis on safety. It is a language with fewer and safer mechanisms, but with powerful functionality delivered by a well-chosen set of built-in features and a large collection of sensibly and consistently designed library classes. Its portability has also been a huge plus, especially coupled as it is with the Java Virtual Machine's ability to smoothly merge with internet browsers as a "plug-in." Its relative safety has given it an advantage as a teaching language over C++, which was once the favorite in academic settings. More adventurous programmers may complain that they are more tightly constrained than they would like, and that the emphasis on safety and portability comes at the expense of more run-time overhead. Java is, however, a compiled language; with careful implementation its code can be made surprisingly fast.

In this chapter, we go beyond our initial coverage in Chapter 4, "C++ and Java Commonalities and Similarities," and as we delve into the areas where Java differs radically from C++ we will see that this language has no identity problems; it is well-conceived and consistent and able to offer solutions to most problems that might arise in a commercial, recreational, or even a research environment. Our discussion begins with text input, one of the areas where the customary approach in C++ differs dramatically from that in Java.

Code samples for this chapter are located on the companion CD-ROM.

7.1 TEXT INPUT OPERATIONS AND THE WRAPPER CLASSES

A capability which is taken very much for granted in C++ is console input. It could be said that here we have an instance where Java is much more "honest" than C++, because text input is a fairly complex process, and the streaming operators of C++ make it look easier than it really is. Java, however, forces the programmer to think of text input operations as lexical analysis operations, which is in fact the correct view. Several ingredients go into this more complex view of input, and we discuss them in the sections that follow. First, however, we need to say a word about the language we intend to use in talking about the necessary classes.

An important OOPL colloquialism we often see is the use of the verb "to wrap" in the context of calling a constructor. For example, the expression

```
new Integer(38)
```

is in fact a call on a conversion constructor. But the language we typically use is that we are "wrapping" an `Integer` object around the primitive `int` value 38. For this reason we call `Integer` a "wrapper class." The "wrap" terminology is also commonly used in talking about files and I/O, where one kind of file processing class object is often used as input to the constructor of another such class.

In a related consideration, it also happens that the numeric wrapper classes `Integer`, `Double`, etc., are used extensively to do the parsing that is necessary to convert data from its external text form into a form suitable for computations. There is a series of parsing operations which take the form of static methods in these classes, for example the `parseInt()` method of class `Integer`. These can be valuable in completing the transition from external numeric literal to internally stored primitive numeric value.

7.1.1 Stream Readers, Buffered Readers, and the readLine() Method

A very useful input operation from the console or from a text file is to read an entire line of text into a string. Unfortunately, neither the standard input object `System.in` nor any other object which can be simply constructed in Java is able to perform this function for us. The `readLine()` method which performs this task resides in class `BufferedReader`, which is not the type assigned to `System.in`, nor is it a class that `System.in` has any kind of inheritance relationship with. What *is* true is that there is a constructor for class `BufferedReader` which takes a parameter of type `Reader`, and there is a class descended from `Reader` called `InputStreamReader`, which has a conversion constructor for parameters of type `InputStream`, which is the type assigned to `System.in`. In short, to obtain the capability to read lines of input from the console, we must (1) wrap an `Input-StreamReader` around `System.in`, then (2) wrap a `BufferedReader` around that. The actual Java code is as follows:

```
BufferedReader consoleReader = new BufferedReader(
    new InputStreamReader(System.in)
);
```

After the above instantiation of the object `consoleReader`, we can fetch lines of text from the console with the statement `str = consoleReader.readLine()`, where `str` is a variable of type `String`. If the line is empty, the empty string will be stored at `str`.

A similar strategy will open a text file for us, but this time we wrap a `BufferedReader` around a `FileReader` object. For example, to read from a text file named *input.txt* we can use the following reader:

```
BufferedReader fileReader = new BufferedReader(
    new FileReader("input.txt")
);
```

Here, if we attempt to read past the end of file the call `fileReader.readLine()` will return `null`.

In both cases above, we must keep in mind that sending the `readLine()` message to a `BufferedReader` object can cause an `IOException` to be thrown.

7.1.2 The StringTokenizer Class

Once we have a line of input stored in a string, how do we mine it for content? With input operations a string must usually be searched for patterns, and those patterns must be converted to the correct internal values. This could be done by writing a character-by-character lexical analyzer, but much of that functionality already exists in the Java library, and we might as well take advantage of it. The two crucial capabilities are (a) using whitespace and/or other delimiting characters to define the boundaries of substrings, and (b) converting those substrings into a form suitable for storage in a program variable. The latter capability is furnished by the numeric wrapper classes, and the former can be accomplished by the `StringTokenizer` class.

Two strings are provided to the `StringTokenizer` constructor at instantiation time: (1) the string to be tokenized, and (2) a string of delimiter characters. Thus, if we instantiate `tokenizer` as

```
StringTokenizer tokenizer = new StringTokenizer(
    "98**75.3    #48",
    " *#"
);
```

then the tokenizer uses the space, asterisk, and "sharp" symbols as separators. Now successive executions of the method call `tokenizer.nextToken()` will yield the strings `"98"`, `"75.3"`, and `"48"`, in turn.

> **NOTE**
>
> *A similar class to StringTokenizer is the Scanner class, which has a constructor that wraps around a string to be parsed, but which, instead of the generic nextToken() method, provides a set of type-specific methods: next() for next string, nextInt() for the next int value, nextFloat() for the next float value, etc. A Scanner object, like a StringToken object, can be configured to use different delimiters, in this case by sending the useDelimiter() message. The operand to useDelimiter is a pattern or a string describing a pattern. Exercise 3 asks the reader to investigate the form and use of such patterns.*

7.1.3 "Parsing" with the Wrapper Classes

When we tokenize a line of text in a generic way, i.e., as a sequence of strings, then we can complete the input process by appealing to the static wrapper class methods. Each is able to convert a string into a stored primitive value. For example, the value of `Double.parseDouble("7.813")` is the stored double-precision value which would be represented in Java code by the literal `7.813`.

Let's put this capability in the context of a small test application. Recall the binary search tree example in Chapter 5, "Additional Concepts from the C++ Language," where we made a string stream and alternately read a `string` key and a `double` value and stored them in a binary search tree. We will expand that example by reading a series of (*key, value*) pairs from text file *properties.txt*. Suppose, for example, that the *properties.txt* file contains the following:

```
Age:  33;    Exemptions:  3
GrossIncome:  90710;  TaxesWithheld:  15878
```

```
DOBYear:  1975;  DOBMonth: 11;  DOBDay: 3
```

We wish to read the file, place all the (*property name, property value*) pairs in a `TreeMap` object, and echo each pair back to the console in alphabetical order by property name. The following application class will accomplish this:

```java
import java.io.BufferedReader;
import java.io.FileReader;
import java.util.Iterator;
import java.util.Map;
import java.util.StringTokenizer;
import java.util.TreeMap;

public class StringTokenizerTest {

    public static void main(String args[]) {
        TreeMap<String, Integer> m =
            new TreeMap<String, Integer>();
        try {
            BufferedReader reader = new BufferedReader(
                new FileReader("properties.txt")
            );
            String line = reader.readLine();
            while (line != null && !line.equals("")) {
                StringTokenizer tokenizer =
                    new StringTokenizer(line, " :;");
                while (tokenizer.hasMoreTokens()) {
                    String key = tokenizer.nextToken();
                    int value = Integer.parseInt(
                        tokenizer.nextToken());
                    m.put(key, new Integer(value));
                }
                line = reader.readLine();
            }
        }
        catch (Exception e) {
            e.printStackTrace();
        }
        Iterator i = m.entrySet().iterator();
        while (i.hasNext()) {
            Map.Entry<String, Double> e =
                (Map.Entry<String, Double>) i.next();
            System.out.println(
```

```
                    e.getKey() + ": " + e.getValue());
        }
    }
}
```

Here we use spaces, colons, and semicolons as delimiters, meaning that the string tokenizer completely ignores them except as separators between the strings of interest, and we read the entire text file into the `TreeMap<String, Integer>` object `m`. The program assumes the property name will come first, followed by an integer literal giving the property value. The object `tokenizer` delivers both as strings, but the string containing the value is converted to type `int` using `Integer.parseInt()`. Once the file has been completely processed we extract the (*property, value*) pairs, each of type `Map.Entry<String, Integer>`, and iterate through them, echoing them to the screen one pair to a line. (The file name *properties.txt* is not qualified with path information, and so it must be placed in the project directory or the instantiation of the reader will fail.)

7.2   JAVA INHERITANCE AND POLYMORPHISM

Classes in Java must always have exactly one direct base class, or superclass. If none is explicitly given, then the base class is always *Object*. Residing in the *Object* class are some powerful capabilities common to all first-class objects, including the ability to hash themselves, to make shallow copies of themselves, and to notify and wait on threads currently executing or attempting to execute methods inside themselves.

Polymorphism in Java, as in Smalltalk, is the default behavior. Overriding a method in a derived class will always cause polymorphic behavior. For example, as it exists in the `Object` base class the `equals()` method only compares pointers. Thus, if each of `p` and `q` is a first-class object of a given type, and that type provides no override of `equals()`, then the result of `p.equals(q)` is precisely the same as the result of `p == q`. The clear expectation is that the programmer will override the `equals()` method, because as it is implemented in `Object` it is redundant. For example, the `Point` class below has overridden the method to give it a more useful meaning:

```
public class Point {
    public int x, y;
    public boolean equals(Object o) {
        if (o == null) return false;
```

```
        Point p = (Point)o;
        return x == p.x && y == p.y;
    }
  }
```

In general, the `equals()` method is expected to be overridden in such a way as to involve the *values* of its two operands, even though the version in `Object` does not.

There is a type of method in Java which cannot be overridden. If a method is declared `final`, then it may not be redefined in derived classes. The `wait()` method of class `Object` is an example, where the actions taken by a thread in order to wait for exclusive access to an object are defined. In that case, allowing the programmer to redefine these actions could be catastrophic. The Java compiler may elect to translate calls to final methods inline, because there is no possibility of polymorphic behavior by a final method.

Note that the above use of keyword `final` differs from but is related to its use in data member declarations, where it means that the value of the member is fixed at instantiation time and cannot be changed during the lifetime of the object. Another meaning of the keyword is that when a *class* is declared final then it cannot be used as a superclass. All the methods of such a class are implicitly final and are candidates for inline implementation.

Java inheritance is always public inheritance, meaning that anything which is public in the base class will always be public in the derived class. Thus, Java derived classes are true subtypes.

7.3   JAVA INTERFACES

Java does not allow more than one base class, but a Java class may implement as many *interfaces* as the programmer wishes. Implementing an interface, however, typically does not gain resources for the implementing class. On the contrary, it incurs an obligation. An interface does not have any active content, but consists only of instance method prototypes and static data; any class which implements the interface must supply definitions for all the methods which are declared in the interface.

Some of the most important entities in the Java library are interfaces, including `Collection`, `List`, and `Queue`. Interfaces have no constructors, and they share with abstract classes the property that objects cannot be directly instantiated in a conventional way using their type names. However, once an object of a type which implements an interface has been instantiated, it can be transmitted as an argument to a method which has a parameter of the interface type. The declaration

```
Queue q;
```

is acceptable, but its value will be `null` until an assignment is made to it, and any object assigned to it must implement the `Queue` interface. Because `LinkedList` is one of the implementers of the interface, the assignment

```
q = new LinkedList();
```

is perfectly correct.

7.3.1 Sorting and Interface Comparable

Let us use sorting an array as an example. There is a class called `Arrays` in the Java library that is capable of sorting into a prescribed order any array of values of a built-in type, and also arrays of first-class objects if the object type in question has been properly constructed. `Arrays` sorts the built-in types by overloading the static `sort()` method once for each such type. The algorithm it uses is a variant of the *quicksort* algorithm, which although very sophisticated is still a "compare and swap" algorithm. For built-in types, all comparisons can be done with the native operators <, <=, etc. But these operators are not defined and cannot be defined for first-class objects in Java. Instead, inside the `sort()` overload with parameter type `Object[]` the code is written in such a way as to require that the actual type assigned to the array elements implement the `Comparable` interface, reproduced below:

```
public interface Comparable {
    public int compareTo(Object o);
}
```

If `x` and `y` are objects of a class type which implements the `Comparable` interface, then the expression

```
x.compareTo(y)
```

should return –1 if the value of `x` is considered "less than" that of `y`, 0 if it is considered the same, and 1 if it is considered greater. Let's suppose, then, that we are comparing two objects `a[i]` and `a[j]` of type `Object`. The following code sequence makes no sense because operator < is not defined for such operands:

```
if (a[i] < a[j]) {
    //    ^ Syntax error.
    Object temp = a[i]; a[i] = a[j]; a[j] = temp;
}
```

Instead, we code the following:

```
if (((Comparable)a[i]).compareTo(a[j]) < 0) {
    Object temp = a[i]; a[i] = a[j]; a[j] = temp;
}
```

So in order to make a class, say `EmployeeRecord`, plug into this framework, it is only necessary that the class (a) claim to implement the `Comparable` interface in its declaration, and (b) actually make good on the claim by providing a definition for `compareTo()`. An outline of a conforming class is given below:

```
class EmployeeRecord implements Comparable {
    String firstName, middleName, lastName;
    int employeeID;
    ...
    public int compareTo(Object o) {
        EmployeeRecord emp = (EmployeeRecord)o;
        if (employeeID < emp.employeeID) return -1;
        else if (employeeID == emp.employeeID) return 0;
        else return 1;
    }
    ...
}
```

Now an array of employee records can be sorted into increasing order based on ID number as follows:

```
EmployeeRecord emps[] = new EmployeeRecord[n];
... // Fill the array 'emps' with data on employees.
Arrays.sort(emps); // 'emps' is now sorted.
```

Using the scheme demonstrated above, a generic sort can be accomplished without using "generics" as such. In fact, Java for much of its history has incorporated nothing like the C++ templates, relying for genericity on interfaces. A class which has some utility function to perform as a service for client classes simply separates all the capabilities it needs from those client classes into an interface, then performs its services only on objects of a class for which that interface is implemented. The implementing classes are never mentioned by name in the "generic" utility code. All parameters and local variables are declared using the interface as a type, but of course all instantiated objects must either be received as parameters or be constructed using utility classes which implement the interface.

7.3.2 Example: Interfaces for a Radix Sort

For an example, let us consider the radix sort scheme. In a radix sort, the records are never actually compared; rather they are repeatedly sorted into queues called *bins* based on the value of a single digit in the key, and after being so distributed all the queues are concatenated back into one large queue in a manner which keeps them sorted on that particular digit. When all the digits in the key have been used in this way, from least significant to most significant digit, the list is sorted.

To write a generic radix sort, then, we need our elements to have the capability to inform clients concerning the radix of the key (e.g., base 10 for zip codes, base 36 for part numbers with mixed base-10 digits and upper-case alphabetic characters), the number of digits in the key, and the individual digits of the key. The `RadixSortElement` interface below suffices:

```
package OOPLS;

public interface RadixSortElement {
    int radix();        // Radix r.
    int digitsInKey();  // Width w of key.
    int getDigit(int i);// i must be between 0 and w-1,
                        // inclusively. Digit 0 is the
                        // rightmost (lowest order) digit.
                        // Returns a value between 0 and r-1.
}
```

We construct now a class which implements this interface.

```
package OOPLS;

public class PostalRecord implements RadixSortElement {
```

```
    int zip;
    String name, address1, address2, city, state;
    public int radix() { return 10; }
    public int digitsInKey() { return 5; }
    public int getDigit(int i) {
        int digit = zip;
        while (--i > 0) digit /= 10;
        return digit % 10;
    }
    public PostalRecord(String name, String address1,
                        String address2, String city,
                        String state, String zip)
            throws Exception {
        this.name = name;
        this.address1 = address1;
        this.address2 = address2;
        this.city = city;
        this.state = state;
        this.zip = Integer.parseInt(zip);
    }
}
```

Happily, we do not have to individually tailor a radix sort to work only on collections of `PostalRecord` objects. It is straightforward to write a 'generic' radix sort which works for any class implementing interface `RadixSortElement`.

We perform the sort on a `Queue`, not an array, because direct access to elements by their positions in the array is unnecessary in a radix sort. Note that `Queue` is, again, not a class but an interface. From that interface we will be using methods `add()`, which adds an element to the rear of the queue, `element()`, which returns the element at the front, and `remove()`, which removes the element at the front. When we create our bins we will instantiate objects of type `LinkedList`, a class which implements the `Queue` interface but also has other capabilities we will use, namely `addAll()`, which adds all the elements of one `LinkedList` object onto the end of another, `clear()`, which removes all elements, and `isEmpty()`, which returns `true` exactly when there are no items remaining.

```
package OOPLS;

import OOPLS.RadixSortElement;
import java.util.LinkedList;
import java.util.Queue;
```

```java
public class RadixSorter {
    public static void sort(Queue masterQ) {
        RadixSortElement rse =
            (RadixSortElement)masterQ.element();
        LinkedList[] subQ = new LinkedList[rse.radix()];
        for (int i=0; i<rse.radix(); ++i)
            subQ[i] = new LinkedList();
        int binNumber, digitPosition = 1;
        RadixSortElement currentItem;
        while (digitPosition <= rse.digitsInKey()) {
            while (!masterQ.isEmpty()) {
                currentItem =
                    (RadixSortElement)masterQ.element();
                masterQ.remove();
                binNumber =
                    currentItem.getDigit(digitPosition);
                subQ[binNumber].add(currentItem);
            }
            for (int k=0; k<rse.radix(); ++k) {
                masterQ.addAll(subQ[k]);
                subQ[k].clear();
            }
            digitPosition++;
        }
    }
}
```

With all the other parts already in place, the coding of the above sort is straightforward. Below is a client class encapsulating a main program and some test data:

```java
import OOPLS.PostalRecord;
import OOPLS.RadixSorter;
import java.util.LinkedList;
public class RadixSortTester {
    static String[][] trialData = {
        {"Zachariah Malachi", "101 Holy Lane",
         "Apartment 3B", "Jerusalem", "GA", "35109"},
        {"Cody Kadiddlehopper", "5967 Old Horse Lane",
         "", "Badlands", "KS", "50505"},
        {"Curtis Plemmons", "Route 7",
         "", "Turkey Trot", "PA", "16678"},
        {"Melinda Jabbers", "11234 Fifth Avenue", "",
         "Manhattan", "OK", "77789"},
```

```
                  {"Smyrna Figs", "200 Locust Avenue", "",
                   "Richmond", "KY", "40475"},
                  {"Allyson Krauts", "421 Mockingbird Lane",
                   "Box 277", "Nashville", "TN", "37205"}
            };
            public static void main(String[] arg) {
                LinkedList mainQueue = new LinkedList();
            try {
                for (int i=0; i<trialData.length; ++i) {
                    mainQueue.add(new PostalRecord(
                        trialData[i][0], trialData[i][1],
                        trialData[i][2], trialData[i][3],
                        trialData[i][4], trialData[i][5]
                    ));
                }
                RadixSorter.sort(mainQueue);
            }
            catch (Exception e) {
                System.err.println(e.toString());
            }
            while (!mainQueue.isEmpty()) {
                PostalRecord record =
                    (PostalRecord)mainQueue.element();
                if (record != null) {
                    System.out.println(record.zip);
                    mainQueue.remove();
                }
            }
        }

    }
```

7.3.3 Interface Inheritance

Interfaces can inherit, but only from other interfaces. The syntax which signifies
that one interface inherits from another is exactly the same as that which signifies class inheritance. Thus, the first line of an interface definition for interface
A will appear as

```
    interface A extends B
```

if its base interface is B. If A is defined in that fashion, then any class which
implements interface A must also implement interface B. In other words, interface inheritance tends to lead to an accumulation of obligations. The deeper in

the interface inheritance chain we go, the more requirements are placed on the classes which implement those interfaces.

Interface inheritance is unrelated to class inheritance. Two classes related by inheritance may implement two totally unrelated interfaces, and no inheritance relationship need be present between two classes which implement the same interface or related interfaces.

7.3.4 Iterating through a Collection

One interface is so important that a control structure is built around it. The "for-each" control structure dispenses with the need for an explicit mention of an iterator or an index when making a pass through a Java container or array. In the following array example, the variable x is used as a placeholder and varies over all the values `a[0], a[1], ..., a[n-1]`.

```
int a[] = new int[n];
...
for (int x: a)
    System.out.println(x);
```

There is an attractive elegance to this control structure, and we would like to use it in more settings than just in making a pass through an array. Fortunately, here Java employs a cooperation between library design and language design. The language allows this control structure to be used with any class which implements the `Iterable<>` interface. Because the only method in that interface is the `iterator()` method, nearly all the containers in the Java library qualify. Here is an example:

```
TreeMap<String,String> spouse = new TreeMap<String,String>();
spouse.put("Henry", "Maude");
spouse.put("Theodore", "Minerva");
spouse.put("Carol", "Joe");
for (Map.Entry couple: spouse.entrySet())
    System.out.println(couple.getKey() + " is married to " +
        couple.getValue());
```

Output is as follows:

```
Carol is married to Joe
Henry is married to Maude
Theodore is married to Minerva
```

7.3.5 Interface Cloneable—the Ramifications of Pointer Semantics

Java is not completely "locked in" to pointer semantics. Yes, when we make the assignment a = b where a and b are first-class objects of type MyClass, we always create an alias, meaning that a and b now refer to the same object. However, it is perfectly possible and acceptable to use a separate copy of a Java object as a new value for another Java object. The clone() method resides in the ultimate base class Object, and is endowed with the capability to make a shallow copy of the object which is executing it, place that copy on the heap, and return a handle to it. So, if the data members of the class to which a and b belong are all of primitive types such as int, char, double, etc., then the statement

```
a = (MyClass)b.clone();
```

accomplishes our objective, *if* it is legal. But the programmer who designs the class must take explicit action to "legalize cloning" for the type! (This does not require congressional action and is not controversial.)

Why should the class designer have to give explicit thought to whether the class should be allowed to be cloned? The answer is rooted in the cautiousness with which Java was designed. It was recognized that, generally speaking, it is a complicated thing to mix value semantics with pointer semantics, and there is a lot of potential for grievous error. That error potential comes primarily from the confusing of shallow copies with deep copies. For example, suppose class MyClass has three data members, two of them primitive and the third a first-class object. Then a shallow copy will make completely separate copies of the first two data members, but will only copy the handle of the third. We have pushed the "pointer semantics" a little deeper, but it is still there. So the Java designers thought it best that the programmer be forced to make a specific decision whether or not to "turn on" the cloning capability for a class.

Interface Cloneable is the means for turning on cloning. Its definition is simple, and goes as follows:

```
public interface Cloneable {
}
```

In other words, it is an empty interface. What possible use can it be, then? It is there to provide a means by which the JVM can perform a run-time check before executing the value-copying code in method clone(). When the clone() message is sent to an object, the first thing the method does is access the run-time type information provided with the object to see whether that object imple-

ments `Cloneable`. If it does not, then an exception of the type `CloneNotSup-`
`portedException` is thrown. This mechanism, although only slightly expensive
in terms of run-time overhead, would not be considered in a language with the
C++ design philosophy, which is to do a minimum of run-time checks, but here
it makes perfect sense. We are not maximizing run-time speed; rather, we are
putting protection mechanisms into place to make the language safer.

Thus, if we change our `Point` class to the following, then we can make
clones:

```
public class Point implements Cloneable {
    public int x, y;
    public Object clone() throws CloneNotSupportedException {
        return super.clone();
    }
}
```

Now if we code

```
Point p = new Point(), q = (Point)p.clone();
```

then the assignment `p.x = 5` changes `p` but does not change `q`. It is easy to
see that we might often want this type of behavior. Suppose `p` and `q` were larger,
more complicated objects; this pattern makes it easier to give `p` and `q` values
which are "mostly alike," with minor differences. The object `q` starts out with
the same value as `p`, but continues on its own path afterward.

The override of `clone()` in the `Point` class seems unnecessary, because all it
does is return the same thing the version in class `Object` would return. We had
to include it, however, in order to allow clients to clone `Point` objects, because
`clone()` is a `protected` method in class `Object`.

But what of the "deep copy" issue? How can we achieve the ability for objects
to make deep copies of themselves? We need no new mechanisms for this. Polymorphism provides us the capability to *redefine* the `clone()` method so that it
makes a deep copy, if we wish. For instance, let us recall the `BasedFigure` class
of Chapter 4. Suppose we make the following naïve attempt to add cloning support to that class:

```
public class BasedFigure implements Cloneable {
    private Point base;
    public BasedFigure(Point base) {
        this.base = base;
```

```
        }
        public Point getBase() { return base; }
        public Object clone() throws CloneNotSupportedException {
            return super.clone();
        }
    }
```

This simple solution does not work, of course, because the `clone()` method in class `Object`, being a shallow cloning mechanism, will only copy the handle of the member called `base`. To get a true deep copy, we must be more careful in our override of `clone()`, as follows:

```
    public Object clone() throws CloneNotSupportedException {
        BasedFigure copy = (BasedFigure)super.clone();
        copy.base = (Point)base.clone();
        return copy;
    }
```

Here again the call `super.clone()` invokes the shallow copy mechanism, in which a new object will be created on the heap having its `base` member (in fact, its only member) constructed as a copy of the current one. We then immediately overwrite that member with a clone, completing the deep copy, and return the constructed copy.

To be a true deep copy, the cloning mechanism may need to be separately defined for all first-class types involved: all base classes, all classes of data members, all base classes of those classes, etc. If we stop short of that we risk having a copy which is partially separate but partially merged with the original value.

The issues above are complex, but they are not unique to Java. C++ gives us the first level (the shallow copy) for free for some classes with its "default memberwise copy" assignment semantics. For a true deep copy, however, we often must rewrite the assignment operator and take into account all the above considerations. There are no protection mechanisms in C++ to make the programmer think twice about the safety of his definition of "deep copy," however.

7.4 JAVA ENUMERATIONS

Much of which could be said about Java enumerations in Chapter 4 was left unsaid because the emphasis there was on the similarities between the two languages. Actually, Java enumerations are a totally different concept from C++

enumerations. As we said in Chapter 4, C++ enumerations are a handy way to bind a whole group of named constants to a local scope and to give that group a type name. Although the same use can be made, somewhat awkwardly, of Java enumerated constants, the Java enumerated type concept is quite different. In Java, objects of an enumerated type are first-class objects and can have attributes and behaviors. Consider, for example, the following chess piece type:

```java
public enum ChessPiece {
    WHITEPAWN(1,1), WHITEKNIGHT(1,3), WHITEBISHOP(1,3),
    WHITEROOK(1,5), WHITEQUEEN(1,9), WHITEKING(1,1<<30),
    BLACKPAWN(0,1), BLACKKNIGHT(0,3), BLACKBISHOP(0,3),
    BLACKROOK(0,5), BLACKQUEEN(0,9), BLACKKING(0,1<<30);
    private int side, value;
    private ChessPiece(int side, int value) {
        this.side = side;
        this.value = value;
    }
    public int getSide() { return side; }
    public int getValue() { return value; }
    public String toString() {
        String rv;
        if (getSide() == 0) rv = "Black ";
        else rv = "White ";
        switch(getValue()) {
            case 1: return rv + "Pawn";
            case 3:
                if (this==WHITEKNIGHT || this==BLACKKNIGHT)
                    return rv + "Knight";
                else return rv + "Bishop";
            case 5:
                return rv + "Rook";
            case 9:
                return rv + "Queen";
            case 1<<30:
                return rv + "King";
        }
        return rv;
    }
}
```

Note that this enumerated type has a constructor. But an enumerated type cannot actually have its constructor called by a client, because the constructor is required to be `private`. Instead, the arguments to the constructor for a given enumerated type value are listed in parentheses after that value's name. (Hence, for example, after the WHITEQUEEN constant the constructor arguments are listed as 1 for the side and 9 for the value associated with that piece.) There are in fact only a limited number of values of any given enumerated type, and the client does not create objects having these values; they already exist.

Each enumerated type is derived from the same base type, namely Enum. With that base type come some inherited behaviors, one of which is a static method called values(), and if we invoke that behavior we obtain an Iterable object which is capable of enumerating the various values of the type. Thus, the output from…

```
for (ChessPiece piece: ChessPiece.values())
    System.out.println(piece);
```

is the following, in which each piece's value is printed on a separate line using the toString() override provided.

```
White Pawn
White Knight
White Bishop
White Rook
White Queen
White King
Black Pawn
Black Knight
Black Bishop
Black Rook
Black Queen
Black King
```

Java enumerated types can implement interfaces but cannot inherit from any class but Enum, nor can they be used as base classes.

7.5   INNER CLASSES IN JAVA

Java shares with C++ the capability of nesting classes within classes within classes, to as deep a level as the programmer wishes. We did not give that capability any specific attention when we covered C++, however, because the capability is not much used in that language and there are no particular semantic peculiarities when it is used. On the other hand, inner classes are much relied upon in Java and are heavily used in event-driven programming. The reason is found in a curious and unexpected "surprise" which the C++ programmer (new to Java) gets when he takes a close look at Java inner classes!

7.5.1 Nonlocal References in Inner Classes

Consider the following example, in which class `ASquared` is contained inside class `A`.

```
package OOPLS;

public class A {
    int a;
    public class ASquared {
        int get() { return a*a; }
    }
    public A(int a) {
        this.a = a;
    }
    int get() { return a; }
}
```

The corresponding code would not be legal in C++, because there is a nonlocal reference in the inner class `ASquared` to the data member `a` of `A`. Such a nonlocal reference seems nonsensical, because `a` is an instance variable and there could be any number of instances of class `A` at any given time, each with its own copy of `a`, and there does not seem to be any way to specify to which of those copies the reference applies. The reference is legal here, however, so how are we to make sense of it? Some client code will help. Here is an example in which an `A` object and an `ASquared` object are created, and their encapsulated values printed:

```
import OOPLS.A;

public class AClient {
    public static void main(String args[]) {
        A a_obj = new A(5);
        A.ASquared asqr_obj = a_obj.new ASquared();
        System.out.println("a = " + a_obj.get() +
            ", and a*a = " + asqr_obj.get());
    }
}
```

The key difference between C++ and Java is seen in the one line of code

```
A.ASquared asqr_obj = a_obj.new ASquared();
```

This is very odd syntax if your background is in C++. Notice that here the `new` operation is coded as if it is a message to the object `a_obj`. The reason is that this instantiation of the class `A.ASquared` is directly linked to that object. Inside the storage representation of `asqr_obj` there is a stored pointer to the object `a_obj`, and that pointer is used to resolve any nonlocal references when messages are sent to `asqr_obj`. For that reason, when we send the message `asqr_obj.get()`, the statement `return a*a;` refers to the copy of `a` inside `a_obj`, which has the value 5. The output from our main program is then

```
a = 5, and a*a = 25
```

Note that we cannot statically resolve the nonlocal reference to *a* in `A.ASquared.get()`, but must employ a level of indirection. The slight extra cost in execution time is worth it here, as we shall see, because Java makes extensive use of this mechanism.

We do have the option in Java to dispense with the link to the outer object, by simply declaring the inner class `static`. Thus, if we replace the first line of the definition of `A.ASquared` with

```
public static class ASquared {
```

then the references to `a` in `get()` become illegal. The instantiation in the main program is also illegal and should be coded as

```
asqr_obj = new A.ASquared();
```

7.5.2 Using an Inner Class to Export an Interface

We now come to another curious thing about interfaces. Not only is it true that we cannot instantiate interfaces, but sometimes we must use objects whose types are hidden from us and about which all we know is that they implement the interface we need. For example, the method `listIterator()` in class `LinkedList` returns an object of unknown type which implements the `ListIterator` interface. In reality, its type is unimportant, because all we need from it are the behaviors in the interface. However, it is instructive to note here that the type of the object returned is `LinkedList.ListItr`, and that `ListItr` is a `private` inner class of `LinkedList`. Because of the link to the outer object, the iterator returned by `listIterator()` will have access to the storage representation of the linked list and can deliver the needed functionality.

Let us show how this works by implementing a simple linked list. We do not often, in practical programming, want to "reinvent the wheel" like this, preferring to use the library `LinkedList` class. It is instructive, however, to show how a list and its iterator might be built from scratch. Moreover, the class below will be slightly more efficient than the library class in performing its methods, because it only maintains pointers in one direction. When a library class requires more overhead than is needed, and performance is an issue, we may be called upon to build our own tools.

Because this is only a teaching exercise, we will build our list in a type-specific way, as a list of objects of type `Point`. A generic version would be nearly as simple to build.

```java
package OOPLS;

import java.util.Iterator;

public class PointList {
  static class node {
      Point p;
      node link;
      public node(Point p) { this.p = p; }
      public node(Point p, node link) {
          this.p = p; this.link = link;
      }
  }
  node front, back;
  public void push_front(Point p) {
      if (front == null) front = back = new node(p);
      else {
          front = new node(p,front);
      }
  }
  public void push_back(Point p) {
      if (front == null) push_front(p);
      else {
          back = back.link = new node(p);
      }
  }
  public Point getFront() {
      if (front == null) return null;
      else return front.p;
  }
```

```
        public Point getBack() {
            if (back == null) return null;
            else return back.p;
        }
        public Iterator<Point> iterator() {
            return new PointItr();
        }
        class PointItr implements Iterator<Point> {
            node last, current;
            public PointItr() { last = current = front; }
            public boolean hasNext() { return current != null; }
            public Point next() {
                Point rv = current.p;
                last = current;
                current = current.link;
                return rv;
            }
            public void remove() {
                if (current != null) {
                    if (current == front) {
                        front = last = current = current.link;
                        if (front == null) back = null;
                    }
                    else last.link = current = current.link;
                }
            }
        }
    }
```

Notice how easy it is to build the inner class `PointItr`, because its methods can freely reference the members of the outer class, specifically the private data type `node` and the pointers `front` and `back`. Note also that the instantiation of the inner class object, because it occurs inside one of the methods of the outer class, namely method `iterator()`, could have been coded as **this.new** `PointItr()`, but the use of **this** as a qualifier is redundant at class scope unless there is a need to resolve a name conflict. The point is that the link to the outer class object which will be imbedded in the `PointItr` object will be pointing to whatever object received the `iterator()` message.

The following test code should confirm that the class behaves as expected:

```
import OOPLS.PointList;
import OOPLS.Point;
import java.util.Iterator;
```

```
public class PointListClient {
    public static void main(String args[]) {
        int [][] data =
            {{345,78}, {890,987}, {23,56}, {0,700}};
        PointList pl = new PointList();
        for (int i=0; i<data.length; ++i)
            pl.push_back(new Point(data[i][0],data[i][1]));
        Point fp = pl.getFront(), bp = pl.getBack();
        System.out.println(
            "Front = (" + fp.x + ", " + fp.y + ")");
        System.out.println(
            "Back = (" + bp.x + ", " + bp.y + ")");
        System.out.print("All = ");
        Iterator<Point> i = pl.iterator();
        boolean first = true;
        while (i.hasNext()) {
            if (!first) System.out.print(", ");
            first = false;
            Point p = i.next();
            System.out.print("(" + p.x + ", " + p.y + ")");
        }
        System.out.println();
    }
}
```

7.5.3 Anonymous Inner Classes

In the above example, the inner class name `PointItr` seems entirely superfluous. It is true that it provides a mechanism for instantiating an object for the `iterator()` method to return; however, if we could do so without burdening the symbol table with a name clients will never see, we might be better served. In fact, Java provides a mechanism called *anonymous inner classes* which does exactly that. An anonymous inner class is a type constructed dynamically, in order to instantiate an object conforming to some interface or deriving from some class. To illustrate how this is done, we note that the `PointList` class could have been written without the `PointItr` inner class and with the `iterator()` method coded as follows:

```
public Iterator<Point> iterator() {
    return new Iterator<Point>() {
        node last, current;
        { last = current = front; }
        public boolean hasNext() { return current != null; }
        public Point next() {
```

```
                    Point rv = current.p;
                    last = current;
                    current = current.link;
                    return rv;
            }
        public void remove() {
            if (current != null) {
                if (current == front) {
                    front = last = current = current.link;
                    if (front == null) back = null;
                }
                else last.link = current = current.link;
            }
        }
    }; // Note semi-colon.  This ends the return statement!
}
```

The method coded in this way delivers precisely the same functionality, without introducing a new type name. (In a sense we "lied" when we said that interfaces cannot be instantiated, because it is legal to do so if we provide inline definitions for all the methods of the interface at the point of instantiation!)

7.5.4 Adapters

For the most part it is best to keep an interface small, because (a) smaller interfaces tend to be more intuitive, and (b) the larger the interface the more annoying it is for the client programmer who is tasked with implementing it. Often the programmer needs an object which implements an interface, but he only needs a small part of the functionality of that interface. For those cases, there is a type of class called an *adapter*. The Java library has a number of these classes, whose role is to minimally satisfy the requirements of an interface. For example, the interface `MouseListener` has five methods, but those who use it often need only one of those methods, namely `mouseClicked()`. So the library provides the class `MouseAdapter`, which has empty bodies for all five methods. The programmer then *extends* `MouseAdapter`, instead of *implementing* `MouseListener`. Now the one needed method can be included as an *override* of the method in the adapter, rather than an *implementation* of the method in the interface. This can work extremely well for anonymous inner classes, because it shortens a piece of code that can look somewhat awkward if it is too voluminous. Compare the code segment

```
new MouseListener() {
```

```
    public void mouseClicked(MouseEvent e) {
        // Do something useful.
        ...
    }
    public void mouseEntered(MouseEvent e) {
    }
    public void mouseExited(MouseEvent e) {
    }
    public void mousePressed(MouseEvent e) {
    }
    public void mouseReleased(MouseEvent e) {
    }
}
```

with the segment

```
new MouseAdapter() {
    public void mouseClicked(MouseEvent e) {
        // Do something useful.
        ...
    }
}
```

7.6   JAVA GENERICS

Heterogeneous container classes have limited usefulness in practical software development. Most containers need to have a fairly good idea of the properties of the objects they contain. Although the old-style heterogeneous Java containers are quite flexible in that they are able to store any first-class object, using them can be annoying. The programmer using such a container (who hopefully knows the types of objects stored there) must systematically cast each object into the appropriate type every time he needs it to perform one of its more specialized functions. Generic containers, on the other hand, allow the programmer to dispense with casting, because the compiler is informed in advance about the type of the objects it will contain. Thus, for example, `LinkedList<Double>` is to be preferred over a `LinkedList` object if it is known that every object in the container will be of type `Double`. So the Java "generic" container classes are quite valuable, as they provide a facility for creating type-specific containers.

7.6.1 Defining a Generic Container Class

Let us investigate how we would define a Java generic class. We will use as an example a container class which has a simple and well-understood interface, which we will call a "leaky stack." The public interface to our leaky stack will be the same as that of the library generic container `Stack<>`, but our leaky stack will have a size limit. Each leaky stack object will be given a capacity when it is created, and when the stack exceeds that capacity the object which has been in the stack for the longest time will disappear in order to accommodate the newly pushed item.

The implementation of the `LeakyStack<>` class below is similar to that of a "wrap-around queue." The items in the stack are actually maintained in a fixed-size `Vector<>` object, and the `top` index advances, in a circular fashion, to accommodate `push` operations. If `top` and `bottom` collide after a push, then `bottom` is advanced and the element which it now indexes "drops out" of the stack. If they collide after a pop, the stack is empty. The size of the vector of elements is one more than the size of the stack, so that a full stack always has one unused location, namely the location identified by the `bottom` index.

```java
package OOPLS;

import java.util.Vector;
import java.util.EmptyStackException;

public class LeakyStack<E> {
    Vector<E> elements;
    int n, top, bottom;
    public LeakyStack(int m) {
        this.n = m+1;
        elements = new Vector<E>();
        elements.setSize(n);
        elements.trimToSize();
        top = bottom = 0;
    }
    public E push(E e) {
        top = (top + 1) % n;
        if (top == bottom) bottom = (bottom+1) % n;
        elements.set(top,e);
        return e;
    }
    public E pop() throws EmptyStackException {
        if (empty()) throw new EmptyStackException();
        E rv = elements.get(top);
```

```
            top = (top + n - 1) % n;
            return rv;
    }
    public E peek() throws EmptyStackException {
            if (empty()) throw new EmptyStackException();
            return elements.get(top);
    }
    public boolean empty() {
            return top == bottom;
    }
    public int search(Object o) {
            int i = top, ord = 1;
            while (i != bottom) {
                    if (elements.get(i).equals(o)) return ord;
                    ++ord;
                    i = (i+n-1) % n;
            }
            return -1;
    }
}
```

Notice that when an element is popped the `top` must "decrement," but if we were to code this action in the obvious way, as

```
top = (top - 1) % n;
```

then we would run afoul of the ugly fact that the `%` operator does not behave properly for negative numbers. Instead, we must code

```
top = (top + n - 1) % n;
```

and we get the correct result even if the value of `top` is zero.

The type parameter `E` in the above example is typical of the style employed for Java generics. Normal Java style uses identifiers that begin with capitals as type names, and because the parameter to the generic class is a type we follow that convention. On the other hand, it is an unknown type, so we cannot be expected to associate any intuition with its name. It is best to keep such names short and abstract. Single character capital letters or short all-caps names are commonly used.

The following code puts the class through some paces:

```
import OOPLS.LeakyStack;
```

```java
public class LeakyStackClient {
    static int[] a = {67, 93, 70, 12, 49, 34, 78, 55, 32, 88};
    public static void main(String args[]) {
        LeakyStack<Integer> s = new LeakyStack<Integer>(7);
        // The stack holds at most seven elements at any time.
        for (int i=0; i<a.length; ++i) s.push(a[i]);
        System.out.println("78 is number " + s.search(78)
            + " on the stack.");
        System.out.print("Top:");
        while (!s.empty()) {
            System.out.println("\t"+s.pop().intValue());
        }
    }
}
```

Output from the test program should look as follows:

```
78 is number 4 on the stack.
Top:    88
        32
        55
        78
        34
        49
        12
```

Here the class `Integer` is transmitted to the type parameter `E`. The mechanism for performing this transmission is radically different from that of C++ template instantiation. Instead of generating a new class for every use of the `LeakyStack<>` pattern, that pattern is compiled and placed in a file with the `class` extension, just as a nongeneric class would be, and the same code is used in executing all method calls. This is possible because type parameters are restricted to first-class types, and the stack representations of local and class variables of these unknown types are just handles, to be used to access run-time–allocated heap objects. Everything a compiler needs in order to do a proper translation is present.

Normally, the only messages that can be sent to an object of a type identified only as a type parameter are those messages that are valid for any first-class type. We can help this situation if we decide that a particular generic type parameter can only correspond to a subtype of some particular type. For example, if the parameter `E` above were expected to implement `Cloneable`, we could have coded the first line as

```
public class LeakyStack<E extends Cloneable> {
```

Again, note that the keyword is `extends`, not `implements`. Here we say that the parameter `E` is *bounded* by the `Cloneable` interface.

7.6.2 Type Relationships Revisited

Let us now revisit the issue of types and subtypes, because interfaces and generics have changed the landscape dramatically. If we admit that an interface is a type, and if we define subtyping in terms of parameter compatibility, we must admit that any class which implements an interface is a subtype of that interface. Even though an interface is never the primary type of any particular object, it is still a type, and it still has subtypes.

How do generics change the complexity of type relationships? For example, is Vector<List> a supertype of Vector<LinkedList>? In general, if A is a subtype of B, is Vector also a subtype of Vector? For that matter, is Vector a supertype of both? It seems reasonable at first glance to answer "yes" to all these questions. Let us consider the ramifications that design decision would have, however.

Suppose that `v` is a vector of type `Vector<Integer>`, and suppose that in some class, say `Utility`, there is a static method with the following definition:

```
public static void addQuacker(Vector<Object> v) {
    v.add(new Duck());
}
```

If `Vector<Integer>` is to be considered a subtype of `Vector<Object>` then the call `Utility.addQuacker(v)` is legal, and places a duck in our vector of integers! Given what we know about Java's cautious philosophy, and given that we have already said that an advantage of the type-specific containers is that we do not have to cast their elements when we reference them, we are led to the conclusion that Java would certainly not allow this feathered impersonator. We are then led to the conclusion that there can, in fact, be NO relationship between any two different classes constructed from the same generic class. Similarly, there can be no relationship between these classes and their nongeneric counterpart.

We seem to be leading toward the conclusion that there has been no change in the way types relate to each other as a result of introducing generics. That is not the case, however. Seeing the advantage of introducing some compatibility between all these types, the designers of Java introduced the concept of *wildcard* types, which use a question mark as a "stand-in" for a type. Thus, a supertype of all types created from the `Vector<>` generic class is the class `Vector<?>`. Such wildcard types will not allow us to call any of their methods which use a type parameter of the generic class as the type of one of the method's parameters. Thus, if `lstack` has a declared type of `LeakyStack<?>`, then we may not call `lstack.push()`, but we may call `lstack.pop()`. This guarantees that we cannot add any inappropriate objects. For example, we cannot add an `Integer` object to a container of the type `LeakyStack<Double>`.

A downside to the use of wildcard types is that the only messages we can send, without casting, to an object whose type is only known as a wildcard are messages to the base type `Object`. Thus, the following static method is illegal, because it tries to send the `compareTo()` message to the top element of a stack of type `LeakyStack<?>`.

```
public static int compareTopTwo(LeakyStack<?> s) {
    Object topElement = s.pop();
    return s.peek().compareTo(topElement); // Illegal
}
```

We can overcome the above difficulty by casting the result of `s.peek()` to type `Comparable`, but the following is a more elegant solution, using a so-called *bounded wildcard*:

```
public static int compareTopTwo(LeakyStack<? extends Comparable>
s) {
    Object topElement = s.pop();
    return s.peek().compareTo(topElement); // Works now
}
```

Because `Comparable` is an interface, not a class, it seems odd to use the keyword `extends` here. The meaning of the keyword is overloaded, however, and it does not mean the same thing here as it would in a class definition. It indicates a supertype relationship, but it does not imply an inheritance relationship. With the syntax

```
? extends Comparable
```

we are *bounding* the wildcard type, restricting it to a smaller collection of values, namely those of a type which implement the `Comparable` interface.

7.7   JAVA HASH TABLES

Because all first-class objects can hash themselves using the `hashCode()` method of class `Object`, any first-class object can be installed in a hash table. There are a number of hash table types in Java, including `Hashtable`, `HashSet`, and `HashMap`. Each of these is available as a generic class or as an old-style heterogeneous container. Using the default constructor of one of these hash tables will initially provide constant-time store and retrieve operations, but as the table fills with data it will become less efficient and a reallocation and rehashing operation will ultimately be triggered. Because these hash tables are so easy to use, the client may tend to use them without a great deal of knowledge about hash tables. Here is a simple code segment which illustrates the use of `HashMap`.

```
HashMap<String,Double> payRate = new HashMap<String,Double>();
payRate.put("Louise", 15.67);
payRate.put("Ted", 12.89);
payRate.put("Helen", 11.78);
payRate.put("Marvin", 12.50);
System.out.println("Ted earns " + payRate.get("Ted") +
                " an hour.");
for (Map.Entry e: payRate.entrySet())
    System.out.println(e.getKey() + " earns " +
                        e.getValue() + " an hour.");
```

The observant reader will note that this code snippet could just as well have been coded using `TreeMap`. In fact, both implement the `Map` interface, and all the method calls above are from that interface. The difference here is that in the `for` loop the keys should come out in random order, whereas with `TreeMap` they would be sorted in order on the key values. In general, we choose hashing over a tree in order to achieve constant time storage and retrieval efficiency, as opposed to logarithmic efficiency from a tree structure.

The serious programmer will usually want to pay careful attention to the characteristics of the key set before using the default `hashCode()` method in the `Object` base class. It may be that the designer's special knowledge of the key set will provide a much better hashing function. Thanks to polymorphism, all that is necessary to have a hash table use a different hashing algorithm is to implement that algorithm as an override of `hashCode()`. The following example illustrates a hashing algorithm for strings:

```
public class StringForHashing {
```

```
        String s;
        public StringForHashing(String s) {
            this.s = s;
        }
        public int hashCode() {
            int sum=0, term=0, mod4=0;
            for (int j=0; j<s.length(); ++j) {
                term |= s.charAt(j);
                mod4 = (mod4 + 1) % 4;
                if (mod4 == 0) {
                    sum ^= term;
                    term = 0;
                }
                else term <<= 8;
            }
            if (mod4 != 0) sum ^= term;
            return sum;
        }
        public String get() { return s; }
    }
```

The goal in writing `hashCode()` is to *scramble* the key, i.e., to map it into an integer in such a way that the resulting values for a random set of strings are as uniformly distributed as possible. The above algorithm tries to do this by losing as little of the variability of its keys as possible. It packs four characters at a time into the 32-bit integer *term*, and XOR's all these 32-bit chunks into *sum*. The packing process loses no information if the characters are ASCII, and "exclusive or" operations keep as much or more information as additions.

Other behaviors of hash tables can be overridden as well, by using different constructors. The *capacity* of the hash table is the number of buckets currently assigned to it, where a bucket is an individually indexable location in the table. The initial capacity of the hash table can be specified in a constructor, an important option because the larger the hash table the more efficiently searches can be performed. The capacity will automatically increase when the current population of the table exceeds a certain fraction of its current capacity. This fraction is called the *load factor*. The load factor can be specified as the second parameter of yet another constructor. Thus, the declaration

```
    HashMap<StringForHashing,Double> payRate =
        new HashMap<StringForHashing,Double>(20000, 0.85);
```

allocates a hash map with an initial capacity of 20000 (`StringForHashing,Double`) pairs, which will reallocate and rehash its elements when the population exceeds 17,500 records (85% of 20,000). Reallocation is an expensive operation, and the programmer usually is better served to avoid it.

`Hashtable` and `HashMap` are very similar, but there is an important difference. `Hashtable` is *fail-fast*, meaning that when there is an iterator actively sequencing through it then the only operations which can modify the table without throwing an exception are the iterator's own methods.

7.8 INTRODUCTION TO THE SWING LIBRARY

At this point, we have seen enough of the language to begin our discussion of some of its facilities for graphics and event-driven programming. We will begin with some simple graphics primitives.

7.8.1 The Graphics and Component Classes

The Java class on which we will rely in this text for drawing capabilities is called `Graphics`. Like the device context in MFC, a `Graphics` object maintains some resources for drawing, including a clip rectangle, a font, and a color. It also maintains as one of its resources a handle to the object within which it is expected to draw. This object is of a type derived from `Component`, and objects of that class have the capability to create a `Graphics` object. (`Graphics` is an abstract class, and each object which instantiates an object of that class uses a subtype suitable to itself.)

> _____
> **NOTE** *The interested reader will want to investigate Graphics2D, a newer and more sophisticated class of drawing objects, but we will stick with the older and better known Graphics class for this introduction.*

The painting of a component is performed in response to a paint message, and that message can either originate with the host system or with the programmer. In either case, the event handler ultimately invokes the `paint()` method of the affected component. That method has one parameter, which is a `Graphics` object.

`Component` is the base class for a variety of on-screen entities, including edit boxes, buttons, scroll bars, and simple windows. We will be using the component class `JPanel` as our basic building block for custom-designed components. It is akin to the `CView` class in MFC in that `JPanel` objects are intended to be contained inside a larger window. Moreover, like Smalltalk morphs, other components, including other `JPanel` objects, can be placed inside a `JPanel` object.

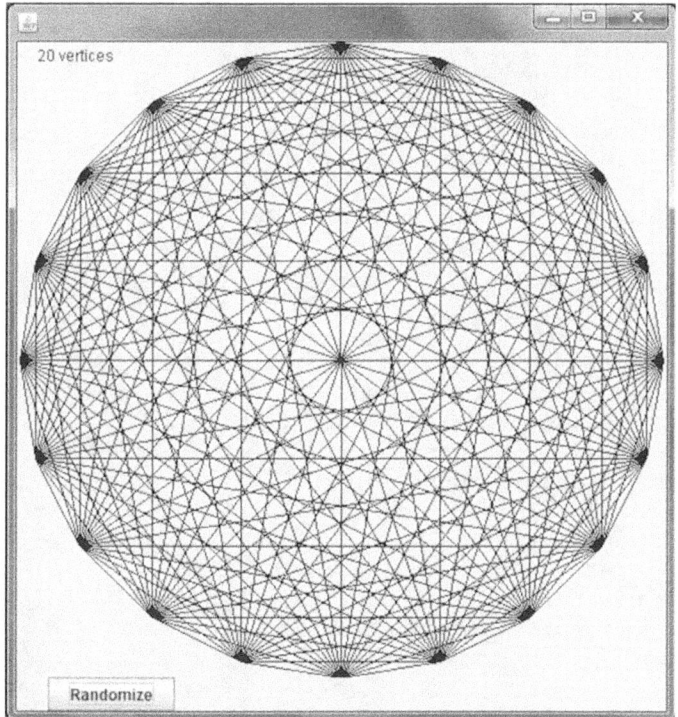

FIGURE 7.1 A `CompleteGraphPanel` application

For now, though, we will simply draw directly to our panel. We include below the source file for a "complete graph" panel to illustrate the structure of a programmer-defined component and some of the capabilities of the `Graphics` class. A complete graph on n vertices is drawn, where the value of integer n is supplied as a parameter to the constructor or with a separate call to `setNumVertices()`. A complete graph has exactly one edge for every pair of vertices, as seen in the screen shot in Figure 7.1, in which twenty vertices are arranged as points around a circle and each edge is drawn as a line joining two vertices. In the program, our complete graph panel appears as the most prominent portion of the display, with a push-button for randomizing the number of vertices below it. We will shortly demonstrate how to incorporate our panel into the program, but for now let us look at the panel itself.

```
package OOPLS;
import java.awt.Graphics;
import javax.swing.JPanel;
import java.awt.Rectangle;
import java.awt.Point;

public class CompleteGraphPanel extends JPanel {
    int n;
    public CompleteGraphPanel(int initialN) {
        setNumVertices(initialN);
    }
    public int getNumVertices() { return n; }
    public void setNumVertices(int n) {
        this.n = n>=3?n:3;
    }
    public void paint(Graphics g) {
        super.paint(g);
        Rectangle rect = g.getClipBounds();
        Point center = new Point(rect.x+rect.width/2,
            rect.y+rect.height/2);
        int radius = Math.min(rect.width/2, rect.height/2);
        Point p[] = new Point[n];
        for (int i = 0; i<n; ++i) {
            double theta = 2*i*Math.PI/n;
            p[i] = new Point(
                (int)(center.x+radius*Math.cos(theta)),
                (int)(center.y+radius*Math.sin(theta)));
        }
        for (int i = 0; i<n; ++i) {
            for (int j=i+1; j<n; ++j)
                g.drawLine(p[i].x,p[i].y,p[j].x,p[j].y);
        }
        g.drawString(n + " vertices", 15, 15);
    }
}
```

The `drawLine()` and `drawString()` methods of class `Graphics` in the example are straightforward. The forms of such messages sent to a `Graphics` object `g` are

```
g.drawLine(x1,y1,x2,y2);
```

to draw a line from coordinates `(x1, y1)` to pixel coordinates `(x2, y2)`, and

```
g.drawString(string,x,y);
```

to draw a string on the panel. In the latter case, the string will be positioned *above* and to the right of the point (x, y), not below as in MFC. Another difference is that these coordinates are considered to be coordinates of the corners where (square) pixels meet, not coordinates of the pixels themselves. Such a view usually plays a minor role, but we will keep it in mind for when we need it. Positive directions are down and to the right, as we expect.

7.8.2 Top-Level Components

Panels are *lightweight* components, meaning they live inside heavyweight components and "borrow" their screen real estate. The operating system has no knowledge of a lightweight component, because all operations of a lightweight component are managed by the JVM. In contrast, a *heavyweight* component is a Java wrapper around an externally defined entity, such as an operating system window or a browser panel. In order to start an application, we need such a heavyweight component, called a *top-level* component. There are three Java classes from which a top-level component can be derived, namely JFrame, JDialog, and JApplet. The first of these is of immediate interest to us, and we will cover the others in due course.

A JFrame object is a stand-alone window, roughly equivalent to the CFrameWnd class of *MFC*. It comes with a border and a title bar, and can support a menu. Its client area corresponds to an object called its *content pane*, and it is to this content pane we must add our panels and other components. We will build our complete graph application as a JFrame subclass called CGClient.

One additional ingredient will be added to our complete graph application, namely the button which randomizes the number of vertices. Its class is JButton, and it is, of course, another lightweight component. Like all components, it is capable of responding to paint events, mouse and keyboard events, and timer events, but its "canned" response is typically the only one in which we are interested. Specifically, the only thing that concerns us here is the button's response to a mouse click event, which it refashions into a "button push" event, of type ActionEvent, which it, in turn, places in the JVM's event queue. The fact that the event gets placed there is of no use to us, however, if we do not establish an event handler for it. For this type of event the JVM wants to see as a "handler" an (*object, method*) pair satisfying two requirements: (a) the object must implement the ActionListener interface, and (b) the method must be named actionPerformed() and have the correct parameter interface. Because Java provides enough run-time information to find the method having that name and interface given the object, the only thing we really have to supply is a handle to the `ActionListener` object. Because the presence of the `actionPerformed()` method is required before the object's class can legally claim to implement the interface, we know in advance that the method will be found.

Once we have registered the listener object, the JVM will automatically call the method every time it takes off the event queue an `ActionEvent` object associated with that particular button. The way we register the event handler is to send the `addActionListener()` message to the `JButton` object, passing as a parameter a handle for an object implementing the required interface. The response of the button object is to add that handle to a list of action listeners which it maintains. When an `ActionEvent` is removed from the event queue, it will contain a handle to its source component (in this case the button component), and that component will have attached to it the list of action listeners we just mentioned. The Java event handling sequence is completed by calling the `actionPerformed()` method for every listener on that list.

In the example below, the `JFrame` object itself is made to implement the `ActionListener` interface, and so the handler is established with the line of code

```
randomizeButton.addActionListener(this);
```

This and other important initializations take place inside the method *initComponents()*.

```
import OOPLS.CompleteGraphPanel;
import java.awt.BorderLayout;
import java.awt.Point;
import java.awt.event.ActionEvent;
import java.awt.event.ActionListener;
import java.util.Random;
import javax.swing.JButton;
import javax.swing.JFrame;
import javax.swing.WindowConstants;


public class CGClient extends JFrame
                      implements ActionListener {
    Point DEFAULTBASE = new Point(50,50);
    final int DEFAULTWIDTH = 500, DEFAULTHEIGHT = 500,
              MAXVERTICES = 50, MINVERTICES = 3;
    Random rnd = new Random();
    JButton randomizeButton = new JButton("Randomize");
    CompleteGraphPanel cgPanel = new CompleteGraphPanel(8);
```

```
public CGClient() {
    initComponents();
}
private void initComponents() {
    setDefaultCloseOperation(
        WindowConstants.EXIT_ON_CLOSE);
    setBounds(DEFAULTBASE.x,DEFAULTBASE.y,
        DEFAULTWIDTH,DEFAULTHEIGHT);
    getContentPane().add(cgPanel);
    randomizeButton.addActionListener(this);
    getContentPane().add(
        randomizeButton,BorderLayout.SOUTH);
}
public void actionPerformed(ActionEvent e) {
    cgPanel.setNumVertices(
        Math.abs(rnd.nextInt())
        % (MAXVERTICES - MINVERTICES + 1) + MINVERTICES);
    cgPanel.repaint();
}
public static void main(String args[]) {
    java.awt.EventQueue.invokeLater(new Runnable() {
        public void run() {
            new CGClient().setVisible(true);
        }
    });
}
}
```

An essential change in state is effected with the first line of initCompo-
nents(). JFrame windows normally disappear from view but do not disappear
as operating system entities when a close operation is performed by the user.
More specifically, the normal default close operation is HIDE_ON_CLOSE, and in
order to make the window act like a stand-alone application we must change it
to EXIT_ON_CLOSE with setDefaultCloseOperation(). On the second line,
we establish the initial location and size of the frame window. On the third, we
establish the parent/child relationship between the frame window and the complete graph panel by adding the panel to the frame window's content pane. The
fourth line is the establishment of the event handler, as explained above. Finally,
the last line of initComponents() adds another lightweight component to the
frame, namely the button which causes the number of vertices to change to a
new randomly selected number. The location of this button is to the "south" of
the panel, and there is clearly more than meets the eye in the code which estab-

lishes that location. We will say more about this in the context of layouts below.

The `actionPerformed()` method is the event handler for the button push. It uses the `Random` object `rnd` to generate a number between 3 and 50, and sets this number as the number of vertices of the panel. It then causes a redrawing of the complete graph by executing the `repaint()` method.

The main program has an odd form. Actions taken here are to (a) instantiate an object of an anonymous inner class type implementing the `Runnable` interface, (b) schedule the `run()` method of that object to be executed in the dispatch thread of the JVM, and (c) exit the main thread. The `run()` method creates an instance of `CGClient` and makes it visible on the screen. From here the message loop takes over, and the window will continue to interact with the user until it is closed. Work gets done via messages being sent to the window and its components and the dispatch thread executing their handlers. All our main programs which create `JFrame` windows will have this form.

7.8.3 Timer Example: A "Dropped Ball" Panel

In our Smalltalk discussion, we presented a bouncing ball example in which the ball continued to bounce off the edges of the client rectangle without any effects of friction or gravity. To illustrate the use of animation and timers in Java, we will use a similar example but will subject our ball to both gravity and the damping effects of bouncing and friction. Below is a "business class" which models the ball itself, giving it a randomly chosen initial location and speed. Our physics is not perfect, but is close enough for our current purposes.

```
package OOPLS;
import java.awt.Color;
import java.awt.Graphics;
import java.awt.Point;
import java.awt.Rectangle;
import java.util.Random;

public class DroppedBall {
    double centerx, centery; // Exact coordinates of center.
    double dx, dy;   // Exact speed in x and y directions,
                     // respectively.  Units are pixels per
                     // second.
    int ddy = 400;   // Gravitational acceleration in pixels
                     // per second per second.
    int radius = 20;  // Radius of ball.
    double bouncePct = 0.95; // Bouncing damps vertical
                             // speed using this fraction.
```

```java
double rollPct = 0.70;    // Rolling damps horizontal
                          // speed using this fraction.
double epsilon = 1.0E-2; // Ball is considered to be
                          // touching bottom edge of win-
                          // dow if it is this close.
Color ballColor;
Random rnd = new Random();
Rectangle rectangle = new Rectangle();
public final void randomizeLocationAndSpeed() {
    centerx = Math.abs(rnd.nextInt()) % 200 + 100;
    centery = Math.abs(rnd.nextInt()) % 100;
    dx = rnd.nextInt() % 100 + 100;
    dy = rnd.nextInt() % 50;
}
public DroppedBall() {
    randomizeLocationAndSpeed();
    float red = rnd.nextFloat(),
          green = rnd.nextFloat(),
          blue = rnd.nextFloat();
    ballColor = new Color(red, green, blue);
}
public void setRectangle(Rectangle rect) {
    rectangle = rect;
}
public void setColor(Color c) {
    ballColor = c;
}
public void cycle(int elapsedMillis) {
    centerx += dx * elapsedMillis/1000.0;
    centery += dy * elapsedMillis/1000.0;
    double leftx = centerx - radius,
        rightx = centerx + radius,
        bottomy = centery + radius;
    if (leftx <= rectangle.x ||
        rightx >= rectangle.x + rectangle.width)
        dx = -dx;
    if (bottomy >= rectangle.y + rectangle.height) {
        centery = rectangle.y + rectangle.height - radius;
        dy = -bouncePct * dy;
    }
    dy += ddy * elapsedMillis/1000.0;
    if (Math.abs(bottomy - rectangle.height) < epsilon
        && dy >= 0)
        dx *= rollPct;
}
public void draw(Graphics g) {
```

```
        g.setColor(ballColor);
        int leftx = (int)(centerx-radius),
            topy = (int)(centery-radius);
        g.fillOval(leftx, topy, 2*radius, 2*radius);
        g.setColor(Color.BLACK);
        g.drawOval(leftx, topy, 2*radius, 2*radius);
    }
    public Point getCenter() {
        return new Point((int)centerx, (int)centery);
    }
}
```

Very few of the ideas in this class are specific to Java or Swing, but the `draw()` routine has some new things for us to think about. Notice that `Graphics` objects in Swing, unlike device contexts in MFC, do not differentiate between colors for drawing lines and colors for filling regions. There is only one color associated with the `Graphics` object at a time, and to switch colors requires a call on the `setColor()` method of `Graphics`. Colors can be constructed from scratch, as we see in the following code excerpted from the constructor:

```
float red = rnd.nextFloat(),
      green = rnd.nextFloat(),
      blue = rnd.nextFloat();
ballColor = new Color(red, green, blue);
```

Here the `nextFloat()` method of class `Random` meshes nicely with what we wish to do in constructing a random color for our ball. It returns a randomly chosen real number between 0 and 1, in other words a random fraction. Because the red, green, and blue components of the `Color` constructor require such fractions, we have only to pass them on. The result is similar to the `RGB` macro of MFC, where smaller numbers indicate darker colors. Thus, `new Color(0f,0f,0f)` is black, `new Color(1f,1f,1f)` is white, and `new Color(0.7f,0.5f,0f)` is brown.

In the `draw()` routine, in order to obtain the effect of a colored ball with a black circular edge, we had to use `g.setColor(ballColor)` to switch to our randomly generated ball color, call `fillOval()`, switch to black using `g.setColor(Color.black)`, and call `drawOval()`. Note that the color black is a "pre-mixed" public static data member of class `Color`, as are red, green, blue, yellow, magenta, pink, and several others. The `fillOval()` and `drawOval()` routines have identical parameter lists. Thus, `fillOval(x,y,width,height)` fills a rectangle `width` pixels by `height` pixels in size located below and to the right of the coordinates `(x, y)`.

The `cycle()` method would contain similar logic in any language, and is intended to be called many times per second, along with `draw()`, in order to achieve the desired animation. This animation requires a timer, which is encapsulated in the following panel class:

```java
package OOPLS;

import java.awt.Graphics;
import java.awt.event.ActionEvent;
import java.awt.event.ActionListener;
import java.awt.event.ComponentAdapter;
import java.awt.event.ComponentEvent;
import java.awt.Color;
import javax.swing.JPanel;
import javax.swing.Timer;
import java.util.Random;

public class DroppedBallPanel extends JPanel
                                implements ActionListener {
    final int FREQUENCY = 30; // Timer events per second.
    Timer timer = new Timer(1000/FREQUENCY, this);
    DroppedBall ball = new DroppedBall();
    public DroppedBallPanel() {
        ball.setRectangle(getBounds());
        addComponentListener(new ComponentAdapter() {
            public void componentResized(ComponentEvent e) {
                ball.setRectangle(getBounds());
            }
        });
    }
    public void actionPerformed(ActionEvent e) {
        ball.cycle(1000/FREQUENCY);
        repaint();
    }
    public void paint(Graphics g) {
        super.paint(g);
        ball.draw(g);
    }
    public void drop() {
        Random rnd = new Random();
        ball.setColor(
            new Color(
                rnd.nextFloat(),
                rnd.nextFloat(),
                rnd.nextFloat())
```

```
        );
        ball.randomizeLocationAndSpeed();
    }
    public void start() {
        timer.addActionListener(this);
        timer.start();
    }
    public void stop() {
        timer.removeActionListener(this);
        timer.stop();
    }
}
```

The timer is instantiated inline, at the point where it is declared, with a constructor that has one integer parameter, the number of milliseconds between timer interrupts, and one `ActionListener` parameter, the panel itself. The former parameter, the number, is computed as `1000/FREQUENCY`, i.e., the number of milliseconds per second divided by the number of timer events per second, which makes the units come out milliseconds per timer event—exactly what is needed.

The dropped ball is also instantiated inline, in the process of which it is given a random color, speed, and direction by its constructor. The panel's constructor passes on to the dropped ball the dimensions of its client area, as the rectangle within which the ball is to bounce. Then a `ComponentListener` object is constructed and attached to the panel to take action when the panel is resized. It is constructed as an anonymous inner class extending the `ComponentAdapter` class and overriding the only method in the interface which concerns us, namely the `componentResized()` method. The action of the override is simply to supply the new panel bounds to the dropped ball object so that it knows where the walls and floor are against which it is supposed to bounce.

The `actionPerformed()` method, being the only method in the `ActionListener` interface, is next. Recall that a handle to the panel object is passed as the second parameter of the *Timer* constructor, and as a consequence the `actionPerformed()` method will be called with every timer event generated by that timer. Several times a second, then, this method will execute, and each time it will send a `cycle()` message to the ball (causing it to change its position) and repaint the panel.

Four methods remain. The `paint()` method first executes the version of itself in the superclass, then requests the ball to draw itself on the panel. Using the `drop()` method the client can "pick up" the ball, randomize its color, and give it a new random direction and speed. The `start()` and `stop()` methods which follow make it possible for a client class to control the animation. Until the `start()` method is called, no timer events will be generated.

A panel must have a host in order to be seen, so let us construct a `JFrame` object into which we may embed a `DroppedBallPanel` object.

```java
import OOPLS.DroppedBallPanel;
import java.awt.event.WindowAdapter;
import java.awt.event.WindowEvent;
import javax.swing.JFrame;

public class DroppedBallClient extends JFrame   {
    DroppedBallPanel panel = new DroppedBallPanel();
    public DroppedBallClient() {
        initComponents();
    }
    public void initComponents() {
        setDefaultCloseOperation(
            javax.swing.WindowConstants.EXIT_ON_CLOSE);
        setBounds(100,50,600,500);
        getContentPane().add(panel);
        panel.start();
    }
    public static void main(String args[]) {
        java.awt.EventQueue.invokeLater(new Runnable() {
            public void run() {
                new DroppedBallClient().setVisible(true);
            }
        });
    }
}
```

This client class is minimal, being nothing more than a frame into which to place our dropped ball panel. The frame's initial location and size are arbitrarily set, and can be readjusted as desired by the user. The panel, being the only occupant of the frame's content pane, will expand and contract to fill the frame as the user adjusts its size. The client class begins the animation with the `start()` message, and the timer will cease operation when it is garbage-collected after the panel to which it is attached is destroyed.

In some situations, it may be necessary for the programmer to take more explicit control of stopping the timer. This can be accomplished in the above example by replacing the `initComponents()` method by the following:

```
public void initComponents() {
    setDefaultCloseOperation(
        javax.swing.WindowConstants.DISPOSE_ON_CLOSE);
    setBounds(100,50,600,500);
    getContentPane().add(panel);
    addWindowListener(new WindowAdapter() {
        public void windowClosed(WindowEvent e) {
            panel.stop();
        }
    });
    panel.start();
}
```

By specifying `DISPOSE_ON_CLOSE` as opposed to `EXIT_ON_CLOSE`, the programmer guarantees that a `WindowEvent` will occur when the user closes the window, at which time the `windowClosed()` handler in the anonymous inner class will explicitly stop the timer by sending the `stop()` message to the `DroppedBallPanel` object.

7.8.4 Layouts

In the `CGClient` class of Section 7.8.2, our `initComponents()` function contained the following line of code:

```
getContentPane().add(randomizeButton,BorderLayout.SOUTH);
```

The purpose of this is clear, which is to add the button component to the frame, just below the visible manifestation of the `CompleteGraphPanel` object. What is this `BorderLayout` class, and what does it have to do with this positioning process? It is one of several layout classes, and one of the most useful. It is, in fact, the default layout for content panes.

A *layout* is an object which is attached to a content pane with a `setLayout()` message and governs the relative positions of components which are placed there. A number of schemes are available, from the haphazard arrangement governed by class `FlowLayout`, to the relatively controllable `BoxLayout` and `BorderLayout` classes, to the more complex `GroupLayout` and the inflexible `AbsoluteLayout`. All these can be managed with hand-coding, but `GroupLayout` and `AbsoluteLayout` are usually managed with code generators accompanying an IDE such as *NetBeans* or *Eclipse*. On the other hand, `FlowLayout` gives us almost no control over where things are placed and how they look, so we will concentrate on `BorderLayout` and `BoxLayout`.

```
┌─────────────────────────────────────────────┐
│                    NORTH                      │
├──────┬────────────────────────────┬──────────┤
│      │                            │          │
│      │                            │          │
│      │                            │          │
│ WEST │          CENTER            │   EAST   │
│      │                            │          │
│      │                            │          │
│      │                            │          │
├──────┴────────────────────────────┴──────────┤
│                    SOUTH                      │
└─────────────────────────────────────────────┘
```

FIGURE 7.2 The regions of `BorderLayout`

The scheme represented by class `BorderLayout` divides a content pane into five regions, corresponding to the five public static constants, `NORTH`, `SOUTH`, `CENTER`, `EAST`, and `WEST`. The relative positions of these are illustrated in Figure 7.2. Relative sizes of these regions will depend on what is placed there, but once the four outer regions have been given their minimal sizes the center region gets all the remaining space. As the user resizes the frame these regions will grow and shrink but will maintain their relative positions. The `CGClient` frame is organized like this, but with only the center region and the south region occupied. A more embellished version of that frame appears below. In that version, buttons have been placed at the four points of the compass, with the complete graph panel in the center.

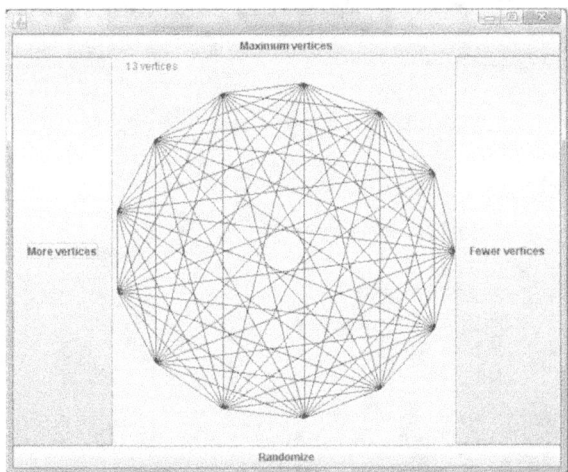

FIGURE 7.3 Illustrating `BorderLayout` with the complete graph panel

The `BoxLayout` class splits the content pane into sequentially ordered subregions, arranged either vertically or horizontally. The constructor requires a content pane as its first operand, and either `BoxLayout.X_AXIS` or `BoxLayout.Y_AXIS` as its second operand. If the former, then the components are arranged horizontally, and if the latter they are arranged vertically. Because panels can be nested inside panels, and each panel has its own layout, there is room for quite a bit of creativity. The following frame class constructs the display as a vertical box layout with three components, the first being a dropped ball panel, the last a complete graph panel, and the middle another panel with two buttons laid out horizontally.

```java
import OOPLS.CompleteGraphPanel;
import OOPLS.DroppedBallPanel;
import java.awt.Container;
import java.awt.EventQueue;
import java.awt.event.ActionEvent;
import java.awt.event.ActionListener;
import java.util.Random;
import javax.swing.BoxLayout;
import javax.swing.JButton;
import javax.swing.JFrame;
import javax.swing.JPanel;
import javax.swing.WindowConstants;

public class DualClient extends JFrame {
    DroppedBallPanel dbp = new DroppedBallPanel();
    CompleteGraphPanel cgp = new CompleteGraphPanel(17);
    JButton ballDropButton = new JButton("Drop ball");
    JButton randomizeButton = new JButton(
        "Randomize vertices");
    JPanel buttonPanel = new JPanel();
    public DualClient() {
        initComponents();
    }
    public void initComponents() {
        setDefaultCloseOperation(
            WindowConstants.EXIT_ON_CLOSE);
        setBounds(10,10,500,600);
        Container cp = getContentPane();
        cp.setLayout(new BoxLayout(cp,BoxLayout.Y_AXIS));
        cp.add(dbp);
        dbp.start();
        buttonPanel.setLayout(
            new BoxLayout(buttonPanel,BoxLayout.X_AXIS));
        buttonPanel.add(ballDropButton);
        ballDropButton.addActionListener(
            new ActionListener() {
```

```
                    public void actionPerformed(ActionEvent e) {
                        dbp.drop();
                    }
                });
            randomizeButton.addActionListener(
                new ActionListener() {
                    public void actionPerformed(ActionEvent e) {
                        int numVertices =
                            new Random().nextInt() % 48 + 3;
                        cgp.setNumVertices(numVertices);
                        cgp.repaint();
                    }
                });
            buttonPanel.add(randomizeButton);
            cp.add(buttonPanel);
            cp.add(cgp);
        }
        public static void main(String args[]) {
            EventQueue.invokeLater(new Runnable(){
                public void run() {
                    new
                        DualClient().setVisible(true);
                }
            });
        }
    }
```

Figure 7.4 is a screen shot of the resulting layout. As the window is resized, the panels will expand and contract to conform to their relative positions in the frame.

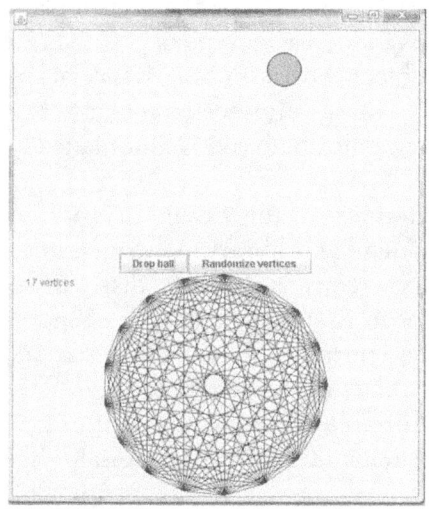

FIGURE 7.4 The DualClient frame

7.9 SERIALIZATION

Persistence of objects is relatively easy to achieve in Java. Java's facilities for persistence in fact represent a reversal of the stand which Java has taken on text input, which is to be more honest about the difficulties of that process. The actual implementation of persistence is in fact far more complex than the parsing and conversion of literals on a line of input, but Java's facilities utterly hide that complexity. This is in fact a great favor to the programmer and could only be achieved in a language with complete type information available at run-time.

7.9.1 Introduction to Java Serialization

Unlike the SDI pattern in MFC, where an archiving operation must be incrementally constructed for each C++ class for which persistence is desired, all that is necessary to make saving and restoring an object of a Java class possible with existing library facilities is to declare that the class implements `Serializable`. Like the `Cloneable` interface, `Serializable` is an empty interface and is only used for run-time checking. The routine which does that checking is the `writeObject()` method of class `ObjectOutputStream`. If `obj` is an object of a class implementing `Serializable`, and `ooStream` is an object of type `ObjectOutputStream`, then the instruction

```
ooStream.writeObject(obj);
```

causes two run-time actions. First, the actual type of `obj`, which the compiler only knew as `Object`, is looked up, and the JVM makes sure that it is a class which implements `Serializable`. If the class is indeed a subtype of `Serializable`, then the JVM will attempt to save the object to disk in binary format, in the file associated with `ooStream`. The `Serializable` interface is similar to the `Cloneable` interface in that any subtype of a serializable type is automatically serializable.

What is so remarkable here is the unexpectedness of this design decision in light of other decisions of like kind in this language and library. As we read the documentation, instead of finding that a shallow copy is saved to disk, as we would expect after wrestling with that concept in the context of the `clone()` method, we find that the `writeObject()` method purportedly saves a *deep copy*. Indeed it can and will do this if (a) the object's class is a subtype of `Serializable`, and (b) all its data members are of serializable types. Note that this is a recursively defined criterion, in the sense that a data member will be serializable provided it satisfies the same two criteria.

> *To serialize an object, it is necessary to be able to fully explore at run-time its type structure, which means the serializing algorithm must explore all the types involved in its definition. If anywhere in this arbitrarily complex directed graph of types we encounter a first-class type that is not serializable, there is still a possibility that serialization can be completed. If it is an unserializable field in an object being serialized, it will normally cause a NotSerializableException to be thrown. But if it is a supertype of a serializable type, then it can still be serialized if it provides a writeObject() and a readObject() method. These methods turn the interface inside out. Instead of ooStream.writeObject(obj), the call is obj.writeObject(ooStream). The intent is the same, but now the programmer takes charge of the details. There are some fairly complex rules that apply in this case, which require careful study. On the other hand, the procedure is very clean if we make sure, from the bottom up, that all involved classes are simply declared serializable.*

Think about what must be done to achieve deep copy serialization. In response to `ooStream.writeObject(obj)`, the JVM must iterate through all the fields of `obj` and write their binary representations to the stream. But all fields of first-class type are in fact represented by handles, and essentially represent links in a directed graph. These links must be saved to the file in a way which is independent of the involved objects' current locations in memory. Because these links may imply circular relationships, we must be careful not to store the same object more than once. What is saved to the file is in fact a persistent representation of a directed graph.

7.9.2 Wrapping for Storage

Binary stream instantiation code has a rather baroque appearance, but that cannot be helped. In order to obtain an object capable of writing another object (of any serializable type) to a stream, we must wrap three times. Here is the general pattern for outputting in binary:

```
import java.io.BufferedOutputStream;
import java.io.FileOutputStream;
import java.io.ObjectOutputStream;
...
    try {
```

```
            ObjectOutputStream ooStream =
                    new ObjectOutputStream(
                    new BufferedOutputStream(
                    new FileOutputStream(file name)));
            ...
            ooStream.writeObject(any serializable object);
            ...
            ooStream.flush();
            ooStream.close();
        } catch (Exception exc) {
            exc.printStackTrace();
        }
```

A similar pattern must occur on input, as follows:

```
    import java.io.BufferedInputStream;
    import java.io.FileInputStream;
    import java.io.ObjectInputStream;
    ...
        try {
            ObjectInputStream oiStream =
                    new ObjectInputStream(
                    new BufferedInputStream(
                    new FileInputStream(file name)));
            ...
            ASerializableType obj =
                (ASerializableType)oiStream.readObject();
            ...
        } catch(Exception exc) {
            exc.printStackTrace();
        }
```

Obviously, objects saved to a file must be read in the same order in which they were written. Commonly, however, exactly one large object will be written.

7.9.3 Some Simple Examples

All library containers are serializable; for example, if an object is of type LinkedList<Type> and Type is serializable, then we get serializability of the container object for free. Programmer-defined containers are trickier. If the class has no first-class objects as data members, then we only need to add implements Serializable to the first line of the class definition, as in the following example, which encapsulates a pair of indices for a two-dimensional array. (We will need this class in Section 12.10 as a representation of the location of a "room" in a maze.)

```
package OOPLS;

import java.io.Serializable;

public class Indices2D implements Serializable {
    int i, j;
    public Indices2D() {
        i = j = 0;
    }
    public Indices2D(int i, int j) {
        this.i = i;
        this.j = j;
    }
    public boolean equals(Object obj) {
        Indices2D opnd = (Indices2D) obj;
        return opnd.i == i && opnd.j == j;
    }
}
```

Like cloning a deep copy, serializing a more complex class requires that we make all its constituents serializable. Our `PointList` class of Section 7.5.2 is an example of such a class. There is a simple and short list of things which must be done to make that class serializable:

1. We must make `PointList` itself implement `Serializable`, by adding

   ```
   import java.io.Serializable;
   ```

   to our imports in *PointList.java* and replacing the first line of the definition with

   ```
   public class PointList implements Serializable {
   ```
2. We must make the inner class `node` serializable, by changing the first line of its definition to

   ```
   static class node implements Serializable {
   ```
3. We must make the `Point` class serializable by making changes to file *Point.java* similar to those in step 1.

Once these things have been done, we may write to a file a binary representation of a `PointList` object and read that representation back into a memory-resident object. The `writeObject()` method will traverse the links and copy all the nodes and all the links to the file, and the `readObject()` method will perform the reverse function.

7.10 MENUS, DIALOGS, AND A COMPLETE APPLICATION

In this section, we develop an application that generates a maze and interacts with a user attempting to solve the maze. It is a complete application in the sense that it presents a menu to the user and guides him through a sequence of actions, then allows him to save his work to a file and return to it later. We will see the power of serialization, which makes saving the state of a complex object to a file a surprisingly simple task.

We will be building some dialogs along the way for the purpose of gathering data from the user, and we will show how to attach a menu bar and menu items to a `JFrame` object. But before we do so we will introduce the `JOptionPane` class, which has some useful static methods for displaying brief messages to the user.

7.10.1 The JOptionPane Class

There are occasions when a condition arises internally which require a user to be informed or to give some simple feedback to the program. For situations such as these, it is common to use the static methods of `JOptionPane`. The simplest use of these is shown in the archetypical "Hello, world" application below:

```java
import javax.swing.JOptionPane;

public class HelloWorld {
    public static void main(String args[]) {
        JOptionPane.showMessageDialog(null, "Hello, World!");
    }
}
```

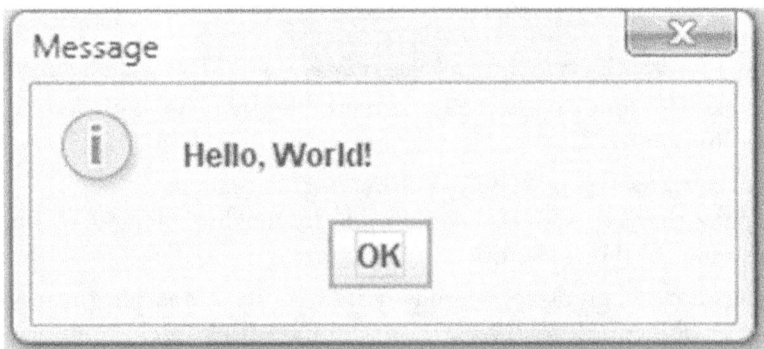

FIGURE 7.5 A `JOptionPane` dialog box

The result of running this program is the little dialog box in Figure 7.5. There are many other quick and easy dialog boxes which can be generated on the fly. For example, we can use `showConfirmDialog()` to display a message to which the user can reply by pressing a *Yes*, *No*, or *Cancel* button. Or we can do prompted text input with `showInputDialog()`. We will leave it up to the user to investigate these capabilities in the Java documentation pages for `JOptionPane`.

7.10.2 Building a Maze

Building an arbitrarily complex randomly generated maze is easy if one has the right programming tools. To make an m by n maze, we start with mn rooms organized in an m by n rectangular arrangement, each totally isolated from the others. Figure 7.6 is a drawing with m = 6 and n = 8.

FIGURE 7.6 Initial maze state

Note that there are initially mn regions in the maze, no one of which is reachable from any other. In order to make it a more entertaining maze, we need to have exactly one region, and we need to remove as few walls from the original configuration as possible in order to achieve this state. There is a very clear way to look at this: every time we remove an interior wall which separates two different regions, the number of regions goes down by one; therefore, if we find and remove such a wall $mn - 1$ times we will be left with exactly one region. In other words, we need to use the following algorithm:

```
Build the initial rectangular configuration:
    m rows by n columns of isolated rooms.
Repeat until mn - 1 walls have been removed:
    Randomly select an interior wall.
    If the cells on either side of the selected wall are in
    different regions,
        Remove the wall.
```

The algorithm is simple enough conceptually, but how are we to know when two rooms are in the same or different regions? For that matter, when we remove a wall, how do we combine the two regions on either side into one? These operations are characteristic of a type of problem called a "Union-Find" problem, and the answers are surprisingly simple after we study the commonly employed solutions.

The technique which works for mazes is to build an m by n array of links (or pointers, handles, references, or whatever you wish to call them), and use those links to identify which region each cell is currently associated with. Initially each cell points back to itself, as indicated in Figure 7.7(a) for the 2 by 3 case. Removing a wall amounts to resetting one of those links. For example, if we remove the two interior walls on the first row, in order, we might obtain the configurations 7.7(b) and 7.7(c), in order.

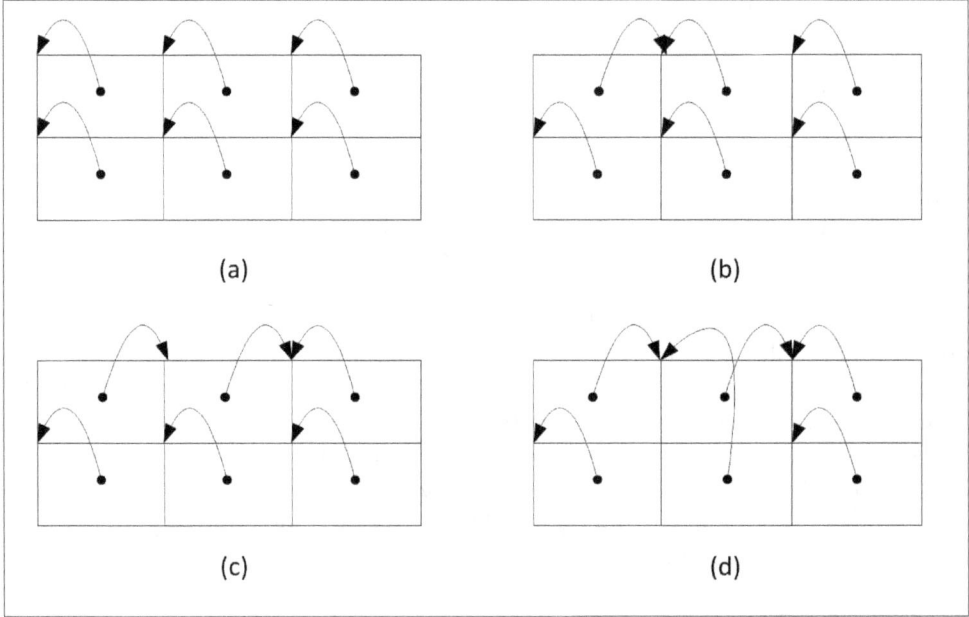

FIGURE 7.7 Various pointer configurations in the maze data structure

Now removing the wall in the very middle could yield the configuration 7.7(d), in which all pointer chains end at the upper-right cell, except for the two bottom corners.

There is a certain arbitrariness to this scheme, as any of the configurations in Figure 7.8(a), (b), and (c) is logically equivalent to the one shown in 7.7(d).

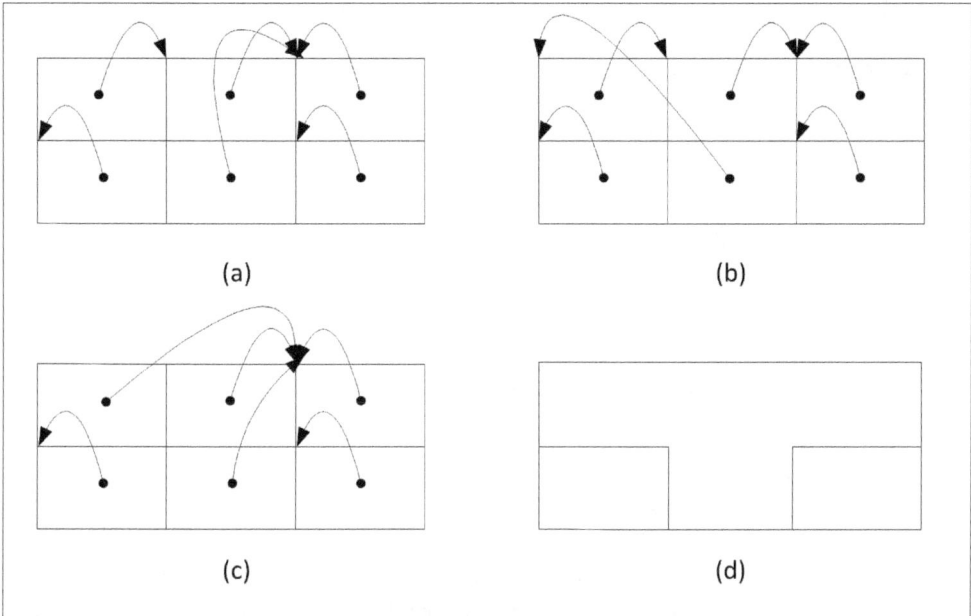

FIGURE 7.8 Multiple representations equivalent to Figure 7.7(d)

The point we are making is that all of the above link settings indicate the same partially constructed "maze" in Figure 7.8(d). They do so because the pointers in the two isolated cells in all the above cases will never take us out of those cells, and following a chain of pointers from any other cell always leads to the upper-right-hand cell, which is acting as the "representative" of its region.

The best arrangement of pointers is clearly 7.8(c). In that configuration, the number of links we must follow from any given room in the region to reach the "representative room" of the region (being the only room whose pointer points back at itself) is a minimum, namely exactly one.

7.10.3 The Maze Class

In this section, we present the source file *Maze.java* in segments, interspersed with discussion. The first segment consists of the `package` statement and a group of imports, followed by a definition of the link type `RoomLink` and the top part of the class, containing the private data. The `RoomLink` class is odd-looking and would be illegal in a language with value semantics, because the only data member it has is another object of the same type. In Java, however, where all first-class objects are just handles, it makes perfectly good sense.

```
package OOPLS;

import java.awt.Color;
import java.awt.Graphics;
import java.util.Random;
import java.awt.Rectangle;
import java.io.Serializable;

class RoomLink implements Serializable {
    public RoomLink link;
}

public class Maze implements Serializable {
    int m, n, iStart, jStart, iFinish, jFinish;
    final static int NORTH = 0, EAST = 1, SOUTH = 2, WEST = 3;
    RoomLink[][] room;
    boolean[][][] wall;
    Random rnd = new Random();
```

Here we see the data member `room` declared as a rectangular array of `Room-Link` objects, i.e., an array of pointers like that described in the previous section. It is this array which we will use to build our maze. The walls of the maze are represented by the three-dimensional `boolean` array `wall`. If, for example, `wall[i][j][EAST]` is `true`, then we cannot travel east from the cell in the i-th row, jth column because there is a wall in that direction. Note there is some redundancy here, because `wall[i][j+1][WEST]` actually represents the same location and must have the same value. Integer values `m` and `n` are the dimensions of the maze, and the coordinates (`iStart`, `jStart`) and (`iFinish`, `jFinish`) give the wanderer's initial position and desired destination, respectively. The constructor below gives these locations randomly chosen values, then passes control to the maze-constructing `initialize()` routine.

```
public Maze(int m, int n) {
    this.m = m;
    this.n = n;
    iStart = rnd.nextInt(m);
    jStart = rnd.nextInt(n);
    do {
        iFinish = rnd.nextInt(m);
        jFinish = rnd.nextInt(n);
    } while(Math.abs(iStart-iFinish)+
            Math.abs(jStart-jFinish) < 0.25*(m+n));
    initialize(m, n);
}
```

Note that the start and finish locations are chosen so that the sum of the distance apart of their x-coordinates and the distance apart of their y-coordinates is no less than a quarter of the sum of the two dimensions of the maze. This makes it less likely that the maze will be too easy.

Some simple access functions are next, including the routine `hasWall()`, which gives public read-only access to the `wall` array. Following these is the maze allocation routine `initialize()`, which first "builds" walls along the outside and between all adjacent rooms by setting all entries of the `wall` array to true. It then ends with a call to `buildMaze()`, which will implement the random wall-removal algorithm. Notice that the `getStart()` and `getFinish()` routines return objects of the type `Indices2D`, which we introduced in Section 7.9.3. Abstractly, we could have used the `Point` class here, because it also encapsulates a pair of integers, but it is best to reserve that class in our minds as representing a pixel location. There is less risk this way of confusing the order of the two integer indices, which in that case would have to be referred to as `x` and `y`.

```java
public int getNumColumns() { return n; }
public int getNumRows() { return m; }
public Indices2D getStart() {
    return new Indices2D(iStart,jStart); }
public Indices2D getFinish() {
    return new Indices2D(iFinish,jFinish); }
public boolean hasWall(int i, int j, int k) {
    if (i >= 0 && i < m && j >= 0 && j < n && k >= 0 && k < 4)
        return wall[i][j][k];
    else return false;
}
public void initialize(int m, int n) {
    room = new RoomLink[m][n];
    wall = new boolean[m][n][4];
    for (int i=0; i<m; ++i)
        for (int j=0; j<n; ++j) {
            room[i][j] = new RoomLink();
            room[i][j].link = room[i][j];
            for (int k=0; k<4; ++k)
                wall[i][j][k] = true;
        }
    buildMaze();
}
```

The `buildMaze()` routine below very simply implements the wall removal algorithm, by "punting" the major part of the work to the `randomlyEliminateWall()` routine.

```
void buildMaze() {
    int numRegions = m*n;
    while (numRegions > 1) {
        randomlyEliminateWall();
        --numRegions;
    }
}
```

The `buildMaze()` function is appropriately private, as is the following `randomlyEliminateWall()` routine, which *must* not be invoked unless the maze is still under construction, because if it were it would enter an infinite loop.

```
void randomlyEliminateWall() {
    boolean wallFound = false;
    while (!wallFound) {
        int i=0, j=0, k = -1;
        while (k < 0) {
            i = rnd.nextInt(m);
            j = rnd.nextInt(n);
            k = randomInteriorWall(i,j);
        }
        wallFound = eliminateWall(i,j,k);
    }
}
```

The inner loop above, governed by the condition `k < 0`, continues to execute until indices i, j, and k are found for which `wall[i][j][k]` actually represents an interior wall which has not yet been removed. With each execution, the loop will choose a room and `randomInteriorWall()` will make exactly one random guess at a direction, and if that does not work it will return `-1`. The value of `k` coming out of the inner loop could still fail its purpose if `room[i][j]` and the room on the other side of `wall[i][j][k]` are in the same region, in which case `eliminateWall()` will return `false`. Let us take a closer look at these two methods.

```
int randomInteriorWall(int i, int j) {
    int k = rnd.nextInt(4);
    if (i==0 && k == NORTH) return -1;
    if (i==m-1 && k == SOUTH) return -1;
    if (j==0 && k == WEST) return -1;
    if (j==n-1 && k == EAST) return -1;
    if (wall[i][j][k]) return k;
    else return -1;
}
```

```java
boolean eliminateWall(int i, int j, int k) {
    int i2=0, j2=0;
    switch(k) {
        case NORTH:  i2 = i-1; j2 = j;   break;
        case EAST:   i2 = i;   j2 = j+1; break;
        case SOUTH:  i2 = i+1; j2 = j;   break;
        case WEST:   i2 = i;   j2 = j-1; break;
    }
    if (!inSameRegion(room[i][j],room[i2][j2])) {
        wall[i][j][k] = false;
        int oppositeOfK = (k+2) % 4;
        wall[i2][j2][oppositeOfK] = false;
        join(room[i][j], room[i2][j2]);
        return true;
    }
    else return false;
}
```

The `randomInteriorWall()` routine chooses exactly one of the four compass points and asks first if the wall in that direction is an exterior wall, in which case it returns −1. It then asks if there is indeed a wall there, in which case it returns true. After that the `eliminateWall()` function computes the indices of the adjoining room as (`i2`, `j2`) and asks if that room is in the same region as the room with indices (`i`, `j`). If they are in the same region, the routine returns false, but if they are not the two representations of that wall, `wall[i][j][k]` and `wall[i2][j2][(k+2)%4]`, will be set to false, removing the wall. The function then returns true, indicating a successful wall removal. It is important to note, however, that along the way we take explicit action to "join" the two regions, by calling the `join()` function below:

```java
void join(RoomLink l1, RoomLink l2) {
    while (l1.link != l1) l1 = l1.link = l1.link.link;
    while (l2.link != l2) l2 = l2.link = l2.link.link;
    l1.link = l2;
}
```

The most obvious task of `join()` is to find the two rooms which are acting as 'representatives' of the two regions, and set the link in one to point to the other. It is unimportant which direction we do this, meaning the last statement could just as well have been `l2.link = l1`. It is also important for efficiency to 'reorganize' the `room` array by shortening the chain of links leading from any room to its representative room. Thus, even though `l1 = l1.link` would have been sufficient in the first iteration for the obvious purpose of the function, we code 11 = 11.link = 11.link.link instead, which allows us to both find the representative room and also do some work to shorten those chains.

The method inSameRegion() is written recursively, and is very simple. If the link fields in the two rooms are the same, they are obviously in the same region. Failing that, if the two links each point back to themselves, they are in different regions. If both these tests fail, we punt to a recursive call.

```
boolean inSameRegion(RoomLink l1, RoomLink l2) {
    if (l1.link == l2.link) return true;
    else if (l1 == l1.link && l2 == l2.link) return false;
    else return inSameRegion(l1.link,l2.link);
}
```

This completes the maze construction code. We have also given the maze the capability to "draw itself," given a Graphics object and a bounding rectangle. That code is included below:

```
public void draw(Graphics g, Rectangle rect) {
    int cellWidth = (int)(rect.getWidth()/n);
    int cellHeight = (int)(rect.getHeight()/m);
    for (int i=0; i<m; ++i)
      for (int j=0; j<n; ++j)
        for (int k=0; k < 4; ++k)
          if (wall[i][j][k])
            switch(k) {
              case Maze.NORTH:
                g.drawLine(j*cellWidth, i*cellHeight,
                           (j+1)*cellWidth, i*cellHeight);
              break;
              case Maze.EAST:
                g.drawLine((j+1)*cellWidth, i*cellHeight,
                           (j+1)*cellWidth, (i+1)*cellHeight);
              break;
              case Maze.SOUTH:
                g.drawLine(j*cellWidth, (i+1)*cellHeight,
                           (j+1)*cellWidth, (i+1)*cellHeight);
              break;
              case Maze.WEST:
                g.drawLine(j*cellWidth, i*cellHeight,
                           j*cellWidth, (i+1)*cellHeight);
              break;
            }
    drawSpot(g,iStart,jStart,Color.GREEN,cellWidth,cellHeight);
```

```
        drawSpot(g,iFinish,jFinish,Color.RED,cellWidth,cellHeight);
    }
```

Notice that all the interior walls are "drawn twice." Inserting tests to avoid this would accomplish little in terms of efficiency, and would clutter the code. Computing `cellWidth` and `cellHeight` as integers requires truncating the fractional part, which means the maze will always fit into the drawing rectangle but, depending on the dimensions involved, could leave nearly half of each dimension of the rectangle as a blank margin. That will not happen, however, unless `m` and `n` are large enough to produce a maze which is impossible to solve, both mentally and visually!

We finish the `Maze` class with the `drawSpot()` function, which is used to draw a green disk at (`iStart`, `jStart`) and a red disk at (`iFinish`, `jFinish`).

```
    void drawSpot(Graphics g, int i, int j, Color color,
                  int cellWidth, int cellHeight) {
        g.setColor(color);
        int y = i*cellHeight + 1, x = j*cellWidth + 1;
        g.fillOval(x, y, cellWidth-2, cellHeight-2);
        g.setColor(Color.BLACK);
        g.drawOval(x, y, cellWidth-2, cellHeight-2);
    }

} // End of Maze class
```

7.10.4 The MazePanel Class

The `MazePanel` class encapsulates a `Maze` object and its user-provided complete or partial solution, along with a keyboard event handler for user-controlled navigation of the maze. Serialization of the maze also occurs in this class.

```
    package OOPLS;

    import java.awt.Color;
    import java.awt.Graphics;
    import java.awt.event.KeyAdapter;
    import java.awt.event.KeyEvent;
    import java.util.LinkedList;
    import javax.swing.JPanel;
    import java.awt.Rectangle;
    import java.io.BufferedInputStream;
    import java.io.BufferedOutputStream;
```

```java
import java.io.FileInputStream;
import java.io.FileOutputStream;
import java.io.ObjectInputStream;
import java.io.ObjectOutputStream;
import java.util.Iterator;
import javax.swing.JOptionPane;

public class MazePanel extends JPanel {
    final static int DEFAULT_ROWS = 30, DEFAULT_COLUMNS = 40;
    final static Color PATH_COLOR = Color.MAGENTA,
            FINISHED_PATH_COLOR = new Color(0f, 0f, 0.8f);
    int cellWidth, cellHeight;
    Rectangle rect;
    Maze maze;
    LinkedList<Indices2D> solution =
        new LinkedList<Indices2D>();
    boolean spaceDown = false;
```

Figure 7.9 shows an example maze panel. (Default size for the maze is 30 rooms by 40 rooms, but the one in the figure is 15 by 30.) The user's partially constructed path is colored magenta, while a fully constructed correct path will turn a shade of dark blue when the user enters the target room. The `cellWidth` and `cellHeight` attributes have the same interpretation here as in the `draw()` routine of the `Maze` class, but are computed as needed rather than passed back and forth between classes. The `rect` data member is a handle to the panel's bounding rectangle; it is passed in to the maze's `draw()` routine so it can properly draw itself.

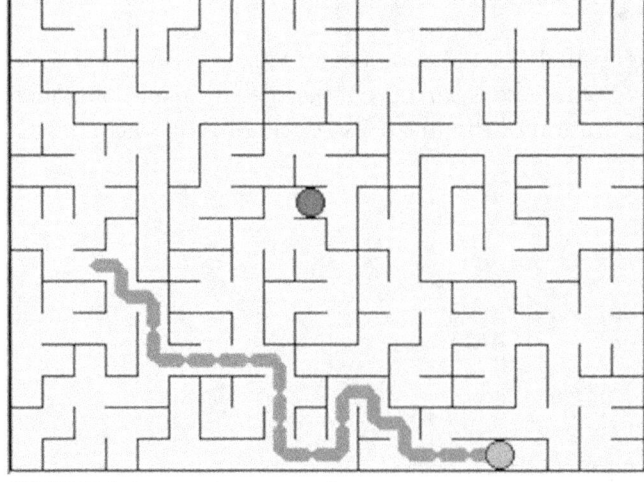

FIGURE 7.9 An example maze panel

The remaining three members are: (1) `maze`, a handle to the maze itself, which the maze panel will construct and reconstruct as needed; (2) `solution`, the user's solution entered using arrow keys, represented as a linked list of `Indices2D` pairs; and (3) `spaceDown`, a flag which when set to `true` informs the `paint()` routine that the user has pressed and not released the space key and therefore needs some help locating the start and finish locations. The constructor below constructs the maze using the default dimensions, then starts the `solution` list by adding the indices of the maze's 'start' room to it. (It is an essential invariant of any object of this class that at the conclusion of any method the `solution` list should not be empty, but should contain at least the maze's start position.) After initializing `solution`, the constructor establishes the panel's ability to respond to keystrokes by calling the `setFocusable()` method from its indirect superclass `Component`. It then attaches a `KeyListener` object constructed as an extension of the `KeyAdapter` class.

```java
public MazePanel() {
    maze = new Maze(DEFAULT_ROWS,DEFAULT_COLUMNS);
    solution.add(maze.getStart());
    setFocusable(true);
    addKeyListener(new KeyAdapter() {
        public void keyPressed(KeyEvent e) {
            if (maze.getFinish().equals(solution.getLast()))
                return;
            Indices2D current = solution.removeLast();
            Indices2D last = null;
            if (!solution.isEmpty())
                last = solution.getLast();
            solution.add(current);
            switch(e.getKeyCode()) {
                case KeyEvent.VK_UP:
                    goNorth(current,last); break;
                case KeyEvent.VK_RIGHT:
                    goEast(current,last); break;
                case KeyEvent.VK_DOWN:
                    goSouth(current,last); break;
                case KeyEvent.VK_LEFT:
                    goWest(current,last); break;
                case KeyEvent.VK_BACK_SPACE:
                    if (solution.size() > 1)
                        solution.removeLast(); break;
                case KeyEvent.VK_SPACE:
                    spaceDown = true;
        }
    }
```

```
            repaint();
        }
        public void keyReleased(KeyEvent e) {
            if (spaceDown) {
                spaceDown = false;
                repaint();
            }
        }
    });
}
```

The methods we are overriding from the `KeyAdapter` class are `keyPressed()` and `keyReleased()`. Our override of `keyPressed()` will perform the following actions. (1) It first checks to see if the solution is already complete, in which case it will return without responding to the keystroke. (2) If the solution is not complete, it removes the last position from *solution* and saves it as the `Indices2D` object `current`. (3) The variable `last` is then defined as an `Indices2D` object to keep track of the previous position visited, which is now the last item on the list if the list is nonempty. If it is empty, `last` is set to `null`. (4) Now `current` is replaced on the back of the list, and (5) a numeric code identifying the key which was pressed is obtained from the `KeyEvent` object `e` with the call `e.getKeyCode()`. This code is used to control a `switch` statement. The `switch` (6) compares the key's code to the codes `VK_UP`, `VK_RIGHT`, `VK_DOWN`, `VK_LEFT`, `VK_BACK_SPACE`, and `VK_SPACE`, all of which are static constants inside `KeyEvent`. If it is one of the first four, then the respective choice is made to call one of the private methods `goNorth()`, `goEast()`, `goSouth()`, and `goWest()`. If the code is `VK_BACK_SPACE`, and the `solution` list contains more than just the start square indices, then the last element of `solution` is deleted. If it is `VK_SPACE`, the `spaceDown` flag is set to `true`. The last action is to (7) repaint the panel. The `keyReleased()` override checks to see if `spaceDown` is set, and if so clears it and repaints.

The four routines `goNorth()`, `goEast()`, `goSouth()`, and `goWest()` are similar to each other and have the task of (a) determining if it is legal to go in that direction, and (b) extending the solution in that direction if it is legal.

```
    void goNorth(Indices2D current, Indices2D last) {
        if (current.i > 0 &&
                !maze.hasWall(current.i,current.j,Maze.NORTH))
            if (last == null || last.i != current.i - 1)
                solution.add(new Indices2D(
                    current.i - 1,current.j));
```

```
        else solution.removeLast();
    }
    void goEast(Indices2D current, Indices2D last) {
        if (current.j < maze.getNumColumns()-1 &&
                !maze.hasWall(current.i,current.j,Maze.EAST))
            if (last == null || last.j != current.j + 1)
                solution.add(new Indices2D(
                    current.i,current.j + 1));
            else solution.removeLast();
    }
    void goSouth(Indices2D current, Indices2D last) {
        if (current.i < maze.getNumRows() - 1 &&
                !maze.hasWall(current.i, current.j, Maze.SOUTH))
            if (last == null || last.i != current.i + 1)
                solution.add(new Indices2D(
                    current.i + 1,current.j));
            else solution.removeLast();
    }
    void goWest(Indices2D current, Indices2D last) {
        if (current.j > 0 &&
                !maze.hasWall(current.i, current.j, Maze.WEST))
            if (last == null || last.j != current.j - 1)
                solution.add(new Indices2D(
                    current.i,current.j - 1));
            else solution.removeLast();
    }
```

Four public functions now follow which give the client some control over the maze and its solution. There are two versions of a `newMaze()` function, one which keeps the same dimensions as the old maze and one which explicitly specifies the dimensions. The `eraseSolution()` method puts `solution` in its one-element start state, and `getMaze()` returns a handle to the maze so that the client can manipulate it through its public interface.

```
    public void newMaze() {
        newMaze(maze.getNumRows(),maze.getNumColumns());
    }
    public void newMaze(int m, int n) {
        maze = new Maze(m,n);
        eraseSolution();
        repaint();
    }
    public void eraseSolution() {
        solution.clear();
```

```
        solution.add(maze.getStart());
    }
    public Maze getMaze() { return maze; }
```

The `paint()` routine for the panel follows, which first draws the user's complete or partial solution using a series of calls to the (user-defined) `drawThick-Line()` function, then requests the maze to draw itself. Finally, if the `spaceDown` flag is set, the paint routine draws a large green circle around the start square and a large red circle around the finish square.

```
public void paint(Graphics g) {
    super.paint(g);
    rect = getBounds();
    cellWidth = (int)(rect.getWidth()/maze.getNumColumns());
    cellHeight = (int)(rect.getHeight()/maze.getNumRows());
    if (solution.getLast().equals(maze.getFinish())) {
        g.setColor(FINISHED_PATH_COLOR);
    }
    else {
        g.setColor(PATH_COLOR);
    }
    Iterator<Indices2D> i = solution.iterator();
    Indices2D last = i.next();
    while (i.hasNext()) {
        Indices2D next = i.next();
        int i1=last.i, j1=last.j, i2=next.i, j2=next.j;
        drawThickLine(g,
            j1*cellWidth+cellWidth/2,
            i1*cellHeight+cellHeight/2,
            j2*cellWidth+cellWidth/2,
            i2*cellHeight+cellHeight/2);
        last = next;
    }
    g.setColor(Color.BLACK);
    maze.draw(g, rect);
    if (spaceDown) {
        int radiusOfCircle =
            Math.max(rect.width/20, 2*cellWidth);
        g.setColor(Color.GREEN);
        g.drawOval(
          maze.getStart().j*cellWidth +
              cellWidth/2 - radiusOfCircle,
          maze.getStart().i*cellHeight +
              cellHeight/2 - radiusOfCircle,
```

```
      2*radiusOfCircle,2*radiusOfCircle);
    g.setColor(Color.RED);
    g.drawOval(
      maze.getFinish().j*cellWidth +
          cellWidth/2 - radiusOfCircle,
      maze.getFinish().i*cellHeight +
          cellHeight/2 - radiusOfCircle,
      2*radiusOfCircle,2*radiusOfCircle);
  }
}
```

The `drawThickLine()` function draws the "line" connecting one room to its adjacent room in the list *solution*. Instead of using the `drawLine()` function of class *Graphics*, we are using an elongated ellipse. This gives the representation on screen of the user's solution a "daisy-chain" appearance.

```
void drawThickLine(Graphics g, int x1, int y1,
                               int x2, int y2) {
    if (x1 == x2) {
        int width = cellWidth/2;
        int height = y2>y1?(y2-y1+1):(y1-y2+1);
        g.fillOval(x1-width/2,Math.min(y1,y2),width,height);
    }
    else {
        int height = cellHeight/2;
        int width = x2>x1?(x2-x1+1):(x1-x2+1);
        g.fillOval(Math.min(x1,x2),y1-height/2,width,height);
    }
}
```

The last two methods in class `MazePanel` implement persistence. Function `saveMaze()` serializes the maze and the user's complete or partial solution to the file specified by its `String` parameter `filename`, and `openMaze()` reads those serialized objects back into memory from a file. In either case, if something goes wrong with the file operation the routine first uses `JOptionPane` to display a notification to the user, then returns `false` to the client.

```
public boolean saveMaze(String filename) {
    try {
        ObjectOutputStream binaryOut =
                new ObjectOutputStream(
                new BufferedOutputStream(
                new FileOutputStream(filename)));
```

```
            binaryOut.writeObject(maze);
            binaryOut.writeObject(solution);
            binaryOut.flush();
            binaryOut.close();
            return true;
        } catch (Exception exc) {
            JOptionPane.showMessageDialog(this,
                "Could not save to '"+filename+"'");
            return false;
        }
    }

    public boolean openMaze(String filename) {
        Maze oldMaze = maze;
        LinkedList<Indices2D> oldSolution = solution;
        try {
            ObjectInputStream binaryIn =
                    new ObjectInputStream(
                    new BufferedInputStream(
                    new FileInputStream(filename)));
            maze = (Maze)binaryIn.readObject();
            solution =
                (LinkedList<Indices2D>)binaryIn.readObject();
            repaint();
            return true;
        } catch(Exception exc) {
            JOptionPane.showMessageDialog(this,
                "Could not open '"+filename+"'");
            maze = oldMaze;
            solution = oldSolution;
            return false;
        }
    }
} // End of class MazePanel
```

Again, note that in order to implement serialization all we did was to make sure that all involved classes were declared to be (and therefore were!) serializable. At this point all we had to do to save was to call `writeObject()`, and all we had to do to load was to call `readObject()`.

7.10.5 Menus on a JFrame Object—The Maze Application

A menu is just a tree with "buttons" at its leaves. Actually, the leaves are not buttons but objects of type `JMenuItem`; they are like buttons in that they are there to be clicked on, and in response to the click an `ActionEvent` is manufactured and sent to a list of listeners. So just as with buttons, we need only attach an `ActionListener` to make the menu item work.

In the Swing framework, we build a menu from the top down. At the root is a `JMenuBar` item, which must be attached to the `JFrame`-derived application class using `setJMenuBar()`. The first-level items are each either of type `JMenu` or of type `JMenuItem`. Each `JMenu` object can have multiple objects "added" to it, each of which can be either a `JMenu` or a `JMenuItem` object. We illustrate the construction of a menu by completing our maze application, in which we add a main class which is a subtype of `JFrame` and employ a menu to give the user control of all operations on the maze.

```java
import OOPLS.Maze;
import OOPLS.MazeConfigurationDialog;
import OOPLS.MazeHelpDialog;
import OOPLS.MazePanel;
import java.awt.EventQueue;
import java.awt.FileDialog;
import java.awt.event.ActionEvent;
import java.awt.event.ActionListener;
import javax.swing.JFrame;
import javax.swing.JMenu;
import javax.swing.JMenuBar;
import javax.swing.JMenuItem;
import java.awt.FileDialog;
import java.awt.event.WindowEvent;

public class MazeApplication extends JFrame {
    MazePanel mp = new MazePanel();
    JMenuBar menuBar = new JMenuBar();
    JMenu fileMenu = new JMenu("File");
    JMenuItem saveItem = new JMenuItem("Save");
    JMenuItem saveAsItem = new JMenuItem("Save As");
    JMenuItem loadItem = new JMenuItem("Open");
    JMenuItem exitItem = new JMenuItem("Exit");
    JMenuItem newItem = new JMenuItem("New");
    JMenu editMenu = new JMenu("Edit");
    JMenuItem eraseSolutionItem =
        new JMenuItem("Erase solution");
    JMenuItem configurationItem =
        new JMenuItem("Reconfigure maze");
    JMenuItem helpMenu = new JMenuItem("Help");
```

All the components of the menu to be attached to the `JFrame` are declared in the code above, at the top of the class definition. As they are declared and instantiated, they are given names and text descriptions. They do not yet constitute a menu, because their dependencies have not been defined. In order to do that, we need to take run-time action in the form of a series of `add()` operations, culminating in the `setJMenuBar()` message to the `JFrame` itself.

```
String filename = "";
public MazeApplication() {
    setBounds(0,0,700,500);
    initComponents();
}
```

Above we see the declaration for data member `filename`, which is an important part of the state of the frame. The string in this variable is always visible to the user, because it is displayed in the title bar of the window. If the maze currently on screen is a freshly generated maze which has not been saved to a file, this string's value will be the empty string. Once a maze has been saved to a file, or once an old maze has been read from a file, this string will take on the fully qualified file name to which the maze was saved or from which the maze was read.

The constructor appears next, which merely establishes a reasonable initial size and location for the window with a `setBounds()` message, then calls the `initComponents()` routine in order to set up the menu.

Setting up a menu is a long process, but the pattern is simple and repetitious and quite clear and familiar to the experienced Java programmer. Our `initComponents()` routine below sets up the menu one menu item at a time, beginning with the response to *File...New*.

```
public void initComponents() {
    fileMenu.add(newItem);
    newItem.addActionListener(new ActionListener() {
        public void actionPerformed(ActionEvent e) {
            mp.newMaze();
            filename = "";
            setTitle("");
            repaint();
        }
    });
```

When the user selects *File...New*, a new maze is randomly generated with the same dimensions as before. In keeping with the fact that the new maze does not reside on disk, the current file name is blanked out, along with the frame window's title bar.

```
fileMenu.add(saveItem);
saveItem.addActionListener(new ActionListener() {
    public void actionPerformed(ActionEvent e) {
        if (filename.length() == 0) saveAs();
        else mp.saveMaze(filename);
    }
});
```

The response to *File…Save* is to see if there is currently a file associated with the maze on display. If not, then the `saveAs()` routine is called (see below). If there is such a file, its fully qualified file name is passed on to the maze panel's `saveMaze()` function, which serializes the maze, along with the user's solution, to that file.

```
fileMenu.add(saveAsItem);
saveAsItem.addActionListener(new ActionListener() {
    public void actionPerformed(ActionEvent e) {
        saveAs();
    }
});
```

The response to *File…Save As* is to call the `saveAs()` method, which we will elaborate on at the end of this section. We now examine the actions taken when the user decides to load a previously saved maze from disk.

```
fileMenu.add(loadItem);
loadItem.addActionListener(new ActionListener() {
    public void actionPerformed(ActionEvent e) {
        FileDialog lfd =
                new FileDialog(MazeApplication.this,
                        "Load Maze",FileDialog.LOAD);
        lfd.setFile("*.maz");
        lfd.setVisible(true);
        if (lfd.getDirectory() != null &&
            lfd.getFile() != null &&
            lfd.getFile().length() > 0) {
            String oldFilename = filename;
            filename = lfd.getDirectory()+lfd.getFile();
            if (mp.openMaze(filename)) setTitle(filename);
```

```
            else filename = oldFilename;
        }
        mp.repaint();
    }
});
```

When the user makes the menu choice *File…Open*, we bring up a canned file dialog to help the user navigate the file system and find the file where the desired maze is stored. This requires class `FileDialog`, and the constructor we use here has three parameters. The argument passed to the first parameter is `MazeApplication.this`, establishing the frame window object (not the object of anonymous class type to which `this` alone would refer) as the parent window. The second argument is the title to be used in the dialog box's title bar, and the argument to the third parameter is a code specifying that the intent is to load from a file and not to save. Before the dialog is made visible on the screen, the file name is passed in as "`*.maz`", which insures that, at least initially, the only file choices presented to the user will be files ending with `.maz`. If the user ends the dialog by clicking on the *Cancel* button, one or both of `getDirectory()` and `getFile()` will return null values, and no action will be taken. Otherwise an attempt will be made to read a maze from the chosen file. If that attempt is successful, the `filename` attribute changes and the title bar of the window changes to match it, and the previously stored maze and solution are displayed. If not, the old file name will be restored.

The next menu item corresponds to the menu choice *File…Exit*, assumedly made when the user wishes to exit the program. To achieve this it suffices to place a "window closing" event on the event queue. The user will interact with this dialog in the usual way, and when finished will click on either the *OK* or the *Cancel* button.

```
fileMenu.add(exitItem);
exitItem.addActionListener(new ActionListener() {
    public void actionPerformed(ActionEvent e) {
        dispatchEvent(
            new WindowEvent(
                MazeApplication.this,
                WindowEvent.WINDOW_CLOSING));
    }
});
```

The file menu is now complete, and we can attach it to the menu bar.

```
menuBar.add(fileMenu);
```

Next is the *Edit...Erase Solution* menu choice, which only requires that we pass the request on to the maze panel, then repaint the panel.

```
editMenu.add(eraseSolutionItem);
eraseSolutionItem.addActionListener(new ActionListener() {
    public void actionPerformed(ActionEvent e) {
        mp.eraseSolution();
        mp.repaint();
    }
});
```

Edit...Reconfigure Maze requires two user inputs, the number *m* of rows and the number *n* of columns to be used in constructing new mazes. We will use a custom-constructed dialog box called `MazeConfigurationDialog` to obtain those inputs from the user. The complete definition of that dialog will be given in the next section.

```
editMenu.add(configurationItem);
configurationItem.addActionListener(new ActionListener() {
    public void actionPerformed(ActionEvent e) {
        Maze oldMaze = mp.getMaze();
        MazeConfigurationDialog mcd =
new MazeConfigurationDialog(mp);
        mcd.setModal(true);
        mcd.setVisible(true);
        if (mp.getMaze() != oldMaze) {
            filename = "";
            setTitle("");
        }
        mp.repaint();
    }
});
```

The maze configuration dialog only needs to be passed a handle to the maze panel in order to begin its work. It is configured using the `setModal(true)` message so that it will operate as a modal dialog box, and because it has a direct link to the maze panel it will make its own modifications to that panel, as we shall see in the next section. If it makes modifications it will do so by reconstructing the maze, so that the old maze handle is no longer the one held by the panel. In that case, the test `mp.getMaze() != oldMaze` succeeds, whereupon we clear out the `filename` attribute and the title bar.

The remainder of the `initComponents()` function is given below. First we add the edit menu and the `helpMenu` menu item to the menu bar, then we attach the menu bar to the frame. On the way out, we establish the `EXIT_ON_CLOSE` behavior as always, then attach the maze panel to the content pane. Notice that `helpMenu` is actually not a menu but a menu item, but it is attached directly to the menu bar. It has an action listener attached which brings up a custom dialog having no purpose other than to communicate some simple instructions to the user.

```
menuBar.add(editMenu);
helpMenu.addActionListener(new ActionListener() {
    public void actionPerformed(ActionEvent e) {
        MazeHelpDialog helpDialog = new MazeHelpDialog();
        helpDialog.setVisible(true);
        mp.repaint();
    }
});
menuBar.add(helpMenu);
setJMenuBar(menuBar);
setDefaultCloseOperation(EXIT_ON_CLOSE);
getContentPane().add(mp);
}
```

Following `initComponents()` is the `saveAs()` method, called from the former in two places.

```
void saveAs() {
    FileDialog sfd = new FileDialog(
            MazeApplication.this,"Save Maze", FileDialog.SAVE);
    if (filename.length() == 0) filename = "untitled.maz";
    sfd.setFile(filename);
    sfd.setVisible(true);
    if (sfd.getDirectory() != null && sfd.getFile() != null
        && sfd.getFile().length() > 0) {
        String oldFilename = filename;
        filename = sfd.getDirectory() + sfd.getFile();
        if (!filename.substring(
            filename.length()-4).equals(".maz"))
                filename += ".maz";
        if (mp.saveMaze(filename))
            setTitle(filename);
        else filename = oldFilename;
    }
}
```

```
        mp.repaint();
    }
```

This code is very similar to that in the `actionPerformed()` function of the action listener attached to the `loadItem` menu item. Some points of difference are: (1) the file dialog is configured to save, not load; (2) if no file name is currently assigned the name `"untitled.maz"` is given; and (3) code is inserted to insure that the file name ends in `.maz`.

7.10.6 Custom Dialog Boxes

In the previous section, we made reference to two custom dialog classes, to be used for (1) inputting new dimensions for the maze and (2) displaying help instructions. We give the definitions for those dialog boxes here. First, the file *MazeConfigurationDialog.java* is presented below in its entirety.

The construction of a `JDialog`-derived class is very similar to that of a `JFrame`-derived class. The major difference is that the `setModal(true)` message cannot be sent to the latter. Once that message has been sent to a dialog object, not only is its parent window frozen as soon as it becomes visible, but its existence is tied to its visibility. In other words, when it receives the `setVisible(false)` message, it is destroyed.

```java
package OOPLS;
import java.awt.event.ActionEvent;
import java.awt.event.ActionListener;
import javax.swing.BoxLayout;
import javax.swing.JButton;
import javax.swing.JDialog;
import javax.swing.JLabel;
import javax.swing.JPanel;
import javax.swing.JTextField;

public class MazeConfigurationDialog extends JDialog {
    JTextField rowsField = new JTextField();
    JTextField columnsField = new JTextField();
    JButton okayButton = new JButton("OK");
    MazePanel mp;
    int m, n;
    public MazeConfigurationDialog(MazePanel mp) {
        this.mp = mp;
        m = mp.getMaze().getNumRows();
        n = mp.getMaze().getNumColumns();
        setBounds(100,100,250,120);
```

```
        initComponents();
    }
    public void initComponents() {
        setLayout(
            new BoxLayout(getContentPane(),BoxLayout.Y_AXIS));
        JPanel topPanel = new JPanel();
        topPanel.setLayout(
            new BoxLayout(topPanel,BoxLayout.X_AXIS));
        topPanel.add(new JLabel("Number of Rows:         "));
        rowsField.setText(new Integer(m).toString());
        rowsField.setSelectionStart(0);
        rowsField.setSelectionEnd(3);
        topPanel.add(rowsField);
        getContentPane().add(topPanel);
        JPanel middlePanel = new JPanel();
        middlePanel.setLayout(
            new BoxLayout(middlePanel,BoxLayout.X_AXIS));
        middlePanel.add(new JLabel("Number of Columns:    "));
        columnsField.setText(new Integer(n).toString());
        columnsField.setSelectionStart(0);
        columnsField.setSelectionEnd(2);
        middlePanel.add(columnsField);
        getContentPane().add(middlePanel);
        JPanel bottomPanel = new JPanel();
        bottomPanel.setLayout(
            new BoxLayout(bottomPanel,BoxLayout.X_AXIS));
        bottomPanel.add(new JLabel(""));
        bottomPanel.add(okayButton);
        okayButton.addActionListener(new ActionListener(){
            public void actionPerformed(ActionEvent e) {
                int newM =
                    Integer.parseInt(rowsField.getText());
                int newN =
                    Integer.parseInt(columnsField.getText());
                if (newM > 1 && newN > 1 && m != newM ||
                    n != newN)
                    mp.newMaze(newM,newN);
                setVisible(false);
            }
        });
        bottomPanel.add(new JLabel(""));
        getContentPane().add(bottomPanel);
    }
}
```

The appearance of the dialog box on the screen is as illustrated in Figure 7.10. Note that the `setSelectionStart(0)` and `setSelectionEnd(2)` messages were sent to the two text boxes, without which the user would have had to backspace over the old values before typing the new.

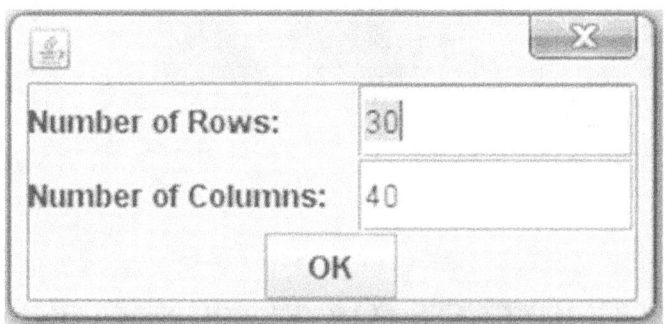

FIGURE 7.10 Appearance of a `MazeConfigurationDialog` object

```
package OOPLS;

import javax.swing.JDialog;
import javax.swing.JLabel;
import javax.swing.JTextArea;

public class MazeHelpDialog extends JDialog {
  JTextArea helpText = new JTextArea();
  public MazeHelpDialog() {
    setBounds(20,20,400,250);
    this.setResizable(false);
    helpText.setBounds(getBounds());
    initComponents();
  }
  public void initComponents() {
    helpText.setLineWrap(true);
    helpText.setWrapStyleWord(true);
    helpText.setEditable(false);
    helpText.setText(
    "  Use the arrow keys to navigate "
  + "from the green 'start' room \n"
  + "  to the red 'stop' room.  Use "
  + "backspace to erase one link at\n"
  + "  a time from your solution.\n\n"
  + "  'File...New' generates a new maze.\n"
  + "  'File...Save' saves the "
  + "maze and your complete or partial solution.\n"
```

```
+   "   'File...Open' opens a new maze.\n"
+   "   'Edit...Erase solution' removes "
+   "all moves so you can start from\n"
+   "           scratch on a new solution.\n"
+   "   'Edit...Reconfigure maze' allows "
+   "you to change the number of rows\n"
+   "           and columns of the maze.\n\n"
+   "   If you have difficulty locating "
+   "the start and finish locations,\n"
+   "   press and hold the space key.");
    getContentPane().add(helpText);
  }
}
```

7.11   GAINING RUN-TIME ACCESS TO TYPE INFORMATION

We have mentioned many times that nonprimitive objects in Java "know" their types and can be asked for type information at run-time, but we have only mentioned that capability in connection with checks made by the Java Virtual Machine. In fact, we can make such inquiries with client code. Given an object `obj` whose type could only be ascertained by the compiler as `Object`, we may obtain its precise type with the call `obj.getClass()`. This call is the gateway to gaining extensive knowledge about the object. We sometimes use the term *reflection* to refer to this ability of an object to deliver complete run-time information concerning its attributes and behaviors, and languages that allow reflection are called *reflective*.

But what type of object is returned by the `getClass()` method, and how may we use it? There are some obvious answers to the second question, such as the following pattern to discern whether two first-class objects are of the same type.

```
if (obj1.getClass() == obj2.getClass()) {
    // Come here if obj1 and obj2 are exactly the same type.
    ...
else {
    // Come here if obj1 and obj2 are of different types.
    ...
}
```

> *The explicit test of an object's type, although enabled by the Java language and by just about any language that provides run-time type information, is not considered good programming practice and is probably evidence of a flaw in a program's design. Reliance on polymorphism is almost always a viable alternative and a better alternative to explicit run-time type testing.*

NOTE

This is very rudimentary, however, and does not come near to showing us the full power of the run-time information available to us. Actually, a Java object can furnish full information concerning not only its type but also all its attributes and behaviors. The `getClass()` method resides in the ultimate base class `Object`, and returns an object of type `Class`. Every Java type has such an associated object, including primitive types. Because we cannot send messages to primitive types, we access their associated class objects by using the *class* static attribute, as in `int.class`.

Where there is one "meta-type" there must be others, in order to give complete information. So in addition to `Class`, there are types called `Constructor`, `Method`, and `Field`, among others. For example, in order to obtain an array containing the methods associated with object `obj`, we can use the declaration

```
import java.lang.reflect.Method;
...
Method[] methods = obj.getClass().getMethods();
```

Then we can cycle through the methods with a loop, if we wish. For example, the following code sequence steps through all the methods associated with the object, calls the ones which are parameterless, and attempts to display the `toString()` representation of the value returned.

```
int numMethods = methods.length;
for (int i=0; i<numMethods; ++i) {
    TypeVariable tv[] = methods[i].getTypeParameters();
    System.out.println("Method " + i + " is " +
                        methods[i].getName());
    int numParms = methods[i].getParameterTypes().length;
    if (numParms == 0) {
        try {
            Object returnValue =
                methods[i].invoke(obj, new Object[]);
            System.out.println(
                "Value returned is " +
```

```
                    returnValue.toString());
        }
        catch (Exception e) {
            System.out.println(
                "Return value could not be displayed");
        }
    }
}
```

7.12   COMPONENT-LEVEL PROGRAMMING

The fact that *everything* about Java types and Java objects is run-time accessible makes it easy to do component-level programming. IDEs like *NetBeans* and *Eclipse* provide interactive design capabilities where the programmer can build a "drag and drop" interface by choosing tools from a pictorial menu. This is certainly not a capability unique to Java, but the ease with which that menu can be changed to incorporate programmer-defined components called *JavaBeans*™ is striking.

All of the `JPanel`-derived classes we have developed, i.e., `CompleteGraph-Panel`, `DroppedBallPanel`, and `MazePanel`, some with slight changes, are eligible for use as "beans" and for incorporation into the *NetBeans* tools menu. However, to make them more configurable it is desirable to give them more *properties*.

7.12.1 Bean Properties

The Java Bean model for component-level programming is based on a simple naming convention. For example, to define a `boolean` property called `lefthanded`, we would have to provide public `getLefthanded()` and `setLefthanded()` methods. The actual existence of a field named `lefthanded` is not necessary. If (1) a "get" and a "set" routine are present, are both public, and are similarly named, (2) the return type of the get routine is the same as that of the single parameter of the set routine, and (3) that type is either primitive or one of a restricted collection of types the IDE recognizes, then the IDE will present the property as an attribute for direct manipulation in the properties dialog associated with a component, once it has been added to the interface. (If there is only a "get" method, then the item will appear on the "Properties" list as a read-only item.) For example, the attribute `leftHanded` would appear along with a checkbox. If the box is checked, then the value is `true`, and if not, the value is `false`.

An important feature of properties is their association with *property change events*. A property change event (type `PropertyChangeEvent`) should be "fired" whenever a property changes and that property might be "interesting" to clients. The simplest way to add support for property change events is to provide in the bean class a `PropertyChangeSupport` data member, say `pcs`, and configure it so that it (a) is advised when clients register their interest in property changes and (b) fires the events when they occur. Requirement (a) is achieved by overriding the bean's `addPropertyChangeListener()` method so that it calls the method of the same name in `pcs`, and requirement (b) is achieved by calling the `firePropertyChange()` method of `pcs` when the appropriate "setter" is called. The argument to `firePropertyChange()` can be a newly instantiated `PropertyChangeEvent`, whose constructor needs (1) the bean within which the change occurs, (2) a string giving the name of the property (e.g., `leftHanded`), (3) the property's old value, and (4) the property's new value. Simpler versions of `firePropertyChange()` exist, however, which use some subset of those four parameters and create the event object internally.

We illustrate below by providing an expanded definition for the `DroppedBallPanel` class, in which the properties `minimumSize`, `maximumSize`, `preferredSize`, `color`, `bounce`, and `moving` are introduced.

```
package OOPLS;

import java.awt.Color;
import java.awt.Dimension;
import java.awt.Graphics;
import java.awt.event.ActionEvent;
import java.awt.event.ActionListener;
import java.awt.event.ComponentAdapter;
import java.awt.event.ComponentEvent;
import java.beans.PropertyChangeEvent;
import java.beans.PropertyChangeListener;
import java.beans.PropertyChangeSupport;
import java.util.Random;
import javax.swing.JPanel;
import javax.swing.Timer;

public class DroppedBallPanel extends JPanel
                            implements ActionListener {
    final int FREQUENCY = 30; // Timer events per second.
    DroppedBall ball = new DroppedBall();
    Timer timer = new Timer(1000/FREQUENCY, this);
```

```
boolean moving = false,
        bounced = false;
PropertyChangeSupport pcs =
    new PropertyChangeSupport(this);
public DroppedBallPanel() {
    ball.setRectangle(getBounds());
    addComponentListener(new ComponentAdapter() {
        public void componentResized(ComponentEvent e) {
            stop();
            ball.setRectangle(getBounds());
            start();
        }
    });
    start();
}
public void addPropertyChangeListener(
    PropertyChangeListener pcl) {
    pcs.addPropertyChangeListener(pcl);
}
public void actionPerformed(ActionEvent e) {
    ball.cycle(1000/FREQUENCY);
    repaint();
    if (ball.bounced())
        pcs.firePropertyChange("bounce", false, true);
}
public void paint(Graphics g) {
    super.paint(g);
    ball.draw(g);
}
public void drop() {
    if (!moving) start();
    Random rnd = new Random();
    ball.setColor(
        new Color(rnd.nextFloat(),
                  rnd.nextFloat(),
                  rnd.nextFloat())
    );
    ball.randomizeLocationAndSpeed();
}
public void start() {
    if (!moving) {
        timer.addActionListener(this);
        timer.start();
        moving = true;
        pcs.firePropertyChange(new PropertyChangeEvent(
            this,"moving",false,true));
```

```java
            }
        }
        public void stop() {
            if (moving) {
                timer.removeActionListener(this);
                timer.stop();
                moving = false;
                pcs.firePropertyChange(new PropertyChangeEvent(
                    this,"moving",true,false));
            }
        }
        public void setColor(Color c) {
            ball.setColor(c);
        }
        public Color getColor() {
            return ball.getColor();
        }
        public Dimension getPreferredSize() {
            return new Dimension(400,300);
        }
        public Dimension getMinimumSize() {
            return new Dimension(200,150);
        }
        public Dimension getMaximumSize() {
            return new Dimension(1024,768);
        }
        public boolean getMoving() {
            return moving;
        }
        public void setMoving(boolean isMoving) {
            if (moving != isMoving) {
                if (moving) stop();
                else start();
            }
        }
        public boolean getBounce() {
            return ball.bounced();
        }
    }
```

The property change support which is built into the above class focuses on the `moving` property and the `bounce` property, but in neither case does the actual generation of events occur inside a "set" method. Property change events for `moving` are generated inside the `start()` and `stop()` routines, which are the only methods which actually produce changes in the `moving` property. In both cases, the property change support object *pcs* is told (in two different ways, for variety) to "fire" a `PropertyChangeEvent`, which simply means that `pcs` will traverse its list of listeners and call the `propertyChange()` method in each listener, providing the event in question as its operand in all cases. Property change events for `bounce` occur when the ball bounces off the bottom edge of its bounding rectangle, and we will need to make a couple of small changes to the `Dropped-Ball` class so that we can detect that eventuality from a `DroppedBallPanel`. Specifically, we (a) add the following line of code inside the `DroppedBall` class

```
boolean bounced = false;
```

and (b) modify the `cycle()` function so that it sets `bounce` to `true` every time `dy` changes sign and sets the same flag to `false` when `dy` does not change its sign. The resulting `cycle()` function appears as follows, with the added code in italics:

```
public void cycle(int elapsedMillis) {
    centerx += dx * elapsedMillis/1000.0;
    centery += dy * elapsedMillis/1000.0;
    if (centerx - radius <= rectangle.x ||
        centerx + radius >= rectangle.x + rectangle.width)
        dx = -dx;
    bounced = false;
    if (centery + radius >= rectangle.y + rectangle.height) {
        centery = rectangle.y + rectangle.height - radius;
        dy = -bouncePct * dy;
        if (Math.abs(dy) < 15) dy = 0; //
        else bounced = true;
    }
    dy += ddy * elapsedMillis/1000.0;
    if (Math.abs(centery+radius - rectangle.height) < epsilon
        && dy >= 0)
        dx *= rollPct;
}
```

Recompiling the `DroppedBall` and `DroppedBallPanel` classes with these additional behaviors and attributes makes the latter class file well suited for use as a Java Bean. In *NetBeans*, the menu choices *Tools...Palette...Swing/AWT Components* bring up the Palette Manager dialog, which allows the programmer to change the tools palette (visible via *Window...Palette*) to incorporate the bean. Clicking the *Add from Project...* button brings up a file directory browser, which allows the programmer to navigate to the directory containing the project that produced the compiled class file. Once that project directory has been selected the user clicks the *Next>* button and a list of the successfully compiled components from that project is presented. Selecting `DroppedBallPanel` from this menu and again clicking on *Next>*, the user is presented with a choice of submenus within the tools palette to which the new component can be added. Here, the user selects the *Beans* palette category and clicks on *Finish*. If all has gone well, when the user inspects the tools palette the `DroppedBallPanel` bean appears as one of the choices.

Clicking on the *DroppedBallPanel* bean icon on the tools palette and dragging it onto a `JFrame` form actually causes an object of type `DroppedBallPanel` to be instantiated. Its initial size will be determined by the `preferredSize` property, but it can be resized once it is dropped onto the frame. Using reflection, the IDE populates the panel's "properties window" with the actual values of those properties which have been defined by the naming conventions above. Thus, the `color` property appears on the menu, and because the IDE recognizes the type `Color`, which is specified as the return type of method `getColor()` and the type assigned to the parameter of `setColor()`, it presents the IDE user with a button on that line of the properties window that, if pushed, brings up a color choice dialog. The ball, whose color was randomly assigned when the panel was instantiated, can thus be ordered to dynamically change its color. Similarly, the `moving` property can be changed by checking or unchecking its check box.

7.12.2 A "Drag and Drop" Example

In this section, we develop a simple application which makes use of the bean we created in the previous section. We will have *NetBeans* generate for us an application which coordinates the states of a complete graph panel and a dropped ball panel, by (a) having the number of vertices of the complete graph reset to a random value every time the ball bounces and (b) dropping the ball every time that number of vertices is a multiple of ten. Before we do this, we must convert the `CompleteGaphPanel` class to a bean class.

Only one obstacle prevents `CompleteGraphPanel` from qualifying as a bean. In order to be selected from a palette and dropped onto a frame or applet, a `JPanel`-derived class must have a default constructor. This is because dropping a bean on to a form requires that we instantiate from its class a default-constructed object, so that we can populate its properties dialog with actual values. For this reason, we add to the `CompleteGraphPanel` definition the following code:

```
public CompleteGraphPanel() {
```

```
    this(3);
 }
```

Once this has been done, `CompleteGraphPanel` can be added to the Beans subpalette using the menu interactions described above.

To construct our application, we ask *NetBeans* to create a `JFrame` application with the menu choices *File…New File…*. In the resulting dialog, we select *Swing GUI Forms* in the left-hand panel and *JFrame Form* in the right-hand panel, then click on *Next>*. We name our class *BeansApp* and click on *Finish*.

We have now entered a forms editor in which there is a form depicted as a gray rectangle with a light violet border. On the right should appear the tools palette. Assuming the two beans have been added to the palette as described above, we can navigate to the Beans subpalette, and using that palette drop a `DroppedBallPanel` on the left and a `CompleteGraphPanel` on the right of the form, then resize them so that between them they occupy all of the frame's area. A right-click on the left-hand panel brings up a pop-up menu, from which we can choose *Change Variable Name…* and give the left-hand panel the name `ballPanel`. Similarly, we can change the variable name for the right-hand panel to `cgPanel`.

We can now use the menu choices *Run…Run File…Run "BeansApp.Java"* to see the resulting application in which the two panels appear side by side. The ball should be bouncing, but because no event handling has been introduced, the complete graph is just pictured as a triangle and is not changing state.

In order to use the ball's bounces as occasions for modifying the complete graph panel, we go back to the forms editor and right-click on the dropped ball panel on the left. In the resulting pop-up menu, we choose *Events…PropertyChange…propertyChange*. This changes our view from the forms editor (i.e., the "design view") to the text editor ("source view"). We can go back and forth between these two views using the "Source" and "Design" buttons on the tool bar above the editor pane.

Currently the text cursor should be in the `ballPanelPropertyChange()` method of the `JFrame` form, a method which was automatically generated by our latest menu choices. As generated, this is just an empty method, but it is called from the `propertyChange()` event handler of an anonymous inner class which the `JFrame` form has attached to the panel as a property change listener. We can therefore get the behavior we seek by adding the following lines of code:

```
import java.util.Random;  // Top of file
...
```

```
        Random rnd = new Random(); // Just inside class definition
    ...
        private void ballPanelPropertyChange(
            java.beans.PropertyChangeEvent evt) {
            // TODO add your handling code here:
            if (evt.getPropertyName().equals("bounce")) {
                cgPanel.setNumVertices(rnd.nextInt(48)+3);
                repaint();
                if (cgPanel.getNumVertices() % 10 == 0)
                    ballPanel.drop();
            }
        }
```

Again, we can see the program in operation with the menu choices *Run...
Run File*. The number of vertices in the complete graph should change with every bounce of the ball, but also whenever that number is a multiple of 10 the ball will change color and be dropped again with a randomly chosen angle and speed. The timer continues to generate events even when the ball rolls to a stop, so the visual effects can be renewed at any time by resizing the window.

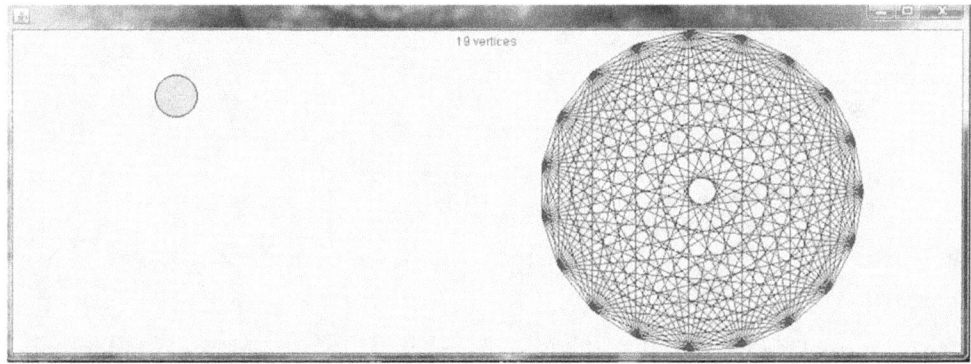

FIGURE 7.11 A `DroppedBallPanel` bean and a `CompleteGraphPanel` bean on the same `JFrame` form, with coordinated events

7.13 APPLETS

It should be mentioned in passing here that much of the initial appeal of the Java language was due to the ease with which Java code could be embedded into a Web page to give that page "active content." The keys to this capability were (a) the applet classes `Applet` and `JApplet`, which are designed to construct active panels for use on Web pages, and (b) the incorporation of an applet loader and Java Virtual Machine into a Web browser.

Creating an applet is not terribly different from creating a `JFrame` form. The most striking difference is that there is no `main()` method in an applet. This is because it is not the JVM but the browser which initiates the applet, and the browser follows a different protocol, first loading the applet class, then instantiating the object, and finally calling specific methods of the applet object according to an established pattern described below. Instead of a `main()` routine, the browser requires that there be four methods, as indicated in the following skeleton:

```
package OOPLS;

import javax.swing.JApplet;

public class MyApplet extends JApplet {
    public void init() {
        super.init();
    }
    public void stop() {
        super.stop();
    }
    public void start() {
        super.start();
    }
    public void destroy() {
        super.destroy();
    }
}
```

As the reader may surmise, the base class `JApplet` already has implementations for all four of these routines, so the above class could be totally empty and have the same effect. However, each of these methods has a specific role in the management of the applet's appearance and behavior within a Web page, and the programmer should carefully consider the actions germane to his particular application's needs.

The `init()` method is a "view initialization" routine and often is used to perform the duties of a constructor as well, because the browser will call this method immediately after instantiating the applet object. The `stop()` method is called when the user navigates away from the Web page. One useful thing to do here would be to kill any timers currently running in the applet. Conversely, `start()` is called with every visit to the page, both immediately after `init()` and also when the user navigates back after visiting other pages. Here the programmer should restart the timers associated with the applet, if there are any. Finally, `destroy()` is called when the page becomes inaccessible and the applet leaves memory.

7.13.1 The Maze Application as an Applet

Let us use the `MazeApplication` class as an example, and investigate the changes necessary in order to transform it into an applet, say `MazeApplet`. We enumerate those changes below:

1. We will insert the applet into our library package OOPLS. Consequently, we can remove the four import statements which refer to classes in the OOPLS package, and replace them with the statement:

    package OOPLS;

2. We will, however, need the following additional import statement:

    import java.swing.JApplet;

3. Now the first line of the class definition should be changed from

    public class MazeApplication **extends** JFrame {

    to

    public class MazeApplet **extends** JApplet {

4. The `MazeApplication()` constructor can now be deleted, and replaced with the following `init()` method:

    ```
    public void init() {
        initComponents();
    }
    ```

    Note that this does away with the `setBounds()` call, which is appropriate because the size of the applet is determined by the surrounding HTML code.

5. Delete all calls to `setTitle()`. An applet does not have a title bar, and cannot tell the Web browser to change its title bar.

6. In all `FileDialog()` constructors, replace the first parameter, `MazeApplication.this`, with `(JFrame)null`.

7. Delete the call

    setDefaultCloseOperation(EXIT_ON_CLOSE);

which appears on the next-to-last line of the `initComponents()` routine. The applet will automatically exit when its page cannot be navigated back to.

8. Delete the `main()` method.

The above transformation will indeed convert our maze application into an applet. Once the applet is compiled to a class file, it can be loaded into a Web browser. Hand-coding an HTML file is not necessary, as Web page editing software can automatically handle the insertion of the applet at the desired location on the page and the resizing of the maze applet to the desired dimensions.

To test the applet from *NetBeans*, use the menu choices *Run...Run File... Run "MazeApplet.java."* This will do two things: it will generate an HTML file properly constructed to display the applet, and it will run the applet using the *AppletViewer* application distributed with the JVM.

7.13.2 Security and the "Sandbox"

The above section rather dishonestly represents the maze applet as being fully functional. It is completely functional when run from the applet viewer, but not quite so when run from within a Web browser. If the purpose is to run the applet from a Web browser (and that is certainly the only reason for writing an applet instead of a stand-alone application) the code which loads and saves mazes could just as well be deleted, unless the applet is signed. A Web browser runs an applet in a "sandbox," meaning that there is a restricted set of capabilities provided to that applet. None of those capabilities involves reading files or storing files in the client's directory. Attempting to save a maze causes our applet to throw an exception, which will result in a *JOptionPane* message similar to the one in Figure 7.12.

FIGURE 7.12 Attempting to do a file save from an applet

The reason this restriction is made is for the sake of security. Web pages which contain active content are a potential threat to the safety of the machine on which the client browser is running, because such content constitutes an active running program which may demand system resources and cause changes in the state of the system. Depending on the level of access granted, the system could be accidentally or deliberately harmed. For this reason, the default status of applets is that they are given no access to the file system. There are ways of enclosing an applet (or, for that matter, the original JFrame-derived maze application) in a "signed" JAR file, which allows the browser user to inspect the signature and express either confidence or a lack of confidence in that signature. If the user approves the signature, the application continues to run and has access to the file system.

7.13.3 Applets and Threads

Strictly speaking, the actions undertaken by init() and the other three "milestone" methods should be scheduled on the event-dispatching thread, using SwingUtilities.invokeAndWait(). The needed changes are indicated below:

```
import javax.swing.JOptionPane;
import javax.swing.SwingUtilities;
    ...
    public void init() {
        try {
            SwingUtilities.invokeAndWait(new Runnable() {
                public void run() {
                    initComponents();
                }
            });
        }
        catch (Exception e) {
            JOptionPane.showMessageDialog(
                getContentPane(),
                "Applet initialization failed."
            );
        }
    }
```

The reason for this alteration is that init() is executed on the *initial thread*, whereas Swing component constructors and Swing event handling methods are supposed to execute on the *event dispatch* thread. The initComponents() routine builds a GUI out of Swing components, and so in order to maintain the convention of using the event handling thread for such activities we create a thread and use `invokeAndWait()` to schedule it on the event handling queue. We use that routine rather than `invokeLater()` because it is important that the `start()` routine, which will be executed on the initial thread, not be executed until the construction of the GUI is complete.

7.14 SUMMARY

Using C as a base, C++ and Java have diverged in remarkable ways, and illustrate for us the magnitude of the design space in which we operate when we attempt to design a programming language. For its part, Java aims for controlled expansion of functionality using safe and consistent strategies. An odd inconsistency seems to show up in the issue of shallow versus deep copy mechanisms, because Java's `clone()` mechanism defaults to shallow copies and its serialization technique produces deep copies. The combination works well in practice, however. In particular, Java's features for serialization are strikingly powerful and easy to use.

Java takes a rather fine-grained approach to the packaging of string input and parsing capabilities, so that several library classes and strategies must be used in order to transform lines from a text file containing numeric literals into internal form. Thus, a `BufferedReader` object can be "wrapped around" a `Stream-Reader` or `FileReader` object to give us the `readLine()` capability, and the string-oriented `StringTokenizer` class or the more comprehensive `Scanner` class can then be used to separate tokens from a line. The wrapper classes provide type-specific string-to-primitive-value conversions, for example `Integer.ParseInt()`.

Because Java's containers permit only first-class objects as members, and because all such objects have the ability to hash themselves with the `hashCode()` method, Java includes three varieties of hash table among its standard containers, namely `HashTable`, `HashSet`, and `HashMap`. All will dynamically reallocate if their load factor goes beyond a specific limit which can be set in the constructor. Overriding the `hashCode()` method is advised if the key set has peculiarities known to the programmer.

Three Java features introduce a certain amount of genericity into Java programming. (a) *Interfaces* provide a natural way of abstracting exactly what capabilities are needed from objects with which an application needs to collaborate. Interfaces have their own inheritance framework which is totally orthogonal to class inheritance relationships, so that two totally unrelated objects could serve the role of that collaborator as long as they implement the required interface. (b) All Java classes inherit from the ultimate base class `Object`, so that inherently generic tasks such as those performed by container classes are quite naturally performed. (c) Java *generics* allow the programmer to take advantage of (b) without requiring client programmers to perform explicit casts in order to invoke more specific behaviors.

Java classes may be nested, one within another, and the implied dependencies in that relationship by default are passed on to the objects which belong to those types. Normally, it is not possible to instantiate an object of an inner class type without specifying explicitly or implicitly an object of the outer class type whose referencing environment encloses that of the first object. On the other hand, if the inner class is declared *static*, then the only thing shared between objects of that class and objects of the outer class is the collection of static members and methods. Objects of a static inner class type may be instantiated without making reference to any particular object of the outer class type. *Anonymous* inner classes can be declared and instantiated simultaneously, by implementing an interface or extending a class with inline definitions. These anonymous inner class objects are extremely useful as event handlers.

Java's *Swing* graphics library uses messages to a `Graphics` object to draw on components, i.e., objects of type `Component`. Examples of components are objects of type `JButton`, `JTextField`, `JLabel`, and `JPanel`. The last is a blank canvas on which the programmer draws by overriding the `paint()` method in derived classes. Such panel objects can be nested, one inside the other, a fact which is the basis for "drag-and-drop" programming in Java. Panels are lightweight components, meant to live inside heavyweight components of type `JFrame`, `JApplet`, or `JDialog`. A heavyweight component is called such because it corresponds to a window defined by an outside entity, either a browser or the operating system.

Java event handlers are objects called *listeners*, which implement a particular interface. For example, an object which implements the `ActionListener` interface must be supplied in order for a `JButton` object to respond to a mouse click. The mouse click creates an `ActionEvent` object, which is passed to the `action-Performed()` method of all action listener objects on the button's action listener list. The programmer can add as many such listeners as are needed using the `addActionListener()` method of the button object. Timers (type `Timer`) also have an `addActionListener()` method and react to action events, but in this case the events are automatically generated at regular intervals; the length of the interval is specified at the time the `Timer` object is instantiated. There are many of these specialized listener interfaces. An example is `ComponentListener`; a listener object of this type can be added to a component, and the object's `componentResized()` method will be called every time the component changes size.

A *layout* may be associated with a component, such as a panel. A layout object directs the placement of subcomponents within the component. For example, an object of type `BorderLayout` places components in one of five positions, called `NORTH`, `SOUTH`, `EAST`, `WEST`, and `CENTER`. A `setLayout()` message can be sent to the container, with a layout object as argument, after which the particular layout object directs placement in the manner for which it is designed.

Complete information concerning the type of a Java object can be obtained, in the form of an object of type `Class`, in response to the message `getClass()`. An object of unknown type can be asked for its `Class` object in this fashion, and that object in turn can furnish at run-time a list of methods, constructors, and fields, each of which can furnish their names, parameters (if applicable), and all other information concerning themselves. In this way, methods can be discovered and called dynamically.

The capability of Java objects to furnish information about themselves makes it a natural thing for IDE's like *NetBeans* to allow programmers to fashion their own "drag and drop" components. Such components are derived from class `JPanel`, and can be designed by the programmer and placed in the *NetBeans* toolbox menu.

REVIEW QUESTIONS

1. Explain what it means to "wrap" one object around another. Does wrapping entail an inheritance relationship? What kind of relationship is engendered by "wrapping," typically?

2. Describe three different meanings for the keyword `final`. How are the three meanings related to each other?

3. What implementation option is available to the compiler in the case of a `final` method, which is not available for other types of instance methods? Explain.

4. What is an interface? What does it mean for a class to implement an interface?

5. How does multiple implementation of interfaces avoid the complications of multiple inheritance? Why is it not a complete substitute for multiple inheritance? Explain.

6. Is an interface a type? Explain your answer.

7. Can a variable be declared to be of an interface type? If so, how can it be initialized, and how can it receive a value?

8. Explain the content and usage of interface `Comparable`.

9. "Inheritance" has similar syntax for interfaces as for classes, but a different meaning. What does it mean for one interface to "extend" another?

10. What is the reason that interface `Cloneable` exists? How can it be of use, since it is empty? Explain.

11. The method `clone()` is not a part of the `Cloneable` interface, but it is often overridden in classes which implement that interface. Why?

12. How is it that inner classes in C++ are not allowed to reference instance data members of the enclosing class, whereas those of Java are allowed to do so? Explain carefully using Java code.

13. What is the "link to the outer class object," and how is it initialized at construction time?

14. Why is the Java default semantics for inner classes so useful when a method needs to export an interface (such as an iterator) which has access to the internal state of the exporting object? Describe an example.

15. Give an example of the use of an anonymous inner class, using correct syntax. Explain your example.

16. Why is the Java anonymous inner class used so extensively? Describe an application type which makes heavy use of this pattern.

17. What are adapters, and why are they needed?

18. There is a type of inner class in Java which is equivalent to an inner class in C++. What is this type of inner class called? What sort of nonlocal references to outer class entities are valid in such an inner class? What is different about the way an object of such an inner class type is instantiated?

19. Explain why generic classes are not a difficulty for compilers, in that they provide no more of a challenge in translation than ordinary classes.

20. Suppose we are designing a generic class `MyClass<T>`. How are we restricted when we send messages to objects of type `T` from class scope inside `MyClass`?

21. What type relationships hold between the three types `Vector`, `Vector<Object>`, and `Vector<Integer>`?

22. What harm is there in allowing an argument of type `Vector<Integer>` to be transmitted to a parameter of type `Vector<Object>`? Explain.

23. What are the subtypes of `LinkedList<?>`? Can a method with a wildcard type as a parameter be constructed which allows us to place a noninteger in a collection of type `LinkedList<Integer>`? If so, how? If not, why not?

24. Suppose `MyInterface` is an interface. What are the subtypes of the bounded wildcard type `TreeSet<? implements MyInterface>`? What advantage accrues to the use of this type over the use of `TreeSet<?>`? ... over the use of `TreeSet<MyInterface>`?

25. Name the three Java hash table classes mentioned in the text, and distinguish between them. In what sense can we say that these are as generally applicable in applications as the tree-based collections? How do the hash table classes differ in their characteristics from the tree classes?

26. How is `hashCode()` used? Why is it sometimes advisable to override the `hashCode()` method?

27. Describe the purpose of class `Graphics`, and give examples of messages which might be sent to an object of type `Graphics`.

28. Describe the Java view of pixel coordinates. What does an `(x, y)` pair in that coordinate system denote? If `g` is a `Graphics` object and `(x0, y0)` and `(x1, y1)` are pixel coordinates, which pixels are actually "drawn" in response to the call `g.drawLine(x0,y0,x1,y1)`?

29. Where does a `Graphics` object position the text in response to the message `drawString()`? Illustrate with an example.

30. Describe the purpose of class `JPanel`. How are `JPanel` objects used in the definition of graphical user interfaces (GUIs)?

31. Objects of types derived from `Component` are *lightweight* windows. What is a lightweight window? Give some examples.

32. What is a *top-level*, or *heavyweight*, window? What three Swing library classes are they associated with, and how are these classes different from each other?

33. Describe the protocol which governs communications between a "listener" object and an object which generates the event in which the listener is interested.

34. Describe the `ActionListener` interface, and name some of the *Swing* classes which implement it. Describe the general category of events to which an action listener might respond.

35. Describe and explain the structure of the `main()` method for a `JFrame`-based application. How is it able to accomplish anything useful?

36. Explain how to use a timer object. What arguments are used in the constructor call? What type of event does it cause, and what type of listener should be added to a timer object? How can we make sure our timer has been stopped before exiting the program?

37. What is a layout? How is a layout used? Give some examples of layouts.

38. Explain `BorderLayout` in detail, with an example.

39. What do the interfaces `Cloneable` and `Serializable` have in common? How are they different?

40. What must be true before objects of a class which implements `Serializable` can be properly serialized? How is serialization accomplished, and how is the serialized object restored to memory?

41. Explain how menus are built by establishing at run-time a relationship between objects of type `JMenuBar`, `JMenu`, and `JMenuItem`.

42. What type of event is raised by selecting a menu item, and how is an event handler established for such an event?

43. Explain why the code below succeeds in what it is attempting to do, in view of the fact that `==` compares only for identity, not for value:

```
if (obj1.getClass() == obj2.getClass()) {
    // Come here if obj1 and obj2 are exactly the same type.
    ...
}
else {
    // Come here if obj1 and obj2 are of different types.
    ...
}
```

44. If `obj` is a first-class object, what type of object is returned by the method `obj.getClass()`? How is it used? How is the information it contains determined by a program unit for types which are not first-class types?

45. The types `Constructor`, `Method`, and `Field` are types used in a programming pattern called *reflection*. Describe the purpose of reflection.

46. What is component-level programming? How is reflection used in component-level programming? What is a Java component called?

47. What is a bean property? Give prototypes for a "getter" and a "setter" for property "Weight" of type `double`.

48. What is a property change event? Do property change events arise synchronously or asynchronously? Describe how a class can be set up with proper protocol to allow listeners to establish an interest in a property change event, and how a listener can register such an interest.

49. Why must a Java bean have a default constructor? Explain.

50. Explain what makes Java applets different from `JFrame` applications. Although the visible manifestation of a Java applet is a top-level window, it is not an operating-system-defined window. Why?

51. Describe the purpose of the methods `init()`, `start()`, `stop()`, and `destroy()`, of class `JApplet`.

52. Explain the "sandbox," and why it is necessary. How may it be circumvented?

EXERCISES

1. Write a complete Java program which (1) instantiates a `BufferedReader` to read from the console, (2) requests the user's date of birth in the form `99/99/9999`, (3) inputs the date of birth, (4) determines the month, day, and year, and (5) displays on the console the same data, separated out into lines as in the following example:

   ```
   Month:   9
   Day: 30
   Year: 1990
   ```

2. How would you change the code in the preceding question if the data was to come from the first line of the text file *personalData.txt* and the output to be placed in the file *report.txt*?

3. Research the `Scanner` class, then write the code to instantiate a `Scanner` object capable of separating the numbers out of a string `dataString` containing data such as the following (where the number of data items is unknown), then list the names on one line and the numbers on the second, separated by spaces. You may assume the data come in (string, integer) pairs as indicated, and always use the indicated delimiters.

   a. String:
   ```
   "George - 188; Claudia - 133; Abe - 244; Gertrude - 117;"
   ```
   b. Output:

```
George Claudia Abe Gertrude
188 133 244 117
```

4. Using the `StringTokenizerTest` class from Section 7.1.3 as your model, rewrite the program so that it has the same functionality but uses a `Scanner` object instead of a `StringTokenizer` object. Use the online Java documentation (or a local copy if you have installed one) to guide your use of the `Scanner` class.

5. Write the definition of a class called `MutableInt` which "wraps" around an `int` value, but which default-constructs with a value of zero. Your class should provide `get()` and `put()` access functions, plus an override of the `toString()` function. It should also provide `add`, `subtract`, `multiply`, and `divide` member functions which accumulate the value internally and return as their values the object receiving the message. Thus, if `x` is instantiated as `new MutableInt(37)`, then after `x.subtract(13).divide(3)` the call `x.toString()` should return the value "8". Provide also a public constructor which converts a string to a `MutableInt` object by "parsing" the string and storing it internally as an `int` value.

6. Why should the `equals()` method from class `Object` be overridden in class `MutableInt`? Describe how this would be done. Also describe the difficulties in using this class with classes like `HashMap` and `TreeMap`, which use the values of the objects they contain as lookup keys.

7. What type relationships are always known to exist between objects in Java bound to different variables of the same interface type? Explain why you answered as you did.

8. Explain the content and usage of interface `Iterable`. How does it relate to the `for` statement? Give an example of a `for` statement which iterates through a container `myContainer` of type `MyIterable` and outputs each object in the container to `System.out` using the `toString()` method.

9. Write an `IntArray` class for Java similar to the one you wrote in C++ for Exercise 16 of Chapter 5. Note that you will have to do a complete redesign, because the features available in Java are not the same as those for C++. Explain all the changes you had to make, and why you had to make those changes. The test code given in Chapter 5 must also be rewritten for Java, as follows:

```
IntArray a = new IntArray(), b, c;
a.put(5,77);
```

```
a.put(7,99);  // a's content is now the sequence
              // 0, 0, 0, 0, 0, 77, 0, 99.
b = a.clone();
c = b.clone(); // a's, b's, and c's contents are the same.
```

10. Modify the class you wrote in Exercise 9 so that it implements `Iterable`.

11. Write a generic class called `HeterogeneousPair` which has two type parameters `T1` and `T2`. An object of this type should store two objects internally, of those two respective types, and its constructor should take two such objects of those respective types as parameters. Both objects should be `null` when such a pair is first instantiated. Provide `getFirst()`, `getSecond()`, `setFirst()`, and `setSecond()` methods. The latter two should return as their values the object receiving the message. Finally, supply a `toString()` method which calls `toString()` for each of the contained objects in turn and formats the result string as an ordered pair (i.e., as the two strings separated by a comma and enclosed in parentheses).

12. What happens in Exercise 11 when you attempt to add an `initialize()` method which causes each of the two contained objects to be default-constructed? Can you think of a reason why this is the case?

13. Construct a derived class of `JPanel` called `DiamondPanel` for which the representation on the screen is a diamond formed by joining the four midpoints of the four sides of the panel. Your class should have a constructor which requires two colors `c1` and `c2`. Color `c1` is used to fill the outside of the diamond, and color `c2` is used to fill the inside of the diamond, with the border of the diamond always drawn in black. You will need the `fillRect()`, `drawPolygon()`, and `fillPolygon()` messages. When the window is resized, the diamond should grow and shrink to conform to the new window.

14. Write a complete `JFrame`-based program which incorporates a `DiamondPanel` as described in Exercise 13. Set it up initially to show a red diamond in a green window, but have the colors reassigned randomly each time the frame is resized.

15. Write an `initComponents()` method which establishes a menu bar and attaches it to a `JFrame`. Your menu should have three items attached, labeled *File*, *Edit*, and *About*. The *File* menu should have four items attached, labeled *New*, *Open*, *Save*, and *Exit*. The *Edit* menu should have two items attached, labeled *Copy* and *Paste*. *About* should be a leaf item,

with nothing attached. Do not associate any handlers with these choices, but choose between the three types JMenuBar, JMenu, and JMenuItem in such a way that event handlers can be attached to the leaves of the tree.

16. Modify *CGClient.java* to add the three new buttons in Figure 7.3, then give them ActionListener objects which perform the indicated actions.

17. The class BorderFactory can be used to create a JPanel object with a particular kind of border. For example, the code

```
JPanel panel = new JPanel();
panel.setBorder(
    BorderFactory.createLineBorder(Color.black)
);
```

creates a panel with a black line as border. Create a derived class of JPanel called TTTSquarePanel, all of whose instances have such a border assigned to them in the initComponents() method. Each instance of TTTSquarePanel should also have an instance variable of type char, and the value of this variable should determine how the panel is drawn. If the panel contains a lowercase or capital "x", it should be drawn in a way that indicates that fact, for example with two drawLine() messages each drawing a line from corner to corner. On the other hand, if it contains "o", then a single drawOval() message should suffice. Provide "get" and "set" methods for the contained character value.

18. Supply a single instruction which, when added to the initComponents() method in Exercise 17, reacts to a mouse click by causing the panel to change to an "o" if it contains an "x", to change to a blank if it contains an "o", and to change to an "x" if it contains anything else.

19. Use BoxLayout and a 3 by 3 arrangement of TTTSquarePanel components (see Exercise 17) to construct a JPanel-derived class called TTT-Panel which resembles a Tic-Tac-Toe board. Design TTTPanel so that it takes set() messages which change the way a given panel is drawn. To illustrate, if tttPanel is a TTTPanel object, then tttPanel.set(1,1,"x") should change the contents of the middle panel, and it should be drawn in any subsequent "paints" so as to indicate its contents.

20. Modify the PointList class from Section 7.5.2 by giving it a save() member function that serializes the list to a binary file whose name is provided as a String parameter.

21. Use the Java documentation to learn more about JOptionPane. Write a short application which uses JOptionPane to prompt for and obtain a

number n, then prompt for and obtain n pairs of int values. Your application should create a Point object from each such pair, put each point into a single PointList object, and save the list to the file *PointList.bin*.

22. Write a client program which reads the file *PointList.bin* created in Exercise 21 and displays its contents on the console.

CHAPTER 8

C# AND THE COMMON LANGUAGE INFRASTRUCTURE

Programming languages come about in various ways: through one individual's insight, through government initiatives, and sometimes through commercial initiatives. The language we discuss in this chapter is an example of the latter. C# was commissioned by the Microsoft Corporation, but now exists as a separate standard and has multiple implementations. It is another C-derived language, borrowing features of both C++ and Java, with innovations of its own. It has had considerable popularity, taking over much of the market where Visual Basic was once dominant. Programmers who enjoyed the latter as a quick and powerful application generator, but did not like the legacy influence of the BASIC language, were immediately drawn to the pragmatic and sometimes elegant C# language.

Code samples for this chapter are located on the companion CD-ROM.

8.1   INTRODUCTION TO THE COMMON LANGUAGE INFRASTRUCTURE

To a large extent, the story of C# is the story of the Common Language Infrastructure (CLI), which is a standardized specification for a virtual machine and, like the Java Virtual Machine, is designed explicitly to be a platform on which to implement a language. Unlike the JVM, however, the CLI was designed from the beginning to accommodate multiple languages, including C++, C#, Visual Basic, and J# (a Java variant), among others. The byte code which constitutes the "machine language" for the CLI is called *Common Intermediate Language*, or CIL. It is designed for "just in time" (JIT) compilation, meaning that the original source code for a program unit is translated into the CIL byte code, and that rather than directly interpreting the byte code the CLI translates it piecemeal into native code and executes that code, as needed. If the same code segment is revisited later, it is no longer necessary to translate that segment because the native code translation already exists and can be directly executed on the target machine.

The CLI is a common platform on which Microsoft's .NET (pronounced "dot-net") framework executes. The .NET framework is a collection of services and libraries, encompassing language run-time support, operating system services, collection classes, Internet services, and event handling. Porting the CLI to a new machine allows that machine to host all the .NET languages and to support any of the .NET libraries which are not specific to a different operating system. This ambitious project has achieved much success as a powerful rapid deployment framework.

Like the Java Virtual Machine, the CLI encompasses support for dynamic memory management, including garbage collection. All the CLI languages tap into this resource, even those which traditionally have been associated with purely stack-based or programmer-controlled memory management. It is necessary that they do so, because all the .NET library classes are designed for dynamic memory management. Therefore, even C++ programs targeting .NET typically use primarily "managed classes," i.e., those whose objects will be automatically reclaimed by the run-time system. Conversely, however, C# programs may make use of unmanaged types which employ "unsafe" features of the language, patterned after similar features in C++.

NOTE *In this chapter, we will attempt to follow the accepted conventions for naming program entities in the C# culture, in which identifiers which name methods of a class routinely begin with a capital letter, so that typically only data members have names which begin with a lower-case letter.*

8.2 SOME INTERESTING C# DESIGN CHOICES

Rather than basing the .NET framework entirely on existing languages, Microsoft decided to design and engineer its own high-level language, which would leverage the CLI to maximum advantage. C# (pronounced "CSharp"), like Java and C++, is a C-derived object-oriented programming language with good data abstraction facilities. Like Java, subscripted variables are checked for range violations. As in C++, programmer-defined operator overloading is permitted, and (in carefully isolated program segments) C# also allows "unsafe" direct manipulation of memory addresses and unchecked subscripting. Like Java, the language uses pointer semantics for its types defined as classes, meaning that an object whose type is constructed explicitly by a class definition is represented by a "handle," or a pointer, and that assignments to variables of such types can create aliases. C# also extends its value semantics beyond primitive types and enumerated types, however, bringing in the *struct* data typing facility. The behavior of variables of struct types is defined in a manner similar to the way it is defined in C++.

To the programmer familiar with Java or C++, the language is relatively easy to begin to use. As we gain more experience with it, however, we find that it is an interesting mix of the two, with additional ideas showing up in unexpected places. Some of those ideas are totally new, and some are a blend of old and new. In this chapter, we will rely on the user's familiarity with C++ and Java to avoid repeating very similar discussions of syntax and semantics, and we will concentrate on C#'s differences from those two languages. Accordingly, let us put the spotlight on some of those differences before we broaden our view and look at what it is like to develop event-driven applications in C#.

8.2.1 C# Control Flow

The `if`, `if…else`, `switch`, `while`, and `do…while` structures survive essentially intact from the C language. Like Java, C# normally requires the conditions upon which these structures depend to be Boolean (type `bool`) expressions, and forbids any conversions from `bool` values to numeric values or vice versa. If, however, an expression is of a type which has been furnished with `true` and `false` operators or with an implicit `bool` operator (see Section 8.2.9), then that expression may be used as a condition on which a control structure is dependent.

The container-oriented Java `for` loop appears in a more readable form in C#, called a `foreach`. Again, the necessity of using an integer index to step through an array is removed, as in the following code segment, which displays each element of an array on the console.

```
int [] a = new int[n];
...
foreach (int x in a)
    Console.WriteLine(x);
```

In the corresponding Java `for` construct, assigning a value to `x` is allowed, but because `x` is just a local variable in the range of the `for` such an assignment has no effect on the members of the array. In C#, such an assignment is forbidden.

The `foreach` construct, like the corresponding Java `for` variant, is integrated into the library classes via an interface. To be specific, if a type (library or programmer-defined) implements the `IEnumerable` interface or its generic version `IEnumerable<>`, then any container of that type can be used in the above fashion in a `foreach` loop. An example follows where the generic `List<>` class is used to instantiate a collection of doubles. Because `List<>` implements `IEnumerable<>`, the `foreach` statement can be used to sequence through any list of a type constructed using that generic class.

```
using System.Collections.Generic;
    ...
    List<double> list = new List<double>();
    ...
    double sum = 0;
    foreach (double x in list) sum += x;
```

NOTE

It should be mentioned here that the requirement for the container to implement the IEnumerable interface is uniform. In fact, all array types do implement that interface, and that fact is why the first example worked.

Iteration without the `foreach` construct is possible, but yields little advantage. For example, the following is equivalent to the above `foreach` loop:

```
    IEnumerable<double> i = list.GetEnumerator();
    while (i.MoveNext()) sum += i.Current;
```

Note that this is similar to Java's iteration pattern, with the significant design difference that Java combines increment with access in the `next()` method, whereas C# combines increment with test in the `MoveNext()` method. A consequence is that a newly instantiated C# enumerator is not positioned at the beginning, but rather "just before the beginning" of the enumerated collection, and an attempt to access the `Current` property before executing `MoveNext()` causes a run-time exception.

The `break` and `continue` loop control facilities again survive from C intact. Unlike the Java language, C# retains the `goto`'s and labels of the C language, as does C++.

Only minor differences exist between C# built-in operators and precedence levels and those of Java and C++, so we will not exhaustively discuss those features here. It is interesting and useful to note here, though, that Java's `instanceof` operator appears here as the `is` operator, and is more generally applicable. The right-hand operand of the C# `is` operator is a type, as in

```
expression is type
```

The difference here is that `type` is not restricted to reference types, but is applicable to all safe types. Thus, `5 instanceof int` would be incorrect code in Java, where `5 is int` compiles in C# and evaluates to `true`.

Similar to the Ada language is the idea of incorporating two types of logical connectives. Besides the "short-circuit" `&&` and `||` operators of Java and C++, which C# retains and calls "conditional logical operators," the designers added the operators `&` and `|`, which are called "Boolean logical operators." These latter operators also take two `bool` expressions as operands, and the two classes of operators are very similar in their effects. In fact, in cases where a result is successfully computed, operator `&&` always produces the same result as operator `&` and operator `||` always produces the same result as operator `|`. But operators `&` and `|` *always evaluate both operands*, so that if the programmer wishes the evaluation of the right-hand expression to take place in order to make sure that some side effect occurs, he can use these operators. This is a fine point which most Java and C++ programmers with any experience will appreciate, as it is often important to remember that the expression `E1 && E2` is evaluated by first testing whether `E1` is false. If it is `false`, then a `false` value will be returned for the entire expression, and `E2` will not be evaluated. If it is `true`, then and only then will the code which evaluates `E2` be executed. A similar rule applies to the expression `E1 || E2`, meaning that if `E1` evaluates to `true` then a value of `true` will be returned, and only if it evaluates to `false` will `E2` be evaluated. For the expressions `E1 & E2` and `E1 | E2` both `E1` and `E2` will be evaluated before the overall result of the expression is computed.

We hasten to point out here that `&` and `|` are overloaded and, when applied to fixed numeric types, retain their original meanings from C as bitwise Boolean operators. Thus, `27 & 32` evaluates to `0`, and `27 | 32` evaluates to `59`.

C# incorporates `try...catch`, `try...finally`, and `try...catch...finally` blocks for exception handling. These are not substantially different from the corresponding features in C++ and Java.

8.2.2 Value and Reference Types

In C#, enumerations and variables of primitive numeric type denote values, not references. (Recall that Java enumeration types are references, while numeric types are values.) There is a large variety of numeric types, all of which are defined in a platform-independent manner. Signed integer types range from the 8-bit `sbyte` type to the 64-bit `long`, and include the familiar 32-bit `int` and the 16-bit `short`. Unsigned types include a 16-bit `char`, the 8-bit `byte`, and the 64-bit `ulong`, as well as the 16-bit `ushort`. The floating point types are a 32-bit `float` and a 64-bit `double`, both of which are IEEE standards.

To all these more or less familiar numeric types C# adds a `decimal` type, the values of which occupy 128 bits. Decimal values incorporate 28-29 decimal digits of precision, nearly twice as many as `double`, and allow for precise computations with decimal fractions. A decimal literal may incorporate a decimal point and must end with the suffix character `m`. Decimal literals can accommodate an exponential part, for example `-71.024e-16m`. By way of illustration, the code sequence

```
decimal x = 64.78990283785203402934785023478E10m;
double z = (double)x;
Console.WriteLine(x);
Console.WriteLine(z);
```

produces the output

```
647899028378.52034029347850235
647899028378.52
```

in which we see that the `double` variable is relatively close in value but holds only about half the number of significant digits. The explicit cast in the example is necessary, because C# does not implicitly coerce `decimal` to `double` or vice versa.

The `struct` construction is, as it is in C++, similar to a class in its appearance. In contrast to C++, however, in C# there are major differences between structs and classes, not the least of which is that variables whose types are constructed in this fashion represent values, not references. Let us illustrate with an example, the familiar `Point` data type we have used in the past. If we define it as a struct, it appears as follows:

```
struct Point {
    public int x, y;
    public Point(int x, int y) {
```

```
        this.x = x;
        this.y = y;
    }
  }
```

Note that, as in Java, no semicolon is required after the definition, nor is there an "initialization part" in the constructor, so the initialization of variables takes place as it would in Java. Also, as in Java, each attribute or behavior must individually be labeled `public` if it is to appear in the client interface of the type. A cursory examination would lead us to the conclusion that the only difference from Java is in the use of the keyword `struct`, which does not appear in that language. However, there are some restrictions that seem arbitrary at first glance, such as the fact that structs inherit implicitly from the library type `ValueType` (which inherits from `Object`) and may not inherit from other classes or structs, nor may they be used as a base type for any other type. This is not such an arbitrary restriction when you consider that in C# culture structs are true "value types," intended to represent smaller, encapsulated packages of data and operations whose application is very targeted, limited, and clear. A base type for an inheritance hierarchy is often intentionally vague and sometimes incomplete, and for such a type we use a class construct.

Even the initialization of a `struct` object can be made to appear as it would in Java, for instance

```
    Point p;
    ...
    p = new Point(200,350);
```

The notation above is a very large break from convention, because the pattern *new type_name(parameters)*, because the time of Simula, has always denoted a pointer. Java and C++ both maintain that convention. Here, the meaning must be different, because `p` denotes a value, not a pointer. The effect, if taken literally without optimizing, should be to create a temporary on the stack of type `Point`, call the constructor to initialize it, then copy the value of the temporary thus created into the storage for `p`. Pragmatically, however, both space and time can be saved by allowing the compiler to generate code to simply call the constructor to initialize `p`'s space directly.

NOTE *As confirmation of the "value semantics" interpretation, note that p's constructor in the example need not be called at all. The code below is perfectly correct.*

```
Point p;
p.x = 200;
p.y = 350;
```

This code would never do if `Point` were defined as a class, because it would denote `null` and therefore the two references `p.x` and `p.y` would be invalid. Curiously, then, this code segment would be illegal both in Java (where `Point` would have to be a class and `p` would again be `null`), and also in C++, where the one constructor provided for `Point` must be called every time an instance is created.

C# performs compile-time checks to ensure that all variables are initialized before they are used. Thus, the following code would not compile:

```
Point p;
p.x = 200;
Console.WriteLine(p.y); // Illegal.  p.y is not initialized.
```

All the primitive types have corresponding library types. These are not "wrapper classes," however, as they exist in Java, but structs. These types are in fact simply aliases of the corresponding primitive types. Some of these library type names are obvious, such as `Double`, but the library type for `float` is `Single`, and the discrete numeric types are named according to their sizes. For example, the alias for `int` is `Int32`, and that for `ulong` is `UInt64`. Unlike the Java wrapper classes, these C# library types are not immutable and are assignment-compatible with their primitive counterparts. Thus, the following code is valid and uses stack space allocated for `w` at block entry—it does not reallocate space when `w` changes values.

```
UInt64 w = new UInt64(); // Initializes w to zero.
...
w = 352052795028570275UL;
w += 1;
```

All "safe" C# types are "unified," meaning that all types are considered to descend from the base type `object`, even value types. The keyword `object` is also an alias for a library type, namely `Object`.

Any value type can be "boxed," in preparation for storing it in a library container or transmitting it to a parameter of type `object`. This is a very Java-like idea, but it has a different appearance here. Because there are no wrapper classes, the "ultimate base class" `object` is used as the type of the 'box,' and as objects are removed from their containers they are "unboxed" and viewed once more as values. Boxing is implicit, but unboxing must be explicitly represented using a cast operation. An example follows:

```
ArrayList a = new ArrayList();
a.Add(21);  // Autoboxes 21 as Object.
foreach (object obj in a) {
    int x = (int)obj; // Explicit "unboxing" is necessary.
    Console.WriteLine(x);
}
```

We emphasize here that although a boxed quantity "knows" its type, it cannot legally be sent any messages via the methods specifically associated with its contained value type. The following code illustrates:

```
object o = 5;  // o is a "box" containing the integer 5.
if (o.CompareTo(5) == 0) Console.WriteLine("o is 5");
// Illegal.  An 'object' doesn't understand 'CompareTo'.
if (5.CompareTo(5) == 0) Console.WriteLine("5 is 5");
// Legal, and displays '5 is 5'.
if (o is int) Console.WriteLine("o is integer");
// Legal, and displays 'o is integer'.
```

Every value type in C# has a corresponding *nullable* type which can be represented in code with the type name followed by a question mark, for example `int?`. The nullable types are actually struct "wrappers" with an extra Boolean flag indicating whether or not a value has been assigned. The default initial "value" of an uninitialized variable of a nullable type is `null`. For a type `T`, the notation `T?` is actually shorthand for the library type name `System.Nullable<T>`.

8.2.3 Arrays and Multidimensional Arrays

The notation for declaring and allocating a C# array is a notation also acceptable in Java, for example…

```
double [] eigenVals = new double[n];
```

Note that with C# the square brackets *must precede* the identifier in the declaration. Both this form and the form where the brackets follow the identifier are allowed in Java, but in C# there is no choice. In both Java and C++, we view a two-dimensional array as an "array of arrays," a natural approach. Recall that the Java declaration

```
int scoreOnTest[][] = new int[3][30];
```

declares and constructs an array of three 30-element arrays. A similar thing can be done in C#, but we must iterate in order to allocate each array, as follows:

```
int [][] scoreOnTest = new int[3][];
for (int i=0; i<3; ++i) score[i] = new int[30];
```

The awkwardness of requiring a loop to allocate the above array is ameliorated by the fact that there is a *separate data type* for two-dimensional arrays, as illustrated below:

```
int [,] scoreOnTest = new int[3,30];
```

Now the entry in row 4, column 10 of this array would be denoted by score-OnTest[4,10]. This notation is un-C-like, but it is a very old notation. It was not used in C or C++, and indeed it would have been awkward to use it because the comma operator makes comma-separated subscripts ambiguous unless we make arbitrary restrictions on what kinds of expressions can be used as subscripts. It was used, however, in older languages like FORTRAN and Pascal, where a(i,j) and a[i,j] were, respectively, the correct ways to refer to the entry in row i, column j of a two-dimensional array a.

Here the designer of the language chose pragmatic proliferation of features over economy, with the result that there are now two ways to allocate and use two very similar categories of data structures. What is even more interesting is that when we move up to three dimensions we see *four* similar type possibilities for a base-type int array, namely int[][][], int[][,], int[,][], and int[,,]. Although they seem "equivalent," they are not in fact (because the issue of "raggedness" must be factored in), and there is no type equivalence relationship between these choices. If we wish to allocate an n-dimensional array where the sizes of dimensions are homogeneous, however, the number of possible ways to do this increases exponentially as n increases (see Exercise 4).

The size of each dimension of a multiply dimensioned array can be obtained by sending the GetLength() message. Specifically, for an n-dimensional array a, the message a.GetLength(0) returns the size of the first dimension, and in general a.GetLength(i-1) returns the size of the i-th dimension. For a one-dimensional array, the property a.Length has the same value as that returned by a.GetLength(0). Thus, for a five-dimensional array b with the allocation pattern [,,,,] the size of the third dimension is `b.GetLength(2)`, but for allocation pattern `[,][,][]` it would be considered an ill-posed question to ask for that size, because there are multiple "copies" of that dimension. The size of `b[0,0]` could be different from that of `b[0,1]`, for example. If `b` were homogeneous, however, we could refer to the size of the third dimension using any subscripted variable, for example

```
b[0,0].GetLength(0).
```

8.2.4 Strings and Parsing

Strings are reference types, but like the built-in value types there is both a keyword (`string`) and a library name (`String`) to refer to the type. As expected, a `+` operator is used to concatenate strings. Escape sequences are used in string literals, as is the norm in C-derived languages, so that `"\n"` represents a string containing only a line separator. However, the programmer is given the option of suppressing such escape sequences by using the `@` prefix. In a string literal introduced by that symbol, each backslash character simply represents itself. Thus, while `"\\\\"` denotes a string of two backslash characters, the literal `@"\\\\"` denotes a four-character string.

There are some useful parsing and formatting capabilities built into the `string` type. For example, the `Split()` instance method is provided for the purpose of splitting a string into an array of strings. If `Split()` is used without parameters then the tokens in the string are assumed to be separated by white space. If one parameter is used, that parameter is an array of characters to be used as separators. (There is also a two-parameter form which includes as its second parameter a count of the number of tokens desired.) The following code uses the one-parameter form:

```
String sentence = "He said, \"Control yourself!\"";
char [] separators = {' ', '"', ',','!'};
String [] tokens = sentence.Split(separators);
```

The response to the above code segment is to store the strings `"He"`, `"said"`, `""`, `""`, `"Control"`, `"yourself"`, `""`, and `""` in the array `tokens`. To see this, note that `Split()` by default puts an empty string between any two consecutive separators and that it views a string which ends with a separator as having an empty token following that separator. These empty strings could have been avoided by sending the message as `Split(StringSplitOptions.RemoveEmptyEntries)`.

Parsing capabilities also reside in the library classes accompanying the primitive numeric types. Thus, in the same way the Java wrapper class `Integer` "knows how" to parse an integer literal stored in a string, so does `Int32` know how to perform that parse for the C# language. As an example, we can use the following program to add up all the numbers on a single line of console input:

```
using System;

public class AddLine {
    public static void Main() {
        string line = Console.ReadLine();
        string[] tokens = line.Split();
        int sum = 0;
        foreach (string token in tokens)
            if (token != "") sum += Int32.Parse(token);
        Console.WriteLine(sum);
    }
}
```

Recall that `int` and `Int32` are aliases, even though one is a keyword and one is the name of a library class, so that `Int32.Parse(token)` could also have been written as `int.Parse(token)`. When we run the above program, we will see a console window displayed, with a blinking text cursor. If we then enter, say,

```
100  300  40  500
```

we will obtain the output

```
940
```

Note that it is comparatively easy to obtain a line of input from the keyboard, using the static `ReadLine()` method of class `Console`. `Console` resides in namespace `System` and also contains a `Read()` method for reading one character at a time. It provides console output via its `Write()` and `WriteLine()` methods, which again are a little more sophisticated than the corresponding facilities in the Java language.

For converting objects to strings, the `ToString()` method exists in the base class `object` and can be overridden for programmer-defined types. For more specialized purposes, there is a static `Format` method in class `string` which aids the process of mixing literals with labeling information. Thus, if integers `x` and `y` have the values 47 and 62, respectively, then the statement

```
string s = string.Format("x = {0} and y = {1}.", x, y);
```

places in variable s the string "x = 47 and y = 62.". Similar capabilities are built into special overloads of the Write() and WriteLine() methods of Console, so that the statement

```
Console.WriteLine("x = {0} and y = {1}", x, y);
```

compiles successfully, and when executed produces a line of output containing the string in the previous example. In general, in both forms, the first parameter is a string which may have multiple occurrences of the pattern {n}, where n is a non-negative integer literal. Here n = 0 corresponds to the second parameter, n = 1 to the third, etc. When the output string is produced, a literal corresponding to the value of that parameter replaces the pattern.

_____

NOTE

We should mention here that the programmer has considerable control over how data is displayed with the above features. For example, ToString() can be given a string parameter which affects the way the target is converted to a string, so that 11.ToString("X") evaluates to "B." This happens because the parameter "X" specifies that the string is to be formatted as a hexadecimal literal. Further investigation of these facilities is left to the reader.

8.2.5 Parameter Transmission in C#

Just as in Java, the only active components in a C# program are methods in structs and classes. These methods may be ordinary instance methods, or they may be static methods, distinguished by the keyword static given as one of the attributes, as in C++ and Java. When a method is called, information may be transmitted into and out of that method by means of its parameters. C# retains value transmission as its primary mechanism for passing data in, but like C++ it adds additional mechanisms for the purpose of causing side effects in the arguments passed to its parameters. However, the accompanying notations borrow more from Ada than from C++.

Recall from our study of Java that it does implement generics but does not provide sufficient mechanisms to construct a generic "swap" function, because the only parameter transmission mechanism is call by value. C# incorporates both generics and call by reference, so that it does allow the definition of a generic swap utility, as seen in the following example:

```
public class Utility {
    ...
```

```
public static void swap<T>(ref T a, ref T b) {
    T temp = a;
    a = b;
    b = temp;
}
...
}
```

What is odd in C#'s notations for call by reference is that special syntax is also needed *on the call side* when parameter transmission by reference occurs. Thus, a call to swap the values of byte quantities x and y could appear as

```
Utility.swap<byte>(ref x, ref y);
```

or just as

```
Utility.swap(ref x, ref y);
```

in which the compiler infers the type byte from the types of variables x and y. Notice that if the type being swapped is a reference type, such as string, the effect is that the parameters are *references to references*. For example, for string variables s and t the effect of

```
Utility.swap(ref s, ref t);
```

is to swap the handles associated with those variables. No actual copying of values occurs.

Another transmission technique new to C-derived languages is *out* transmission. This technique is similar to that for reference parameters and is identical in effect to a technique in the Ada language which has exactly the same denotation. In short, an out parameter requires no initialization incident to the call, and its value cannot be used in the text of the subprogram before it is initialized. Before returning to the caller, it is the obligation of the subprogram to supply a value for each out parameter. As in the call by reference technique, we are required to use a special notation on the call side. The following static method illustrates this technique for the purpose of "filling up" a list of integers using input from the console:

```
using System.Collections.Generic;

public class Utility {
    ...
```

```csharp
public static void GetIntegers(out List<int> a) {
    // Read a line of integers from the console into the
    // list a. Each integer must be separated from the
    // next by white space or a comma.
    String buffer = Console.ReadLine();
    char [] seps = {'\t', ' ', ','};
    String[] tokes = buffer.Split(seps);
    a = new List<int>();
    foreach(string token in tokes) {
        try {
            a.Add(Int32.Parse(token));
        }
        catch(Exception e) {
            // Ignore non-integers on the input line.
        }
    }
}
...
}
```

The `List<>` generic collection is from the .NET library and so is accessible from any of the .NET languages. It is not a simple list at all, but is very much like the C++ `vector<>` and the Java `Vector<>`. In the example, we split the input line into tokens, and then attempt to parse each token as an integer. Every time the parse succeeds, we add the resulting integer to our list. The example we gave earlier, in which a series of integers is read from the console and their sum is displayed, can now be rewritten to take advantage of this utility routine, as follows:

```csharp
using System;
using System.Collections.Generic;
using OOPLS;

public class AddLine {
    public static void Main() {
        List<int> numbers;
        Utility.GetIntegers(out numbers); // Note the call-side
'out'
        int sum = 0;
        foreach (int x in numbers) sum += x;
        Console.WriteLine(sum);
    }
}
```

NOTE *The requirement for a special notation on the call side is not arbitrary. Having that requirement makes it possible to use the out and ref parameter attributes for the purpose of overloading functions. Thus, void f(ref int), void f(out int), and void f(int) can all coexist without ambiguity.*

8.2.6 Variable-Sized Parameter Lists

Something about the version of the `WriteLine()` method of class `Console` which we used in Section 8.2.3 may nag at the edges of the reader's consciousness as being vaguely unconventional. Let us look again at that line of code.

```
Console.WriteLine("x = {0} and y = {1}", x, y);
```

To give voice to the reader's misgivings, let us state the obvious. There is no clear limit to the number of parameters that could be needed in such an expression, so no matter how many overloads of `WriteLine()` we define in the conventional way there is no way we could do justice to the intent of this pattern of usage. What is needed, and what therefore must be present in the language, is some facility for variable-sized parameter lists. This facility is provided in C# using array parameters preceded by the `params` keyword. An example follows:

```
public class Utility {
    ...
    public static int Sum(params int[] a) {
        int result = 0;
        foreach (int x in a) result += x;
        return result;
    }
    ...
}
```

Once this definition has been made, we can apply the `Sum` function to any number of integer parameters. For example, the value returned from `Utility.Sum(34,33,33)` is 100, as is that returned from `Utility.Sum(25,25,25,25)`.

A similar facility, present in the C language, is included in C++. Because that version is a patently "unsafe" and low-level facility, we chose not to cover it in this text. The reader should realize, however, that the safety with which we are able to use this feature in C# is purchased at a price, because run-time attribute checking is integrated into this feature. Again the design goals of safety and efficiency have come into conflict, as they must often do.

8.2.7 Properties—Access Functions in Disguise

When we referred earlier to the current item selected by the `IEnumerable` object `i`, we used the notation `i.Current`. A misleading notation, this is not a reference to a public member variable of the object `i`, but a special kind of parameterless function call. `Current` is what C# calls a `property` of the object `i`. Properties are meant to be a more syntactically pleasing approach to access functions, i.e., what many Java people refer to colloquially as "getters and setters." As an example, let us consider the following simple Java class:

```
public class RubberBall {
   ...
   double bounceCoeffient;
   public double getBounceCoefficient() {
      return bounceCoefficient;
   }
   public void setBounceCoefficient(double bc) {
       if (bc >= 0 && bc <=1) bounceCoefficient = bc;
   }
   ...
}
```

This has become such a prevalent pattern in Java that IDEs such as *NetBeans*, which integrate into their interfaces the Java Beans component construction regimen, are specifically designed to look for that pattern. When both `getX()` and `setX()` methods with the correct interfaces are observed in a user-defined component placed by the programmer in the IDE's toolbox, the IDE will place a single "property" called `x` in the property dialog for that component. If `RubberBall` were a Java Bean component, it would be presented to the user as having a `BounceCoefficient` property.

C# has taken this pattern to the logical conclusion, obviating the need for "getters and setters" by providing special notations for "properties" in the interface to a class. In C#, we can code functionality equivalent to that shown above into a class as follows:

```
public class RubberBall {
   ...
   double bounceCoefficient;
```

```
public double BounceCoefficient {
    get {
        return bounceCoefficient;
    }
    set {
        if (value >= 0 && value <= 1)
            bounceCoefficient = value;
    }
}
    . . .
}
```

Supposing, then, that item `MikeysBall` is defined as

```
RubberBall MikeysBall = new RubberBall();
```

we no longer have to code

```
MikeysBall.setBounceCoefficient(0.8);
```

but can instead code

```
MikeysBall.BounceCoefficient = 0.8;
```

The latter code will trigger an invocation of the `set` portion of the property `BounceCoefficient`, with `value` bound to 0.8. We can access the value of this property, now, with the simple reference `MikeysBall.BounceCoefficient` instead of the call `MikeysBall.getBounceCoefficient()`. Such a reference, in a setting where a value is required, triggers the `get` portion of the property's definition.

8.2.8 Indexers—Programmer-Defined Subscripting

C++ takes an approach to programmer-defined subscripting which uses the operator overloading features of the language. Java eschews programmer-defined operators and does not have a facility for programmer-defined subscripting, going so far as not even to allow subscripting operations on library containers. The designers of C# felt that programmer-defined subscripting was important—so important that they designed special features in support of it, called *indexers*. The syntax for the definition of an indexer method has a similar appearance to that for properties, in that it a `get` and/or a `set` portion. As with properties, if there is a `set` component then the keyword `value` is bound at call time to a value to be stored.

Let us take as an example a class called `Primes` for the generation, storage, and retrieval of prime numbers. For a positive integer `i`, we have in mind to access the `i`-th prime number by subscript, so that if `p` is an object of type `Primes` then `p[i-1]` will yield the `i`-th prime. Thus, `p[0]` will evaluate to 2, `p[1]` to 3, `p[2]` to 5, etc. The example follows:

```csharp
using System.Collections.Generic;

public class Primes {
    List<int> primes = new List<int>();
        // Cache of computed primes.
    public Primes() {
      // Constructor adds the first two primes to the cache.
        primes.Add(2);
        primes.Add(3);
    }
    int getPrime(int i) {
        // Called only if i >= primes.Count.
        int candidate = primes[primes.Count - 1] + 2;
        while (i >= primes.Count) {
            int primeIndex = 1;
            int divisor = primes[primeIndex];
            bool couldBePrime = true;
            while (couldBePrime &&
                    divisor * divisor <= candidate) {
                if (candidate/divisor*divisor == candidate)
    couldBePrime = false;
                else divisor = this[++primeIndex];
            }
            if (couldBePrime) primes.Add(candidate);
            candidate = candidate + 2;
        }
        return primes[i];
    }
    public int this[int i] {
        // This is the indexer.  It is read-only, since there
        // is no 'set' part.
        get {
            if (i < 0) return 0;
            else if (i < primes.Count) return primes[i];
            else return getPrime(i);
        }
    }
}
```

Notice the form of the indexer, which of course has only a `get` portion because we can't allow the client to change the value associated with the `i`-th prime number. Instead of a property name the keyword `this` is used, followed by one or more parameters in square brackets, separated by commas. Using this syntax multiple subscripting patterns may be defined for the same class, using different subscript types and different numbers of subscripts. Overload resolution can then be used to select a specific indexer to match the types of the subscripts for a given subscripted variable.

The following console application uses the `Primes` class to allow the user to examine the `i`-th prime number, for any positive integer `i`.

```
using System;
using System.Collections.Generic;
using OOPLS;

class PrimesClient  {
    static string Ordinal(int i) {
        switch (i) {
            case 1: return "first";
            case 2: return "second";
            case 3: return "third";
            default: {
                string suffix;
                if (i > 20 && i%10 == 1 && i%100 != 11)
                    suffix = "-st";
                else if (i > 20 && i%10 == 2 && i%100 != 12)
                    suffix = "-nd";
                else if (i > 20 && i%10 == 3 && i%100 != 13)
                    suffix = "-rd";
                else suffix = "-th";
                return i.ToString()+suffix;
            }
        }
    }
    static void Main(string[] args) {
        Primes p = new Primes();
        int i = 1;
        while (i >= 1) {
            Console.WriteLine(
                "Enter a positive integer i, please.");
            string line = Console.ReadLine();
            line = line.Split()[0];
            i = Int32.Parse(line);
```

```
        if (i >= 1) {
            Console.WriteLine(
                "The {0} prime number is {1}.",
                Ordinal(i), p[i - 1]);
        }
    }
}
```

8.2.9 Operator Overloading

Many of C#'s operators may be overloaded, but fewer choices are given to the C# programmer than are given to the C++ programmer. For example, the unary operators ++ and -- may only be overloaded once, so that the programmer may not define both a prefix and a postfix version. Once such an overload is provided, both the prefix and postfix forms will call that same overload.

Programmer-defined operators must be defined as static methods, and at least one operand of such an operator must be of the type to which the method belongs. This latter requirement prevents the programmer from redefining existing operator meanings for primitive or library types.

For operators that have an associated assignment operator (for example +, which has the associated assignment +=), when the ordinary operator has been supplied C# will automatically provide the assignment operator as well. Consider, then, a coordinate-wise + operator for the Point class below:

```
public Point {
    public int x, y;
    public Point(int x, int y) { this.x = x; this.y = y; }
    public Point operator + (Point p, Point q) {
        return new Point(p.x+q.x, p.y+q.y);
    }
}
```

Between two Point variables p and q, now, the assignment

```
p += q;
```

takes place as if it had been coded

```
p = p + q;
```

One reason for this design is that there is no "return by reference" mechanism in C#, so that assignment semantics cannot be defined inside a method and must be defined by a convention such as the above. In a related issue, the assignment operator = cannot be redefined, and always causes a bit-for-bit copy, either of a handle (for reference types) or of a value (for value types).

The unary operators that permit programmer-defined overloads in C# include the following:

```
+    -    !    ~    ++    --    true    false
```

The latter two are intended for cases in which the programmer wishes to use an object as if it were of type `bool`, as in the following code:

```
if (x) Process(x);
```

It may seem odd to the reader that a language which forbids the routine implicit conversion to type `bool` of primitive numeric types would encourage the user to define ways to institute such conversions for his own types, considering that those types may in fact be made to look indistinguishable from built-in types. That is the case, however. Consider the following simplified `Rational` type:

```
using System;

public class Rational {
    public class ZeroDivideException: Exception {}
    private int num, den;
    public Rational(int num, int den) {
        if (den == 0) throw new ZeroDivideException();
        if (den < 0) { num = -num; den = -den; }
        this.num = num;
        this.den = den;
        lowestTerms();
    }
    public Rational(int num): this(num,1) {}
    public Rational(): this(0,1) {}
    private void lowestTerms() {
        int d = den, n = Math.Abs(num);
        while (d > 0) { int temp = n % d; n = d; d = temp; }
        int gcd = n;
        den = den / gcd;
```

```
        num = num / gcd;
    }
    public static bool operator true(Rational r) {
        return r.num != 0;
    }
    public static bool operator false(Rational r) {
        return r.num == 0;
    }
    public override string ToString() {
        if (den == 1) return num.ToString();
        else return num.ToString()+"/"+den.ToString();
    }
}
```

Here we see programmer-supplied overloads of both operators `true` and `false`. In fact, if one is present then both must be present. The following code will cause only one line of output, because the default-constructed `s` will have the value 0, interpreted as `false` because operator `true` returns `false`.

```
Rational r = new Rational(10,-15), s = new Rational();
if (r) Console.WriteLine("r = {0}.", r);
if (s) Console.WriteLine("s = {0}.",s);
```

The binary operators that permit programmer-defined overloads in C# include the following:

```
+   -   *   /   %   &   |   ^   <<   >>   ==   !=   >   <   >=   <=
```

As with C++, the precedence and associativity of an operator reside with the operator symbol, not with any particular definition of that symbol's meaning.

The interplay between the so-called "Boolean conditional operators" and "logical conditional operators" comes into play again here, in an odd way. Note that the operators `&&` and `||` do not appear in the above list. They cannot be directly overridden, but if binary operators `&` and `|` and unary operators `true` and `false` are overridden, then `&&` and `||` can be used in expressions involving the type in question. For example, the expression `p && q` is evaluated by first sending the `false` message to `p`. If the result comes back `true`, then the expression evaluates to `false`. If not, then the computation `p & q` is initiated, and the result of that computation is sent the `operator true` message. If that message returns `true`, the result of the short-circuit `&&` is `true`. If not, the result is `false`.

Programmer-defined type conversions are also allowed in C#, and those conversions can either be allowed to be implicit or require explicit casts. The following list type provides an implicit type transfer to type *int* by identifying the list with its count when an integer is required:

```
class MyList : List<int> {
    public static implicit operator int (MyList m){
        return m.Count;
    }
}
```

8.2.10 C# Compilation Units

C# source code is contained in only one kind of file, typically with the *cs* extension. There are no header files. On the other hand, a C# compilation extends over a *compilation unit*, which may consist of multiple source files. The compiler works with all source files in the compilation unit at once, and each file may reference identifier associations in any other file in the project, even if the pattern of those references is circular (e.g., file A needs the x defined in file B, which needs the y defined in file A).

NOTE

The reader should take care not to confuse a C# compilation unit with the C++ compilation unit, which is a "virtual text file" consisting of one source file blended together with zero or more include files, with additional textual changes applied to it by the preprocessor. The C# compilation unit is a collection of source files, and is never combined into one text file.

If a name is intended to be restricted to a single compilation unit and not available to client code, it can be given the access modifier internal. This is somewhat similar to the Java "friendly" access, which in that language has no associated keyword and is considered the default access level for any class-scope entity. There are two important points of clarification here, however. The first is that the default access characteristic of class members in C# is private, not internal. The second is that a compilation unit is not identical with a directory, and other compilation units may share the directory yet not have access to the internal attributes of other compilation units.

The protected internal access modifier may be attached to a class member for the purpose of making it accessible only to derived classes within the same compilation unit. This is a very fine-grained access level, not seen in any of the other C-derived languages.

8.3   C# TYPES AND NAMESPACES

Namespaces in C# are not married to directory names as are Java packages, nor are class, struct, or interface names. In fact, the situation more resembles that of C++, in which file and directory organization is almost entirely orthogonal to program structure. However, there is no such thing as a header file, because C# compilation units which are not intended to provide an entry point for execution are compiled to a library file with a *dll* extension, a file which like the Java *class* file can provide to the C# compiler or to the CLI all the necessary information concerning its accessible contents. Thus, just as is the case with Java, one type of file provides both compile-time and run-time information.

A C# compilation unit which is designed to generate an application is compiled to a file with the *exe* extension. The reader must keep in mind that the content of such a file is not native code, but CIL code intended for JIT compilation. This is a somewhat misleading situation in the Microsoft Windows environment, where native code executable file names also have the *exe* suffix. Clearly, more than a simple operating system loader is required to load and begin to execute a CIL code file, and the user will notice the difference in the time it takes to execute a CIL file as opposed to a native code file. The same thing, of course, is true of Java *class* files, but because the operating system's interface is not designed to recognize such files there is clear indication of the fact: the user must explicitly invoke the JVM by its name, *java*. In contrast, Windows integrates the .NET framework into its operating system interface when .NET is installed, so that its CIL files appear to Windows users to have the same properties as native code files.

How, then, do files, namespaces, and types relate to each other? Let us examine that question, starting with the program entity that object-oriented programmers are most interested in: classes.

8.3.1 C# Classes and Partial Classes

A C# class resembles, more than anything, a Java class. Access levels such as `public`, `protected`, and `private`, and the additional access levels `internal` and `protected internal`, must be individually assigned to each class member, whether it is a method, a field (data member), a property, an index, or a nested type.

Member functions may be overloaded as long as their parameter interfaces are different, and constructors may be included for initialization purposes. Destructors are allowed and use the same syntax as C++, but the programmer should keep in mind that because C# employs garbage collection he may have no direct control over when an object is destroyed.

A facility called a static constructor, which functions like a Java static initialization block, is permitted, and has the same syntax as a constructor except that instead of an access modifier the keyword `static` is used, as in the following:

```
public class BabyNames {
    static List<string> mostPopularGirlNames,
                        mostPopularBoyNames;
    static BabyNames() {
        mostPopularBoyNames = new List<string>();
        mostPopularBoyNames.Add("Michael");
        mostPopularGirlNames = new List<string>();
        mostPopularGirlNames.Add("Jennifer");
        . . .
    }
    . . .
}
```

The assignments in the static constructor will be made once, before any instantiations of the class.

As in Java, objects of class type are represented by references, so that assignment to variables of such types is explained using pointer semantics. Also as in Java, multiple inheritance is not permitted, but a class may implement as many interfaces as is necessary.

As in Java, classes may be declared `abstract`, which has the effect of forbidding any instantiations of the type. Methods may be declared abstract as well, and if a method is abstract then it is a compiler error not to declare the enclosing class abstract. Abstract classes are not required to contain abstract methods, but just as in Java, a class derived from an abstract class must either provide implementations of all the abstract methods or be itself declared abstract.

A class may be declared `static`, in which case all its methods and nonconstant data members must also be declared static. Such a class cannot participate in inheritance, neither as a base class nor a derived class, and objects of the class type cannot be instantiated.

If a class is declared `sealed`, then it may not act as a base class for any other class. Such a class resembles a Java class which is declared `final`.

Because only public inheritance is permitted, the syntax for declaring a base class is simple. To declare that class `B` is directly derived from `A`, we use the notation

```
class B: A {
    . . .
}
```

If class B also implements interfaces C, E, and F, the notation expands to the following:

```
class B: A, C, E, F {
    . . .
}
```

C# classes may contain type definitions, including inner classes. On this issue, however, C# differs from Java. Objects constructed from C# inner classes do not have a link to an outer class object, and code in inner class methods cannot refer to nonstatic members in the containing class.

A class which has the modifier `partial` is open and can be added to by other program units. Several partial classes of the same name may be encountered by the compiler in one compilation unit, and the compiler combines those into one class. (This facility provides one practical way for a programmer to add his own contributions to a class which is supplied by a code generator.) No forward declaration is needed in order to resolve references to class members not declared in the current file, as long as every needed member definition is present in some file which is included in the project being compiled.

8.3.2 C# Structs

Much discussion has already occurred in Section 8.2 concerning structs. They are given a special status in C# which they did not have in C++, because variables of a type declared as a struct use value semantics, not reference semantics. A struct cannot name its own base class, nor can it be used as a base class, so a type fashioned using this facility represents an old-fashioned abstract data type, not a class in the object-oriented sense. Nothing prevents a struct from implementing any number of interfaces, however.

Because structs are "autoboxed" as needed, their objects are candidates for inclusion in any of the .NET container classes. The procedure for doing so is very simple and natural if the generic containers are used, and does not in fact differ in any way from that used for generic containers of reference types. The programmer should keep in mind, however, that every time an autoboxing operation occurs a copy of the struct object is made on the heap, and every time an unboxing occurs another copy is made from the heap to the stack.

The base type for all structs is `ValueType`, which interestingly enough is not a value type but a class. The base type for `ValueType` is `object`.

8.3.3 Interfaces

The meaning of a C# interface is exactly that of a Java interface, namely a contract which implementers must honor. Thus, if a method signature is present in an interface then any class or struct which claims to implement the interface must provide an implementation of that method. The syntax is very similar to that of a Java interface. No access modifiers may be used on the methods of an interface, because each is implicitly public.

Other than methods, C# interfaces may also contain properties, events, and indexers. These elements are represented in the natural way, as seen in the following example:

```
interface IdentifiedValue {
    int Identity { get; }
    double Value { get; set; }
}
```

In the example, the property `Identity` must be furnished by any implementer, and must at least provide read access. It may also provide write access with a `set` part, but that is not required by the interface. However, the `Value` property must be furnished with both read and write access. As with methods, no access modifier is present in the specification of a property in an interface, but the implementer is required to provide the `public` access modifier.

The reader may easily surmise from the above example the proper appearance of an indexer in an interface. We leave the discussion of events for later.

8.3.4 Enumerations

Enumerations, like structs, are value types. The syntax for declaring an enumeration is a mixture of that used in Java and that used in C++. As in Java, an enumeration always defines a named type, not just a list of integer constants (as C++ would allow). As in C++, individual values may be assigned in the enumeration list, as in the following example:

```
enum SizeNameType {TEN = 10, ELEVEN, TWELVE };
```

Unlike Java, however, C# permits us to convert the type of a named constant in an enumeration list into a numeric type. Such a type transfer requires an explicit cast.

```
int size1 = SizeNameType.TEN;         // Does not compile.
int size2 = (int) SizeNameType.ELEVEN; // Compiles.
```

The base type for all enumerated types is `Enum`, which is a reference type. The base type for `Enum` is `object`.

8.3.5 Namespaces and Namespace Aliases

A namespace is a portion of the referencing environment. However, namespaces can contain nothing which would not be allowed in the global referencing environment, which means that in C# a namespace must consist of only type definitions and other namespaces. Conversely, the only thing which can contain a namespace is another namespace.

Accessibility attributes such as `public` and `private` cannot be applied to namespaces, and the contents of a namespace may not be declared `private`. All namespaces are implicitly public, and that access level cannot be changed. The individual items in the namespace are public by default. The only attribute which can be applied to a class inside a namespace is `internal`.

The global referencing environment is an unnamed namespace which we refer to as the "global namespace." If *X* is a namespace or type defined in the global namespace, then it is visible anywhere in the program using the notation `global::X`, or just `X` if there does not exist a more local association for `x` which applies at that point in the program.

As in C++, a namespace is open and may be "added to" by any source file, or the namespace may be reopened repeatedly in the same source file. This rule applies to all namespaces at all levels of nesting.

Nesting of namespaces is a natural and convenient way of partitioning the referencing environment in useful ways. It may, however, lead to long and complex names, as in fact it does in the .NET library. A `using` statement such as

```
using System.Collections.Generic;
```

can obviate the need to make direct reference to a long and involved namespace name, but this has the potential for introducing name conflicts, because everything in the namespace is now available for unqualified referencing. A convenient halfway measure is to introduce a namespace *alias*. The notation is similar to the above but introduces a new identifier which may be used as an alias for the namespace throughout the source file, for example

```
using SCG = System.Collections.Generic;
```

If the above statement is made at the beginning of a source file, then references to the entities declared inside the namespace must still be qualified, but rather than the lengthy qualification required when no *using* statement appears, we may use the qualifying prefix `SCG::`, as in the following example:

```
SCG::Console.WriteLine();
```

This syntax is not valid for ordinary namespace names, which use the "dot" operator for qualification. The two colons may only be used with namespace alias qualification and with the keyword `global`.

8.3.6 Partial Methods

A method which is declared `partial` need not be supplied with a body. For example, in the following partial class the method, `Superfluous()` is declared partial.

```
partial class Interesting {
    void Necessary() {
        // Essential stuff.
    }
    partial void Superfluous();
}
```

All calls on a partial function will be ignored unless a definition is given for that method, either later in the same file or in another file in the same compilation unit. Given the nature of a C# compilation unit, consisting of multiple files containing fragments of namespaces and partial classes, this facility makes incremental and modular development easier, because we can gracefully "stub" a method as partial and add its definition later in a separate file, removing that file if we no longer want the functionality contained therein. For example, we could provide the following definition for `Superfluous()` in a separate file.

```
partial class Interesting {

    partial void Superfluous() {
        // Actual definition follows.
        ...
    }
}
```

```
    }
```

If the file containing the definition is present in the project, then all the calls on `Superfluous()` will invoke the behavior indicated. If that file is removed, then the project will still compile and the calls on `Superfluous()` will be ignored.

8.4 ADDITIONAL INHERITANCE CONSIDERATIONS

As we stated above, inheritance patterns in this language resemble those of Java. Multiple inheritance is not permitted, but a class may implement as many interfaces as desired. Inside a derived class, the keyword `this` refers to the object through which a method invocation was initiated, as expected. If the programmer wishes to refer to that object as an instance of its direct base class, the keyword `base` is supplied for that purpose. Inside an overridden method `f`, the call `base.f()` should invoke the version of `f` in the immediate base class. To reach further back in the inheritance chain for an earlier definition of `f`, casting `this` to the appropriate type and sending the message to the resulting expression may succeed, depending on other characteristics of the function. Postponing the binding of a particular reference to `f` until run-time, so that it may be associated with a definition of `f` appearing *later* in the inheritance hierarchy, is what we have called run-time polymorphism, and C# has chosen to provide this capability in a familiar but subtly different way.

8.4.1 Run-Time Polymorphism

Polymorphism is not the default run-time behavior in C# programs. In that respect, the language resembles C++, and it even borrows the `virtual` keyword from that language, with a similar meaning. If a method in a C# class is *not* declared `virtual`, then calls to that method are resolved statically by the compiler, taking into account the declared type associated with the identifier in the method invocation, *not* the actual type of the object it names. This seems strange, because only reference types can be base types for inheritance, so we are used to thinking of an identifier naming an object of such a type as nothing more than a name for a handle, so that the true "type" resides with the object on the end of that handle. This view would seem to lend a certain naturalness to the idea of polymorphism as default behavior, because we think of messages as being sent to objects, not typed handles. The whole idea of interfaces is indeed based on that assumption, and the fact that the language allows interfaces implies that the mechanisms for implementing polymorphism as default behavior are in place. However, that mechanism is *not* the default. Let us look at an example:

```
public class MyBase {
    public int f(int x) {
        return x*x;
    }
}
public class MyDerived: MyBase {
    public int f(int x) {
        return base.f(x)*x;
    }
}
```

Now the client code

```
MyBase b = new MyDerived();
Console.WriteLine(b.f(3));
```

outputs the number 9 to the console. An equivalent code segment in Java would output 27.

In order to obtain the Java behavior in the example, we must add the keyword `virtual` as an attribute of the method `f` in the base class, as follows:

```
public class MyBase {
    virtual public int f(int x) {
        return x*x;
    }
}
```

That change alone would cause the client code to output 27. We would get a warning, however, from the compiler, which wants to see an explicit indication in the derived class that a polymorphic override is occurring. This simply means we attach the keyword `override` as an attribute of method `f` in the derived class.

```
public class MyDerived: MyBase {
    override public int f(int x) {
        return base.f(x)*x;
    }
}
```

So C#, like C++, is designed to give the programmer a choice whether or not to give a particular method polymorphic behavior. C# goes even further with this design idea, however, pushing the decision down into the derived classes by giving the programmer a limited ability to individually specify which "incarnations" of the method are to be considered polymorphic overrides and which are to be resolved statically by the compiler. The syntactic trigger to this decision is the choice of the keyword `override`, as seen above, versus the keyword `new`. If `new` is used in place of `override` in the above example then no polymorphism actually takes place. In fact, when `new` is used in this way, no derived class from that point forward in the inheritance hierarchy can polymorphically override the method, and the method itself can only be invoked directly by compiler-generated code in which the compiler has resolved the reference to the method statically. Let us expand the above example for the purpose of explaining more fully.

```
public class MyIndirectBase {
    virtual public int f(int x) {
        return x;
    }
}
public class MyBase: MyIndirectBase {
    override public int f(int x) {
        return x * x;
    }
}
public class MyDerived: MyBase {
    new public int f(int x) {
        return base.f(x)*x;
    }
}
```

Here we have gone two classes deep in the inheritance hierarchy to give `f` polymorphic behavior, but have stopped at the third level. In this example, a message sent via method `f` to an object named by an identifier bound to type `MyIndirectBase` or to type `MyBase` will be resolved dynamically, but a message sent in that way to an object named by an identifier bound to `MyDerived` or to any of its derived classes will be resolved statically by the compiler.

8.4.2 Inline Implementation

Any method which is not an event handler and cannot be overridden in the polymorphic sense is a candidate for inline implementation. This is true because in that case the compiler has sufficient information with which to translate each call, and the binding of the call to the sequence of statements which defines the routine being called can just as well take the form of an inline translation as that of an explicit transfer of control. C# compilers often make this choice, and can do so in several circumstances.

An obvious case in point is static methods. Static methods are associated with the class itself, not an instance of the class. For that reason, if the compiler has access to the method's source code it may choose to make an inline translation of any call to that method. But even instance methods can sometimes be identified as being ineligible for overriding. Methods of a struct, for example, cannot be overridden because the struct can have no derived types. A class declared `sealed` also cannot be used as a base class for any other class and so none of its methods can be overridden. Finally, if a method is declared `new` then calls to it can be resolved statically. All of these situations permit inlining of methods.

It is not the province of the programmer to dictate whether a method should be inlined, and in C# the programmer cannot even request it. The decision is entirely that of the compiler. All the cases described above, in which a method might be inlined, are trumped by any circumstance that will require a code pointer identifying the actual location of the byte code for the translated method. A case in point is that in which a method is used as an event handler. All the above types of methods could in fact be used as event handlers, and so might need an actual byte code translation corresponding directly with the method's definition. (Recall that event handlers must always be invoked indirectly, because the association of the event with its handler is a run-time action.)

8.5   C# TYPE PARAMETERS

A Java-style "generic programming" facility is provided in C#, but it is stronger for a couple of reasons. One is the fact that in C# all safe types derive from `object`, so that the C# system of generics, based like that of Java on inheritance relationships, encompasses a wider range of types. The other is that a variety of constraints can be placed on type parameters using the `where` clause. One or more `where` clauses may follow the parameterized class name in the definition of a class with type parameters, but only one such clause may be used for each type parameter. Here is a sample pattern:

```
public class Widget<S,T>
    where S: struct, IEnumerable, IComparable
    where T: new() {
    ...
}
```

In the example, parameter S can only be matched by a value type which implements the interfaces IEnumerable and IComparable, whereas type T must be furnished with a default constructor. A base class may also be specified, but the relationships indicated by where clauses must be legal relationships; for example, they cannot imply multiple inheritance or circular inheritance patterns. A C# compiler cannot be considered standard-compliant unless it can flag all such illegal combinations in where clauses as errors. For example, the combination struct, new() is illegal because a value type cannot be given a programmer-defined default constructor.

Let us use as an example the following translation into C# of our Java radix sort:

```csharp
using System.Collections.Generic;

public interface RadixSortKey {
    int DigitCount { get; } // Number of digits in key.
    int this[int i] { get; }  // Subscript 1 returns least
                              // significant digit.
    int Radix { get; }  // Returns the base for the radix
                        // representation.
}


public interface RadixSortElement<K>
        where K: struct, RadixSortKey {
    K Key { get; }
}
```

Here we are using two interfaces, namely RadixSortKey and RadixSortElement<>, and we are using properties and a programmer-defined subscripting operation instead of access functions. For example, if key is an object of a type which implements RadixSortKey and which represents a decimal key, then key.Radix should return 10, key[1] should return the value of the ones digit, key[2] should return the value of the tens digit, etc.

The class which performs the sort is parameterized over the key type and the record type.

```csharp
public class RadixSorter<K,E>
        where K: struct, RadixSortKey
        where E: RadixSortElement<K> {
    public static void sort(Queue<E> masterQ) {
        E rse = masterQ.Peek();
        Queue<E>[] subQ = new Queue<E>[rse.Key.Radix];
        for (int i=0; i<rse.Key.Radix; ++i)
            subQ[i] = new Queue<E>();
```

```
int binNumber, digitPosition = 1;
E currentItem;
while (digitPosition <= rse.Key.DigitCount) {
    while (masterQ.Count != 0) {
        currentItem = masterQ.Peek();
        masterQ.Dequeue();
        binNumber = currentItem.Key[digitPosition];
        subQ[binNumber].Enqueue(currentItem);
    }
    for (int k=0; k<rse.Key.Radix; ++k)
        while (subQ[k].Count != 0)
            masterQ.Enqueue(subQ[k].Dequeue())
    digitPosition++;
    }
  }
}
```

Note that, as before, we are sorting a queue, not an array. The .NET generic container `Queue<>` is not an interface as in Java, but a class with a default constructor. We use the member function `Peek()` to determine the element at the front of the queue in a nondestructive manner, whereas the `Dequeue()` operation supplies that functionality while at the same time removing the examined item from the queue. The `Enqueue()` operation adds an item to the rear of the queue.

It is instructive here to finish the example by converting the Java test program into C#.

```
using System;
using System.Collections.Generic;
using OOPLS;

public struct ZipCode: RadixSortKey {
    int zip;
    public ZipCode(int zip) {
        this.zip = zip;
    }
    public int Radix { get { return 10; } }
    public int this[int i] {
        get {
            int digit = zip;
            while (--i > 0) digit /= 10;
            return digit % 10;
        }
```

```
    }
    public int DigitCount { get { return 5; } }
    public int Value { get { return zip; } }
}

public class PostalRecord: RadixSortElement<ZipCode> {
    ZipCode zip;
    string name, address1, address2, city, state;
    public PostalRecord(string name, string address1,
                        string address2, string city,
                        string state, string zip) {
        this.name = name;
        this.address1 = address1;
        this.address2 = address2;
        this.city = city;
        this.state = state;
        this.zip = new ZipCode(Int32.Parse(zip));
    }
    public ZipCode Key {
        get { return zip; }
    }
}

public class RadixSortTester
{
    static string[,] trialData = {
        {"Zachariah Malachi", "101 Holy Lane",
         "Apartment 3B", "Jerusalem", "GA", "35109"},
        {"Cody Kadiddlehopper", "5967 Old Horse Lane",
         "", "Badlands", "KS", "50505"},
        {"Curtis Plemmons", "Route 7", "",
         "Turkey Trot", "PA", "16678"},
        {"Melinda Jabbers", "11234 Fifth Avenue", "",
         "Manhattan", "OK", "77789"},
        {"Smyrna Figs", "200 Locust Avenue", "",
         "Richmond", "KY", "40475"},
        {"Allyson Krauts", "421 Mockingbird Lane",
         "Box 277", "Nashville", "TN", "37205"}
    };
    public static void Main(string[] arg) {
        Queue<PostalRecord> mainQueue =
            new Queue<PostalRecord>();
        try {
            for (int i=0; i<trialData.GetLength(0); ++i) {
                mainQueue.Enqueue(
```

```
                    new PostalRecord(
                        trialData[i,0], trialData[i,1],
                        trialData[i,2], trialData[i,3],
                        trialData[i,4], trialData[i,5]
                    )
                );
            }
            RadixSorter<ZipCode,PostalRecord>.sort(mainQueue);
        }
        catch (Exception e) {
            Console.WriteLine(e.ToString());
        }
        while (mainQueue.Count != 0) {
            PostalRecord record = mainQueue.Dequeue();
            Console.WriteLine(record.Key.Value);
        }
    }
}
```

As in C++ and Java, methods can also incorporate parameterized types. In the case of a call to a parameterized method, we may explicitly represent the type to be transmitted to the parameter, as in `swap<int>(ref x, ref y)`, or we can sometimes omit explicit mention of that type and allow the compiler to infer it, as in `swap(ref x, ref y)`, in which the `int` type transmitted to the type parameter is inferred from the types of the variables `x` and `y` in the call.

The implementation of generics in C# is similar to that of Java, in that the class or method with parameterized types cannot be a 'template' for inline code substitution which disappears after the compile phase, but is actually translated into CIL code using base classes and casts.

8.6 SOME IMPORTANT LIBRARY INTERFACES

Interfaces play as important a role in C# as they do in Java. We have already seen that certain interfaces are "language-integrated," meaning that without the presence of those interfaces in the library certain built-in language features do not have meaning. For example, only classes which implement `IEnumerable` can be used as the container type in a *foreach* loop. That interface is quite simple, requiring only that there be a `GetEnumerator()` method returning an `IEnumerator` object capable of delivering elements of a container. But `IEnumerator` is also an interface and is also language-integrated. Let us take a closer look at this and several other very important C# interfaces.

8.6.1 IDisposable and the using Statement

Before we talk about enumeration it is convenient to first explain the `IDisposable` interface, because that interface must be implemented by any type which implements `IEnumerator<>`. `IDisposable` is a very short interface, containing only the method signature `void Dispose()`. A type which implements `IDisposable` is often a *resource*, meaning that it "owns" operating system or language run-time resources and is capable of freeing those resources in its `Dispose()` method. (That interpretation does not necessarily have to be given to `Dispose()`, because its meaning is up to the designers of all the particular implementations of the method.)

There is, however, an integration of this library interface into the language proper, via the `using` statement. The `using` statement is a particular kind of block, in which an object of a type which implements `IDisposable` is allocated, used, and then disposed of. For example, if `Widget` is a type which implements `IDisposable`, then a `using` block involving a particular use of a `Widget` object might appear as follows:

```
using (Widget w = new Widget()) {
    // Code which uses object w.
    ...
}
```

The block encapsulated above will not explicitly call `w.Dispose()`. That call will be generated by the compiler and executed just before the block is exited. The call on `Dispose()` is executed as if it appeared in a `finally` block, so even if there is an exception thrown the resources held by `w` will be properly disposed of.

8.6.2 Anonymous IEnumerable Objects and yield Statements

The easiest way to use the `IEnumerable` interface is *not* to do a direct implementation of that interface, which would require the construction of an object of a type that implements `IEnumerator`. We will momentarily discuss the more difficult approach, but first let us look at another language integration of these interfaces which is paradigm-challenging but extremely easy to use.

Let us use as an example the class `Primes` described earlier. That class allows access to individual primes via a non-negative integer subscript, so that if `p` is an object of type `Primes` then `p[0]` has the value 2, `p[1]` the value 3, `p[2]` the value 5, etc. The object `p` keeps an internal cache, so that if it has already found the prime with subscript j, and if i £ j, then it has only to subscript the cache to find the prime corresponding to subscript i. The cache is a private instance variable of type List<int> named primes.

Suppose we wish to give the client the ability to sequence through the cache using a *foreach* statement. We could make the class itself implement IEnumerable<int>, an approach that certainly works, or we could give the class a method, say cache(), which returns an anonymous IEnumerable<int> object, as follows:

```
public IEnumerable<int> cache() {
    for (int i = 0; i < primes.Count; ++i)
        yield return primes[i];
}
```

On the one hand, this is an extremely simple solution, and very easy to use. If p is a Primes object, then the loop

```
foreach (int prime in p.cache()) Console.WriteLine(prime);
```

displays all the primes in p's cache, one to a line.

On the other hand, the thoughtful reader may question what is going on here. We seem to be dealing, in the case of the yield return statement, with a mechanism that cannot be explained in terms of the sequence control mechanisms seen in C++ and Java. That is exactly what we are dealing with, but it is not a new idea, nor is this the first language to implement this idea. Python has a very similar feature, and Simula-67 incorporated the foundational idea. In fact, C# is much more subtle and limited in its use of that idea than Simula-67, which incorporated *coroutines* in its design. Recall from Chapter 1, "A Context-Sensitive Introduction," that a coroutine is like a subroutine, but there is no caller/called distinction between two coroutines. A group of cooperating coroutines enjoy a symmetric relationship, wherein each can at any time yield control to another without losing its context. When the coroutine which yielded is resumed at a later time, it will not have to execute from scratch but will resume execution from the point at which it last surrendered control.

What happens in the interplay between the body of the foreach loop in the client code and that of the for loop in the cache() method is that with each execution of the statement

```
yield return primes[i];
```

in the latter, execution does not actually return from the method, but is suspended while control is transferred to the point where a reference was made to the `foreach` variable `prime`. The reference is resolved using the value returned by the `yield return`, and the next iteration of the `foreach` loop will cause an implicit resumption of the `for` loop in `cache()`, right after the last `yield return`. The variable `i` will be incremented and tested, and if the loop is exited then the `MoveNext()` method in the anonymous `IEnumerable<int>` object will return `false`, which will end the `foreach`. If the loop is not exited, then the next `yield return` performs another coroutine transfer and the `foreach` body is repeated with a new value for `prime`.

There is another way in which the *yield* keyword is used. If an early exit is desired from the coroutine interaction, a full return can be accomplished using the statement

```
yield break;
```

8.6.3 Implementing IEnumerable<> and IEnumerator<>

Supposing we wish to implement `IEnumerable<>` directly, rather than through the `yield return` coroutine interaction, we must furnish a `GetEnumerator()` function which returns an `IEnumerator<>` object. Accordingly, let us acquaint ourselves with the `IEnumerator<>` interface. Because it implements `IDisposable`, it must have a `void Dispose()` function. But it must also have `MoveNext()` and `Reset()` methods, as well as a `Current` property. The following example, although not very useful, is sufficient to illustrate the necessary techniques:

```
class Triple<T> {
    T x, y, z;
    public Triple(T x, T y, T z) {
        this.x = x; this.y = y; this.z = z;
    }
    public IEnumerator<T> GetEnumerator() {
        return new TripleEnumerator<T>(this);
    }
    public class TripleEnumerator : IEnumerator {
        int current = 0;
        Triple<T> triple;
        public TripleEnumerator(Triple<T> triple) {
            this.triple = triple;
        }
        public void Dispose() { } // Do nothing. No resources
                                  // are used.
```

```
        public bool MoveNext() {
            if (current == 3) return false;
            else {
                ++current;
                return true;
            }
        }
        public void Reset() { current = 0; }
        public object Current {
            get {
                switch (current) {
                    case 1: return triple.x;
                    case 2: return triple.y;
                    case 3: return triple.z;
                    default:
                        throw new InvalidOperationException();
                }
            }
        }
    }
    class TripleEnumerator<U> :
            Triple<U>.TripleEnumerator, IEnumerator<U> {
        public TripleEnumerator(Triple<U> triple) :
            base(triple) { }
        public new U Current {
            get { return (U)base.Current; }
        }
    }
}
```

Because the first enumerator must have access to the private members of its
instance variable `triple`, it must be an inner class. Two enumerator classes are
needed because any class implementing `IEnumerator<T>` must also implement
`IEnumerator`, and just as in Java there is no relationship between those two types.
Therefore, the first inner class implements `IEnumerator` and the second extends
the first as well as implementing `IEnumerator<T>`. Because it inherits the proper
forms of `Dispose()`, `MoveNext()`, and `Reset()` from the base class, as well as a
version of the property `Current` which is associated with a return type of `object`,
all the second inner class must do to implement `IEnumerator<T>` is to provide a
version of that property which is parameterized over the type. The following client
code should execute correctly and output `23 5 7` on the console:

```
Triple<int> t = new Triple<int>(23, 5, 7);
foreach (int i in t)
```

```
Console.Write(i + " ");
```

8.6.4 The ICloneable Interface

The `ICloneable` interface performs a function similar to that of `Cloneable` in Java, but its use is discouraged because of the high likelihood that programmers will confuse shallow copying with deep copying. Like Java objects, all C# objects have the ability to make shallow copies of themselves. Whereas Java furnished the `clone()` method, in C# the function of shallow copying is accomplished by the method `MemberwiseClone()`, a protected method which resides in the base class `Object`.

Recall that in Java, a message sent via a call to the `clone()` method in base class `Object` instigates a run-time check to ensure that the `Cloneable` interface is implemented by the class of the object to which the message was sent. No such requirement exists here, so that any class or struct may call `MemberwiseClone()` from any of its methods regardless of whether or not it implements `ICloneable`.

In fact, all a class needs to do in order to implement a shallow copy is to provide the following method definition:

```
object Clone() { return MemberwiseClone(); }
```

If such a method appears then the programmer has the right to add `ICloneable` to the list of interfaces implemented by the class, but the method will "work" whether or not he does so.

Just as described in the Java chapter, we can proceed "from the bottom up" to provide all classes on which our "cloneable" class depends with their own cloning mechanisms, and thereby carefully construct a complete or partial deep copy facility. This process is fraught with error potential, however, and the .NET committee has probably done the right thing in deprecating this interface.

We will see later that C#, like Java, provides a convenient and error-free deep copying facility in its serialization mechanism, so that if we truly wish a deep copy we can tap into this language-defined process. Although serialization is usually associated with the use of auxiliary storage, there are ways to serialize to a memory buffer. Deserializing from that same buffer will then provide us with a deep copy.

8.6.5 The IComparable Interface

To take part in a sort or to be used as a type parameter to `SortedDictionary` or `SortedList`, a type must implement the `IComparable` interface. Only one method is necessary, namely the `CompareTo()` method, a call to which takes a single operand of type `object` and returns an `int`. The forms with type parameter `T` require that the parameter in `CompareTo()` be of type `T`. For objects `o1` and `o2`, `o1.CompareTo(o2)` should return –1, 0, or 1 depending respectively on whether `o1` should logically be considered less than, equal to, or greater than `o2`. The relationship thus implied should be a *total order*, i.e., not only must it be reflexive, symmetric, and transitive, but any two elements of the universe of possible values represented by the type `T` should be comparable.

8.7   FUNCTION TYPES IN C#

In C++, functions are not first-class objects, but can be manipulated using pointers. In Java, the mechanism of reflection gives us the `Method` library type, which is indeed a first-class type and allows a method to be used as data and even to be dynamically invoked. However, that type has no language-defined structure to support a natural manipulation of its instances in ways one would hope to be able to manipulate methods. C# has the similar class `MethodInfo` and other associated classes for reflection purposes, but again that class is not a convenient abstraction of a method type. The reason we say this is that although the reflection types allow methods to be treated as data, they are not assignment-compatible with methods in the sense that C++ pointers are. C# addresses this issue with three features intended to incorporate some aspects of functional programming into the language: delegates, lambda functions, and expression trees.

8.7.1 Delegates

The C# delegate type is the platypus in the family tree of programming language features. It is like an oddly viable two-headed lizard. The apparent purpose of the delegate feature, at first glance, is to provide types whose variables may be assigned method values. It is in fact that, but it is more. Let us look at a simple example. The declaration

```
public delegate double DoubleToDouble(double x);
```

declares a simple delegate type `DoubleToDouble`, whose values are methods with one `double` parameter returning `double` values. The instantiation

```
DoubleToDouble mathFunction = new DoubleToDouble(Math.Abs);
```

associates the delegate variable `mathFunction` with the absolute value function, so that now the evaluation `mathFunction(-3.76)` produces the value 3.76. A reassignment such as

```
mathFunction = new DoubleToDouble(Math.Ceiling);
```

would now cause `mathFunction(-3.76)` to evaluate to -3. The language syntax allows us to save some writing here, because the assignment

```
mathFunction = Math.Ceiling;
```

has exactly the same meaning and produces the same effect.

All this seems to be straightforward design, and probably produces no discomfort or confusion for a novice student of C#. But one simple question may already be forming in the reader's mind. The use of `Math.Abs` and `Math.Ceiling` in a situation in which they appear to be used as parameters in a constructor suggests that they already have types. If so, why can we not instantiate variables of those types? The fact is that the only place in C# in which we are allowed to treat methods as if they were data is in the above syntax, in which they are used to instantiate delegates, or in a situation in which they can be "autoboxed" to have that same interpretation. Methods *per se* are not first-class objects in C#, and in fact are not directly associated with types. The constructor call

```
new DoubleToDouble(Math.Ceiling);
```

does not invoke a programmer-defined or library-defined constructor method, but is in fact a language-defined syntactic construct with a context-sensitive meaning. The name in parentheses is classified by the compiler as a *method group* and has no actual type, neither named nor constructed, associated with it. It may be the name of a class or instance method of some class or struct, and when the method is invoked through the delegate variable, it behaves in the same way as if it had been invoked using a statically constructed name. In general, a method group may not statically identify a single function, because polymorphism may be involved. Therefore, a delegate instance creation may involve the same sort of dynamic method lookup which occurs when a call to a virtual function occurs.

The fact that delegate objects can be associated with either class methods or instance methods is intriguing, because normally class methods are statically invoked and hence can be inlined by the compiler. Clearly any method which has been associated with a delegate cannot be inlined when called through that delegate, a fact which complicates the compiler writer's implicit charge to discern which methods need actual translated machine subroutines associated with them and which ones do not.

8.7.2 Multicast Delegates

The view of delegates one gets from looking at the introduction in the above section is that they are nothing more than type-safe function pointers (in the case of delegates instantiated from static methods), or (object, method) pairs (in the case of instance methods). In fact, however, this language gives them a much stronger status than that. The impetus for including them comes largely from the desire to provide language-defined support for event handlers. Thus, the language goes "all the way" in support of event handling, expanding the delegate idea to incorporate a similar capability to that of the Java "listener" lists.

Recall that in Java some classes which provide event handler functionality maintain lists of listener objects, each of which is an object of a type which implements a certain interface, such as `ActionListener`. In the case of C#, a class which provides event handler functionality provides a single delegate object which corresponds to the event to be handled. This does not imply, however, that only one method can fire in response to the occurrence of that event. In fact, the base class for all delegate types in C# is `MulticastDelegate`, and this type name gives an indication of what is actually the case: a delegate variable may be associated with not just one, but any number of methods.

To illustrate, let us use a class called `Cheers` containing multiple functions with a minimal interface, and a delegate type to match that interface.

```csharp
public class Cheers {
    public static void Generic() {
        Console.WriteLine("Yay!");
    }
    public static void LongGeneric() {
        Console.WriteLine("Yaaaaaaaaay!");
    }
    private string teamName;
    public Cheers(string teamName) {
        this.teamName = teamName;
    }
    public void Specific() {
        Console.WriteLine("Yay, {0}!", teamName);
```

```
        }
        public void LongSpecific() {
            Console.WriteLine("Yaaaaaaaaaay, {0}!", teamName);
        }
    }

    public delegate void VoidFunction();
```

We can instantiate a new delegate object using the `VoidFunction` type and one of the static functions in `Cheers`, as follows:

```
    VoidFunction cheerleader = new VoidFunction(Cheers.Generic);
```

It should come as no surprise that the call `cheerleader()` now causes the output

```
    Yay!
```

to appear on the console. But if we execute the statements

```
    cheerleader += Cheers.LongGeneric;
    Cheers irish = new Cheers("Irish");
    Cheers bama = new Cheers("Bama");
    cheerleader += irish.Specific;
    cheerleader += bama.Specific;
    cheerleader += irish.LongSpecific;
    cheerleader += bama.LongSpecific;
```

then the single call `cheerleaders()` produces the output

```
Yay!
Yaaaaaaaaaay!
Yay, Irish!
Yay, Bama!
Yaaaaaaaaaay, Irish!
Yaaaaaaaaaay, Bama!
```

Functions can be removed from a delegate in a similar fashion. Thus,

```
    cheerleader -= Cheers.LongGeneric;
    cheerleader -= Cheers.Generic;
```

removes the two static functions.

The reader should not miss the recursive nature of this design. The notation

```
cheerleader += bama.LongSpecific;
```

actually creates a delegate and "adds" that delegate to the delegate `cheerleader`. In other words, the above is short for

```
cheerleader += new VoidFunction(bama.LongSpecific);
```

Thus, the right-hand operand of `+=` is a delegate. This implies, and it certainly is true, that delegates can be nested inside delegates to any level of nesting, and the run-time structure of a delegate object is that of a directed graph. For example, consider the following program:

```
using System;

class DelegateTree {
    void A() { Console.Write("A"); }
    void B() { Console.Write("B"); }
    void C() { Console.Write("C"); }
    void D() { Console.Write("D"); }
    void E() { Console.Write("E"); }
    void F() { Console.Write("F"); }
    void G() { Console.Write("G"); }
    void H() { Console.Write("H"); }
    void I() { Console.Write("I"); }

    delegate void VoidFunction();

    static void Main() {
        DelegateTree dt = new DelegateTree();
        VoidFunction a = dt.A;
        VoidFunction b = dt.B;
        b += dt.C;
        VoidFunction c = new VoidFunction(b); // Here the explicit
        // use of 'new' avoids simply copying a handle.
        VoidFunction e = dt.E;
        e += dt.G;
        e += dt.H;
        e += dt.I;
        c += dt.D;
        c += e;
```

```
        a += c;
        a += dt.F;
        a();
    }
}
```

This program builds the tree in Figure 8.1, then produces the output ABC-DEGHIF, indicating that the call pattern follows that of a depth-first traversal of the leaves of the tree. But keep in mind that there is no reason this relationship should be constrained to a tree shape. For example, the assignment e+=a creates a cycle in the graph! (Exercise 8-56 invites the student to explore the ramifications of this oddity.)

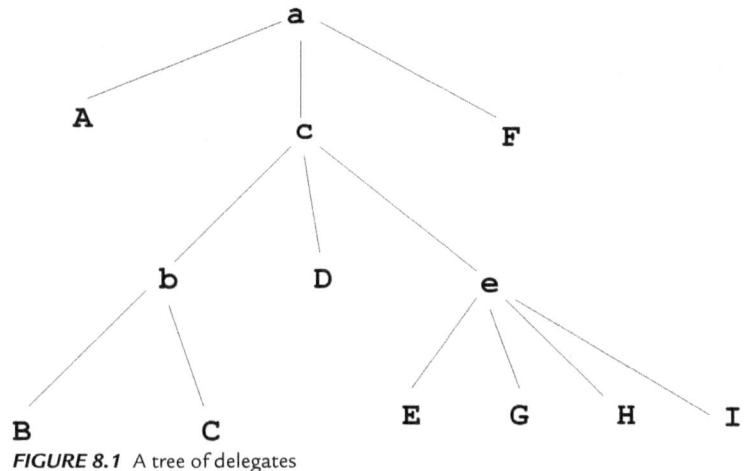

FIGURE 8.1 A tree of delegates

8.7.3 Lambda Expressions and Anonymous Methods

A lambda expression provides a way to instantiate a delegate based on an unnamed method or to add to a delegate an unnamed method. The syntax is based on Church's Lambda Calculus, which would represent the function $x^2 + 5x + y$ as $\lambda xy.x^2 + 5x + y$. The idea is to convert an expression with unbound variables into a function. A C# lambda expression similar to this example is

```
    (x, y) => (x*x + 5*x + y)
```

Like the method names used to instantiate delegates, the lambda expression is a syntactic construct which is not directly associated with a type and cannot be used for any purpose except to instantiate a delegate object or an expression tree object (see below). In the above example, the types of parameters x and y are inferred from the context. Thus, the following code

```
delegate double TwoParameterMathFunction (double x, double y);
TwoParameterMathFunction f = new TwoParameterMathFunction(
    (x, y) => (x*x + 5*x + y)
);
Console.WriteLine(f(2,3));
```

compiles and outputs the number 17. Types can be associated with the parameters in a lambda function, and those parameters may even be given the ref or out attributes, but those types and attributes must match those associated with the delegate being instantiated.

Multiple statements may be associated with the definition of a lambda expression, by using a block instead of an expression. Thus, after the instantiation

```
VoidFunction FranklinQuotes =
    (() => {
        Console.WriteLine("A penny saved is a penny earned.");
        Console.WriteLine("Honesty is the best policy.");
    });
```

the call FranklinQuotes() yields the output

```
A penny saved is a penny earned.
Honesty is the best policy.
```

A lambda expression executed via a delegate will execute in the context where it was constructed. Consider the following code:

```
int [] countList = {2, 4, 6, 8};
VoidFunction cheer = (()=> {
    foreach (int x in countList) {
        Console.Write(x);
        Console.Write(", ");
    }
    Console.WriteLine(" who do we appreciate?");
});
```

In this example, references are made to variables not declared in the block of the lambda expression, and those references are bound at the time the lambda expression is evaluated and stored as CIL code, so that the output from the call `cheer()` appears as

```
2, 4, 6, 8, who do we appreciate?
```

This output will occur any time a delegate call is issued to the handle associated with `cheer`, whether or not that call occurs in the same context in which the lambda expression was constructed. Thus, the same output would occur if `cheer` were passed as a parameter to a function and the function made the call using that parameter, or if `cheer` were a nonlocal variable which was referenced after the block in which the lambda expression occurred was exited.

An *anonymous method* is similar to a lambda expression in that it signifies an unnamed function. An anonymous method begins with the keyword `delegate` and is followed optionally by a parameter list and finally by a block. For example, the initialization of the delegate `cheer` in the above example could have been accomplished using an anonymous method instead of a lambda function, as follows:

```
VoidFunction cheer = delegate {
    foreach (int x in countList) {
        Console.Write(x);
        Console.Write(", ");
    }
    Console.WriteLine(", who do we appreciate?");
};
```

C# terminology lumps lambda expressions and anonymous methods into the single-term *anonymous functions*. The major difference between the two is that anonymous methods cannot be defined using an expression; they must incorporate a body in the form of a block.

8.7.4 Captured Local Variables

In the example above, we say that the anonymous function used to instantiate the delegate variable `cheer` has *captured* the local variable `countList`. What happens if the delegate so created *outlives* the block to which `countList` is local? Normally when a block is exited the space occupied by its local variables is reclaimed. Because `countList` is a reference type, that only means that the handle by which it is referenced is reclaimed; clearly it will not be available for garbage collection, because there are still active references to it within the code for the delegate. But what if a local variable of a value type were captured, or what if we were dealing with an anonymous function which made assignments to a local variable? Consider the following example:

```
public class CaptureExample {

    delegate void VoidFunction();
    static VoidFunction haha;

    delegate int IntGetter();
    static IntGetter getCount;

    static void tryCapture() {
        int laughCount = 0;
        haha = delegate { laughCount++; };
        getCount = () => laughCount;
    }

    public static void Main() {
        tryCapture();
        for (int i=1; i<=200; ++i) haha();
        Console.WriteLine("Count stands at {0}", getCount());
    }

}
```

Here the local variable `laughCount` is of a value type and would normally be destroyed by the process of stack unwinding when `tryCapture()` returned from its call. But because that call has bound `laughCount` to each of the two delegate objects `haha` and `getCount` through the references made to it in the two anonymous functions, `laughCount` has been captured and will not be available for storage reclamation until both of those two delegates become eligible for garbage collection. So we have engineered an example where a local variable outlives its block and is used as an invocation counter for a delegate. The class compiles successfully and outputs

```
Count stands at 200
```

In C# terminology, the capturing of `laughCount` has transformed it from a *fixed* variable into a *moveable* variable. The compiler writer is tasked with doing whatever is necessary to make sure that any future references to `laughCount` continue to refer to the same value while at the same time relocating it to some place other than the stack frame assigned to the routine `tryCapture()`. The obvious way to do this is to move `laughCount` to the heap, and that is what the C# compiler will do, by bundling all free variables captured by a given delegate type into an object called a *closure*.

8.7.5 Parameterized Delegates

Orthogonality was not a major goal when C# was designed. Combining features in creative ways is not always allowed, even if doing so might in some cases be useful. However, C# did see fit to allow the programmer to combine type parameters with delegates, and that combination is often productive. Consider the following parameterized delegate type:

```
public delegate T BinaryOperation<T>(T x, T y);
```

This type is a perfect abstraction of the idea of a binary operation. (Other than the distraction that delegates are also containers!) However, because many such operations are primitives and are not explicitly associated with named methods usable in a delegate constructor, how can we actually use it for the purpose for which it is most suited? The answer is to use a lambda expression. For example,

```
BinaryOperation<int> integerDivide =
new BinaryOperation<int>((x,y)=>x/y);
```

instantiates a delegate variable `integerDivide` which can be used as a dynamic representative of the integer divide operation, meaning that it can be transmitted to any parameter of type `BinaryOperation<int>` and when called via that parameter will behave as an integer divide.

Let us expand on this example. Recall the static `Sum` method which we used to illustrate variable-sized parameter lists, reproduced below:

```
public static int Sum(params int[] a) {
    int result = 0;
    foreach (int x in a) result += x;
    return result;
}
```

Suppose we wished to generalize this code so that it would compute the sum of any collection of numbers, no matter what type. Our first attempt might appear as follows:

```
public static T Sum<T>(params T [] a) where T: new() {
    T result = new T();
    foreach (T x in a) result += x;   // Error!
    return result;
}
```

The problem with this is that the compiler must translate it into CIL code, and it has no idea how to translate the `+=` operation, because that is a primitive which only applies to certain types, and there is no guarantee that the type transmitted to `T` actually has such an operation. Even if it did, the compiler has no way to generate code to invoke it. (If this were a C++ template we could postpone the binding of `+=` to machine code until the template is referenced by a call. Java and C# do not use that strategy for their generics.)

Let us widen our view a little. Accumulating a sum is not that different from accumulating a product or a string. We start with an initial value, and then apply the same operation over and over in order to augment that value. In the case of products, we start with 1 and apply the multiply operation. In the case of strings, we start with the empty string and apply the concatenation operation. Because all these are binary operations, we can achieve a generalization of our goal by renaming our method `Accumulate()` and adding two new parameters: an initial value and a delegate of type `BinaryOperation`. We can also help the cause of generalization by using as a collection *any* container class that implements `IEnumerable`. The result is the following code:

```
public static T Accumulate<T>(T initial, BinaryOperation<T> op,
                              IEnumerable<T> a) {
    T result = initial;
    foreach (T x in a) result = op(result,x);
    return result;
}
```

By using the `IEnumerable` interface, we have gained the ability to "accumulate" all the elements of practically any .NET container as well as those of an array, but we have lost the capability to accommodate a variable-sized parameter list. We can easily regain that capability with an overload, as follows:

```
public static T Accumulate<T>(T initial, BinaryOperation<T> op,
                              params T [] a) {
    return Accumulate<T>(initial, op, (IEnumerable<T>) a);
}
```

The rest is done with lambda functions, as seen in the following calls:

```
decimal sum = Utility.Accumulate(0.0m, (x,y)=>x+y,
2929597524.78m,
9284729752.89m,
9857437734.29m
  );
  long product = Utility.Accumulate(1L, (x,y)=> x*y,
      98129L, 8529L, 67L, 874L, 23L);
  string bigString = Utility.Accumulate("",(x,y) => x+y,
      "Fours", "core ", "and ", "seven ", "years ago our ",
      "fathers ", "brought forth on this continent a ",
      "new nation, ", "conceived in ", "liberty and ",
      "founded on the ", "proposition that ", "all men ",
"are created equal ", "and are endowed by their creator ",
"with ", "certain inalienable rights."
  );
```

In all of the above, the argument transmitted to the delegate parameter is a lambda function, which is converted to the appropriate delegate type incidental to the call.

8.7.6 Expression Trees

The ability to treat code as data is not a programming language feature one expects to find in compiled languages, even those implemented on virtual machines. That ability implies keeping around at run-time a lot of machinery one does not expect to need beyond compile time. But this language does provide a limited capability of that sort, called *expression trees*.

Certain types of lambda expressions are convertible into expression trees, which are data objects whose structure is that of a parsed expression. Because they are data objects, they can be manipulated as data in dynamic ways, and they can be compiled into delegate objects and executed as needed. We will look at an example, but note that it is an example to illustrate the mechanics of creating an expression tree, converting it into a delegate, and executing that delegate. The example does not hint at the actual application of such trees, which would take some time to develop.

```
using System.Linq.Expressions;
...
delegate T Function<S, T>(S s);
```

```
...
Expression<Function<int, double>> exprTree =
    (int x) => Math.Sqrt(x + 1);
    // Created an expression tree
Function<int, double> f = exprTree.Compile();
    // Converted the tree to a delegate object.
Console.WriteLine(f(8));
    // Executed the delegate
```

A lambda expression cannot be converted into an expression tree if it is defined by a block or if its definition contains assignment operators.

8.8 .NET FRAMEWORK COLLECTION CLASSES

The `System.Collections` and `System.Collections.Generic` namespaces house a number of collections of a more or less standard type. We have already used the `Queue<>` class in our radix sort example, and we made mention of the fact that the `List<>` class is not a linked list but resembles what C++ calls a vector. The linked list class in the .NET generic collections library is called `LinkedList<>`. It is a doubly linked list and gives the programmer access to individual nodes via the associated node type `LinkedListNode<>`. For example, if we wish to find the value 47 in a linked list of integers called `intList`, then the call `intList.Find(47)` returns either null (if 47 is not in the list) or a handle to an object of type `LinkedListNode<int>` which is the actual node containing that value. The `Next` and `Previous` properties of that node then give us access to the neighboring nodes.

The hash table generic container class is similar to Java's `HashMap<>` class and is called `Dictionary<>`. Recall that in Java every first-class object has the ability to hash itself via the `hashCode()` method of class `Object`. The C# `Object` class also has a hashing method, called `GetHashCode()`, and because all types in C# descend from `Object`, whether they are reference types or value types, in C# *every* object of a safe type can be hashed. For example, the code `0.79.GetHashCode()` compiles and (in Visual C#) returns the value 731096806.

NOTE

Although one would certainly almost never have any desire to use double values as keys in a hash table, and in fact it would likely be a poorly advised decision to do so, the example illustrates the comprehensiveness of the incorporation of hashing into the language. Also, the programmer should always be aware that the object class's hashing algorithm may not be a good algorithm for his particular key set, and an override of GetHashCode() may be advisable.

Dictionary<>, like all the containers mentioned here, implements the IE-numerable<> interface, but it enumerates over objects of type *KeyValuePair<>*. Each of those objects has a Key property and a Value property. The following code illustrates:

```
Dictionary<string, decimal> salary =
    new Dictionary<string, decimal>();
salary.Add("Lou", 88578.97m);
salary.Add("Mary", 55555.00m);
salary.Add("Rhoda", 38000.00m);
salary.Add("Sue-Ann", 65000.00m);
salary.Add("Ted", 72000.00m);
salary.Add("Murray", 50000.00m);
foreach (KeyValuePair<string, double> p in salary)
    Console.WriteLine("{0} makes ${1}.", p.Key, p.Value);
```

The Dictionary<> type is accompanied by an indexer, so that the line

```
salary.Add("Lou", 88578.97m);
```

could just as well have been coded as

```
salary["Lou"] = 88578.97m;
```

As we would expect with a hash table, there is no predefined order in which the (*key, value*) pairs are stored. That order is affected by the hash function being used and by the size of the hash table, which can be supplied as a constructor argument, if desired. If the number of pairs inserted in the table exceeds the capacity specified, the hash table will automatically reallocate and the contents of the table will be redistributed, a process that also may affect order.

The binary search tree class is called SortedDictionary<>. It has a similar interface to that of Dictionary<>, but stores its contents in order by key.

The .NET equivalent to Java's hash-table-based set class is a relatively recent addition to the collection, and uses the identical name HashSet<>. It includes an Add() method for adding individual elements, as well as UnionWith() and IntersectWith() for forming unions and intersections. Each of UnionWith() and IntersectWith() can take any IEnumerable operand, and each produces a HashSet<> result. The class KeyCollection<> is also a set type, but it represents the set of keys in a dictionary and cannot be instantiated as a separate container.

> *Although the pure set data types of the form HashSet<T> were added fairly recently, the Enumerable class has been around for a while and includes static methods Union() and Intersect() which, for any type T, take two IEnumerable<T> operands and produce an object implementing the IEnumerable<T> interface.*

NOTE

8.9   WINDOWS FORMS AND CONTROLS

Visual C#, like MFC, depends heavily on code generators to give programmers developing windowed applications a quick start on a new project. It is possible, but practically and culturally almost impossible, to avoid using those generators for anything other than console projects. The option of using header files to help in keeping hand-coded elements of a program physically separate is not available, because C# does not use such files. However, we have a powerful tool for that purpose in the *partial class*.

Let us briefly walk through the development of a windowed application using Visual Studio, wherein we will outline a strategy and methodology for maintaining the integrity of hand-coded files.

8.9.1 Starting a Windows Application in Visual Studio

The library class `Form`, residing in namespace `System.Windows.Forms`, can be used in much the same way as we used the `CView` class in MFC, as a basis for quick development of Windows applications, but we do not need a separate frame window object because the same `Form` object serving as the view window is also the frame window. `Form` is the base class for all .NET application windows, including dialog-based applications, single-view applications, and multiple document interface (MDI) applications, as well as for child windows within an MDI application. We will use it for now as a base class for a quick and simple beginning application.

From the Visual Studio interface, make the menu choices *File...New...Project*. In the resulting dialog, under *Project Types*, choose *Visual C#*, then *Windows*. Under *Templates*, choose *Windows Forms Application*. Use the name `GrowingDisks` for the application name. There is a check box to allow you to either add this project to an existing solution or make a new solution file for it. After you have made that choice, click on OK, and the editor panel will display a form in "Design view," meaning that a drawing of a frame window will appear in that panel. The drawing will show only a framed window with a title bar showing the title "Form1" and a small client area, with a light gray background.

There is already a working program behind this unimpressive window design, consisting of three source files: *Form1.cs*, *Form1.Designer.cs*, and *Program.cs*. For better mnemonics, let us rename those first two files. In the *Solution Explorer* window, right-click on *Form1.cs*, select *Rename* from the resulting pop-up, and give the file the new name *GrowingDisksForm.cs*. When asked whether you wish to rename all references, respond by clicking *yes*.

When we compile and execute the project, it displays a window that can be resized, minimized, and moved around on the desktop, but there is no interesting functionality to it. All the same, we should look at some of this generated code and analyze what it is doing, beginning with the *Program.cs* file.

```
using System;
using System.Collections.Generic;
using System.Linq;
using System.Windows.Forms;

namespace GrowingDisks
{
    static class Program
    {
        /// <summary>
        /// The main entry point for the application.
        /// </summary>
        [STAThread]
        static void Main()
        {
            Application.EnableVisualStyles();
            Application.SetCompatibleTextRenderingDefault(
                false);
            Application.Run(new GrowingDisksForm());
        }
    }
}
```

All the code for this application will be placed by the code generator in a namespace having the same name as the project, in this case `GrowingDisks`. The entry point for execution is, as usual, entitled `Main()`, and resides in a static class simply entitled `Program`. In the `Main()` routine, three messages are sent to the class `Application`, to get the ball rolling. The last of these messages calls the `Run()` static method of that class and sends to it a newly instantiated object of our window class, named `GrowingDisksForm`. The `Run()` method makes the window visible on the screen, initializes the event-handling mechanisms, and raises the *Load* event.

The code for the wizard-generated `GrowingDisksForm` class is in two files: *GrowingDisksForm.cs* and *GrowingDisksForm.Designer.cs*. Both of these will be modified by the wizard as the programmer manipulates the screen representation of the application's window in the edit panel of the IDE, and it is best to make only minimal hand-coded changes to these files. The *GrowingDisksForm. cs* file is quite short and appears as follows:

```
using System;
using System.Collections.Generic;
using System.ComponentModel;
using System.Data;
using System.Drawing;
using System.Linq;
using System.Text;
using System.Windows.Forms;

namespace GrowingDisks
{
    public partial class GrowingDisksForm : Form
    {
        public GrowingDisksForm()
        {
            InitializeComponent();
        }
    }
}
```

All of the above `using` statements except the last one are at this time superfluous, and are generated "just in case they are needed." What is defined in this file is a *partial class*, which is augmented in the *GrowingDisksForm.Designer.cs* file. That file contains as its salient feature the definition of the `InitializeComponent()` method which is called in the `GrowingDisksForm` constructor. The programmer is heavily discouraged from modifying this method, as evidenced by the fact that the editor does not initially display it, instead collapsing it to a gray box labeled "Windows Form Designer generated code." If we click on the plus sign to the left of that box, then the following method definition appears:

```
private void InitializeComponent()
{
    this.components = new System.ComponentModel.Container();
    this.AutoScaleMode =
```

```
        System.Windows.Forms.AutoScaleMode.Font;
    this.Text = "Growing Disks";
}
```

All of this code is ultimately quite understandable, but is technical and somewhat of a distraction for our purposes. As the window in "design view" is modified, by adding components and event handlers, it will become more and more technical. We do not need to become embroiled in these technicalities, and indeed we are encouraged by the interface itself not to modify this file by directly editing the source code.

We are, however, encouraged to modify the *GrowingDisksForm.cs* file, and indeed we must do so. The problem with that, however, is that the wizard also will be modifying that file, and it is important for portability's sake to avoid making major modifications to it. The pattern we will employ for our modifications is this: we will use the properties box and its associated wizards to create wizard-generated methods with the general naming pattern OnEventName(), which the wizard will insert into *GrowingDisksForm.cs*, and we will provide a partial method declaration with the same name, except with the first letter lower cased. We will add the actual definitions of those methods in a hand-coded file, but let us go ahead and "stub" the hand-coded event handlers here. To do this, we add two lines inside the partial class GrowingDisksForm, as follows:

```
partial void onPaint(Graphics g);  // For the paint event.
partial void onClick(Point p);  // For the mouse click event.
```

These stubs will be fleshed out in the hand-coded file, which we will add to the project later. Before we can do this, we must introduce some drawing tools.

8.9.2 Drawing on a Form

The library classes encapsulating drawing tools for .NET are Color, Brush, Pen, and Graphics. Their operation is quite standard. As in MFC, we fill regions with brushes and outline regions with pens. A number of standard colors come as public properties of class Color, such as Color.Red, Color.SpringGreen, Color.AntiqueWhite, etc. If, however, we wish to create a custom color by mixing red, green, and blue as we have in previous projects, we encounter the problem that Color does not have a simple (red, green, blue) constructor. There is, however, a class called ColorTranslator which provides the static call FromWin32(), and that call can create a color from an integer. We will describe how to accomplish this shortly.

Brushes also come in premixed colors, and we can get one of these pre-fabricated brushes by accessing public properties of class `Brushes` (`Brushes.SpringGreen`, for example). If we wish to instantiate a brush having a custom-mixed color, we must create an object of a derived class type, because `Brush` is an abstract class. Typically we use `SolidBrush` to create a custom brush class, and pass to it the color we have mixed.

Here we need to get a little technical. Hexadecimal literals are coded in C# exactly as in C++, so that `0x2F`, for example, is the number 2 × 16 + 15. To prepare an integer representing a desired color, hexadecimal notation is handy because the three bytes in the low-order 24 bits of an individual word line up nicely as bit patterns. For example, the chocolate brown color we mixed in Chapter 3, "Smalltalk and the Squeak Environment," as (140, 100, 0), would use the 8-bit quantity 140 = 0x8C as a red level and 100 = 0x64 as a green level, so that the integer we need in order to represent that color is `0x00648C`. Note that the colors line up reversed, so that the low-order eight bits provide the red level.

To obtain a brown brush, then, the following code suffices:

```
Color Brown = ColorTranslator.FromWin32(0x00648C);
Brush BrownBrush = new SolidBrush(Brown);
```

The *Pen* class has a one-parameter constructor which just needs a color, so that

```
new Pen(Color.Black)
```

instantiates a black pen.

The `Graphics` class provides methods for drawing, such as `DrawRectangle()`, `FillRectangle()`, `DrawEllipse()`, and `FillEllipse()`. All these have similarly formed parameter lists. For example, if `g` is a `Graphics` object then the call

```
g.FillEllipse(BrownBrush, 100, 150, 50, 80);
```

will paint with brown the interior of an ellipse inscribed in the 50 by 80 rectangle whose upper-left-hand corner is at (100, 150). The call

```
g.DrawEllipse(new Pen(Color.Black), 100, 150, 50, 80);
```

will outline that region with a black border.

Drawing text on the screen requires the explicit use of a font and a brush (for color). Thus, to display "Hello, World!" on the screen in a bounding rectangle with upper-left-hand corner at (70, 55), we must use

```
g.DrawString("Hello, World!", Font, Brushes.Black, 70, 55);
```

The above assumes the call came from inside class scope in a class derived from *Form*. In that class, *Font* is a property, so that the message as coded causes g to draw the string using the font currently selected by the form.

Lines are easy, but `DrawLine()` must be furnished with a pen, as evidenced by the following code intended to draw a black line from (20, 30) to (100, 10).

```
Pen blackPen = new Pen(Color.Black);
g.DrawLine(blackPen, 20, 30, 100, 10);
```

Like an MFC device context, a C# `Graphics` object can draw a Bezier curve, which is a curve with four "guide points." The four points determine three lines, because the last line (which would determine a quadrilateral) is never used. The curve drawn will be tangent to the first line at the location of the first point and to the third line at the location of the last point, and the position of the middle line determines the depth and inclination of the curve. The drawing in Figure 8.2 illustrates, and if `p` is an array containing the points indicated by the black dots in the picture and `g` is a `Graphics` object, then the call

```
g.DrawBezier(new Pen(Color.Red), p[0], p[1], p[2], p[3]);
```

will draw the curve.

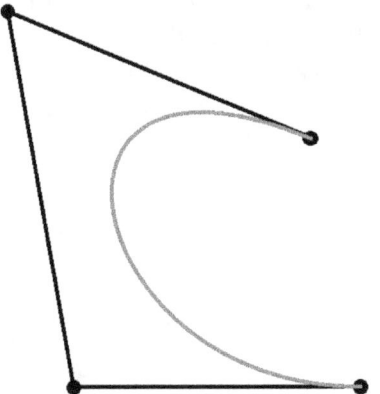

FIGURE 8.2 A Bezier curve

8.9.3 Events in C#

C# events are always implemented as delegates. This fact has the confusing effect of seeming to identify the event and the handler as the same thing. That confusion must be tolerated in the C# culture, and in the same discussion we may refer to the delegate object implementing the event as the "handler," and also to one of the methods attached to the delegate as a "handler."

Because a delegate is a directed graph of delegates in which methods are stored as pendant vertices, and because executing a delegate executes the methods by traversing the graph, we can observe two things about C# event handling. The first is that the association of multiple event handlers with an event is clearly accommodated by the design. The second is that all handlers for the same "event" are forced to conform to the interface indicated by the particular delegate type that defines the event.

The standard delegate type for event handling is `System.EventHandler`, defined as follows:

```
public delegate void EventHandler(object sender, EventArgs e);
```

We are not forced to conform to this interface, however, because we can create delegate types with any desired signature. Note that (in contrast to Java "listener" interfaces) we cannot make subtypes from `EventHandler`, because delegates do not participate in inheritance.

The accepted pattern for C# library classes which expose events in their interface is to make them available as public properties. For example, the `Timer` class in `System.Windows.Forms` has a property entitled `Tick`. A timer which has been started will call at regular intervals all the methods encapsulated in the delegate exposed by its `Tick` event. To register an interest in that event for timer `t`, an object may simply add a method which conforms to the `EventHandler` interface to `t`'s `Tick` event. The following class definition illustrates the use of a timer:

```
using System.Windows.Forms;

public class Seconds {
    int seconds, goal;
    Timer t = new Timer();
    void bump(object sender, EventArgs e) {
        seconds++;
        if (seconds == goal) t.Stop();
```

```
    }
    public void SecondCount(int goal) {
        this.goal = goal;
        seconds = 0;
        t.Interval = 1000;
        t.Tick += bump;
        t.Start();
    }
    public int Count { get { return seconds; } }
}
```

Events in the properties box of a Windows form or other user interface component are exactly what is described above. They are public properties which expose delegates. For example, the `Form` class from namespace `System.Windows.Forms` has a number of such properties, such as `Click`, `Paint`, `DoubleClick`, and `Key-Down`. When we select such a property from the *Properties* table, a combo box with a text box and a drop-down list is visible to the right of the property name. The list is usually empty, however, and what we are expected to do is to key into the text box a method which will be used as an event handler inside the `Form`-derived class. After keying in the name, pressing the *Enter* key will cause the wizard to generate an empty instance method by that name, usually conforming to the `EventHandler` interface. The wizard will also generate code inside the `InitializeComponents()` method which adds the generated method to the delegate which is the event handler for the chosen event. Multiple handlers may be established by continuing to enter new names in that same text box.

8.9.4 An Application Using Mouse Events and a Timer

Let us pick up our `GrowingDisks` project again now. When we left off we had generated a new Windows Forms project and projected a need for some event handlers, which we stubbed off with partial function declarations. Let us use the wizard to generate some event handlers for class `GrowingDisksForm`. Accordingly, go to the *Solution Explorer* window, right-click on the file name *Growing-DisksForm.cs*, and select *View Designer* from the resulting pop-up window. Now make the menu choices *View…Properties Window*, or click on the *Properties* tab. Click on the lightning bolt at the top of the properties window, and a listing will appear of all the events which can be raised by the user's interactions with the form. Find the *Paint* event and key in the name `OnPaint` in the text box to its right. This will take you out of design view and into code view with the text cursor inside the newly-generated `OnPaint()` routine. This routine deviates a little from the `EventHandler` interface in that the second argument is of the type `PaintEventArgs`, which means that the second parameter `e` can access a `Graphics` object. Key in the call

```
onPaint(e.Graphics);
```

This is the only code needed inside the body of the wizard-generated handler.

Return to the properties box of the form, and find the `Click` property. Key in `OnClick` and press return. Place in the generated code the two lines

```
MouseEventArgs me = (MouseEventArgs)e;
onClick(me.Location);
```

The cast to derived type `MouseEventArgs` is necessary, because the delegate accessed via event property `Click` is of type `EventHandler`, so that even though the second argument on the call side is of type `MouseEventArgs`, it is received by a parameter of the base type `EventArgs`. The `Location` property was needed, and it is not an attribute of objects of the `EventArgs` class.

The final version of the modified wizard-generated partial class `Growing-DisksForm` inside file *GrowingDisksForm.cs* should now look as follows:

```
public partial class GrowingDisksForm : Form
{
    public GrowingDisksForm()
    {
        InitializeComponent();
    }

    partial void onPaint(Graphics g);
    partial void onClick(Point p);

    private void OnPaint(object sender, PaintEventArgs e)
    {
        onPaint(e.Graphics);
    }

    private void OnClick(object sender, EventArgs e)
    {
        MouseEventArgs me = (MouseEventArgs)e;
        onClick(me.Location);
    }
}
```

Because of the partial method declarations, the project should still compile and run, but it does not have any more functionality than it did before.

We wish to incorporate all our application-specific functionality into a hand-coded file. That functionality is summarized as follows. When the program loads it should display only the message

```
Click anywhere.  Each mouse click will produce a growing disk
```

in the upper-left-hand corner of a white-background client area. With the user's first mouse click, the message will disappear and a painted disk with a randomly chosen interior color will appear, with center at the mouse click, and over a period of a few seconds it will grow to a maximum size. Each successive click will generate a new such disk.

For this project, we will maintain all our source code in the hand-coded file *HCGrowingDisks.cs*. To create this file, make the menu choices *Project...Add new item*, and in the resulting dialog box under *Templates* choose *Code File*. Fill in the file name *HCGrowingDisks.cs* at the bottom and click the *OK* button. The editor panel is now blank, showing an empty text file. The content we add to this file will extend namespace `GrowingDisks` by adding to it the new class `Disks` and the remainder of the class `GrowingDisksForm`.

We must now issue this warning: in a *Windows Forms* project, when the IDE is asked to edit a source file containing a class derived from class *System.Windows.Forms.Form*, it assumes the programmer desires to open the file in "design view." The editor gets confused if we open a design view for the same class using more than one source file. So instead of double-clicking on *HCGrowingDisks.cs* when it is desired to open that file via the Solution Explorer window, it will be necessary to right-click on the file name, then select *View Code* from the resulting pop-up.

Let us go over the contents of the hand-coded source file *HCGrowingDisks.cs* in segments. First comes the block of `using` directives and the reopening of namespace `GrowingDisks`.

```
using System;
using System.Drawing;
using System.Windows.Forms;
using System.Collections.Generic;

namespace GrowingDisks {
```

Next is the workhorse class, named `Disk`. Each disk is accompanied by a `ra-dius` which begins at a declared minimum value and grows as the disk ages. The `age` of the disk is a milliseconds count, and will not proceed past the value `age-WhenFullGrown`, just as `radius` will not grow past `maxRadius`. Other attributes of a `Disk` object are a `brush` for coloring its interior, the location of its `center`, a `Timer` object named `timer` which is started in order to animate the disk's growth, and a reference `parent` to the form on which the disk is to be drawn. One static random number generator `rnd` is shared by all instances of the class.

```
public class Disk {
    const int MAXRADIUS = 100, MINRADIUS = 10,
             MAXFULLGROWNAGE = 5000, MINFULLGROWNAGE = 1000,
             TICKINTERVAL = 50;
    private int radius;
    private int maxRadius;
    private Point center;
    private int age, ageWhenFullGrown;
    private Brush brush;
    private Timer timer;
    private Form parent;
    static Random rnd = new Random();
```

Instead of a constructor, we will be using the static "factory method" `random-Disk()` to create our disks.

```
public static Disk randomDisk(Point center, Form parent) {
    Disk result = new Disk();
    result.radius = MINRADIUS;
    result.maxRadius = result.radius +
        rnd.Next(MAXRADIUS - result.radius + 1);
    result.age = 0;
    result.ageWhenFullGrown = MINFULLGROWNAGE +
        rnd.Next(MAXFULLGROWNAGE-MINFULLGROWNAGE+1);
    result.center = center;
    Color randomColor =
        ColorTranslator.FromWin32(rnd.Next(0xFFFFFF));
    result.brush = new SolidBrush(randomColor);
    result.parent = parent;
    result.timer = new Timer();
    result.timer.Interval = TICKINTERVAL;
    result.timer.Tick += result.onTimer;
    result.timer.Start();
    result.draw(parent.CreateGraphics());
```

```
        return result;
    }
```

Here the timer's association with the event handler onTimer() is being set up by hand, with no help from wizards. The forms editor toolbox has a timer which can be dragged onto the form, and the wizard will generate a handler for it, but timers and their handlers do not need a visual display and there is no need to use a code generator. Certainly there is no way we could use "drag and drop" techniques to allocate and initialize timers in the way we are doing that here, because we are giving each dynamically generated disk its own timer. At the same time, we must acknowledge that a timer is a resource, and that resource should be freed when it is no longer needed. Accordingly, when a disk is "full-grown" we will stop its timer, then null out its handle so that it can be reclaimed.

The first of the instance methods of `Disk` is `ageBy()`, which increases the age of the disk by an integer `span`, then recomputes the radius to reflect the new age of the disk. Following it is the `draw()` routine, which uses different variants of the `FillEllipse()` and `DrawEllipse()` methods from those discussed above to draw the colored disk.

```
public void ageBy(int span) {
    age += span;
    radius = (int)(
        MINRADIUS + age/
            (float)ageWhenFullGrown * (maxRadius-MINRADIUS)
    );
}
public void draw(Graphics g) {
    Rectangle rect = new Rectangle(
        center.X-radius, center.Y-radius,
        2*radius, 2*radius);
    g.FillEllipse(brush, rect);
    g.DrawEllipse(new Pen(Color.Black), rect);
}
```

The `onTimer()` hand-coded event handler follows. Note that this ends class `Disk`.

```
public void onTimer(object source, EventArgs e) {
```

```
if (age < ageWhenFullGrown) ageBy(TICKINTERVAL);
else {
    timer.Stop();
    timer = null;
}
draw(parent.CreateGraphics());
}
```

Finally, comes the remainder of class `GrowingDisksForm`. Very little remains for it to do.

```
partial class GrowingDisksForm: Form {
    LinkedList<Disk> disks = new LinkedList<Disk>();
    partial void onClick(Point p) {
        Disk newDisk = Disk.randomDisk(p, this);
        disks.AddLast(newDisk);
        Refresh();
    }
    partial void onPaint(Graphics g) {
        if (disks.Count == 0) g.DrawString(
            "Click anywhere. Each mouse click will " +
            "produce a growing disk.",
            Font, Brushes.Black, 10, 10);
        else foreach (Disk d in disks) d.draw(g);
    }
}
} // End of namespace GrowingDisks.
```

The disks are kept in a `LinkedList`, and with each new mouse click the routine `onClick()` is called by the form's `Click` handler, whereupon it manufactures a new random disk and adds it to the list. The call to base class `Form`'s instance method `Refresh()` at the end of `onClick()` raises a `Paint` event. The event handler initiated by that event calls `OnPaint()`. The latter routine, every time it is invoked, checks to see if there are any disks then either invites the user to click on the client area or sequences through the linked list and asks each disk to draw itself.

With this file completed and the project compiled, the program executes as expected.

8.10   PROGRAMMER-DEFINED EVENTS

Like properties and programmer-defined subscripts, programmer-defined events in C# have their own special syntax. Recall that when a class exposes a property on the client interface, it may provide either read access, write access, or both. When an event is so exposed, it must provide the ability to add delegates to that event using the `+=` operator or to remove delegates with the `=` operator. The way such an event is defined is similar to the way a property is defined, except that instead of `get` and `set`, the event definition uses the keywords `add` and `remove`.

8.10.1 Event Syntax

The event definition is preceded by an access modifier (such as `public`), the keyword `event`, a delegate type name, and the name by which the event is to be known to clients. Inside the definition, the keyword `value` denotes the delegate object which was used as the right-hand side of the `+=` or `=` operator. Thus, a class called `Baby` might have the following event defined:

```
public event EventHandler Burp {
    add {
        burpHandler += value;
    }
    remove {
        burpHandler -= value;
    }
}
```

Inside an object with instance variable `baby`, the following code might be used to register an action to be taken in response to the event.

```
baby.Burp += delegate (object o, EventArgs e) {
    wipeMouth(baby);
    putDown(baby);
};
```

The parameters are ignored by the anonymous method, because they are not needed. A more appropriate design would be to use the `VoidFunction` delegate type defined earlier instead of `EventHandler`, in which case the anonymous method would not need a parameter list (not even a set of empty parentheses). In any case, the call by the client to the `+=` operator invokes the `add` portion of the event, whereas using `-=` would invoke `remove`.

8.10.2 A Bouncing Ball Class with a "Bounce" Event

We have used two varieties of the bouncing ball class in previous chapters, and here we will introduce another to further familiarize the reader with some of the concepts we have been discussing. In previous versions, we have incorporated no gravity at all (in the Smalltalk version) and constant gravity in the "down" direction (in the Java version). In this version, we will incorporate gravity which changes direction and strength with every bounce. Our `BouncingBall` class will be part of a library project called `OOPLS` and of a namespace by the same name.

To begin the project, use Visual Studio menu choices *File...New...Project*, and in the resulting dialog box choose the project type *Visual C#* and the template *Class Library*. Fill in the name `OOPLS` and choose *Add to Solution* from the drop-down box next to the *Solution:* label. Click on *OK*.

Now in the *Solution Explorer* panel, right click on the *OOPLS* project and select *Add...New Item....* In the *Templates* panel, click on *Code File*. Fill in the name *BouncingBall.cs* and click on *OK*. You will be confronted with a blank editor panel, into which you must enter the code for the *BouncingBall* class, the beginning portions of which appear as follows:

```csharp
using System.Drawing;
using System;

namespace OOPLS {

    public delegate void BounceHandler();

    public class BouncingBall {
        float x, y, // Pixel coordinates must accommodate a
                    // fractional part for animation.
    dx, dy, // Units are pixels per second.
    ddx, ddy; // Units are pixels per second per
            // second.
        int radius = 20;
        Rectangle rect;
        Color color;
        BounceHandler bounce;
        Random rnd = new Random();
        const int MAXSPEED = 200, MAXGRAVITY = 150;
```

Into the `OOPLS` namespace, we have now introduced two entities, both of them types. The first is the delegate type `BounceHandler`, which corresponds to parameterless `void` methods. The second is the `BouncingBall` class. Necessary attributes for the class include the current position coordinates of the center, `x` and `y`, speeds in the `x` and `y` direction `dx` and `dy`, and `x` and `y` gravity components `ddx` and `ddy`. Also necessary are the ball's `radius`, a Rectangle object `rect` within which the ball is to bounce, a `color` with which to fill the ball's representation on the screen, a `BounceHandler` delegate named `bounce`, and a random number generator. Constants `MAXSPEED` and `MAXGRAVITY` set limits on how fast the ball can move and how fast its velocity can change.

The constructor initializes `x` and `y` to positon the ball just below and to the right of the upper-left-hand corder of the window, then makes random choices for speed and gravity.

```
public BouncingBall() {
    x = y = 2*radius;
    dx = (float)rnd.NextDouble()*MAXSPEED;
    dy = (float)rnd.NextDouble()*MAXSPEED;
    ddx = MAXGRAVITY - (float)rnd.NextDouble() * 2 * MAXGRAVITY;
    ddy = MAXGRAVITY - (float)rnd.NextDouble() * 2 * MAXGRAVITY;
}
```

The `Bounce` event handler takes into account the possibility that delegate member `bounce` may be `null`.

```
public event BounceHandler Bounce {
    add {
        if (bounce == null) bounce = value;
        else bounce += value;
    }
    remove {
        if (bounce != null) bounce -= value;
    }
}
```

Three properties, `BallColor`, `Radius`, and `Rect`, are now placed on the public interface. Each is a direct representation of a corresponding instance member.

```
public Color BallColor {
    set {
        color = value;
    }
    get {
        return color;
    }
}
public int Radius {
    set {
        radius = value;
    }
```

```
    get {
        return radius;
    }
}
public Rectangle Rect {
    set {
        rect = value;
    }
    get {
        return rect;
    }
}
```

BounceX() and BounceY() are private methods which will be called by Cycle() when it is time to bounce the ball horizontally or vertically, respectively. Note that both make new random choices for the gravity variables ddx and ddy. This has the effect of changing the direction of "down" and the strength of the gravitational attraction, which makes the motion of the ball less predictable and more interesting to the user.

```
void BounceX(int newx) {
    dx = -dx;
    ddx = MAXGRAVITY -
            (float)rnd.NextDouble() * 2 * MAXGRAVITY;
    ddy = MAXGRAVITY -
            (float)rnd.NextDouble() * 2 * MAXGRAVITY;
    x = newx;
    if (bounce != null) bounce();
}


void BounceY(int newy) {
    dy = -dy;
    ddy = MAXGRAVITY -
            (float)rnd.NextDouble() * 2 * MAXGRAVITY;
    ddx = MAXGRAVITY -
            (float)rnd.NextDouble() * 2 * MAXGRAVITY;
    y = newy;
    if (bounce != null) bounce();
}
```

The Cycle() method will be called at regular intervals, the size of which is determined by a timer. In this design, the timer does not reside with the ball but with the form (to be designed presently) on which the ball will reside.

```
public void Cycle(int msecs)
{
    x += dx * msecs / 1000.0f;
    y += dy * msecs / 1000.0f;
    if (x - radius < rect.Left) BounceX(rect.Left + radius);
    if (x + radius > rect.Right) BounceX(rect.Right - radius);
    if (y - radius < rect.Top) BounceY(rect.Top + radius);
    if (y + radius > rect.Bottom)
        BounceY(rect.Bottom - radius);
    dx += ddx * msecs / 1000.0f;
    if (Math.Abs(dx) > MAXSPEED) dx = MAXSPEED*Math.Sign(dx);
    dy += ddy * msecs / 1000.0f;
    if (Math.Abs(dy) > MAXSPEED) dy = MAXSPEED*Math.Sign(dy);
}
```

The ball is able to draw itself with the following method, given a `Graphics` object `g`. Note that here the brush is not an attribute of the ball but is created and disposed of with every `Draw()` operation.

```
public void Draw(Graphics g) {
    using (Brush fillBrush = new SolidBrush(color)) {
        g.FillEllipse(fillBrush, (int)x - radius,
                                        (int)y - radius,
                      2*radius, 2*radius);
        g.DrawEllipse(Pens.Black, (int)x - radius,
                                        (int)y - radius,
                      2*radius, 2*radius);
    }
}} // End of class BouncingBall and namespace OOPLS
```

8.10.3 Reacting to the Event—A Bouncing Ball Application

A good hand-coded application to show off our bouncing ball class needs just a few event handlers. Let us begin such an application in the same way we began the `GrowingDisks` application. Section 8.9.1 summarizes that process, and the reader who is still struggling with the interface should return to that section and repeat the steps there, using the name `BouncingBall` instead of `GrowingDisks`. For the purpose of this section, we will assume the reader has already constructed a `BouncingBallClient` application containing only wizard-generated code which has been placed in files *BouncingBallForm.cs*, *BouncingBallForm. Designer.cs*, and *Program.cs*. The reader should select the *properties* tab and click on the "lightning bolt" button, then add to the form class some empty event handlers for the `Load`, `Resize`, and `Paint` events, entitled `OnLoad`, `onResize`, and `OnPaint`.

Recall that the `BouncingBall` class has no timer, and that our plan was to put the timer inside the form class. To do this, bring up *BouncingBallForm.cs* in designer mode and select the *Toolbox* tab. In the toolbox, find the timer icon, then drag it onto the form. There will now be a gray strip at the bottom of the editor pane with a clock icon, indicating the presence of a timer. The name currently assigned to it is `timer1`, but because we only have one timer, let us rename it to `timer`. Do this by right-clicking on it, selecting *Properties*, and then editing the text beside the label *Name*.

To add an empty handler for the timer, click on the timer icon, and then click on the *Properties* tab. In the properties window for the timer, click on the lightning bolt icon and you will see that the only event associated with the timer is `Tick`. To the right of that entry, key in `OnTick` and press *Enter*. The wizard-generated form class now has all the handlers it needs, but there is no functionality there. We prepare to add our own hand-coded functionality by adding partial function declarations and calls for each of the three handlers. The resulting contents of the file *BouncingBallForm.cs* are included below:

```
using System;
using System.Collections.Generic;
using System.ComponentModel;
using System.Data;
using System.Drawing;
using System.Linq;
using System.Text;
using System.Windows.Forms;

namespace BouncingBallClient
{
    public partial class BouncingBallForm : Form
    {
        public BouncingBallForm()
        {
            InitializeComponent();
        }

        partial void onLoad();
        partial void onResize();
        partial void onPaint(Graphics g);
        partial void onTick();
```

```csharp
        private void OnLoad(object sender, EventArgs e)
        {
            onLoad();
        }

        private void OnResize(object sender, EventArgs e)
        {
            onResize();
        }

        private void OnPaint(object sender, PaintEventArgs e)
        {
            onPaint(e.Graphics);
        }

        private void OnTick(object sender, EventArgs e)
        {
            onTick();
        }
    }
}
```

The reader should now add the empty hand-coded file *HCBouncingBall-Form.cs*, into which we will insert the rest of the partial class. Before we edit that file, however, there is an important connection to be made between this project and the OOPLS project.

As we edit the hand-coded file, we will declare and continually make reference to a `BouncingBall` object. Accordingly, the reader should add to the project a reference to the project containing the `BouncingBall` class, which we called OOPLS. This is accomplished by right-clicking on the `BouncingBallClient` project in the solution explorer window, selecting *Add Reference...*, clicking on the *Projects* tab, selecting OOPLS from the resulting list, and clicking the *OK* button. At this point, a reference to OOPLS.`BouncingBall` in our hand-coded file can be correctly resolved. Of course, to reference `BouncingBall` without qualification requires the `using OOPLS;` statement.

We now construct file *HCBouncingBallForm.cs*. The first segment below includes the necessary `using` statements and begins the namespace and partial class, into which are inserted the declaration of a single bouncing ball and the `onLoad()` function.

```csharp
    using OOPLS;
    using System.Drawing;
```

```
using System.Windows.Forms;

namespace BouncingBallClient {
    public partial class BouncingBallForm: Form {
        BouncingBall ball;
        partial void onLoad() {
            ball = new BouncingBall();
            ball.BallColor = Color.Green;
            ball.Rect = ClientRectangle;
            timer.Interval = 30;
            timer.Start();
        }
```

The instantiation of the object `ball` has been delayed until load time, so that the property `Rect` can be initialized with the correct value, which can at that time be obtained using the `ClientRectangle` property of the `Form` object. That assignment is repeated each time the form is resized, as indicated below. The remaining code is straightforward.

```
        partial void onResize() {
            ball.Rect = ClientRectangle;
        }
        partial void onPaint(Graphics g) {
            ball.Draw(g);
        }
        partial void onTick() {
            ball.Cycle(timer.Interval);
            Refresh();
        }
    }
}
```

The motion of the ball when we execute this application is interesting, because the "down" direction changes with every bounce. The motion is smooth, but odd and sometimes unexpected.

8.11 UNSAFE CODE

C++ is designed for speed, power, and low-level interfacing, with few concessions made for the sake of safety and security; Java is designed for understandability, safety, dependability, and maintainability. These are the two endpoints between which the design of C# was intended to fall. Some believe it errs too much on one side or the other, but it certainly seems to be a language of compromises. To answer those who criticize C++ for its lack of safety, C# provides many of the same safeguards as does Java. To answer those who desire some of the low-level, machine-oriented features of C++, the designers of C# included features which can only be used in a textual context labeled `unsafe`, features such as pointers, pointer arithmetic, and the "address of" and dereferencing operators.

Any class, struct, block, or method which is marked `unsafe` is called an *unsafe context*. In an unsafe context, the address-oriented features familiar to the C++ programmer may be used, such as the prefix `&` and `*` operators and the `->` pointer selection operator, which have the same meaning as in C++ (see Chapter 5, "Additional Concepts from the C++ Language"). There are some restrictions, however, on what a pointer is allowed to point to. A pointer may only point to a *fixed* variable, defined as a variable which has a stable address. Any variable subject to garbage collection and compaction is known as a *moveable* variable, and before we try to take its address, we must fix it using a `fixed` statement.

An example will illustrate. Following is a `shuffle` method, which attempts to place an array into random order by randomly selecting and swapping elements.

```
class Utility {
    ...
    public static void shuffle(int [] a, int n,
                               int swapCount) {
        Random rnd = new Random();
        for (int count = 1; count <= swapCount; ++count) {
            int i = rnd.Next(n), j = rnd.Next(n);
            swap(ref a[i], ref a[j]);
        }
    }
    ...
}
```

Suppose we wish to "speed up" the code by doing away with subscript range checking. Because subscripts on C# arrays are *always* checked to ensure they are in the correct range of values, we cannot use arrays and achieve our goal. So instead we try an unsafe block and a pointer, but the following attempt falls short because it tries to take the address of a reference type.

```
public unsafe static void shuffle(int [] a, int n,
                                  int swapCount) {
```

```
      Random rnd = new Random();
      int *p = a;  // Illegal.  Can't point to a reference
                   // type variable.
      for (int count = 1; count <= swapCount; ++count) {
          int i = rnd.Next(n), j = rnd.Next(n);
          swap(ref p[i], ref p[j]);
      }
  }
```

The solution is to *fix a's* address with a `fixed` statement, as follows:

```
public unsafe static void shuffle(int [] a, int n,
                                  int swapCount) {
    Random rnd = new Random();
    fixed (int *p = a) {
        for (int count = 1; count <= swapCount; ++count) {
            int i = rnd.Next(n), j = rnd.Next(n);
            swap(ref p[i], ref p[j]);
        }
    }
}
```

> **NOTE**
>
> *The fixed statement is similar to the using statement, which allocates an object for the duration of a block, and upon exit from that block the resources used by the object are freed via an implicit call on Dispose(). At the end of the block the variable goes out of scope and its space may be reclaimed. Similarly, in the above fixed block, the pointer p is only valid during the execution of the block and goes out of scope after that. While the block is executing the garbage collector may not relocate the space for a.*

There are other ways to allocate a block of memory, set a pointer to it, and use that pointer to step through it. If we wish to use stack memory, we can do so with the `stackalloc` operator, an unsafe operator which returns a pointer to typed memory. An example follows:

```
unsafe {
    void *p = stackalloc char[2000];
    ...
}
```

The example uses a *void ** pointer. Just as in C++, *void ** is compatible with all pointer types. Stack space is usually more limited than heap space, so the programmer is well advised to be careful of this facility. To obtain a really large block of space, it is usually necessary to use a moveable (heap-allocated) object in a `fixed` block (typically we would use an array whose elements are of a value type, as illustrated earlier).

Just as in C++, C# is very uncritical of `void *` casts inside unsafe blocks. For example, to set a pointer and begin to make reads and stores aligned at absolute memory addresses, the strategy outlined below works.

```
unsafe {
    void *p = (void *) 0x05F45678;
    ... // Access the block of memory beginning at address
    ... // 0x05F45678 using pointer p and offsets from it.
}
```

C# retains the C++ conventions and notations concerning subscripting of pointer variables and the use of the dereferencing operator `*`, so that `p[i]` and `*(p+i)` refer to the same object. A `void *` pointer cannot be dereferenced but can be copied to any typed pointer, which can then be dereferenced. This, of course, defeats the type structure of the language, as was intended. The situation is not as drastic as in C++, however, because in C# one cannot declare a pointer to, or obtain the address of, a reference type. Only value types can have pointers set to their variables.

8.12   FILE I/O AND SERIALIZATION

The classes for text input and output in C# are `StreamReader` and `StreamWriter`. The workhorse methods for `StreamReader` are `Read()` and `ReadLine()`, and for `StreamWriter` we make heavy use of the overloaded methods `Write()` and `WriteLine()`. All these are similar to the familiar static routines by the same names in `System.Console`, and the output routines are capable of handling any of the primitive value types, so that for example a `Dictionary<string,decimal>` object might be created and written out to disk as follows:

```
Dictionary<string, decimal> salary =
  new Dictionary<string, decimal>();
salary["Lou"] = 88578.97m;
salary["Mary"] = 55555.00m;
salary["Rhoda"] = 38000.00m;
salary["Sue-Ann"] = 65000.00m;
```

```
salary["Ted"] = 72000.00m;
salary["Murray"] = 50000.00m;
using (StreamWriter writer = new StreamWriter("salary.txt")) {
    foreach (KeyValuePair<String, decimal> p in salary)
        writer.WriteLine("{0} {1})", p.Key, p.Value);
    writer.Flush();
}
```

As implied by the above `using` statement, the `StreamWriter` class implements `IDisposable`, so that the operating system resources tied up by the `StreamWriter` object `writer` can be freed by an explicit call such as `writer.Dispose()` or by an implicit call resulting from falling out of a `using` block.

Symmetrically, we can in a separate program read the file created above back into a dictionary as follows:

```
Dictionary<string, decimal> salary =
    new Dictionary<string, decimal>();
using (StreamReader reader = new StreamReader("salary.txt")) {
    string line;
    while ((line = reader.ReadLine()) != null) {
        string[] tokens = line.Split();
        string key = tokens[0];
        string valueString = tokens[1];
        salary[key] = Decimal.Parse(valueString);
    }
}
```

As an alternative to calling constructors, the programmer could have used the static methods in class `System.IO.File` to open a `StreamReader` or a `StreamWriter`, using the calls

```
StreamReader reader = File.OpenText("salary.txt");
```

and

```
StreamWriter writer = File.CreateText("salary.txt")) {
```

The `File` class is a convenient resource for creating commonly configured text files and binary files, and for some rudimentary operating system level operations, such as file copy and move operations, testing for the existence of files, and testing and setting file attributes.

Serialization in C#, just as in Java, involves saving deep copies of in-memory objects to files in binary format. Programmer-defined serializable types should have the necessary run-time information added to them; the programmer can achieve that aim by adding the attribute decoration `[Serializable]` by itself on the line of code preceding the definition of the type. If the programmer wants to provide the details of serialization, he can have his class implement the interface `ISerializable`.

The simplest way to serialize is to use the facilities of the `BinaryFormatter` class from namespace `System.Runtime.Serialization.Formatters.Binary`. A default-constructed object of this class contains the operations `Serialize()` and `Deserialize()` which can write and read, respectively, any serializable object to or from a binary file associated with a `FileStream` object. The following code writes our dictionary object from the previous example to a binary file, destroys the access path to the dictionary object, then reads back an identical copy of the object from the file.

```
BinaryFormatter formatter = new BinaryFormatter();
using (FileStream outStream = File.OpenWrite("binary.txt")) {
    // Save an exact "deep" copy to disk.
    formatter.Serialize(outStream, salary);
}
salary = null; // Old dictionary is now inaccessible.
using (FileStream inStream = File.OpenRead("binary.txt")) {
    // Restore using the copy on disk.
    salary = (Dictionary<string, decimal>)
formatter.Deserialize(inStream);
}
```

The example works because dictionaries, like all .NET library containers, are serializable. More than one object can be serialized to the same file, but the typical pattern is to save one serializable object to one file.

8.13 SUMMARY

C# is the language which shows off to greatest advantage the Microsoft .NET application development framework, which is a multi-language framework built around a virtual machine called the Common Language Infrastructure (CLI). A large collection of libraries accompanies that framework, containing valuable reusable code, some of it specific to the *Windows* class of operating systems and some of it more generic. The designers were not content, however, to let the libraries take center stage, choosing to involve the C# language intimately with the semantic concerns of key .NET library classes. Certain aspects of C# syntax and semantics cannot be understood without any knowledge of those classes, and vice versa.

Involvement of the libraries in language semantics is not new. For example, all the object-oriented languages we have studied in this book, except C++, have used a single library class (`ProtoObject` in Squeak Smalltalk, `Object` in Java and C#) as the ultimate base class for all classes. C# has simply used this concept on a wider scale, by not only making all primitive types library types (as does Smalltalk), but also involving library classes and interfaces in the explanation of the meaning of key language concepts such as `foreach` iteration and the `using` statement.

Like Java, C# divides types into value types and reference types. Unlike Java, however, C# (a) allows programmers to define their own value types using the `struct` facility, and (b) knits all the value types into one inheritance hierarchy, giving them all the base type `ValueType`, whose base type in turn is `Object`. The primitive value types all have two names, one of which is a reserved word in the language and one of which is a library type name. Although the value types are routinely "autoboxed," as they are in Java, they are simply boxed as type `Object`, and there is not a parallel set of "wrapper classes."

As we examine C#'s design, we see a pragmatic eagerness to accumulate features. Arrays are handled similarly to the way they are handled in Java, but multidimensional arrays can be built using two orthogonally applicable principles. The Java use of "arrays of arrays" is allowed, but there is also a separate facility using comma-separated subscripts. Parameter transmission by value is the default, but reference transmission and out transmission are permitted using special notations on both the calling and the called side. Variable-sized parameter lists are accommodated with a special notation involving an array parameter preceded by the keyword `param`. Access functions, programmer-defined subscripting operations, and events all have their own notations. Programmer-defined operators and programmer-defined casts are allowed, but these features have some curious idiosyncrasies when applied to the logical operators. Simula-style coroutines are used in a limited fashion and in disguised form, for the purpose of providing a flexible way for an object to deliver up successive values for a `foreach` loop.

As in Java, the predefined cloning operation is a shallow copying operation, whereas serialization produces a deep copy. C#'s integration of cloning facilities into its class hierarchy rests, as it does in Java, on an interface, in this case named `ICloneable`, and on a protected cloning method in class `object`. That method is named `GetMemberwiseClone()`, and produces a shallow copy. `GetMemberwise-Clone()` is not linked to the `ICloneable` interface in the same way that Java's `clone()` is linked to its `Cloneable` interface, meaning that in C# any method may call `GetMemberwiseClone()` to get a shallow copy of its containing object, whether or not it implements `ICloneable`. Serializable classes are expected to implement `ISerializable`. Many library container classes are serializable, and programmer-defined types may be provided with that capability, but building it into a new class can be difficult and error-prone unless all involved types have been designed from the ground up with serialization in mind.

More so than C++, C# has minimized the effect of the operating system concept of the "file" on its source code organization. Using namespaces, partial classes, and partial methods, it is possible to divide up a program into files in a way that is largely independent of the logical organization of the program entities defined in those files. Yet C# has only one type of source file, and a C# compilation unit may not span multiple directories.

Both compile-time and run-time polymorphism are present. Polymorphism is not the default behavior for method calls however, and the keyword `virtual` is used, as in Simula and C++, to mark a method as having that behavior. Additional keywords `override` and `new` are used to propagate and to terminate polymorphic behavior, respectively, down the inheritance graph. Java-style generic classes and methods have more clout, because all types (except unsafe types) descend from `object`.

C# has re-introduced the concept of code as data, which was present in Smalltalk but previously absent from the compiled object-oriented languages. Delegate types and expression trees make it possible at run-time to manipulate certain forms of function definitions, compile them, and execute the compiled functions.

Syntactically, C# has a disturbing appearance to some because of its use of expressions which have a syntactic category but no type, and which require context-sensitive rules for correct parsing. Method groups used in delegate instantiations and lambda functions fall into this category.

The .NET collection classes provide no substantially new concepts. As in Java, hashing is integrated into the class hierarchy, with base class `object` defining the `GetHashCode()` method and with derived types having the ability to override that definition. There are two associative collections, `Dictionary<>` and `SortedDictionary<>` which store (*key*, *value*) pairs, and `HashSet<>`, a comparatively recent addition to .NET, uses hashing techniques to store sets of keys.

Event-driven windowed applications for MS Windows operating systems make heavy use of the `Form` class, which is the base class for a framed window class and also for a nestable panel class. As with *NetBeans* and MFC, there is heavy reliance on code-generating "wizards" for rapid development of such applications, but wizard-generated code is easily kept apart from hand-coded source files using partial classes and partial methods.

The "unsafe" features which C++ is known for, namely pointer data types, pointer arithmetic, and the "address" operator, are present to a limited extent in C# and form a separate set of features which are carefully "walled off" from the rest of the language. For example, pointer types do not participate in the `object` inheritance hierarchy. These features do not blend well with other features of the language, so that they must be contained in special "unsafe contexts" which are syntactically marked as such.

REVIEW QUESTIONS

1. Describe what is meant by each of the following abbreviations: CLI, CIL, JIT. Explain how they relate to the C# language.

2. Describe the .NET framework. What is a "managed class," and why are they important in the .NET framework?

3. Describe a difference in the way the iteration variable is allowed to be used in a C# `foreach` loop and the way such a variable may be used in the corresponding Java construct.

4. Describe the initialization, test, access, and increment operations as they are typically used with C# `IEnumerable<>` "enumerators." How do these differ from Java iterators?

5. What are the two types of logical "and" and "or" connectives in C#? Explain why both are included in the language.

6. Describe the difference between the interpretation of `new` when it is used to allocate a class, as opposed to its interpretation when it is used to allocate a struct. Give at least one additional meaning of the `new` keyword in C#.

7. Does C# permit uninitialized variables? Explain carefully.

8. Explain the difference between the library types associated with C# primitive types and the "wrappers" of Java.

9. Describe how value types fit into the inheritance framework of C#.

10. What is a nullable type? Why are nullable types needed? To what library generic type do the nullable types correspond?

11. Describe the two different facilities in C# for multidimensional arrays, and how they interact.

12. What is a "property"? What standard method types is it meant to replace? Explain.

13. How does a programmer create overrides for operators in the C# language? What restrictions apply?

14. How is C# compilation different from C++ and Java compilation? Describe carefully.

15. Describe the access levels `internal` and `protected internal`. Compare to Java's "friendly" access.

16. What is a static constructor? Why does a static constructor not have an access modifier?

17. How do C# destructors differ from C++ destructors? Explain.

18. Investigate whether you can use a destructor with a struct. Whether or not it is allowed, does it make sense to use destructors with structs? Explain why you do or do not think so.

19. Do C# inner classes have a "link to the outer class," like Java classes? Why do you think the language was designed this way?

20. How does C# differentiate syntactically between implementation of an interface and inheritance from a class? Do you think the syntax provides enough of a differentiation? Why or why not?

21. What is a partial class? Why do you think this kind of a structure is not allowed in Java or C++?

22. How does "autoboxing" in C# differ from the mechanism of the same name in Java? Describe the overhead involved in autoboxing an object of struct type, and in unboxing that object.

23. Namespaces are implicitly public, no matter how deeply one is nested inside another. Standard qualification of names allows us to make reference to deeply nested entities such as `System.Collections.Generic.LinkedList`. Give two forms of the `using` statement which allow us to avoid using very long qualified names, and show examples of how these forms of `using` appear in a program and how referencing of names is affected by them. What advantage does each of the two notations have over the other?

24. What kinds of entities may be referenced using the qualifier `global::`?

25. Explain what partial methods are and how they can be used.

26. Partial methods must have a void return type. Why do you think this is the case? Is this restriction absolutely necessary for language consistency?

27. Can an overridden method `f()` in a direct base class be called from within its override in the derived class? How? Given an object `obj` of the derived class type, referenced in an unrelated client class, can all the versions of the method `f()` be invoked by sending messages to casts of `obj`? On what issue does the answer to this question ride?

28. What do we mean when we say run-time polymorphism is not the default behavior in C#? What syntactic elements are used to achieve this type of polymorphism, and what precisely is the effect of using them?

29. The following example is repeated from the text...

```
public class MyIndirectBase {
    virtual public int f(int x) {
        return x;
    }
}
public class MyBase: MyIndirectBase {
    override public int f(int x) {
        return x * x;
    }
}
public class MyDerived: MyBase {
    new public int f(int x) {
        return base.f(x)*x;
    }
}
```

Given the definitions above, what is output by the following code? Explain why this happened.

```
MyIndirectBase b = new MyDerived();
Console.WriteLine(b.f(3));
```

30. What C# methods are candidates for inline translation? Is the programmer allowed to make this decision? What about methods which are to be used as event handlers? Explain your answers carefully.

31. Describe the ways in which C# generics differ from Java generics.

32. Why will the following generic class fail to compile?

```
class A<T,U,V> where T: U where U: V where V: T {
    public void anotherMethod() { }
```

```
}
```

33. Explain the way in which the `IDisposable` interface from the .NET library is integrated into the C# language.

34. Explain the way in which the `foreach` and `yield return` statements cooperate to allow one object to sequence through the contents of a container owned by another object.

35. Compare and contrast the Simula coroutine control protocol with the interaction between `foreach` and `yield return`.

36. Java's `clone()` method makes a run-time check to ensure that the class of the object to which it was sent as a message implements `cloneable`. Explain why, given that C# makes no such run-time check as a result of a similar call on `MemberwiseClone()`, it is still true that special measures must be take to give clients access to that method. What measures must be taken by the designer of a class in order to give clients access to `MemberwiseClone()`?

37. The C++ standard library uses `operator <` to define the order in some of its containers. The other relations can be automatically derived from it, for example by using `b < a` to define `a > b` and using `a < b || b < a` for "not equals." What do you think about this approach to defining order, as opposed to using an ordering interface such as `IComparable`? Which of these works better if the ordering is not required to be total? Which works best to ensure the programmer is aware that a total order is needed? Why do you think so?

38. What is a delegate? Do your best to explain. Why has this author characterized delegates as both odd and viable? Do you think there are pitfalls for the programmer built into the "oddity" of this feature? Are there software engineering principles it violates? Explain your answers.

39. Are delegates more, or less, convenient for event handling than the Java "listener list"? Why or why not? Are they more, or less, secure? Why or why not? Are they more, or less, flexible? Why or why not?

40. What is the major difference, other than syntax, between lambda functions and anonymous methods?

41. Explain the concept of captured local variables in a lambda function or anonymous method. What are the difficulties for the compiler writer attempting to implement this feature?

42. What is an expression tree? How are expression trees related to lambda functions and delegates?

43. What container in .NET corresponds to the Java `Vector<>` class?

44. How does searching an object of a .NET `LinkedList<>` type differ from searching a Java `LinkedList<>` or a C++ `list<>`? Specifically, what is returned from a `Find()` message, what can be done with it, and how does this capability differ from the capabilities of the returned value in the other two cases?

45. Normally, enumerating over a container class for objects of type `T` involves using a `foreach` statement which iterates over objects of type `T`. How do types `Dictionary<>` and `SortedDictionary<>` differ from other containers in that respect? Give an example.

46. If the developer of a Windows Forms project follows the protocol suggested in this chapter for inserting hooks into a hand-coded file, the project should compile even if we remove that hand-coded file. Why? What will happen when we execute the project compiled without that file?

47. Logically there is no difference between a file and a sequential list. If a programmer has a number of items he desires to serialize, is there an advantage in first placing them all into a `LinkedList<object>` container, then serializing the container to a file, as opposed to serializing each item into that file in turn? Explain.

EXERCISES

1. Research or speculate on the exact storage format of the `decimal` data type, and account for its usage of 128 bits. Explain (1) why it is capable of storing 28-29 decimal digits and a sign, as well as (2) how it keeps up with the placement of the decimal point.

2. Show how to construct C# code which inspects the type of a boxed object `obj`, then uses casts to send the message `a()` if the type is `A`, but message `b()` if the type is `B`. From a software engineering perspective, does this seem to be a good way to construct code? Why or why not? Can you suggest alternatives?

3. Given integers `i`, `j`, and `k`, and integer arrays `a`, `b`, `c`, and `d`, of varying types, the subscripted variables `a[i,j,k]`, `b[i,j][k]`, `c[i][j,k]`, and

`d[i][j][k]` have a similar yet different look. If all these are valid references, then the storage formats for the four different arrays will certainly be different. What is potentially the only *logical* difference in the four types associated with these arrays, and what is the major difference in the protocol for allocating these arrays?

4. In the context of the previous question, how many "logically equivalent" ways are there to declare a homogeneous `int` array with four dimensions? List them all. Can you make a conjecture about how many ways there are to declare such an array with n dimensions, for an arbitrary positive integer n? Justify your conjecture, informally.

5. Assuming homogeneity, give expressions for the sizes of the fourth and fifth dimensions of the array `a` with allocation pattern `[,][][,]`.

6. What is the value of the expression `"Aaargh! Avast ya squab!".Split()`? How would that value be different if we were to put two spaces, instead of one, after the first exclamation mark?

7. Write three different C# statements capable of producing the output

   `x is value`

   where `value` is a literal denoting the current value of variable `x`. Use the static `WriteLine()` method of class `Console` in all three cases, but (a) in the first solution use the one-parameter version of `WriteLine()`, string concatenation, and the `ToString()` method, then (b) in the second solution use the one-parameter `WriteLine()` again, but first format the string using the `Format()` method, and (c) finally in your third solution use the multiparameter version of `WriteLine()`.

8. Write a generic `RotateRight()` static method for class `Utility`, designed so that the call

   `Utility.RotateRight(`**`ref`**` x, `**`ref`**` y, `**`ref`**` z);`

   results in x receiving z's value, y receiving x's value, and z receiving y's value.

9. In question 8-16, we successfully sent a `Split()` message to a string literal. Investigate and determine which messages can be sent to an `int` literal. For example, is `6.Parse("7")` a valid expression? Why or why not, do you think? What about `6.GetHashCode()`?

10. Write a generic `Hash()` static method with a variable-sized parameter list for the `Utility` class that sums up the hash codes for multiple objects,

all passed as parameters, and returns the sum of those hash codes *modulo* *n*, where *n* is the first parameter of the `Hash()` method. Thus, `Utility.Hash(50,"Bruno",389.7,new Widget())` returns a number between 0 and 49.

11. Rewrite the following Java class in C#, so that it uses a property called `ID`, instead of "getters and setters."

    ```
    class Employee {
        int employeeID;
        public Employee(int id) { employeeID = id; }
        public int getID() { return employeeID; }
        public void setID(int id) { employeeID = id; }
    }
    ```

12. Investigate the integration of properties with other features of the language. Is a property with both `get` and `set` portions compatible with `ref` parameters in a method call? Is a property with a `set` portion compatible with `out` parameters in a method call? Construct some sample C# code illustrate how you would use this capability, whether or not it exists, and report on whether or not the code compiles.

13. Design a generic class called `Triple<>` which stores its three components, all of the type determined by the class's type parameter, using member variables `x`, `y`, and `z`, but provides access to them using an indexer. Your class should have a constructor which provides values for each of the three components, so that if `t` is defined by

    ```
    Triple<double> t =
        new Triple<double>(23.4, 98.3, -74.1) ;
    ```

    then `t[0]` will have the value 23.4, `t[1]` the value 98.3, and `t[2]` the value -74.1. An attempt to use any other index value should case an `IndexOutOfRangeException` object to be thrown.

14. Provide the `Rational` class from Section 8.2.9 with an `operator +`, an `operator -`, an `operator *`, and an `operator /`.

15. Provide the `Rational` class from Exercise 14 with an `operator ==`, an `operator !=`, an `operator <`, an `operator <=`, an `operator >`, and an `operator >=`.

16. Investigate and discuss the extent to which it is true that supplying both `operator true` and `operator false` methods to a class can be equivalent to supplying a single `operator bool` type conversion method. Why do you think both mechanisms are there?

17. Write a generic C# interface called `I3D<>` which has only one element, a three-dimensional indexer with three integer parameters. Your indexer should require read access and allow write access.

18. Write a declaration for an enumeration type called `Limits` containing a constant called `MIN` with value -2^{30} and one called `MAX` with value 2^{30}.

19. Propose an implementation strategy for delegates. How is it possible that a delegate can be a "member" of an object of its own type? How would a storage strategy be formulated to support this relationship?

20. Recalling the example at the end of Section 8.7.2, draw a tree structure to illustrate the way the delegate `a` would be stored if it were created with the following sequence:

```
VoidFunction d = dt.A;
VoidFunction c = dt.C;
d += dt.B;
d += dt.G;
VoidFunction b = new VoidFunction(d);
VoidFunction e = dt.D;
VoidFunction a = dt.E;
a += dt.F;
b += dt.H;
b += c;
e += b;
a += e;
a += dt.I;
```

21. In the previous question, what does the delegate call `a()` produce on the console?

22. In Exercise 20, add the final line of code

```
a += a;
```

Does this code compile? If so, what is produced by the call `a()` after the change has been made? Is it possible to enter an infinite loop if this kind of injudicious use is made of delegates? What algorithm do you think is used, in general, to traverse a delegate?

23. Give a C# lambda expression for the function which computes the hypotenuse of a right triangle given the lengths of the legs of the triangle, i.e., the square root of the sum of the squares of those two lengths. What is needed to "activate" the lambda function so that it can actually be called? Be specific, using code examples.

24. Write a hand-coded source file for a Windows Forms class which draws a Japanese flag. Your window should allow resizing but always maintain an 8 to 5 aspect ratio, and should consist of a white rectangle in which is centered a red disk inscribed in a square which is 3/5 the size of the window's vertical dimension.

FIGURE 8.3 The Danish Flag application

25. Write a hand-coded source file for a Windows Forms class which draws a Danish flag. Your window should allow resizing, and should at all times consist of four red rectangles, with the gaps between them forming a white Nordic Cross, as in Figure 8.3. The flag should be drawn in such a way that, if we consider the client rectangle to have the aspect ratio 27 by 19 (width by height), then the corresponding number for the width of each of the two stripes is 3, the upper-left and lower-left rectangles are each 9 by 8, and the upper-right and lower-right rectangles are each 15 by 8. For this application, when the window is resized you should not maintain the aspect ratio, but you should still keep the same relative proportions in the x and y directions.

26. Modify your program from Exercise 25 so that it responds to mouse clicks by cycling the display between various countries which use similar flags; for example, go from Denmark to Sweden, Finland, Iceland, and Norway, then back to Denmark. Display on the window's title bar the name of the country represented.

CHAPTER 9

PYTHON

Although not explicitly designed as a scripting language, Python has from the beginning incorporated an interpreted implementation and rich library resources for interfacing with operating systems. These attributes have made Python a natural candidate when a scripting language is needed, so Python is often used for scripting and tends to get classified as that type of language. This is one reason Python is sometimes overlooked as an example of language design because the structure of a scripting language is usually somewhat rudimentary. One expects that the major purpose and use of such a language should be to orchestrate a relatively small number of operating-system-level or browser-level actions and to bind that series of actions into a "program." In other words, scripting languages are viewed as "glue" for the purpose of pasting together the actions of several programs, which may have been developed in multiple languages. As design models, they have not attracted much attention. Python is far more than a scripting language, however. It is an intriguing combination of pragmatics and sophistication, with clean and elegant syntax, powerful language constructs, and abundant library resources.

NOTE *At the time of this writing, there are two active lines of development for the Python language, the 2.x line and the 3.x line. Because ultimately the plan is to move to the latter, all discussion in this chapter will use 3.x syntax.*

The reader will recognize some ideas in this language that are similar to ideas we have discussed in earlier chapters of this book, but should keep in mind that, of the languages to which we have devoted chapters in this text, only Smalltalk and C++ are older than Python. Although Python has continued to evolve, it is generally safe to say that the ideas encountered here come from independent sources, not from Java or C#.

Code samples for this chapter are located on the companion CD-ROM.

9.1 PYTHON: A HIGHLY SIMULATED OOPL WITH UNOBTRUSIVE SYNTAX

Python syntax is in some sense a "throwback" to an earlier time, when whitespace was significant and instructions often had column dependencies. Consider that in "modern" languages the only reasonable use for whitespace (when it does not occur inside comments or string literals) has been as a separator between tokens. But in the older language SNOBOL, whitespace was used to denote string concatenation, pattern concatenation, or pattern matching, depending on where it occurred. In this language, whitespace has meaning, but in a rather unique sense.

9.1.1 Indentation

Python makes whitespace "significant" in a totally different way. What its design does is to make dependencies between certain syntactic constructs a function of indentation. For example, whereas in most languages the consistent indentation of loop bodies and conditional blocks is a convention, considered to be "good citizenship" on the part of the programmer, in Python it is required because it is syntactically significant. Each statement in a sequence of statements which constitutes a loop or conditional block body, or a method definition, must be indented in precisely the same way the others at the same level are indented. Spaces or tabs or a combination of them must be used, but the sequence of tabs and space characters on the left must be exactly the same in each dependent element. Similarly, each method assigned to a class must be indented in a manner identical to the way in which the other methods are indented.

As a result of this requirement, function bodies need no bracketing syntax. A definition which implements the function $f(x, y) = xy^2 - 3x^2 + 7$, for example, might appear as follows:

```
def f(x, y):
    w = x*y*y
    z = 3*x*x
return w - z + 7
```

Note the absence of explicit delimiters to indicate where the function body begins and ends. Such delimiters are unnecessary because the three lines of the definition are indented identically.

<table>
<tr><td>

NOTE
</td><td>

The above is a simple value-returning function, and illustrates the fact that Python supports old-style procedural programming, just as does the C++ language. Like C++, then, Python is a multi-paradigm language.
</td></tr>
</table>

Often, it is a syntactic necessity when we make whitespace significant to use a *continuation character*. For example, in early versions of FORTRAN, if we wanted to make a statement span multiple lines we had to alert the compiler to this situation by placing a nonblank character in a certain column of the line being used as a continuation. In Python, the continuation character is a backslash, but we place it on the line *being continued*, and we are free to place it anywhere on that line as long as it is the last nonblank character. Python does not always need this continuation character, but we use it "when necessary" in cases where the translation might run into ambiguities without it. In what follows, we will freely use the backslash for continuations where they are needed.

9.1.2 Keyword Arguments

In compiled languages, tokenizing an identifier generally yields one of two things: (1) if the identifier is the name of a keyword, then the token representing it will be an integer code which is used by the parser to discover the structure of the language construct in which it is imbedded; (2) if the identifier is not a keyword, then it is either already in the symbol table or will be immediately entered into the symbol table, and the token sent on to the parser will be a pointer to that symbol table entry. This presents a problem in the case of keyword arguments, which appear in a function call like the following example:

```
f(y=6, x=3)
```

If `f` is the function defined in the last section, then this call is the same as `f(3, 6)`. The parameter names `x` and `y` are being used to disambiguate the call. The syntax `y=6` denotes a *keyword argument*, which has the form `parameter_name = expression`. This strategy for matching arguments to parameters is flexible and perhaps less error-prone than the usual positional correspondence, where the first argument is passed to the first parameter, the second to the second, etc. A compiler for a language like C++ might have a problem with this, because the names `x` and `y` are being used out of context. They are not keywords, so they would be looked for in the symbol table. But they would not be found there because they would only exist during the compilation of function `f`'s definition. Nor could they be installed in the symbol table, because the information needed to do that would either already have been discarded (in case f's definition has already been compiled) or would not yet have been seen. But keyword parameters make perfectly good sense in Python, where the parameter names are actually attributes of a created object, a first-class function object serving as the run-time representation of the function.

These few syntactic oddities are mentioned up front, before we start our discussion of the salient features of the language, because by these preliminary examples we hope to prepare the reader for an innovative design which started with few preconceptions, and which makes little concession to convention.

9.2 THE IDLE ENVIRONMENT AND CONSOLE I/O

All that is necessary for Python programming is the Python interpreter and libraries, a text editor, and an interactive console or console window. These, and a simple development environment called IDLE, are available as a free download from www.python.org. IDLE offers a Python-specific text editor as well as a specialized console window, which displays a line prompt (>>>) and maintains a read, evaluate, print (REP) loop. A sample session is shown below:

```
>>> 21 + 34
55
>>> from math import factorial
>>> factorial(48)
12413915592536072670862289047373375038521486354677760000000000
```

At the top of the interactive REP window there are menu choices for debugging and for opening source files for editing, and within the file windows there are menu choices for executing a file as a program. These are the major capabilities needed by the programmer.

9.2.1 Console Output

Console I/O operations are included in Python, both for the purpose of providing an elementary interactive capability and for testing. Output to the console is achieved via the `print` statement, a built-in language feature. The number of arguments to `print` is variable, and any object of any type may appear in a print list. The appearance of each object on the console is dictated by its `str` representation, so that for any object x,

```
    print(x)
```

And

```
    print(str(x))
```

should produce the same effect on the console window. All Python objects have a string representation, accessed via the `str` primitive, and programmer-defined types can override this representation.

Multiple arguments are separated in the print list by commas, and (by default) on output by spaces. Thus, if `s1` contains 'super' and `s2` contains 'man', then the output produced on the console by **print**(s1,s2) is super man.

> **NOTE** *One can avoid the space separator by using strings and concatenation, as in **print**(str(obj1)+str(obj2)), or by using the keyword argument sep=" in the last position of the print list. If it is desired to suppress the generation of a new line character, the keyword argument end=" can be used.*

9.2.2 Console Input

Input from the console is string-oriented, as in Java and C#. A parameterless `input()` call pulls in a sequence of characters, terminated by a line-feed, and the latter is not part of the input. Thus, if in response to

```
x = input()
```

the user enters the line of input

```
Fourscore and seven years ago
```

then the value returned from the call on `input()`, and therefore the value stored at `x`, is the string "Fourscore and seven years ago". Such string values must be converted into the proper types, using the `split()` behavior which strings possess (similar to that seen in the C# language), along with various parsing and value-construction capabilities possessed by the various primitive and programmer-defined types being exercised. For example, if the line of input is then the code

```
line = input()
values = line.split()
payGrade = int(values[0])
hourlyPay = float(values[1])
weeksPay = 40*hourlyPay
print("Pay grade", payGrade,
      "is associated with an hourly rate of $", hourlyPay,
      ",\nresulting in a gross income of $", weeksPay,
      "per week")
```

produces the output

```
Pay grade 8 is associated with an hourly rate of $ 17.25 ,
resulting in a gross income of $ 690.0 per week
```

Here we see illustrated the fact that the primitive types `int` and `float` (discussed immediately below) are capable of lexically analyzing a string, recognizing whether or not that string contains a proper literal representation of one of its values, and (if so) constructing and storing the value. All other primitive types possess similar abilities, and the programmer may need to provide a corresponding ability for any types he creates.

If type is unknown, the `eval` primitive (discussed in more detail later) is able to examine a string, determine whether it constitutes a valid literal in the language, and return a value of the appropriate type. Thus, in the example the sequence

```
payGrade = eval(values[0])
hourlyPay = eval(values[1])
```

correctly translates the input and would produce the same results as the corresponding statements used above.

9.3   PYTHON DATA TYPES

Just as in Smalltalk, types are attributes attached to objects, not to names. The same name (in the same scope) which had been associated with an integer at an earlier time may later be associated with a real number, a complex number, or an object of a programmer-defined type. The perceptive reader will correctly conclude, then, that there are no declarations in the language which bind variables to types. (But keep in mind that although types are not very strongly a part of the programmer's mental model when constructing correct syntax elements, they figure strongly in the semantics of a Python program.)

Another thing about Python types which minimizes their role in syntactic considerations is that not every stored value of a given primitive type will necessarily have a corresponding literal. That peculiarity of the language is somewhat of a "card trick," because other notations always exist for computing the desired stored value—notations that are very like literals. The best illustration is signed integers. The notation `-37` does not qualify as an integer literal, but instead is an expression denoting the negation of the literal `37`. (Because this expression is statically computable, the reader could justifiably argue that whether or not it is considered a literal is a moot point.) Pushing the example a little further gives us expressions like `2.0 - 3j`, which has a `complex` value but according to the language documentation is actually a statically evaluable expression, not a literal. There are `float` literals such as `2.0`, and there are `complex` literals such as `3j`, but the combination of the two is an expression to be computed, and not a "literal" in the Python sense.

The data types provided to the programmer by the Python language, and the operations accompanying them, are fairly conventional but have a few twists, as we shall see. A significant assortment of container classes is provided as built-in types rather than via a library, strings are immutable but quite sophisticated, and even the numbers have some surprises in store for us.

In Python, all types are themselves objects of type `type`, and every object can be queried as to its type using the `type()` primitive. For an object `obj`, the call `type(obj)` returns an object of type `type` which is the run-time representation of the type of `obj`.

9.3.1 Numeric Types

Python has made a rather unique choice when it comes to its implementations of numeric types. Recall that in C++ the built-in numeric types are usually native machine types and that in Smalltalk all such types are library classes which can be modified by the programmer. These choices reflect the priorities of the two languages, on the one hand a priority in favor of efficient execution and on the other hand a priority in favor of giving the programmer more flexibility. The Python built-in numeric types are a mix of software-simulated and machine types. For example, the `int` type must be software-simulated because it is indefinite-precision, meaning that the result of operations which yield `int` results is not limited in size by considerations such as machine word size but may be as large in magnitude as is necessary to store the result of an operation, as long as there is sufficient memory to store that result. On the other hand, the `float` type is a native floating point type, usually the same type into which the C++ `double` maps. Python holds to the near-universal convention that a numeric literal is stored as floating point if and only if it (a) contains a decimal point or (b) contains an exponential part. Thus, `3.145` and `3145e-3` represent the same floating point value; on the other hand, `300` is of type `int`, while `3e2` is of type `float`.

> **NOTE**
>
> *Because Python has no variable declarations, type names like float are not highly visible, but they are used to cast values to a different type and to explicitly check the type of an object, as well as to default-construct an object. For example, the expression float() evaluates to the same value as the literal 0.0.*

Python also supplies a built-in `complex` type, as noted above. Internally, a `complex` value is a pair of `float` values, called its real and imaginary parts. The literal `5j` represents a `complex` value with a real part of `0.0` and an imaginary part of `5.0`, and the expression `5+1j` evaluates to a `complex` value with a real part of `5.0` and an imaginary part of `1.0`. In any arithmetic expression, if one of the operands is `complex` then the result is `complex`. If no `complex` values are involved in a numeric computation, the result is `float` whenever any of the constituent arguments is a `float`.

The standard complement of built-in numeric operations is available, with some extras. The familiar forward slash `/` denotes exact division and always returns a `float` value when its two operands are taken from the two real types `int` and `float`. The double-slash operator `//`, if applied to a pair of `int` values, returns an `int` result. The mathematically inclined reader will be pleased to learn that the result of such an operation is a proper "quotient," even when the dividend is negative, and the result of the `%` operation is a proper "remainder." In other words, if `a` and `d` are `int` values, `q` is the result of the operation `a//d`, `r` is the result of the `a%d` operation, and `d` has a positive value, then it will always be true that `a` is equal to `d*q + r`, `0 <= r`, and `r < d`. For example, `-7//3` yields `-3` and `-7%3` yields `2`. (Reflecting the fact in mathematics that $(-7) \bmod 3$ is 2.) This is not the pattern in any of the C-derived languages, which always truncate the quotient toward zero and return negative "remainders" when the dividend is negative and the divisor positive.

Curiously, the `//` operator (called *floor division*) and the modulo operator `%` may be used in Python with `float` data. The former always returns an `int` result, but the latter may return a `float`, because in the case where one of the divisor and dividend is a noninteger the remainder may in fact have a fractional part. Using these operators on real data is hazardous and does not have the same guarantee of accuracy as the corresponding `int` operations, due to the possibility of representation errors and/or roundoff errors.

Python has included the exponentiation operator, `**`, used in FORTRAN, and extended it to include complex operations. Thus, `3**2` yields the `int` value `9`, and `2.0**3` yields the `float` value `8.0`, while `1j**2` yields the `complex` value `-1+0j`.

All Python numeric types are immutable, even those which, like `int`, may require heap space to store their values. But the following sequence is correctly coded and prints `False` on the console:

```
x = 2038209745029730427034572097520730270527305277820
y = x
x += 1
print(x == y)
```

The reason `False` is displayed is that as a result of the statement `x += 1` the heap object being referenced by `x` has changed. The statement has the same meaning as `x = x + 1`, in which a new `int` object is created on the heap having value `x + 1`, and the new association for `x` is the newly created object, whereas `y` still references the original object created by the translation and storing of the large integer literal.

9.3.2 NoneType and the Value None, and Uninitialized Variables

A number of special-purpose singleton types, i.e., types with only one possible value, are included in the language. One of these is the type `NoneType`, whose only value is denoted by the reserved word `None`. This type is available for the programmer to use for any desired purpose, and usually the fact that a variable has been given this value can be used as a notification that no useful value is available yet. In this way, it is similar to the Java value `null`, except that the latter is automatically assigned to uninitialized Java variables declared to be of class type. No such special status is afforded to `None`. (The value does have special status in other ways, however. For example, every function call returns `None` implicitly if no explicit result is returned.)

The existence of `None` and its lack of language-imposed significance with respect to uninitialized variables brings up the question of how Python approaches the issue of uninitialized variables. Interestingly, this is a nonissue, because an uninitialized variable is a nonexistent variable. A variable exists if and only if it is stored in some part of a run-time symbol table, and it will not be stored if it has not been given a value. Therefore, the relevant run-time check employed in Python when a variable's value is referenced is not a check of whether or not the variable has been given a value, but of whether or not the variable exists at all. If it does, then it will have a value. If not, an exception will be raised.

9.3.3 Sequence Types

Python employs pointer semantics, but for all the types above the aliasing issue is moot, because immutable types cannot cause the kind of trouble that we associate with aliases. In this section, we introduce a number of types, all styled *sequence* types, some of which are mutable.

In Python, a "sequence" is a collection whose elements are arranged with ordinal positions and the name of which can be subscripted (C-style) with a non-negative integer value in order to pick out individual elements. (Negative subscripts are also allowed, as we shall see shortly.) The student who has been educated in a C-derived language will immediately think of arrays, but curiously there is no "array" type in Python which is comparable to that found in those languages. (An extension module called "arrays" provides a library type similar to a C array, however, and in fact it is easy to build an array type from scratch.) Instead, there are several built-in sequence types, two of which are "mutable," i.e., which will allow their sizes to be changed or allow a different object to be placed in a given ordinal position after the sequence object is created.

The built-in `list` type is the more useful of Python's two mutable sequence types. It is comparable to the vector types in the C++ and Java libraries. Unlike those types, however, it has its own list-construction notation, namely a comma-separated list enclosed in square brackets. The entities listed between the brackets can be arbitrary expressions, whose values are determined by run-time evaluation. Such a notational entity is not called a "literal" in Python documentation, but when its elements are statically evaluable it meets the definition given in this book. Thus, `[4, 'Ralph', True]` is a literal by our definition because it is a name which fully specifies its value, but `[4+x, y / z]` is a nonliteral expression evaluating to a two-element list, provided x, y, and z have been given numeric values. `[]` denotes an empty list, the same list value returned by the call `list()` on the default constructor.

The fact that lists are mutable is illustrated by the code sequence

```
myList = [2, 3, 4]
myList.append(0)
```

```
myList[1] = 7
```

which results in `myList` having the value `[2, 7, 4, 0]`.

The string type `str` is a built-in type whose values are Unicode strings, and its literals are somewhat familiar to programmers with C experience, with some exceptions. A string literal in Python may be enclosed either in single quotes or in double quotes. Thus, the two literals `'Hello, World'` and `"Hello, World"` have the same type and the same value. Just as in C, a backslash escape character may be used to denote special characters such as tabs, new lines, etc. Two different delimiters for strings gives us more flexibility, however, because (for example) instead of the notation `"\""` one can use the more readable `'"'`, which has the same value. The backslash loses its special significance in string literals which begin with `r` or `R` (for "raw"), so that `r'\n'` is a two-character string consisting of the backslash character followed by the letter `'n'`.

Another type of string literal in Python is delimited by two identical tokens, each composed of three consecutive double-quote characters. A string so delimited allows for the inclusion of literal end-of-line characters, as follows:

```
lincolnQuote = """
    Fourscore and seven years ago, our fathers brought forth
    upon this continent a new nation, conceived in liberty and
    dedicated to the proposition that all men are created
    equal.
"""
```

The stored string includes the five end-of-line characters as well as the indicated text.

NOTE *Because the language accepts expressions as statements and does automatic storage reclamation for unnamed objects, the multiline string notation is routinely used for commenting code. The other comment notation begins with the # character and ends with an end-of-line.*

Strings in Python are immutable, so that the second statement of the code sequence

```
s = "Mandy"
s[1] = "i"  #Illegal!
```

will cause a run-time error. Strings behave like `int` values, meaning that all string operations produce newly computed string values and do not alter old string values.

NOTE *Ordinarily Python's strings are composed of a sequence of 16-bit Unicode characters. If the programmer desires 8-bit ASCII characters, the appropriate literal to use is one prefixed with the character 'b' or 'B' (for "byte"). Thus, the value named by the literal "literal" occupies fourteen bytes, whereas b"literal" occupies only seven bytes. The latter object would be referred to in Python documentation as a byte string, and the type name associated with it is bytes. Objects of type bytes are immutable.*

A very useful notation, which can be used with all sequence types, is the *slice* notation. This notation is similar to subscript notation, but denotes a subsequence rather than an individual element. The form most often used for a slice of a sequence accessible via the name `name` is `name[i:j]`. Here `i`'s value is the (zero-based) ordinal location in the sequence which marks the first element in the subsequence, and `j`'s value is the ordinal location just beyond the final element of the subsequence. For example, suppose the following string assignment has been made:

```
a = "Rumpelstiltskin"
```

Then the expression `a[0:6]` will evaluate to the string `"Rumpel"`, and `a[4:8]` will evaluate to `"elst"`.

There are some other curious and useful notations for accessing portions of a sequence. For example, to access elements of a sequence based on their distance from the end of the sequence rather than from the start, we can use negative subscripts. In the above example, the expression `a[-1]` evaluates to `"n"`, and `a[-4:-1]` evaluates to `"ski"`.

The number of elements in any sequence can be obtained using the built-in function `len`, so that if `a`'s value is as given above then `len(a)` evaluates to `15`. In the same way `len([6,x,12])` is `3`, and `len([])` is zero.

Here the value `None` has a useful meaning. If `s` is a sequence, then when in the slice notation we use `None` on the right-hand side of the colon, as in `s[i:None]`, the resulting expression denotes the remainder of the sequence from `s[i]` on. (When `i` is non-negative this is the sequence whose elements are `s[i]`, `s[i+1]`, `s[i+2]`, ..., `s[n-1]`, where `n == len(s)`.) Thus, in the above example, `a[4:None]` evaluates to 'skin'. Also, for any sequence s, whenever it is true that `j` is greater than or equal to `len(s)`, then `s[i:j]` evaluates to the remainder of the sequence from position `i` on. Finally, to obtain this same remainder the right-hand side of the colon can simply be omitted, as in `s[i:]`.

The slice notation can be used to extract a noncontiguous subsequence from a sequence value, by using a step size larger than 1. For example, `"abcdefghijklmnopqrstuvwxyz"[0:26:3]` has the value `"adgjmpsvy"`. Negative step sizes reverse order, so that `"Rover"[4::-2]` evaluates to the string `"rvR"`.

A type very closely related to `bytes` is `bytearray`, the other mutable sequence type. The fact that a `bytearray` object is mutable is illustrated by the following code sequence:

```
a = bytearray()
a[0:None] = \
    b'All these characters will be stored in a byte array.'
a[0:5] = b'T'
```

Note that in the example, it is necessary to do slice assignments. Assigning to the variable `a` would have changed its type to `bytes`. As it is, when execution of this sequence of statements is completed the value of the string stored at `a` will be the same as that indicated by the literal `b'These characters will be stored in a byte array.'`, but that value will be stored as a mutable `bytearray` object.

NOTE

Python has no type comparable to the char type in the C-derived languages. In all cases where the programmer would use that type, in Python he would use a one-character string. Such strings have no numeric value, but the built-in function ord() is supplied, which will convert a one-character string into an integer code. Conversely, the function chr() converts a numeric character code into a one-character (Unicode) string. The two functions are inverses of each other, so that chr(ord(s)) should evaluate to the same value as s, provided that value is a one-character string, and for an integer-valued quantity m the expression ord(chr(m)) should have the same value as m provided that value is a non-negative integer in the appropriate range.

The final built-in sequence type in Python is the immutable type `tuple`. A value of type `tuple` is identical (in the abstract) to a value of type `list`, meaning that it is a subscriptable, heterogeneous sequence of objects. Immutability of tuples is the central difference between the types. The fact that a tuple is immutable means that (a) the size of a tuple is fixed at creation time and may not be made larger or smaller, and that (b) the `i`-th location in a tuple must continue to be associated with the object placed there at creation time for the tuple's lifetime. If the `i`-th object is sent a message, however, it is permitted for the object to change its value (its internal state) in response to the message; it is the *identity* of the `i`-th object that cannot be allowed to change.

A `tuple` expression is very similar to a `list` expression, except that it is enclosed in parentheses rather than brackets. The assignments in the following text give tuple values to the variables `dad` and `monthLengths`.

```
dad = ("Jones", "Melvin", 46, "Male", "Married")
monthLengths = (31, 28, 31, 30, 31, 30, 31, 31, 30,
                31, 30, 31)
```

When there is no syntactic ambiguity, the parentheses around a tuple expression may be omitted. Thus, the assignment

```
dad = "Jones", "Melvin", 46, "M", "Married"
```

has the same effect as the corresponding one in the previous example.

The notation for a one-element tuple presented a syntax challenge in the design of Python, because parentheses enclosing a single expression merely indicate grouping for the purpose of controlling order of evaluation of operations within that expression. For that reason, it was decided that a one-element tuple would be represented with the enclosing parentheses notation but with a closing comma inside the parentheses. Thus, `(6)` represents the value `6`, but `(6,)` represents a one-element tuple containing only the value `6`.

There is an interesting form of assignment in Python, called *tuple assignment*, which allows the individual elements of a sequence to be assigned to corresponding variables on the left-hand side of the assignment operator. Some examples are given below:

```
(dad, mom) = ("George", "Martha")
jan, feb, mar, apr, may, jun, jul, aug, sep, oct, nov, dec = \
    31, 28, 31, 30, 31, 30, 31, 31, 30, 31, 30, 31
(pi, e) = 3.14159, 2.71828
vegetable, meat, drink, dessert = \
    [ 'carrots', 'steak', 'tea', 'pie' ]
```

This relaxed syntax presents a mental parsing challenge for the programmer who is well-versed in C-language notations. An illustration of this problem is seen in the statement

```
r = a, b = 34, 45
```

which is a valid expression in C and in C++ with a drastically different meaning in Python. In these and some other C-derived languages, the commas would be right-trivial operations (meaning the value of the expression is the value of the right-hand side) which evaluate both sides and which have lower precedence than the assignment operator. So in those languages r would receive a's value, b would receive the value 34, and the final result of the computation would be 45. But in Python the effect is quite different: a receives the value 34, b is assigned the value 45, and r is assigned the tuple value (34, 45).

There is another reason why these notations cause confusion, a reason which does not involve the precedence of operators. The comma-separated list has already been established as the means of denoting a tuple value. However, when that same notation appears on the left-hand side of an assignment operator it does not denote a tuple at all. The parser categorizes it as a "test list," a syntactic category also used to parse tuples, but does not try to construct a tuple object from it. Instead, it does a context-sensitive check to determine whether each of the notations in the list actually denotes a proper target for an assignment. If each of the left-hand notations is a valid name for a stored value, and if the right-hand side evaluates to a sequence value with the same number of elements as there are entries in the left-hand list, then all of the indicated assignments will be made.

This interpretation of assignment provides an interesting way for a function to return more than one value. As an example, consider the following function:

```
def divide(dividend, divisor):
    return dividend//divisor, dividend%divisor
```

This function returns a two-element tuple and could be called as follows:

```
quo, rem = divide(25, 7)
```

Here the result of executing the statement is to store the values 3 and 4 into the variables quo and rem, respectively.

9.3.4 String Operations

Because scripting has from Python's early days been one of the major uses of the language, and because powerful text manipulation facilities are very useful in scripting, it is natural that Python should come with some sophisticated string-manipulation capabilities. For example, the `%` operator, which denotes the modulo operation as discussed above when used with numeric data, is overloaded to also denote a formatting operation which produces a computed string. More specifically, if the left-hand operand of `%` is a string, and if this string operand contains certain formatting codes, then the result is a string incorporating a literal representation of the value of the right-hand side. For example, if the value of x is 27, then "x = %d" % x evaluates to the string "x = 27". C programmers will recognize this style of formatting, in which `%d` is replaced by a decimal integer literal equaling or approximating the value of the corresponding expression. Other codes are `%f` for decimal notation with a fractional part, `%e` for scientific notation, and `%s` for strings. These codes allow precise specification of width and of the format of decimal literals; for example, `%14.5f` specifies a field width of fourteen characters, with five decimal digits to the right of the decimal point.

More than one value can be represented in the resulting formatted string if we make the right-hand side a tuple. For example,

```
"The square root of %d is %8.5f" % (10, math.sqrt(10))
```

evaluates to the string

```
'The square root of 10 is 3.16228'
```

Here the assignment of format codes is from left to right, in order, so that `%d` is paired with 10 and `%8.5f` is paired with the square root of 10.

A similar, even seemingly redundant, feature of Python allows strings to be sent the `format` message, in response to which they will return a suitably formatted string. Here, instead of using the `%` format codes we use a specifically designed formatting language which incorporates the use of keyword arguments, multiple references to the same value, and various other mechanisms which, like the `%` format codes, define a "language within a language." The first example above can be reformulated in this way as "x = {0}".format(27) and will return exactly the same result. Another example is shown below:

```
labeling = \
    "{0} cares nothing for {1}; she only cares for {0}."
```

```
print(labeling.format("Emma", "Paul"))
```

The output to the console is:

```
Emma cares nothing for Paul; she only cares for Emma.
```

Note that the algorithm here is somewhat different from that of the `%` operation, which owes its inspiration to the C language and which is geared to the primitive types of the language. For example, if `e` is an object of some programmer-defined type, then there is no format code for `e`, whereas the expression

```
"The employee record for {0} is '{1}'.".format(e.name, e)
```

would always make sense. The reason is that the `format` behavior of `str` works by applying `str()` (here performing something like a "conversion constructor") to each of the operands in the argument list and concatenating the resulting strings with the surrounding text. Because every object has a string representation, there is no way this strategy can fail.

Late bindings mean that functionalities which usually belong to the translation phase can be freely combined in flexible ways with run-time operations. For example, the parsing and evaluation capabilities of the language can be explicitly invoked and applied to an arbitrary string at run-time. Thus, if the string `s` denotes a Python expression with a value, then `eval(s)` will evaluate to that value. Only value-returning expressions can be used, and assignment operations inside a string will cause `eval` to throw an exception. Thus, `eval("78 + 22")` evaluates to 100, `eval(' "Hello, " + "world!" ')` evaluates to "Hello, world!", and if `x` has the value 32 in the current referencing environment the expression `eval('x // 2')` evaluates to 16. A similar capability to that of `eval` is provided for strings encompassing a sequence of Python statements, in the `exec` primitive. The following example illustrates:

```
preliminaryActions = \
    'print("Have the donor bare his or her arm.")\n' + \
    'print("Prepare the site by swabbing with iodine.")'
exec(preliminaryActions)
```

The result, of course, is that the two `print` statements inside the string will execute in sequence and send the indicated text to the console.

9.3.5 Hashing and the Built-In Keyed Collections

As with Java and C#, the ability of an object to "hash itself," i.e., to produce a hash code for itself, has been built into Python. All languages which provide such a facility are faced with an inherent problem, however. The hash code for an object is derived from its value, and is used to determine its position in a hash table. Once an object has been placed into a hash table, a change in its value can make it unreachable, because its logical hash address has changed. Languages with value semantics have much less to worry about with this issue, but when a reference object is placed in a hash table there is a high likelihood that it will still be accessible via an independent access path which is not known to the routines which maintain the hash table. If after an object has been installed in the table, the program issues a value-changing message to it, its logical hash value changes. Because the hash table itself will not be informed of this message, it is unaware that the object in question now resides at the wrong location in the hash table. If the table is now searched to determine if the object is present, the search will probably fail; conversely, if the table is searched to determine whether an object is present which has the same value as that which the stored object currently has, that search will probably also fail.

Python's solution to this problem is to only allow objects of an immutable type to be used as keys in its hash table-based collections. This means we can use objects of type `int`, `float`, `complex`, `str`, `tuple`, and `bytes` as keys in a Python hash table, for example, but we cannot use objects of type `bytearray` or `list` in such a way. This policy does not totally shield the programmer from responsibility in this area, however, because the language does not incorporate a facility for checking whether or not *programmer-defined* types are immutable. Objects of a programmer-defined type can be placed into hash tables, and when this happens it is up to the programmer to define a policy that works to avoid the problems described above.

_____

NOTE *Just as with Java and C#, the ability of an object to hash itself is defined in the base class object, but the usual syntax for invoking that behavior is not object-oriented. The call to obtain the hashed value of object x is the procedural-looking hash(x). This is just syntactic sugar, though, for the call x.__hash__(). This message will cause a run-time exception if it is found that x is an object of a type known to be mutable, but if it succeeds then x is a valid candidate for acting as a key in the key-oriented messages associated with hash table types.*

Type `set` is a hash table-based set type. As such it differs radically from the C++ `set<>` class template types and the Java `TreeSet` and `TreeSet<>` types, which are binary-search-tree-based. (No binary-search-tree types are provided as built-in types in Python.) Like lists, sets have their own literal notation, which is identical to that for lists and tuples except that the bracketing symbols are the set brackets `{` and `}`. The following code sequence creates a set and dumps its contents out on the console:

```
s = set()
s.add(78)
s.add(7+2j)
s.add("Jeff")
print(s)
```

The value printed is `{(7+2j), 78, 'Jeff'}`, although the order in which the elements are listed will depend on the particular implementation of Python. No particular order is required for hash table implementations.

Objects of type `dict` are dictionaries, i.e., sets of (*key*, *value*) pairs stored in no particular order, implemented as hash tables. Notation for storing a new pair in a dictionary is identical to that used for the C++ standard library types crafted from the template `map<>`; i.e., the dictionary's name is subscripted with the *key*, and the resulting expression evaluates to the *value* half of the pair, i.e., the object corresponding to the key in the table. For example, to create the dictionary `match` and store the pairs (`"Fred"`, `"Marge"`) and (`100`, `200`) in it we can use the sequence of statements

```
match = dict()
match["Fred"] = "Marge"
match[100] = 200
```

The difference from C++, of course, is that the Python dictionary type is heterogeneous, meaning that for a given dictionary neither the key nor the value is restricted to any particular data type, provided the key is immutable.

Like sets, dictionaries have their own literal notation. The single statement

```
match = {"Fred":"Marge", 100:200}
```

accomplishes the same thing as the previous code sequence. Also, any number of keyword arguments may be added as parameters to the `dict` constructor call, as in the following example:

```
dad = dict(age=45, sex='M', spouse='Molly', first='Frederick',
    middle='Samuel', last='Boggs')
```

After the above assignment, the value of `dad["age"]`, for example, will be 45.

Because sets and dictionaries are mutable, they may not themselves be used as keys for hash tables. On the other hand, there is a built-in type named `frozenset` that is immutable and whose instances have hash values. To build a frozen set, we first build a set and then use that set as the argument to the constructor of a `frozenset`, as follows:

```
fs = frozenset({2, 3, 5, 7, 11, 13})
```

Now we can use `fs` as a key, as in...

```
s = dict()
s[fs] = "Primes under 15"
```

9.4 PYTHON SCOPES AND INFORMATION LAYERING

Python does not provide an obvious facility for information hiding. By default, if the programmer is able to construct a legitimate name (access path) for an object, and if the reference to the object is made during its lifetime, both read and write access to the object are granted. There are no private class or instance variables, and all attributes and behaviors of an object are accessible from outside that object.

Without diminishing the value of explicit mechanisms for information hiding, we should point out that the hierarchical pattern of naming in this as in any object-oriented language naturally encourages a self-imposed abstraction regimen on the part of the programmer. The "layering" effect achieved by requiring names to be composed from the "outside in" using a component-selection operator makes it quite natural for the programmer to deliberately ignore the internal details of an object if he only needs access to a specific behavior or high-level attribute of that object for his purposes. (Even so, unrestricted access to all the components of a high-level abstraction is dangerous because it invites programmers with incomplete knowledge of those components to misuse them.)

Along with hierarchical naming comes nesting of scopes. In Python, this nesting has a similar appearance to other OOPLs—a global scope incorporating all predefined identifier associations and some additional programmer-defined associations forms the outer level, then class, function, or module scope, then smaller scopes defined by inner functions or classes. Although Python takes seriously the idea of static scopes, it has no true static declarations for ordinary variables, not even in the minimalist sense of a Smalltalk declaration (variable names only, no type given). Let us examine the scope-defining constructs of the language, and we will attempt to point out the intricacies of Python's scoping mechanisms as we do so.

9.4.1 Function Definitions and Function Objects

Although more limited and more expansive scopes exist, it is useful for us to begin our discussion of Python scopes with those delimited by function definitions. A variable in Python is not bound to a scope at translation time by a specific statement designed for that purpose, so that variables are not declared in the usual sense. But practically speaking a variable is "declared" when it is first given a value. So the variables local to a function are simply those which are (a) parameters of the function, (b) targets of an assignment in the body of the function, or (c) variables which are bound in certain special-purpose control structures, such as `for`, `with`, and `except` (to be discussed later). Besides variable bindings, of course, there are bindings of names to function and class definitions, and to modules, but for now we will restrict ourselves to thinking about variable bindings.

A variable which is referenced in a function but which has no "declaration" in that function, i.e., for which no binding is made inside the function, is considered a nonlocal reference if it exists in an enclosing scope. Because function definitions can be nested inside other function definitions, the following code is sufficient to illustrate the point. In the example, a 5 is displayed on the console.

```
def doLittle():
    x = 5
    def doLess():
        print(x) # Refers to nonlocal x
    return doLess()

doLittle() # Returns None, but causes console output.
```

Curiously, as soon as we add an assignment to `x` in the inner function `doLess`, references to `x` in that function are no longer nonlocal. If during a single invocation of that function we perform the first assignment to variable x *after* the first reference is made to x, we have invalidated the program, and the interpreter will throw an exception. The following simple modification to the above example will illustrate:

```
def doLittle():
    x = 5
    def doLess():
        print(x) # Illegal.  Local variable x is used before
                 # it is "declared"
        x = 10
    return doLess()

doLittle()
```

This example raises an `UnboundLocalError` exception because there has been an attempt to print the value of local variable x in `doLess()` before such a value exists. The error goes away in the following version, however, because the reference to x in the inner block is specifically declared to be `nonlocal`.

```
def doLittle():
    x = 5
    def doLess():
        nonlocal x
        print(x)
        x = 10
    return doLess()

doLittle()
```

In the above example, the inner assignment x = 10 no longer constitutes a "declaration," because it is not the first assignment to the nonlocal variable x.

> **NOTE** *A similar declaration, global x, can be made in any scope, and specifies that x, when used in this scope, refers to a global association for the identifier x.*

Overloading of function names is not permitted in Python, partly because parameters are not declared as to type. Because no declared sequence of parameter types is available as a tool for disambiguation, a natural question to ask is whether overloading might be allowed using the number of parameters to differentiate between different functions with the same name. (But note that because

Python allows the use of default arguments that strategy would be of limited usefulness.) Let us consider what happens when we try to define multiple functions with the same name, with the following as an example:

```
def f(x): return x*x
def f(x,y): return x+y
```

Here we have attempted to overload the identifier **f** with two different function definitions, reasoning that there can be no confusion because one version of f has a single parameter and the other is a two-parameter function. But the actual effect in Python is similar to the following sequence of two assignments:

```
x = 32
x = 57.8
```

Only the second assignment "sticks," and that does not surprise us. But exactly the same mechanism is used for "executing" the two different function definition operations—the first definition installs a symbol table entry for f which is changed by the second definition; i.e., the old association for f is over-written. No syntax error is committed, and only the two-parameter form of f remains in the symbol table. The call f(8), for example, would now raise a TypeError exception, but f(3,4) would return 7.

A very useful facility is provided in Python for variable-sized parameter lists. The function designer has the choice to place an asterisk before the final parameter in the list, in which case that parameter will bind at call time to a list of the arguments which were not matched to parameters. Thus, the function definition

```
def f(x, *args):
    for a in args: print(a)
```

when called as f('a',29,(5,6)) will display

```
29
(5,6)
```

Similarly, when a parameter is prefaced by two asterisks then it will bind at call time to a dictionary of (*keyword, argument*) values. The keys in the dictionary will be strings representing the keywords used in the call which are *not* names of parameters. Thus, if the definition is

```
def g(x, **kwargs):
    for a in kwargs.keys(): print(a,"=",kwargs[a])
```

and it is called as `g(count=29,pair=(5,6), x='a')` then the output will be

```
count = 29
pair = (5,6)
```

These "catch-all" parameters must occupy the last parameter positions, and if both are used then the argument list (single-asterisk) parameter must precede the keyword-arguments (double-asterisk) parameter.

These notations can be used on the call side, as well. Thus, the code

```
fList = ['a',29,(5,6)]
f(*fList)
gDict = {'count':29,'pair':(5,6),'x':'a'}
g(**gDict)
```

would achieve similar results to the calls described above.

9.4.2 Class Definitions

Although many Python scripts are written using only procedural aspects of the language, Python is a legitimate object-oriented language, with its own approaches to the features we expect to find in such a language. A class definition defines a scope, and at the same time binds the class name to the class, which is both a type in the conventional sense and a run-time object of type `type`. The familiar example of the `Point` data type will illustrate:

```
class Point:
    def __init__(self, x=0, y=0):
        self.x = x
        self.y = y
    def norm(self):
        return (self.x**2 + self.y**2)**0.5
```

The definition as given defines class `Point` with instance variables `x` and `y`. The first parameter in each of the two instance methods, here named `self` according to the usual Python convention, refers to an instance of class `Point`. The `__init__()` method is an initialization routine similar to those often used in Smalltalk, and will automatically be called every time a `Point` object is constructed. Coding =0 after the parameter names as we did in the example guarantees that if the client code fails to supply arguments for either or both of the two parameters, a default argument of 0 will be supplied.

> **NOTE** *Because of the lack of overloading, Python classes cannot have multiple constructors. This one is able to do double duty as both a default constructor and a conversion constructor by using default arguments.*

The norm() method uses the instance variables x and y to compute the distance of the point from the origin. Access functions such as getX() and getY() could be added, but would be absurdly contrary to the spirit of this language, because x and y are public by default and there are no mechanisms for hiding them.

In the example, we see an explicit syntactic representation of what we already know to be true: The first argument in any method call, implicitly, is a reference to the object receiving the message. Here we see the parameter self being used in each method definition as an explicit representation of the parameter receiving that implicit argument.

The following code segment instantiates some Point objects and echoes their values and their norms to the console:

```
def displayDistance(pt):
    print("(", pt.x, ',', pt.y, ") is at a distance of ",
        pt.norm(), " from the origin.", sep = '')

p = Point(234, 507)
q = Point()
r = Point(y = 100, x = 50)
s = Point(x = 5)
p.x = 400
displayDistance(p)
displayDistance(q)
displayDistance(r)
displayDistance(s)
```

Note the explicit references pt.x and pt.y in the definition of the displayDistance function, and the assignment to p.x below it, illustrating the lack of information hiding. The above code produces the following output:

```
(400,507) is at a distance of 645.793310588 from the origin.
(0,0) is at a distance of 0.0 from the origin.
(50,100) is at a distance of 111.803398875 from the origin.
(5,0) is at a distance of 5.0 from the origin.
```

> **NOTE**
>
> *There is a "back door" technique which can be used to partially achieve the effect of private variables. Variables whose names begin with two underscores will have their names "mangled" during translation, so that they cannot be referenced by client code unless the client programmer knows the mangling scheme. The mangling is accomplished with a very simple string-manipulation algorithm, and the intent is clearly to accommodate the willing software engineer voluntarily complying with good practice, not to keep serious hackers at bay.*

Method references can be made in two different ways, by referencing a *method object* or a *function object*, in Python terminology. In the above example, `Point.norm` is a function object, but `p.norm` is a method object. The difference is that the method object incorporates a stored pointer to an instantiation, which it plugs into the first argument position when it is called. The function object, on the other hand, must be explicitly passed such a pointer. Thus, in the above, `Point.norm(p)` results in the same function call as `p.norm()`.

It should be pointed out here that there is very little type checking performed in Python, and it is a mistake to assume too much sophistication in the static or dynamic checking mechanisms of the language. In particular, `self` is not a keyword, and the use of the parameter name `self` as the first parameter for a method does not imply that there will be a type check which might insure that the message was delivered through the appropriate type of object. For example, if `q` is an object of a type totally unrelated to the type `Point` described above, but which has real-number attributes `x` and `y`, then the call `Point.norm(q)` succeeds and returns the distance from the origin of the point in the plane with coordinates (`q.x`, `q.y`).

Inner classes in Python are like those of C++, i.e., they are types belonging to types, as illustrated below:

```python
class Outer:
    x = 12
    class Inner:
        def __init__(self):
            self.x = 10
    def __init__(self):
        self.x = 8
```

The statements

```
outer = Outer()
inner = Outer.Inner()  #Here outer.Inner() does the same thing.
                       #This is not Java!
print(outer.x, Outer.x, inner.x)
```

create two independent objects, with three different versions of the variable x. The `print` statement displays the following output on the console:

```
8 12 10
```

A big difference in Python over the other languages we have studied is the flexibility of nesting class and function definitions. Neither of these two program organization tools has the ascendancy over the other, so that, for example, a class can be nested inside a function, inside another function, inside a class, etc., to any level and in any combination.

9.4.3 Modules

Modules come in two flavors, and are either represented by compiled object code (typically translated from a C source file) or by separate Python source files. We will restrict our discussion to the latter. The Python source file containing the entry point for execution is called the *main module,* and it is "executed" by the Python interpreter in response to an operating system-level command or a command issued to an IDE. Before this execution begins, a dictionary is created for inserting global variable associations and for resolving global references, into which is inserted the pair ("__name__", "__main__"). For this reason, a common coding convention is for every Python source file to include a code block at the very end with the following form:

```
if __name__ == "__main__":
    """
    Module test code or application main program follows.
    """
    ...
```

All the code which precedes this block is typically executed for the purpose of making name associations and initializing the module. What makes this colloquialism work is that if a module named A, say, is imported instead of being executed as a main program, the imported module hides the outer association for variable __name__ by replacing it with the inner association ("__name__", "A"), as long as the import operation is executing. Other than this, there is no difference between executing a Python source file as an application and importing that file.

There are two different syntaxes for imports. The simplest is to import the module's dictionary with a statement of the form `import module_name`. Thus, if the module resides in file *A.py* then the statement

```
import A
```

will "execute" the file and thereby create an association for the identifier A. The type associated with A is `module`, but the major attribute of that value is its dictionary, i.e., the dictionary resulting from the module-level declarations and computations made during the import. Because an import is a computation, it may result in any of the side effects which we associate with computations— screen displays, console I/O, file I/O, and even network traffic. The new association for A is made in the scope in which the `import` statement appears. If x is a variable bound in A's outer scope, then the name A.x makes sense in the importing scope after the import operation and will be resolved by doing a lookup in the dictionary which is associated with A's value, i.e., the top-level dictionary of the module A. The name of this dictionary is A.__dict__ and, in fact, at this point the name A.x is an alias for A.__dict__["x"].

NOTE

It is useful when attempting to understand the effects of import to ignore the translation aspects for the most part, because Python translation is mostly limited to tokenizing and basic static syntax checking, and to think of the interpreter as directly executing the source file. Thus, for example, we can think of a class definition inside a module as being "executed," whether it is encountered during the execution of the module or during an importation of the module by another module. The result of this "execution" is the storing of the class's name and value (a class object of type type) in the importing module's run-time dictionary (if the execution of the file is due to an import statement) or the global dictionary (if the file represents the main module). This dictionary is an object of type dict and is used for referencing operations. Importing a module simply augments the referencing environment by adding the module's name as one more entry in the appropriate dictionary.

On the other hand, we have the option of dispensing with the use of the module name A for referencing purposes, by importing with a `from` statement, as in ...

```
from A import x, y , z
```

or ...

```
from A import *
```

If we choose to use the `from` statement, then instead of adding the single identifier A to the currently active referencing environment, we add one or more of the associations which reside in A. If we use the wild-card `*`, we insert *all* of A's top-level identifier associations into the current referencing environment.

When all or part of a module is imported which has already been initialized with a previous `from` or `import` statement, the actions associated with module initialization are not repeated. The effect of the new import operation is merely to change the current referencing environment by introducing new associations into the appropriate scope.

This is an interesting mechanism, because unlike similar import facilities in other languages we have studied in this text, the effect of the import can be localized, so that it only modifies a *local* referencing environment. Although a `from` statement using the wildcard `*` placeholder can only be used at the module level, all other forms of the `from` and `import` statements have no restrictions on their placement and are subject to Python's rules of scope.

9.4.4 Decorating an Object

Python provides direct support for the "decorator" pattern, meaning that any module, function, class, or object of class type can have additional attributes and behaviors added to it dynamically. For example, the following function definition is perfectly legal, but the proper use of the function depends on a particular sequence of "decorations" being applied to the `rand()` function before its first call.

```
def rand():
    rand.seed = (rand.multiplier*rand.seed + \
                 rand.increment)%rand.modulus
    return rand.seed
```

The definition can be made workable with the following additional statements, or ones like them. (Again, the author makes no guarantees that the resulting pseudo-random number generator has the proper random properties!)

```
rand.multiplier = 26873
rand.increment = 23234
rand.modulus = 2**31-1
rand.seed = 67889
```

By using decorator attributes instead of local variables, we have now made the internals of the function accessible to client code, so that not only can the client change the seed, he can actually change the number-theoretic properties of the random number sequence. The extent to which multiple calls on `rand()` will produce a sequence of integers which appears to be random depends on the sophistication with which the client manipulates the internals of the function.

Decorator attributes are an extension to the referencing environment and are stored in the built-in `__dict__` attribute, possessed by all first-class objects, so that (for example) in the above example `rand.__dict__["seed"]` is an alias for `rand.seed`.

9.4.5 Storage Management and Dynamic Variable Deletion

As one would expect in a highly simulated language with many late bindings, Python employs dynamic storage management, including garbage collection techniques. Ordinarily garbage collection is performed incrementally using reference counts, a fact that puts a performance tax on variable assignments but obviates the need for asynchronous invocations of the compute-heavy "mark and release" garbage collection algorithm. In its place is a cycle-detection algorithm which also runs asynchronously but is more lightweight. Complicating the picture, however, is the introduction into this language of a feature that seems very C++-like at first glance, a feature which allows the destruction of the correspondence between heap objects and their access paths.

More precisely, we can say that the dynamic nature of referencing environments in Python is made complete by the fact that the programmer has the power not only to create identifier associations at arbitrary points during execution, but also to delete such associations. This facility is not to be compared with the `delete` primitive in C++, in which the programmer explicitly commands the heap to reclaim the space on the end of a pointer but retains the pointer variable. In Python, a delete operation (specified by the keyword `del`) actually removes its target from the referencing environment. This will result in a deletion of an associated object from the heap only if the removal of the variable leaves the object with no more access paths by which it may be reached.

To illustrate, if `x` and `y` are local variables, then after the statement

```
del x, y
```

any future references to those variables will be invalid, unless those variables appear as left-hand side arguments in assignments or in other types of operations that cause a new value to be associated with `x` or `y`, in which case the name will be re-inserted in the current dictionary.

This same keyword `del` is used for deletions from Python's mutable built-in container types `bytearray`, `list`, and `dict`. Each of these uses subscript notation to specify an element of the container. Subscripted variables and slices can be deleted from these types of containers with notation similar to the above. The following code illustrates:

```
myList = ["loaf of bread", "bologna", "jug of wine", "thou"]
del myList[1]
print(myList)
```

In the example, the value `['loaf of bread', 'jug of wine', 'thou']` is printed. This example is different in kind from the first, however, because after this deletion the "variable" `myList[1]` still exists. All that has changed is the contents of the container `myList`.

What Python has done is to make explicit to the programmer the fact that every formal grouping of identifier associations in the language has a run-time representation as a symbol table. Not only local associations, but class-level and module-level associations are subject to the same usage of the `del` primitive. A deletion operation occurring in a scope properly nested inside the scope of the variable being deleted is illegal because it is interpreted as an attempt to reference a local variable before it is defined.

```
def doLittle():
    x = 5
    def doLess():
        del x    # Illegal
    return doLess()
```

In the example, the statement `nonlocal x` before the deletion would make the inside reference to `x` legal and would allow the deletion.

Deletion is allowed for methods, instance variables, and class variables of a class. For example, if `C` is a class with class variable `x`, instance method `f`, and instance variable `y`, and if `cee` is an instance of `C`, the statement

```
del C.x, C.f, cee.y
```

removes all three associations from their respective dictionaries. Similar kinds of actions remove associations from module dictionaries.

9.5 SEQUENCE CONTROL IN PYTHON

Sequence control is for the most part conventional in Python, with expression-level control governed by precedence and associativity rules, with flow of control between statements dictated using specialized statement forms, and with function composition and run-time polymorphism dictating the sequence of actions due to function and method calls. Python incorporates a limited form of coroutine interaction, similar to that seen in C#. (But remember that Python predates C#.) We will start our discussion, however, with a feature similar to those we have already seen in C++, Java, and C#, a feature that is associated with error detection and recovery but in fact can also be categorized as a sequence control mechanism.

9.5.1 Exception Handling

The simplest example of exception handling in Python is a single `try` block and a single "generic" handler, as follows:

```
try:
    print("Attempting to divide by zero")
    x = 5/0
    print("Successfully divided by zero")
except:
    print("Error!")
```

Here the expression `5/0` cannot be evaluated. But, in Python, the programmer does not have to insert code to specifically test whether or not a zero divide is about to happen. The language itself will catch the error and throw a `ZeroDivisionError`.

The above example shows a generic response, meant to catch any exceptional condition. As with other languages having this feature, Python allows multiple `except` blocks targeting different exception types. The exceptional condition may be caught by the Python run-time, as in the example above, or it can be explicitly tested for by the programmer, who can then "raise" the error. The `raise` statement is provided for this purpose, and it corresponds to the `throw` statement in C++ or Java. Some examples of `raise` statements follow, with comments explaining the meaning.

```
raise RuntimeError
    # Argument is an exception type.

raise Exception("Something unusual happened")
    # Argument is an instance of an exception type.

raise
    # An exception is in the process of being handled.  Raise
    # the same exception in the immediately containing scope,
    # or in the caller.
```

All exception types must be types derived from the `BaseException` class. Correspondingly, there are multiple types of `except` blocks. Some examples of different kinds of `except` headers are listed below:

```
except Exception:      # No exception object is used.

except RuntimeError as rte:
    # The exception type is RuntimeError, and the exception
    # object is transmitted to parameter "rte".
```

The form of these two alternatives suggests that the first would be used in case the parameter of the `raise` statement is an exception type and the second in case that parameter is an *object* of an exception type. Actually, either style of `except` statement can be used, no matter how the exception was raised. If an exception object is needed and is not specified in the `raise` statement, one will be default-constructed from the exception type.

Python does not check to make sure that exception handlers are "in the right order." If a base-type exception handler appears before a derived-type handler, and if the derived type or an object of that type is raised, then the base-type handler will handle the exception. Even though the derived-type handler is unreachable code, no error will be detected.

No new scope is introduced by a `try` block or an `except` block. Any variables introduced there will be bound in the most closely enclosing scope. A `finally` block may be incorporated, which will execute every time the `try` block executes, whether or not an exception is raised. The `finally` block must follow all `except` blocks.

9.5.2 The `with` Construct

When it is desired to manage a resource in a localized way, it is often desirable to use a `with` block. For example, the following block creates a file and writes some numeric literals to it:

```
with open("file.txt",'w') as file:
    for x in range(30):
        file.write(x*5)
```

This is not as general purpose a construct as it might at first appear to be. Certainly it is true that the header does in fact accomplish the work of the assignment

```
file = open("file.txt",'w')
```

and that the file associated with variable `file` is automatically closed upon exit from the `with` block. On the other hand, there is more going on than this.

In the `with` header, the expression after the `with` keyword must be a *context manager*. Mechanically, all this means is that it must be an object with an __enter__() method and an __exit__() method, and, in fact, the `open()` primitive as used above does return such an object. In Java, this requirement could be formally met by specifying that the object should implement a certain interface. But Python performs no static checks here. The required methods are searched for and executed only when needed. Thus, when the `with` block is executed the __enter__() message is sent, and if there is no such method there will be an exception thrown. The __exit__() message will be sent upon exit from the block, whether or not the block exits normally.

9.5.3 Operator Precedence

Python documentation treats the list-formation, set-formation, and tuple-formation notations as "operators," and includes those notations in the list of most tightly binding operator symbols. This point of view is unnecessary, of course, because these special syntactic forms can never be ambiguous if they are formed properly. The reason it is there is that some operators can be applied to these container objects. For example, any two sequence objects of the same type can be concatenated with the + operator, and operator * can be used to compute a list or tuple having multiple copies of the contents of another such object. Thus, for example `2*(1,2)` is `(1,2,1,2)`.

Putting those issues aside, that leaves the component-selection operation (`.`) as the most tightly binding, a fact that should surprise no one. Subscripting and slicing operations (using the square brackets "operator") occupy the second highest precedence level.

Next come the mathematical operators. In keeping with the accepted conventions of algebra, the most tightly binding operator symbol in this classification is the `**` operation, i.e., exponentiation. Python provides right-to-left associativity for this operator. After this come the prefix unary operators `+`, `-`, and `~`, the latter being a bitwise "not" operation. As with all prefix operators, the only way to interpret associativity for these is right to left. (There are no unary "increment" or "decrement" operators, so that `--7` evaluates to `7`.) Two more levels of arithmetic operations follow, namely the multiplicative operators `*`, `/`, `//`, and `%`, followed by the additive operators, i.e., the binary `+` and `-` operators. As expected, the arithmetic operators associate left to right, as do the remaining operators in our discussion here.

The remainder of the bitwise operators follow, with the highest precedence going to the shift operators `<<` and `>>`. After these, in descending order of precedence come bitwise "and" (`&`), bitwise "exclusive or" (`^`), and bitwise "or" (`|`).

The next grouping is composed of the relational operators. These are all in one precedence group and include all tests for equality, order, and inequality. The order relations use the conventional notations, i.e., the operator symbols `<`, `>`, `<=`, and `>=`. The two equality operators are `is` and `==`, with the former comparing the identities and the second testing the values of the two operands. The operators which are the negations of these two are `is not` and `!=`, respectively.

Occupying the next three levels of precedence are the Boolean operators. In order beginning with the highest precedence, these are the unary `not`, binary `and`, and binary `or`.

Certain prefix operators, some of which might in other languages be library references, appear as built-in operators. These include `abs`, `type`, and `len`. Python documentation does not address the question of where function-call operations go in the precedence hierarchy, but pragmatically they can be viewed as sharing the same precedence as the subscripting and slicing operators.

9.5.4 Statement-Level Sequence Control

Assignment, represented by the `=` operator symbol as in C, is not considered an expression-level operation but a statement type. Thus, although an expression can be used as a statement (in the C tradition), a statement such as `a = b = c = 7` is not an expression statement but a form of the assignment statement. It has the same effect as that of a C assignment of the same form, however. Special forms of assignment exist for each of the binary operators, as in C. Thus, `x += 1` is an assignment statement, termed an *augmented* assignment statement, but the language definition specifies that unlike the statement `x = x + 1`, which has the same ultimate result, the augmented form is specifically limited to one evaluation of the name `x`.

Python provides some conventional forms of conditional execution and looping constructs, as well as some more sophisticated forms. The two-way `if` statement looks exactly as one might expect, as illustrated by the following code:

```
if baby.sex == 'F':
    baby.firstName = "Jennifer"
    baby.middleName = "Lynne"
else:
    baby.firstName = "John"
    baby.middleName = "David"
```

A one-way `if` can be formed by omitting the `else:` portion of the construct. The programmer may insert as many "else if" blocks as needed after the `if` portion, using the `elif` keyword as in the following routine:

```
def monthString(n):
    if (n == 1): return "JAN"
    elif (n == 2): return "FEB"
    elif (n == 3): return "MAR"
    elif (n == 4): return "APR"
    elif (n == 5): return "MAY"
    elif (n == 6): return "JUN"
    elif (n == 7): return "JUL"
    elif (n == 8): return "AUG"
    elif (n == 9): return "SEP"
    elif (n == 10): return "OCT"
    elif (n == 11): return "NOV"
    elif (n == 12): return "DEC"
```

Note that there is no C-style `switch` statement, so the above code cannot be improved without storing the alternatives in a tuple or list and using a subscript to fetch the needed string.

The conditional expression that is so cryptic in C-derived languages has a more straightforward syntax in Python. To illustrate, the statement

```
valu = x + y if x <= y else x - y
```

is equivalent in its effects to the sequence below.

```
if x <= y:
    valu = x + y
else:
    valu = x - y
```

The `while` statement is straightforward and is illustrated in the code below, which has as its purpose to place in variable `x` an approximation to the constant `e`.

```
x = n = 1
lastX = 0.0
while abs(x-lastX) > 1.0E-15:
    lastX = x
    n *= 2
    x = (1 + 1/n)**n
```

As in C-derived languages, there is a `break` statement which provides immediate exit from the most closely enclosing loop, and a `continue` statement which provides immediate transfer to the loop continuation test of that loop.

NOTE *Python has a "no-op" at the statement level which can be handy for inserting statement-level "stubs" to be filled in later. This is the pass statement, used below to code an empty primary alternative for an if statement.*

```
if stillLooping:
    pass
else:
    break
```

There is, as is to be expected in a language of this sort, a counter-controlled loop introduced by the keyword `for`. But it is based on a form which in previous chapters we have considered an alternative, i.e., a special case. That form is in fact quite similar to the C# `foreach` statement, and has the syntax indicated by the following example:

```
for x in ["dwight", "sandy", "melvin", "horace", "percy"]:
    print(x)
```

The example prints each of the names in the list to the console on a separate line.

The counter-controlled loop is a special case, and is constructed using *ranges*, as illustrated below:

```
for i in range(n):
    # Perform some action with the current value of i.  This
    # action will be repeated for each value of i in the set
    # {0, 1, 2, …, n-1}.
```

An important question to ask about the above code pattern, one we should always ask about loops which introduce a variable, is whether or not the scope of the variable i is restricted to the loop body. If it is, then the exit value of i will be unavailable in the following code. But in the case of Python, a statement-level control structure does not introduce a new local scope, so the variable i will belong to the scope immediately enclosing the for statement. Its value will be accessible to the code which follows the loop. So what is that value to be? Assuming the loop exited normally, and not because of a break statement, the value in i will be n-1, not n. This is because the iteration is defined by a range, not by an "initialization, test, increment" protocol.

A range is not a sequence, but an object of type range. It is a legitimate argument to the constructor of a sequence, however, so that list(range(5)) constructs the list [0,1,2,3,4]. Ranges do not have to begin with 0 or consist of consecutive integers, as the following examples show:

```
range(12,15)    # Represents the integers 12, 13, 14.
range(0,10,2)    # Represents the integers 0, 2, 4, 6, 8.
```

When stepping through a dictionary, the variable in the for header iterates through the keys. Consider the following code:

```
opposites = {"dog":"cat", "up":"down", "right":"left",
            "black":"white"}
for k in opposites: print("The opposite of", k, "is",
                            opposites[k])
```

The output from the example shows the "scrambling" effect the hash table implementation has on the order in which things are stored:

```
The opposite of right is left
The opposite of black is white
```

```
The opposite of dog is cat
The opposite of up is down
```

Any range, sequence, set, or dictionary can be used on the right-hand side of `in`, but in fact this control structure does not require any of these, specifically. What is required is an *iterator*, and in all the above examples the right-hand side was converted to an iterator by the Python run-time. But Python iterators are not of the same stripe as the iterators in C++ and Java, as we are about to see.

9.5.5 Generators, Iterators, and Comprehensions

The only things required for an object to be an iterator is that (1) it has a `__next__()` behavior which returns the next object or value in some logical sequence, and that (2) it raises the `StopIteration` exception when there is nothing left in the sequence. Range objects and containers all have `__iter__()` behaviors which return iterators based on their elements. But there is a more exotic way to create an iterator.

A function or method which possesses a `yield` statement always returns a *generator*, which is an iterator by our definition but is in fact also a coroutine based on the function's code. Python uses the coroutine interaction to produce the logical sequence of values required by an iterator. Let us use the following as an example, a function returning a generator which steps through Pythagorean triples.

```python
def pythagoreanTriples(n):
    """
        Returns an iterator which sequences through all the
        triples of integers x, y, z, where x < y < z <= n and
        x**2 + y**2 == z**2
    """
    for y in range(4,n):
        for x in range(3,y):
            for z in range(5,n+1):
                if x**2 + y**2 == z**2:
                    yield (x, y, z)
```

This generator defines an iterator object, which is controlled using the primitive `next()` and the exception handling mechanism. The following code displays all the Pythagorean triples where all three integers are no larger than 15:

```python
try:
```

```
        iter = pythagoreanTriples(15)
        while (True):
            x, y, z = next(iter)
            print(x, y, z)
    except:
        pass
```

The call `pythagoreanTriples(15)` does not execute the function in the normal sense, but rather it produces an iterator which (abstractly) is positioned at the beginning of a list of triples defined by the call. In fact, there is no such list— the iterator is simply an object whose active part is an invocation of the function, but for which execution has been suspended. With the first call on `next(iter)` (syntactic sugar for `iter.__next__()`), the invocation of the `pythagoreanTriples()` function which was constructed by the original call executes until it reaches the first `yield`, and the call returns the tuple sent back by the `yield` statement. Execution of the function is suspended, then, until the next call on `next`, at which point it commences where it left off. When a call on `next` does not lead to the execution of a `yield` statement, a `StopIteration` exception is raised. The code as given should display the following results:

```
3 4 5
6 8 10
5 12 13
9 12 15
```

NOTE *Effectively, next and yield are acting as coroutine transfers, swapping control back and forth between the iterator client and the iterator. But the above example was presented in the given form only for the purpose of giving a more precise feel to the reader for the way in which iterators work in Python. The following accomplishes the same purpose and works in precisely the same way, but is much more elegant:*

```
for x, y, z in pythagoreanTriples(15):
    print(x, y, z)
```

A *comprehension* is an expression-level concept, but we discuss it here because it is so closely related to `for` iteration. It bears a relationship to `for` statements which is similar to the relationship between the expression-level `if...else` operator and the `if...else:` statement. Comprehensions come in three flavors: `list` comprehensions, `set` comprehensions, and `dict` comprehensions.

A list comprehension is an expression whose result is a list, formed from an expression and one or more `for` clauses, each optionally followed by an `if` clause, with the whole expression enclosed in list brackets. A simple example is a list of strings containing literals which are approximations to the square roots of integers, as follows:

```
["%5.3f" % math.sqrt(x) for x in range(7)]
```

The above evaluates to

```
['0.000','1.000','1.414','1.732','2.000','2.236','2.449']
```

A `list` comprehension can be much more complex than this, as the following example illustrates:

```
listVal = [x + 2*y + 3*z
    for x in range(3)
    for y in range(3) if x+y <= 4
    for z in range(4) if x+y+z < 4]
```

Note the nesting of `for` clauses, two of which have been qualified with `if` clauses. The example is rather randomly constructed, and the result would be difficult to compute by hand. The value computed by Python is `[0,3,6,9,2,5, 8,4,7,1,4,7,3,6,5,2,5,4]`, precisely the same as that computed and stored in variable `listVal` by the code below:

```
listVal = []
for x in range(3):
    for y in range(3):
        if x+y <= 4:
            for z in range(4):
                if x+y+z < 4:
                    listVal.append(x + 2*y + 3*z)
```

Set comprehensions have nearly identical syntax, except that they are enclosed in set brackets, not square brackets. They compute sets, not lists, so that the expression

```
{x + 2*y + 3*z
    for x in range(3)
    for y in range(3) if x+y <= 4
```

```
for z in range(4) if x+y+z < 4}
```

evaluates to the set {0, 1, 2, 3, 4, 5, 6, 7, 8, 9}.

Finally, `dict` comprehensions are enclosed in set brackets and begin not with a single expression but with two expressions separated by a colon. For example, if `selectedSet` is the name of a particular set of values from the domain of some function `f`, consider the following line of code, in which `fCache` is assigned as its value a dictionary containing (`x`, `f(x)`) pairs where the `x` values are the values in `selectedSet`.

```
fCache = {x: f(x) for x in selectedSet}
```

NOTE

Computing the dict comprehension for the assignment to fCache involves evaluating f(x) for every x in the given set and storing it in a hash table using x as a key. This is a good technique if values of this form are needed many times and in random patterns, and if repeated computation of f is costly. After the hash table fCache has been constructed, the programmer can use fCache[x] instead of f(x) and obtain linear performance. This technique is best limited to discrete values of x, because roundoff error can make it unlikely one would find a particular floating-point value in a hash table.

Comprehensions mesh seamlessly with other comprehensions and with the `for` statement. Consider the following cryptic but powerful combinations:

```
for value in {f(x) for x in selectedSet}:  print(value)
[{x: y for x in selectedSet if x > 70}
    for y in [t+f(t) for t in range(5)]]
```

9.5.6 Operator Overloading

Operator overloading is accomplished in Python via a set of naming conventions for instance methods. For example, to overload the "subscript operation" in a class, we give that class instance methods entitled __getitem__() (for read access) and/or __setitem__() (for write access). An example follows, in which a class called `Orderer` is defined. An `Orderer` object is supplied a `dict` object at construction, and provides ordered read access via an integer subscript to the (*key, value*) pairs stored in that dictionary.

```
class Orderer:
    def __init__(self,d):
        self.d = d
        self.keys = list(d.keys())
        self.keys.sort()
    def __getitem__(self, i):
        return self.keys[i], self.d[self.keys[i]]
```

The following client code provides an illustration of the way this class is used:

```
d = dict()
theKeys = [8797, 7787, 3456, 9000, 2234, 1099, 7007]
theValues = ['x', 'y', 'z', 'w', 'r', 'a', 'q']
for i in range(len(theKeys)):
    k = theKeys[i]
    v = theValues[i]
    d[k] = v
od = Orderer(d)
```

After the above assignments, the (*key, value*) pairs of dictionary d are now accessible in order by key through the Orderer object od, and the mechanism the client is able to use for that purpose is an integer subscript. Thus, the expression od[0] evaluates to (1099, 'a'), and the code

```
for i in range(len(theKeys)):
    print(od[i])
```

displays the following on the console:

```
(1099, 'a')
(2234, 'r')
(3456, 'z')
(7007, 'q')
(7787, 'y')
(8797, 'x')
(9000, 'w')
```

It should be noted that proper behavior of an Orderer object as given requires that there be no more changes to the dictionary object around which it is wrapped, because the sorting of the pairs by key occurs at instantiation.

TABLE 9.1 Examples of operators and their associated instance methods

Operator	Instance Method
+	__add__
-	__sub__
*	__mul__
/	__truediv__
//	__floordiv__
**	__pow__
%	__mod__
<	__lt__
>	__gt__
<=	__le__
>=	__ge__

Some examples of other overloadable operators and their corresponding instance method names are given in Table 9.1. These are just a few of the overloadable operators, however. For example, the meanings of built-in prefix operators such as `len()` and `repr()` can also be overloaded, and it is possible to make objects of a given type "callable" by defining the instance method `__call__()`.

9.6 INHERITANCE AND POLYMORPHISM

Inheritance is strictly public, and is accomplished syntactically by placing the base-class name in parentheses after the derived-class name in the class definition. The following code illustrates the syntax:

```
class Disk(Point):
    def __init__(self, x = 0, y = 0, radius = 1):
        Point.__init__(self, x, y)
        self.radius = radius
    def area(self):
        return 3.1416*self.radius**2
```

Note the explicit form of the call on the base-class `__init__()` method here. We may view these initialization routines as "constructors," and this is the same sense in which the term is used in the other languages we have studied—i.e., constructors are initialization routines which are called incidental to instance creation.

NOTE

An alternative to the syntax Point.__init__(self, x, y) is the more abstract super(Disk,self).__init__(x, y). The latter syntax relieves the programmer of the burden of tracking down and hard coding the name of the base class and makes it unnecessary to change this line of code if the base class changes. However, it will not call multiple base-class constructors in the case of multiple inheritance (see below).

As in Smalltalk, run-time polymorphism is the default and is the only option, because there are no static declarations which bind identifiers to types. A message is always delivered to a specific object, and if that object has a method which can respond to the message that method will be called. If it has no such method, then its superclasses are searched for an appropriate method, in a particular order. But this order may not be obvious, as we shall see immediately.

Multiple inheritance is allowed in Python, and has the expected attendant complications. References to instance variables or instance methods may seem to be ambiguous and need a nontrivial resolution procedure. In general, whether or not those references can be satisfactorily resolved depends on the requirements placed by the language designers on the properties of the resolution results. For a given example, the scope in which a reference is resolved will depend on both the particular inheritance pattern and the search algorithm. Python uses the C3 algorithm ([Barrett96]) to attempt to resolve class-level identifier references in super-classes when no definition exists in the object where execution currently resides. The algorithm cannot always resolve ambiguities, and hence some attempts to derive classes from multiple bases may throw the `TypeError` exception.

The reason inheritance sometimes fails in Python is that more recent versions of the language have recognized the need for the search order to be *monotonic*. A monotonic search order is a topological sort of the directed graph determined by the inheritance patterns involved. But not every directed graph can be topologically sorted; more precisely stated, not every directed graph defined by the constraints on search order dictated by the Python language can be topologically sorted. The simplest example where no monotonic search order exists is one like that given in [Barrett96]. Their example was given in the Dylan language, but the class relationships can be stated nicely in Python as follows:

```
class grid_layout: pass
class horizontal_grid(grid_layout): pass
```

```
class vertical_grid(grid_layout): pass
class hv_grid(horizontal_grid, vertical_grid): pass
class vh_grid(vertical_grid, horizontal_grid): pass
class confused_grid(hv_grid, vh_grid): pass
```

The search order established for method resolution in Python is guided by two simple rules: (1) proceed backwards along the inheritance hierarchy, and (2) when multiple inheritance is involved, proceed from left to right in the coded list of base classes. Because of rule 2, in the example above, a search for an attribute or behavior which began because of a reference in vh_grid would search for a resolution in vertical_grid before it searched in horizontal_grid. Similarly, a search beginning in hv_grid would search in horizontal_grid before vertical_grid. For this reason, the last line of code raises a TypeError exception.

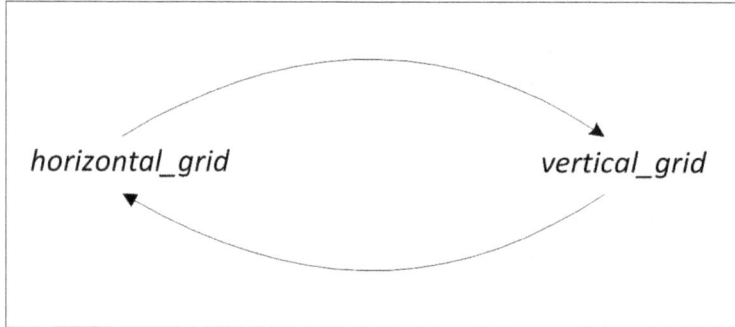

FIGURE 9.1 A cycle in the search dependencies graph

NOTE

It is only the last line of the code above that produces an error. The directed graph defined by the first four lines can easily be linearized. But once we add the last line, we introduce the two-cycle indicated in Figure 9.1. No directed graph containing a cycle can be topologically sorted, so no monotonic method resolution order exists for class confused_class.

In Python 2.x, there are no implicit type relationships. Python 3.x changes this by providing an ultimate base class from which all types derive, so that all programmer-defined types which do not explicitly give a base type are implicitly subtypes of object.

9.7   FUNCTIONAL FEATURES OF PYTHON

Python functions are first-class objects, with attributes, so that once a function has been defined the name of the function becomes a "variable" whose value is an object of type *function*. That value may be copied into another variable, used as an argument in a function call, or returned as the value of another function.

For example, the following function takes as parameters a one-parameter function *f* and two numbers *a* and *b*. It returns as a result another one-parameter function—one which calls the other using the argument passed to it, multiples the result by *a*, and adds *b*.

```
def combine(f, a, b):
    def g(x):
        return a*f(x) + b
    return g
```

Now after

```
import math
```

the assignment

```
h = combine(math.sqrt,5,10)
```

places in variable *h* the function $h(x) = 5\sqrt{x} + 10$.

For situations in which an unnamed function must be created on the spot, we can use the `lambda` operation. Thus, the call

```
k = combine(lambda x: x**2, 4, 3)
```

places in variable *k* the function $k(x) = 4x^2 + 3$.

It is important here to distinguish the difference between the lambda expressions of C# and the `lambda` operation in Python. In the former, a lambda expression is not run-time evaluable but is only a syntactic construct used to create a delegate object. Here the `lambda` operation actually computes and returns, at run-time, an object of type `function`. Thus, the two constructs

```
def g(x,y):
    return x**3*y**2 - 5*x + 7
```

And

```
g = lambda x, y: x**3*y**2 - 5*x + 7
```

have very similar effects. The type of `g` is `function` in both cases, but in the first case the value assigned to `g.__name__` is `'g'` while in the second case that value is `'<lambda>'`.

9.8   THE EXTERNAL ENVIRONMENT

Python's libraries constitute a rich collection of facilities for dealing with the external environment that extends beyond basic OS facilities and file systems to internet communications and multimedia. For our immediate purposes, we will restrict ourselves to (1) facilities for opening, processing, and closing a text file, and (2) facilities in support of persistence of objects.

9.8.1 Files and I/O

The `open()` primitive of the language, like many of its library-defined capabilities, is detailed and customizable. Much of its functionality matches corresponding options available in C-library routines. We will cover only enough to provide an introduction and to allow us to write some interesting programs.

The object returned by the simplest use of the globally accessible `open()` primitive is of type `io.TextIOWrapper`, a subclass of `io.TextIOBase`. After

```
textFile = open("existingFile.txt")
```

the `TextIOWrapper` object `textFile` can be used to read text data from the indicated file. It will do so using string-oriented input methods such as `readline()`, `readlines()`, and `read()`, two of which return strings and one of which returns a list of strings.

The method `readline()` reads from the current position of the file pointer through the end of the line. Thus, the effect of a sequence of `readline()` messages will be to return a corresponding sequence of strings, those being the individual lines in the file. The action of `readline()` is therefore somewhat like the action of the `input()` primitive, except that the string returned by `readline()` includes the trailing end-of-line character or characters, if such exists. The empty string `""` will only be returned by `readline()` when the data in the file has been exhausted, because an empty line shows up as `"\n"`.

The `read()` and `readlines()` methods are similar in that both read from the current file pointer to the end of file. The difference is that the former reads the entire file into a single string and the latter reads into a list of strings. Thus, if `textFile` has been opened as in the above example, then the statement

```
lines = textFile.readlines()
```

is equivalent to the following code sequence:

```
lines = []
line = textFile.readline()
while line != "":
    lines.append(line)
    line = textFile.readline()
```

There is no input method associated with text files which breaks out "tokens" from a line. To accomplish that objective the programmer must send the `split()` message to each of the individual lines. The default behavior of `split()` is to treat all white space as delimiters, so that if the content of `line` is "The quick brown fox\n", then `line.split()` returns the list ["The", "quick", "brown", "fox"].

NOTE *Providing a delimiter string operand to split() will modify this behavior. For example, if labelAndList contains the string*

```
"Items to be sold:  clothing, linens, furniture, jewelry"
```

then the evaluation of the expression `labelAndList.split(":  ")` causes all the occurrences of the two-character string ": " to be found, then uses those as delimiters. Thus, the expression evaluates to the two-element list consisting of the string "Items to be sold" and the string "clothing, linens, furniture, jewelry". A second operand may also be provided: an integer giving the maximum number of times to use the delimiter. Thus, `labelAndList.split(" ",3)` returns the value

```
['Items','to','be',
 'sold: clothing, linens, furniture, jewelry'].
```

To write to a text file, again all messages must be string-oriented. After the initial open-for-output command

```
outFile = open("newFile.txt", 'w');
```

the messages `write()` and `writelines()` can be sent, the former simply sending a string to the output file and the latter sending each of a list of strings. In either case, no whitespace character is sent unless it is embedded in the string. Thus,

```
outFile.writelines( ["The","quick\n","brown","fox\n"] )
outFile.close()
```

produces the output file with contents as follows:

```
Thequick
brownfox
```

9.8.2 Python Features for Persistence—pickle and shelve

The import command `import pickle` brings into the program's namespace Python's `pickle` package for saving and restoring persistent objects to and from binary files. In the simplest case, the use of this package is quite straightforward. For example, suppose we have made the binding...

```
sandwich = ['bread', 'mayo', 'cheese', 'ham', 'lettuce']
```

and we wish to save this object to a binary file named *lunch.bin*. Then we must "pickle" the object by (a) creating the binary file with an `open()` statement, (b) dumping the object to the file using `pickle.dump()`, and (c) closing the file. The following sequence accomplishes these actions:

```
outfile = open('lunch.bin','wb')
pickle.dump(sandwich, outfile)
outfile.close()
```

As a result of executing this code, a copy of the `list` object stored at `sandwich` is saved (in binary form) to file *lunch.bin*. To gain access to the copy we must (a) open another file object based on the same file name *lunch.bin*, this time for binary read access, (b) load the object from the file using `pickle.load()`, and (c) close the file. Here is the code...

```
infile = open('lunch.bin','rb')
```

```
sandwichCopy = pickle.load(infile)
infile.close()
```

Now the variable `sandwichCopy` contains a reference to an identical deep copy of the list associated with `sandwich`.

Most library types create serializable objects (but there are some exceptions, notably `_io.TextIOWrapper`). Any programmer-defined type whose members are serializable should be serializable with `pickle`. More than one object can be pickled in the same file, and all such objects will load in the same order they were saved. If, on the other hand, it is desired to have keyed access to multiple objects in the file using a string-valued key, then we can use the `shelve` module.

As we did with the `pickle` module, we will cover only the basic functionality of `shelve`. After the initial `import shelve` statement, we may open a "shelf" with the class method `open()`. An example follows:

```
zoo = shelve.open('dolittle.bin')
```

If the file did not previously exist, it will be created. If it existed before it must be a properly formed "shelf" or an error condition will be raised. If the open went smoothly we can now "write" (*key, value*) pairs to the file by subscripting `zoo` and making assignments. The keys must always be strings, but the value stored may be any Python object. Here are some examples:

```
zoo["mammals"] = ["lion", "giraffe", "tapir", "zebra"]
zoo["reptiles"] = ["python", "crocodile", "sea turtle"]
zoo["other"] = ["tarantula", "newt", "eagle"]
```

Here we are treating `zoo` as if it were a `dict` object, although technically its type is `shelve.DbfilenameShelf`, and we are safe in doing so because the latter type recognizes and appropriately responds to all the messages recognized by `dict`. We can persistently save the contents of `zoo` to the file *dolittle.bin* by calling its `close()` method:

```
zoo.close()
```

Now any program can have access to this "dictionary" via the stored file. Besides `close()`, there is another important message which can be used to save `zoo`'s contents, namely

```
zoo.sync()
```

The `sync()` message should be sent periodically when a shelf is open for extended processing because if the value associated with a key is sent a message which causes it to change, then the wrong value may ultimately be saved to the file.

The same call which created the file can be used to reopen it:

```
zooToo = shelve.open('dolittle.bin')
```

The messages `keys()` and `values()` work here exactly as they do for a `dict` object. For example, executing the following code...

```
for key in zooToo.keys():
    print('The',key,'in the zoo are:\n  ',zooToo[key])
```

produces the output...

```
The mammals in the zoo are:
  ['lion', 'giraffe', 'tapir', 'zebra']
The other in the zoo are:
  ['tarantula', 'newt', 'eagle']
The reptiles in the zoo are:
  ['python', 'crocodile', 'sea turtle']
```

The restriction on keys is the same as that with a `dict` object: they must be immutable. No restrictions are placed on the value associated with each key. When the `close()` message is sent, a deep copy is made of each value, and that copy is saved in the binary file. The keys are also saved, of course, and the correspondence between the key and its associated value is encoded in the file. If it is desired to keep the file synchronized with its associated (*key, value*) pairs in memory, the file can be opened with the keyword argument `writeback = true`. If this is done, then periodic `sync()` messages may be sent, in response to which the contents of the particular values will be synchronized with deep copies in the file. This synchronizing will not close the file, and additional changes can be made before closing the file.

9.9   THE TKINTER LIBRARY AND GUI APPLICATIONS

Python was not created with event-driven programming in mind. Its functional features do, however, make it easy to associate events with their handlers, and there are a number of GUI packages available for use with Python. The most accessible and portable of these is actually distributed and installed with Python. It is `tkinter`, a package adapted from a product originally designed for the `Tcl` scripting language. As a matter of fact, `tkinter` has been implemented by imbedding in Python a `Tcl` interpreter and using that interpreter to execute the `tkinter` commands.

9.9.1 Creating a Root Window in tkinter

After the obligatory

```
from tkinter import *
```

we can instantiate a root window and start its message loop using the sequence

```
root = Tk()
root.mainloop()
```

This root window has little functionality except to allow the user to move, resize, minimize, maximize, and destroy it. Figure 9.2 is a depiction of the root window.

FIGURE 9.2 A root window

9.9.2 Adding a Button and a Label

Here we augment the root window created in the previous section by adding a `Label` object, a `Button` object, and an event handler for the button. The complete program appears as follows:

```
from tkinter import *
root = Tk()

label = Label(root, text = '')

def respond():
    if label['text'] == '': label['text'] = "Not so hard!"
    else: label['text'] = ''

button = Button(root, text = "Push me!", command = respond)

button.pack()
label.pack()
root.mainloop()
```

Here the `text` parameter to the `Button` constructor receives a string to be used as a label, and the `command` parameter receives a function object capable of responding to the button push event. Notice that each of the `Button` constructor and the `Label` constructor has a first parameter which identifies the parent window in which it will appear, which we have called `root` in the example. Running this program now produces a window which appears at first to contain only the button object with the text `Push Me!` displayed on the face of the button. When the user clicks on the button the label field, which before was invisible, now displays the message `Not so hard!` The result is shown in Figure 9.3.

FIGURE 9.3 A window with a button and a label

The programmer should be aware that sending the `mainloop()` message to the root window as we have done it here causes the main thread to enter the window's message loop, and that thread will not return from executing the loop until the window is destroyed. For this reason, the `mainloop()` message was not sent until all the window's components had been put in place and initialized.

One of the key ingredients to the process of window initialization is the "packing" of components. Even though the constructors for the label and button objects have already fired and have identified those two objects as being components of the `root` window, they must be made visible in the window by sending them a `pack()` or `grid()` message. In the example, the two messages `label.pack()` and `button.pack()` are used to place the two components in the window in order. The `grid()` message provides more control, but we will leave it for the reader to investigate that particular way of laying out a display.

9.9.3 Threads and Windows

The following class encapsulates the functionality of the previous section in a more elegant fashion, and will allow us to do some experimentation:

```python
from tkinter import *

class TouchyButton:

    def __init__(self):
        self.root = Tk()
        self.label = Label(self.root, text = '')
        self.button = Button(self.root, text = "Push me!",
                            command = self.respondToPush)
        self.button.pack()
        self.label.pack()
        self.root.mainloop()

    def respondToPush(self):
        if self.label['text'] == '':
            self.label['text'] = "Not so hard!"
        else: self.label['text'] = ''
```

Now the Python constructor call `TouchyButton()` will bring up a window like the above, and multiple calls will bring up identical copies of the window. But the two-statement sequence below may not behave in the way the reader thinks.

```python
TouchyButton()
TouchyButton()
```

Here, what actually happens is that the first window appears on the screen and behaves in the manner expected, but the second does not make its appearance until after the first has been closed. This is because the `mainloop()` call is executed inside the current thread, and the first constructor call does not return until the message loop for the corresponding window has exited.

Now consider the following class, which is similar to the previous one but encapsulates only a single button, which when pushed causes a `TouchyButton` object to be created.

```
class TouchyButtonMaker:

    def __init__(self):
        self.root = Tk()
        self.button = Button(self.root, text = "Touch me!",
                        command = self.respondToTouch)
        self.button.pack()
        self.root.mainloop()

    def respondToTouch(self):
        TouchyButton()
```

Here the construction of the `TouchyButton` object is made to occur as a response to a button push event. This is quite different from simply calling the `TouchyButton()` constructor twice in sequence, because event handlers in Python execute in separate threads. This means that multiple pushes of the "Touch me!" button will create multiple `TouchyButton` objects, all visible and active at the same time. Each such copy corresponds to a separate invocation of the `respondToTouch()` method, each of which has its own stack and is waiting for the window to close so that the top stack frame can be popped and the thread can die.

9.9.4 "Modal" Windows

The technique illustrated in the previous section is a common way of creating "dialog boxes" in `tkinter`. But notice that all our `TouchyButton` "dialogs" were modeless, meaning that when they came up they did not block the receipt of messages by the "parent" `TouchyButtonMaker` window. Turning the `Touchy-Button` class into a class which spawns a modal window is simple, and can be done as follows:

a. Make `TouchyButton` a derived class of `Toplevel`.

b. Have the `__init__` function (constructor) in `TouchyButton` call its base class constructor.

c. Remove the `self.root` member and the assignment to it. The class is now its own root window.

d. Call `self.grab_set()` in the constructor in order to route all mouse and keyboard events to this window.

e. Replace `self.root.mainloop()` with `self.wait_window(self)`.

f. Replace `self.root` with `self` wherever it occurs in the remainder of the class.

Once this is done, the same `TouchyButtonMaker` client class which was used in the last section should cause the `TouchyButton` dialog to be invoked in a modal fashion.

9.9.5 Widgets and Events in tkinter

Besides labels and buttons, many other light-weight screen artifacts, called "widgets," can be created and placed in a `tkinter` top-level window, including the familiar components we have seen in previous chapters—list boxes, scroll bars, text boxes, etc. In particular, instances of the `Frame` class can be crafted which have the "nestability" quality we saw in Smalltalk's `Morph` class, Java's `JPanel` class, and the `Form` class of Windows Forms: frames can be nested inside other frames using a layout manager, to any level of nesting. Other widgets can be dropped onto such frames, or a frame can be associated with a `Canvas` object and drawing messages sent in order to customize the appearance of the frame (see below).

The "canned" push event associated with the `Button` object above was given a handler by passing a function object to the `command` parameter in the constructor. A more general mechanism for establishing such a correspondence is the `bind()` message, which can be sent to any widget. The general form of such a message is...

```
w.bind("event name", method or function object)
```

where `w` is the name of some widget. For example, the constructor call given in the above example as...

```
self.button = Button(self.root, text = "Touch me!",
                     command = self.respondToTouch)
```

could have been shortened and the binding of the button push event to its handler put off until the next statement, as follows:

```
self.button = Button(self.root, text = "Touch me!")
self.button.bind("<Button-1>", self.respondToTouch)
```

There are a large number of events which can be specified in this fashion. The string used as the first parameter to `bind()` has a structure, which is parsed in order to precisely specify the particular event which should result in a call to the handler. In the above example, we see two of the components which can be ascertained by such a parse. First, the *event type* is "`Button`". This does not mean the high-level `Button` widget, but rather a mouse "button down" event. The "`-1`" substring specifies a *detail*, which in this case narrows the event to a *left* mouse button. (A right mouse button would be specified with the detail "`-3`".) In addition to these two components there is an optional series of *modifier* components which, if used, can specify combinations of events. An example is "`<Control-KeyPress-i>`". Here the event type is "`KeyPress`", "`-i`" is a detail, and "`Control-`" is a modifier. A handler bound to this event will be invoked whenever the associated widget has the focus and the user presses the two indicated keys simultaneously. See the `tkinter` manual (distributed with Python installations) for details.

9.9.6 Canvas Objects and How to Draw with Them

The functionality of a drawing object and a memory bitmap have been combined in `tkinter` into one class called the `Canvas` class. An instance of this class is an object capable both of storing memory representations of drawn objects and of responding to commands to draw such objects. But there is an additional surprise with canvases: they not only draw and represent figures, but they *identify* each drawn object with an integer ID, and such objects can be made to change their attributes by routing messages to them through their containing `Canvas` object. Such a canvas is therefore not only an active drawing component and a bitmap, but also a container of sorts. The "objects" contained in it are not true objects in the Python sense, but each has a set of attributes that can be modified in a limited way by the `Canvas` object in response to messages sent to that object.

Actually, a `Canvas` object can be placed inside any widget, and once it is "packed" and set up to respond to the `<Configure>` event, the messages sent to it will immediately cause changes in the appearance of the widget. For the present, in our examples, we will attach the canvas directly to the top-level widget and draw our figures in it. For example, the code below produces a "Japanese flag" drawing in a top-level widget.

```python
from tkinter import *

class JapaneseFlag:
    def __init__(self):
        self.root = Tk()
        self.canvas = Canvas(self.root,bg="white",
                             width=700,height=500)
        self.canvas.bind('<Configure>',self.draw)
        self.canvas.pack(expand=YES,fill=BOTH)
        self.circleID = None
        self.root.mainloop()

    def draw(self,event):
        w, h = self.canvas.winfo_width(),
               self.canvas.winfo_height()
        self.radius = 0.3*min(w,h)
        self.center_x = self.canvas.winfo_x() + w/2
        self.center_y = self.canvas.winfo_y() + h/2
        self.drawSpot("red")

    def drawSpot(self,color):
        if self.circleID != None:
            self.canvas.delete(self.circleID)
        self.circleID = self.canvas.create_oval(
            self.center_x - self.radius,
            self.center_y - self.radius,
            self.center_x + self.radius,
            self.center_y + self.radius,
            fill = color
        )

if __name__ == "__main__":
    JapaneseFlag()
```

The example displays a "Japanese flag" window in which the red spot stays in the center of the window and maintains a radius equal to three-tenths of the size of the smallest dimension of that window, no matter how it is moved or resized. This is because the `<Configure>` event is raised whenever any of the dimensions of the window are changed, and that event is bound to the `draw()` method which redisplays the red spot. Note that the old spot is deleted from the canvas first, to prevent multiple spots from appearing in the window.

Some of the messages we have used in the example deserve closer scrutiny. For example, (1) the "winfo" (`winfo_width()`, `winfo_height()`, `winfo_x()`, `winfo_y()`) messages sent to the canvas object can actually be sent to any widget in order to access specific information about that widget. (2) The `create_oval()` message, also sent to the `Canvas` object, is one of a class of messages which can be sent in order to create graphics objects identified by an integer ID, including `create_line()`, `create_rectangle()`, `create_text()`, `create_polygon()`, etc. As in the other libraries we have studied, the message which creates an ellipse (oval) has an identical parameter interface to that which creates a rectangle. The first two parameters are the (x, y) pixel coordinates of the upper-left corner of the rectangle, and the third and fourth parameters give the coordinates of the lower-right corner. The `fill` parameter receives a string stipulating the interior color. When an oval is created, it will be inscribed within the indicated rectangle.

Note also that the `pack()` message sent to the canvas object specifies `fill` and `expand` parameter values. The keyword argument `fill = YES` specifies that the canvas should expand beyond its current dimensions if necessary, to fill the containing widget. Similarly, `expand=BOTH` specifies that the canvas should expand in both the x and y dimensions.

9.10 A POSTSCRIPT: PYTHON, SMALLTALK, AND A CULTURE OF REUSABILITY

It should be noted that of all the other languages covered in this text Python most resembles Smalltalk. Both languages employ a lot of late bindings, use reference semantics, and allow identifier associations to dynamically change type. But the Smalltalk designers were immersed in a vision, and were creating not just a language but a complete application development environment. For that reason, the language and its library are one holistic organism, consisting of a tiny core of functionality surrounded by a sea of library classes, all of which are open to inspection and tinkering, with the proviso that the data items in a class are accessible only via the insertion of access functions.

Python's evolution was quite different. The development environment for which it was constructed was nothing more than a simple text editor and interpreter. It does not hold the core structure of the language sacred but has evolved and changed, integrating those changes with the surrounding library. All the same, it too depends for its functionality on a huge class library, also open-source and regularly receiving contributions from an active and growing user community.

Perhaps the biggest triumph of the object-oriented languages is this universally successful incorporation, in all the major OOPLs, of a culture of reusability. No longer is the "reinvention of the wheel" considered acceptable practice, because not only is there a large library of reusable classes distributed with these languages, but in all cases there are many well-known commercially available and open-source class libraries. Add to this the fact that organizations routinely produce in-house libraries for internal use, and it can truthfully be said that these OOPLs cultures have taken us to the next level in software productivity.

9.11   SUMMARY

Python is an interpreted and heavily simulated language, incorporating ideas from a mixture of organizational paradigms—procedural, object-oriented, and functional. It has powerful built-in features and a streamlined, if unconventional, syntax. It also has a very large and growing set of libraries, which (like the language itself) mix procedural and object-oriented elements. Its information-hiding is odd and somewhat weak, defaulting to a "name it and claim it" kind of openness, where any component of any object is accessible to any other object whose author has the requisite knowledge to build and use a legitimate name for that component. Many capabilities of the language appear to be procedural in nature but only because the language incorporates "syntactic sugar" for a more complex object-oriented form (for example, `len(s)` versus `s.__len__()`).

There are no declarations in Python in the true sense of the word; an action which associates a value with a new variable is called a "declaration" in the language documentation, but there are no translation-time actions which either declare a type or establish a scope for a variable. Run-time type checking, although permissible, is usually not performed; existence checking replaces it, because a type error usually manifests itself as an attempt to send a message to an object for which no corresponding method exists. Because there are no declared types, there is no overloading of function or method names.

The built-in data types of the language are divided into two types: mutable and immutable. Many of the collection types (lists, vectors, tables, *etc.*) we are accustomed to seeing in libraries are provided in Python as built-ins. Some of these built-in collections are *sequence* types, meaning that each element is identifiable by an ordinal position. The immutable sequences are `tuple`, `str`, and `bytes`. All of these are useable as keys for sets and hash tables. The mutable sequences are `list` and `bytearray`. The latter two are not useable as keys because their hash addresses would necessarily be computed based on their current values, and those values are subject to change. The keyed collections are hash table types, called `set` and `dict`, and the immutable `frozenset`, the objects of which can themselves be used as keys. Of the collection types, literal notations are provided for `tuple`, `str`, `bytes`, `list`, `set`, and `dict`. No binary search tree type is provided, neither as a built-in nor with any of the libraries distributed with the installation. All Python collections are necessarily heterogeneous.

The numeric types are standard, with a few twists. Type `int` is indefinite-precision, `float` varies from machine to machine, and a `complex` type is provided and has its own literal notation for imaginary numbers. Integer operations are standard except that integer division (symbol `//`) and the integer modulo operation (symbol `%`) obey the Division Algorithm theorem even when the dividend is negative.

Python scoping mechanisms illustrate the balance in the language between procedural and object-oriented thinking. Class definitions establish scopes which may include member functions, member variables, and inner classes. The scope defined by a function or method may include local variables, inner classes, and inner functions. Modules can be defined as separate source files which include any number of definitions, and importing a module has the effect of dynamically modifying the importing environment by executing the code in the corresponding file. Complicating the issue of local referencing environments is the ability of external entities to add or delete identifier associations from those environments.

Sequence control mechanisms are relatively standard, consisting of C-style operator precedence rules on the expression level and special statement forms such as `if` and `while` at the statement level. The `for` statement uses iterators exclusively, and so has a rather unexpected form but is quite powerful. Iterators can be constructed from functions using the coroutine-like `next` and `yield` interaction. Message handling is necessarily governed by run-time polymorphism, because a message cannot be statically associated with its corresponding method in any reliable way. Exception handling uses `try` blocks similar to those seen in C++, Java, and C#, but no static checking is performed to enforce proper order of handlers.

Reference counts are used to detect inaccessible objects, which are automatically reclaimed as soon as they are detected. An asynchronously scheduled cycle detection algorithm completes the Python dynamic storage management strategy.

Multiple inheritance is allowed in Python and has a similar interpretation to that of C++, but improper inheritance patterns may arise and are dynamically checked at class definition time (a class definition is a late binding in Python).

Functions are first-class objects and come in two flavors: function objects and method objects. A method object differs from a function object in that it has an associated object pointer which is used as the first parameter in any method call. Unnamed function objects may be constructed using lambda expressions.

Persistence is provided by two packages, called `pickle` and `shelve`. The former provides facilities for saving deep copies of objects to a binary file, whereas the latter is able to treat a file as a persistent dictionary, storing binary (*key, value*) pairs for which the associated value is a deep copy of a memory object. The interface to a shelf file is similar to that of a `dict` object.

The `tkinter` package provided with Python distributions is based on a GUI package designed for the `Tcl` scripting language. It takes advantage of Python's functional features, passing function and method objects as parameters and so allowing dynamic manipulation of event handlers. There is no provision which allows multiple handlers to be simultaneously attached to the same event. Graphics primitives are messages to objects of type `Canvas`, each of which is a collection of light-weight "objects" which are created, modified, and deleted by sending such messages.

REVIEW QUESTIONS

1. What is different about the status of whitespace in Python, as opposed to the other languages in this text? Explain.

2. Explain the idea of keyword arguments. How do they differ from positional arguments?

3. Recall from our study of C++ that it is permitted in some compiled languages to completely omit the names of parameters in a function or method declaration, but it is absolutely necessary to include their types. On the other hand, in a Python function definition one is *not allowed* to include types, but *must* include parameter names. What language rules and implementation strategies have led to these opposing sets of rules?

4. Explain how the `eval()` and `exec()` primitives are alike, and how they are different.

5. What are the numeric types of Python? How do Python's numeric types differ from those of other languages you have studied?

6. Describe the way in which Python's "floor division" is similar to and different from Java or C++ integer division. Relate your answer also to the modulo (`%`) operation.

7. In a Python arithmetic expression, what are the rules governing the type of the final result?

8. Explain what happens when the following sequence of Python statements is executed. Why is `False` displayed on the console, even though `x` and `y` are references? Explain carefully.

   ```
   x = 20382097450297304270345720975207302705273057820
   y = x
   x += 1
   print(x == y)
   ```

9. If `obj` is an object, what is the result of the expression `type(type(obj))`? Explain.

10. What are the sequence types in Python? Which of them are mutable? Give examples of "literals" for all types except `bytearray` types. How can one construct a `bytearray` object with a known value?

11. Describe the two formatting operations (the `%` operation and the `format()` message) which can be performed on strings. Do these two similar capabilities indicate a needless redundancy in the language? Why or why not? Explain carefully.

12. Unlike the situation in Smalltalk, the type of a "primitive" numeric operation in Python can usually be determined by knowing the operation and the types of its operands. Is this a rule which is hard-wired into the Python language, or can programmer-defined functions or methods be designed to return values of different types based on run-time decisions? Regardless, `eval()` is an exception to the above-stated rule about operations on primitive types. Why?

13. Why would it be dangerous to use a mutable object as a hash table key? Are all mutable objects banned from being used as such? If not, describe an exception to the rule and comment on the safety of your example.

14. Describe a kind of set which is a valid key for a hash table, and give an example of its use.

15. Discuss information hiding in Python. What decisions about this issue were made by the designers, and what kind of reasoning do you think went into those decisions?

16. Discuss variable declarations in Python. Although there is no explicit declaration syntax, the language does have static scope rules and speaks about the declaration of variables in its documentation. What does Python documentation refer to when it speaks of a "declaration," and how is it different from a declaration in the usual sense?

17. Why is overloading of functions, in which the same name is used for two different function definitions, not permitted in Python?

18. Is `self` a keyword in Python? Explain the significance of the identifier `self` in Python.

19. Is the idea of an "access function" a significant concept in Python culture? Why or why not?

20. When is an instance variable "private" in Python? Experiment with such variables to ascertain the mangled forms of their names. (You can use the `__dict__` attribute to see all the instance variables of any object of class type.) Determine whether you have read and/or write access to the variable using the mangled form of the name. Comment on the security aspects of using such "private" variables.

21. Explain the difference between a method object and a function object. Can every method object be associated with a function object? If not, why not? If so, how? Can every function object be associated with a method object? If not, why not? If so, how?

22. Explain the difference in the way Python source code can be split between multiple files and the way that C++ and/or Java programs are split between multiple files. Why does it seem so much simpler in Python? What is the central difference between the two approaches?

23. For a module `M`, explain all the differences you know between the patterns of usage and the effects of the two statements below:
```
import M
from M import *
```

24. Describe the actions initiated by each of the `import` statements below, assuming the first import is the first statement in the source file.
```
import M
...    #other statements
def f():
      from M import f, g
     ...    #other statements
```

25. In the code below, suppose that the only content in module `M` is the assignment statement `x = 0`. What is output by the code segment? Explain.
```
import M
M.x = 5
def f():
```

```
import M
print(M.x)
  f()
```

26. Explain the difference between the `del` primitive in Python and the C++ `delete` statement.

27. Describe the ways in which the pattern of interaction between the Python `try` block, `except` block, and `raise` statement differ from that between the `try` block, `catch` block, and `throw` statement of C++ and/or Java. Discuss correct construction, static and run-time checking, and run-time actions.

28. How does Python differ from C++ and Java in its handling of the "division by zero" error?

29. Explain the purpose, form, and execution of a `with` block. What must be true of the `with` operand?

30. Does Python operator precedence resemble that of Java and C++, or does it resemble that of Smalltalk? Do you find the answer to this question surprising? Why or why not?

31. Compare and contrast augmented assignment operations in Python with the corresponding features in C++. For example, if `x` is an object of type `XType`, where `XType` is a class, in each case how does the programmer provide a meaning for the syntax `x += 1`? How does each language avoid multiple access operations for the name `x`?

32. In the standard "initialize, test, increment" style of counter-controlled loop, the issue of the exit value of the loop variable is explained in terms of a flow graph. How do we explain the exit value of a Python `for` loop variable for a counter-controlled loop, i.e., for a loop where the variable iterates over a range? For programmers, is there a practical difference between the two approaches to defining the exit value?

33. Most uses of the Python `for` statement involve the use of ranges or sequences, but the language does not define the meaning of the statement in those terms. How is the meaning defined, and how do we relate that meaning to the more specialized forms of the `for` statement?

34. What is the technical definition of the term *generator* in Python? Of the term *iterator*? Explain how `yield` and `next` work together to achieve a specialized kind of coroutine interaction. How can the programmer avoid explicit use of `next`?

35. What is a `list` comprehension? A `set` comprehension? A `dict` comprehension? Give an example of each.

36. How is programmer-defined operator overloading accomplished in Python? Explain.

37. Explain the details of how Python inheritance is regulated. Is private or protected inheritance allowed? How about multiple inheritance?

38. How are constructors coded in Python? What other Python feature does this look like? Relate the two features to each other.

39. What rules govern the situation in which a reference is made to a class member not defined in the class, so that the base class(es) must be searched for an appropriate environment in which to resolve the reference? Which base classes are searched first, and how does the search progress?

40. What status is given to functions in Python? What is the difference between function objects and method objects? Explain and give examples.

41. What kind of object is returned by the Python `open` operation? What messages can it be sent? How do they operate, and how do they differ from the facilities for console input and output?

42. What two modules provide for the saving and restoring of persistent objects in Python? How are they different? Explain.

EXERCISES

1. The conventional idea of a "token" is that it is an atomic element of syntax composed of some string of characters and used to detect the grammatical structure of a program. Conventionally, tokens are flanked by white space or file boundaries. How can we still use the "tokenization" idea with the Python language, where whitespace is used for more sophisticated purposes than simply to separate tokens? Would Python tokens differ from tokens in a more conventional language?

2. Comment on what is necessary to implement keyword arguments. What actions are necessary when the function is defined? What actions are necessary when a call to it involves keyword arguments?

3. The `split()` behavior of type `str` has two optional parameters. *Use them both* to write Python code which evaluates the data in the string

stored in variable `matchDataString`, to determine the winner of a tennis match. The string will consist of a sequence of dash-separated pairs, where each pair is separated from the next by a comma, as in "`Bobbi-Eileen,6-2,7-5`". As the example implies, the first dash-separated pair indicates the names of the participants and the remaining pairs represent scores in each set. Your code should work with any number of sets and should output the result in the form indicated by the following example:

```
Bobbi wins 6-2,7-5
```

4. Have IDLE evaluate the expression "`ss`".`split('s')`. What is the result, and what do you conclude from it?

5. Which of the following are valid Python statements? For those which are valid, what types are involved, how does the execution of the statement proceed, and what values are assigned to the variables? For the others, explain why they are invalid.

a. `x, y, z = 1, 2, 3`
b. `x, y = 1, 2, 3`
c. `x = 1, 2, 3`

6. In what language(s) that we have studied does the syntax

```
return x, y+1, z/2
```

make sense? How does its meaning in Python differ from that in the other language(s)?

7. Determine by experimentation the shortest string which will be correctly processed by `exec()` but not by `eval()`. Are there strings which `eval()` evaluates but which are rejected by `exec()`? If so, what are they? If not, why not?

8. In the following code, the order of the first two statements in the inner function `doLess()` is important. (a) What happens if we switch the order of those first two statements, and why does it happen? (b) Explain how we can switch the order and insert the statement *nonlocal x* and have a correctly formed function definition. (c) How does the result of the call `doLittle()` change from the result of that call in the original code, when we make the changes in (b)?

```
def doLittle():
    x = 5
    def doLess():
        x = 10
        print(x)
```

```
            return x
        return doLess() + x
```

9. What is printed by the following code? Why?

```
    class Outer:
      x = 4
      class Inner:
          x = 13
          def __init__(self):
              self.x = 15
          x = 9
      def __init__(self):
          self.x = 5

  outer = Outer()
  inner = outer.Inner()
    print(outer.x, inner.x, Outer.x, outer.Inner.x)
```

10. Write a class definition for a class `MyIteratorClass` whose instances are valid iterators. Write it so that it imitates a range. Specifically, for any integer `n`, `MyIteratorClass(n)` should behave exactly like `range(n)` when it is used as the iterator in a `for` loop.

11. Give an expression for a `list` comprehension containing all the two-character strings consisting of consecutive lower-case letters, i.e., which evaluates to `['ab', 'bc', 'cd', 'de', 'ef', 'fg', 'gh', 'hi', 'ij', 'jk', 'kl', 'lm', 'mn', 'no', 'op', 'pq', 'qr', 'rs', 'st', 'tu', 'uv', 'vw', 'wx', 'xy', 'yz']`.

12. Give an expression for a `dict` comprehension which evaluates to a dictionary consisting of the twenty-five pairs `'a':'b'`, `'b':'c'`, `'c':'d'`, ..., `'y':'z'`. It should require only a slight modification to your answer for the previous exercise.

13. Write a class definition for a mutable type `MyChar` which encapsulates a single-character string and provides an addition operation which adds an integer value to the ordinal value of the stored character. For example, if `x` is an object encapsulating the string `'A'`, then the call `x + 1` should first modify x's stored string, then return `x`, which should now encapsulate the string `'B'`. Also, provide a definition of the `str()` operation which returns the encapsulated string.

14. Rewrite the code in Exercise 13 so that `MyChar` is immutable, specifically so that the `+` operator does not modify the `MyChar` object which is executing it, but rather computes and returns a new `MyChar` object.

15. In either of Exercises 13 or 14, suppose that after providing the + operation we want to also give `MyChar` the operation `+=`, so that if `m` is a `MyChar` object then `m += 1` causes the ordinal value of the one-character string associated with `m` to be increased by 1. What must we do? Explain.

16. C++ uses a similar algorithm to that used by Python for discovering inconsistencies in inheritance patterns due to multiple inheritance. Python notices an inconsistency as soon as it "executes" the first class definition which introduces an inconsistency. When does C++ discover such an inconsistency? Experiment by constructing the inheritance pattern in section 9.6 with C++ classes.

17. Construct example class definitions, with constructors, to discover the effect of using `super` to call a base class constructor from a derived class constructor, in the case where the derived class has more than one direct base class. Is such usage allowed? If so, which base class is referred to by `super`? How can the other base class constructor(s) be called? Give the code for your example, including driver code, describe the results of executing the driver.

18. Write a two-parameter Python function called `compose` which forms and returns as its result the composition of two one-parameter functions `f` and `g`, where `g` is to be called first and its value used as input to `f`. Do not use a lambda expression in your definition of `compose`. Test your function by computing the composition of $f(x) = \sqrt[3]{\left|\dfrac{x}{x+1}\right|}$ and $g(x) = \sin\left(\dfrac{x^2}{7}\right)$. The call `compose(f,g)(5.7)` should give the result 7.3456217421001515.

19. Do Exercise 18 using a lambda expression.

20. Write a Python class with base class `list` which encapsulates a list of strings from a file. Name the class `tokens`, and give it a two-parameter constructor. The first parameter of the constructor is a string `fname` to be used as a file name, and the second is a delimiter string `delims`. The default argument of the second parameter should be the null string. In the constructor, the `tokens` object opens the file having the name stored in `fname`, splits each line into substrings, and appends each nonempty substring to itself. No additional instance variables should be used beyond those in the base class. If the argument provided to `delims` is an empty string, the calls on `split()` should provide no parameter; otherwise, `delims` should be the parameter to `split()`.

21. For Exercise 20, write test code to read a file name from the console, tokenize the file having that name using the `tokens` class, read another file name from the console, and write the tokens from the first file into the second file, one to a line.

22. Suppose `stringList` is a list of strings and `fname` is the name to be given to an output file. Write a sequence of Python statements which accomplishes the same task as the statements

    ```
    outFile = open(fname, 'w')
    outFile.writelines(stringList)
    outFile.close()
    ```

    but does not use the `writelines()` method.

23. In this exercise, you will test the ability of the `pickle` module to store and retrieve an object of a programmer-defined type. Create a text file, or choose an existing text file, convert it to a list of strings using the `tokens` class described in Exercise 20, then pickle the resulting `tokens` object to a file. Now close IDLE, reopen it, and try to retrieve the pickled object. If you are able to successfully retrieve it, experiment with it to make sure that it really is a deep copy of the pickled object. Describe the steps you took to be successful at retrieving the pickled file, along with any mistakes you made along the way.

24. Choose a text file and convert it to a list of strings using the `tokens` class described in Exercise 20. Now import `shelve` and create a new shelf file called `tokenShelf`, based on the file *tokenShelf.bin*. Store the tokens in your shelf using the string representation of the ordinal position as a key, so that `tokenShelf["0"]` is the first token, `tokenShelf["1"]` is the second, *etc.* Close IDLE, reopen it, and reopen the shelf. Experiment to make sure the shelf has the desired contents. Describe the steps you took and any mistakes you made along the way.

25. Although `tkinter` does not include a timer widget, there is an `after()` message which can be sent to a root window, which schedules a function to be called after a certain delay. If that function then schedules itself, it will behave somewhat like a timer event handler. Investigate the `after()` message in the `tkinter` documentation, then use this strategy to write a `Timer` class. When a `Timer` object is created, the constructor should receive as its list of parameters (1) a count `ms` of the number of milliseconds to delay between calls, (2) a callback function `f`, and (3) a `*args` parameter which encapsulates whatever additional parameters are

necessary to constitute an argument list for `f` (see the discussion at the end of Section 9.4.1). When the constructor executes, it should save its parameters as instance variables and construct a `Tk` object `tk`. It should start only when it receives a `start()` message, at which time it should send an appropriate `after()` message to the window `tk`, withdraw `tk`'s screen representation with the command `tk.withdraw()`, and start `tk`'s message loop. `tk` will then be capable of handling events, though it is invisible, so it can respond to the `after()` callback. (Note that the thread which sent the `start()` message will be suspended, so `start()` should not be issued from the main thread, but from an event handler.) Finally, provide a `kill()` method which kills the timer by destroying the window.

26. Modify the `Timer` class you built in Exercise 25 by giving it a member function `setTimeLimit()` which imposes a time limit, killing the timer at the end of that time limit. Design it so that the limit is a millisecond count, but if that count is negative the timer does not stop until it is killed from outside.

27. Use the `Timer` class you created in Exercise 25 to construct a `BouncingBall` class similar to the examples used at various places in the text. Determine a speed randomly at construction time, using a minimum of 50 and a maximum of 500 pixels per second.

28. Rewrite Exercise 25 from Chapter 8, the Danish flag application, using Python and `tkinter`.

REFERENCES

[Barrett96] Barrett, Kim, et al., "A monotonic superclass linearization for Dylan," *Proceedings of the 11th ACM SIGPLAN conference on Object-oriented programming, systems, languages, and applications* (October 1996): pp. 69–82.

A

EVENT-DRIVEN PROJECT IDEAS

NOTE

Many of the projects in this appendix could be attacked on various levels. The specification is somewhat loose in most cases, and the emphasis for all these should be the building of a nice interface with a direct-manipulation feel. Much difficulty can be added to several of these projects, based on the extent to which more sophisticated business logic is incorporated. For example, the programmer may choose to incorporate some intelligent strategies for solving puzzles or playing games. Making the project more challenging in this way is certainly worthwhile, but what is to be learned in doing so is less relevant to programming languages and event-driven programming, and more relevant to object-oriented analysis and design and artificial intelligence. The building of distinct business classes and view classes is mentioned explicitly in Project 2, but the instructor may choose to require this kind of "separation of concerns" approach in any of these projects.

PROJECT 1: BASEBALL GAME SIMULATION (SMALLTALK-SPECIFIC)

Place the files *Rangen.st*, *Pitcher.st*, and *BaseballScore.st* in your Smalltalk directory, and merge them into a morphic "world" with the *fileIn* menu choice. Then create a `BaseballScoreMorph` that maintains a display depicting the state of the game at any given time, as is done by the `BowlingScoreMorph`. Your morph should show which team is at bat and which runners are on which bases, and it should reproduce somewhere in the window a display similar to that generated by the `displayOnTranscript` method in class `BaseballScore`.

This means that you need to set up pitches on a schedule and animate the game with the **step**, **stepTime:**, and **startStepping:** methods. The result of each pitch should show up on the screen, and pressing the space key should cause the speed of the game to increase. It should be possible in this way to see the entire game in a few seconds.

To get an idea what the score portion of your display should look like, paste the following into your Workspace window and execute it:

```
cal := Pitcher new: 78324.
"Adjust random number seed so your team wins!"
jose := Pitcher new: 96987.
s := BaseballScore new.
s setTeamName: 1 to: 'Reds'.
s setTeamName: 2 to: 'Cards'.
s setPitcherForTeam: 1 to: cal.
s setPitcherForTeam: 2 to: jose.
Transcript show: Character cr.
[ s gameOver ] whileFalse: [
  s playInning.
  s displayOnTranscript.
  Transcript show: Character cr
]
```

Your display should incorporate a graphic depiction of the runners, as in the example in Figure A.1. The color of an occupied base should change when the team at bat changes. Home base should always be colored with the color of the team at bat.

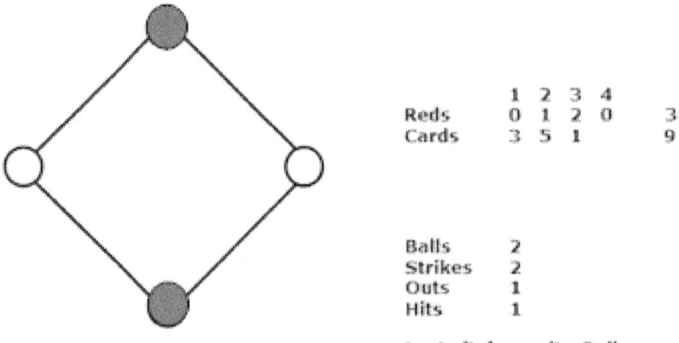

	1	2	3	4	
Reds	0	1	2	0	3
Cards	3	5	1		9

Balls	2
Strikes	2
Outs	1
Hits	1

Last pitch result: Ball

FIGURE A.1 Screen Display for a `BaseballMorph`

PROJECT 2: TIC-TAC-TOE

Part 1: Design a business class called `TicTacToeScore` for playing Tic-tac-toe. Your class should only keep score; it need not have any knowledge of strategy. For example, in the Smalltalk language a series of messages such as the following might be used by a client to create a game and apply a series of moves.

```
game := TicTacToeScore exes: 'Mary' oes: 'Ted'.
game moveRow: 1 column: 1. "Move for X"
game moveRow: 2 column: 2. "Move for O"
etc.
```

Your class should also contain methods for determining whether or not a square is occupied, whether or not the game is over, and the result of a game.

Part 2: Create a `TicTacToeGame` class which maintains a graphical view of the game state and allows users to play Tic-tac-toe with mouse clicks. The view object should keep the display current at all times and should announce when a game is over and who won. There should also be controls in the interface for beginning a new game and for entering the names of the players.

PROJECT 3: THE "DOTS" GAME

Design an application which allows two players to play the dots game using mouse actions. Your view object should begin by displaying a rectangular array of dots, and the players move using a "click and drag" motion, from one dot to the dot immediately to its north, east, west, or south side. The game continues until all possible connections have been made. When one of the small rectangles is completed by a move, that rectangle is re-colored using the color of the person making the move, and the same player must now make another move. When a rectangle can be completed in this fashion, the player with the move is obliged to do so. The player with the largest number of rectangles wins.

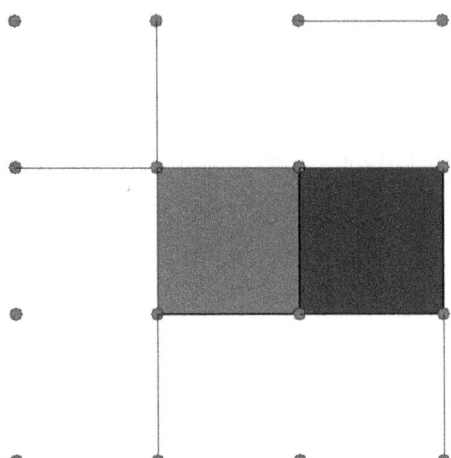

FIGURE A.2 The Dots game

Your application should allow the users to specify the dimensions of the array and to choose their colors. It should announce the winner using a pop-up window.

PROJECT 4: TWO-PLAYER GAME SIMULATION

Using the descriptions of Projects 2 and 3 as a model, write a graphical user interface that allows two players to play a game, such as Chess, Checkers, or Nine-Men's Morris.

PROJECT 5: THE EIGHT PUZZLE

In the Eight Puzzle, the puzzle solver slides tiles one space either horizontally or vertically in order to achieve the state in Figure A.3. Design a view object which allows the user to play the Eight Puzzle with mouse clicks or with click-and-drag motions. Your view should incorporate a button or some other control to allow the user to randomize the state of the puzzle at any time, in order to start a fresh game. Be careful, however, because not every puzzle state allows a solution. The simplest way to make sure that your puzzle can be solved is to set up your internal data structure so that it is initially solved, then to perform some large number of randomly chosen sliding moves in order to achieve a challenging starting position.

1	2	3
4	5	6
7	8	

FIGURE A.3 A solved eight puzzle

PROJECT 6: EIGHT PUZZLE GENERALIZATION

The Fifteen Puzzle is exactly like the Eight Puzzle, but is played on a four by four grid. Generalize your puzzle application from Project 3 so that it accommodates the Fifteen Puzzle and *any such puzzle* played on an n by n grid, for reasonable values of n.

PROJECT 7: SUDOKU

In a Sudoku puzzle, the puzzle solver is confronted with a nine-by-nine array of squares, as seen in Figure A.4. Some of those squares have numbers in them, and some are blank. The object of the game is to place numbers in all the blank squares in a very specific way, as we describe below.

1	4		8	3				
				6		2		
8		7	2			3		
			5	6				
5	7			2			9	6
			1	4				
	1				3	9		4
	5			1				
				7	9		1	5

FIGURE A.4 A Sudoku puzzle

The puzzle has three organizational units, namely (1) the rows, each divided into nine squares, (2) the columns, also divided into nine squares each, and (3) nine three-by-three arrays of squares, specifically those framed with bold lines in the figure. The rule for a solved puzzle is the same in all three of these units— each of the nine squares in the unit must be assigned a number between one and nine, inclusively, and all the numbers in that range must appear within the unit. This means no unit may contain the same number twice. Design an application that allows the user to enter and solve Sudoku puzzles. Figure A.5 shows the solution to the puzzle in Figure A.4.

1	4	2	8	3	5	7	6	9
9	3	5	7	6	1	4	2	8
8	6	7	2	9	4	5	3	1
3	2	1	9	5	6	8	4	7
5	7	4	3	2	8	1	9	6
6	9	8	1	4	7	3	5	2
2	1	6	5	8	3	9	7	4
7	5	9	4	1	2	6	8	3
4	8	3	6	7	9	2	1	5

FIGURE A.5 A solved Sudoku puzzle

Your application should have a distinct puzzle entry mode and a distinct puzzle solution mode, and should be able to save and restore puzzles.

PROJECT 8: PUZZLES

Design an event-driven application to solve your favorite puzzle, using Projects 5-8 as your inspiration. Include the ability to start a new puzzle, an announcement of results, and the ability to save and restore partially solved puzzles.

PROJECT 9: GRAPHICAL DATA COLLECTION

The visual thesaurus at http://www.visualthesaurus.com is an excellent example of a graphical interface to an interesting data collection. Using it as your inspiration, design a data collection and a graphical interface to that collection which demonstrate one or more relationships between the data items as links in a directed graph. Your application should have the following attributes:

1. The view should incorporate at least one area to which you draw directly with graphics commands, and at least one mouse event should be handled which interacts with your drawing.

2. It should allow interactive additions to the database using mouse clicks or buttons and text boxes.

3. It should make all the data visible, although not necessarily all at once.

4. It should have a menu attached, with at least a save/restore capability.

PROJECT 10: CALCULATOR

Write a calculator application. Your calculator should at least perform all the basic arithmetic operations plus square root, reciprocal, y^x, natural logarithm, and common (base 10) logarithm. Other enhancements might include trig functions, degrees/radians, precision control, factorial, memory, parentheses, history of operations, and just making the overall appearance of the display attractive.

ANSWERS TO ODD-NUMBERED EXERCISES

CHAPTER 1

1. (a) Java, C++, and C# all permit overloading, which is the reuse of a name that already has one association in order to give it an additional association. In all cases, the context in which the name is used will provide an unambiguous meaning. For example, in Java, C++, or C# the name f may be introduced in the same class, say class A, with two different bindings as a member function, as long as their parameter lists are substantially different (for instance, the one having two int parameters and the second having a double parameter and an int parameter).

(b) Overriding occurs when a new association is introduced for a name, and the new binding makes the old one inaccessible in certain contexts in which it would have been accessible if the new association had not been introduced. The standard example is that in which a member function is introduced in a derived class with the same name *and the same interface* as in the base class. So if class B inherits from class A, and class A has a definition for member function f requiring two int parameters, class B can be given a member function f with the same interface. The new definition overrides the old in the sense that everywhere within B's scope any unqualified reference to f which uses the two int parameters will be resolved inside B. The override also always occurs if f is sent as a message to a B object. What differentiates languages is whether the override happens if f is sent as a message to an object which has been declared to be of type A, but is also of type B. (This cannot happen except in compiled languages, where such fine-grained declarations are commonly used.) The one school of thought, from the days of Simula, is that the programmer should have the opportunity (through the use or nonuse of virtual methods) to make the choice. The other is that it should always be the object itself which fields the message, and that is in fact the only choice in languages like Smalltalk, in which there is no other candidate. In the compiled language Java, the override still occurs (the programmer has no choice), but C++ and C# use the Simula approach; i.e., the override only occurs if special measures are taken by the programmer to enable it.

3. The standard algorithm for evaluating a postfix expression is to read the expression from left to right, and to push operands on a stack as they are encountered. If each token is precisely identified as representing either an operand or an operation (i.e., function), if the value of each operand can be obtained, and if the arity of each operation is unambiguously known, then we can evaluate any postfix expression by performing the following steps for each token:

a. If the token represents a value, push that value on the stack.

b. Otherwise, if the token represents a function f, then ascertain its arity, say n, and…

    i. Pop n operands off the stack and form a correctly ordered argument list.

    ii. Call f with the argument list built in step i.

    iii. Push the value returned from the call of f onto the stack.

        a. Otherwise the postfix expression has an error.

c. Once each token has been processed in this manner, the correct value of the expression should be on the stack.

Example: `34 5 * 7 12 + +`

Here the actions are:

```
Push 35
Push 5
Pop two and multiply to obtain 175
Push 175
Push 7
Push 12
Pop two and add to obtain 19
Push 19
```

```
Pop two and add to obtain 194
Push 194
```

The answer, 194, is now on top of the stack.

5. A Python solution is as follows. It assumes `m` and `n` are non-negative.

```
def gcd(m,n):
    large = max(m,n)
    small = min(m,n)
    if small == 0:
        return large
    else:
        return gcd(large-small,small)
```

7. Note: The simplified notation for describing tokens in the text has some limitations, so a small liberty has been taken in the solutions below. Specifically, the + sign is used to denote concatenation of symbols and also as a literal representing itself. The instructor may want to introduce the students to some more powerful notations.

   a. A decimal integer literal, allowing leading zeros:
```
digit = 0 + 1 + 2 + 3 + 4 + 5 + 6 + 7 + 8 + 9
unsigned = digit (digit)*
integer_literal = unsigned + (-unsigned) + (+unsigned)
```
   b. A double literal:
```
unsigned_fixed = (. unsigned) + (unsigned .)
                             + (unsigned . unsigned)
fixed = unsigned_fixed + (-unsigned_fixed) +
                        (+unsigned_fixed)
exp_part = (e+E)integer_literal
double_literal = fixed + (fixed exp_part)
                      + (integer_literal exp_part)
```

9. The following Java code segment illustrates:
```
int c[] = new int[10];
int x = 55;
for (int i=0; i<=10;++i) c[i] = i;
```
Java will throw an `ArrayIndexOutOfBoundsException` on the last iteration of the loop, because `c[10]` does not exist. On the other hand, if we replace the first line by
```
int c[10];
```
then the code becomes syntactically valid in C++, and running it causes no obvious errors unless it was compiled in a special debug mode. If no

debug routines were compiled into the code, then the absence of any run-time error is no guarantee that the code which follows will run correctly, however. For example, it is possible, depending on the way the compiler organizes the stack frame, that the value 55 in the variable x will be over-written with some other value.

11. The C++ language has reference parameters, which are of the *in out* classification. For example, the following routine receives an argument by reference and returns to the caller after squaring the argument's value.

```
void square(double &z) { z = z*z; }
```

Now if x has the value 1.1, the call

```
square(x);
```

has the effect of storing `1.21` at x. The Java language has no *in out* parameter transmission, so the effect above can only be achieved by a definition such as

```
double squareOf(double z) { return z*z; }
```

whereupon the call

```
x = squareOf(x);
```

achieves the desired effect.

13. Although transmission by reference qualifies as an *in out* technique, it can be used in places where *out* transmission is desired. Thus, if c is a C++ char variable, then the call

```
cin.get(c);
```

ignores the prior value of c, discarding it and placing in c the value of the next character in the standard input stream cin. Curiously enough, the get member function is overloaded to allow a "Java style" input operation, namely

```
c = cin.get();
```

In the latter case, the value returned is actually of type int, and will be coerced into the char type as a side effect of the assignment.

15. Java derives all first-class types from class Object. The latter class defines an instance method called toString(), which when called returns a character string representation of the value of the receiving object. All derived types for which the base type does not provide a reasonable representation of the value are expected to provide an override of toString(). All operations one would consider to be "output operations," i.e., which need to display or store a textual representation of a value,

will send the `toString()` message to whatever value is to be output, and the string of characters resulting from that call will be sent to the output device or file. If the value to be output is a primitive value, it will first be wrapped using the appropriate wrapper class. For output in binary, the member function `writeObject()` of class `ObjectOutputStream` can be used (see Section 7.9.1).

17. The following Java class contains the desired elements, plus an augmented `add()` facility (implemented using overloading) that allows adding a single element, an array of elements, or another `IntArray` onto the end of the existing `IntArray` object. Also included is a `dump()` routine for debugging purposes, and a static `main()` function for testing.

```java
import java.io.PrintStream;

public class IntArray {
    int elts[];
    private static void copy(int a[], int b[], int begin) {
        // Copy all of a into b[begin], b[begin+1], etc.
        if (a.length + begin <= b.length)
            for (int i=0; i<a.length; ++i)
                b[begin + i] = a[i];
    }
    public IntArray() {
        elts = new int[0];
    }
    public IntArray(IntArray a) {
        elts = new int[a.elts.length];
        copy(a.elts,elts,0);
    }
    public IntArray(int a[]) {
        elts = new int[a.length];
        copy(a,elts,0);
    }
    public void add(int x) {
        int oldElts[] = elts;
        elts = new int[elts.length+1];
        copy(oldElts,elts,0);
        elts[oldElts.length] = x;
    }
    public void add(IntArray x) {
        add(x.elts);
    }
    public void add(int x[]) {
        int oldElts[] = elts;
```

```
        elts = new int[elts.length+x.length];
        copy(oldElts,elts,0);
        copy(x,elts,oldElts.length);
  }
  public int get(int i) {
      if (i >= elts.length) throw new ArrayIndexOutOfBound-
sException();
      return elts[i];
  }
  public void put(int i, int val) {
      if (i >= elts.length) throw new ArrayIndexOutOfBound-
sException();
      else elts[i] = val;
  }
  public void dump(PrintStream out){
    for (int i=0; i<elts.length; ++i) out.print("\t"+elts[i]);
      out.println();
  }
  public static void main(String [] args) {
      IntArray a = new IntArray();
      int initial[] = {4, 5, 6};
      a.add(initial);
      IntArray b = new IntArray(a);
      a.add(7);
      int more[] = {8, 9, 10};
      IntArray c = new IntArray(more);
      b.add(c);
      System.out.println("Contents of a:");
      a.dump(System.out);
      System.out.println("Contents of b:");
      b.dump(System.out);
      System.out.println("Contents of c:");
      c.dump(System.out);
  }
}
```

CHAPTER 2

1. Python considers a method associated with an object to be a first-class object of type *function* and identical in type to an old-fashioned procedure. Thus, in the following code, the values of variables a.f, b.f, and g are all of the same type and are parameterless functions returning an integer.

```
class A:
    def __init__(self, x):
        self.x = x
    def f(self):
        return self.x

def g():
    return 2

a = A(3)
b = A(5)
```

These functions can be placed into an indexable table `h` (of type `list`) as follows:

```
h = [a.f, b.f, g]
```

Now the call `h[0]()` invokes `a.f` and returns 3, where the call `h[2]()` invokes `g` and returns 2. A table could be formed in this fashion and used as a callback table.

3. The author's Java solution to Exercise 2 sorted n randomly generated integers with a selection sort and produced the following results:

```
Largest n for 10 microseconds is 49
Largest n for 100 microseconds is 243
Largest n for 500 microseconds is 537
Largest n for 1000 microseconds is 775
```

4. Interpolating linearly in the resulting table gives the following results:

a. If a time slice is 500 microseconds, a third of that is 167, which is in the interval [100, 500], yielding a value of n somewhere between 243 and 537. The slope of the line in that interval is $\frac{537-243}{500-100} = .735$, yielding an approximation of 243 + .735(67), or around n = 292.

b. If a time slice is one millisecond, or 1000 microseconds, our time limit is 333 microseconds and a similar reasoning will yield n = 414.

c. If a time slice is 10 milliseconds, then our time limit is 3333 microseconds. We have to extrapolate outside the table, and we obtain n = 1201.

5. A Smalltalk solution could be a new instance method for class `Integer`. The given example would be coded as follows:

```
1000000 separate
```

and the method definition would look like this:

```
separate
```

```
|color red green blue quotient|
color := Array new: 3.
red := self \\ 256.
quotient := self // 256.
green := quotient \\ 256.
blue := quotient // 256.
color at: 1 put: red.
color at: 2 put: green.
color at: 3 put: blue.
^color
```

Here the \\ operation is "remainder modulo n," and // is "quotient modulo n." The keyword self refers to the object (i.e., the Integer object, 1000000 in the example) that received the message. The ^ operation in the last line returns the array of three color levels as the result of the call.

CHAPTER 3

1. The solutions follow, and in both cases the parentheses are necessary for a proper evaluation.

    a. Solution for f(x, y) = 3 + xy + y^2
    ```
    f := [:x :y | 3 + (x*y) + (y*y)]
    ```

    b. Solution for $g(x) = \sqrt{1 + \sin x}$
    ```
    g := [:x | (1 + x sin) sqrt]</LL>
    ```

3. No parentheses are needed in the solutions that follow.

    a. Solution for f(2.3, 7.9)
    ```
    f perform: #value:value: with: 2.3 with:7.9
    ```

    b. Solution for $g(x) = \sqrt{1 + \sin 5\pi/7}$
    ```
    g perform: #value: with: 5*Float pi / 7
    ```

5. The solution below should work.

    ```
        [a < b] whileTrue: [a := 2*a. b := b - epsilon]
    ```
    To check your answer, try evaluating the expression in the workspace (select it, then inspect its value with ctrl-i) after first setting a to 0.0123 and b to 3.7, with epsilon set equal to 0.001. The final value of a should be 6.2976 and that of b should be 3.691.

7. **moveDisksTo:** target **from:** source **using:** temp
    ```
    "Display on the transcript instructions for moving this
    number (i.e. the number represented by self) of disks
    ```

from the source peg to the target peg in the Towers of
Hanoi game, using temp for temporary storage."
        self <= 0 **ifTrue**: [^nil].
        self = 1 **ifTrue**: [
            Transcript **show:** 'Move a disk from ', source, ' to ',
                target, Character **cr**.
        ] **ifFalse**: [
            (self - 1) **moveDisksTo:** temp
                        from: source **using:** target.
            1   **moveDisksTo:** target
                        from: source **using:** temp.
            (self - 1) **moveDisksTo:** target
                        from: temp **using:** source.

        ]

9. **cycle**
    y := y + x.
    Count := Count + 1.
    ^y

11. Three ways of creating the desired rectangle object are as follows. There
    are many other ways besides these.

    Rectangle **origin:** 200@220 **extent:** 200@150.

    200@220 **extent:** 200@150

    Rectangle **left:** 200 **right:** 400 **top:** 220 **bottom:** 370.

13. a. self **bounds:** (200@250 **extent:** 500@300)
    b. A search engine turns up several RGB triples for the color mauve, one
       of which is (224, 176, 255). So the following message should have the
       desired effect.
       self **color:** (Color **r:** 224.0/255 **g:** 176.0/255 **b:** 1)
    c. self **borderColor:** Color **black**.
    d. self **borderWidth:** 1.

15. a. The green spots get drawn at each mouse click, as expected. However,
       when the morph is resized, moved, or minimized and restored, all the
       green spots disappear. This is because the morph is redrawn by the dra-
       wOn: message every time any one of those actions occur, and no override
       has been defined for that method in GreenSpotsMorph. Also, no infor-
       mation is being created within GreenSpotsMorph which would allow us to
       remember where the spots are.

    b. The changes in Section 3.11.2 provide an override for drawOn: and
       move all the drawing actions to that method. They also provide an Or-
       deredCollection object, stored in instance variable spots, which is able

to remember all the spots, storing each as a `Point` object representing the offset of the point from the upper-left-hand corner of the morph. The value of `spots` is initialized to an empty collection in a new instance method `initialize`, an override of a base class method. Subsequently, the `mouseDown:` method stores the required offset every time it fires, but does not itself draw the spot. Instead of drawing, `mouseDown:` sends the `changed` message to the morph, which indirectly causes `drawOn:` to be invoked.

CHAPTER 4

1. The C++ "Hello, World!" program can be written as follows:

```
#include <iostream>
using std::cout;

int main() {
    cout << "Hello, World!\n";
    return 0;
}
```

The Java version goes like this:

```
public class HelloWorld {
    public static void main(String args[]) {
        System.out.println("Hello, World!");
    }
}
```

A major difference can be seen in the way libraries are viewed. In C++, the vehicle for involving library code is the "include file." Each `include` file is a collection of definitions and declarations which provide the compiler with sufficient information to generate the correct code references to library entities when it builds the object file. Those references are further followed up during the link step. Hence, the line of code

```
#include <iostream>
```

brings in a large number of additional source code lines which must subsequently be compiled, most of which will never be used. A similar facility exists in Java with the `import` statement, but there is one package which never needs importing, namely `java.lang`. Because the `System` class resides in `java.lang`, it does not need to be imported, so the reference to `System.out.println()` is properly resolved without an `import` statement. (In fact, `out` is a static class member of `System` of type `Print-Stream`, and `println()` is an instance method of `PrintStream`.)

This points out a major difference between C++ and Java, the idea of language-integrated libraries. Although C++ has extensive libraries, none of them are given "special status." The core C++ language is library ignorant.

In C++, we have the `using` statement, which allows us to make unqualified reference to certain namespace entities, and it is because of the `using` statement above that we can refer to `cout` as such, and not as `std::cout`. Similar things can be done using Java's `import` statement, but that statement can never be used to make *objects* visible without qualification. Because `cout` is in fact an object, not a type, this is a difference between the two languages illustrated by our sample code.

Another difference is the fact that in C++ the entry point for program execution is in a file-scope function, usually identified as the only global association for the identifier `main`. Java requires the entry point to be in a public static method of some class, again with the name `main`. C++'s main program must return an integer completion code, while Java's `main` methods are `void` functions. C++ allows its main function to have an empty parameter list, but has another form (not used in the example) with two parameters, intended to communicate to the program a command line parameter list. The Java version of `main` requires a string array for the same purpose, which (in spite of the requirement that it be there) is often unused.

The final difference noticeable in the above code segments is that the output of the string `"Hello, World!"` in the C++ program is achieved by invoking the library-defined operator `<<`, a facility that cannot exist in Java, which eschews programmer-defined operators.

3. (a) The following C++ loop copies all the characters in a C-style string (i.e., a character array with trailing null character) stored at `source` to a similar array (at least as large as `source`) stored at `dest`.

```
int i = 0;
while (source[i] != '\0') {
    dest[i] = source[i];
    i = i + 1;
}

dest[i] = '\0';
```

(b) The following accomplishes the same purpose in a much more succinct way, but the novice programmer may have to study it carefully in order to understand its operation:

```
for (int i=0, j=0; dest[i++] = source[j++];);
```

Even more cryptic is the following version, which uses features discussed in Chapter 5.

```
for (char *p = source, *q = dest; *q++ = *p++;);</LL>
```

5. The Java code is as follows:

```
Vector<MyClass> v = new Vector<MyClass>();

for (int i=0; i<n; ++i) v.add(new MyClass());
```

In C++, a similar purpose is accomplished with

```
vector<MyClass> v(n);
```

The two code segments are quite different, for several reasons. One reason is that the Java Vector<> generic class does not have a constructor that provides the initial size of the vector, as does the C++ vector<> class template. We could have set the Java vector's size on the very next line, with v.setSize(n), but that would only have allocated n null handles. We would still have needed a for loop to construct each of the MyClass objects. In Java, the only stack storage used is for a handle providing access to the vector v, which is allocated on the heap along with all its elements. C++ allocates v on the stack and uses heap space for the elements.

7. There is no way to do this in Java. Suppose the base class is Base and the derived class is Derived. An obvious thing to try is ((Base)obj).f(), but when we compile and run we see that it has the same behavior as obj.f() because polymorphism cannot be overridden. That same syntax does in fact work in C++, whether or not f is a virtual function.

9. (a) The Java version is as follows:

```
Iterator<Integer> i = s.iterator();
while (i.hasNext())
    System.out.println(i.next());
```

(b) The C++ version is different:

```
set<int>::iterator i = s.begin();
while (i != s.end())

    cout << *i++ << endl;
```

(c) In both cases, the integers will be displayed on standard output in ascending numerical order.

11. Suppose the linked list is called s in both cases. Java would use the following two lines of code:

```
int i = s.indexOf(3479);
s.remove(i);
```

These two lines of code are quite understandable, but require two linear traversals of the list. The C++ version would appear as follows:

```
list<int>::iterator i = find(s.begin(),s.end(),3479);
s.erase(i);
```

Here only one traversal is required, because the iterator i marks the place where the value was found, and it is now a constant-time operation to remove the integer stored there. This code is quite technical and cryptic to the novice, however.

13. The part of the question which is irrelevant concerns the comparison of the TreeSet and the TreeSet<Integer> containers. C++ has only the set<> class template, and its STL container library was designed from the beginning to use templates. The most natural C++ solution is to use file-scope procedures instead of static member functions, as follows:

```
#include <set>
using std::set;
#include <iostream>
using std::cin;
using std::cout;

double median(set<int> &s) {
    int n = s.size();
    set<int>::iterator m = s.begin();
    for (int i=0; i<n/2; ++i) ++m;
    if (n%2 == 1) return *m;
    else return (*--m + *++m)/2.0;
}

int main() {
    set<int> s;
    int n;
    do {
      cout << "How many integers? (Enter a positive number) ";
        cin >> n;
    } while (n <= 0);
    for (int i=0; i<n; ++i) {
```

```
        cout << "Enter integer number " << i+1 << ":   ";
        int x;
        cin >> x;
        s.insert(x);
    }
    cout << "The median value is " << median(s) << ".\n";
}
```

15. The required Java code is as follows:

```
    Iterator<Map.Entry<String,String>> i =
        manAndWife.entrySet().iterator();
  while (i.hasNext()) {
     Map.Entry<String,String> pair = i.next();
     String man = pair.getKey();
     if (man.charAt(0) == 'P')
        System.out.println(
            man + " is married to " + pair.getValue() + "."
        );
  }
```

17. (a) The Java code below constructs an object of an anonymous type which implements interface `Comparator`, in such a way that the normal order of strings is reversed. It passes that object as a parameter to the `TreeMap<>` constructor, causing that container to store its pairs in the opposite order.

```
    TreeMap<String,String> manAndWife =
        new TreeMap<String,String>(
            new Comparator() {
       public int compare(Object o1,
                        Object o2) {
            String s1 = (String)o1,
                   s2 = (String)o2;
            return s2.compareTo(s1);
       }
        }
    );
```

(b) A C++ `map<string,string>` object uses operator `<` to guide its storage order. However, we can provide a third template parameter which overrides that order, which is a class whose objects are *function objects* capable of comparing two strings in a different way. The library class `greater<string>` (from header file *xfunctional*) is such a class, and it redefines the order on strings using its instance method `operator ()`, which receives two string parameters `s1` and `s2` and returns `true` if and only if `s1 > s2`. All that is necessary is that we instantiate `manAndWife` as follows:

```
    map<string,string,greater<string> > manAndWife;    </LL>
```

CHAPTER 5

1. The expressions which *do* have l-values are: `x`, `a[0]`, `*&x`, `*(a+1)`, and `*p`.

3. Such a pattern can be achieved in C++ using a "pointer to a pointer," as follows:

```
float **b = new float*[2];
b[0] = new float[3];   // First row has three elements
b[1] = new float[5];   // Second row has five elements
```

5. Whether the string `"I am a string"` is stored once, and all occurrences refer to that one location, or whether each occurrence is stored separately, is a compiler decision. (For example, in Visual Studio 2010, each project can be set to "pool" literal strings or not.) If the literal string is stored only once, i.e., if such strings are pooled, the program will display `"Same"`. If not, it will display `"Different"`.

7. The following code receives the address of (a pointer to) an integer, and squares the value stored at that address:

```
void square(int *p) {
    *p = (*p)*(*p);
}
```

9. (a) The code will not compile because the call `c1.f(c2)` in `main()` supplies a `c2` object as the parameter to the call on `c1.f`, and that method requires a `c1` object. C++ will automatically convert if it has a `c1` constructor with a `c2` parameter, or if it has an `operator c1()` in class `c2`. It gives no preference to either of these mechanisms, however, and because both options are available the code is ambiguous. (b) Removing either the conversion constructor from `c1` or the `operator c1()` from `c2` would allow the code to compile. (c) Removing the constructor causes 48 to be output; keeping the constructor and removing `operator c1()` causes 13 to be output.

11. The code will not compile. Any of the three definitions of `f` would be compatible with the call, and only standard conversions are necessary—specifically the conversions from `int` to `double` and `double` to `int`. But because these are both considered the same type of conversion for the purpose of overload resolution, neither is preferred over the other. With respect to the call, using *e* for exact match and *s* for standard conversion, the three argument-to-parameter matching patterns are (a) *ese*, (b)

sss, and (c) *ees*. Because exact match is superior to standard conversion for argument matching purposes, both (a) and (c) are superior to (b). However, neither of (a) and (c) is preferred over the other, so the call is considered ambiguous.

13. The following solution is made more elegant by the use of `stringstream` temporaries, which make character-by-character processing unnecessary:

```
#include <iostream>
using std::cin;
using std::cout;
using std::endl;
#include <fstream>
using std::ifstream;
#include <string>
using std::string;
#include <sstream>
using std::stringstream;

int main() {
ifstream fin("textin.txt");
string s;
getline(fin, s);
while(!fin.eof() && !fin.fail()) {
        stringstream(s) >> s;
        cout << s << endl;
        getline(fin,s);
}
return 0;
}
```

The effect in the above of `stringstream(s) >> s` is to replace s by the first word in s.

15. The following order is a valid total order on points:

```
class Point {
    ...
public:
    ...
    bool operator < (Point p) const {
        if (x < p.x) return true;
        else if (x == p.x && y < p.y) return true;
        else return false;
    }
    ...
};
```

Using this order, nine pairs of points were placed in a map called `point-Pairs`. Specifically, the map $(x,y) \rightarrow \left(\dfrac{x+y}{2}, \dfrac{x-y}{2} \right)$ was applied for even values of x and y between 0 and 4, inclusively, using the following code sequence:

```
Point p(x,y);
Point q((x+y)/2,(x-y)/2);
pointPairs[p] = q;
```

When the mapped points were output, the result was as follows:

```
(0, 0)->(0, 0)   (0, 2)->(1, -1)  (0, 4)->(2, -2)
(2, 0)->(1, 1)   (2, 2)->(2, 0)   (2, 4)->(3, -1)
(4, 0)->(2, 2)   (4, 2)->(3, 1)   (4, 4)->(4, 0)
```

Visual inspection confirms the mapping was correct. The experiment was then repeated, with the order redefined as

```
bool operator < (Point p) const {
    return x < p.x && y < p.y;
}
```

This order is not total; for example, the two points (0, 2) and (2, 0) are incomparable. The output in this case was as follows:

```
(0, 0)->(2, 2)   (0, 2)->(2, 2)   (0, 4)->(2, 2)
(2, 0)->(2, 2)   (2, 2)->(3, 1)   (2, 4)->(3, 1)
(4, 0)->(2, 2)   (4, 2)->(3, 1)   (4, 4)->(4, 0)
```

Note that only the last row of mapped points is correct.

17. The following private recursive utility method makes the order operators easier to write. The elements of the array are on the heap and are accessible via the pointer `elts`. The current size of the array is in instance variable `n`.

```
class IntArray {
    int *elts; // Pointer to array of elements.
    int n;     // Current size.
    ...
    bool lessThan(int start, const IntArray & a) const {
        // Recursively evaluates whether the portion of
        // elts beginning at start is lexographically less
        // than a.elts, beginning at the same position.
        const int infinity = 1<<30;
        int thisStart, aStart; // These will begin at start
            // and stick at the first nonzero entries in elts
            // and a.elts, respectively, or at infinity.
        for (thisStart = start;
```

```
                thisStart < n && elts[thisStart] == 0;
                thisStart++);
        if (thisStart >= n) thisStart = infinity;
        for (aStart = start;
                aStart < a.n && a.elts[aStart] == 0;
                aStart++);
        if (aStart >= a.n) aStart = infinity;
        if (thisStart == aStart) {
            if (aStart == infinity) return false;
                // Both contain nothing but zeros.
            else if (elts[aStart] == a.elts[aStart])
                return lessThan(aStart+1, a);
            else return elts[aStart] < a.elts[aStart];
        }
        else if (thisStart < aStart)
            return elts[thisStart] < 0;
        else return a.elts[aStart] > 0;
    }
```

Now the operators can be defined as follows:

```
public:
    ...
    bool operator < (const IntArray &a) const {
        return lessThan(0,a);
    }
    bool operator > (const IntArray &a) const {
        return a.lessThan(0,*this);
    }
    bool operator == (const IntArray &a) const {
        int i;
        for (i=0; i<a.n; ++i) {
          if ((i < n) && elts[i] != a.elts[i]) return false;
            if (i >= n && a.elts[i] != 0) return false;
        }
        for (i; i<n; ++i) if (elts[i] != 0) return false;
        return true;
    }
    bool operator != (const IntArray &a) const {
        return !(*this == a);
    }
    bool operator >= (const IntArray &a) const {
        return !(*this < a);
    }
    bool operator <= (const IntArray &a) const {
```

```
        return !(*this > a);
    }
};
```

19. The output in response to a declaration like

```
    D d;
```

is as follows:

```
    B's A B C's A C D
```

The output shows the order of initialization of the five constituent portions of d's storage map. First, the A portion of B's storage map is initialized, then B's storage map, then the A portion of C's storage map, then C's storage map, then finally D's storage map is initialized last.

If we make each of B and C inherit virtually from A, the new output is as follows:

```
    D's A B C D
```

Here we see that an A object has been default constructed. It will be initialized first, and it will be the only A portion of d's storage map, used by all three of the other classes as well.

21. Following is the complete header file, beginning with the interface to the class template, followed by the definitions of the individual methods:

```
#ifndef __RATIONALTEMPLATE_H
#define __RATIONALTEMPLATE_H

template <class intType>
class Rational {
public:
    Rational(intType numerator=0, intType denominator=1);
    Rational<intType> operator*(Rational<intType> b);
    Rational<intType> operator/(Rational<intType> b);
    Rational<intType> operator-(Rational<intType> b);
    Rational<intType> operator-();
    Rational<intType> operator+(Rational<intType> b);
    intType getNumerator() { return numerator;}
    intType getDenominator() { return denominator; }
private:
    intType numerator, denominator;
    void lowestTerms();
};

template <class intType>
```

```
Rational<intType>::Rational(
    intType numerator, intType denominator):
        numerator(numerator), denominator(denominator) {
    // Constructor needs only a numerator and denominator.
    if (denominator == 0) throw "Attempt to divide by zero";
    lowestTerms();
}

template <class intType>
intType gcd(intType m, intType n) {
    // Greatest common divisor function.
    if (m == 0 && n == 0) throw "Attempt to compute gcd(0,0)";
    if (m < 0) m = -m;
    if (n < 0) n = -n;
    if (m > n) {
        intType t = m;
        m = n;
        n = t;
    }
    while (m != 0) {
        intType t = m;
        m = n % m;
        n = t;
    }
    return n;
}

template <class intType>
void Rational<intType>::lowestTerms() {
    // Implementation of private member function for reducing
    // to lowest terms.
    intType divisor = gcd(numerator,denominator);
    numerator = numerator / divisor;
    denominator = denominator / divisor;
    if (denominator < 0) {
        numerator = -numerator;
        denominator = -denominator;
    }
}

template <class intType>
Rational<intType> Rational<intType>::operator * (
        Rational<intType> b) {
    // Multiplication operation.
    return Rational<intType>(numerator*b.numerator,
                            denominator*b.denominator);
```

```
    }

    template <class intType>
    Rational<intType> Rational<intType>::operator / (
            Rational<intType> b) {
        // Division operation.
        if (b.numerator == 0) throw "Attempt to divide by zero";
        return Rational<intType>(
            numerator*b.denominator,denominator*b.numerator);
    }

    template <class intType>
    Rational<intType> Rational<intType>::operator - (
            Rational<intType> b) {
        // Subraction operation.
        return Rational<intType>(
            numerator*b.denominator - denominator*b.numerator,
            denominator*b.denominator);
    }

    template <class intType>
    Rational<intType> Rational<intType>::operator + (
            Rational<intType> b) {
        // Addition operation.
        return Rational<intType>(
            numerator*b.denominator+denominator*b.numerator,
            denominator*b.denominator);
    }

    #endif
```

CHAPTER 6

1. On each iteration of the message loop, Win32 asks if there is a message pending. If there is, then the first message is dequeued and interpreted, and its callback function is called. On the other hand, if there are no messages in the queue then idle processing may occur. Because idle processing is inserted into the middle of the message dispatching process, it must conform to the same restrictions one observes when writing event handlers. It should perform a relatively small amount of work on the current thread, because if it monopolizes the processor then normal processing is interfered with. Only tasks that can be partitioned into small chunks of work which are accomplished sporadically should be performed here. (In

MFC, this is accomplished by generating an `OnIdle()` override in the application class.)

3. The "mapper" application randomly chooses a set of locations within the client window, where it draws a small black spot and labels it with a city name, in the same manner in which cities are marked on a highway map. The city names are in a fixed array, but the choice of locations is performed randomly every time the window is redrawn. When the client area is redrawn, then, all the city locations change. This happens every time the window is resized, maximized, or minimized and restored.

5. The data structure `history` is a stack of "place markers," each of which is a pair consisting of a pointer to a category and an iterator marking a place within the list of subcategories. If the `place` object being pushed on the stack were not a value but a reference, then the next statement after the push, which is intended to begin the process of modifying `place` so that it advances into the tree, would also advance the place marker on the stack, thereby undoing the important work of keeping track of the previous location.

7. Both an `OnDraw()` override and an `OnLButtonDown()` event handler must be generated, so the solution below provides hand-coded routines to be called from those generated methods.

```
#include <afxwin.h>
#include <list>

#ifndef __HCDRAWGRAPH_H
#define __HCDRAWGRAPH_H

using std::list;

class HCDrawGraph {
    list<CPoint> vertices;
    enum {RADIUS = 10};
public:
    void onDraw(CDC *pDC) {
        list<CPoint>::iterator i;
        for (i = vertices.begin(); i != vertices.end(); ++i) {
            list<CPoint>::iterator j;
            for (j = i; ++j != vertices.end();) {
                pDC->MoveTo(*i);
                pDC->LineTo(*j);
            }
```

```
        }
        CBrush redBrush(RGB(255,0,0));
        CBrush *oldBrush = pDC->SelectObject(&redBrush);
        for (i = vertices.begin(); i != vertices.end(); ++i)
            pDC->Ellipse(i->x - RADIUS, i->y - RADIUS,
                         i->x + RADIUS, i->y + RADIUS);
        pDC->SelectObject(oldBrush);
    }
    void onLButtonDown(CWnd *pWnd, CPoint point) {
        vertices.push_back(point);
        pWnd->Invalidate();
    }
  };

#endif
```

CHAPTER 7

1. The file below accomplishes all the stated objectives:

```
import java.io.BufferedReader;
import java.io.IOException;
import java.io.InputStreamReader;
import java.util.StringTokenizer;

class Exercise_7_1 {
    public static void main(String args[])
            throws IOException {
        BufferedReader reader =
            new BufferedReader(
                new InputStreamReader(System.in));
        System.out.println(
            "Please input your date of birth in the form " +
            "99/99/9999");
        String line = reader.readLine();
        StringTokenizer tokenizer =
            new StringTokenizer(line,"/");
        int month = Integer.parseInt(tokenizer.nextToken());
        int day = Integer.parseInt(tokenizer.nextToken());
        int year = Integer.parseInt(tokenizer.nextToken());
        System.out.println(
                "Month: " + month +
                "\nDay: " + day +
                "\nYear: "+ year);
    }
```

```
   }
```

3. The following program illustrates the technique of using a scanner; in the program, the string " *; *| * *" matches a delimiter consisting of either a semicolon flanked by spaces or a hyphen flanked by spaces.

```java
import java.io.BufferedReader;
import java.io.InputStreamReader;
import java.util.Scanner;
import java.util.Vector;

class Exercise_7_3 {
    public static void main(String args[]) {
        BufferedReader reader =
            new BufferedReader(
                new InputStreamReader(System.in));
        String line =
            "George - 188; Claudia - 133; Abe - 244; " +
            "Gertrude - 117;";
        Scanner scanner = new Scanner(line);
        scanner.useDelimiter(" *; *| *- *");
        Vector<String> names = new Vector<String>();
        Vector<Integer> numbers = new Vector<Integer>();
        while (scanner.hasNext()) {
            String name = scanner.next();
            names.add(name);
            int number = scanner.nextInt();
            numbers.add(number);
        }
        for (String name: names) System.out.print(name + " ");
        System.out.println();
        for (Integer number: numbers)
            System.out.print(number + " ");
        System.out.println();
    }
}
```

5. The class definition follows…

```java
public class MutableInt {
    private int x;
    public MutableInt() {
        this.x = 0;
    }
    public MutableInt(int x) {
        this.x = x;
    }
    public MutableInt(String s) {
```

```
        this.x = Integer.parseInt(s);
    }
    public MutableInt add(int y) {
        x += y;
        return this;
    }
    public MutableInt subtract(int y) {
        x -= y;
        return this;
    }
    public MutableInt multiply(int y) {
        x *= y;
        return this;
    }
    public MutableInt divide(int y) {
        x /= y;
        return this;
    }
    public String toString() {
        return new Integer(x).toString();
    }
    public int get() { return x; }
    public MutableInt put(int x) {
        this.x = x;
        return this;
    }
}
```

7. Two objects, each bound to a variable of the same interface type, need not have any other type relationships. Each is a subtype of the interface type, but any other type relationship they may have is independent of that fact.

9. The code below is a modification of that given in this appendix for Exercise 17 of Chapter 1. Because Java is unable to provide an override for the subscripting operator, we have instead provided `get()` and `put()` methods. Also, to approximate the value semantics of operator =, we have made the class cloneable and provided a `clone()` override. No destructor is necessary because of Java's use of garbage collection.

```
public class IntArray implements Cloneable {
    private int elts[];
    private static void copy(int a[], int b[], int begin) {
        // Copy all of a into b[begin], b[begin+1], etc.
        if (a.length + begin <= b.length)
            for (int i=0; i<a.length; ++i) b[begin + i] = a[i];
```

```
        }
    public IntArray() {
        elts = new int[0];
    }
    public IntArray(IntArray a) {
        elts = new int[a.elts.length];
        copy(a.elts,elts,0);
    }
    public int get(int i) {
        if (i >= elts.length) {
            int oldElts[] = elts;
            elts = new int[i+1];
            copy(oldElts,elts,0);
        }
        return elts[i];
    }
    public void put(int i, int val) {
        get(i);
        elts[i] = val;
    }
    public Object clone() {
        IntArray a = new IntArray(this);
        return a;
    }
    public int size() {
        return elts.length;
    }
}
```

11.
```
    class HeterogeneousPair<T1,T2> {
    private T1 o1;
    private T2 o2;
    public T1 getFirst() { return o1; }
    public T2 getSecond() { return o2; }
    public HeterogeneousPair<T1,T2> setFirst(T1 o) {
        o1 = o;
        return this;
    }
    public HeterogeneousPair<T1,T2> setSecond(T2 o) {
        o2 = o;
        return this;
    }
}
```

13.
```
    public class DiamondPanel extends JPanel {
    Color c1, c2;
    public DiamondPanel(Color c1, Color c2) {
```

```
            this.c1 = c1;
            this.c2 = c2;
        }
        public void paint(Graphics g) {
            Rectangle rect = getBounds();
            int w = rect.width;
            int h = rect.height;
            int xPoints[] = {
                rect.x, rect.x + w/2, rect.x + w, rect.x + w/2
            };
            int yPoints[] = {
                rect.y+h/2, rect.y, rect.y+h/2, rect.y+h
            };
            g.setColor(c1);
            g.fillRect(rect.x, rect.y, w, h);
            g.setColor(c2);
            g.fillPolygon(xPoints,yPoints,4);
            g.setColor(Color.BLACK);
            g.drawPolygon(xPoints,yPoints,4);
        }
    }
```

15.
```
        public void initComponents() {
        JMenuBar menuBar = new JMenuBar();
        JMenu fileMenu = new JMenu("File");
        JMenu editMenu = new JMenu("Edit");
        JMenuItem aboutItem = new JMenuItem("About");
        menuBar.add(fileMenu);
        menuBar.add(editMenu);
        menuBar.add(aboutItem);
        JMenuItem newItem = new JMenuItem("New");
        JMenuItem openItem = new JMenuItem("Open");
        JMenuItem saveItem = new JMenuItem("Save");
        JMenuItem exitItem = new JMenuItem("Exit");
        fileMenu.add(newItem);
        fileMenu.add(openItem);
        fileMenu.add(saveItem);
        fileMenu.add(exitItem);
        JMenuItem copyItem = new JMenuItem("Copy");
        JMenuItem pasteItem = new JMenuItem("Paste");
        editMenu.add(copyItem);
        editMenu.add(pasteItem);
        setJMenuBar(menuBar);
    }
```

17.
```
    class TTTSquarePanel extends JPanel {
```

```java
        char contents;
        public TTTSquarePanel() {
            initComponents();
        }
        public void initComponents() {
            setBorder(BorderFactory.createLineBorder(Color.black));
        }
        void set(char val) {
            contents = val;
        }
        char get() { return contents; }
        public void paint(Graphics g) {
            super.paint(g);
            Rectangle rect = g.getClipBounds();
            int epsilon = Math.min(rect.width/10, rect.height/10);
            int xl = rect.x +  epsilon,
                xr = rect.x + rect.width - epsilon,
                yt = rect.y + epsilon,
                yb = rect.y + rect.height - epsilon;
            if (contents == 'x' || contents == 'X') {
                g.drawLine(xl, yt, xr, yb);
                g.drawLine(xr, yt, xl, yb);
            }
            else if (contents == 'o' || contents == 'O')
                g.drawOval(xl, yt, xr - xl + 1, yb - yt + 1);
        }
    }
19.     class TTTPanel extends JPanel {
        public TTTPanel() {
            initComponents();
        }
        TTTSquarePanel square[][] = new TTTSquarePanel[3][];
        public void initComponents() {
            for (int i=0; i<3; ++i) {
                square[i] = new TTTSquarePanel[3];
                for (int j=0; j<3; ++j)
                    square[i][j] = new TTTSquarePanel();
            }
            setLayout(new BoxLayout(this, BoxLayout.Y_AXIS));
            for (int i=0; i<3; ++i) {
                JPanel rowPanel = new JPanel();
                 rowPanel.setLayout(new BoxLayout(rowPanel,BoxLayout.X_
    AXIS));
                for (int j=0; j<3; ++j)
                    rowPanel.add(square[i][j]);
```

```
                add(rowPanel);
            }
        }
        public void set(int i, int j, char val) {
            square[i][j].set(val);
        }
    }
21.   import OOPLS.PointList;
    import OOPLS.Point;
    import java.util.Iterator;
    import java.util.StringTokenizer;
    import javax.swing.JOptionPane;

    public class PointListClient {
        public static Point getPointFromUser() {
            boolean correctInput = false;
            int num1=0, num2=0;
            while (!correctInput) {
                try {
                    String line = JOptionPane.showInputDialog(
                        "Please enter a point as two integers " +
                        "separated by a space");
                    StringTokenizer tokenizer =
                        new StringTokenizer(line);
                    num1=Integer.parseInt(tokenizer.nextToken());
                    num2=Integer.parseInt(tokenizer.nextToken());
                    correctInput = true;
                }
                catch(Exception e) {}
            }
            return new Point(num1,num2);
        }
        public static void main(String args[]) {
            PointList pl = new PointList();
            int numPoints = Integer.parseInt(
                JOptionPane.showInputDialog("How many points?"));
            for (int i=0;i < numPoints; ++i)
                pl.push_back(getPointFromUser());
            pl.store("PointList.bin");
            System.out.println();
        }
    }
```

CHAPTER 8

1. The reader may consult the MSDN description of `System.Decimal`, which gives some of the detailed specification, but that will not describe the actual format. The following dump methods for Visual C# are constructed using unsafe code, and will help the reader experiment to find out more about the storage format:

```
public unsafe static void dumpWord(void* p) {
    // Dump the word pointed to by pointer p, assuming the
    // high-order bits are in the high-address byte.
    byte* pb = (byte*)p;
    pb += 3;
    for (int i = 1; i <= 4; ++i)
    {
        int lobyte = *pb % 16;
        int hibyte = *pb-- / 16;
        Console.Write(hibyte.ToString("X") +
                        lobyte.ToString("X"));
    }
}
public unsafe static void dump(decimal d) {
    byte* p = (byte *) &d;
    Console.WriteLine(d + " is stored as follows: ");
    dumpWord(p);
    dumpWord(p + 4);
    dumpWord(p + 12);
    dumpWord(p + 8);
    Console.WriteLine();
    Console.WriteLine();
}
```

By calling the dump routine with an assortment of values, some large, some small, some positive, some negative, some with fractional part, and some without, the reader will discover that the last three 32-bit words contain the significant digits of the decimal value, a total of 96 bits. He will also discover that the value is stored in binary format, not binary-coded-decimal. Because 96 bits hold 2^{96}, or roughly 7.9×10^{28} possible bit patterns, this explains the precision limit of 28 or 29 decimal digits. The reader should also discover that the first bit of the first word is a sign bit and that the remaining 31 bits of the first word are more than enough to store the position of the decimal point.

3. The only logical difference in the four arrays is in their shapes. The array `a` must be an m by n by p array, for some constants m, n, and p.

The b array, on the other hand, is an *m* by *n* array of arrays, and each of those *mn* arrays will be assigned its own size. c is an *m*-element array, and each of those *m* elements is a rectangular array. Finally, d is an array of "ragged arrays," meaning that for each i, d[i] is an array of arrays. Each d[i] can be a different size and shape, and for each i and j, d[i][j] can have its own size. The major difference in the protocol for allocating these arrays is that where there are multiple sizes we must make an individual allocation for each of the variable-sized elements. Thus, a can be allocated with one instruction, whereas d requires one instruction to allocate, followed by a loop allocating each of the two-dimensional ragged arrays d[i]. Within this loop, there will be a loop allocating each of the one-dimensional arrays d[i][j]. The arrays b and c will need different protocols because their shapes are different. For example, if c is to be allocated with m elements, so that each element c[i] is an n[i] by p[i] array, where n and p are int arrays, the following code suffices:

```
c = new int[m][,];

for (int i=0; i<m; ++i) c[i] = new int [n[i], p[i]];
```

5. `a[0,0][0].GetLength(0)` and `a[0,0][0].GetLength(1)`

7. (a) `Console.WriteLine("x = " + x);`

   (b) `Console.WriteLine(string.Format("x = {0}", x));`

   (c) `Console.WriteLine("x = {0}", x);`

9. Attempting to code `6.Parse("7")` in Visual Studio, we get the message, "Member int.Parse(string) cannot be accessed with an instance reference; qualify it with a type name instead." Given this response we might be inclined to conclude that no class messages may be sent to literals of int type. Further evidence to support that comes to light when we try `6.Equals(7,8)`, in which case we get a similar message. But the fact that messages are being sent to int literals is not the issue, because `6.GetHashCode()` compiles fine, as does `6.CompareTo(7)`. In fact, a little digging in the C# documentation quickly turns up the rule that static messages must always be sent to the class, not to instances of the class. This makes plenty of sense, but it is one case in which C# is more restrictive than Java, which has no problem allowing static messages to be sent to instances. (C++ also allows such usage.)

11.  ```
     class Employee {
     int employeeID;
     ```
     ```

```
    public Employee(int id) { employeeID = id; }
      public int ID {
          get {
              return employeeID;
          }
          set {
              employeeID = value;
          }
      }
  }
}
```

13.
```
    class Triple<T> {
    private T a, b, c;
    public Triple(T a, T b, T c) {
        this.a = a;
        this.b = b;
        this.c = c;
    }
    public T this[int i] {
        get {
            switch(i) {
                case 0: return a;
                case 1: return b;
                case 2: return c;
                default:
                    throw new IndexOutOfRangeException();
            }
        }
        set {
            switch(i) {
                case 0: a = value; return;
                case 1: b = value; return;
                case 2: c = value; return;
                default:
                    throw new IndexOutOfRangeException();
            }
        }
    }
}
```

15. The following works as long as the numerator and denominator are kept in lowest terms and the denominator is always positive:

```
public static bool operator ==(Rational r, Rational s) {
    return r.num == s.num && r.den == s.den;
}
public static bool operator !=(Rational r, Rational s) {
```

```
        return r.num != s.num || r.den != s.den;
    }
    public static bool operator < (Rational r, Rational s) {
        return r.num * s.den < s.num * r.den;
    }
    public static bool operator > (Rational r, Rational s) {
        return s < r;
    }
    public static bool operator <= (Rational r, Rational s) {
        return r.num * s.den <= s.num * r.den;
    }
    public static bool operator >= (Rational r, Rational s) {
        return s <= r;
    }
```

17.
```
    public interface I3D<T> {
    T this[int i, int j, int k] {
        get;
    }
}
```

19. Actually, any class which includes as an instance member a list of objects of its own type will have many of the same capabilities as a delegate, as the following example illustrates:

```
class DelegateLike {
    private string id;
    private List<DelegateLike> members =
        new List<DelegateLike>();
    public DelegateLike() { this.id = "Anonymous"; }
    public DelegateLike(string id) { this.id = id; }
    public static DelegateLike operator +(DelegateLike d1,
                                          DelegateLike d2) {
        d1.members.Add(d2);
        return d1;
    }
    public string ToString()
    {
        return id;
    }
}
```

Here, the + operator has an odd effect, because it modifies its left-hand operand, but the real intent here is to allow the use of +=, and that goal is achieved. In fact, += has the same effect as +, i.e., it causes the right-hand argument to be included in the list encapsulated by the left-hand argument. Reference semantics is at the heart of this, of course.

21. EFDABGHCI

23. The required C# lambda expression is `(x,y)=>(Math.Sqrt(x*x+y*y))`. It must be used to instantiate a delegate, as in the following code:

```
delegate T BinaryOperator<T>(T a, T b);

public static void Main(){
    BinaryOperator<double> d = (x,y)=>Math.Sqrt(x*x+y*y);
    ...
```

Now, for example, the call `d(3,4)` should invoke the function defined by the lambda expression and return the value 5.0.

25. The code below has been tested and, when integrated into a properly configured Windows Forms project, produces the application pictured in Figure 8.3:

```
using System;
using System.Drawing;
using System.Windows.Forms;

namespace Danish_Flag {
    public partial class DanishFlagForm: Form {
        void onResize() {
            Invalidate();
        }
        void onPaint(Graphics g) {
            Rectangle box = ClientRectangle;
            int width1 = 9 * box.Width / 27;
            int width2 = 15 * box.Width / 27;
            int height = 8 * box.Height / 19;
            Size smallSize = new Size(width1, height);
            Size largeSize = new Size(width2, height);
            Point NWBase = box.Location;
            Point NEBase =
                new Point(box.X + 12*box.Width/27, box.Y);
            Point SEBase = new Point(
                box.X + 12*box.Width/27,
                box.Y + 11*box.Height/19);
            Point SWBase = new Point(
                box.X, box.Y + 11*box.Height/19);
            g.FillRectangle(Brushes.Red,
                            new Rectangle(NWBase, smallSize));
            g.FillRectangle(Brushes.Red,
                            new Rectangle(SWBase, smallSize));
            g.FillRectangle(Brushes.Red,
                            new Rectangle(NEBase, largeSize));
```

```
        g.FillRectangle(Brushes.Red,
                        new Rectangle(SEBase, largeSize));
      }
    }
  }
```

CHAPTER 9

1. Python would need a whitespace token with two attributes, (1) its type ("whitespace token"), represented as a small integer code, and (2) its character sequence, a sequence of spaces and tabs. Like the identifier token or the integer literal token, its type is not enough to fully specify it. The use of such a token in a lexical analysis prepass allows the parser to function somewhat like a conventional parser. Unfortunately, the way this token is used cannot be explained with simple context-free rules. Like the rule that says a variable must be declared before it is used, the rules about indentation must be enforced by context-sensitive considerations.

3.
```
matchDataList = matchDataString.split(',',1)
    namesString = matchDataList[0]
    name = namesString.split('-')
    scoresString = matchDataList[1]
    scoresDataList = scoresString.split(',')
    setsWon = [0,0]
    for scores in scoresDataList:
        score = scores.split('-')
        s1 = int(score[0])
        s2 = int(score[1])
        if (s1 > s2): setsWon[0] += 1
        elif (s2 > s1): setsWon[1] += 1
    if (setsWon[0] > setsWon[1]): print(name[0], end='')
    else: print(name[1], end='')
    print(" wins " + scoresString)
```

5. Both of (a) and (c) are valid, but for two different reasons. Statement (a) is a tuple assignment and assigns the values 1, 2, and 3 to the variables x, y, and z, respectively. Statement (c) is equivalent to x = (1, 2, 3) and assigns to x a tuple value. Finally, (b) is invalid, because the number of variables to the left of the = symbol is not the same as the number of values to the right.

7. The string "x = 0", when evaluated by exec(), assigns to variable x the value 0. That string cannot be evaluated by eval(), because assignment

is not an expression-level operation. On the other hand, because expressions are valid statements, any string which constitutes a valid expression can be evaluated by both, the difference being that `eval()` returns as its value the value of the expression, whereas `exec()` returns `None`. Clearly, then, `exec()` is of no use unless side effects are produced by executing the string.

9. The four variables are all named `x`, but each belongs to a different scope. The first two are instance variables in the classes `Outer` and `Outer.Inner`, respectively, while the last two are class variables in the same two respective classes. (Note that `outer.Inner` could have been coded as `Outer.Inner`.) Output to the console is…

```
5 15 4 13
```

11. One solution is…

```
[chr(x) + chr(x+1) for x in range(ord('a'),ord('a')+25)]
```

13.
```
class MyChar:
    def __init__(self, c='\0'):
        self.c = c
    def __add__(self, x):
        self.c = chr(ord(self.c) + x)
        return self
    def __str__(self):
        return self.c
```

15. Nothing needs to be done. The assignment `x += 1` will be translated as `x = x+1`, and the desired effect will be achieved in both cases.

17. It is allowed, and will call the constructor for the first base class mentioned in the list of base classes. The other base classes' constructors can then be called by using the appropriate function objects (`B.__init__()` in the example below).

```
class A:
    def __init__(self, c='\0'):
        self.c = c
    def __str__(self):
        return self.c

class B:
    def __init__(self, x = 0):
        self.x = x
    def __str__(self):
        return str(self.x)
```

```
class C(A, B):
    def __init__(self, c='\0', x = 0):
        super(C,self).__init__(c) # Calls A constructor.
        B.__init__(self,x)        # Calls B constructor.
    def __str__(self):
        return A.__str__(self)+B.__str__(self)
```

The driver code **print**(C('x',4)) instantiates an object of type C and prints its string representation. Here the output is x4. Note that the language allows the constructors to be called (or not called) in any order.

19.
```
def compose(f, g):
    return lambda x: f(g(x))


def f(x):
    return abs(x/(x+1))**(1/3)


def g(x):
    import math
    return math.sin(x*x/7)


print(compose(f,g)(5.7))
```

21.
```
print("Please enter the name of the input text file:  ",
        end = '')
inFileName = input()
print("Please enter the name of the output file:  ",
        end = '')
outFileName = input()
outFile = open(outFileName,'w')
for x in tokens(inFileName):
    outFile.write(x+'\n')
outFile.close()
```

23. The text describing this exercise was stored in file *exercise23.txt*. The tokens object was then created and stored in file *tokens.bin* using the following code:

```
from Exercise20 import tokens

tokes = tokens("Exercise23.txt")
import pickle
jar = open("tokens.bin","wb")
pickle.dump(tokes,jar)
jar.close()
```

Here a problem was discovered with the tokens class as it was created by the author. That class as written was storing the result of its open()

operation, a `TextIOWrapper` object, as an instance member, and such objects cannot be serialized. When the variable referencing the `TextIO-Wrapper` object was made to be local to the block and therefore no longer a part of the `tokens` object, serialization was successful. The following code then successfully retrieved the `tokens` object and displayed the "tokens" in the file, one to a line, on the console window:

```
from Exercise20 import tokens

import pickle
jar = open("tokens.bin","rb")
tokes = pickle.load(jar)
jar.close()
for toke in tokes: print(toke)
```

25. Caution—Sending the `start()` message to a timer constructed using the code below locks the thread of the caller. Initiate the timer from a dedicated thread only.

```
class Timer:
    def __init__(self, ms, callback, *args):
        from tkinter import Tk
        self.tk = Tk()
        self.ms = ms
        self.countLimit = -1
        self.args = args
        self.callback = callback
    def start(self, event=None):
        self.tk.after(self.ms, self.executeCallback)
        self.tk.withdraw()
        self.tk.mainloop()
    def executeCallback(self):
        self.callback(*self.args)
        self.tk.after(self.ms, self.executeCallback)
    def kill(self):
        try:
            self.tk.destroy()
        except:
            pass
```

27. Note in the solution below that rather than calling `startBall()` in the constructor that call is scheduled as a reaction to `<Configure>`, so that it will be executed in a separate thread. If it had been called in the constructor, the constructor would have locked and the root window's polling loop would not have started.

```
from tkinter import *
```

```python
from Timer import Timer

class BouncingBall:
    def __init__(self, color, radius):
        self.color = color
        self.radius = radius
        self.x = self.y = 2*radius
        self.ballID = None
        self.timeInterval = 1/30
            # 30 frames per second
        self.root = Tk()
        self.canvas = Canvas(self.root, bg = 'white',
                             width = 700, height = 500)
        self.canvas.pack(expand=YES, fill=BOTH)
        self.root.bind('<Configure>', self.startBall)
        self.root.bind('<Destroy>', self.destroy)
        self.root.mainloop()
    def startBall(self, event):
        import random
        self.root.unbind('<Configure>')
        self.dx = random.randrange(50, 500)
        self.dy = random.randrange(50, 500)
        self.timer = Timer(int(self.timeInterval*1000),
                           self.cycle)
        self.timer.start()
    def draw(self):
        if self.ballID != None:
            self.canvas.delete(self.ballID)
        self.ballID = self.canvas.create_oval(
            self.x-self.radius, self.y-self.radius,
            self.x+self.radius, self.y+self.radius,
            fill=self.color)
    def cycle(self):
        w, h = self.canvas.winfo_width(),
               self.canvas.winfo_height()
        self.x += self.timeInterval*self.dx
        if self.x < self.radius:
            self.x = self.radius
            self.dx = -self.dx
        if self.x > w-self.radius:
            self.x = w-self.radius
            self.dx = -self.dx
        self.y += self.timeInterval*self.dy
        if self.y < self.radius:
            self.y = self.radius
```

```
                  self.dy = -self.dy
            if self.y > h-self.radius:
                  self.y = h-self.radius
                  self.dy = -self.dy
            self.draw()
      def destroy(self,event):
            try:
                  self.timer.kill()
            except:
                  pass

if __name__ == "__main__":
      BouncingBall("red",20)
```

ABOUT THE CD-ROM

MINIMUM SYSTEM REQUIREMENTS

All the software required for this book should run without difficulty in a current install of Windows XP, Windows Vista, Windows 7, or Windows 8, having 2 gigabytes of RAM and 4 gigabytes of free space on the hard drive. The most strenuous requirements are brought into play when powerful IDEs such as NetBeans® and Visual Studio® are used. Squeak Smalltalk and Python both make much smaller demands on memory and hard drive resources.

CONTENTS OF DIRECTORIES *CHAPTER 1* **AND** *CHAPTER 2*

These directories contain only figure files; there are no significantly large code segments in Chapters 1 and 2, except for some Simula 67 code. The author was unable to get a Simula compiler, so that code has not been tested, but is included only to give the reader a feel for the language.

CONTENTS OF DIRECTORY *CHAPTER 3*

This directory contains figure files (extension *.tif*) and Smalltalk source files (extension *.st*) needed for Chapter 3 ("Smalltalk and the Squeak Environment"). The files can be used by executing *filein* operations from the Squeak environment. Squeak Smalltalk is available as a free download from http://www.squeak.org/.

CONTENTS OF DIRECTORY *CHAPTER 4*

This directory contains figure files and Java and C++ source files (extensions *.java*, *.h*, and *.cpp*) needed for Chapter 4 ("C++ and Java Commonalities and Similarities"). A C++ compiler, a Java compiler and the Java virtual machine, and a text editor are needed here.

CONTENTS OF DIRECTORY *CHAPTER 5*

This directory contains figure files and C++ source files (extensions *.h* and .cpp) needed for Chapter 5 ("Additional Concepts from the C++ Language"). Any C++ compiler will suffice for this chapter; the author used a commercial install of Microsoft Visual Studio C++, but there are free downloads for C++ compilers available.

CONTENTS OF DIRECTORY *CHAPTER 6*

This directory contains figure files and C++ source files (extensions *.h* and *.cpp*) needed for Chapter 6 ("Visual Studio and the Microsoft Foundation Classes"). The reader will need the code generators in Visual Studio for this chapter. Please note that MFC is not included in the free downloads of Visual Studio Express.

CONTENTS OF DIRECTORY *CHAPTER 7*

This directory contains figure files and Java source files (extension *.java*) needed for Chapter 7 ("Java and the Swing Library"). The reader will need NetBeans (available as a free download from http://netbeans.org) and Java (available as a free download from http://www.java.com/en/download/index.jsp).

CONTENTS OF DIRECTORY *CHAPTER 8*

This directory contains figure files and C# source files (extension *.cs*) needed for Chapter 8 ("C# and the Common Language Infrastructure"). The reader will need the .NET framework and the C# language. The author used Visual Studio Professional, but Visual Studio C# Express is available as a free download and should suffice (http://www.microsoft.com/visualstudio/en-us/products/2010-editions/visual-csharp-express).

CONTENTS OF DIRECTORY *CHAPTER 9*

This directory contains figure files and Python source files (extension *.py* or *.pyw*) needed for Chapter 9 ("Python"). Python and the IDLE environment are available as a free download from http://www.python.org/getit/.

INDEX

www.ingramcontent.com/pod-product-compliance
Lightning Source LLC
Chambersburg PA
CBHW080401190526
45161CB00003B/97